Advances in Titicaca Basin Archaeology-1

Edited by

Charles Stanish,
Amanda B. Cohen, and
Mark S. Aldenderfer

Cotsen Institute of Archaeology at UCLA
Los Angeles, California

Library of Congress Cataloging-in-Publication Data
Advances in Titicaca Basin archaeology / edited by Charles Stanish, Amanda B. Cohen, and Mark S. Aldenderfer.
    v. cm. — (Monograph / Cotsen Institute of Archaeology, University of California, Los Angeles ; 54-)
    Includes bibliographical references.
    ISBN 1-931745-15-3 (alk. paper)
    1. Indians of South America—Titicaca Lake Region (Peru and Bolivia)—Antiquities. 2. Tiwanaku culture—Titicaca Lake
        Region (Peru and Bolivia) 3. Excavations (Archaeology)—Titicaca Lake Region (Peru and Bolivia) 4. Titicaca Lake Region
        (Peru and Bolivia)—Antiquities. I. Stanish, Charles, 1956- II. Cohen, Amanda B. III. Aldenderfer, Mark S. IV. Monograph
        (Cotsen Institute of Archaeology at UCLA) ; 54-
    F3319.1.T57A38 2005
    984'.1201—dc22

                                                    2004028970

ISBN 1-931745-15-3 (paper)
ISBN 1-931745-19-6 (cloth)

Contents

Authors' Affiliations

Mark S. Aldenderfer
University of California, Santa Barbara

Elizabeth Arkush
University of California, Los Angeles

Matthew S. Bandy
Institute of Andean Studies, Berkeley

Cecilia Chávez
Programa Collasuyu, Puno, Peru

Lisa M. Cipolla
University of California, Santa Barbara

Lawrence S. Coben
University of Pennsylvania, Philadelphia

Amanda B. Cohen
University of California, Los Angeles

Edmundo de la Vega
Programa Collasuyu, Puno, Peru

Kirk L. Frye
University of California, Santa Barbara

Christine A. Hastorf
University of California, Berkeley

John W. Janusek
Vanderbilt University, Nashville

Cynthia J. Klink
University of California, Santa Barbara

Joel Myres
University of California, Irvine

Rolando Paredes
Instituto Nacional de Cultura, Puno, Peru

Aimée Plourde,
University of California, Los Angeles

Matthew T. Seddon
SWCA Environmental Consultants, Salt Lake City

Charles Stanish
University of California, Los Angeles

Tiffiny Tung
Vanderbilt University, Nashville

List of Figures

All figures are by the authors unless otherwise noted.

List of Tables

Preface

THIS VOLUME REPRESENTS the first in a planned series of edited volumes on the archaeology of the Titicaca Basin. Stretching over 50,000 km^2, the Basin is an enormous area with a long and rich archaeological past. The actual region that was directly or indirectly influenced by Titicaca Basin cultures covers almost four times as much area from northwest Argentina to San Pedro de Atacama and into the Amazonian drainage. Over the last 100 years, scholars have painstakingly pieced together the fragments of that past. This series is intended to provide a venue in which new data and interpretations from the circum-Titicaca region can be published.

The editors thank the individual authors for their contributions and patience in producing this very complicated but important volume. Some of the papers were submitted several years ago. The editors and the authors have updated the chapters as necessary. In matters of style and convention, we follow the guidelines for publication at the Cotsen Institute. In matters of orthography, we permitted each author to use their preferred spellings and conventions.

Many people have provided assistance in the long process of preparing this volume for publication. We would like to thank Karen Doehner for her assistance in the earlier stages of manuscript preparation. She also translated some of the text. Matthew Bandy provided much technical support throughout the project as well as contributing a paper. We thank our superb copyeditor, Dr. Janet Dunn, who proved to be exacting and diligent. Ms. Carol Leyba designed this volume, and we once again thank her for her outstanding work. The Director of Publications of the Cotsen Institute of Archaeology at UCLA, Dr. Julia Sanchez, has provided immense professional help in this work. Finally, we thank Mr. Lloyd Cotsen for his generous support of the Institute's mission, including the publication of archaeological monographs and books.

1.

Introduction to "Advances in Titicaca Basin Archaeology-1"

Charles Stanish and Amanda B. Cohen

THE TITICACA BASIN represents one of the last great understudied areas in the Americas where indigenous state societies developed (Figures 1.1–1.4). Throughout the western hemisphere, regional research and intensive excavations have been conducted for several generations in the centers of early state development, such as the central basin of Mexico, the Maya lowlands, the Cusco valley, and the north coast of Peru. In contrast, the Titicaca Basin was not an area of widespread and intensive research until the late 1970s. The two monumental sites of Pukara and Tiwanaku are exceptions. During the sixteenth century, scholars commented on the great ruins in and around these two important centers. Both Pukara and Tiwanaku have been the subject of systematic research for generations. Carlos Ponce Sanginés (1995) summarizes the research at Tiwanaku over the years. He likewise was a major figure in the history of Tiwanaku studies. Pukara was excavated by Alfred Kidder in the 1930s (S. Chávez 1992) and more extensively in the 1970s by Elías Mujica (1978, 1985, 1987, 1988). Clark Erickson (1988a, 1988b, 1996) conducted reconnaissance, survey, and excavations in raised-field areas and associated Pukara sites in the northern Titicaca Basin throughout the 1980s. Alan Kolata (1986) conducted some reconnaissance in the Koani Pampa in the late 1970s and early 1980s and then moved onto Lukurmata and Tiwanaku (1993, 1996, 2003). Likewise, sporadic research was conducted on other monuments such as Chiripa (K. Chávez 1988; Kidder 1943), Qaluyu (K. Chávez 1977), Sillustani (Bandelier 1910), Pajchiri (Bennett 1936), the Islands of the Sun and Moon (Bandelier 1910), Tankatanka (Vásquez 1940), Iskanwaya (Arellano López 1975), and Chucuito (M. Tschopik 1946). A few scholars conducted nonsystematic and nonintensive reconnaissance in the region, including Vásquez (1937, 1939), Bennett (1933, 1934a), Kidder (1943), Chávez-Ballon,

FIGURE 1.1. Map of South America

Neira (1967), Hyslop (1976), and Faldín Arancibia (1985, 1991). This work, combined with ethnohistorical research on the later periods of prehistory, provided a broad outline of the culture history of the region (e.g., Bouysse-Cassagne 1991; Lumbreras 1974b; Lumbreras and Amat 1968). Work outside of the far northern and far southern areas of the basin was very rare until the late 1980s. The systematic analysis of raised

fields in the Huata area by Erickson, as mentioned above, and the rescue excavations by Núñez and Paredes at Isla Esteves (1978) represented the first intensive research away from either Pukara or Tiwanaku core areas.

In spite of this work, research in the Titicaca Basin has been surprisingly sparse compared to other areas of the world where first-generation states developed. It is important to remember

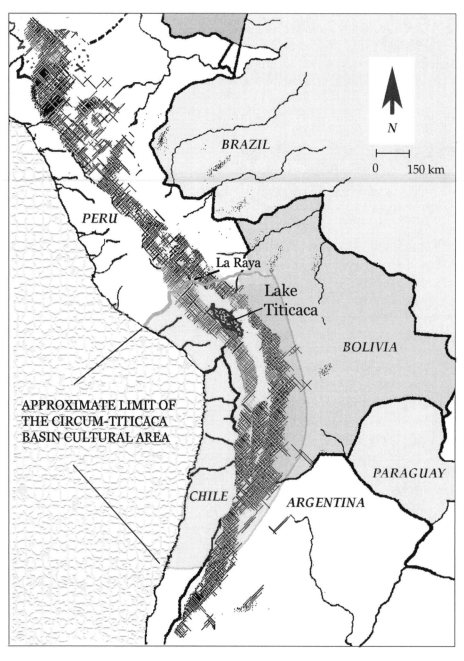

FIGURE 1.2. Map of western South America

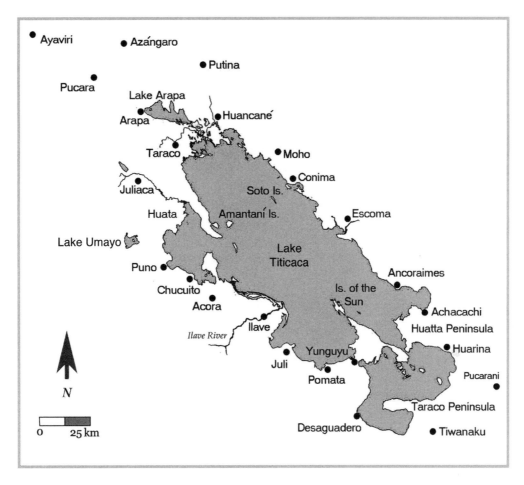

FIGURE 1.3. Political map of the Lake Titicaca area

that the Titicaca Basin, conservatively defined as just the hydrological boundaries, is twice the size of the country of Belize. Defined in cultural-geographical terms as the maximum area of Tiwanaku influence, the circum-Titicaca cultural region is almost four times larger than its hydrological boundaries. In fact, the south-central Andes, the area that corresponds to this cultural-geographical definition, is as large or larger than most of the areas of the world where first-generation states developed. It is not unprofitable to view the Andes as comprising three largely autonomous areas of first-generation states—the north coast of Peru, the central highlands where Wari developed, and the Titicaca Basin where Tiwanaku evolved (e.g., Stanish 2001a).

Whether one accepts this distinction or not, it is clear that we have just begun to grasp the nature and range of the prehistoric settlement of the Titicaca Basin outside of the Pukara and Ti-

wanaku areas. Most archaeologists who work in other areas of the world where complex societies evolved would be amazed at the number of undiscovered sites in the Titicaca Basin. In both systematic surveys and nonsystematic reconnaissance, we routinely find unreported sites that are over 5 ha in size, and sometimes up to 15 ha in size, with sunken courts, low pyramids, monoliths, hundreds of diagnostics on the surface, and so forth. Areas such as the Azángaro and Ayabacas River Valleys in the north remain unsurveyed, yet they most certainly contain significant sites. The same can be said for virtually the entire eastern side of Lake Titicaca on the Peruvian and most of the Bolivian side. The archaeology of the eastern slopes of the Andes, with the exception of some work by Juan Faldín Arancibia (1985, 1991) and that of Jorge Arellano López (1975), is virtually unknown. Huge fortified sites and settlements with obvious artificial

FIGURE 1.4. Map of the Lake Titicaca area with selected sites mentioned in text

modification and architecture can be seen in air photos of the region. Wendell Bennett (1933, 1950) noted large sites in the southeast region, but they remain largely unreported. In short, huge tracts of land in the Titicaca Basin remain completely unvisited by professional archaeologists.

Throughout the last decade, the western and northern Titicaca Basin has been surveyed by members of the Programa Collasuyu. This is a research program jointly administered by Mark Aldenderfer, Edmundo de la Vega, and Charles Stanish. Housed in Puno, it evolved out of the Proyecto Lupaqa that was located in Juli and administered by Stanish. The Program is modeled after the Programa Contisuyu, originally created

and administered by Michael Moseley and Fernando Cabieses. The Programa Contisuyu continues today, with its seat in Moquegua. Since the mid-1990s, Programa Collasuyu has housed and/or supported dozens of research projects in the region.

In the past fifteen years, members of Programa Collasuyu have discovered literally hundreds of new sites. We have begun the slow but immensely satisfying work of documenting, excavating, and theorizing about the entire Titicaca region, not just Pukara and Tiwanaku. This book is intended to be the first in a multiple series of reports on research throughout the circum-Titicaca Basin.

CHRONOLOGY

Two kinds of chronologies are employed in the Andes. One is historical, characterized by the famous "horizon" marker methodology. The most common one, of course, is that of John Rowe, developed in collaboration with Dorothy Menzel from the analysis of pottery from Ica on the south coast of Peru. The second chronology is a stage-based one, first developed in detail by Luis Lumbreras (1974b, 1981). There has been a large literature on the strengths and weaknesses of these kinds of chronologies and this debate will not be repeated here.

In general, most contemporary archaeologists working in the Titicaca region utilize the stage chronology for a number of reasons as outlined in Stanish (2003). Alongside the stage chronology, many of us use a historical chronology as well for specific areas of the Titicaca Basin. That is, following traditions from around the world, we have a broad, anthropologically informed stage chronology for the region as a whole, with a series of historical chronologies for local sequences. Such a dual approach permits us to control for the organizational characteristics of the most complex cultures at any one time throughout the region, while also controlling for the specific differences in style in the many subareas of the region. The general stage chronology is seen in Figure 1.5. The specific chronologies for separate areas of the Titicaca Basin are listed in many of the chapters.

Chronology in the Titicaca Basin

	North	West	South	Isla del Sol	Stage	Ica
1500	Inca	Inca	Inca	Inca	Expansive Inca	Late Horizon
1000	Colla / Late Huaña / Tiwanaku	Lupaqa / Tiwanaku	Pacajes / Tiwanaku V	Altiplano / Tiwanaku	Regional Period / Tiwanaku Expansive	Late Intermediate / Middle Horizon
500	Early Huaña / Pukara	Late Sillumocco	Tiwanaku IV / Qeya / Kalasasaya / Late Chiripa	Late Titinhuayani	Upper Formative	Early Intermediate Period / Early Horizon
AD/BC						
500	Cusipata	Early Sillumocco	Middle Chiripa	Early Titinhuayani	Middle Formative	
1000	Qaluyu	Pasiri	Early Chiripa	Pasiri		
1500					Early Formative	
2000					Late Archaic	

FIGURE 1.5. General chronology used in the Titicaca Basin

ADVANCES IN
TITICACA BASIN RESEARCH

This volume follows a traditional chronological ordering of articles. In Chapters 2, 3, and 4, Mark Aldenderfer, Cindy Klink, and Lisa Cipolla discuss recently discovered Archaic sites in the region. The work by Aldenderfer and his colleagues from the University of California, Santa Barbara, has substantially changed our understanding of the Titicaca Basin Archaic. Aldenderfer and Klink's contributions represent the first point typology in the region, indicating that there were Early, Middle, Late, and Terminal Archaic occupations. (To date, no Paleo-Indian sites have been found in the Lake Titicaca Basin.) Klink's and Cipolla's work represent some of the first analyses of systematically collected reconnaissance data on Archaic period settlement distribution published for the region. Klink discovered over 150 Archaic period sites in the western Titicaca Basin of the Huenque drainage, while Cipolla discusses and analyzes almost 100 sites in the Huancané-Putina region located in the north.

The work of Klink and Cipolla indicates that there were heavy concentrations of Archaic period peoples up the rivers away from the lake. Their work, both here and in other versions yet to be published, suggest that the immediate lake area was not as conducive to human occupation as were the river valleys and dry puna in the uplands. Around the Terminal Archaic at 4400–3600 BP, Klink sees a shift toward the present lake edge marking, perhaps, "...the initial shift toward greater use of more lakeshore-oriented land-use systems" that were characteristic of all later periods (Klink, Chapter 2, this volume). The data from the Huancané-Putina region reported on by Cipolla in Chapter 4 support this model as well. Likewise, excavations at an open-air site on the Island of the Sun indicate initial occupations during the Terminal Archaic that also support this model (Stanish et al. 2002).

Cipolla's chapter represents the first systematic presentation of Archaic data from the northern Titicaca region. She notes the similarities and differences between the northern and the western basin, comparing her data to that of Aldenderfer and Klink. Like the Ilave area in the west, Early, Middle, Late, and Terminal Archaic sites are found in the north. Certain differences in the projectile point styles in the assemblage suggest to Cipolla that the well-known north-south cultural-geographical division of the basin so obvious in Qaluyu/Chiripa and Pukara/Tiwanaku times may have actually begun in the Late Archaic. The Archaic period data from the north basin are also critical for understanding the relationship between the northern Titicaca Basin and the Cuzco region further to the north over the pass of La Raya.

The transition from the Archaic to the Early Formative appears to be broadly correlated to some significant changes in climate. Unfortunately, paleoclimate data are ambiguous, and interpretations vary too much at this time to make any empirically sound assertions about the relationship between culture and environment. However, there does seem to be a consensus that a major mid-Holocene drought episode ended sometime between the beginning and the middle of the second millennium BC in the south-central Andes (e.g., see Abbott, Binford, Brenner, and Kelts 1997; Abbott, Seltzer, Kelts, and Southon 1997; Seltzer 1990, 1993; Seltzer et al. 1998). It is probably not a coincidence that greater reliance on agriculture, increasing sedentism, and modest population growth correlate to the higher precipitation levels at this time.

The Early Formative corresponds to a general settling of the population along the lake edges in small, undifferentiated villages. There is no evidence of corporate architecture or other indicators of rank. Survey data from various sources (e.g., Albarracin-Jordan 1992; Stanish and Plourde 2000; Stanish et al. 1997) suggest that largely sedentary villages first appeared around 2000–1500 BC. Many of these developed out of their Terminal Archaic predecessors. On the Island of the Sun, excavation data indicate a very smooth transition from the Terminal Archaic to the Formative, based upon analysis of a single midden from a multicomponent site. Pottery first developed by at least 1500 BC on the mainland and probably earlier (see Steadman in press) in the region as a whole. On the Island of the Sun, excavations at the single midden indicate that pottery was adopted a little later on the island than on the mainland.

The first ranked societies constitute the Middle Formative in our stage chronology. The most prominent Middle Formative political centers are Qaluyu in the north and Chiripa in the south. The earliest Chiripa and Qaluyu pottery dates to at least 1400 BC. These well-made vessels appear to be associated with a new emphasis on feasting and possibly the development of prestige-good economies in simple chiefly societies. Middle Formative societies rose and fell with some regularity throughout the region (Stanish 2003). By 800 BC or so, the sites of Pukara and Tiwanaku developed as two of a number of important chiefly centers in the region. By 200 BC, if not earlier, these two sites rose in prominence among their peers and constituted two of several major centers. The period in which complex regional polities (complex chiefdoms in some typologies) developed is defined here as the Upper Formative. Stanish (1999, 2003) defines these polities as complex chiefdoms. They are characterized by the development of two groups, elites and commoners, plus a distinctive corporate architecture, a regional settlement system, heightened economic exchange, and increased production of preciosities.

Christine Hastorf (Chapter 5, this volume) provides an exhaustive review of Upper Formative period settlements for the Titicaca region. She characterizes the period as one defined by the emergence and consolidation "...of multiple community ceremonial centers around the basin." She goes on to note that the time period is also dominated by "regional ethnic polities with a cohesive iconography" (Hastorf, Chapter 5, this volume). She marks the end of the Upper Formative with the shift to Tiwanaku dominance around the middle of the first millennium AD. Based upon a superb data set from her work at Chiripa (Hastorf 1999a, 1999b), she is able to divide the Upper Formative into Early, Late, and Terminal phases. Her chapter nicely summarizes the iconography, architecture, economy, and settlement distributions of Upper Formative sites.

Joel Myres and Rolando Paredes in Chapter 6 provide a report about one of the major islands on the northern side of the lake. Their chapter describes a fascinating pattern not described in any other area of the basin—paired sunken courts. In our survey of the west (Stanish et al. 1997) and north Titicaca Basin (Stanish and Plourde 2000), we never found any architectural pattern similar to that described by Myres and Paredes as the Isla Soto Archaeological Complex. The site of Pukara has three principal courts at its summit. Myres and Paredes place the Isla Soto courts in the Pukara tradition, dating the occupation of the site to the end of the Pukara period, around AD 200–400.

The Isla Soto remains are significant. We know that other islands in the lake—such as the Islands of the Sun and Moon, Isla Esteves outside of Puno, and possibly Amantaní—have pre-Inca architecture. Other islands, such as Pallalla near the Island of the Sun and many of the small islands in the little Lake Huiñamarca, have later remains as well (Bauer and Stanish 2001; Stanish and Bauer 2004). Islands were a very important part of the economic and cultural life of the region. Work on the Island of the Sun indicates that the first occupation dates back at least 4000 years. No systematic survey of the rest of the islands of Lake Titicaca has been conducted. This contribution by Myres and Paredes represents an important new data set for our nascent understanding of the island archaeology of the Titicaca region.

The collapse of the Pukara polity occurred no later than AD 400. Around AD 600, a phenomenon never before experienced in the Titicaca region—the first and only archaic state—developed in the Tiwanaku area. Tiwanaku expanded over a large area, incorporating adjacent territories up to the Ilave and Escoma Rivers. Beyond this area, Tiwanaku seems to have controlled roads and enclaves in strategic locations (Stanish 2002, 2003). Chapter 7 summarizes the Tiwanaku period in the northern and western Titicaca Basin. We learned that south of the Ilave River, the Tiwanaku occupation was generally built on the same settlements and architectural patterns as the earlier, pre-Tiwanaku sites. North of the Ilave River, Tiwanaku sites are far more scattered. In a few areas—such as the Puno Bay, Paucarcolla, Juliaca, and Taraco—Tiwanaku established enclaves or colonies. In between these areas we were unable to locate substantial Tiwanaku settlements at the densities seen in the Juli-Pomata or Pacajes (southern Titicaca region) areas. Chapters 8 and 9 provide insight into the Tiwanaku occupation on the Island of the Sun and the pre-Tiwanaku and Tiwanaku occupations at a major site on the western lake edge.

John Janusek provides a very important insight into the nature of Tiwanaku urbanism in Chapter 10. His summary of excavation data allows us a detailed view of domestic life in different sectors of the city. He illustrates the diversity of domestic life, discusses data about craft specialization, and details some of the patterns of growth of the urban complex. He notes, for instance, that occupation outside of the core area of Tiwanaku did not occur before AD 600. This is quite significant given Seddon's contribution in Chapter 9. Seddon's carbon dates from the major Tiwanaku ritual site on the Island of the Sun come in after AD 600 as well. These data, combined with the data presented in Chapter 7 suggest strongly that Tiwanaku did not expand out of its core territory until the seventh century AD. This is several centuries later than the date argued by Ponce Sanginés and others in earlier publications and serves to alter our understanding of Tiwanaku expansion. Parenthetically, we note that the very close development in time of Tiwanaku and the Wari state is indeed intriguing. Not a single Wari sherd has been found in the Titicaca Basin. However, the seemingly parallel rise and fall of Wari and Tiwanaku political dominance is indeed an important area for future research.

The Island of the Sun was home to almost thirty Tiwanaku sites. It was also almost certainly one of the first areas outside of the Tiwanaku Valley to be incorporated into the Tiwanaku state. Seddon's chapter discusses the Tiwanaku occupation of the Island of the Sun. He notes the very close ties to the Tiwanaku core, based upon ceramic analysis. Seddon's observation that the full range of Tiwanaku vessel types is found on the island is significant. Analysis of Tiwanaku sites in other areas, such as Moquegua (Goldstein 1989), suggest that other "provincial" assemblages were more selective. The significance of this empirical pattern remains to be more fully understood.

A significant observation is that Tiwanaku sites on the Island of the Sun align along a road that was later used by the Inca for the famous pilgrimage to the Sacred Rock area (Bauer and Stanish 2001; Stanish and Bauer 2004). This raises the intriguing possibility that the sandstone outcrop known as the Titikala and worshipped by the Inca was actually constructed during Tiwanaku times. Bauer and Stanish (2001) arrived at this conclusion, arguing that the pan-regional pilgrimage destination was a product of state ideologies. States only controlled the Island of the Sun during the Tiwanaku and Inca periods, and these were the only times in which elaborate architecture was associated with the Titikala area. Seddon (1998) takes a slightly different view, but still sees the Tiwanaku use of the island as linked to Tiwanaku state ideology.

Kirk Frye and Edmundo de la Vega provide us an excellent overview of the Late Intermediate or Altiplano period in the region in Chapter 11. This time in the Titicaca Basin is noted for the dramatic shifts in material culture and settlement patterns from the previous Tiwanaku period. In fact, it is no exaggeration to say that the Altiplano period represents the end of a cultural tradition that began at least two, and possibly three thousand years earlier. The art, architecture, and other cultural patterns that culminated in the Tiwanaku state began at least in the Middle Formative, if not as early as the Early Formative. The sunken court tradition, for instance, began in the early Middle Formative and became more elaborate and complex up through Tiwanaku. Flat-bottomed bowls, most likely linked to elaborate competitive feasting among elites, also started in the early Middle Formative and evolved into the *kero* of the Tiwanaku (Stanish 2003). Stone sculpture carving essentially stopped with the collapse of Tiwanaku. Settlement patterns shifted from a predominance of nucleated settlements with villages and hamlets in the Tiwanaku period and earlier, to a highly dispersed settlement system in which massive fortified hilltop sites were built to protect people living in hundreds of hamlets scattered over the landscape. Raised-field agriculture dramatically declined, pastoralism increased, and most forms of high-value commodity production ceased. Above-ground burials, known as *chulpas*, developed for the first time in the region as well.

The collapse of the Tiwanaku state ushered in truly momentous changes in the Titicaca region. We know from ethnohistoric documents that the Titicaca Basin was divided into a number of politically distinct groups. These included the Pacajes in the south, Lupaqa to the southwest, the Colla to the north and northeast, and a number of smaller polities to the east. The eastern groups were occasionally referred to as Omasuyos. Frye and de la Vega document many of these changes, focusing in particular on the Lupaqa.

Frye and de la Vega argue that climate change was a major factor in the shift from intensive agriculture to an agro-pastoral economy. They nicely note that the settlement data "...indicate a relatively fluid political landscape, characterized by alliance building and warfare between ever changing corporate groups" (Chapter 11, this volume). Ethnohistorical documents (e.g., the *Garci Diez Visita* as analyzed by Murra [1964, 1972]) suggest that Lupaqa political organization was highly complex, characterized by state societies. Frye (1997a) and Frye and de la Vega (Chapter 11, this volume) demonstrate that this interpretation is not supported by the archaeological data. Rather, they argue for intense factional competition between societies characterized by chiefly levels of organization. Such research serves to provide an important warning that historical documents are culturally filtered and can be biased, if not outright false in some cases (Stanish 1989c).

In 1994 a spectacular cave site with hundreds of basket burials was found in the Acora region inland from the lake. In the Aymara dictionary of Ludovico Bertonio, published in 1612, one entry defines a "chulpa" as a "basket" (*serón*) where bodies are kept. This enigmatic reference is apparently resolved with the discovery of numerous mummy bundles found in the cave of Molino-Chilacachi. Similar burials have been sporadically reported from around the circum-Titicaca Basin as well throughout Peru and Bolivia. This cave was excavated by de la Vega and Frye as a rescue operation a few years ago; and the results are described in Chapter 12. They discovered the remains of 166 individuals placed inside a cave with a restricted entrance. The cave materials date to the Altiplano period. Physical anthropological analyses by Tiffiny Tung indicate a wide range of

cranial deformation styles. The cave represents a type of burial practice that was most likely much more widespread throughout the region.

The Inca occupation of the Titicaca Basin represents the first time that an outside power controlled the Aymara-speaking lands. In Chapter 13, Frye offers a new summary of the region that incorporates regional data from the Pacajes, Lupaqa, and Colla areas. He nicely shows the similarities and differences between regions. Most significantly, he points out that the northern Colla area was more militarized than the Lupaqa area. This review article represents the first systematic attempt to work out the differences in Inca administrative policies within the Titicaca Basin, as opposed to differentiating the region with other areas of the central Andes (e.g., Stanish 1997). It is a welcome beginning to exciting new research.

Elizabeth Arkush offers the first systematic assessment of Inca ritual sites in the southwestern and southern Titicaca Basin in Chapter 14. She conducted a systematic reconnaissance of the region, beginning in the Copacabana area and moving to the west and north. She documented dozens of new and underreported sites in the area. In particular, she describes a number of carved rock sites that were located in several distinct locations. The lack of any strict spatial pattern of the numerous carvings along the known Inca road is important. As Arkush notes, the carvings "...clearly refer to Inka, rather than indigenous, ceremonial styles, yet they are highly varied in location, size, labor investment, and technical skill" (Arkush, Chapter 14, this volume). She notes that such a pattern would require, in at least four sites, a major detour from the main road. Six other sites would have required minor detours. A handful of others were directly on the road. The lack of any strict association between the road and the Inca-imposed ritual styles provides a fascinating look into the nature of local and imperial interactions as mediated by ideology during the Inca occupation.

One of the least-known archaeological regions in the Andes is the eastern slopes of the Titicaca Basin. The area in Bolivia known as Larecaja and the province in Peru known as Carabaya constitute some of the most remote places in the region. This area is famous in the alternative literature as the home of Paititi and Akakor, lost cities built in the forests perched above the mysterious Amazon. In Chapter 15, Lawrence Coben and Charles Stanish discuss the results of a brief reconnaissance into the area. This reconnaissance was facilitated by the construction of a new road to the hydroelectric plant at San Gabán. The results of just a few days' observations were striking. Vast numbers of late prehistoric sites were discovered along an ancient road. The pre-Hispanic road generally followed the course of the modern road, with some obvious differences where foot bridges could pass over streams and other topographic features.

The Carabaya region is outside of the Titicaca Basin hydrological drainage but is clearly part of the circum-Titicaca Basin in cultural terms. Sites with Colla- and Lupaqa-related pottery abound along the roads. One site in particular, first noticed by Coben and Stanish in a photograph in the office of the alcalde of Ollachea, is a fairly large and well-preserved Inca site that is located in a similar topographical location as Machu Picchu. The site of Illincaya (also spelled Illingaya) is perched above a protected hill at the edge of a road. Below the site are hot springs. The high-forest/low-forest ecotone begins just below the town of Ollachea, as it does at Machu Picchu. In fact, the existence of a major road with Late Intermediate and Inca period sites that cuts directly into the forest suggests a pattern that is similar to the settlement system from Cusco to Machu Picchu. These data raise the compelling possibility of more settlement systems created by late prehistoric polities up and down the eastern slopes of the Andes. Certainly, the Carabaya region was known to be a major source of gold for the Inca state. It is significant that the first major use of the road is pre-Inca, associated with northern Titicaca Basin polities. Our understanding of the eastern slopes is essentially nonexistent, and this chapter raises exciting new possibilities for future work.

Matthew Bandy and John Janusek provide a fascinating look at early Colonial period settlement shifts and demographic trends in Chapter 16. They first offer a refinement of the Late horizon and Early Colonial ceramic chronology of the Pacajes area. They then provide a very so-

phisticated analysis of the archaeological indicators of household size and material correlates of household artifact dispersals as they relate to assessing population estimates. Their analysis of the demographic and settlement shifts provided some very surprising results. While they did in fact discover substantial drops in the population of the Tiwanaku Valley and Katari Basin, they found that the population of the Taraco Peninsula increased during the Early Colonial period. They attribute this to the differences in administration between these areas. While the areas that experienced population decline were held by individual Spaniards as *encomiendas*, the Taraco area was a direct Crown holding. Their data therefore indicate that indigenous peoples preferred to live outside of the *encomienda* system in favor of living in Crown territories. The political tensions between *encomenderos* and the Spanish Crown are legion in the historical literature. Such archaeological data serve to complement and enhance our understanding of the complexities of early Colonial life, again providing a wholesome check on the often biased documentary data.

Chapter 17 of this volume catalogs and describes a number important sites found throughout the western and northern basin areas. Reconnaissance has been conducted by Programa Collasuyu members over many years. Most of these sites are outside of individual members' research areas but are too important to not be published.

Work continues in the Titicaca Basin at an ever-increasing rate. This volume reflects a small portion of the exciting results that continue to come out. At the present time, very important work is focused on the Formative period occupations in the northern basin. Excavations by Elizabeth Klarich (2004) at Pukara have uncovered domestic elite areas. Amanda Cohen (2003a, 2003b, 2004) has excavated two Formative period sites in the Pukara Valley including both ceremonial and domestic contexts. Rolando Paredes and his colleagues continue to work in the northern Basin. In the southern basin, survey projects are ongoing, including investigations by Matthew Bandy and Carlos Lémuz. Excavations at sites in the south are currently being conducted by John Janusek, Javier Escalante, Deborah Blom and Nicole Couture, and by Christine Hastorf and Matthew Bandy. Aimée Plourde (2004) has finished the analysis of settlement and excavation data from the site of Cachichupa near Putina. Carol Schultze has finished a project in the Puno Bay. Work on the Archaic and Early Formative periods, continues in the western and northern basin by Aldenderfer and his team. Future volumes in this series will highlight these new data and continue to build on our understanding of the archaeology of this fascinating area of the world.

2.

Archaic Period Research in the Río Huenque Valley, Peru

Cynthia J. Klink

INTRODUCTION

OUR UNDERSTANDING of the Archaic[1] period in the Lake Titicaca Basin[2] remains limited, hampered by a lack of research aimed specifically at illuminating this early prehistoric period in the region. Nearly all archaeological investigations in the region have focused exclusively on Formative period and later complex societies (see this volume; also Bermann 1994; Kolata 1996b; Mujica 1987; Stanish and Steadman 1994; Stanish et al. 1997). Preceramic period research on the Altiplano, while still in an incipient stage, began with Aldenderfer's Proyecto Ch'mak Pacha, a long-term archaeological project centered in the Río Ilave Valley, Peru (Aldenderfer 1996). I present in this paper the initial data from another recently initiated Archaic period research project, situated in the Río Huenque Valley in the southwestern lake basin, Peru (Figure 2.1).

The Río Huenque research project has two goals: to develop a firmer understanding of Preceramic settlement and adaptations on the Peruvian Altiplano, and to examine the process of initial human movement into and settlement of the region. Field research took place in two phases. The first phase (1997–98) involved intensive, systematic survey of four survey blocks in the river valley, and was aimed at obtaining a representative sample of sites and documenting their general characteristics and distribution. The second phase (1998) entailed intensive surface collection at a series of Early through Late Archaic period sites, and enables more detailed examination of changes in the use of specific lo-

cations within the valley over time. While data analysis is ongoing, the following summarizes the initial results of the 1997–98 survey phase.

THE PROJECT SETTING

The Modern Environment

The Río Huenque originates at the base of the western Cordilleran Mountains and flows northward across the Altiplano before emptying into the Río Ilave near Lake Titicaca (Figure 2.1). The region lies within the puna ecological zone, a high-elevation tundra-like grassland of low plant diversity and productivity (Aldenderfer 1989; Brush 1982; Molina and Little 1981; Thomas and Winterhalder 1976). Major subsistence resources are available year-round, and either cluster around *bofedales* (swamps) and other permanent water sources, or are found more widely dispersed throughout the surrounding mountains. The region's distinct wet/dry climatic seasonality results in seasonal size fluctuations in many streams, lagoons, and bofedales throughout the project area. Modern land-use within the Huenque Valley is almost exclusively pastoralism, with very limited agriculture occurring only on the northern periphery (downstream end) of the survey zone.

Dry and wet puna subtypes occur within the survey area (Aldenderfer 1989; Brush 1982; Molina and Little 1981; Thomas and Winterhalder 1976). Dry puna occurs in the higher-elevation southern and western rim of the Titicaca Basin, and is found in the upstream section of

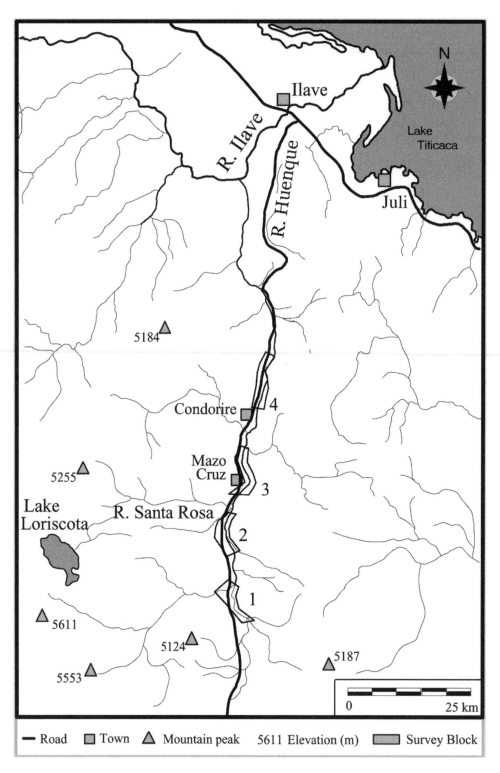

FIGURE 2.1. The Río Huenque Valley, with the location of the 1997 survey blocks

the Huenque Valley. Annual precipitation here is very low (300–800 mm), and may fall as snow, hail, or rain. While most precipitation typically falls during the November-to-March wet season, the onset and duration of the rainy season and total amount of rainfall can be quite unpredictable, and intense storms can occur at any time of year. Mean annual temperatures (1–6° C) are quite cold. Night frosts are common throughout the year, but extreme frosts are a typical daily occurrence during the dry season. These conditions create a marginal environment, and modern settlement in the dry puna zone is minimal. Wet puna occurs in the lower-elevation zone closer to Lake Titicaca, and is found in the middle to lower Huenque Valley. Annual precipitation is higher (700–1200 mm) and typically falls as rain, although hail and snow are possible. Mean annual temperatures are also higher (3–8° C), and night frosts occur primarily during the dry season. Modern settlement in the Huenque Valley is much greater in the wet puna zone.

Survey blocks 1 and 2 are located within the dry puna upstream section of the Río Huenque Valley. The valley bottom in Block 1 is poorly defined, and only a single, low river terrace is present. Extensive valley bottom bofedales are common, fed by high groundwater table seeps and springs along the Cordilleran Mountain base, and are clearly augmented by modern canal systems. Small groves of *queñua* trees occur in the mountains along the valley's western margin. Elevations in the Block 1 survey area range between 3995 and 4200 m. Within Block 2 the river valley is moderately developed, with typically two terrace flights present along the channel margins. Stream bottom bofedales remain common, but are smaller and appear to be partially replaced by small lagoons. Mountains immediately flank the valley's eastern margin. Elevations in the Block 2 survey area range between 3980 and 4135 m. Survey blocks 3 and 4 occur within the wet puna zone. The valley widens considerably just south (upstream) of Block 3, at the confluence of the Río Huenque and an important tributary, the Río Santa Rosa. Two to three terrace flights mark the river channel margin here. On the river's western margin, the upper terrace merges into a broad pampa whose surface con-

tains small, shallow pans that temporarily hold water during the rainy season. Mountains again flank the river to the east. Block 3 contains a couple of small lagoons and discontinuous, small, stream-side bofedales. Elevations in the Block 3 survey area range between 3960 and 4100 m. Within block 4, the river enters a gap cut through an anomalous east–west-trending mountain range. Caves and rock shelters are abundant, and terraced agricultural plots are scattered high among the rock outcrops. Small mountain-slope and *quebrada*-bottom bofedales appear, again apparently fed by mountain springs and seeps. Small queñual groves occur in more sheltered pockets on the mountain slopes. Elevations in the Block 4 survey area range between 3940 and 4200 m.

The Paleo-Environment

The 12,000 to 8,000 BP period, although for the most part cooler and moister than modern conditions, marked the onset of a long-term drying trend that began in fits and starts and accelerated more rapidly after 9000 BP. The transition from Late Pleistocene to Holocene conditions was more pronounced in the Bolivian than in the Peruvian Cordillera, due to the greater extent of glacial cover in the former (Baied and Wheeler 1993; Seltzer 1990, 1993). Glacial retreat in the Bolivian Cordillera began around 12,000 BP, and was marked by a series of still stands and readvances until about 10,000 BP (Abbott, Seltzer, Kelts, and Southon 1997; Seltzer 1993). After this time, glaciers rapidly retreated to near-modern limits by 9000 BP, and most valleys were completely deglaciated before 8000 BP (Abbott, Seltzer, Kelts, and Southon 1997; Seltzer 1990, 1993). Bofedales and small lakes formed in deglaciated terrain in both the Bolivian and Peruvian Cordilleras (Abbott, Seltzer, Kelts, and Southon 1997; Baied and Wheeler 1993; Graf 1981). Paleo-lake Tauca (Titicaca) began to drop from its high stand at 5–10 m above modern levels sometime after 11,000 BP (Clapperton 1993), and likely approached modern levels around 9000 BP (Abbott, Seltzer, Kelts, and Southon 1997). Recently deglaciated areas underwent pioneering vegetation stages (Graf 1981), and nonglaciated areas developed more extensive vegetation cover, which consisted of mixed grass-shrub lands likely with interspersed pockets of queñual forests (Baied and Wheeler 1993).

The 8000–4500 BP period is the extreme peak of Holocene aridity. The 8000–7000 BP portion marks the establishment of notably drier-than-present conditions. Beginning around 8000 BP, grasses increased at the expense of other vegetation, and at 7000 BP evidence for queñual forests essentially disappeared (Baied and Wheeler 1993). Lake Titicaca dropped in level from about 15 m below present at 8100–7700 BP (Wirrmann and Fernando de Oliveira 1987; Wirrmann and Mourguiart 1995; Wirrmann et al. 1988) to perhaps as much as 50 m below present by 7200 BP, and evaporate deposits formed across sections of the lake basin at this time (Wirrmann and Fernando de Oliveira 1987; Wirrmann et al. 1988). Between about 7000 and 5400 BP, many smaller lakes went through multiple periods of desiccation (Abbott, Seltzer, Kelts, and Southon 1997; Graf 1981), and vegetation cover decreased in extent (Graf 1981). By 5400 BP, many smaller lakes were completely desiccated and eroded (Abbott, Seltzer, Kelts, and Southon 1997), and extensive portions of Lake Titicaca had been exposed and erosionally truncated, with river channels cut into the newly exposed lake bottoms at depths up to 85 m below modern lake levels (Seltzer et al. 1998). The water chemistry in Lake Titicaca was quite saline, and closely resembled that of the modern brines in Lake Poopó, located further south on the Altiplano in the salt puna ecozone (Wirrmann and Mourguiart 1995).

Conditions began to ameliorate somewhat during the 4500–3000 BP period, although change apparently occurred very gradually. Lake Titicaca began to rise in level after circa 4500 BP (Wirrmann et al. 1988), but likely first came within 15–20 m below present around 3500–3300 BP (Abbott, Binford, Brenner, and Kelts 1997). Peat formation reoccurred in some previously desiccated bofedales around 4000 BP (Graf 1981). Small mountain glaciers reformed, an indicator of increased precipitation, beginning perhaps as early as 4000 BP, but most clearly between 3000 and 2500 BP in the eastern Cordillera (Abbott, Seltzer, Kelts, and Southon 1997; Seltzer 1990, 1993).

METHODOLOGY

The 1997–98 survey phase utilized a probabilistic, systematic, and intensive survey design. The locations of the four survey blocks were selected such that two blocks were located in each environmental zone. The blocks were evenly spaced along the valley and were of approximately equal size; each also contained roughly comparable features (mountains, terraces, bofedales or lagoons, etc.). All terrain within each block was systematically examined by pedestrian survey, with typically 10-m and no greater than 15-m intervals between crew members. "Sites" were operationally defined as locationally discrete artifact clusters, and their borders typically delimited based on where artifact densities fell below two to three artifacts within 10 m. Isolated projectile point finds were also recorded. "Components" refer to the chronological distinctions perceptible within the archaeological materials recovered at a site. Three artifact collection strategies were used, depending on site preservation, size, and content: grab samples, transect collections, and point-provenience collecting. Information on site size, artifact density, geomorphic and environmental setting, the kinds and distribution of artifacts or structures present, and state of preservation was recorded for all sites. Locations were fixed using a Global Positioning System (GPS).

The data analysis and interpretation generally follow the Preceramic periodization established by Aldenderfer (1998) at the site of Asana in the adjacent Peruvian high sierra, as modified for the Peruvian Altiplano by Aldenderfer and Klink (Aldenderfer and Klink 1996; Klink and Aldenderfer 1996). The Río Huenque project's chronological scheme has four Archaic periods: the Early Archaic, circa 10,000–8,000 BP; the Middle Archaic, circa 8000–6000 BP; the Late Archaic, circa 6000–4400 BP; and the Terminal Archaic, circa 4400–3600 BP. Projectile point style cross-dating provides the means for identifying chronologically distinct Archaic components at individual sites, and utilizes the projectile point typology defined by Klink and Aldenderfer (Chapter 3, this volume). This typology is based on excavation data from the sites of Asana (Aldenderfer 1998), Quelcatani, located in the Río Huenque watershed (Aldenderfer in press), Jiskairumoko, located in the Río Ilave Valley (Aldenderfer 1997), and other excavated sites within the broader region (Dauelsberg 1983; Lavallée et al. 1982; Neira 1990; Ravines 1967, 1972; Rick 1980; Santoro 1989; Santoro and Chacama 1984; Santoro and Nuñez 1987).

PROJECT RESULTS

Four blocks totaling 32.87 km^2 were surveyed during 1997–98 (Block 1, 8.33 km^2; Block 2, 8.51 km^2; Block 3, 8.39 km^2; Block 4, 7.64 km^2), and 300 sites were recorded. Of these, 151 sites contained one or more Archaic components, resulting in an Archaic period site density of 4.59 sites per km^2. The remaining sites contained only evidence of Formative period and later components (n = 122), or did not contain culturally or temporally diagnostic artifacts or features (n = 27). The majority of Archaic sites are multicomponent (n = 110, 73%). Open-air sites overwhelmingly predominate, with only a few cave or rock shelter sites clearly containing Archaic components (n = 3, 2%).

Archaic Period Site Densities

One of the major surprises of the Río Huenque project was the extremely high density of Archaic sites. While Aldenderfer's (1996) Río Ilave survey had reported an Archaic site density of 4.99 sites per km^2, this was considered inflated due to the opportunistic and judgmental survey methodology used. In contrast, Stanish and colleague's (1997) systematically designed Juli-Pomata survey along the Lake Titicaca shore recorded an Archaic site density of 0.02 sites per km^2. However, this density was considered too low for what could be expected in the Huenque project, since no major river valleys fell within the boundaries of Stanish's survey zone, and Aldenderfer's Ilave survey recorded a notable drop in the Archaic site density in the zone closest to Lake Titicaca (Klink and Aldenderfer 1996; Stanish et al. 1997). The results of Rick's (1980) Junin survey in the central Peruvian puna were also examined in an attempt to find another comparable systematically designed survey data set oriented to the Archaic period. His Archaic

site density of 0.13 sites per km^2 (Rick 1980), while comparable to Stanish and colleagues' (1997) density, was assumed to be lower than could be expected for the Río Huenque project, since vegetation cover in central Peru is heavier than in southern Peru and since Rick used less intensive survey methods than those used in the Huenque project.

Averaging the densities reported by these projects, an expected Archaic site density of 1.71 sites per km^2 was considered reasonable. The recorded Huenque Valley density of 4.59 sites per km^2 is significantly higher than expected, and is very similar to that reported by Aldenderfer (1996) for the Ilave Valley, despite notable differences in some of the survey methods used between these two projects. The high comparability of these results lend considerable support to the contention that Archaic period human settlement and land use concentrated within the interior valleys of the Lake Titicaca Basin, while the more lakeshore-oriented settlement pattern documented for the post-Archaic period and in the ethnohistoric record developed relatively late in prehistory (Aldenderfer and Klink 1996; Klink and Aldenderfer 1996).

General Component Trends

Among the 151 Archaic period sites, 205 distinct components were recognized. These include 29 Early Archaic components, 70 Middle Archaic components, 69 Late Archaic components, 22 Terminal Archaic components, 9 components that span the Early/Middle Archaic transition, and 6 components that straddle the Middle/Late Archaic transition. The transitional components will not be discussed further here. Table 2.1 presents the basic component data.

The first observation we can make is that there is a dramatic rise in component counts between the Early and Middle Archaic, a pattern also reported for the Río Ilave Valley (Aldenderfer 1996; Klink and Aldenderfer 1996). Two factors, perhaps working in concert, could account for the more than doubling of component counts between these periods. The first is population movement into the Lake Titicaca Basin. While areas such as the high sierra zone around the site of Asana saw continued use during the Middle Archaic (Aldenderfer 1998), this period in other

TABLE 2.1. Archaic period component counts and densities

	Sites with Archaic Components[#]	Early Archaic	Middle Archaic	Late Archaic	Terminal Archaic
Count	151	29	70	69	22
Density (per km^2)	4.59	0.88	2.13	2.10	0.67
Time-calibrated count*		7.25	17.50	21.56	13.75
Time-calibrated density (per km^2)*		0.22	0.53	0.67	0.42

\# Because of sites with multiple components, the total count is greater than the total number of sites.
* The time-calibrated count and calibrated density are calculated as the component count or the component density divided by the number of 500-year blocks comprising each Archaic period. They account for the variable time lengths of different periods and facilitate direct inter-period comparisons.

adjacent regions, such as the far southern Peruvian coast (Sandweiss et al. 1998) and the northern Chilean highlands (Santoro 1989; Santoro and Nuñez 1987), is marked by a notable decline or general absence of sites. Middle Archaic period migration into the Lake Titicaca Basin may have been one response to environmental changes associated with the onset of notable early to mid-Holocene climatic warming. The high degree of similarity in Early and Middle Archaic projectile point styles between the lake basin, the Chilean highlands, and the Peruvian coast minimally argue for cultural contact between these areas at this time (Klink and Aldenderfer 1996). The second possibility is the reorganization of settlement and mobility patterns within the basin, with greater mobility potentially contributing to higher site frequencies during this period. The shift to drier conditions on the Altiplano likely would have reduced environmental productivity in the lake basin (but to a lesser extent than in other, already relatively drier areas such as the coast, or the more southerly Chilean highlands), and would have increased resource patchiness. These environmental responses could have fostered either more frequent residential moves (lower productivity) or greater logistical mobility (increased patchiness).

Other than a modest increase in component count and density, there is relatively little difference between the Middle and Late Archaic components. The Terminal Archaic marks a period of more pronounced change, with component count and density decreasing substantially. Like the earlier increase, this pattern could have re-

sulted from either migration out of the Huenque survey zone and/or reduced mobility within it. Climatic conditions had begun to improve during the Terminal Archaic, and the likely resultant increase in resource productivity could have supported a land-use pattern oriented toward use of longer-term residential bases. Lake Titicaca also began to rise from its mid-Holocene low level, with water chemistry becoming increasingly fresh during this period. This should have increased the attractiveness of the near-shore zone, and could have fostered the initial shift toward more lakeshore-oriented settlement during this time. This period also marks a time of notable cultural change. Distinct, more geographically localized projectile point styles developed within the south-central Andes at this time, and multiple styles appeared (and overlapped temporally) within the basin, some of which suggest the first use of bow and arrow technology (Klink and Aldenderfer, Chapter 3, this volume). Ceramics were being used, and the first settled villages also likely began to appear, at least in portions of the basin, by the end of the Terminal Archaic (Aldenderfer 1997; Steadman in press). Together, these data more strongly support an interpretation of substantial settlement pattern reorganization and cultural change, rather than an interpretation of uniform population decline across the entire lake basin.

Environmental and Geographic Component Distribution Data
Another surprising result is the somewhat greater use of the dry puna rather than the wet puna en-

TABLE 2.2. Component distribution across environmental zones

	Early Archaic (n = 29)	Middle Archaic (n = 70)	Late Archaic (n = 69)	Terminal Archaic (n = 22)
Dry puna	55%	54%	58%	50%
Wet puna	45%	46%	42%	50%
Dry/wet puna density ratio*	1.17	1.13	1.31	0.94

* This ratio is calculated as the site density in the dry puna zone divided by the site density in the wet puna zone. It accounts for the slight size difference in total survey area coverage between the two zones. Values greater than 1.00 indicate greater use of the dry puna; values less than 1.00 indicate greater use of the wet puna.

TABLE 2.3. Component distribution by survey block*

	Early Archaic (n = 29)	Middle Archaic (n = 70)	Late Archaic (n = 69)	Terminal Archaic (n = 22)
Block 1	48%	39%	39%	18%
Block 2	7%	16%	19%	32%
Block 3	21%	27%	30%	45%
Block 4	24%	19%	12%	5%

* Percentages do not add up to 100 due to rounding error.

TABLE 2.4. Component distribution by resource-access zone[#]

	Early Archaic (n = 29)	Middle Archaic (n = 70)	Late Archaic (n = 69)	Terminal Archaic (n = 22)
Mt./upland*	34%	15%	13%	10%
Permanent water**	45%	52%	55%	64%
Other/ephemeral resources***	20%	33%	32%	27%

\#   Percentages do not add up to 100 due to rounding error.
*   Mountaintops, slopes and fans.   ** River terrace, bofedal, or lake margins.   *** Hills, pampas.

vironmental zone, a robust pattern that endures throughout most of the Preceramic period (Table 2.2). The relative use of the dry puna consistently hovers around 55% from Early through Late Archaic times. The distribution first becomes slightly skewed toward greater use of the wet puna zone during the Terminal Archaic period, which suggests that this period may indeed mark the initial shift toward greater use of more lakeshore-oriented land-use systems.

This pattern, the opposite of what was initially expected, has a couple of implications. First, the greater use of the dry puna rather than the wet puna during most of the Preceramic indi-

cates an erroneous assessment of the early prehistoric settlement potential of these zones, which was based on relative differences in modern climatic conditions and population distributions. Second, the persistence of this pattern, despite other major changes in Preceramic settlement, implies that such large-scale environmental variability played a relatively minor role in Archaic period developments in the Titicaca Basin, until perhaps Terminal Archaic times. Instead, it seems that geographic position within the valley and local environmental variability exerted greater influence (see Tables 2.3 and 2.4).

The distribution of components by survey block (Table 2.3) provides a means of examining changing site distributions along a transect from the Río Huenque headwaters at the base of the western Cordillera (Block 1) toward Lake Titicaca (Block 4). Over the course of the Preceramic period, the relative intensity of land use shifted from the upper watershed (Block 1) to the more downstream reaches (Blocks 2 and 3). However, the use of Block 4, which exhibits a general pattern of relatively low use-intensity, also declined over time. The relative drop of use-intensity in Blocks 1 and 4 may be related to the shift away from mountain/upland resource-access zones (see below), which, at least currently, are richest in Blocks 1 and 4.

The Early Archaic components are strongly clustered in Block 1, with nearly half of all components from this period found here. The percentages of Early Archaic components are much lower in all other blocks, but their proportions do rise moving in the downstream direction. This highly skewed distribution suggests that the initial use of the valley was concentrated in the higher-elevation areas closest to the western Cordillera and sierra valleys, with substantially lower use of other areas. It also implies that the initial entry into the southwestern Titicaca Basin may have come from the western Andean flanks, as proposed by Aldenderfer (1993, 1998).

In contrast, during the Middle Archaic, the components have a stronger bimodal distribution, concentrating primarily in Blocks 1 and 3. Compared to the Early Archaic, the relative use of Block 1, and to a lesser extent Block 4, declined while the use of Blocks 2 and 3 rose. This pattern suggests that new settlement shifted in the downstream direction toward previously lightly used areas, and perhaps were preferentially oriented toward Block 3. The Late Archaic pattern strongly resembles that of the Middle Archaic, indicating little alteration in settlement strategies during these periods.

A dramatic change took place during Terminal Archaic times. Components show a strong unimodal distribution, but for the first time the greatest use was concentrated in Block 3 and decreased in the upstream (interior) direction. This supports the hypothesis that the Terminal Archaic represents a significant reorientation in settlement strategies and the initial shift toward relatively greater use of the zone closer to Lake Titicaca (Aldenderfer 1996; Aldenderfer and Klink 1996). Comparison of Terminal Archaic and Post-Archaic site densities between the Río Ilave (Aldenderfer 1996) and Río Huenque survey zones solidly buttresses this argument. The Terminal Archaic component densities are slightly higher in the Ilave Valley (0.81 sites/km^2) than in the Huenque Valley (0.67 sites/km^2), and this density differential increases even more substantially in the Post-Archaic period. The Post-Archaic component density in the Río Ilave Valley (14.05 sites/km^2) is double that of the Huenque Valley (6.94 sites/km^2).

The distribution of components by resource-access zone (Table 2.4) also reveals notable changes over the course of the Archaic. Resource-access zones were defined based on geomorphic site settings. Mountain/upland settings—which include mountaintops, mountain slopes, and fans at mountain bases—should provide access to dispersed resources such as taruca (deer) and vicuña in queñual forest and tola shrub land (Aldenderfer 1998), and to smaller, rocky-habitat animals such as viscacha and some ground-nesting birds. Permanent water settings include river terrace margins and the immediate edges of lakes and bofedales, and would have provided access not only to water, but to all animals found habitually using these habitats, particularly the vicuña (Aldenderfer 1998), and likely a variety of birds. All other geomorphic settings, such as the lower-elevation hills and ridges interspersed across the pampas and the pampas themselves, likely would have provided access to limited and more unpredictable resources. The bunch-grass-dominated plant communities found in these areas have very low productivity and generally provide only low-grade forage for herbivores (Aldenderfer 1998), although rodents such as chinchilla can be found here. During the wet season, shallow pans on the pampas surface fill with water and provide temporary camelid grazing areas for modern-day pastoralists.

Throughout the Preceramic period, the use of mountain/upland areas decreased while the use of permanent water settings increased. The Early Archaic components are the most evenly distributed, with the greatest use of upland-oriented settings during this period. This suggests that resource use likely was most diversified, perhaps indicating a random-encounter foraging strategy, but one focused on those habitats with the highest likely resource productivity and predictability. The use of upland habitats decreased substantially during the Middle Archaic, and was replaced primarily by the greater use of ephemeral resource habitats and to a lesser extent by the use of permanent water habitats. The onset of drier conditions in the early to mid-Holocene likely reduced the extent and/or productivity of upland vegetation communities, lowering the attractiveness of this resource zone. This land-use trend continued for the remainder of the Preceramic, with Terminal Archaic land use appearing most focused on permanent water resource settings. This notable focus on habitats best suited for vicuña suggests that resource acquisition may have become much more strongly focused on these animals over time. The same habitats preferred by vicuña are also those best suited for domesticated camelids, and these land-use patterns may also signal the onset of herding and camelid domestication by the Terminal Archaic times or during the Terminal Archaic period. However, the Terminal Archaic pattern differs dramatically from that for the post-Archaic period, when pastoral economies should have been firmly in place. The Post-Archaic component distribution (mountain/upland 35%, permanent water 29%, other/ephemeral 36%) most closely resembles the highly diversified pattern of the Early Archaic period. This pattern could have resulted from either the shift to substantially wetter conditions after circa 3600 BP, or the emergence of fully pastoral economies, which would have allowed people to use a more diverse range of habitats because they could ensure access to animal resources by moving herds with them.

Site Size and Density Trends

Until more detailed analyses of the contents and structures of individual sites can be completed, general site size and artifact density data provide the only means of examining changes in settlement pattern and organization over time. Size and density are examined using two data sets: all sites, and single-component sites only. The first has the advantage of larger sample sizes, but site sizes and artifact densities are likely inflated due to multiple reoccupations. Using only single-component sites reduces, but does not eliminate, this potential source of error. Unfortunately, the single-component site samples are extremely small and therefore likely do not constitute representative samples. Several simplifying assumptions must be made in order to interpret the results of these analyses. First, site size is assumed to serve as a reasonable proxy measure of the size of the co-residential group, with larger site sizes indicating larger residential groups. Second, artifact density is presumed to be a reasonable indicator of site-use intensity, with higher artifact densities indicating longer-duration occupations and/or more frequent site reuse during each period.

Examining quantitative changes in average site size (Table 2.5), both data sets are in agreement for certain general trends. These robust patterns include the following. Mean site size decreases between the Early and Middle Archaic, and again between the Late and Terminal Archaic. Mean size increases from Middle to Late Archaic times, but does not attain the level noted for the Early period. Reliable assessment of absolute size changes is hampered by notable variability between the two data sets, but the single-component data suggests site size changes may have been quite substantial.

Mean site sizes were highest during the Early Archaic, suggesting that co-residential group sizes may have been largest at this time. This conflicts with the stereotypical image of small bands of early hunter-gatherers, but as data from Monte Verde (Dillehay 1997) indicates, some very early foragers also lived in relatively large groups. Larger co-residential group size may have been an adaptive strategy used by early colonists in the Titicaca Basin to decrease the risk of reproductive failure (Beaton 1991) or lower the risk of subsistence failure by pooling individual risk (Kelly 1995). The reduction in mean site size from the Early to Middle Archaic suggests that the significant

TABLE 2.5. Quantitative site size data (in m^2)

	Early Archaic	Middle Archaic	Late Archaic	Terminal Archaic
All sites[1]				
Mean	6963	5092	5855	5341
Standard deviation (m^2)[2]	*6625*	*4795*	*6287*	*4485*
n	24	66	63	18
Single component[3]				
Mean	5084	2672	3325	1383
Standard deviation (m^2)	*0*	*2046*	*1237*	*915*
n	1	7	2	5

1. All single- and multicomponent sites with diagnostic material for a specific component, not including isolated point finds, when quantitative data were recorded. One exceptionally large Ceramic period site overlying a much smaller Preceramic occupation was not included because it significantly skewed average size computations.

2 Standard deviations nearly equal or exceed the mean in cases when the size distribution does not conform perfectly to a normal distribution.

3. Sites with material diagnostic of only a single Archaic period, not including isolated point finds, when quantitative data were recorded.

TABLE 2.6. Qualitative artifact density distributions

All Sites[1]	Early Archaic (*n* = 25)	Middle Archaic (*n* = 68)	Late Archaic (*n* = 65)	Terminal Archaic (*n* = 20)
Low-density sites	8%	18%	18%	20%
Moderate-density sites	40%	35%	34%	25%
High-density sites	52%	47%	48%	55%
Single-component sites[2]	Early Archaic (*n* = 1)	Middle Archaic (*n* = 7)	Late Archaic (*n* = 2)	Terminal Archaic (*n* = 5)
Low-density sites	0%	29%	100%	40%
Moderate-density sites	100%	57%	0%	60%
High-density sites	0%	14%	0%	0%

1. All single- and multicomponent sites with diagnostic material for a specific component, not including isolated point finds, when artifact density data were recorded. One exceptionally large Ceramic period site overlying a much smaller Preceramic occupation was not included because it significantly skewed average size computations.

2. Sites with material diagnostic of only a single Archaic period, not including isolated point finds, when artifact density data were recorded.

increase in Middle Archaic component counts may be partially accounted for by population dispersal into smaller residential groups. The moderate increases in Late Archaic site sizes imply somewhat greater population aggregations, and this, combined with the modest increase in Late Archaic (time-calibrated) component density, suggests at least some population growth over Middle Archaic times. The Late to Terminal Archaic decrease in mean size is difficult to interpret, given the substantial difference in the apparent magnitude of change between the two data sets. Relying on all sites, change in residential group size may have been minimal. In contrast, the single-component data suggests a significant shift to perhaps the smallest residential group sizes of the entire Preceramic.

The artifact density distributions for the sites (Table 2.6) reveal that the Early Archaic may have been the most sedentary period, as this period had the highest proportion of moderate- and high-density sites (both data sets). Mobility apparently increased in the Middle Archaic, with higher proportions of low-density sites occurring at this time (both data sets). However, the magnitude of this shift is difficult to assess, given the notable differences between the two data sets and the extremely small sample of single-component Early Archaic sites. The single-component data suggests that mobility may have become more complexly organized during the Middle Archaic, with a wider array of longer- and shorter-term sites used, and/or higher reoccupation frequencies at some sites. This greater complexity suggests a shift toward a more logistically organized (sensu Binford 1980) mobility pattern relative to the Early Archaic. Subsequent trends are difficult to discern because of conflicting trends between the two data sets. There was either no change from the Middle to Late Archaic (all sites), or a shift back to a less complex, residentially organized (sensu Binford 1980) mobility pattern more like the Early Archaic, but characterized by higher mobility (single-component sites). The Late to Terminal Archaic trend is clearer, as both data sets indicate a shift toward more longer-term occupations during Terminal Archaic times. However, the magnitude of this change is uncertain, as is whether it was accompanied by a shift from residential to more logistically organized settlement (single-component sites) or not (all sites).

DISCUSSION

The surprisingly high Archaic site densities in the Huenque Valley greatly strengthen the hypothesis that the majority of Archaic period developments played out in the more interior sections of the Lake Titicaca Basin rather than along the lakeshore (Aldenderfer and Klink 1996; Klink and Aldenderfer 1996). This is further supported by comparisons of site densities between the Ilave and Huenque Valleys that indicate that substantially greater use of areas closer to Lake Titicaca first occurred during Post-Archaic times. This shift in land-use focus makes sense within the context of the clearly documented early through mid-Holocene dry phase in the broader region, which first began to ameliorate during the Terminal Archaic and most closely resembled modern conditions after circa 3600 BP. As noted earlier, mid-Holocene warming caused a significant drop in the level of Lake Titicaca and dramatically increased salinity levels and reduced lacustrine productivity (Selt-

zer et al. 1998; Wirrmann and Mourguiart 1995; Wirrmann et al. 1988).

The Early Archaic components represent the first clear human use of the Titicaca Basin. This initial occupation occurred during the period of climatic amelioration developing after the peak of glacial conditions at the end of the Late Pleistocene. The more extensive glaciation in the Bolivian Cordillera, particularly on its eastern flank where large mountain glaciers lasted until circa 10,000–9,000 BP (Abbot, Seltzer, Kelts, and Southon 1997), would have limited the potential for early human entry into the Titicaca Basin from the eastern lowlands. Initial access to the lake basin more likely came from the west. In the Peruvian Cordillera, glaciation was less extensive, deglaciation began earlier (Seltzer 1990, 1993), and faunal and vegetal communities did not experience as radical a change as they did in other areas to the south and east (Baied and Wheeler 1993). The low Early Archaic component count and density, the clear clustering of Early Archaic components in Block 1 near the Río Huenque headwaters, and the strong similarity in projectile point styles between the lake basin and the Peruvian/Chilean coast and sierra valleys at this time all support the hypothesis that the Titicaca Basin was first explored and settled by small numbers of lower-elevation groups from the western flanks of the Peruvian Cordillera (Aldenderfer 1998). These early settlers utilized a broad range of resource zones, but land use focused on more productive and predictable habitats, including mountainous, upland environments. Settlement patterns may have been based on a system of residential mobility, with larger residential groups occupying sites for longer periods of time relative to later Archaic periods.

The notable increase in component count and density during the Middle Archaic suggests greater use of the Titicaca region at this time. Based on the decrease in average site size, at least some of the component increase is likely due to population dispersal into smaller residential groups. However, even the extreme magnitude of the site size change suggested by the single-component data set is insufficient to completely account for the component increase in the Middle Archaic. Some migration into the lake basin likely also occurred, probably by members of groups living in the relatively more arid Peruvian/Chilean coast and western valleys. This hypothesis is supported by the substantial decrease in the number of sites in these areas at this time, and by the similarity of Middle Archaic projectile point styles between these areas and the lake basin. During the Middle Archaic, settlement intensity shifted further downstream in the Río Huenque Valley. Land-use patterns became less focused on mountain habitats and more concentrated around permanent water resources, and the use of lower-quality ephemeral resource zones increased substantially. This was most likely a response to increased aridity that reduced the resource potential of upland habitats as queñual forests and tola shrublands declined, and increased the importance of water. Mobility apparently became more logistically organized as environmental patchiness likely increased.

The Late Archaic period witnessed the continuation of many trends initiated during the Middle Archaic. The time-calibrated component count and density increase, as do the mean site sizes, suggesting in-situ population growth and/or some continued migration into the region. In-migration, however, seems highly unlikely, given that the number of Late Archaic sites in adjacent regions also increased substantially at this time (Sandweiss et al. 1998; Santoro 1989), and that stylistic similarities in projectile points between the Altiplano and other regions decreases at this time (Klink and Aldenderfer, Chapter 3, this volume). Land-use patterns closely mimic those of the Middle Archaic, perhaps becoming slightly more focused on permanent water and less so on upland habitats. It is unclear whether mobility patterns changed, but the artifact density data (for single-component sites) suggests a shift toward greater residentially organized mobility and shorter-term site occupations.

Much more notable changes mark the Late to Terminal Archaic transitions, relative to those from the Middle to the Late Archaic. Terminal Archaic time-calibrated component count and density decreased significantly from Late Archaic levels, while mean site size also decreased, albeit to an unknown degree. For the first time

settlement intensity shifted to the wet puna zone and the downstream survey blocks. These data suggest population dispersal both into smaller residential groups and into areas closer toward Lake Titicaca, likely including areas outside of the Río Huenque survey limits (based on the slightly higher component density in the Río Ilave valley) (Aldenderfer 1996). Within the Huenque Valley, land use during the Terminal Archaic also became heavily concentrated around permanent water settings, more so than at any other point during the Preceramic. This is accompanied by a shift, relative to the Late Archaic, toward more longer-term occupations and perhaps greater logistical mobility. That increased settlement "water tethering" (more longer-term occupations, focused around permanent water sources) actually coincides with improving (wetter) climatic conditions suggests that climate change is not solely or directly responsible for this aspect of settlement change. Instead, better access to reliable, year-round water sources may have become more valuable at this time because of increased sedentism and/or greater economic reliance on herding or plant cultivation.

Conclusion

Our knowledge about Preceramic developments in the Titicaca Basin is in a fairly rudimentary stage. This analysis of the site survey data from the Río Huenque Valley project allows us to propose a firmer outline of Archaic period land-use and settlement trends in the region, and highlights important issues and new directions for future research. Inherent limitations in this data set point out the need for more detailed examinations of site structure for aiding interpretations of changing land-use and settlement strategies over time. Ongoing analyses of data from the 1998 intensive collection research phase should bring these subjects into much sharper focus.

Notes

1. The terms "Archaic" and "Preceramic" are used interchangeably.
2. The terms "Lake Titicaca Basin" and "Altiplano" are used synonymously.

3.

A Projectile Point Chronology for the South-Central Andean Highlands

Cynthia Klink and Mark Aldenderfer

INTRODUCTION

OUR GOAL WITH this chapter is to define a temporally sensitive projectile point typology for the south-central Andean highlands. The past ten to fifteen years have seen an increasing amount of archaeological research in the altiplano and the adjacent puna and high sierra of Peru, Bolivia, and Chile (Albarracin-Jordan 1996a, 1996b; Aldenderfer 1998; Bermann 1994; Hastorf 1999b; Janusek 1999; Kolata 1996b; Mujica 1987; Pärssinen and Siiriäinen 1997; Santoro and Nuñez 1987; Stanish 1997; Stanish and Steadman 1994; Stanish et al. 1997). Most of these investigations have focused on the more recent portion of prehistory—the Formative through Inca periods—and these efforts have produced both better-defined ceramic chronologies and a more refined understanding of cultural developments during these periods. In comparison, the Preceramic period remains relatively unknown, and projectile points in general, regardless of age, have received scant attention. It is becoming increasingly clear that this knowledge gap results from a lack of research focused on these topics. Recent survey projects by the authors document a substantial Preceramic human presence within the region (Aldenderfer 1996; Klink 1998). Other researchers, examining later time periods, not only are encountering Preceramic sites during surveys, but also are finding that projectile points often are common items of post-Preceramic period material culture (Stanish and Steadman 1994; Stanish et al. 1997; Lisa Cipolla, Aimée Plourde, Amanda Cohen, and Matt Bandy, all personal

communication, 1999). However, our ability to understand and interpret these finds, especially those from surface contexts, is limited if we cannot reliably assess their cultural/temporal affiliations. We attempt to rectify this problem with the projectile point typology presented below.

Background

This typology is based on projectile point data from excavated and radiocarbon-dated contexts within the south-central Andean highlands (Figure 3.1), and it should be viewed as directly applicable only within this region. The northern limit of this region is defined by the Río Camana/Majes drainage in the Department of Arequipa, and in the south between the Ríos Camarones and Camiña in northern Chile. The western flanks of the Andes define the western limits of the region, while to the east, it includes the high puna stretching through Peru, Chile, and Bolivia eastward to the continental divide. As more sites in the highlands are added to the database, it will be possible to expand the geographic scope of the typology.

The projectile point assemblages from the sites of Asana (Aldenderfer 1998) and Quelcatani (Aldenderfer, in press), located in southern Peru (see Figure 3.1), are the foundation of this chronology. These sites are the only deeply stratified, well-dated, extensively excavated sites within the region that contain Preceramic through Formative period and later deposits. Asana is a deeply stratified, open-air site located at 3435 m elevation, in the high sierra ecozone of the western Cordillera. Excavations covered

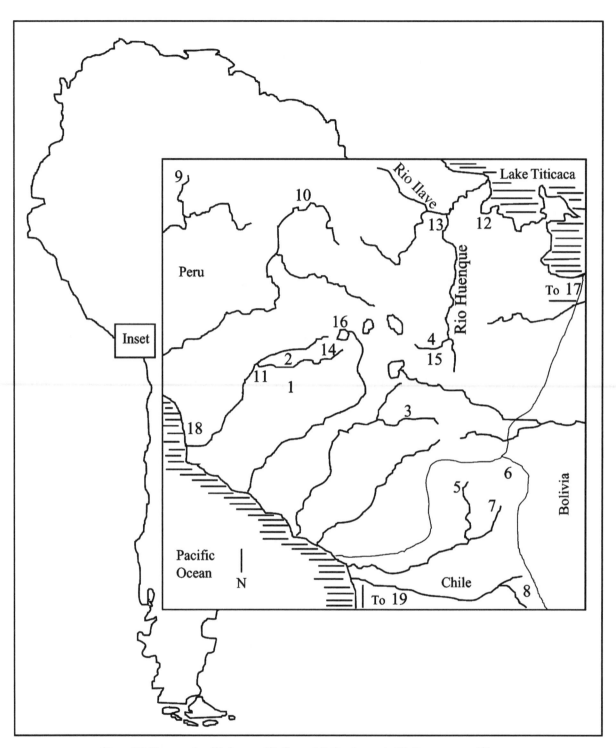

Sites: (1) Toquepala, (2) Asana, (3) Caru, (4) Quelcatani, (5) Patapatane, (6) Hakenasa, (7) Las Cuevas, (8) Tojo-Tojones, (9) Sumbay, (10) Ichuña, (11) Omo, (12) Tumatumani, (13) Jiskairumoko, (14) El Panteon, (15) Tumuku, Quelkata, (16) Titijones, (17) Tiwanaku, (18) Yara, (19) Acha-2, Camarones-14.

FIGURE 3.1. Select sites and locations in the south-central Andean highlands

over 350 m² of area, reaching depths of 3.0 below the surface in portions of the site. Thirty radiocarbon dates document the Early through Terminal Archaic/Early Formative site occupation, spanning a period from ca. 10,000 to 3,400 BP. Quelcatani is a deeply stratified rock shelter situated at 4420 m elevation, in the dry puna ecozone of the altiplano. Excavations here covered 48 m² of area, and attained a maximum depth of 1.5 m below the surface. The suite of 15 radiocarbon dates and diagnostic ceramics indicate use of the site from ca. 7300 to 500 BP, with the most intensive site use occurring during the Late/Terminal Archaic through Inca times. Most other excavated sites in the region have tested only small areas, have only one or two radiocarbon dates to support the proposed site chronologies, and/or encountered archaeological deposits dating to limited periods of prehistory (Aldenderfer 1997; Neira 1990; Santoro 1989; Santoro and Nuñez 1987; Stanish and Steadman 1994). Data from these sites are discussed and integrated as appropriate in the text that follows. We also draw on point type frequency data from survey projects in the Río Huenque (Klink 1998) and Río Ilave (Aldenderfer 1996) Valleys, in the southwestern portion of the Titicaca Basin, in order to assess the prevalence of individual point types within the broader region.

Certain limitations of this typology must be made explicit. First, projectile point styles that are known only from surface finds or from undated excavated contexts are not incorporated into this typology, since our objective is the construction of a temporally sensitive classification scheme. Therefore, this typology does not completely encompass the known range of projectile point variation within the region. Second, most research has been conducted in the southern Lake Titicaca Basin and the adjacent western Cordillera, producing a somewhat geographically skewed data set. Despite these difficulties, we believe that the existing data are more than adequate to outline temporal changes in projectile point forms and attributes for the area, and that the typological format used here is robust and flexible enough to incorporate new data as they become available.

Methods, Definitions, and Measures

Two basic components provide the structural framework for this typology: *series*, which are broad categories defined by a general set of shared attributes, and *types*, which are series subdivisions that are delineated by differences in other characteristics. *Diagnostic characteristics* are the essential attributes a point must exhibit to be classified into a specific series and type. Other shared attributes are mentioned when describing the projectile point examples used to define a type or series, but these are not considered diagnostic characteristics. Some characteristics may ultimately prove to be so, but the definitions intentionally are left more inclusive at this stage.

The descriptive sections for individual point types include brief discussions of comparative data from excavated and radiocarbon-dated sites outside of the south-central Andean highlands and, occasionally, other sites within the region that have less than ideal temporal control. These regional comparisons help us to evaluate the extent of cultural similarities and social interconnections through space and time, and when secure radiocarbon-dated contexts are limited within the south-central Andean highlands these regional comparisons serve to support or augment the age assessments of our point types. In these cases, data from the geographically closest areas are weighted most heavily. Readers seeking more detailed information about these sites should refer to the cited original sources. All radiocarbon dates and age ranges presented here are uncalibrated BP dates. Please note that the terms "Archaic" and "Preceramic" are used interchangeably.

All projectile points minimally have a blade element, for piercing or cutting, and a haft element, for securing and mounting the tool into some type of shaft. Other elements, defined here, may or may not be present. A *shoulder* is the point along the tool margin where there is a clear change in the angle of tool margin orientation, from a straight or expanding blade to a contracting, expanding, or straight haft. This point typically is the point of maximum tool width, and marks the haft/blade transition. If there is no change in tool margin angle, or there is only a general zone of change rather than a single, distinct point, the tool is unshouldered. A *stem* is a characteristic of the haft element. A projectile point is considered stemmed if there is a clear change in the angle of the haft margin along the line running from the shoulder to the base, typically resulting in a reduction of width relative to shoulder width along a portion of the haft. *Blade edge modification* is intentional retouch that creates a toothed or jagged blade margin. This is divided into three qualitatively different types: serration, or very finely spaced retouch; denticulation, or retouch that creates moderately spaced teeth; and spining, or the presence of only a few, widely spaced teeth or projections along the blade margin. A *spine* is a barb or small projection that juts outward from the tool margin. While it may appear as blade edge modification, it may also occur at the shoulder or as a "lashing" feature at the blade/haft transition of unstemmed, unshouldered pieces. Spines at the shoulder of spine-shouldered forms (Series 1, below) may create the spurious appearance of a stem, precisely because a spine by definition projects outward from the tool margin. If the appearance of a stem is attributable solely to the presence of a shoulder spine, the point is considered unstemmed.

Some attribute measurements and ratios should be explained. *Shoulder angle* (Figure 3.2a) is the angle between the longitudinal midline of the tool and the line defined by the proximal side (side toward the haft) of the shoulder. If the shoulders are asymmetrical, the smaller angle is used. An angle less than 90° describes acute-angled shoulders (shoulder apex points more toward the tool tip than toward the tool base). Angles greater than 90° indicate barbed shoulders (the shoulder apex points more toward tool base than toward the tool tip). *Haft angle* (Figure 3.2b) is the angle between a line perpendicular to the longitudinal midline and the line following the haft margin. A 90° haft angle indicates a straight, parallel-sided haft. Values less than 90° denote contracting hafts, with smaller angles indicating more tightly contracting haft margins. *Basal width* is measured as the distance along the base that can be placed flush against a ruler. *Tool length/tool width* and *blade length/tool width* ratios describe general tool form and blade shape, respectively, with values greater than 1.00 indicating more elongated forms. *Haft length/blade length* ratios define how low- or high-waisted the tool is. Values greater than 1.00 indicate a high-waisted haft (haft longer than blade); those less than 1.00 indicate a low-waisted haft (blade longer than haft). *Haft width/tool width* ratios, calculated for stemmed tools only, tell whether the item is broad-stemmed (values greater than or equal to 0.50) or narrow-stemmed (values less than 0.50).

The tables below present quantitative attribute data for individual type specimens. All measurements are given in millimeters. Haft and shoulder angles are in degrees, and are rounded to the nearest five degrees. These data enhance objective description, and facilitate the

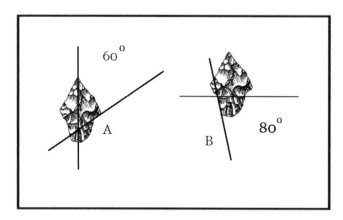

FIGURE 3.2. *(a)* Shoulder angle, *(b)* haft angle

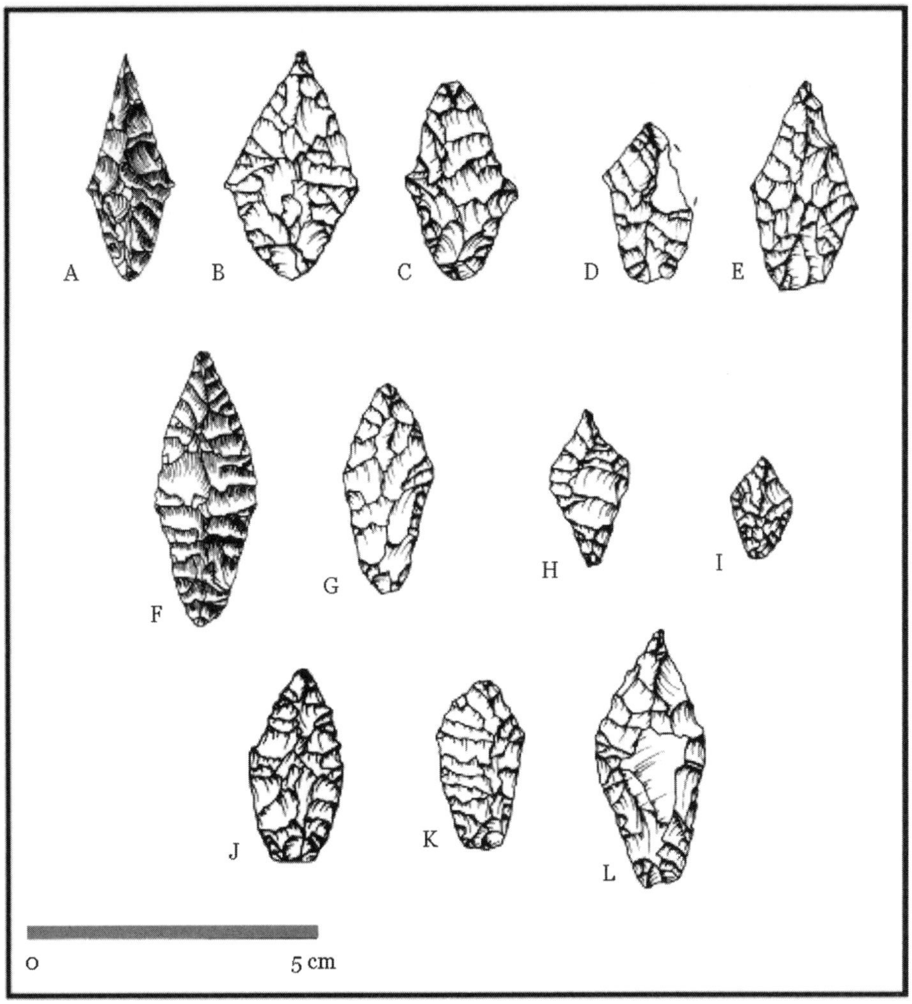

FIGURE 3.3. Types 1A–1B, 2A–2C. Type 1A: *(a)* Asana, level PXXVII, *(b)* Patapatane, after Santoro and Nuñez 1987:Figure 5-13, *(c)* Caru, after Ravines 1967:Figure XXVI-#14. Type 1B: *(d)* Asana, level PXXIV, *(e)* Patapatane, after Santoro and Nuñez 1987:Figure 5-14. Type 2A: *(f)* Asana, level PXXV, *(g)* Quelcatani, level WXXXV. Type 2B: *(h)* Quelcatani, level WXXXI(a), *(i)* Quelcatani, level WXXXI. Type 2C: *(j)* Quelcatani, level WXXXI, *(k)* Quelcatani, level WXXXV, *(l)* Caru, after Ravines 1967:Figure XXVII-17.

assessment of similarities and differences between types. The Asana projectile points were directly examined for this analysis. All measurements for the Quelcatani specimens came from digital photographs. Measurements for tools from other sites were generated from scaled drawings published in the original texts.

SERIES 1. SPINE-SHOULDERED FORMS

The diagnostic characteristics of Series 1 are (1) absence of a stem, (2) presence of a shoulder, and (3) the presence of spines on the shoulder.

The series is divided into types based on overall shape: diamond/foliate (1A), and pentagonal (1B). All of the Series 1 examples share two additional similarities: acute shoulder angles (shoulder angles of 20–55°) and contracting haft margins (haft angles of 65–85°). Spine-shouldered pieces are diagnostic of the Early Preceramic ca. 10,000–8,000 BP.

1A. Diamond/Foliate

This type (Figure 3.3a–c, Table 3.1) is defined based on three examples from Asana, two from Patapatane (Santoro and Nuñez 1987), and two from Caru (Ravines 1967). Its diagnostic characteristic is an elongated, diamond to foliate shape. All examples have straight or very slightly excurvate haft margins that typically contract to convex bases; one has a straight base. All have narrow basal widths (1–2 mm), similar contracting haft angles (65–75°), and moderate-waisted hafts (haft length/blade length ratios of 0.65–1.00). Blade edge modification is present on three specimens. The two Patapatane points differ in having somewhat greater tool widths (24–25 mm). One of these pieces (Santoro and Nuñez 1987:Fig. 5–17) looks transitional between our types 1A, 2A, and 3B. It resembles 2A in having a long haft, and 3B in its large size and blade edge denticulation. However, it differs from the 2A and 3B forms in having at least one clearly spined shoulder.

The Asana pieces come from levels dated to ca. 9400–8600 BP. The Caru and Patapatane examples were recovered from strata dated to ca. 8200 BP at each site. None are known from Quel-catani, which dates to ca. 7300 BP and younger. This form is present, but uncommon, in surface assemblages from the Río Huenque and Río Ilave Valleys. Based on these data and the regional comparisons below, Type 1A is considered diagnostic of the Early Archaic period, or the period dating to ca. 10,000–8,000 BP.

REGIONAL COMPARISONS

Two very similar examples were found at Acha-2, on the far northern Chilean coast, in contexts radiocarbon dated to ca. 8900 BP (Muñoz Ovalle et al. 1993). Neira (1990) recovered one example from basal deposits in the lowest stratum at SU-2, in the Sumbay region of the Arequipa highlands. This stratum is undated, but underlies a stratum containing a diagnostic Arequipa point style cross-dated to ca. 6200 BP at Sumbay SU-3. Santoro and Nuñez (1987) recovered a similarly shaped point at Hakenasa, in the far northern Chilean highlands. It was recovered from an undated level located stratigraphically above a stratum radiocarbon dated to ca. 8300 BP. Similar

TABLE 3.1. Type 1A: Spine-shouldered diamond/narrow foliate

Site	Asana, L. PXXVII, Fig. 3a	Asana, L. PXXV	Asana, L. PXIX	Patapatane, Fig. 3b	Patapatane, Santoro and Nuñez 1987: Fig. 5-#17	Caru, Fig. 3c	Caru, Ravines 1967: Fig. XXVI-#15
Age (BP)	8700–9400	8700–9400	8600	8200	8200	8200	8200
Length	38	38	und	38	53 (est) 47 (frag)	36 (est) 33 (frag)	36
Shoulder angle	35	20	55	45	30	40	45
Tool width	16	17	21	24	25	19	21
Haft length	15	19	17	16	24	15	16
Blade length	23	19	und	22	29 (est)	21 (est)	20
Blade length/tool width	1.54	1.00	und	0.92	1.16 (est)	1.11	0.95
Haft length/blade length	0.65	1.00	und	0.73	0.83 (est)	0.71	0.80
Haft angle	75	70	70	65	75	75	65
Basal width)	2	2	2	1	2	2	2
Tool length/ width	2.38	2.24	und	1.58	2.12 (est)	1.89	1.71

est = Estimated measurement or ratio.   frag = measure of actual fragment.
und = Tool is too fragmentary to assess measure or ratio.

points are also known from Toquepala (Ravines 1972). Here, Ravines' type P2, or "Punta Ichuña" (1972:141) is characterized by "hojas de limbo dentado" and includes two varieties: "una con aletas diminutivas y otra sin aletas." The first variety appears to be what we have called Type 1A, the second our Type 3B. Type P2 occurs in strata 3 and 4, which Ravines estimates to date to ca. 6000–5700 BP and 8700–7900 BP, respectively. Unfortunately, the Toquepala data have limited utility. First, it is impossible to determine whether the P2 varieties occurred sequentially or were contemporaneous at the site, because neither a stratigraphic breakdown of each variety nor specific stratum affiliations for illustrated specimens are provided. Second, the site's chronology is highly problematic because no data are presented that substantiate the proposed ages of individual strata. The entire chronology appears to be based on only two radiocarbon dates, both of which were obtained from material from basal deposits at the site, and only one of which is possibly associated with cultural material (Ravines 1967:54). Given these difficulties, the estimated ages of the strata that Ravines proposes cannot be relied on to help establish the temporal affiliation of any of our point types, although Toquepala's relative chronology remains useful.

Farther north, in the central Peruvian highlands, Rick's (1980) type 2A at Pachamachay—dated to ca. 10,500/11,000 to 9,000 BP—generally resembles our type 1A, although it appears more elongated and has a pointed base. His types 2D and 2E, dated ca. 9000–8000 BP, also generally resemble our type 1A. Lavallée et al. (1985) recovered one similar point from the basal level at Telarmachay, which dates to between ca. 9000 and 7200 BP.

A Possible Transitional Form?

At Patapatane, Santoro and Nuñez (1987:Fig. 5–16) recovered another point nearly identical to the "transitional" style Patapatane point discussed above. This second point derives from an undated level located stratigraphically above the ca. 8200 BP stratum. Spine-shouldered foliates were also recovered at Pampa Colorado, near the Arequipa coast, where they were apparently dated to 8100–7900 BP (Neira 1990). The il-

lustrated Pampa Colorado example very closely resembles the two "transitional" Patapatane specimens in being much wider, longer hafted, and longer bladed, and in having only one clearly spined shoulder, but the Pampa Colorado example lacks blade edge modification. These three examples hint that there may also be a type 1A subvariety (a wider, longer hafted, single spined-shoulder variety) that dates more narrowly to the late Early Archaic/early Middle Archaic transition.

1B. Pentagonal

This type (Figure 3.3d–e, Table 3.2) is defined based on two examples from Asana and two from Patapatane (Santoro and Nuñez 1987). Its diagnostic characteristic is its pentagonal, or 5-sided, form. The fifth "side" refers to the base, which is quite broad (basal widths of 4–8 mm), and either straight or very gently convex. These specimens also differ from the type 1A examples in having less steeply contracting haft angles (75–85°), relatively higher-waisted hafts (haft/blade length ratios of 0.90–1.45), and squatter blade elements (blade length/tool width ratios of 0.69–0.90). No examples have blade edge modification other than the shoulder spines.

At Asana, one point comes from a level dated to ca. 9400–8700 BP, and the other from a level dated to ca. 8700 BP. The two Patapatane specimens are from a stratum dated to ca. 8200 BP. None were recovered from Quelcatani, which dates to ca. 7300 BP and younger. This form is present, but uncommon, in surface assemblages from the Río Huenque and Río Ilave Valleys. Type 1B is considered diagnostic of the Early Preceramic, or the period dating to ca. 10,000–8,000 BP.

REGIONAL COMPARISONS

The undated basal stratum at SU-2 in the Arequipa highlands also contains a point very similar to our type 1B (Neira 1990). As discussed above, this stratum underlies a stratum cross-dated to ca. 6200 BP. Lavallée et al. (1985) also recovered one roughly comparable point from the basal level at Telarmachay, which dates to ca. 9000–7200 BP. None of Rick's (1980) point types at Pachamachay closely match our 1B style. However, some examples of his types 2E (ca.

TABLE 3.2. Type 1B: Spine-shouldered pentagonal forms

Site	Asana, L. PXXVII	Asana, L. PXXIV, Fig. 3d	Patapatane, Fig. 3e	Patapatane, Santoro and Nuñez 1987: Fig. 5-#15
Age (BP)	8700–9400	8700	8200	8200
Length	35	27	35	34 (est) 31 (frag)
Shoulder angle	40	50	45	45
Max. tool width	23	18 (est)	20	19 (est)
Haft length	19	16	17	18
Blade length	16	11	18	16 (est)
Blade length/tool width	0.84	0.69 (est)	0.90	0.84 (est)
Haft length/blade length	1.19	1.45	0.94	1.13 (est)
Haft angle	85	85	80	75
Basal width	4	5	8	5
Tool length/width	1.52	1.50 (est)	1.94	1.79 (est)

9000–8000 BP) and 2B (8000–6500 BP) are reminiscent of our type 1B.

SERIES 2. ANGULAR TO ROUND-SHOULDERED FORMS, UNSTEMMED

The diagnostic characteristics of Series 2 are (1) absence of a stem, (2) presence of a shoulder, and (3) absence of a shoulder spine. Series 1 and 2 are similar; the diagnostic characteristic differentiating them is that Series 2 points have rounded to angular shoulders rather than shoulder spines. All Series 2 examples share some other similarities, including very acute shoulder angles (5–35°) and moderate to high-waisted hafts (haft length/blade length ratios of 0.77–2.11). Subdivision into types is based on overall shape: foliate (2A), diamond to rhomboid (2B), and pentagonal (2C) forms. Type 2A spans the Early/Middle Archaic transition, dating to ca. 9000–7000 BP. Type 2C is diagnostic of the Middle Archaic, or ca. 8000–6000 BP, while Type 2B dates to the later Middle Archaic, or ca. 7000–6000 BP.

2A. Foliate

This type (Figure 3.3f–g, Table 3.3) is defined using three examples from Asana and one from Quelcatani, and its diagnostic characteristic is its foliate shape. All examples have straight to very slightly excurvate haft margins that contract to a convex base. Type 2A also differs from the other Series 2 types in having longer (20–26 mm haft lengths) and more moderately waisted hafts (haft length/blade length ratios of 0.77–1.73), and a much more elongated overall shape (tool length/width ratios of 2.13–2.56). No examples show blade edge modification.

The Asana examples derive from levels dated to ca. 8700–8000 BP. The Quelcatani specimen is from level WXXXV, dated to ca. 7300–7200 BP. Type 2A is present, but uncommon, in surface assemblages in the Río Huenque and Río Ilave Valleys. Based on these data and the regional comparisons below, we consider type 2A diagnostic of the Early/Middle Archaic transition, or the period dating to ca. 9000–7000 BP.

REGIONAL COMPARISONS
Ravines' type P9 at Toquepala closely resembles our type 2A: "una pieza larga y delgada de hoja más o menos oval...la espiga constituye aproximadamente la mitad de la longitud total de la pieza. La base es de forma convexa..." (1972: 147). Type P9 occurs nearly exclusively in strata 4 and 5, the two basal strata at the site. Ravines

TABLE 3.3. Types 2A and 2B: Angular to round-shouldered forms

	2A				2B	
Site	Asana, L. PXXV, Fig. 3f	Asana, L. PXIX	Asana, L. PXII	Quelcatani, L. WXXXV, Fig. 3g	Quelcatani, L. WXXXI(a), Fig. 3h	Quelcatani, L. WXXXI, Fig. 3i
Age (BP)	8700	8600	8000–8100	7200–7300	6000–7000	6000–7000
Tool length	46	32	41 (est)	35	26	17
Shoulder angle	30	25	15	20	5	25
Tool width	18	15	18	15	14	11
Haft length	20	15	26	20	17	10
Blade length	26	17	15 (est)	15	9	7
Blade length/tool width	1.44	1.13	0.83 (est)	1.00	0.64	0.64
Haft length/blade length	.77	0.88	1.73 (est)	1.33	1.89	1.43
Haft angle	75	70	75	80	65	65
Basal width	2	3	2	1	2	1
Tool length/width	2.56	2.13	2.28 (est)	2.33	1.86	1.55

(1967:54) reported a radiocarbon date of ca. 9500 BP from the deepest cultural stratum at Toquepala, although the dated material (carbon and burnt wood) was "sin asociaciones arqueológicas." Santoro and Nuñez (1987) found two points at Patapatane that are transitional in form and attributes between our types 1A, 2A, and 3B. One came from a ca. 8200 BP stratum, the other from an undated, overlying level.

There are several correlates to these types in the central Peruvian highlands. Ricks' (1980) type 3E (ca. 9000–6500 BP) is quite similar, and his 3A (9000–6500 BP) is also reminiscent although it is shorter and squatter. At Telarmachay, a few of Lavallée et al.'s (1985) type 1.4b and their "pointes atypiques" generally correspond to our type 2A. These examples come primarily from levels VI and VII, dating to ca. 9000–6800 BP.

2B. Diamond to Rhomboid

This type (Figure 3.3h–i, Table 3.3) is defined based on two examples from Quelcatani. Its diagnostic characteristics are its diamond to rhomboidal form and small size. Small size is demonstrated by short tool lengths (17–26 mm), short blades (7–9 mm), and narrow tool widths (11–14 mm). The two examples also have nar-

rower bases (1–2 mm) and more noticeably contracting stems (65° haft angles) than other Series 2 examples. Both specimens have rounded shoulders, straight bases, and lack blade edge modification.

Both tools were recovered from levels dating to ca. 7000–6000 BP. Type 2B is absent from Asana and rare in the Río Huenque and Río Ilave Valleys. This limited distribution and the lack of clear regional correlates suggests that type 2B is a localized style diagnostic of the later Middle Archaic, dating to approximately 7000–6000 BP.

REGIONAL COMPARISONS

There are no good correlates for type 2B. Ravines' (1972) type P6 at Toquepala has a diamond-like form similar to our type 2B, but his illustrated examples are noticeably larger, have angular shoulders and pointed bases. Type P6 occurs exclusively in strata 2 and 3 at the site, which Ravines estimates to date to ca. 6000–5000 BP. At Pachamachay (Rick 1980), one illustrated example of Rick's type 3B and one of his type 3A, both dated to ca. 9000–6500 BP, are only vaguely similar to our type 2B. At Telarmachay, some of Lavallée et al.'s (1985) type 1.4b specimens very roughly resemble our type 2B; these

TABLE 3.4. Type 2C: Pentagonal, angular to round-shouldered forms

Site	Quelcatani, L. XXXI(a)	Quelcatani, L. WXXXI, Fig. 3j	Quelcatani, L. WXXXV, Fig. 3k	Asana, L. PX
Age (BP)	6000–7000	6000–7000	7200–7300	8000
Tool length	30	32	28	29
Shoulder angle	25	15	15	5
Tool width	17 (est)	17	15	16
Haft length	17	16	19	19
Blade length	13	16	9	10
Blade length/tool width	0.76 (est)	0.94	0.60	0.63
Haft length/blade length	1.31	1.00	2.11	1.90
Haft angle	70	75	75	80
Basal width	4	5	5	5
Tool length/width	1.76 (est)	1.88	1.87	1.81

examples occur in levels dating to ca. 7200–3800 BP.

2C. Pentagonal

This type (Figure 3.3j–l, Table 3.4) is defined using three examples from Quelcatani and one from Asana. Its diagnostic characteristic is its pentagonal form, with the fifth "side" of the pentagon being the base. The base is quite broad (basal widths of 4–5 mm), and either straight or very gently convex. Other than overall shape and basal width, the 2C specimens do not stand out in any particular way and have "average" metric characteristics compared to other Series 2 examples.

Two Quelcatani examples were found in ca. 7000–6000 BP levels, and the third in a ca. 7300–7200 BP level. The Asana specimen was recovered in level PX, which is dated to ca. 8000 BP. Type 2C forms are relatively common in the Río Huenque and Río Ilave Valleys. We consider type 2C diagnostic of the Middle Archaic, or the period dating to ca. 8000–6000 BP.

REGIONAL COMPARISONS

In his excavations at Caru, Ravines (1967) recovered a similar point, also shown here as Figure 3.3l, from a stratum radiocarbon dated to ca. 8200 BP. This point differs slightly in having a small, shallow basal concavity. Ravines (1972) also illustrates a couple of points from Toque-

pala that closely resemble our type 2C, but no stratum affiliations or point type classifications are provided. In the central Peruvian highlands, Rick's (1980) type 3C (ca. 8000–6500 BP) at Pachamachay strongly resembles our 2C forms, as do some of his 2C (ca. 8000–6500 BP) examples. One of Lavallée at al.'s (1985) "pointes atypiques" recovered from the ca. 9000–7200 BP stratum at Telarmachay also resembles this style.

SERIES 3. UNSTEMMED, UNSHOULDERED FOLIATE FORMS

Diagnostic characteristics of Series 3 are (1) absence of a stem, (2) absence of a shoulder, (3) large size, and (4) elongated shape. These are the generic foliate forms ubiquitous at Preceramic sites across the broader Andean region. We define five major subtypes (3A, 3B, 3C, 3D, 3F) apparently local to the region, based on variation in haft form and blade edge modification. In our presentation of subtype 3D, we also discuss one other potential variant (3E) that occurs rarely in the south-central highlands and seems to be confined primarily to the western Cordilleran flank.

Type 3A spans the entire Early and Middle Archaic, dating to ca. 10,000–6,000 BP. Type 3B is restricted to the Middle Archaic, or ca. 8000–6000 BP. Types 3C and 3D are extremely long-lived forms, enduring throughout the entire Preceramic. The tentative type 3E likely is restricted to the Middle Archaic, or ca. 8000–6000 BP. Type 3F is diagnostic of the Late Archaic, or the period ca. 6000–4400 BP.

3A. Wide Contracting Haft with Straight Base

This type (Figure 3.4a–b) is defined based on two examples from Quelcatani and fourteen from Asana, most of which are basal, or base and blade, fragments. Its diagnostic characteristics relate to haft configuration: straight haft margins that contract to a wide, straight base. The speci-

mens presented in Table 3.5 cover the known range of variation. Those with at least some of the blade element intact (a rare occurrence) lack blade edge modification.

The two Quelcatani points are from a ca. 7000–6000 BP level. At Asana, nearly all points (*n* = 11) are found evenly distributed throughout levels dating to ca. 9400–7100 BP (1–2 points per level for levels PVI through PXVII and levels XX to XXI). Of the remaining Asana points, one derives from level XIV, dated to ca. 6000 BP, and two come from a level (PVI) disturbed by

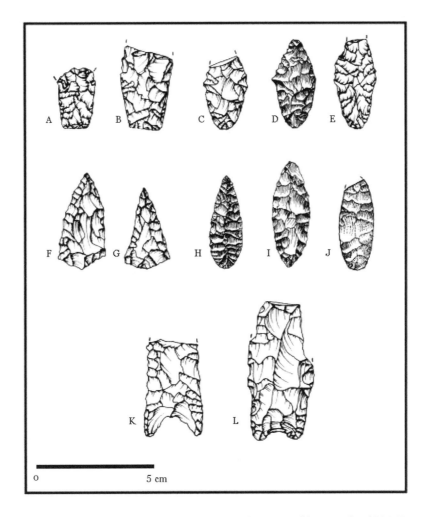

FIGURE 3.4. Types 3A–3F. Type 3A: *(a)* Asana, level PVI, *(b)* Asana, level PXXII. Type 3B: *(c)* Asana, level XVIIc, *(d)* Asana, level XIX, *(e)* Asana, level PI. Type 3C: *(f)* Hakenasa, after Santoro and Nuñez 1987:Figure 8-57, *(g)* Las Cuevas, after Santoro and Nuñez 1987:Figure 4-6. Type 3D/3E: *(h)* Asana, level XVIIb (3D), *(i)* Asana, level XVIIc (3E variant), *(j)* Asana, level XIX (3D). Type 3F: *(k)* Hakenasa, after Santoro and Nuñez 1987:Figure 8-59, *(l)* Sumbay (SU-3), after Neira 1990:36, example B.

TABLE 3.5. Type 3A: Wide contracting haft with straight base

Site	Age (BP)	Width: 15 mm from Base	Width: 10 mm from Base	Width: 5 mm from Base	Basal Width
Quelcatani, L. WXXXI(a)	6000–7000	17	15	13	10
Quelcatani, L. WXXXI(a)	6000–7000	17	15	13	7
Asana, L. XXI	7100	16	15	12	6
Asana, L. PVI, Fig. 4a	6000–7800	16	15	13	10
Asana, L. PVI	6000–7800	18	16	13	9
Asana, L. PXX	8700	16	14	12	7
Asana, L. PXXII, Fig. 4b	8700	20	18	16	10
Asana, L. PXXVI	8700–9400	und	und	12	7

landslide deposits that can only be generally dated to ca. 7800–6000 BP. This point style is fairly common in the Río Huenque and Río Ilave Valleys. We consider Type 3A diagnostic of the Middle through Early Archaic, or the period ca. 10,000–6,000 BP.

Since all examples are fragmentary, it is possible that they may be basal fragments of contracting-haft, straight-based, shouldered, or stemmed forms (Types 1B, 2C, and a few 4D and 4F examples). Only potential similarity to a few 4D and 4F specimens presents a possible problem, as Types 1B and 2C also date to the Early and Middle Archaic, respectively. While types 4D and 4F are characterized by more parallel-sided hafts and convex bases, a few specimens do have slightly contracting margins, and one has a straight base. The data in Table 3.6 indicate that a contracting haft, straight-based basal fragment can be confidently identified as 3A (Early to Middle Archaic), rather than 4D or 4F (Late Archaic stemmed), if (1) basal width is greater than 5 mm, (2) width at 10 mm from the base is greater than or equal to 15 mm, or (3) the blade has not yet been reached at 13 mm from the base.

REGIONAL COMPARISONS

Points with wide, contracting hafts and straight bases (whether from unshouldered, unstemmed forms or not) occur at Early and/or Middle Archaic contexts at several sites. They date to ca. 8200 BP at Patapatane (Santoro and Nuñez 1987) and at Caru (Ravines 1967), and to before 6200

TABLE 3.6. Haft widths for types 3A, and 4D/4F

	3A (n = 11)	4D/4F (n = 5)
Basal width	5–10	3–5
Width at 5 mm up from base	10–16	10–13
Width at 10 mm up from base	12–18	13–14 (n = 2)
Width at 13 mm up from base	16–20	blade element*

* All currently documented type 4D and 4F points have hafts shorter than 13 mm.

BP at SU-2 in Sumbay (Neira 1990). Ravines (1972) illustrates a few tools with these haft characteristics from Toquepala, but unfortunately does not give type affiliations or strata data for these specimens. Further north in the central Peruvian highlands, at Pachamachay, this haft style is found on several point styles dating to ca. 9000–6500 BP (Rick 1980). At Telarmachay this haft style occurs on several points dating to 9000–5700 BP, although the vast majority date to ca. 9000–6800 BP (Lavallée et al. 1985).

3B. Edge Modified Foliates with Straight to Contracting Haft Margins

This type (Figure 3.4c–e) is defined based on ten examples from Asana, and Table 3.7 presents metric data for the most complete specimens.

TABLE 3.7. Type 3B: Edge-modified foliates

Site	Asana, L. XVI	Asana, L. XVIIa	Asana, L. XVIIc, Fig. 4c	Asana, L. XIX, Fig. 4d	Asana, L. XX	Asana, L. PI, Fig. 4e
Age (BP)	6000–6500	6500	6800	7100	7100	6000–7800
Length	45 (est) 34 (frag)	61	38 (est) 28 (frag)	38 (est) 37 (frag)	52 (est) 32 (frag)	49 (est) 37 (frag)
Max. width	18	22	18	20	20	19
Tool length/width	2.50 (est)	2.77	2.11 (est)	1.90	2.60 (est)	2.58 (est)
Basal width	3	4	3	2	2	3

The diagnostic characteristics of type 3B are (1) the presence of blade edge modification, having either serrated, denticulated, or spined blade edges, and (2) haft configuration, having either contracting or parallel-sided haft margins and a convex base. All specimens have an elongated form (estimated tool length/width ratios of 1.90–2.77), and most have contracting hafts. While some type 3B pieces have blade edge spines similar to a few of the Series 1 points, they clearly differ from Series 1 in the lack of an obvious shoulder element.

Nine of Asana's points were found evenly distributed throughout levels dating to ca. 7100–6000 BP (1–2 per level, for levels XVI–XXI). One was recovered from level PI, dated to ca. 7800–6000 BP. None were recovered at Quelcatani, but this style is very common throughout the Río Huenque and Río Ilave project areas. We consider type 3B diagnostic of the Middle Archaic from ca. 8000–6000 BP.

Regional Comparisons

Santoro and Nuñez (1987) found two similar points at Patapatane that appear transitional between our types 1A, 2A, and 3B. One came from a ca. 8200 BP stratum, the other from an undated, overlying level. Dauelsberg (1983) describes finding serrated-edge, convex-based lanceolates at Tojo-Tojone in a small excavation unit that also produced a radiocarbon date of 9580 +1950/−1540 BP. This date must be treated cautiously given (1) the small size and depth of the unit (0.50 x 1.0 m, 40 cm depth), (2) the large sigma range for the date, (3) the uncertain con-

textual relationship between the points and the dated material, and (4) an additional date of 3740 ±130 BP from another small test unit at the site (Dauelsberg 1983). We suggest that the probable age for these 3B-like points is more likely around 8000 BP. Menghin and Schroeder (1957) recovered several pieces strongly resembling type 3B from the basal deposits at the site of Ichuña. While their excavation strategies were quite crude and the site lacks radiocarbon dates, the 3B-like specimens clearly come from levels below those containing Terminal Archaic and younger points (our types 5C and 5D), and either underlie or co-occur with type 4D Late Archaic forms in the basal stratum at the site. Ravines' (1972) type P2, or "Punta Ichuña," at Toquepala includes a variety very similar to our type 3B. As discussed earlier (see Type 1A regional comparisons), the chronometric age of these points cannot be firmly established. However, the site stratigraphy indicates that his type P2 points occur in strata that underlie those containing Late Archaic and younger styles (our types 4D, 5C, and 5D), and overlie or possibly co-occur with a transitional Early/Middle Archaic form (our type 2A).

At Pachamachay in central Peru, Rick's (1980) types 2C (ca. 8000–6500 BP) and 2F (ca. 8500–6500 BP) resemble our type 3B. Telarmachay (Lavallée et al. 1985) contains a number of similar specimens from levels dating to ca. 9000–5000 BP. Cardich's (1958) excavations at Lauricocha recovered 3B-like points from his Horizonte II. The site lacks radiocarbon dates, but Cardich estimated the horizon's age as ca. 8000–5000 BP.

TABLE 3.8. Type 3C: Expanding haft foliates

Site	Hakenasa, Santoro and Nuñez 1987: Fig. 8-#55	Hakenasa, Santoro and Nuñez 1987: Fig. 8-#56	Hakenasa, Fig. 4f	Hakenasa, Santoro and Nuñez 1987: Fig. 8-#58	Las Cuevas, Santoro and Nuñez 1987: Fig. 4-#5	Las Cuevas, Fig. 4g
Age (BP)	4400	4400	4400	4400	8300–9500	8300–9500
Length	44 (est) 24 (frag)	43 (est) 30 (frag)	40	39	30	34
Max width	19	21	19	25	18	21
Tool length/width	2.32 (est)	2.05 (est)	2.11	1.56	1.67	1.62
Width, 20 mm from base	15	15	16	19	11	11
Width, 15 mm from base	16	18	18	22	14	14
Width, 10 mm from base	18	20	19	24	17	17
Width, 5 mm from base	15	21	16	25	16	20
Basal width	5	9	3	17	6	4

3C. Expanding Haft Foliates

Type 3C (Figure 3.4f–g, Table 3.8) is defined based on four examples from Hakenasa and two from Las Cuevas (Santoro and Nuñez 1987). Its diagnostic characteristic is its expanding haft element. All six specimens have straight haft margins that expand to a broad, either convex or straight base. None exhibit blade edge modification. The expanding haft creates an elongated triangular shape vaguely reminiscent of type 5A. However, the two types can be easily differentiated based on 5A's squatter, more triangular form (tool length/width ratios of 1.07–1.43).

No type 3C points were recovered at Asana or Quelcatani, and this style is extremely rare in the Río Huenque and Río Ilave Valleys. The Hakenasa pieces come from a ca. 4400 BP stratum, while the Las Cuevas points derive from a stratum dated to ca. 9500–8300 BP. Given this and the regional correlates below, we propose type 3C occurs, albeit rarely, in the south-central highlands throughout the Preceramic period. This type is diagnostic only at a very general level, serving only as a means to differentiate Preceramic from later occupations.

REGIONAL COMPARISONS

To find correlates for this point type we must look either north to the central Peruvian highlands or south to the Chilean-Argentine salt puna. In central Peru, Rick's (1980) type 4B at Pachamachay, dating to ca. 6500–3500 BP, strongly resembles our 3C specimens. Lavallée et al.'s (1985) type 1.2 at Telarmachay, dating to ca. 9000–5700 BP, also is very similar. Excavations at Lauricocha (Cardich 1958) recovered a couple of comparable points in Horizonte II, estimated to date to ca. 8000–5000 BP. This estimation is supported in part by the co-occurrence within Horizon II of points similar to both our 3C and 3B (Middle Archaic, ca. 8000–6000 BP) forms. To the south, Aschero (1984) found a similar point at Inca Cueva-4, in a stratum dated to ca. 9200 BP. Nuñez Atencio (1992) illustrates two fairly comparable points, one from Tuina (ca. 10,800–9,000 BP) and one from Tambillo (ca. 8600 BP), although these have a more squat shape.

3D. Contracting to Parallel-Sided Foliates Without Edge Modification

Type 3D (Figure 3.4h, j) is defined based on over sixty examples from Asana. Many specimens are fragmentary, and Table 3.9 presents metric data for only some of the more complete pieces. Its diagnostic characteristics are (1) the absence of blade-edge modification, and (2) a haft configuration consisting of parallel-sided to contracting haft margins and a convex base. The more intact specimens also have very elongated shapes (estimated tool length/width ratios of 2.61–2.79).

TABLE 3.9. Type 3D: Convex base foliates without blade-edge modification

Site	Asana, L. XVIIb, Fig. 4f	Asana, L. XVIIc, Fig. 4i (3E variant)	Asana, L. XVIII	Asana, L. XIX, Fig. 4j	Asana, L. XX	Asana, L. XXI	Asana, L. PXXI
Age (BP)	6500–6800	6800	6800–7100	7100	7100	7100	8700
Length	39	46 (est) 44 (frag)	No est 27 (frag)	40 (est) 36 (frag)	47 (est) 39 (frag)	53 (est) 29 (frag)	50 (est) 36 (frag)
Max. width	14	17	22	15	18	19	18 (est)
Tool length/width	2.79	2.71 (est)	no est	2.67 (est)	2.61 (est)	2.79 (est)	2.78 (est)
Basal width	2	1	4	2	1	2	2

No est = Too fragmentary to estimate.

Type 3D is by far the most abundant point style at Asana, where they date to ca. 8700–5300 BP. The vast majority (80%) are found throughout levels dating to ca. 7100–6500 BP (levels XVII–XXII). A notable minority (18%) also occur in Early Archaic levels dating to ca. 8700–8000/7800 BP (levels PVI–PXXIII). One point came from level XII, dated at ca. 5300 BP. None were recovered at Quelcatani, but this point style is ubiquitous in the Río Huenque and Río Ilave Valleys. Based on these data and the regional comparisons below, the 3D style can only be considered diagnostic at a very general level, as it occurs throughout the Preceramic between ca. 10,000–3,600 BP.

REGIONAL COMPARISONS

Type 3D correlates. Essentially identical points occur at many sites across the broader Andean region throughout the entire Preceramic era. Ravines' (1972) type P3 (large) and P4 (small) foliate points at Toquepala occur in all excavated strata at the site, although they tend to decrease in frequency over time. Type 3D-like foliate points are radiocarbon dated to Early to Middle Archaic contexts at Tojo-Tojone (Dauelsberg 1983), a Late Archaic stratum at Hakenasa (Santoro and Nuñez 1987), and Early through Late Archaic contexts at several sites in the Arequipa highlands (Neira 1990).

In central Peru, points essentially identical to our type 3D are found in all three Preceramic horizons at Lauricocha (Cardich 1958). At Telarmachay, Lavallée et al.'s (1985) 3D-like foliate styles (their types 1.1a, 1.1b, 1.1c, 1.5, 1.6) are found in levels IV through VII, dating to ca. 9000–3800 BP. At Pachamachay, similar foliate points (Rick's type 3F, 4A, 4C, 4E, 5A, 5B, 6A, 6B) also date to ca. 9000–3800 BP (Rick 1980). Farther south, the Chilean-Argentine salt puna appears quite different (Nuñez Atencio 1992). Here, type 3D-like foliate points are known only in Late Archaic contexts, dating to ca. 4300 BP at Tulan-52 and 4800 BP at Puripica-I (Nuñez Atencio 1992).

Type 3E (preliminary). We also tentatively define a type 3E, which differs from type 3D by having a pointed, rather than convex, base that creates a bipointed foliate form. There is one obvious bipoint foliate at Asana, found in level XVIIb and dated to ca. 6800–6500 BP (see Figure 3.4i, Table 3.9). None were recovered at Quelcatani, and this form is very rare in the Río Huenque and Río Ilave Valleys. Foliate bipoints, however, are a defined style at Camarones-14, located on the far northern Chilean coast (Schiappacasse and Niemeyer 1984), where they are relatively common in Middle Archaic levels radiocarbon dated to ca. 7400–6600 BP. Dauelsberg (1983) also recovered a couple of bipoints at Tojo-Tojone, but unfortunately has no associated radiocarbon dates. Based on these data we suggest that type 3E is diagnostic of the Middle Archaic, or the period ca. 8000–6000 BP, in the south-central Andes, although it seems to occur primarily along the coast and lower elevations in the western-draining Cordilleran valleys.

For correlates, we can only look north to the central Peruvian highlands. At Telarmachay, Lavallée et al. (1985) recovered bipoints (their

TABLE 3.10. Type 3F: Concave-based lanceolates

	3F Type Specimens		3F Regional Correlates	
Site	Hakenasa, Fig. 4k	Toquepala, Ravines 1972: p. 142	SU-3, Neira 1990: Type Sumbay II-B, p. 36, Example A	SU-3, Fig. 4l
Age (BP)	4400	5000?–5500	5400–6200	5400–6200
Length	60 (est) 39 (frag)	no est 23 (frag)	72 (est) 60 (frag)	78 (est) 57 (frag)
Tool width	25	28	25	27
Basal width	24	19	19	18
Concavity width	18	14	11	12
Concavity depth	7	3	3	4
Tool length/width	2.40 (est)	no est	2.88 (est)	2.78
Haft width*	n/a	n/a	20	22
Haft width/tool width*	n/a	n/a	0.80	0.80

* Calculated for stemmed points only.

types 1.4a and 1.4b) in strata dated to ca. 7200–3800 BP. At Pachamachay, Rick (1980) has one Early Archaic bipoint style, his type 2A, dated to ca. 10,500–9,000 BP. However, bipoint forms are much more common here in the Middle to late Archaic (his types 4C, 4D, 5A, 5B, 6B, collectively dating to ca. 6500–3800 BP).

3F. Concave Base Lanceolate Forms

Type 3F (Figure 3.4k–l, Table 3.10) is defined based on one example from Hakenasa (Santoro and Nuñez 1987), and one from Toquepala (Ravines 1972). Its diagnostic characteristic is its concave base. Both 3F specimens are extremely wide and long, and have parallel-sided to very slightly contracting haft margins. The Hakenasa point has blade edge modification. The Toquepala specimen appears to have denticulation or spines on the haft element, which may have facilitated lashing to the haft.

Type 3F points were not recovered from Asana or Quelcatani, but this style is abundant in surface assemblages in the Río Huenque and Río Ilave Valleys. The Hakenasa example comes from a ca. 4400 BP stratum. The Toquepala specimen is one of Ravines' (1972) type P1 points, which occur exclusively in the upper two strata at the site. Unfortunately, we cannot determine which stratum this point comes from, as the il-

lustration lacks a stratum affiliation. Ravines estimates the combined age of these two strata as ca. 5500–5000 BP. This is substantiated in part by the fact that these strata contain points similar to our Late Archaic type 4D, and overlie strata with points similar to our Middle Archaic type 3B. We consider type 3F diagnostic of the Late Archaic, or the period ca. 6000–4400 BP.

REGIONAL COMPARISONS

Schiappacasse and Niemeyer (1984) recovered two similar points from Camarones-14 that date to ca. 6600 BP. Comparable forms also are known from dated Late Archaic contexts at the site of SU-3 in the Arequipa highlands (Neira 1990). SU-3 contains three prehistoric cultural strata that span the Late Archaic period, the lower two of which produced radiocarbon dates of ca. 5400 BP and 6200 BP, respectively. Neira defines three styles of elongated, lanceolate to triangular points with basal concavities at SU-3, which occur throughout all of the prehistoric strata. Of these, Neira's type Sumbay II-B most closely resembles our type 3F, except for the presence of a very broad stem (see Figure 3.4l). The Sumbay II-C style is also a close match, but has a more triangular form and contracting haft margins.

We are not aware of other excavated and dated correlates for our type 3F. However, surface finds of 3F points are abundant in the south-western Lake Titicaca region. Neira (1990) reports numerous surface finds at the sites of Tumuku and Quelkata, as well as other localities around the community of Chichillape, located in the upper Río Huenque drainage. Aldenderfer (1985) encountered examples at Titijones, in the high puna ecozone of the Río Osmore drainage. Given this, and given its ubiquity in the Río Ilave and Río Huenque project areas, type 3F may be a more localized style occurring primarily in and around the southwestern Titicaca Basin.

SERIES 4. STEMMED FORMS

The diagnostic characteristic of Series 4 is the presence of a stem. Stemmed points are divided into broad-stemmed (types 4A, 4B, 4D, 4F) and narrow-stemmed (types 4C, 4E) forms, with other haft characteristics and overall size serving to further define each type. Types 4A and 4B date to the Early Archaic, or ca. 10,000–8,000 BP. Types 4D and 4F date to the Late Archaic, or ca. 6000–4400 BP. Type 4C dates to the Formative period, and may be a local style in the western-draining Cordilleran valleys. Type 4E dates to Tiwanaku/Middle Horizon times, and may represent an "elite" point style.

4A. Triangular-Bladed, Broad-stemmed Forms with Contracting Hafts

Type 4A (Figure 3.5a–b, Table 3.11) is defined based on one example from Asana, one from Hakenasa (Santoro and Nuñez 1987), and one from Las Cuevas (Santoro and Nuñez 1987). Its diagnostic characteristics are its (1) broad-stemmed form, (2) triangular-shaped blade element, and (3) contracting haft. The two examples with intact bases each have different forms (straight and pointed). The Asana point fragment, and possibly the Las Cuevas point, has finely serrated blade margins. The 4A examples generally resemble those of type 4D, but differ clearly from type 4D in several ways. The 4A specimens have a more triangular-shaped blade element (blade length/tool widths of 0.91–1.33) and a less elongated overall shape (tool length/tool width ratios of 1.27–1.94) than the 4D points. They also typically have a more clearly contracting haft, demonstrated by both haft an-

gle (65–70°) and narrower haft widths at 5 mm above the base (7–8 mm).

The Las Cuevas example is from a stratum radiocarbon dated to between ca. 9500 and 8300 BP. The Hakenasa point derives from a stratum dated to ca. 8300 BP. Asana's point comes from level PXXVII, which dates to between 9400 and 8700 BP. The ca. 9500–8300 BP stratum at Las Cuevas also contained an unfinished point preform that appears generally similar in size and shape to our 4A. No examples are known from Quelcatani, and this style is rare in surface assemblages in the Río Huenque and Río Ilave Valleys. We consider 4A diagnostic of the Early Archaic, or the period dating to ca. 10,000–8000 BP.

REGIONAL COMPARISONS
During excavations at the site of Yara, on the southern Peruvian coast, Rasmussen (1998) recovered a fairly similar point near a hearth radiocarbon dated to ca. 7800 BP. This specimen differs in being much longer and wider than the highland examples, but has the same broad-stemmed, triangular-bladed, contracting haft form. Comparable points apparently also have been found at Tojo-Tojone. Santoro and Nuñez state that:

> Recent excavations in Tojo-Tojone by Santoro and Dauelsberg (ms) recovered diagnostic stemmed, triangular points previously unknown from this site (Dauelsberg 1983). These points were found only in the lowest level of the site, which lacked the thick, lanceolate points diagnostic of the overlying Early Archaic strata. The Tojo-Tojone stemmed triangular points are similar to those from Las Cuevas I (Figure 3.4, nos. 1 and 2). [Santoro and Nuñez 1987:68]

The previously recovered lanceolate points (Dauelsberg 1983) were serrated-edge, convex-based forms similar to our Middle Archaic type 3B and were generally associated with a radiocarbon date of 9580 (+1950, −1540) BP. This suggests that Tojo-Tojone's lower stratum, and the stemmed points it contains, date to some time in the Early Archaic (pre-8000 BP). The results of this more recent work have not yet been published and we cannot evaluate how closely these points resemble our 4A examples.

Outside of the south-central Andes, roughly comparable forms are known only from Pachamachay in the central Peruvian highlands (Rick 1980). Our type 4A does not correlate well with any of the Pachamachay types, but some illustrated examples of Rick's type 2D (ca. 9000–8000 BP) are relatively similar.

4B. Small, Narrow, Broad-stemmed Forms with Contracting Hafts

Type 4B (Figure 3.5c–d, Table 3.12) is defined based on one example from Asana and one from Las Cuevas (Santoro and Nuñez 1987). Its diagnostic characteristics are its (1) broad-stemmed form, (2) small size, (3) narrow width, and (4) contracting haft. Both points also have acute shoulder angles, have convex bases, and lack

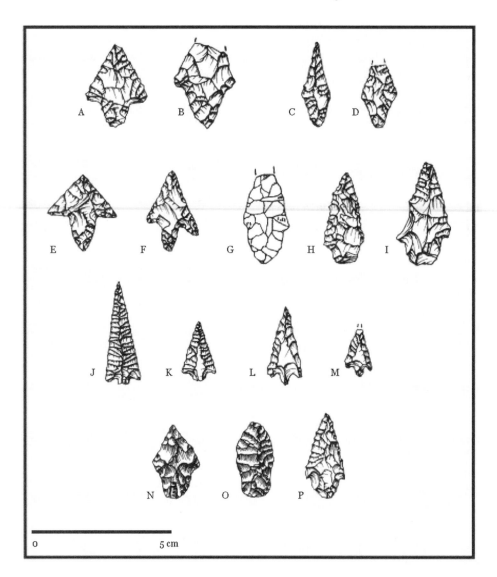

FIGURE 3.5. Types 4A–4F. Type 4A: (a) Las Cuevas, after Santoro and Nuñez 1987:Figure 4-2, (b) Hakenasa, after Santoro and Nuñez 1987:Figure 6-22. Type 4B: (c) Asana, level PXXIX, (d) Las Cuevas, after Santoro and Nuñez 1987:Figure 4-3. Type 4C: (e) El Panteon, level XXII, (f) El Panteon, level XXII. Type 4D: (g) Asana, level VIII, (h) Hakenasa, after Santoro and Nuñez 1987:Figure 7-41, (i) Hakenasa, after Santoro and Nuñez 1987:Figure 7-46. Type 4E: (j) Omo, after Goldstein 1993a:Figure 3.7a (left), (k) Omo, after Goldstein 1993a:Figure 3.7a (center), (l) Tumatumani, after Stanish and Steadman 1994:Figure 174-#0309, (m) Tumatumani, after Stanish and Steadman 1994:Figure 174-#0373. Type 4F: (n) Asana, level VIII, (o) Asana, level VIII, (p) Hakenasa, after Santoro and Nuñez 1987:Figure 7-39 .

TABLE 3.11. Type 4A: Triangular-bladed broad-stemmed forms with contracting hafts

Site	Las Cuevas, Fig. 5a	Hakenasa, Fig. 5b	Asana, L. PXXVII
Age (BP)	8300–9500	8300	8700–9400
Length	28	35 (est) 28 (frag)	und
Shoulder angle	80	60	60
Tool width	22	18	23
Haft width	11	12	17 (est)
Haft width/tool width	0.50	0.67	0.74 (est)
Haft length	8	11	no est
Blade length	20	24 (est)	no est
Blade length/tool width	0.91	1.33 (est)	no est
Haft length/blade length	0.40	0.46 (est)	no est
Haft angle	70	65	no est
Basal width	5	<1	no est
Width, 5 mm above base	8	7	no est
Tool length/width	1.27	1.94 (est)	no est

TABLE 3.12. Types 4B and 4C: Stemmed forms

	4B		4C	
Site	Asana, L. PXXIX, Fig. 5c	Las Cuevas, Fig. 5d	El Panteon, L. XXII, Fig. 5e	El Panteon, L. XXII, Fig. 5f
Age (BP)	9400	8300–9500	3000–3600	3000–3600
Length	29	29 (est) 21 (frag)	26	27
Shoulder angle	50	45	90	90
Tool width	11	13	24	18
Haft width	9	9	10	7
Haft width/tool width	0.82	0.69	0.42	0.39
Haft length	10	9	11	8
Blade length	19	20 (est)	15	19
Blade length/tool width	1.73	1.54 (est)	0.63	1.06
Haft length/blade length	0.53	0.45 (est)	0.73	0.42
Haft angle	80	70	70	75
Basal width	2	2	1	2
Width, 5 mm above base	7	6	7	6
Tool length/width	2.63	2.23	1.08	1.50

blade-edge modification. Within Series 4, type 4B is most similar to 4F. However, besides its contracting haft, type 4B also differs from 4F in having a narrower haft (haft width of 9 mm, basal width of 2 mm), a more elongated form (tool length/width ratios of 2.23–2.63), and rounded shoulders. Overall, type 4B most closely resembles type 1A, with 4B appearing as a smaller, round-shoulder, barely stemmed version.

The Las Cuevas point derives from a ca. 9500–8300 BP stratum. Asana's point comes from level PXXIX, radiocarbon dated to ca. 9400 BP. No examples are known from Quelcatani, and this style is extremely rare in surface assemblages from the Río Huenque and Río Ilave Valleys. We consider 4A diagnostic of the Early Archaic, or the period ca. 10,000–8,000 BP.

REGIONAL COMPARISONS
There are no good correlates for type 4B. The only general comparisons are with Rick's (1980) 2D and 2E (both ca. 9000–8000 BP), and 2B (ca. 8000–6500 BP) styles at Pachamachay, but these are much longer, wider, and do not have rounded shoulders.

4C. Squat, Narrow-stemmed Forms with Contracting Hafts
Type 4C (Figure 3.5e–f, Table 3.12) is defined based on two examples from the site of El Panteon (Aldenderfer 1998), located near Asana. Its diagnostic characteristics are its (1) narrow-stemmed form, (2) small size, (3) wide width, and (4) contracting haft. Both specimens have convex bases, lack blade-edge modification, and have 90° shoulder angles (although one specimen also has one barbed shoulder). Type 4C is most similar to 4E, but clearly differs from it in that 4C is much wider (18–24 mm), higher-waisted (haft length/blade length ratios of 0.42–0.73), and has a notably longer (8–11 mm) and wider (7–10 mm) haft.

The basal level (XXVI) at El Panteon was radiocarbon dated to ca. 3300 BP, but the site is aceramic. These two points derive from a level estimated to date to ca. 3000 BP. No similar points were found at Asana, Quelcatani, or in surface assemblages from the Río Huenque and Río Ilave project areas. We consider 4C a form local to the western draining valleys that likely is diagnostic of the early Formative, or ca. 3600–3000 BP.

REGIONAL COMPARISONS
We are unaware of any good correlates for type 4C. Ravines' (1972) type P5 at Toquepala, which occurs only in the uppermost stratum, bears a slight resemblance, but it is larger, more broadly stemmed, and has ill-defined shoulders.

4D. Large, Broad-stemmed Forms with Parallel-sided Hafts
Type 4D (Figure 3.5g–i) is defined based on one example from Asana, two from Quelcatani, and six from Hakenasa (Santoro and Nuñez 1987). Table 3.13 presents metric attributes for most of these specimens. Diagnostic characteristics include (1) a broad-stemmed form, (2) a wide, parallel-sided haft, and (3) large size. Most of the examples have convex bases ($n = 4$), although two have a straight base. Several show blade-edge modification. Type 4D resembles type 4A, but differs from 4A in having a more elongated blade (blade length/tool width ratios of 1.47–1.79) and elongated overall shape (tool length/tool width ratios of 1.83–2.21). Type 4D typically also has a wider, more parallel-sided haft than type 4A, as shown by its larger haft angles (70–85°) and greater width at 5 mm above the base (10–12 mm).

The Hakenasa points come from a stratum dated to ca. 4400 BP. This same stratum also contained two point preforms and a small point fragment that seem generally similar in size and shape to type 4D. The Asana point is from level VIII, which is dated to ca. 4600 BP. The Quelcatani examples were found in level WXXIX, dating to ca. 5600 BP. This style is very common in surface assemblages from the Río Huenque and Río Ilave Valleys. We consider 4D diagnostic of the Late Archaic, or the period ca. 6000–4400 BP.

REGIONAL COMPARISONS
Ravines' (1972) type P7 at Toquepala strongly resembles our type 4D. The Toquepala P7 style was recovered exclusively in strata 1 and 2, which Ravines estimates to date to ca. 5500–5000 BP. This is substantiated in part by the fact that these strata overlie those containing points similar to our Middle Archaic type 3B. Menghin and Schroeder (1957) recovered several points very similar to our 4D form at the site of Ichuña. While their stratigraphic control was fairly poor and the site lacks radiocarbon dates, they noted that these points came from the lowest excavated deposits. The points recovered from the upper strata resemble our Terminal Archaic to Formative period types 5C and 5D, suggesting that the broad stemmed types in the lower level date to the Late Archaic period.

TABLE 3.13. Type 4D: Large, broad-stemmed, parallel-sided haft forms

Site	Quelcatani, L. WXXIX	Quelcatani, L. WXXIX	Asana, L. VIII, Fig. 5g	Hakenasa, Fig. 5h	Hakenasa, Santoro and Nuñez 1987: Fig. 7-42	Hakenasa, Fig. 5i
Age (BP)	5600	5600	4600	4400	4400	4400
Length	35 (est) 28 (frag)	no est 33 (frag)	37 (est) 30 (frag)	no est 31 (frag)	no est 34 (frag)	37 (est) 35 (frag)
Shoulder angle	70	80	50	75	70	75
Tool width	16	18	17	14	16	19
Haft width	13	15	13	10	11	13
Haft width/tool width	0.81	0.83	0.76	0.71	0.69	0.68
Haft length	8	no est	12	no est	no est	8
Blade length	27 (est)	30	25 (est)	25	26	29 (est)
Blade length/tool width	1.69 (est)	1.67	1.47 (est)	1.79	1.63	1.53 (est)
Haft length/blade length	0.30 (est)	no est	0.48 (est)	no est	no est	0.28 (est)
Haft angle	80	70	80	80	75	85
Basal width	3	no est	2	no est	no est	no est
Width, 5 mm above base	11	no est	10	no est	no est	12
Tool length/width	2.19 (est)	no est 1.83 (frag)	2.18 (est)	no est 2.21 (frag)	(no est) 2.13 (frag)	1.95 (est)

Roughly comparable points have been recovered at SU-3 throughout the ca. 6200–5400 BP levels, and at other sites in the Sumbay region (Neira 1990). However, the Sumbay forms integrate aspects of both our types 4D and 3F. They have the large size, broad stem, and parallel-sided haft of the 4D form, but have basal concavities like type 3F. The Late Archaic SU-3 strata also contained an expanding-haft point form, Sumbay II-E (Neira 1990). Similar broad-stemmed, expanding haft points have been found in undated contexts around Huancané in the northern Lake Titicaca Basin (Lisa Cipolla and Aimeé Plourde, personal communication 2000). Only a few expanding haft forms were recovered during the Río Ilave survey, and none are known from the Río Huenque Valley.

4E. Elongated, Narrow-stemmed Forms with Barbed Shoulders

Type 4E (Figure 3.5j–m, Table 3.14) is defined based on three examples from the site of Omo (Goldstein 1993a, 1993b), located in the Moque-gua Valley's low sierra. Its diagnostic characteristics are its (1) narrow-stemmed form, (2) barbed shoulders, (3) elongated shape, and (4) narrow width. These points have either contracting or parallel-sided hafts. Two have convex bases, the other a straight base. None have blade edge modification.

All three examples were found in Structure 7 at M12, in levels dating to the Omo phase AD 500–650, which was contemporaneous with the later portion of Tiwanaku Phase IV (Classic Tiwanaku). M12 is one component of the larger Omo site complex, a Tiwanaku colony directly occupied by settlers from Tiwanaku (Goldstein 1993a, 1993b). Goldstein suggests that these points were likely imported to M12 from the Tiwanaku heartland because there is no evidence of lithic manufacturing debris, and further notes that they were made of only two material types, including exotic obsidian. Neither Asana nor Quelcatani contained type 4E points, and this style is rare in the Río Huenque and Río Ilave Valleys. Based on these data, and the regional

TABLE 3.14. Type 4: Elongated, narrow-stemmed forms with barbed shoulders

Site	4E Type Specimens			4E Regional Comparisons		
	Omo-M12, Fig. 5j	Omo-M12, Fig. 5k	Omo-M12, Goldstein 1993: Fig. 3.7a (right)	Tumatumani, Fig. 5l	Tumatumani, Stanish and Steadman 1994: Fig. 174-302	Tumatumani, Fig. 5m
Age (AD)	500–650	500–650	500–650	Uncertain	Uncertain	Uncertain
Length	35	20	29	27	14	16
Shoulder angle	115	100	125	130	115	100
Tool width	13	13	13	12	8	9
Haft width	4	5	5	5	3	4
Haft width/tool width	0.31	0.38	0.38	0.42	0.38	0.44
Haft length	3	3	5	4	3	3
Blade length	32	17	24	23	11	13
Blade length/tool width	2.46	1.31	1.85	1.92	1.38	1.44
Haft length/blade length	0.09	0.18	0.21	0.17	0.27	0.23
Haft angle	75	65	90	70	60	70
Basal width	3	2	2	2	1	2
Tool length/tool width	2.69	1.54	2.23	2.25	1.75	1.78

comparisons below, we suggest that type 4E is diagnostic of Tiwanaku IV and V, and may have been an elite style that signaled a higher social or political status.

REGIONAL COMPARISONS

Type 4E points were recovered at the site of Tumatumani (see Figure 3.5l, m, Table 3.14), located along the southwestern shore of Lake Titicaca (Stanish and Steadman 1994). Tumatumani is a major site with artificial mounds that served as an elite/ceremonial settlement during the Late Formative and Tiwanaku IV. Unfortunately, the points cannot be firmly dated to either period because they were recovered from the surface or excavation units consisting of mixed construction fill. However, Seddon (1994) reports that the Tumatumani points are indistinguishable from those recovered from the site of Tiwanaku itself. Goldstein (1993a) also observes that the Omo points are identical to those archived at the Tiwanaku site museum. Like at Omo, the Tumatumani points also were produced on a limited range of materials, including exotic obsidian. The presence of type 4E points

at the site of Tiwanaku itself, Omo (a major Tiwanaku colony), and Tumatumani (an important Tiwanaku satellite center), clearly associates this point type with the growth and spread of the Tiwanaku state. That access to or use of this style may have been reserved for the socio-political elite is implied by both the rarity of 4E points in the Ilave and Huenque Valleys, areas without substantial Tiwanaku centers that likely contained primarily more rural agro-pastoral settlements, and the use of high-quality, exotic materials. The lack of evidence for lithic manufacture at Omo, and the limited range of raw materials used to produce the Omo and Tumatumani points, further suggest controlled production and/or trade.

4F. Small, Broad-stemmed Forms with Parallel-sided Hafts

Type 4F (Figure 3.5n–p, Table 3.15) is defined based on three examples from Asana and four examples from Hakenasa (Santoro and Nuñez 1987). Its diagnostic characteristics are its (1) broad-stemmed form, (2) small size, and (3) parallel-sided haft. Most examples have broad, con-

TABLE 3.15. Type 4F: Small, broad-stemmed, parallel-sided haft forms

Site	Asana, L. VIII, Fig. 5n	Asana, L. VIII, Fig. 5o	Asana, L. VIII	Hakenasa, Santoro and Nuñez 1987: Fig. 7-35	Hakenasa, Santoro and Nuñez 1987: Fig. 7-36	Hakenasa, Fig. 5p	Hakenasa, Santoro and Nuñez 1987: Fig. 7-40
Age (BP)	4600	4600	4600	4400	4400	4400	4400
Length	25	26	29	32	30	29	30
Shoulder angle	35	n/a*	50	60	60	115	90
Tool width	17	14	11	15	16	14	17
Haft width	12	12	8	12	14	10	12
Haft width/tool width	0.71	0.85	0.73	0.80	0.88	0.71	0.71
Haft length	9	10	9	10	10	7	8
Blade length	16	16	20	22	20	22	22
Blade length/tool width	0.94	1.14	1.82	1.47	1.25	1.57	1.29
Haft length/blade length	0.56	0.63	0.45	0.45	0.50	0.32	0.36
Haft angle	80	85	90	85	80	75	65
Basal width	5	5	3	3	5	3	3
Tool length/width	1.47	1.86	2.64	2.13	1.88	2.07	1.76

* Shoulders too rounded to measure angle.

vex bases ($n = 6$); one has a straight base. Several points have blade-edge modification. Type 4F is very similar to 4D, and differs from it primarily in size. Type 4F forms are smaller (25–32 mm tool lengths), primarily due to having shorter blades (16–22 mm blade lengths), but some also have shorter hafts (7–10 mm haft length). While it is possible that 4F specimens are merely extensively resharpened 4D forms, their absence from pre-4600 BP contexts at Asana and Quelcatani suggests they represent a true stylistic shift toward smaller points.

The Hakenasa points come from a stratum dated to ca. 4400 BP, and all Asana examples derive from level VIII, dated to ca. 4600 BP. Although none were recovered at Quelcatani, this style is very common in surface assemblages in the Río Huenque and Río Ilave Valleys. Based on this and the regional comparisons below, we consider 4F diagnostic of the later Late Archaic through Terminal Archaic, or ca. 5000–3600 BP.

REGIONAL COMPARISONS
Aldenderfer has recovered Type 4F points during his 1997–1999 excavations at the site of Jis-

kairumoko, in the Río Ilave Valley. Over 200 m^2 of area have been opened at the site to date, revealing a stacked sequence of domestic structures and associated features. Eight Type 4F points were found in domestic and midden contexts radiocarbon dated to between ca. 4200 and 3600 BP; one was recovered from a ca. 3600–3400 BP level.

Roughly similar points also are known from the salt puna region. Nuñez Atencio (1992) shows several narrow-stemmed versions of our Type 4F point from Tulan-54, where they were dated to the initial agro-pastoral period, or to ca. 3000 BP.

SERIES 5. UNSTEMMED, UNSHOULDERED TRIANGULAR FORMS

The diagnostic characteristics of Series 5 are (1) absence of a stem, (2) absence of a shoulder, and (3) squat, triangular shape. Over 400 Series 5 points were recovered from securely dated contexts at Quelcatani, providing an unparalleled data set for temporal analysis. Initial analyses attempted to define temporally sensitive types using a broad range of attributes, including size, shape, base shape, and depth and width of basal concavity. Unfortunately, the results revealed no fine-grained temporal patterning within the Quelcatani assemblage, demonstrating that many attributes varied continuously and different point variations coexisted for extended periods of time. Here we define only four broad subtypes: ovo-triangular (5A), triangular with straight or convex base (5B), large triangular with concave base (5C), and small triangular with concave base (5D).

In the south-central highlands, Series 5 points developed relatively late in prehistory, with all four types first appearing during the Terminal Archaic period. Type 5A is diagnostic of the Terminal Archaic, or the period ca. 4400–3600 BP. Type 5C spans the Terminal Archaic and Formative, dating from ca. 2400 BC (4400 BP) to AD 500. Types 5B and 5D are longer-lived styles, beginning in the Terminal Archaic ca. 2400 BC (4400 BP) and lasting to AD 1100 and AD 1530, respectively.

5A. Ovo-triangular Forms

Type 5A (Figure 3.6a–c, Table 3.16) is defined based on four examples from Hakenasa (Santoro and Nuñez 1987). Its diagnostic characteristics are its small size and ovo-triangular shape. These are short (less than 30 mm), squat, triangular points whose width, excurvate lateral margins, and convex bases give them a somewhat ovoid appearance. None of the Hakenasa specimens show blade edge modification. One specimen is narrower than the others, and possibly could be an exhausted, extensively reworked Type 3D. However, the data from Asana do not support this idea. The fact that the length of type 3D basal fragments at Asana exceed the length of this Hakenasa example (see Table 3.9) indicates that 3D points were not so extensively reworked and curated, but discarded well before reaching such a small size.

All of the Hakenasa points come from a stratum dated to ca. 4400 BP. None were recovered at Asana or Quelcatani. This type is somewhat rare in surface assemblages in the Río Huenque and Río Ilave Valleys. We propose that Type 5A is diagnostic of the Terminal Archaic, or the period dating to ca. 4400–3600 BP.

REGIONAL COMPARISONS

At Pachamachay in central Peru, Rick's (1980) Types 5B and 8B—dated to ca. 4500–3500 BP and ca. 4500–1500 BP, respectively—are similar in size to our 5A, but have a much more elongated, foliate shape. Further to the south in Chile, 5A-like points apparently date to the Early Preceramic. Nuñez Atencio (1992) recovered one point at Tuina (dated to ca. 10800–9000 BP), which resembles our Type 5A. Another similar point at Tambillo dates to ca. 8600 BP (Nuñez Atencio 1992). Both of these points have the more rounded, squat shape characteristic of our 5A type, but are notably larger than any of our 5A examples.

5B. Straight-based to Convex-based Triangular Forms

Type 5B (Figure 3.6d–e) is defined based on two examples from Hakenasa (Santoro and Nuñez 1987) and forty-four from Quelcatani. Table 3.17 presents metric data for representative

TABLE 3.16. Type 5A: Ovo-triangular forms

Site	Hakenasa, Fig. 6a	Hakenasa, Fig. 6b	Hakenasa, Santoro and Nuñez 1987: Fig. 9-70	Hakenasa, Fig. 6c
Age (BP)	4400	4400	4400	4400
Length	23	20	28	25
Width	20	13	22 (est) 20 (frag)	22
Basal width	5	1	9	7
Tool length/width	1.15	1.54	1.27 (est)	1.14

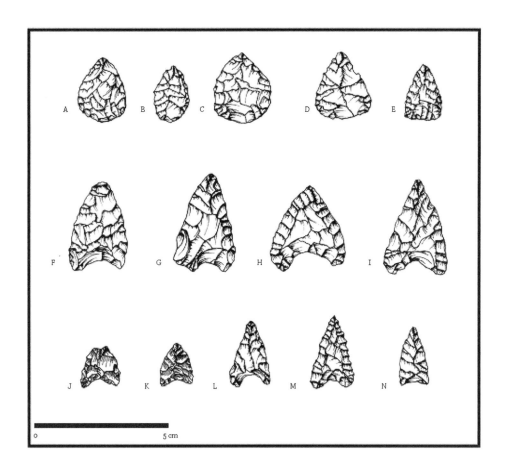

FIGURE 3.6. Types 5A–5D. Type 5A: *(a)* Hakenasa, after Santoro and Nuñez 1987:Figure 9-68, *(b)* Hakenasa, after Santoro and Nuñez 1987:Figure 9-69, *(c)* Hakenasa, after Santoro and Nuñez 1987:Figure 9-67. Type 5B: *(d)* Hakenasa, after Santoro and Nuñez 1987:Figure 9-80, *(e)* Quelcatani, level WXXIV. Type 5C: *(f)* Hakenasa, after Santoro and Nuñez 1987:Figure 9-83, *(g)* Quelcatani, level WXXIV, *(h)* Quelcatani, level WXXV, *(i)* Quelcatani, level WXXV. Type 5D: *(j)* Asana, level IIb, *(k)* Asana, level IIa, *(l)* Quelcatani, level WXVIII, *(m)* Quelcatani, level WXX, *(n)* Quelcatani, level WXVIII .

TABLE 3.17. Type 5B: Straight to convex-based triangular forms

Site	Hakenasa, Santoro and Nuñez 1987: Fig. 9-79	Hakenasa, Fig. 6d	Quelcatani, L. WXXIV	Quelcatani, L. WXXIV, Fig. 6e	Quelcatani, L. WXVIII	Quelcatani, L. WXVIII
Age	4400 BP	4400 BP	3660 BP	3660 BP	2800 BP	2800 BP
Length	31	24	44	20	11	15
Width	24 (est) 22 (frag)	22	34	14	10	14
Basal width	12 (est)	5	15	9	9	8
Tool length/ width	1.29 (est)	1.09	1.29	1.43	1.10	1.07

specimens. The diagnostic characteristics of this type are its triangular shape and a straight to convex base. Lateral margins and bases are typically straight on most examples, but some exhibit very gently convex margins. Blade edge serration or denticulation occurs on a significant minority of specimens. Type 5B generally resembles Type 3C, which also has a somewhat triangular appearance. While Type 5B is typically smaller than 3C, there is some overlap at the large end of the 5B size range. However, the two types are easily differentiated based on overall shape, with 3C having a much more elongated form (tool length/width ratios of 1.56–2.32). Type 5B length/width ratios only begin to approach those of Type 3C when the point length is very small; about 20 mm, which is well below the lower size limit of the 3C type.

The Hakenasa points come from a ca. 4400 BP stratum. At Quelcatani, four points were found in Terminal Archaic levels WWXXV–WXXVII dated to ca. 4400/4000–3700 BP. Two were recovered in Tiwanaku levels WVII and EVI, which are dated to ca. AD 500–1100. However, the vast majority (85%) was evenly distributed throughout levels spanning the entire Formative period (WVIII–WXXIV). Type 5B points were not found at Asana, but are fairly common in the Río Huenque and Río Ilave Valleys. We consider 5B diagnostic of a relatively long period spanning the Terminal Archaic through Tiwanaku, or the period from ca. 2400 BC (4400 BP) to AD 1100, in the south-central highlands.

REGIONAL COMPARISONS
Within the south-central Andean highlands, 5B style points have been recovered from only one other site, Las Cuevas, where one was found in the ca. 9500–8300 BP stratum (Santoro and Nuñez 1987). In the Chilean-Argentine salt puna, 5B-like points appear to be an Early Preceramic style. Aschero (1984) recovered two comparable points from a ca. 9200 BP stratum at Inca Cueva-4. Nuñez Atencio (1992) also shows two analogous points, one from Tambillo dated to ca. 8600 BP and one from Tuina dated to ca. 10800–9000 BP. In central Peru, two of Rick's (1980) Pachamachay styles resemble our type 5B: his type

8C, dated to ca. 3000–2000 BP, and his rare type 1A, dated to ca. 10500–9000 BP.

These data strongly suggest that the prevalence and age of this point style varies geographically. In the central Peruvian highlands, points resembling our 5B style are rare. They appear only at Pachamachay, with three points recovered from Early Preceramic levels and slightly higher numbers in Formative period levels (Rick 1980). In the south-central highlands, 5B points are common and all appear exclusively in Terminal Archaic to Tiwanaku period excavated contexts, except for the single point in the Early Archaic stratum at Las Cuevas. Further south in the Atacama region of Chile and Argentina, 5B-like points also are common, but here they appear exclusively as an Early Archaic style. We suggest that the single early 5B style point at Las Cuevas represents either a heavily reworked type 3C point (which spans the entire Archaic period) or marks the extreme northern limit of Early Archaic influence from the Atacama region.

5C. Large Triangular Forms with Concave Bases
Type 5C (Figure 3.6f–i) is defined based on one example from Hakenasa (Santoro and Nuñez 1987) and thirty from Quelcatani. Table 3.18 presents metric data for representative specimens. The diagnostic characteristics of Type 5C are its (1) triangular shape, (2) concave base, and (3) large size (30 mm or longer). Blade edge modification may or may not be present, including the occasional presence of spines at the haft/blade transition, which likely served as a lashing feature that secured the point to the shaft. Type 5C resembles both the 3F and 5D types, and may be a transitional form between the two. Types 5C and 3F both have concave bases and wide tool widths, but the 3F form has a lanceolate shape, greater length (60–78 mm), and is more elongated (tool length/width ratios of 2.40–2.78) than the 5C type. Types 5C and 5D have the same shape and basal configuration, but the 5D form is, by definition, shorter (less than 30 mm long). Known 5D specimens also appear narrower (less than 20 mm wide).

The Hakenasa point comes from a stratum dated to ca. 4400 BP. At Quelcatani, 5C points oc-

TABLE 3.18. Type 5C: Large triangular forms with concave bases

Site	Hakenasa, Fig. 6f	Quelcatani, L. WXXIV	Quelcatani, L. WXXIV, Fig. 6g	Quelcatani, L. WXXI	Quelcatani, L. WXXV, Fig. 6h	Quelcatani, L. WXXIV, Fig. 6i
Age	4400 BP	3700 BP	3700 BP	3000 BP	3800 BP	3660 BP
Length	31	34	35	30	30	34
Width	21	25	22	26	29	25
Basal width	19	18 (est)	15 (est)	23	23	21
Concavity width	14	13	11	13	18	16
Concavity depth	3	5	4	4	6	5
Tool length/ width	1.48	1.36	1.59	1.15	1.03	1.36

cur in Terminal Archaic through Late Formative levels spanning the period from ca. 2000/2400 BC (4000/4400 BP) to AD 500. A small number (14%) were found in the Terminal Archaic levels WXXV–WXXVII, dated to ca. 4400/4000–3700 BP. The majority (47%) came from the early Formative levels WXX–WXIV, dated to ca. 1500–2000 BP, and their frequency subsequently declined steadily throughout the remaining Formative period levels (WVII–WXIII, EVII–EXIV). Although none were recovered at Asana, type 5C points are relatively common in the Río Huenque and Río Ilave Valleys. We consider 5C diagnostic of the Terminal Archaic through Formative, or the period from ca. 2400 BC (4400 BP) to AD 500.

REGIONAL COMPARISONS

At Jiskairumoko, in the Río Ilave Valley, Aldenderfer recovered a couple of 5C points from levels dating to ca. 3600–3400 BP during his 1997–1999 excavations at the site. At Toquepala, some of Ravines' (1972) illustrated Type P1 points very closely resemble our Type 5C. Type P1 points were found exclusively in the two uppermost strata at the site, with the majority in stratum 1. Unfortunately, we cannot determine whether the 5C-like examples came from one or both strata since the illustrations lack stratum affiliations. Ravines estimates that strata 1 and 2 date to ca. 5500–5000 BP, but we suspect that they also include much younger deposits given

their high frequency of both 5C- and 5D-like points.

Outside of the south-central Andes, comparable points are known only from the more southerly salt puna region. Nuñez Atencio (1992) reports that similar points date to ca. 8600 BP at Tambillo, ca. 8000 BP at Toconce, and 3000–2800 BP at Tulán-54.

5D. Small Triangular Forms with Concave Bases

Type 5D (Figure 3.6j–n) is defined based on two examples from Hakenasa (Santoro and Nuñez 1987), three from Asana, and 345 from Quelcatani. Table 3.19 presents metric data for representative specimens. The diagnostic characteristics of this type are its (1) triangular shape, (2) concave base, and (3) small size (less than 30 mm). Blade edge modification may or may not be present. Type 5C is similar to 5D, but 5C is longer (30 mm or greater) and typically wider (20 mm or greater) than the 5D form.

The two Hakenasa points come from a ca. 4400 BP stratum. At Asana, two were recovered from level IIa—dated to ca. 3600 BP—and one from level IIb, dated to ca. 4300–3600 BP. At Quelcatani, 5D points occur in Terminal Archaic through Late Horizon levels (WIII–WXXVIII, EIII–EXIV), dating from ca. 2400/2000 BC (4400/4000 BP) to AD 1532. The majority (85%) date to the Formative period, with 6% dating to the Terminal Archaic, 6% to Tiwanaku, 2% to the Late

TABLE 3.19. Type 5D: Small triangular forms with concave bases

Site	Age	Length	Width	Basal Width	Concavity Width	Concavity Depth	Tool Length/ Width
Hakenasa, Santoro, and Nuñez 1987: Fig. 9-81	4400 BP	21	15	15	10	2	1.40
Hakenasa, Santoro, and Nuñez 1987: Fig. 9-82	4400 BP	27	15	13	11	2	1.80
Asana, L. IIb, Fig. 6j	3600-4300 BP	17 (est) 14 (frag)	16	15	11	2	1.06
Asana, L. IIa, Fig. 6k	3600 BP	15	13	13	9	2	1.15
Asana, L. IIA	3600 BP	17 (est) 9 (frag)	10	9	7	1	1.70
Quelcatani, L. WXXIV, Fig. 6l	3660 BP	23	16	14	11	4	1.44
Quelcatani, L. WX, Fig. 6m	2400 BP	26	16	14	9	3	1.63
Quelcatani, L. WXVIII, Fig. 6n	2700 BP	21	11	10	9	1	1.91
Quelcatani, L. EXIV	3000 BP	16	9	13	11	1	1.78

Intermediate period, and 1% to the Late Horizon. Within the Formative, frequencies are highest in the later Formative, with 54% of all 5D points found in levels dating to ca. 900 BC–AD 500. Type 5D points are abundant in the Río Huenque and Río Ilave Valleys. We consider Type 5D only a very general temporal diagnostic, serving to differentiate the last 4,400 years (Terminal Archaic through Late Horizon) from the earlier portions of the Preceramic in the south-central highlands.

Type 5D's small size falls within the generally expected size range for arrow points. Shott, working with a lithic collection of 132 arrow points and 39 dart points, calculated a mean arrow size of 31.1 mm length and 14.7 mm shoulder width, and a mean dart size of 51.7 length and 23.1 mm shoulder width (1997:Table 2). However, he points out that his data indicate that while arrows clearly tend to be smaller than darts there is significant size overlap between the two. Based on his data, and calculating out two standard deviations from the dart sample's means, there is only a 5% probability that a point shorter than 23.7 mm and narrower than 13.9 mm is a dart rather than an arrow. Individual length and width measurements were not collected for all Type 5D points at Quelcatani, but all were placed into one of two size classes:

small (20–29.99 mm long) and miniature (less than 20 mm long). Assuming that the Quelcatani miniature size class also includes only points narrower than 13.9 mm, we can say with 95% confidence that the miniature 5D points functioned as arrows.

The distribution of miniature 5D points from secure excavated contexts at Quelcatani (about 100 points) is nearly the same as that seen for all 5D points. A notable minority (11%) were in Terminal Archaic levels dated to between ca. 4400/ 4000 and 3700 BP. Most (85%) came from Formative levels, again with highest concentrations in the later Formative, or ca. 900 BC–AD 500. A few date to Tiwanaku (3%) or Late Horizon (1%) times. None were found in Late Intermediate period contexts. In addition, about twenty-four Type 5B points from solid contexts at Quelcatani are classified as miniature, and they span the Terminal Archaic (ca. 4000–3700 BP) through the end of the Formative. Most of these Quelcatani 5B points (41%) date to the later Formative, or ca. 900 BC–AD 500. These data suggest that use of the bow and arrow in the south-central highlands began by 3700 BP, and perhaps as early as 4400 BP, although significant reliance on this technology may not have developed until the later Formative.

REGIONAL COMPARISONS

Aldenderfer's 1997–1999 excavations at Jiskairumoko in the Río Ilave Valley recovered several 5D points from levels dating to ca. 3600–3400 BP. Type 5D points were also found at the Formative- to Tiwanaku-aged site of Tumatumani, along the Lake Titicaca shore, but cannot be firmly dated because they were recovered from either excavation units containing mixed construction fill or surface contexts (Stanish and Steadman 1994). Many of Ravines' (1972) illustrated Type P1 points at Toquepala are very similar to our Type 5D. Most P1 points were found in the uppermost stratum (stratum 1), with the remainder from stratum 2.

SOME BROADER IMPLICATIONS OF THE TYPOLOGY

Emerging from this work are several patterns that have broader archaeological implications. First, there is a high degree of homogeneity in projectile point styles over relatively broad areas in the early Preceramic. During the Early Archaic, and into the Middle Archaic, the south-central highlands show an extremely strong connection to the adjacent western-draining Andean valleys and coast. All Early Archaic point types known in the south-central highlands (Type 1 series 4A and 4B) have direct correlates with Early Archaic points recovered from sites located in the western Cordillera low sierra and Pacific coastal zone, from Arequipa to northern Chile. These close material culture ties, and the social and/or cultural interactions they imply, continue at least into the earlier Middle Archaic, given the similar geographic distribution of basically identical transitional Early/Middle Archaic (Type 2A) and some Middle Archaic (Types 2C and 3B) styles. This strong link, combined with the facts that the earliest known Preceramic sites in the south-central Andes date to earlier periods along the coast (Keefer et al. 1998; Sandweiss et al. 1989, 1998) than in the highlands, and that the earliest levels at Asana (the oldest known site in the highlands) contain coastal lithic materials, strongly suggest that initial entry into the highlands came from the lower western valleys. More general stylistic similarities link the south-central Andean highlands to central highland Peru. This is most obvious in the distribution of unstemmed, unshouldered foliate points (Series 3 types), which represent long-standing traditions in both regions throughout the Preceramic, as well as in the south-central low sierra and coast.

Second, geographic homogeneity in point styles diminishes substantially through time. Over the course of the Archaic, the number of identifiable styles appears to increase, while the geographic extent of each style decreases. More localized styles first begin to develop in the Middle Archaic (Types 2B and 3E), and this trend accelerates in the Late and Terminal Archaic. During the Late Archaic, most ties to the central Peruvian highlands disappear, and while links to the adjacent western valleys continue, more local highland styles (Type 3F) and variants develop. Local variation is best seen in Type 4D, where different attribute combinations appear in different portions of the south-central highlands. Type 4D-like points have concave bases in the Arequipa highlands, but straight or convex bases in the southwestern Titicaca Basin. The expanding stem 4D variant known from the Arequipa region also appears fairly common in surface contexts in the northern Lake Titicaca Basin, but is rare to nonexistent in the southwestern portion of the basin. This development of more regional styles implies that interaction spheres began to focus within, rather than outside, the south-central highlands and that social-cultural developments increasingly played out over this more localized stage. The proliferation of even more localized styles in the Late Archaic hints that identity markers became more important, or that social or political differentiation intensified at this time.

Third, ties between the south-central highlands and the more southerly salt puna apparently were always very weak, as the entire character of the Preceramic projectile point traditions in these two regions differs sharply. The ubiquitous Archaic period tradition of unstemmed, unshouldered foliate points (Types 3A, 3B, 3D, 3E and 3F) seen in the south-central Andes is rare further south, where unstemmed, unshouldered, triangular forms (Types 3C, 5B and 5C) are common. Most other point types found in the south-central highlands (Series 1 and 2, and Types 4A–4E) are essentially un-known in the salt puna. In addition, the blade and micro-lithic tradition documented in the Atacama region beginning in the Late Archaic—or ca. 5000 BP (Nuñez Atencio 1992)—does not occur in the south-central highlands. This clear divergence suggests that these two regions experienced very different cultural-historical trajectories, likely with only limited contact or interaction, at best, between the two regions throughout most of prehistory.

Finally, it is apparent that projectile point studies also have significant potential to contribute to our understanding of post-Archaic societies. Typically, research emphases move away from lithics toward ceramics, architecture, and settlement patterns when more complex societies are studied, yet clearly projectile points provide additional avenues for investigating these societies and can even help form new questions about them. For example, while it appears that bow and arrow technology developed during the Terminal Archaic, it first becomes heavily integrated into technological systems during the Formative period. It is during this time frame that the first sedentary agro-pastoral villages and complex social and political institutions developed in the Lake Titicaca Basin (Aldenderfer 1997; Hastorf 1999b; Mujica 1987; Stanish and Steadman 1994; Stanish et al. 1997). What role did the bow and arrow play in these developments? At least one important function may have been territorial defense and warfare, as suggested by rock art in the Río Huenque Valley (Klink 1999). However, the bow and arrow never completely replaced other weapon systems. Why were multiple technologies maintained, and what might this reveal about hunting practices and subsistence economies? Projectile point frequencies also appear to drop precipitously in the Titicaca Basin beginning with the expansion of the Tiwanaku state,

and this trend continues through the Late Horizon. How might the reduced use of projectile points relate to state expansion and control? The identification of a probable "elite" Tiwanaku point style (Type 4E) allows an additional means of investigating topics such as social identity and status, and economic issues such as controlled production and trade.

CONCLUSION

Projectile points constitute one of the most abundant material culture indicators of prehistoric occupation and use of the south-central Andean highlands, particularly for the Preceramic period. This is demonstrated by the results of several recent survey projects in the region, which document not only their ubiquity but also their wide range of morphological variability. However, the inability to confidently assess their cultural and temporal affiliations has severely limited the potential to gain insight from these finds. The projectile point chronology presented here moves us considerably closer to not only our immediate goal of being able to use the surface archaeological record as a direct source of information about the prehistory of the south-central highlands, but also our long-term goal of better understanding the history and trajectory of cultural developments in the region. While this typology marks a significant step forward, it should be viewed as a work in progress rather than a final statement. Although its foundation is solid, it is clear that the currently available data set of excavated and radiocarbon-dated projectile point assemblages does not fully reflect the diversity of point forms known from surface contexts. We expect, and hope, that future research will generate additional data and enable refinement and expansion of this typology.

4.

Preceramic Period Settlement Patterns in the Huancané-Putina River Valley, Northern Titicaca Basin, Peru

Lisa M. Cipolla

INTRODUCTION

A SYSTEMATIC SURFACE survey by Stanish and Plourde in 1999 and 2000 recovered almost one hundred Preceramic sites in the Huancané-Putina River Valley of the Titicaca Basin (Stanish and Plourde 2000). The earliest evidence for occupation in the northern basin is indicated by the presence of Early Archaic sites dating to 8000–6000 BC. These dates are consistent with data from the southern and western portions of the basin (Aldenderfer 1998; Aldenderfer and Klink 1996; Klink, Chapter 2, this volume; Stanish et al. 1997), and indicate that the region was not occupied earlier, as no Paleo-Indian period points to date have been found in the Titicaca Basin. Furthermore, the changes in the Preceramic settlement pattern in the northern basin are also consistent with changes seen elsewhere in the basin. While these similarities may not seem surprising, it is useful to note that the Titicaca Basin covers an area of 50,000 km^2, and thus the homogeneity of the data has profound regional implications for understanding the early prehistory of the area. It is not until the Late Archaic period that notable differences between the north and elsewhere in the region appear. Most notable, it is at this time that differences between the northern basin and the southern basin began to form, a pattern that presages the differences seen in the earliest Ceramic periods in the region, such as Qaluyu and Chiripa.

THE SURVEY AREA

The Huancané-Putina River Valley drains from the eastern Cordillera of Peru and Bolivia into Lake Titicaca. It is an entrenched river that meanders widely in many zones leaving existing oxbow wetlands. Tectonic uplift is tilting the basin to the southwest (Bills et al. 1994) at a fairly rapid rate, as the river terraces are actively eroding today. Geographically, the valley can be divided into three main zone types. Zone 1 represents the southern portion of the valley, as it enters into the lake and opens into a wide and marshy zone scattered with small, salty lakes. Surface visibility in this zone is very low, as the land varies between wetland reeds and tall grasses. This area covers approximately 100 km^2 of the survey and is lush agricultural land today, being used for both pasture and raised-field farming.

North of the lakeshore area is Zone 2, where the valley bottom becomes marshy only during the rainy season. This zone covers only about 50 km^2 of the survey area but is distinct in that it is a seasonally wet area today that at times is lush with wetland reeds and grasses around the entrenched Río Huancané.

Zone 3 is the northern end of the survey, where the valley begins to rise and covers approximately 300 km^2. The valley becomes drier and contains two main passes and a number of smaller river tributaries. At the northernmost end of the survey area, the valley narrows again at the edge of an active geologic pass. A hill, named El Volcán, is the source of a large hot spring that overflows into the Putina Pass. The pampa areas surrounding the pass contain groundwater near the surface where modern day artificial lakes, or *qochas*, have been dug to provide water and grasses for pasture animals. At 3900–4000 masl, this is an unusually wet zone with an abundance of available freshwater that makes it ideal for grazing animals and farming highland crops. The natural river terraces in Zone 3 reach as high as 30 m in some areas on one side of the river, with low river-wash terraces on the opposite sides. Because the Putina River is a wide and meandering river, the relict river terraces are actively eroding away.

Distinguishing these three different zones in the survey area is useful for exploring the changes in settlement and subsistence strategies over time, as well as for understanding the nature of the archaeological record that remains on the surface today. The topographic effects that vary throughout the Huancané-Putina River Valley are undoubtedly responsible, in part, for the settlement patterns observed for the Preceramic periods, as surface visibility in some areas is low, and erosion has likely destroyed many sites in the valley.[1]

METHODOLOGY

The survey methodology used by Stanish and Plourde was an intensive, systematic coverage of the entire valley from the ridgetops to the valley bottom. All sites were recorded, and representative samples of all artifact types present on the surface were collected. Relative artifact densities and site sizes were recorded as well. An analysis of all lithic material collected was conducted, with particular attention given to identifying projectile point styles and material types recovered. Artifact densities per site for the Preceramic periods were not calculated for this study, nor were differences in site sizes over time. Most of the Preceramic sites are multicomponent sites, and a detailed study aimed at isolating site size per time period has not been conducted at this time.

The identification of each Preceramic time period for this survey is based on the projectile point typology developed by Klink and Al-denderfer (Chapter 3, this volume). Using their chronology based on point styles, projectile points found during the survey were used to determine time periods. Sites that contained lithic debris only and did not contain either ceramics or diagnostic projectile points are considered "undiagnostic Preceramic" sites. Similarly, some sites yielded fragments of points that are Preceramic in form but do not contain enough of the base of the point to determine its time period. Such sites are also considered to be undiagnostic Preceramic sites. While it is possible that many of the Ceramic period sites that contain lithic debris may also have a Preceramic component, these types of sites were not recorded as Preceramic unless a diagnostic projectile point was found on the surface.

All points found during the survey fall within the typology put forth by Klink and Al-denderfer (Chapter 3, this volume). There are two variant point styles that are common in the northern basin but only occur rarely in the southwestern basin. These styles are variants of Late Archaic points found elsewhere in the basin and always occur on sites with other Late Archaic points. In fact, these points represent almost half of all Late Archaic points found in the Huancané-Putina River Valley, thereby warranting a distinct style type designation that is representative of the Late Archaic for the northern basin.[2]

The two point styles are variants of Type 4D and 4F in the Klink and Aldenderfer typology. In keeping with their typology, these northern basin variants are called Type 4G and 4H. Type 4D is an elongated, broad-stemmed form with parallel-sided hafts; type 4G is similar except that the stems are excurvate and are expanded at the base of the point. The bases themselves are straight to slightly convex. The stems tend to be squat in proportion to the rest of the point, and these points are almost always made of andesite or basalt (Figure 4.1).

Type 4H is a variant of Type 4F. Where Type 4F points tend to be smaller than Type 4D points, Type 4H are typically smaller than Type 4G. Type 4H points are also stemmed points with excurvate hafts, but these points have longer, expanding stems in relation to blade length and their bases are usually slightly to

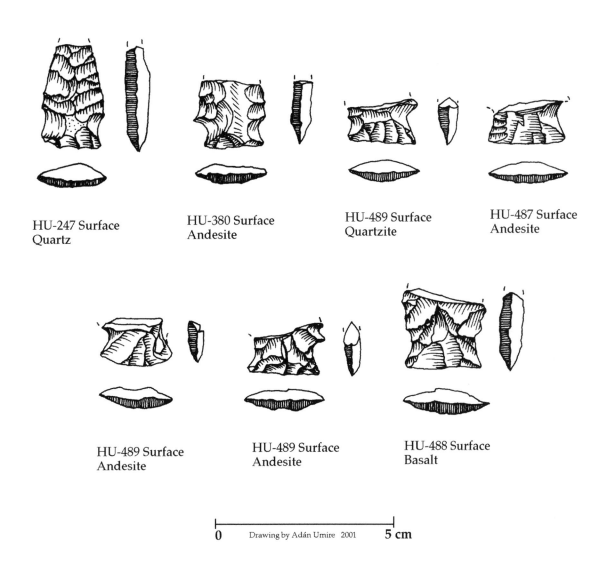

HU-247 Surface
Quartz

HU-380 Surface
Andesite

HU-489 Surface
Quartzite

HU-487 Surface
Andesite

HU-489 Surface
Andesite

HU-489 Surface
Andesite

HU-488 Surface
Basalt

0   Drawing by Adán Umire 2001   5 cm

FIGURE 4.1. Projectile point Type 4G

very convex (Figure 4.2). These points are made of a variety of materials, although they are usually made of chert.

Given the typology identified above, it is possible to understand the settlement pattern for the Preceramic of the Huancané-Putina River Valley. While the existing Preceramic typology is very broad and covers a time span of almost seven thousand years (with three major periods spanning approximately two thousand years each), there are a few point types that have been identified as occurring within a very narrow time frame. Because this information is so spe-

cific, I have chosen to discuss these particular episodes separately where possible.

RESULTS

The Early Archaic Settlement Pattern (10,000–8,000 BP)

Only six sites containing diagnostic Early Archaic points were found in the survey (Figure 4.3). Interestingly, five of the sites are all clustered in Zone 3 along the Río Cala Cala, a tributary of the Río Huancané. The other site is

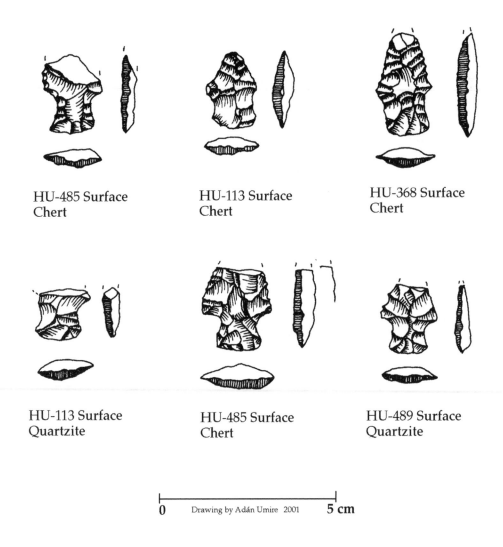

HU-485 Surface
Chert

HU-113 Surface
Chert

HU-368 Surface
Chert

HU-113 Surface
Quartzite

HU-485 Surface
Chert

HU-489 Surface
Quartzite

0   Drawing by Adán Umire 2001   **5 cm**

FIGURE 4.2. Projectile point Type 4H

located in Zone 2. There were a total of eleven points found, with nine of them belonging to either Type 1A or 1B. Most of these points were made from either chert or quartzite, and only one was made of andesite.

In addition to the six Early Archaic sites, three more points were found that could belong to either the Early or Middle Archaic. These points were found at three separate sites, with one occurring in each of the three zones. Two of the points are isolated finds, and another was located on a multicomponent site that had no other Early Archaic points.

The Middle Archaic Settlement Pattern (8000–6000 BP)

Fourteen Middle Archaic sites were found in the valley. Eleven sites were located in the upland areas of Zone 3 and are clustered on the Río Cala Cala and the Río Putina river terraces (Figure 4.4). Two sites are located in the wetland area and only one site is located near the lakeshore. A total of twenty-one Middle Archaic points were recovered, with the majority being made of quartzite. Six points were made of chert, and four were made of nonlocal basalt. Most the points were either Type 2B or 3B. Only two points were Type 2C.

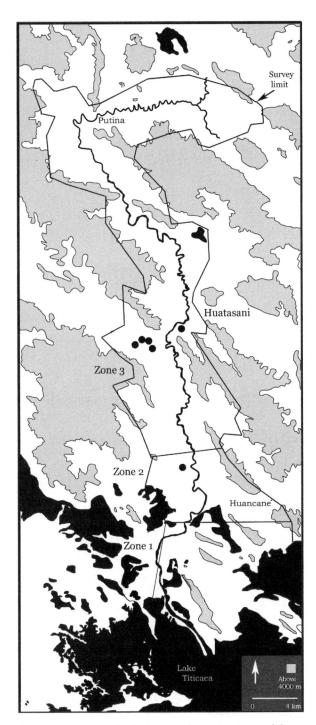

FIGURE 4.3. The Early Archaic settlement pattern of the Huancané-Putina River Valley

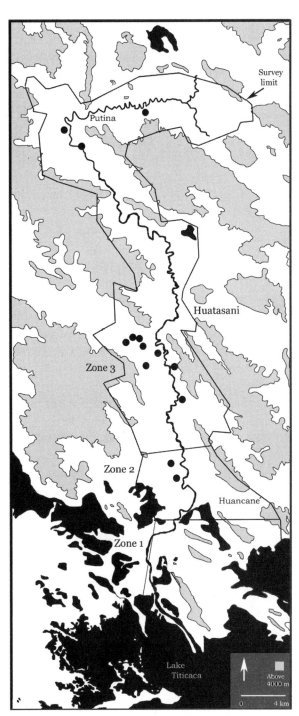

FIGURE 4.4. The Middle Archaic settlement pattern of the Huancané-Putina River Valley

The Late Archaic Settlement Pattern (6000–4400 BP)

A dramatic increase in the number of sites occurred during the Late Archaic. A total of twenty-six sites were found scattered through-

out the entire survey area (Figure 4.5). Eighteen sites are located in Zone 3 in the northern portion of the survey. They are clustered on the river terrace along the western side of the Río Putina and along the Río Cala Cala river terrace in the same locations as the earlier time period sites. Five sites were located in Zone 2 south of Huatasani in various locations ranging from pampa to hilltops. Three more sites were found in Zone 1, with two being along the modern edge of Lake Titicaca south of the town of Huancané. While neither site is located near the Huancané River, it is likely that the river has moved over time and may once have drained into the lake near these two sites. Topographic data show a very wet area just to the north of these sites and is likely to have been the drainage for the river at one point in time.

The point type styles recovered from the survey vary widely, but still work within the typology put forth by Klink and Aldenderfer (Chapter 3, this volume). A total of fifty-one points were found. These were made of a variety of material types, including andesite, basalt, chert, and quartzite. One obsidian point was also recovered. The most striking data regarding the Late Archaic points is the number of excurvate hafted points found in the survey area in comparison to the number found in other regions in the basin. Because twenty-two of the fifty-one points recovered exhibit these features, it is likely that these styles—Types 4G and 4H—are local to the northern basin. These points also occur in each of the three zones of the survey.

The Terminal Archaic Settlement Pattern (4400–3600 BP)

A total of fourteen Terminal Archaic sites were found in the survey (Figure 4.6). Four of these sites are determined by the presence of Type 5A points, with two of the sites being located in the upland area of Zone 3, and two in Zone 2. No sites were found near the lakeshore. A total of five points were found, with two being made of chert, two of quartzite, and one of obsidian.

Of the fourteen sites, five were found with point styles 5B or 5D, which could date to anywhere from the Terminal Archaic to the Late Horizon. No ceramics were found on any of these sites, however, so it is likely that these sites belong to the Terminal Archaic. One site is located in Zone 2, and the others are in Zone 3. No sites were found near the lakeshore, and most of the points found on these sites are made of obsidian.

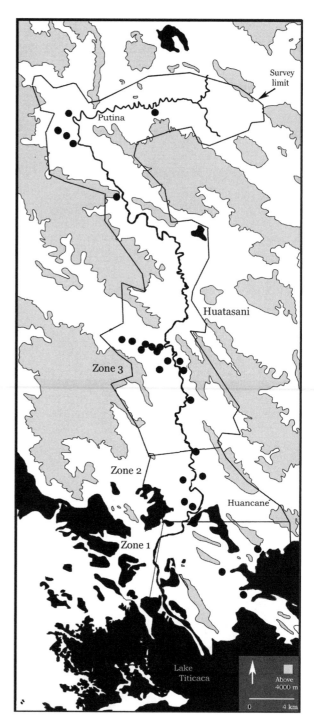

FIGURE 4.5. The Late Archaic settlement pattern of the Huancané-Putina River Valley

Additionally, four sites with Type 5C points were found that could belong to either the Terminal Archaic or Formative periods. One site is an isolated point find in Zone 2, and the other three sites are all large, multicomponent Ce-

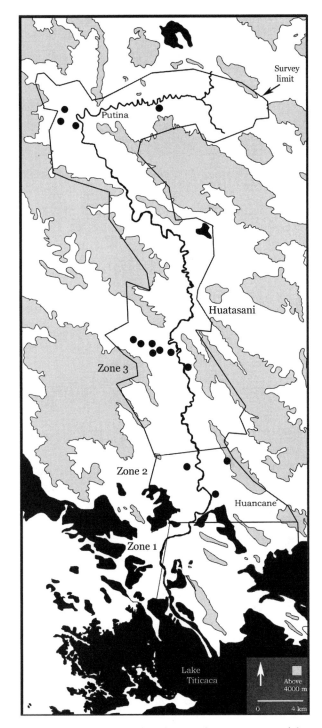

FIGURE 4.6. The Terminal Archaic settlement pattern of the Huancané-Putina River Valley

ramic period sites. Because these points could be associated with the Ceramic period occupations, they are not included in the Terminal Archaic settlement pattern.

Nondiagnostic Preceramic Sites

In addition to the datable Preceramic sites mentioned above, a total of twenty-nine undiagnostic Preceramic sites were identified. Two of these sites contain points that range in time from the Early Archaic to the Late Archaic, and another twenty-seven sites contain either just lithic debris or undiagnostic fragments of Archaic period points. Four sites occur in Zone 1, ten are in Zone 2, and fifteen are located in Zone 3.

DISCUSSION

Overall, at least ninety Preceramic occupations have been found, although many of the sites are multicomponent Preceramic sites. No cave or rockshelter sites were found that could be dated to the Preceramic. All sites recorded were open-air sites, and only a few were found in locations with nearby rockshelters that could have been used occasionally. Many of the rock formations in the valley consist of eroding red sandstone, and very few natural cave or rockshelters have been found.

The change in the distribution of sites over time throughout the Huancané-Putina River Valley is similar to patterns recorded elsewhere in the Lake Titicaca Basin. The earliest occupation of the valley began with a small number of Early Archaic sites located on river terraces and away from the lakeshore. Because of the multicomponent nature of these sites, it is unclear whether these were campsites or isolated hunting zones. Their locations near water sources would be consistent with the interpretation of these sites as having been hunting zones in areas where camelids and deer would have been found, as seen elsewhere in the basin (Klink, Chapter 2, this volume).

The number of Middle Archaic sites is double that of the Early Archaic; however, there are still few sites overall relative to the size of the survey zone. These Middle Archaic sites are located on river terraces in the same areas as the Early Archaic sites, indicating that these zones were probably the most productive in the valley. The Middle Archaic is also the period with the earliest evidence of use of the lakeshore area.

The Late Archaic shows a great increase in the number of sites throughout the valley. These sites are mostly open-air sites along the river terraces. However, a number of sites were also found on hillsides and hilltops, perhaps indicating the diversification of subsistence strategies. In addition, three sites are located near the modern lakeshore area. This pattern is consistent with Klink's data (Chapter 2, this volume) from Río Huenque, where there is a decrease in the number of Late Archaic sites in the uplands and a shift toward the river drainages immediately adjacent to Lake Titicaca. However, the presence of three sites located near the lakeshore margins does not necessarily indicate a greater reliance on lakeshore resources themselves. While the apparent trend toward diversification of subsistence patterns is consistent with this interpretation, there remains the problem of understanding the paleoenvironment during the Late Archaic period. A body of paleoclimatic research in the Titicaca Basin indicates that lake levels were much lower than modern-day levels (Baker et al. 2001). Because of this fact, it is assumed that the sites located near the margins today would probably have not been on the lake edge during the Late Archaic period. Also, these sites are not on the modern-day river terrace but appear to be located along a relict river terrace from where the Huancané River has shifted over time. The shift in the lakeshore environment has likely affected the representation of sites found on the surface during the survey.

The most important difference in the Late Archaic data from the Huancané-Putina survey compared to data from other areas in the basin is the diversity of projectile point styles, particularly the predominance of two types that only rarely occur elsewhere. The similarity in styles of projectile points from the earlier periods with those found elsewhere in the south-central Andes indicates a generalized cultural pattern throughout the region. Whether or not this reflects long-distance transhumance over the region or is an indication of other social factors, it is clear that the localization and diversification of cultural patterns increases significantly during the Late Archaic in the basin. Previous scholars have noted the differences between the northern Titicaca Basin and the southern Titicaca

Basin during the Ceramic periods (Bennett 1950; Burger et al. 2000), and it now seems likely that these differences began in the Preceramic during the Late Archaic period.

There are only half as many Terminal Archaic sites as Late Archaic sites in the valley, but this may be due to the fact that the Terminal Archaic period defines a much narrower time span than does the Late Archaic. As noted by both Klink and Aldenderfer (Aldenderfer 1997; Aldenderfer and Klink 1996; Klink, Chapter 2, this volume), the Terminal Archaic may also represent a truly transitional phase to the Formative period, involving the aggregation of settlements and the appearance of larger, permanently occupied sites in the basin. It is interesting to note, however, that no Terminal Archaic sites have been identified on the lakeshore margins adjacent to the mouth of the Huancané River. Again, this is perhaps due to the change in the lakeshore environment during this period. Baucom and Rigsby (1999) note that during the Terminal Archaic period there was a dramatic increase in rainfall in the basin and the lake level rose anywhere from 25 to 85 m to its present-day level. Because the northern portion of the valley receives more rainfall annually than the southern portion, it is likely that the lakeshore margins were wetter than they are today, and probably were uninhabitable during this period. What is important to note, however, is that the upland portion of the valley contains the largest number of Terminal Archaic sites, indicating that the reliance on upland puna resources continued to be very important during this time. While the subsistence strategies were likely much more diverse than in previous periods, the importance of fresh-water sources and upland grazing land for camelids seems to have continued to be important.

Generally, most of the Preceramic sites found in the valley are located in the low areas along the rivers. In Zone 3, almost of all of the sites are located on the southern and western portions of the rivers. This pattern is striking and indicative of the tectonic uplift in the basin that is moving the rivers in a southwestward direction. The eastern side of the Putina River consists of low river beds and oxbows that likely have destroyed any prehistoric sites in the path of the moving river channel. The river terrace on the western side is very high and, while actively eroding away, contains the only remaining sites in the area. It is entirely possible that many more sites of all time periods existed in the region but have since eroded away. However, it does not appear that population levels were ever very high during the Preceramic periods of the valley.

CONCLUSION

The Preceramic settlement patterns for the Huancané-Putina Valley are similar to those from elsewhere in the region during the Early and Middle Archaic periods. The initial occupation of the northern basin began 10,000–8,000 years ago with a small number of sites and a gradual increase in population over time. Population levels throughout the Preceramic do not appear to have ever been particularly high given the small number of sites in comparison to the size of the valley itself. The subsistence patterns indicate a focus on the upland puna areas of fresh-water sources throughout the entire Preceramic, with increasing diversification of resources not occurring until the Late Archaic period. It is also during the Late Archaic period that significant differences in projectile point styles from elsewhere in the basin occur. The question of why these differences occurred, however, remains to be answered. It is clear that long-distance exchange and interaction occurred throughout the south-central Andes during the earlier Preceramic periods (Aldenderfer 1998; Burger et al. 2000). Therefore, this development alone is not sufficient to explain the nature of the Late Archaic in the northern basin. Whether the explanation for these differences is related to the major environmental shifts in the region or to changes in social organization and other cultural factors is as yet unknown.

NOTES

1. In fact, while our crew was working at site Hu-113 near Putina in November of 2001, we witnessed a portion of a river terrace collapse due to active downcutting of the river terrace on its western edge. A stretch of river terrace, approximately 20 m in length, fell into the Río Putina. Fortunately, no previously recorded sites were at that location. However, we noticed significant erosion along the river terrace at sites HU-101 and 102 in the last two years. Almost 75% of each of these sites had eroded into the Río Putina at the time of this fieldwork.

2. Other points of this same style have been recorded elsewhere in the northern basin, and will be published in the future (Eduardo Arizaca Medina, INC-Puno, personal communication 2002).

5.

The Upper (Middle and Late) Formative in the Titicaca Region

Christine A. Hastorf

INTRODUCTION

THE UPPER FORMATIVE phase (circa 800/600 BC to AD 400) in the south central highlands surrounding Lake Titicaca spans over 1000 years in some locations.[1] This period witnessed the creation of a series of ritually specialized and intensive agricultural-herding polities. Some consider this a time of social stratification with regional yet autonomous long-lived centers. The name for this phase in the Bolivian and Peruvian sequence uses the Formative terminology to describe the first settlements on the landscape as well as evidence of the onset of territoriality (Lumbreras 1974a; Ponce Sanginés 1970, 1971, 1981:13). The Upper Formative Bolivian time span falls within the phasing of the later part of the Early Horizon and the Early Intermediate period of the Rowe Peruvian sequence (Pozorski and Pozorski 1997:7; Rowe 1962). This phase culminates in the marked cultural development of the first pre-Hispanic large-scale polity, Tiwanaku, that expanded throughout the Lake Titicaca region of modern Peru and Bolivia.

There are at least three documented regional centers with civic-ceremonial architecture dated to the beginning of this time phase, and surely more will be uncovered in future systematic surveys. Throughout the first 500 years (contemporaneous with the Early Horizon), on the south coast (particularly the Paracas Peninsula and the Ica Valley) and the northern highlands (e.g., Chavín de Huantar), centers with special architecture were built. These early Titicaca centers are most often located close to the lake shore, like the sites of Chiripa and Incatunuhuiri. (Qaluyu, being an exception, is located along the Pukara River.) These sites grew in local influence with increased exchange and political competition during the latter half of the phase, or the Early Intermediate period (Figure 5.1). All evidence does suggest that they continued to flourish as independent but communicating identities, as seen in their divergent artifact styles. Over time, agricultural and herding production seems to have intensified and broadened, as did trade. This trajectory peaked during the last 400 years of the period, with several central sites gaining prominence over a broader region during this time. In the north, there was Pukara, with regular trading ties to the Nasca and Cusco Valleys that faded before the end of this phase (S. Chávez 1992; Conklin 1983; Mujica 1978, 1987; Rowe and Brandel 1969; Valcárcel 1935; Wheeler and Mujica 1981). In the southern basin, there was Tiwanaku (by the Qeya phase) that superseded the earlier centers like Chiripa, Kala Uyuni, and Santiago de Huata. By the end of this last subphase, around AD 200–400, Tiwanaku had become an active trading center to the south into the Chilean coastal area (Rivera 1991; Rodman 1992), perhaps shifting the balance of trade routes from the previous phase. In the next phase, Tiwanaku began to dominate the region with less obvious competition from other districts around the basin.

Research on this phase has been extensive, informed by not only Formative scholars such as Mark Aldenderfer, Matthew Bandy, Robin Beck, David Browman, Karen Chávez and Sergio

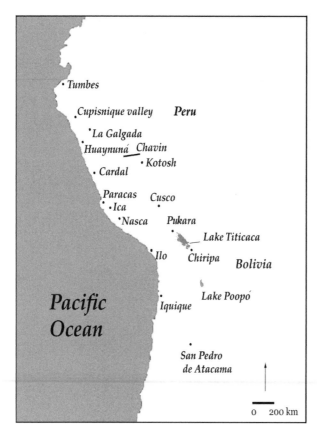

FIGURE 5.1. The central Andes

Chávez, Gregorio Cordero M., Juan Faldín, Alfred Kidder II, Carlos Lémuz, Elías Mujica, Jose Luis Paz Soria, Maks Portugal Zamora, Max Portugal Ortíz, Lee Steadman, Aimée Plourde, Amanda Cohen, Elizabeth Klarich, and William Whitehead, but also the scholars of later phases, including Wendell Bennett, Carlos Ponce Sanginés, Marion Tschopik, Juan Albarracin-Jordan, Sonia Alconini, Marc Bermann, Deborah Blom, Edmundo de la Vega M., Kirk Frye, John Janusek, Alan Kolata, James Mathews, Claudia Rivera Casanovas, Oswaldo Rivera Sundt, Mathew Seddon, and Charles Stanish. We now have a series of ceramic sequences and settlement patterns that give a more realistic sense of the events that occurred during this dynamic time period.

CHRONOLOGY

The dates of the Upper Formative phase in this chapter are 800/600 BC to AD 400 and have been separated into three subphases for this volume. This time span does not equate to the occupation

span of any one site, but rather to the regional cultural development associated with the onset and consolidation of multiple community ceremonial centers around the basin. The beginning of the phase is marked by regional polities that have cohesive iconographies. Its termination dates to the hegemonic shift around AD 400, when the Tiwanaku influence began its expansion northward and westward.

The Upper Formative is divided into three overlapping subphases. Each is culturally consistent, although, since they lack temporal uniformity, the phases overlap in time. The Early Upper Formative (800/600–100 BC) is when the first localized Formative polities and cultures elaborated while gaining influence, yet remained independent. This subphase is most clearly seen at sites like Qaluyu, Chiripa, Incatunuhuiri, and Sillumocco-Huaquina. This phase is the time of the loosely woven, ritually driven, sedentary lineage alliances, where elaborate chthonic lineage rituals are suggested in the architecture, burials, and material remains (Hastorf 2003). The Late Upper Formative (300 BC–AD 200) saw the rise and collapse of the northern center, Pukara; the coalescing of the western Sillumocco sphere (or the Moyopampa Complex [de la Vega, Chapter 8, this volume]); the centralization of the Taraco Peninsula population at Kala Uyuni and probably at Tiwanaku; as well as a series of polities continuing to consolidate their territories (as in the Santiago de Huata Peninsula [Lémuz 2001]). In this subphase, expanded long-distance trade became important, and artifact styles were more broadly distributed. The Terminal Upper Formative (AD 200–400) witnessed Tiwanaku becoming a more formal ritual and political center, as its residents began exercising local power in the southern sectors around the lake. The Formative ends with the Tiwanaku expansion across the basin.

THE ARCHAEOLOGY

The Formative trajectory was an expanding dynamic that began as early as the Early Lower Formative (ca. 2000 to 1500/1100 BC), when the climate became progressively wetter (and perhaps warmer) and the lake level increased, making the Titicaca Basin more arable and hospitable. The evidence for social-political change and stronger ethnic polities, however, is visible in the archaeological record in the Upper Formative times, some 1000–1500 years later, with increased ritual elaboration and concomitant political and ethnic ideologies represented in diverse media, most prominently at settlements with civic ceremonial architecture along the western lake shore. This material evidence for increasing integration does not just mean more people on the landscape, but rather a series of different forms of interaction including long-distance trade, increasing territoriality, and self-identification of group, in addition to more intensive use of procured and produced resources.

These ritual, political, and economic changes are seen in settlement patterns, architecture, lithics, stone imagery, and ceramics. Particularly informative are the major shifts in emphasis of mood and iconographic image on stone and ceramic, associated with a shift in the ideology

FIGURE 5.3. Example of a Pa'Ajano/Yayamama male-female stone carving

seen in the ritual objects. At the beginning of the Upper Formative, the images carved on stone suggest agricultural renewal and fertility animation that continues to have links to water and growth in today's altiplano symbolic world. These early agricultural fertility images are what Browman describes as the Asiruni images of snake, lizard, and frog (Figure 5.2; Browman 1972). Later, the figures tend to be more anthropomorphic, focusing on human heads or whole bodies, often with two sexes on the same figure. The styles are identified by K. Chávez and S. Chávez using the Quechua term *Yayamama* (K. Chávez 1988; S. Chávez and K. Chávez 1975), by Portugal Ortíz using the Aymara term *Pa'Ajano* (1981), and by Browman, similarly, as *Pajano* (1972, but see Browman 1995). These terms refer to the more elaborate back-to-back figures of males and females (Figure 5.3). This group of images imbues a sense of fertility as

FIGURE 5.2. Example of an early Asiruni stone carving

well as lineage and ancestral ties. With the development of Pukara in the Late Upper Formative (the Cusipata phase), there is a shift in image emphasis, with the incorporation of north coastal (Cupisnique) and western Paracas images. These images suggest an active communication with residents of the coast and beyond—a communication that supports status validation, ritual elaboration, and identity building (Helms 1979, 1998).

This Pukara style incorporated the power images of a shamanistic religious cult that is generally associated with the acquisitional power gained from dead enemies and is most notably seen in trophy head images on the coast (Proulx 1999; Williams, Forgey, and Klarich 2001). While heads had been included in the Pa'Ajano images, in the Late Upper Formative they took on a more significant dimension as they were held by kneeling felines or humans, which suggests a stronger sense of unequal power. By the Qalasasaya times, around 200 BC, we begin to see a more overt political authority with controlling civic cults built upon the earlier religious foundations of incorporation and kingroup worship; this authority is reflected in the architecture at the centers that are dotted around the lake.

There is also strong evidence for the intensification of several economic bases throughout the Terminal Upper Formative phase, including intensive raised-field agriculture, a strong lacustrine economy, and herding (Erickson 1988a, 1996; Graffam 1990). Once the lake shore stabilized, sometime around AD 200, and the hydrology was steady (Binford and Kolata 1996), a series of intensive economic strategies were developed, including raised fields, qochas, or artificially enlarged seasonal ponds used to feed and water camelids (Flores Ochoa 1987), and low aqueducts that channeled hillside water for erosion control and water use.

Both the landscape and iconographic evidence suggest an expansion of decision-making control by certain kin or ayllu groups in order to unify and channel labor from a web of nested kin groups scattered across the landscape. The political evidence for these changes is seen in religious manifestations and ancestor ideologies. Toward the end of this phase, the political structures seem to be expanded, as seen in the civic-ceremonial elaboration that bred a sense of centralization. There is evidence for group rituals and feasting, limited access to exotic goods, larger and more active local spheres of influence, and distinctions between centers.

The Early Upper Formative (800/600 BC–250/100 BC)

There are a few key data sets that are useful for the interpretation of this phase. The archaeological record shows social consolidation of scattered but settled populations around ritual sunken enclosures and walled platform mounds during this time. This is a time when several local polities developed their own styles while having basin-wide resonance. The demographic focus on the lakeshore continued, as more and larger settlements are found there. Beginning in this period, the Yayamama religious tradition was found in several locations around the basin. This southern and eastern basin variant of the Upper Formative tradition, as defined by S. Chávez and K. Chávez (1975), includes surreal stone sculptures placed in ritual locations; regular but modest temple centers with ceremonial paraphernalia, including ceramic trumpets, braziers, and serving vessels; feasting; and supernatural iconography with felines, faces with a T eyebrow-nose highlight, prominent and at times divided eyes, tear bands, and rayed heads (Figure 5.4; K. Chávez 1988:17, 21). This tradition suggests a social complex that centers around communal rituals occurring in and around walled sunken enclosures with processions and propitiation surrounding fecundity and spirits. In some ways, this "religious tradition" is simply a combination of traits, because we rarely have these items in situ to be able to discuss the activities involved in this tradition. When we do find these traits, however, they tend to co-occur, suggesting that they do represent a worldview about chthonic deities and their powers. The main sites containing these Yayamama traits were first recognized in the southern basin, but we now know that these occur at settlements around the whole lake circumference.

This phase is when we first see clusters of sites that suggest discrete self-identifying polities. Beck's recent work at Alto Pukara, 4 km

FIGURE 5.4. Example of the "classic" Upper Formative stone carved surreal face

west of Chiripa, allows us to see how a small settlement with only two civic buildings and several hectares of occupation was brought into Chiripa's sphere by around 500 BC (Beck 2004). More excavation work in sites of this time period will allow us to place these enclosures and the associated ritual material into more of a social context through associated residence patterns.

This phase has also been also called the Sunken Court Tradition by Stanish (1994b) because each of the larger sites in this time period has a sunken court, often with an associated raised platform mound. While they are more common in this phase, sunken courts began in the Middle Formative (around 1000 BC), developing from walled ritual burial enclosures. We know that this sunken enclosure tradition was a powerful and important form of ritually marking sacred space and territory, allowing for reunions associated with the ancestors. As such, sunken enclosures continue today, as seen on the island of Amantaní (Niles 1987b; Spahni 1971). Such continuities in the Andes resonate with the long durée of ancestral importance of land claims, fertility, and local power.

The artifact evidence suggests that local alliances were establishing a complex of ritual and economic strategies that led to a more codified life cycle of ayllu boundaries with increasingly stronger ethnic markers. Political leadership is only inferred, but some form of kin-based consolidation and economic accumulation was occurring during these 500 years, as seen in the evolution of increasingly elaborated family burials centered around an adult female at the site of Chiripa (Hastorf 1999a, 1999b, 2003; Steadman and Hastorf 2001).

As these ethnic identities developed and consolidated, it appears that interest in items of exotic status also increased, along with the use of fertility and surreal imagery, entering both from the coast and the eastern forests. These items included sodalite beads, metal jewelry, and warm valley plants.

SITE DISTRIBUTIONS

When Bennett wrote his article surveying the archaeology of the Lake Titicaca Basin in 1950, he mentioned six sites, five of which were dated to the Formative by diagnostic pottery sherds. While today we know of at least a dozen central sites with sunken enclosures potentially dating to this phase, there should be many more as yet unreported sites (Figure 5.5).

A center is defined as a site with a sunken enclosure that also may have a raised platform mound. Sunken enclosures are not found at every site, as is the case at the site of Alto Pukara (Beck n.d., 2004). Clusters of smaller sites, probably farmsteads without special architecture, are found across the landscape, as in the site of San Bartolomé-Viscachani (Herhahn 2001; Stanish and Steadman 1994).[2]

The centers hug the lakeshore and often are in view of the magnificent snow-peaked range of mountains to the east, still important deities today. At least by the end of this phase, the larger sites were regularly spaced around the lake shore in more densely populated regions like the Taraco, Copacabana, and the Huata Peninsulas, as well as along rivers.[3] Charles Stanish (1997) and Clark Erickson (1996) on the western and northern shore, Eduardo Casanova (1942) and Karen Chávez and Sergio Chávez (1997) on the Copacabana Peninsula, Carlos Lémuz (2001)

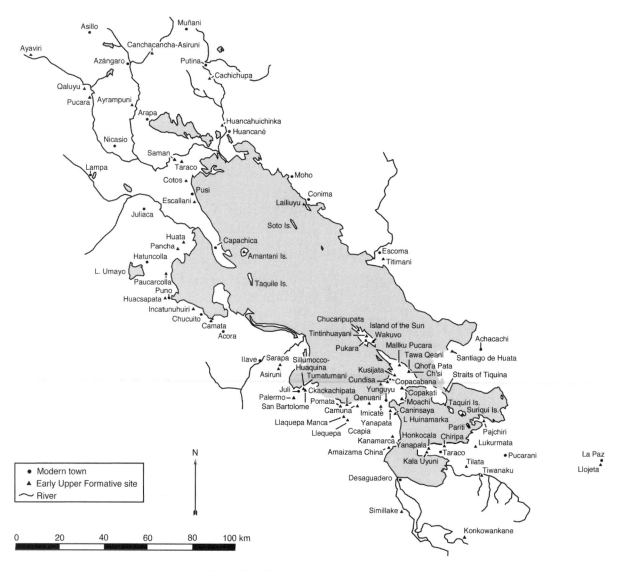

FIGURE 5.5. Map of sites mentioned in text

and José Luis Paz Soría in the Santiago de Huata Peninsula-Achacachi area, and Matthew Bandy (2001b) on the Taraco Peninsula all document the occurrence of these centers about every 6 km or so, with smaller sites in between (Stanish and Steadman 1994; Bandy 2001b). In fact, it is quite clear from some of these more systematic surveys that there are quite dense settlements by the Upper Formative time, at least along the western shore of the lake.

Albarracin-Jordan and Mathews (1990), Albarracin-Jordan (1992), and Mathews (1992a) discovered clusters of sites (about four sites per cluster) dating to this time period in the Tiwanaku Valley, indicating similarities to the ceramics

from Chiripa. These archaeologists suggest that these sites were groups of related kin. In fact, Mathews (1995:93) has gone as far as to suggest that some of these Tiwanaku Valley clusters, the ones on the upper slopes off the valley, are outposts of the Chiripa chiefdom. Albarracin-Jordan (1996b) has constructed a plausible model for local political development in the Tiwanaku Valley. He sees the Formative structure leading up to the Tiwanaku government hinging on the nested relations of kin-based ayllus distributed across the landscape (see also Platt 1986, 1987a).

While there are basin-wide similarities, each known center has slightly different stylistic features, seen most clearly in the recent detailed ceramic study by L. Steadman at Camata (1995) or the new material from Incatunuhuiri (Frye and Steadman 2001). From their studies, we learn that these northwestern lakeshore groups developed their own ceramic traditions, although each was influenced differentially by Qaluyu/Pukara in the north and by the Chiripa styles in the south. It is even possible that these different alliance-ethnic groups spoke different languages or dialects, for there is evidence that there were many more languages spoken around the lake in the past than there are today (Denise Arnold, personal communication 1999).

MAJOR SITES

Chiripa has been the principal site known for this time period for over 50 years. While we now know about more sites, Chiripa continues to stand out as the most elaborately developed site for the phase, in large part because of the archaeological work that has been completed there. Numerous names have been used for this socioreligious development in the southern basin: Classic Chiripa (Bennett 1936), the Lower and Upper House levels (Kidder 1956), Mamani (Browman 1978a, 1980, 1981), and Late Chiripa (K. Chávez 1988; Mohr 1966; Hastorf 1999b; Hastorf et al. 1997). Since these phase names do not share the same dates, I will use the Taraco Archaeological Project's (TAP) most recent absolute dates that are tightly associated with ceramic and architectural dates to discuss Chiripa. Here, the Late Chiripa phase spans the period 800 to 200 BC. This phase will have to be subdivided further, to account for the architectural elaboration that makes this phase rightly famous for the sequence of structures on the ritual mound.

As noted in Hastorf (1999b), the first sunken court that we associate with the Formative period began as early as 1000 BC at Chiripa (Choquehuanca), and is located on the first terrace above the lake. Other sunken enclosures (Llusco and Quispe) were built some time between 500 and 250 BC. One is upslope on the third terrace above the lake, and the other is on the first terrace. These trapezoidal enclosures measure around 13.0 x 11.0 m (Hastorf 1999a; Hastorf et al. 1997; Paz Soría 1999; Whitehead 1999b). Evidence for more elaborate ceramics,

"trumpets," and exotic items suggest that these courts were locations of periodic community gatherings that most probably focused on propitiating the ancestors and associated chthonic earth spirits (Hastorf 2003). In addition to these early sunken courts at Chiripa, there was an elevated platform mound that was initiated off the ground level of the middle terrace as early as 800 BC. The Formative mound is composed of three building stages: the Lower Houses, the Upper Houses, and the "Tiwanaku Enclosure." These early sunken enclosures and the lower mound support the proposition that Chiripa was an early Formative center of the region (Browman 1981). Bandy's (2001b) survey, however, has turned up three other such sites from this time period on the Taraco Peninsula alone, suggesting that this architectural style was repetitive on the peninsula. From our test excavations, in the earliest deposits at the mound we now know that there were many rebuildings and replasterings of the Lower Houses, with less architectural renewal in the later, Upper Houses. These Lower Houses are dated to the early Upper Formative phase (Late Chiripa 2). Our impression is that a series of structures was built on a low mound, which probably was placed around a central space and then enclosed by these little structures. We have evidence about these buildings, not only from Bandy's 1996 excavations (Bandy 1999a), but also from Coe's excavations in Kidder's project (Kidder 1956). After that sequence of ritual closures and rebuildings, the populace altered their architectural style and built fourteen better-formed and coordinated structures that symmetrically encircle a sunken enclosure. These were not rebuilt but were used for ritual storage and small ceremonies for several centuries until around 250 BC. This was the time of ritual change and the building of just one enclosure on the mound, lined with large alternating white and red stone blocks. In the Tiwanaku I phase, there is just one large ritual gathering place at Chiripa.

During this Late Chiripa phase on the peninsula, there are a series of other center-like sites, most notably Yanapata, Honkocala, and Kala Uyuni (Bandy 2001a). These sites each have a sunken enclosure with a larger settlement than those in the surrounding sites (Bandy 2001a). The similar sites of Pachiri, Suriti, and Pariti (Bennett 1936) are located to the north and northeast of Chiripa on islands (or periodic islands during rainy years) in the little lake (Huiñamarca), and the site of Anatayani is found to the southeast.

We know that there are other contemporaneous sites over the Taraco hills, south of Chiripa in the Tiwanaku Valley—sites such as Cerro Choncalla (Bandy 2001b) and T'ijini Pata (Mathews 1992a), with Kantapa (Portugal Ortíz 1992) also in the Tiwanaku Valley, in addition to Konkowankane in the next valley south.

These sites all have architectural evidence. Albarracin-Jordan and Mathews (1990) have further recorded about fifty-five Formative period sites, of as yet unspecified subphases, in the valley. Four small Formative period sites were found in the upper Tiwanaku valley along the southwest hills, along with Kantapa, Qallamarca, Quesani, and Chuu-Chuuni (Albarracin-Jordan et al. 1993:77). Llojeta is located farther to the east, near modern La Paz. We know little about that site except that Bennett found some Chiripa ceramics there (Bennett 1950:90). It is unclear how extensive the settlement was at Tiwanaku in this early Upper Formative time.

Visited sites on islands and the shoreline north of the Taraco Peninsula contain Chiripa-influenced Formative period ceramics (Bennett 1936, 1948, 1950). The extension of Chiripa artifacts throughout the region supports the notion that there was some amount of interaction between the different groups across the landscape. While it is difficult to describe the political relations that such social and artifactual similarities reflect, these sites do seem to have been allied or at least been involved in regular communications, perhaps regularly joining in each other's festivals.

Turning to the northern area of the basin, this Early Upper Formative phase includes not only Qaluyu, located in the northwest side of the basin (S. Chávez 1992; Kidder 1956), but by the end of this phase also includes the beginning of the Cusipata phase (500 to 200 BC) defined at Marcavalle much farther north, and at Pukara, slightly south of Qaluyu (K. Chávez 1977). The Cusipata phase witnessed the first clear civic

building phase at the Early Intermediate period (EIP) center of Pukara (S. Chávez 1992; Franquemont 1986; Mujica 1987; Wheeler and Mujica 1981:26–29). Pukara began with Qaluyu and Cusipata type pottery in the sacred region that first became a sunken enclosure (sector BB in Wheeler and Mujica 1981; K. Chávez 1977).

Amanda Cohen (2000, 2001) has completed a systematic survey and excavations near Pukara and Qaluyu that provide a settlement sequence for this river valley. There are iconographic influences from the south (Chiripa) in these northern sites, including the lower levels of Pukara and Qaluyu. Erickson (personal communication) has reported Formative materials from the site of Pancha, on the northwest shore of the lake. This large site has a stone-lined platform mound, is geographically associated with raised fields, is ceramically associated with Cusipata, and has absolute dates ranging between 800 and 600 BC.

Moving east of the Qaluyu pampa area, we find the sites of Taraco and Saman, but there are probably many more sites, given the high density of human and reptilian Pa'Ajano/Yayamama stone stelae that probably date to this phase (Kidder 1943). The Arapa area would also have had another cluster of associated settlements, with a major site at Huancahuichinka near the modern town of Huancané (S. Chávez 1975; Stanish and Plourde 2000).

At Canchacancha-Asiruni, there is a rectangular sunken enclosure measuring 15 x 20 m, with curving snake carved stelae and other stone blocks in situ (Stanish et al., Chapter 17, this volume). Farther southeast along the lake, Kidder (1943) noted the site of Lailiuyu and Conima. On the opposite side of the lake, Sarapa, located just north of Asiruni, has a large rectangular enclosure as well as a second, smaller sunken enclosure with stone carvings (Kidder 1943). Unfortunately, this site is not securely dated. Myres and Paredes (Chapter 6, this volume) report on a paired sunken court construction on Soto Island in the northeast side of the lake.

Along the northwestern shore is another cluster of sites, the principal site being Incatunuhuiri, which is located between Puno and Chucuito in the Ichu Valley (Kidder 1943; Frye and

Steadman 2001), with the smaller site of Camata or Cerro Cupe nearby (Steadman 1995).[4] While sites in this area seem to be politically independent from Pukara, their artifacts do suggest a northern affiliation, or at least regular contact as far south as the Ilave River. Incatunuhuiri is built on a large terraced hill, with a sunken enclosure on the top that held stone monoliths. There seems to be strong evidence that this settlement was involved in a local exchange network focusing on farming hoes, perhaps explaining its precocious development. Camata spans the entire sequence but has no visible nondomestic architecture. Stanish reports that the Capachica Peninsula has been surveyed by Luperio Onofre, who has found several Formative sites, including Cotos (Stanish et al., Chapter 17, this volume). The presence of ceremonial architecture at the site is undocumented. The Ilave River has a series of Formative sites both inland as well as on the lakeshore (Mark Aldenderfer, personal communication).

Farther south, the next known center consists of three sites within a few kilometers of each other, Sillumocco-Huaquina, Palermo, and Tumatumani, located near the western shore of the lake by the modern city of Juli (de la Vega, Chapter 8, this volume; Stanish 1994b; Stanish and Steadman 1994; Stanish et al. 1997:73–77). The earliest phase of this Formative period site cluster ranges from 800 to 200 BC. Tumatumani has a large artificial step platform mound. Sillumocco-Huaquina sits on a low hill with terraces up to a modest (9.0 x 9.0 m) subterranean enclosure that was built at this time and remodeled in Tiwanaku times, as was Chiripa. Sillumocco-Huaquina is associated with raised fields that also were created at this time. The location of Palermo is unusually inland and the site extends over an area of 12 ha. It seems to have been first settled at the beginning of the phase, as evidenced by a 940 ± 110 BC (calibrated) date that was obtained from construction in the enclosure area. However, the first formal architecture dates to 210 ± 150 BC (calibrated) (Stanish et al. 1997:73). The site is associated with two aqueducts, suggesting that it too had access to water (Stanish 1994b). Also well inland are Llequepa, located between modern Desaguadero and Juli just south of Pomata, and Simillake, along the

Desaguadero River (Hyslop 1976; Posnansky 1938).

These new systematic survey data around the southern shore area indicate that regional ethnic polities were coalescing along the lakeshore during these Formative years, moving from their focus on puna lands to lacustrine resources and farming. By the end of this phase, there is evidence for the construction of sunken enclosures quite regularly and the manufacture of distinctive ceramic types. These data suggest the existence of a separate, independent, and allied group of communities in the basin.

To the south of this Sillumocco (Moyopampa) polity is evidence for another group of associated settlements, based on the presence of several sites with ceremonial architecture and the density of settlements in the region. The largest center is the site of Ckackachipata, near the modern town of Pomata. The sites in the vicinity of the main settlement include Camuna, Llaquepa Mancja, and Llaquepa, and are associated with raised fields (Stanish et. al. 1997:90).

Just south across the Yunguyu Peninsula, Stanish and his colleagues (1997) found a series of sites that they named the southern Ccapia group. Amaizana China and Kanamarca are both located on the southern shores of this peninsula facing the Taraco Peninsula. Habitation evidence exists on a series of domestic terraces. There are large andesite blocks suggesting a sunken enclosure on the top of a hill, although it is not confirmed that this feature is from this same time period. The Caninsaya site has a semisubterrenean enclosure with some carved stone (Stanish et al. 1997). Yanapata has a raised mound with stelae inside. It is unclear if Caninsaya and Yanapata are contemporary or not.

Moving toward the Copacabana Peninsula is the northern Ccapia area, where the land narrows. The two large sites there are Qeñuani and Imicate (Hyslop 1976:248; Stanish et al. 1997:92, 98). Above the terraces of Qeñuani, there is a rectangular structure on a platform. Both sites have evidence of earlier occupation before the Upper Formative and therefore remained locally important for a long time, as did Chiripa (Charles Stanish, personal communication).

The Copacabana Peninsula also has sites that begin in this phase but they begin later than in the zones to the west. Many of these sites were discovered by the Yayamama Project, directed by Karen Mohr Chávez and Sergio Chávez. Recorded sites include Moachi on the southern shore (Browman 1980; Casanova 1942); Mallku Pukara, Ch'isi, Tawa Qeani, and Qhot'a Pata located on the eastern shore (K. Chávez and S. Chávez 1997); Wakkaluyu, found in the center of the Peninsula; and Kusijata, Cundisa, and Copakati situated along the northern shore (S. Chávez, personal communication 1997; Portugal Ortíz 1981; see Figure 5.4). Moachi has a large sunken enclosure along with Pa'Ajano/Yayamama stelae (Casanova 1942). These sites are located primarily along the coastline and suggest a substantial population on the peninsula that was independent from those to the west or the east. Four of these sites have ceremonial sunken courtyards, while others have domestic remains but no sunken enclosures.

Titinhuayani is the early center located on the Island of the Sun, continuing on from the Middle Formative times (Bauer and Stanish 2001). Bauer and Stanish completed a survey on the island that illustrates a detailed settlement pattern shift through time (Bauer and Stanish 2001; Stanish and Bauer 2004). The 4.0-ha site of Titinhuayani includes domestic terraces surrounding a hilltop, like many centers of this time period. The cut stone suggests that this site also had a sunken enclosure. There were two other large sites on the island: Wakuyo (Perrin Pando 1954) and Pukara (Bandelier 1910). All three of these sites are near the modern hamlet of Challa, a beautifully positioned locale. In addition, there are around thirty contemporaneous sites noted across the island, suggesting a solid group of farmsteads, like so many other contemporaneous areas around the lake. An interesting addition from Stanish's survey is the site of Chucaripupata, located where the Incaic sacred rock is (Charles Stanish, personal communication). Matthew Seddon's dissertation of the site noted that this site has early ritual feasting evidence, making this sacred area more long-lived than either the Tiwanaku or Inca empires (Seddon 1998; and see Seddon, Chapter 9, this volume).

Along the eastern shore of the lake in the Escoma region, there is evidence of Formative settlements with mounds and enclosures more similar to the Chiripa style than to the northern style. The most notable center is Titimani, excavated first by Portugal Zamora and later by Portugal Ortíz, his son (Portugal Ortíz 1981; Portugal Ortíz et al. 1993). Titimani includes a platform mound with a sunken enclosure measuring approximately 14 x 17 m. While the semisubterranean court is made of irregular stones (Portugal Ortíz et al. 1993:39), intriguing carved round stones were found within it. Several small structures of undefined age were found around the enclosure; these were thought to have been constructed during this phase or the next. The round stone face carvings are much like historic small deity *conopas* that fall into the Pa'Ajano/Yayamama group of fertility inspired mobile imagery. These stones are cobbles that have been formed into heads. Stanish (2003) notes that there is evidence of a domestic area surrounding the site, making it around 4 ha in size. The pottery is of the southern basin variety, with Chiripa temper, coloring, and treatment. Tikata, Killima, and Chatacolla are among the sites mentioned to be nearby Titimani, but nothing has been reported in the literature about them.

To the east of the Copacabana Peninsula is the Achacachi (Santiago de Huata) Peninsula, where the central site of Santiago de Huata is located. There are a number of sites in this rich zone on the eastern lake shore (Lémuz 2001). The site of Santiago de Huata has a sunken court and anthropomorphic stelae (in a similar style to the Pa'Ajano tradition). The nearby smaller domestic settlements are Carwichkala, Wanchuyo, Pujiti, Kolli Jamachi, Guerra Pata, and Misituta, again suggesting a dispersed population living around these small ritual centers during this time (Cordero Miranda and Portugal Zamora n.d.; Carlos Lémuz, personal communication 1999; Portugal Ortíz 1989:47). In the area called Chigani Alto, Portugal Ortíz (1989) reports possible sites with carved stones, Guerra Pata, Pujiti, Misituta, and Kolli Jamachi. The site of Misituta has a fat cross with camelids, also seen later in the Later Upper Formative phase at Pukara. Like Titimani, this region also has Chiripa style ceramics. Tambo Kusi (Corralpata) is inland along an eastern slope valley (Faldín Arancibia 1985, 1991; Paz Soría 2000; Portugal

Zamora 1967). At Corralpata there are two plat-forms, one of which is within terrace walls (Paz Soría 2000). The Tambo Kusi, Santiago de Huata, and Titimani centers probably expanded throughout this subphase. Their stone anthropo-morphic, camelid, arms, and serpent designs seem most similar to the Chiripa (P'Ajano) style. Unfortunately, these sites do not have absolute dates. Portugal's ceramic, site, and stone de-scriptions place them as Early Upper Formative sites. Based on a theme of sacred deity fertility rituals, their pattern also substantiated a model of the independent but communicating alliances around the lake, much like the Sillumocco, Co-pacabana, and Qaluyu clusters.

ECONOMY

Subsistence at these sites would have been fo-cused on lake resources as well as on the begin-ning of raised-field shoreline farming and herding (de France 1997; Erickson 1996; Kent 1982; Moore et al. 1999; D. Steadman 1997). The centers in this time demonstrate evidence for long-distance trade in permanent goods, which some centers had begun to include in their forms of inter-group competition (Bandy 2001a).

There were also some inland centers on riv-ers during this phase, Qaluyu being one exam-ple. While these inland centers might have focused on herding, they also might have been involved in trade or the production of special goods (such as at Tambo Kusi [Corralpata]), trading into the eastern slopes (Faldín Arancibia 1991; Paz Soría 2000).

Often considered evidence for increasing po-litical consolidation, exotic, imported goods, most notably copper (from an as yet unknown southern source) and obsidian (from the Colca Valley to the north), are found at some of these sites (Browman 1980; Burger et al. 1998a; Burger et al. 1998b; Osgood Brooks and Glascock 1996). Although currently lacking artifactual evidence, we could hypothesize that exotic plants used in hallucinogenic rituals were brought in as well at this time, as is illustrated in Cupisnique ceram-ics in the Early Horizon times and at San Pedro de Atacama in the Middle Horizon. Plants such as coca (*Erythroxylum* sp.), Anadenanthera *(A. colubrina, A. peregrina),* and tobacco *(Nicotiana rustica)* surely would have been present in the

basin by this time, perhaps associated with snuff trays (Angelo Zelada and Capriles Flores 2000), or even certain hardwoods. Such contacts with traders or far-away groups are of particular note when an exotically derived ritual complex is also emerging.

During this time, there were extra-regional stylistic traits that were being brought in and as-similated, although this occurred differentially at each of these site-cluster centers. Influence into the Titicaca Basin could have come from the Alto Ramírez phases of the northern Chilean coast, where we see sedentary villages with re-gional centers and a sense of regular comple-mentarity with the highlands at this time (Rivera 1991). The material suggests that individual groups were adding new activities and associ-ated paraphernalia to augment their ongoing sa-cred rituals, in addition to reaffirming their social relationships.

Taking the Chiripa and the Copacabana area sites as examples of this phase, we can see how settled these people were. Data on domestic oc-cupation are scant for this phase, as few domes-tic structures have been excavated. One house has been excavated and reported on by the Yayamama Project at Tawa Qeani (S. Chávez 1997). An oval semisubterranean stone structure of about 8 x 5 m was uncovered on a terrace about 100 m from the Ch'isi semisubterranean enclosure that dates to 220 BC. It included a small interior hearth. Domestic midden evi-dence has been reported from Camata, Chiripa, T'ijini Pata, Qhot'a Pata, Cundisa, Kusijata, and Ch'isi (Sergio Chávez, personal communication 1997; Hastorf et al. 1997; Mathews 1992a; L. Steadman 1995, 1997). The data obtained by the Yayamama Project suggest that houses were re-moved slightly from the sacred ritual areas at the centers and that they also occurred at small farmstead settlements. In 1996 at Chiripa, we found a curved domestic structure wall that un-fortunately had no intact surfaces. Small sites are also suggested by the Tiwanaku Valley sur-vey data, where most sites are located just above the break in slope of the hills (Albarracin-Jordan and Mathews 1990). Janusek (John Janusek, per-sonal communication 1997) has found a regular pattern of sites running along the edge of the Pampa Koani hillsides.

At Chiripa, both Browman's and TAP's excavations provide evidence for farming and herding (Browman 1978a, 1980, 1986; Hastorf et al. 1997; Moore 1999; Whitehead 1999a). The Chiripa middens have yielded plant and animal food remains. The domestic plant material includes *Chenopodium* seeds and tubers, and both *Solanum* and *Scirpus* from the lake. To date, only one instance of maize has been found at any of these sites. Lee (1997) reports one kernel and one glume uncovered at Ch'isi, which dates to around 200 BC. The many large animal bones are primarily from camelids (Kent 1982; D. Steadman 1997). There is a tremendous amount of fish bone at Chiripa as well as in the Copacabana sites, supporting the interpretation of a strong lacustrine emphasis in the diet (de France 1997; D. Steadman 1997). Both areas have many birds, but these are represented more frequently in the Chiripa collections than on the peninsula overall (de France 1997). At this stage in the research, the same plants and animal taxa turn up in both ritual and domestic settings.

On-site cooking and eating at Chiripa is suggested by the recovery of serving bowls and locally made cooking pots that are burned on the outside (L. Steadman 1999, 2002). Chipped stone, mainly of local origin, is also common, with debitage occurring in the middens and on the site's surface (Matthew Bandy, personal communication). There is regular evidence for stone adzes at the site, which would have been used in woodworking, among other things (Mathews 1992b). This range of material suggests the completion of daily tasks at Chiripa as well as at the other Upper Formative sites, sites that include both ritual centers and farmsteads.

Evidence for the beginning of intensive farming at Chiripa is seen in the nearby raised fields (Graffam 1990) as well as in artificial terreplanes that reach out into the water. Bandy (2001b) reports that there was a large influx of stone hoes from the north onto the Taraco Peninsula at this time. The northern lakeshore region of Pancha also has early evidence of raised fields, as shown by the detailed excavations of Clark Erickson (1996). Intensive herding is indicated at Chiripa by the absence of evidence for large wild animals in the faunal assemblage (Moore et al. 1999). Ecological evidence suggests

that around 800 BC the smaller lake began to shrink during a region-wide drought. If these calculations are correct, then it would seem that at some point during this time period only ponds of water were left in Wiñyamarka on the eastern part of the lake near the Straits of Tiquina.

While we are unclear about activity areas in the specific domestic areas, there is evidence for food display and/or feasting at centers like Chiripa. The domestic rubbish pits that we have excavated show a very different assemblage than those associated with the ritual areas. The domestic pits are filled with fish, bones, charred remains, and many rough cooking pots. The ceremonial rubbish includes more painted pottery and fewer cooking pots (L. Steadman 2002). Such ceremonial activity suggests that these populations were supporting themselves on local produce and perhaps were even increasing their production to aid in the new social interactions that they were developing.

At this time, the southern sites tend to have more painted wares than do the northern sites. If painted wares reflect ceremonial, sacred, public use, then the presence of such painted wares supports the early escalation of ceremonialism in the southern basin, and on the Taraco Peninsula in particular. Although we cannot determine who controlled these feasts and ceremonies, we are learning more about where such events took place.

RITUAL ARCHITECTURE

While we do not know if every center for this time period contains all of the traits listed in K. Chávez's (1988) definition of the Yayamama complex, the centers are defined by having at least one trapezoidal sunken court, approximately 12 x 15 m in size, with one entrance. Furthermore, the enclosure can be lined with stones and may have several stelae, especially at the entrance to the enclosure.

At Chiripa, there are a series of sunken enclosures spanning the period 1000 to 250 BC, and measuring around 11.0 x 13.0 m. The earliest enclosure, Choquehuanca (1000–800 BC), is on the lowest terrace, and has a box at the western end of the rectangle. This has an associated prepared surface to the west where there were a series of burials in what was earlier a sacred burial enclosure (1500–1000 BC) (Hastorf et al. 2001). In the next phase, there are several sunken enclosures. One is located upslope from the mound, on the uppermost terrace (Llusco). It has a small drainage channel in the northwest downslope corner and evidence of a white plaster floor, although the enclosure was unroofed. Another enclosure is located on the lowest terrace, also with a nice drainage ditch (Quispe). The best-preserved example of a semisubterranean enclosure is from the end of this phase, dating to 220 ± 10 BC (Figure 5.6). This is the Ch'isi enclosure that has been completely excavated and reconstructed by the Yayamama Archaeological Project (K. Chávez and S. Chávez 1997). Atop a hill overlooking the eastern lake and the snow-peaked mountains, there is a 14 x 14 m semisubterranean enclosure with an off-center entrance on the southern wall. The walls are stone lined and the floor is made of yellow clay. There is a short canal in the northeast corner to drain the floor. Burials, including one small feline burial, surround the enclosure in quite elaborate corbel-roofed oval pits.

The size of these sunken courts implies that they could accommodate 80 to 100 people at one time, suggesting periodic intra- or even inter-community ceremonies for 20 to 40 families. Artifactual evidence from excavations at Chiripa includes food display and feasting. Feasting is most clearly suggested in certain decorated ceramic types, such as the well-burnished wares of the Late Chiripa ceramics in the enclosures (75 to 85%) (L. Steadman 1997). Many of these are cream-on-red slipped wares of the Upper Formative Chiripa and Yayamama ceramic type (L. Steadman 1997). (This is a switch from the very rare Middle Chiripa red-on-cream ceramics.) In the Early Upper Formative, decorated pottery with geometric design is found at Chiripa for the first time, as are vertical-sided bowls and flat-based open serving jars. A large percentage (36%) of the systematically collected ceramics from the 1996 excavations were drinking bowls for either soups or liquids (Bennett 1936; Mohr 1966:112; L. Steadman 1997). At Chiripa, most ceramics are fiber tempered with external burnishing, the burnishing exposing large white quartz chunks. Although no evidence of in situ activity has been unearthed, we do have many decorated wares, trumpet pieces, and braziers from the enclosures. These ceramic sherds suggest that the food presentation, music, and offering activities that went on in these enclosures probably resembled the activities that take place in contemporary altiplano cemeteries during the All Saints Day feasts for the recently dead souls (Bastien 1995; Spahni 1971). It is likely that families came together to enact rituals that fed the spirits of the earth as they asked their ancestors for help with the crops, the life of the herds, and for the health of the populace in general. These walled, protected spaces were open to the sky. The absence of hearths or fires built within the enclosures suggests that they were intended for meetings, rituals, and feasts, not for food preparation or habitation. Many sunken enclosures had well-prepared, plastered, and colored floors that were cared for (Alconini Mujica and Rivera Casanovas 1993; Bennett 1936; K. Chávez 1988; Hastorf et al. 1992; Hastorf et al. 1997; Hastorf et al. 2001). Ceramic evidence suggests that the space was sacred enough to exclude the preparation of food inside. Based on ritual evidence elsewhere in the Andes and evidence of long-distance exchange at the site of Chiripa, shamanistic ritual acts may have been part of this new, transformed ritual complex.

Significantly, at some of the larger centers we also find a second ceremonial feature—a raised platform—suggesting that there were

FIGURE 5.6. The Ch'isi sunken enclosure that has been completely excavated and reconstructed by the Yayamama Archaeological Project

larger, more primary centers developing in this phase. We see such paired ritual structures at Asiruni, Sillumocco-Huaquina, Tumatumani, Chiripa, Isla Soto, and Titimani, to name a few.

The Lower and Upper Houses, the final Chiripa phase construction of the mound, falls into this Early Upper Formative time period, dating to 800–250 BC (K. Chávez 1988:18; Whitehead 1999b). Clearing off the eastern profile of the mound in 1996, we discovered at least three rebuildings of the Lower Houses. We now know that this famous Upper House building phase has fourteen rectangular structures built around a 26 x 26 m sunken court (Figure 5.7)

Although they varied in size, each building averaged about 7.0 x 5.0 m in size and either abutted or shared a wall with the neighboring building. The structure doorways faced into the courtyard and most walls were either touching each other or had some shared outer walls. The entrances into the interior were narrow, opening both to the north and the south side of the mound. Raised above ground level by being atop the mound, once in the sunken courtyard, people and their activities would not have been visible from outside the mound. And even more hidden would have been the events that were enacted within the rooms that were each surrounded by bins and niches, features that resemble the later Pukara constructions that held stone sculptures (which were probably versions of the ancestors) (Wheeler and Mujica 1981).

An elaborate door jamb system with a double-step fret to allow a solid door (probably wood or woven mat) to be closed and opened would have further restricted movement as well as sight into the stone and mud-brick structures. While this elaborate door system continued into the later Formative at Pukara and even on into Tiwanaku phases, doors were not common elsewhere in the Andes, reinforcing the feeling of secrecy and restriction associated with these special buildings (K. Chávez 1988; John Rowe, personal communication). These are clearly not domestic structures. Rather, as Karen Mohr Chávez has noted, the structures are some form of ritual construction. The walls have a series of niches which, like the earlier Kotosh rooms in the central Andean highlands and in later

Pukara structures, were most likely to have been used for the display of special ritual items, with mummy bundles guarded within the inner chambers (bins). Alternatively, Chávez suggests that almost half of the internal area of each structure was occupied by long narrow bins lining the walls, with the bins having been used for food storage like later qolqa (K. Chávez 1988:figures 2a and 3). The bins themselves have restricted entries and space, and have window-like openings that would have made movement in and out awkward. Chávez reports that Kidder found quinoa and potatoes within these, and we also have found quinoa in one bin from Structure 5 (K. Chávez 1988; Hastorf et al. 1997; Whitehead 1999a). From this, Chávez concluded that both the restricted bins and the niches were surplus storage areas for the chiefly ritual cycle. I prefer to suggest that sacred items, rather than the yearly harvest of food, were stored in these most sequestered spaces. There are precedents for both niches and bins to hold the significant dead ancestors, sacred weavings, conopas, trumpets, or even hallucinogenic drug equipment that was used in the rituals within the small structures themselves and the enclosures. Feasting could have occurred in the courtyard, but at this time the area has not been sufficiently studied to verify the types of activities that might have occurred in that space. If such gatherings were within the houses, only a few people would have been able to comfortably participate. However, if the rituals were in the central plaza, more people could have joined in. This ritual complex represents the last in a long series of building phases involving the construction of separate structures that encircle a sunken court that began around 1000 BC, much like the sequence seen at La Galgada (Greider and Bueno Mendoza 1985).

Like at Kotosh and La Galgada, these elaborately plastered and painted yellow and red structures could have been kin-group rooms for small-scale lineage rituals (Figure 5.1). The larger group activities could have taken place within the central sunken enclosure. Similar ritual buildings have been reported elsewhere in the Andes. Pozorski and Pozorski report small hearth structures with ventilators like the

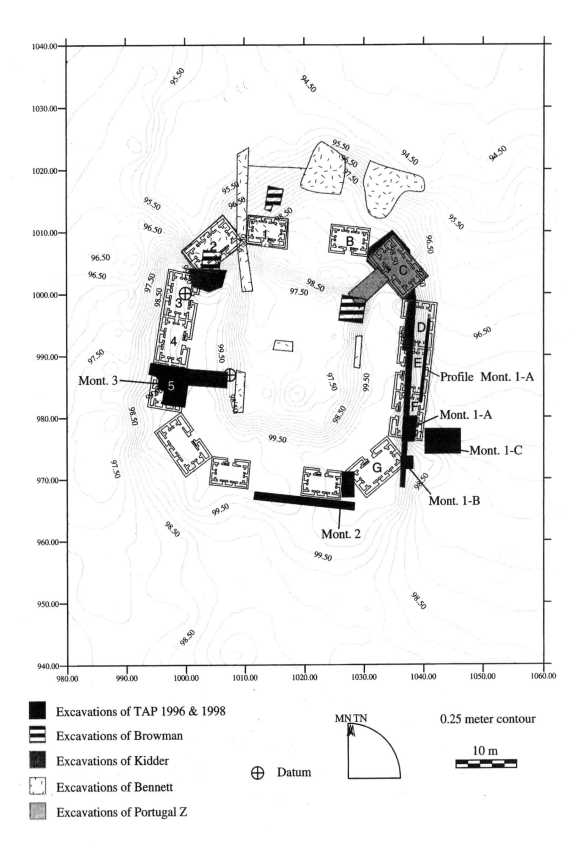

FIGURE 5.7. Plan of Upper Houses at Chiripa with central enclosure and two entrances (Hastorf 1999b)

Huaricoto structures at a number of Casma Valley Initial and Early Horizon sites, dating up to 200 BC (Pozorski and Pozorski 1996). A structure with a central hearth and benches has also been reported in the south coast Acarí Valley at Hachas (Riddell and Valdez 1987:8; Silverman 1996: 116). Continuing on in time, there are a series of later buildings that suggest similar activities as well, most notably Enclosure 2 at Pukara and the Putuni at Tiwanaku (K. Chávez 1988).

One last important point about the ceremonial precinct at Chiripa during the Upper Formative time is that the mound could have had at least two and possibly four contemporaneous sunken enclosures during the lifespan of these Upper Houses. The Amantaní Island in the northern lake (Figure 5.5) continues to have a similar phenomenon today, with a male and a female enclosure simultaneously being used for community rituals (see Arkush, Chapter 14, this volume; for the Pachamama and Pachatata on Amantaní see Spahni 1971; Niles 1987b). Such dualism in ritual architectural designation at Chiripa is illustrated by the two structure types as well as by the two groups of Upper Houses. While this dualism may have originated during the Early Formative and continued throughout the Upper Formative, only further excavations lower in the mound will clarify this.

The continuing evidence of the type of sacred storage discussed above is illustrated in the Upper Houses at Pukara. Nakandarari excavated a truncated step pyramid in sector BG (work reported in Wheeler and Mujica 1981:29). This is quite a small structure and is most like the Upper Houses of Chiripa. Most important, however, is that there were two niches in this Upper Formative (Epoch III) structure, each holding stone sculptures (one a human body and the other a head) (Wheeler and Mujica 1981:29). Both of the plastered and painted statues had been placed in the niches that were then filled in. The stone styles are of a type associated with the transition from the Pa'Ajano/ Yayamama tradition into the Pukara-Tiwanaku stone style. There are probably other structures and even simple sunken enclosures waiting to be uncovered at Pukara that will demonstrate the redundancy we see at Chiripa. This northern Formative tradition has been defined primarily

by two ceramic surface treatments (incised red-on-cream), and one common form (the flat-bottom bowl) (Franquemont 1986; Rowe and Brandel 1969). While these ceramic types share a lip shape with later vessel forms, they reflect an early stage of the ceramic evolution at the site. These ceramics are less similar to the contemporaneous late Qaluyu ceramics (Mujica 1987).

ICONOGRAPHY

Ceramic trumpets with modeled felines found at the Upper Formative centers also suggest elaborate rituals within the courtyards (Bennett 1936; K. Chávez 1988; S. Chávez 1992). Perhaps most significant, although difficult to date, is the evidence for the surreal, carved stone stelae that stood within these enclosures (Browman 1972; K. Chávez 1988, 1997; S. Chávez and K. Chávez 1975; Lémuz 2001; Portugal Ortíz 1981, 1989). The literature has drawings and photographs of the wonderful stone carvings found around the basin's shores.

Although somewhat speculative, there is some logic in the seriation that is discussed by both Browman and K. and S. Chávez. It seems that the first stone figures were made on irregular stones or slabs with what Browman calls Asiruni figures (Figure 5.2; Browman 1972). These have been found in both the north and south of the basin. The images include the frog, lizard, snake, and *suche* (catfish), all of which involve water-earth and amphibian fertility images. These are ethnographically associated with sympathetic agricultural fertility magic (Denise Arnold, personal communication 1999; Browman 1972:Figure 1; S. Chávez and K. Chávez 1975:Figure 11). The images suggest mythic power and mystery, but are not in any way surreal or fearful. They elicit moisture and fertility and are most likely associated with the growing cycle, the lacustrine world, and Pachamama. Chávez and Chávez conservatively date these to pre-Pukara. However, they seem to be earlier, beginning in the Chiripa phases some time after 800 BC.

Increasingly surreal, anthropomorphic faces, in addition to animals (especially camelids), were added on to the imagery of these sculpted stones through time in the Upper Formative. The most notable "classic" images are from the

Copacabana Peninsula (S. Chávez and K. Chávez 1975:Figure 9; Uhle 1912), Chiripa (S. Chávez and K. Chávez 1975:Figure 10a), and the Santiago de Huata Peninsula (Lémuz 2001; Portugal Ortíz 1989). A slab that is often associated with these faces was found at the base of an Upper House on the Chiripa mound and is useful in dating these structures to the Upper Formative phase (Figure 5.3; K. Chávez 1988). Those carvings with faces and eventually whole bodies are the "classic" style of the Pa'Ajano/Yayamama style. This male-female dualism continues on in highland ritual to this day. (For further discussion of the meanings of the deities on the carvings, see Bueno Mendoza 1982; Portugal Ortíz 1981).

The iconography calling for abundance and wealth is seen also in the image of the rayed face that began at this time. Chávez and Chávez suggest that the early imagery has links to the Paracas region and the Ica Valley Ocucaje 9 and 10. However, Silverman (1996) suggests that it actually came to the coast from the altiplano. This argument is still unresolved. Perhaps the iconography actually moved from the eastern slopes west into the basin.

Broad incisions are seen in both Cusipata phase and Qaluyu ceramics, traits suggestive of a northern influence from the Cusco Valley and the site of Chanapata (S. Chávez 1992; Franquemont 1986:11). There is also a southwestern Alto Ramírez connection with heads on the ceramics as well as occurring within burials. The adoption of such images and their importance will continue to inform research in this region for some years.

Also important are the images of front-faced personages with elaborated split eyes that are depicted on ceramic vessels beginning at the end of this phase. These are suggestive of a deity or a shaman that is able to see special things (S. Chávez 1992). Their existence adds to the interpretation that some sort of leaders were involved in the ritual complex at these sites and that they orchestrated and directed people in ritual, sacrificial offerings, libations, drinking, and eating.

Felines are extremely important iconographically throughout the Andes and Amazonia, and if these early faces are the ancestors of the Pukara felines, then this earlier imagery alludes to a powerful force from the jungle, highland, and/or coast. There is no evidence yet from Titicaca Basin sites for drug plant snuffing, but ritual drug taking might have been part of these rituals, for we see evidence of this at coastal sites at this time. To the east, Eduardo Pareja of the Bolivian Institute of Archaeology has been studying and conserving a *yatiri's* (shaman's) pouch that was perfectly preserved in a high eastern valley cave due east of Lake Wiñamarka and the Taraco Peninsula (Pareja, personal communication 1999). In it, there was a quartz crystal and several pelts. The rayed face images and drug taking are evident in the Paracas region at this time period (450 BC to AD 50) (Onuki 1993; Paul and Turpin 1986). In fact, Paul and Turpin make a case in the Paracas textile iconography for the strong impact of a hallucinogen-taking flying shaman cult that eventually incorporated the powerful trophy-head imagery that entered the Titicaca Basin in the next phase with the feline-man theme (S. Chávez 1992). We can posit then that such experimentation in drug-taking shaman ritual activities could have been initiated in this early Upper Formative time, especially where we see ritual architecture.

The Pa'Ajano/Yayamama images continued to include earth/fertility powers, as seen in the semisubterranean stelae and the water loving/growing power images in the mobile figures. These iconographic hints suggest special ritual access not only to drugs, but also to a set of powerful images that are found irregularly across the highlands and the coast. It is in the early part of this time period that Kotosh and Chavín de Huantar were active northern highland centers with internal chambers on top of temple mounds that probably served as sacred precincts for ayllu-based rituals. At Kuntur-Wasi (Figure 5.1), we also see platform mounds, trumpets, monoliths, and trophy-head imagery (Onuki 1993). Across the highlands, there is a sense of selected groups reaching out and expanding their internal powers through links with these exotic and powerful icons (Helms 1993). Sporadically, we see that these Andean shamanistic and ritual concepts were actively brought in to participate in the coalescing of ethnic alliances north and south, forming group identities during this Early Upper Formative phase.

POLITICS

What do these bits of data tell us about the political nature of these times? While there is a clear amplification of more formal ritual ceremony around the lake, we have less direct evidence for the associated politics. There is a kin-based and perhaps even family ritual focus, as seen in Chiripa's fourteen individual structures. These larger groupings were formed into two ayllus or moieties, most likely representing some sort of an extended lineage. Such structures, all at one location, could mean that the Chiripeños developed a stronger nested social order than elsewhere in the basin at this time. In this scenario, certain family lines maintained a structure in the sacred ritual precinct along with its associated ritual cycle and social interaction. With affiliation came communal obligation. How goods were produced remains unclear, but it is possible that since agricultural production was more intensive, labor was extracted, at least periodically, and used in part on the local raised fields, especially as the lake began to retreat around 450 BC. These Upper House mound structures were clearly well maintained, rebuilt often, and replastered even more often (Hastorf et al. 2001; Hastorf 2003). These participatory rituals and feasts would function to cement social units, intensify social authority, provide links to the regional ancestors, and also demonstrate generosity and piety in propitiating the ancestors. The in situ upright stones (as with the Asiruni figures at Arapa, Chiripa, Ch'isi, Santiago de Huata, and elsewhere), the stone female or plant conopas (as at Titimani), and the trumpets that were used in ceremonies all suggest that such rituals took place inside the enclosures. Such an escalation of group consolidation is further seen in the new ritual imagery and paraphernalia that entered the region, the more elaborate ceramics, and the increased presence of exotic goods like obsidian and copper. Due to lack of systematically collected data on economic and political systems, the extent of regional economic production centralization is not yet clear. The subsistence and craft production data we have thus far suggests that people were quite decentralized and community-sufficient. There is little to no evidence for specialization. The notable exception involves hoes that were mined, formed, and traded from Incatunuhuiri (Frye and Steadman 2001).

There is a sense of heightened interdependency and difference between ayllus, families, and genders during this time. Both images and burial evidence place the female at the center of the ritual world, critical for agricultural planting, harvesting, and feasting. Early group burials often center around an adult female (Hastorf 2003; Steadman and Hastorf 2001). Whether there were actual polity leaders beyond lineage spokespersons and ritual organizers is still unclear. While everything, including politics, seems to be colored by ritual, this is not surprising for ritual has always been a powerful force in politics throughout Andean history.

We see these spheres of social-ritual-familial-practice influence growing in different geographic clusters around the lakeshore. People were settled on the landscape with an increasing sense of place and ownership. These separate polities developed their own internal bases of authority and identity through a common language and belief in ancestors, demarcating the sacred on the landscape. Intensification was ongoing in all subsistence realms, especially when the lake retreated. The apparent lack of investment in dwellings on the landscape suggests, like at La Galgada or Kotosh, that these families and communities were more interested in investing time and energy in the construction of communal-spiritual-ritual precincts than in their sleeping quarters (Figure 5.1). The landscape was a large terrain filled with spirit ownership and ancestral memory. Their relations with their ancestors and deities were critical to the well-being of the living, and thus these relations were renewed periodically at ritual locales that brought the nested larger groups together.

The Late Upper Formative (300 BC to AD 200)

As with the previous subphase, we do not have tight control on the chronology of many of the sites of this phase; hence, there is some overlap with the previous phase. Many of the earlier sites are included in this phase, because if they had not become a center in the last phase, they did so in this phase. This subphase is defined by the increased influence and size of Pukara as a center over the northern basin and the beginnings of a ritual settlement at Tiwanaku. The centralizing force of Tiwanaku exerts increasing pressure on its neighbors in the southern basin. This is most evident toward the end of this phase, when the dominant cultural traditions, called the Chiripa culture, diminish and the Tiwanaku traits increase. The phase terminology differs regionally. In the south it is called Qalasasaya, or Tiwanaku I, in the north it is Classic Pukara, and in the west it is Late Sillumocco. Chronologically, the subphase is firmly established in the Early Intermediate period of the Rowe system, reaffirmed by many of the same iconographic attributes that are seen contemporaneously in other parts of the Andes. In the southern basin, this phase was first identified by a certain polychrome incised pottery type (Bennett 1936). Subsequently, the type has only been found in tombs at Tiwanaku, which makes it difficult to use the ceramic type as a diagnostic tool without other chronological indicators.

Overall, there is strong continuity with the previous subphase, with increased evidence for the spread of religious iconography, suggesting local political adoption of the political-ritual paraphernalia as well as increased exchange, especially to the north. Traits associated with Pukara are found from Azángaro to Incatunuhuiri. Hints of these same traits are also evident in the imagery of the Early Intermediate period from the Nasca region, especially the shamanistic death-power imagery. During this time, the scale of ritual increased, as seen in the construction of terraces up the hillsides and elaborate and large enclosures with internal segmented rooms surrounding courtyards, like Court BB at Pukara at the top.

There were also larger communities living on the plains around the ceremonial precincts at Pukara and Tiwanaku. The ritually based political networks that developed during the previous phase continued, but the emphasis of regional influence shifted away from Chiripa and Qaluyu and their fertility images to other sites with their more aggressive iconography and associated festivals.

SITE DISTRIBUTIONS

The sites attributed to this phase have been identified on ceramic stylistic grounds and tend to be similar to Pukara, Tiwanaku, or Sillu-

mocco-Huaquina-Palermo (Figure 5.5). New centers, like Huata and Lukurmata, grew near the lake and were associated with the expansion of raised fields (Bermann 1994; Erickson 1988a, 1996; Lémuz 2001; Stanish 1994b). These developments strongly suggest that intensive agricultural systems were a new focus for these burgeoning centers. The northern region displays an almost classic site hierarchy, with the primary center at Pukara, a series of secondary centers, and many small farmstead-villages across the countryside (Charles Stanish, personal communication). This pattern was hinted at in the previous subphase, but is more strongly prevalent in the Late Upper Formative. The same site pattern seemed to develop in the southwest, with the founding of Lukurmata at the edge of the very productive Pampa Koani (Bermann 1994; Kolata 1986; Kolata, ed. 1996). Even during this subphase, Tiwanaku, with its fancy stone-lined semisubterranean temple and early Qalasasaya raised courtyard, could have been pulling Pajchiri, Tilata, Lukurmata, Kala Uyuni, and Konkowankane within its influence.

Evidence from the Taraco Peninsula provides an informative view of this southern Tiwanaku expansion history. From Bandy's systematic site survey, at this time the peninsula had one major site, Kala Uyuni, on the southwestern side (2001b). There were four secondary sites of about the same size, but these settlements did not grow in size from the earlier phase like Kala Uyuni did. Further evidence from excavations at Chiripa note that the peninsular residents did not join in the Tiwanaku sphere until around 100 BC, continuing with their own ceramic and other cultural traditions, as well as having a discrete political separation, later than the people to the south did (Bandy 2001b; L. Steadman 1999; Whitehead 1999b). Tiwanaku styles and influences finally entered into the peninsula in the Tiwanaku III phase.

At the moment, too little is known about the eastern shoreline to be able to discuss site distributions during this time period. The western shoreline retained its local ceramic stylistic traditions into this time, but there was also an increasing Pukara influence along the western shore (Steadman 1995). The ceramic evidence suggests that while sites such as Incatunuhuiri and Sillumocco were independent, the local elites wanted to gain these exotic images as they were coaxed into participating in the ever-widening exchange and identity networks.

MAJOR SITES

At this time, Pukara grew into a center. Its architectural grandeur confirms the extensive harnessing of labor for the construction of its ritual buildings. The concept behind these buildings was not new, but the number of enclosures (six) on a massive terraced platform, with the visual impact of upslope stairway entrances, would certainly have had an awe inspiring impact on the approaching visitor. The minor centers surrounding Pukara are Ayaviri to the northwest; Ayrapuni, Muñani, and Arapa to the east; Amantaní and Huacsapata to the northeast; and Taraco, Saman, Huancahuichinka, and Escallani southeast toward and on the lake (Charles Stanish, personal communication). A. Cohen's (2000, 2001) new survey around the site of Pukara has identified more settlements from this and earlier time periods. Stanish and Plourde (2000) have now completed a survey to the east in the Huancané-Putina Valley, where they have found the Formative center of Cachichupa along with scores of other Formative sites. Cachichupa covers an area of 5 ha and has one stela within a sunken court that is lined with cut stones, reflecting a very elaborate court for this time period. Here there is a sequence of equidistant sites with sunken enclosures, located near the lake as well as inland near Putina. There are Pukara style influences in this eastern altiplano valley, but the valley has clear political autonomy. An important road to the eastern slopes runs through this region. Hints of trade along this route are in evidence in exotic bone spoons and malachite beads, suggesting the use of hallucinogenic plant snuff.

Farther south along the lakeshore is the well-studied Pancha-Huata complex where many small sites among raised fields surround the two centers of Pancha and Huatta (Clark Erickson, personal communication 1988) as well as Paucarcolla (Steadman 1995).

Still farther south, Incatunuhuiri and Camata continue in this phase. In the large plain of

the Ilave River, there are numerous EIP sites. On the southern edge of the plain, the Sillumocco-Huaquina center expanded, along with the associated Palermo and Tumatumani centers, which are surrounded by thirteen smaller sites. Pomata probably began at this time as well, but it is so cluttered with the remains of later occupations that we do not know much about its earlier times (Lee Steadman personal communication). The Late Sillumocco phase dates from 200 BC to AD 400 (Stanish 1994b). The sites on the Copacabana Peninsula continued into this phase, including Wakkauyu, Copakati, Moachi, Ch'isi, and Cundisa (Figure 5.5) (S. Chávez 1997; Sergio Chávez, personal communication).

The same centers continued to be occupied along the eastern shore. One site that can be dated is Santiago de Huata, because of its famous Pa'Ajano/Yayamama rock stela (Figure 5.4). It has a male figure on one side and a female on the other, with surreal positions of the face and arms (S. Chávez and K. Chávez 1975:Plate 23, Figure 5; Portugal Ortíz 1989).

Research completed by Carlos Lémuz in Santiago de Huata provides new evidence of the dense habitation of this region during this phase (2001). The stepped platform style at Titimani reported by Portugal Ortíz et al. suggests that it might have been built in this phase, if not earlier (Portugal Ortíz et al. 1993). Anatunyani, Pukuro Uyo (Ponce Sanginés 1981), Tambo Kusi (Corralpata), Chojllalla, and perhaps Muccha Cruz are Formative sites (or sites at least with Chiripa phase ceramics) of this time period that were surveyed in 1983 by Juan Faldín Arancibia (1985) and later excavated by José Luis Paz Soría (2000). These sites are notable because of their inland locations, away from the shore and even into the upper eastern slope valleys (Faldín Arancibia 1985). Paz Soría suggests that these are important due to their location on an eastern trade route. Corralpata also has a ceremonial sunken enclosure. Tapia Pineda (1978), Ponce Sanginés (1981), and Portugal all think these sites were formed during the southern basin religious expansion of the Upper Formative phase, though precisely during which of the three subphases still remains less well defined than we would like. While their stelae are Pa'Ajano types

(Portugal Ortíz 1981), dating by the style of image is not accurate enough. We await further research along the eastern side of the lake to fill in information about this region.

In the southwest, we now have evidence of a settlement with civic structures at Tiwanaku. Ponce Sanginés (1971) calls this phase "the village Tiwanaku" or Tiwanaku I phase, suggesting that the site was still comparatively small. The recent Formative evidence from Kolata's and Vranich's projects place the size of the settlement between 1.0 and 2.0 km^2, spread across the center as well as toward the river in the Kkaraña sector of the site (Janusek 2003). Ponce Sanginés first identified this phase, called Qalasasaya, based on thirty-five whole ceramic vessels recovered from burials, which he uncovered in his 1957 excavations while he was refining Bennett's test trench results. There has been some controversy about the stratigraphy and dating of this early Tiwanaku sequence, but the ceramic types that are associated with the phase have been found in other parts of the site, as well as at other sites in the region, and thus both Tiwanaku I and III are still considered real phases. From this Qalasasaya phase we have Pa'Ajano figures in a sunken enclosure that suggest that this site also joined in the same basin-wide ceremonialism. The same range of artifacts spans the adjoining valleys to the north and south of the Tiwanaku Valley. From the Tiwanaku middle- and lower-valley surveys we learn that there were some fairly major settlement pattern changes, consisting primarily of people moving downslope and into fewer settlements, many close to Tiwanaku proper (Albarracin-Jordan and Mathews 1990; Mathews 1995). The secondary site of Tilata was sampled by excavation and found to be occupied during these later Formative times (Mathews 1992b, 1995). Kantapa and Quesani are Tiwanaku Valley sites with continuing occupation (Albarracin-Jordan et al. 1993).

The most detailed domestic Formative excavations at the shoreline site of Lukurmata have been by Marc Bermann (1994). His earliest excavated houses dated to this Tiwanaku I phase. Lukurmata is considered to have developed into an important Tiwanaku center, but its economic focus at this point was probably based on its own local raised-field and rain-fed terrace agriculture. It is clear that the ritual precinct was distinctly separate from the domestic areas at Lukurmata, even at this time (Stanish 1989b; Rivera Sundt 1989). The ceramics are similar, but not identical, to Tiwanaku ceramics, and include nonfiber-tempered, orange plain ware and red banded bowls. Janusek (2003) notes that the burials remain slightly different from the style at Tiwanaku, suggesting that the residents identified locally and retained their own burial heritage of the Taraco Peninsula (Steadman and Hastorf 2001). Bermann uses a different set of phases for his sequencing at the site. I have reassigned his phases to the sequence used in this book.

Despite Browman's suggestion that there was an occupation hiatus at Chiripa, this is not substantiated by recent excavation data. What is suggested now is that the residents did not incorporate the Tiwanaku sphere imagery and the architectural style until the end of this phase, continuing with their earlier religious and social traditions (Bandy 1999b). It is Kala Uyuni farther west on the peninsula that is the largest settlement in the region at this time, on par with Incatunuhuiri (Bandy 2001b). As K. Chávez notes for Chiripa (1988), continued wall alignments suggest strong continuity with the earlier structures. While the site may have lost its centrality in this phase, it did remain a regional ritual center with one sunken court on top of the mound. The Chiripa style persisted longer at Chiripa than at neighboring sites, suggesting that the Upper House enclosures were probably in use throughout the duration of the phase, and that it was only at the end of the phase that they rebuilt the mound in the Qeya Tiwanaku III style. Future sampling and detailed analysis will, we hope, clarify the transition into the Tiwanaku sphere at Chiripa, which occurred sometime between 100 BC and AD 200. Because we do not have as accurate a dating sequence as we would like for this phase, many of these southern regional shifts are not well understood, pending more archaeological research. Overall, the settlements from the different regions seem to share more stylistic similarities during the Late Upper Formative, suggesting that there was more interaction throughout the basin during this subphase.

ECONOMY

The evidence we have suggests that the economic production continued to intensify over this time period around the lake shore. The raised fields near the lake nearest to Pukara were expanded (Erickson 1988a, 1996). Recent Koani Pampa evidence to the north of Tiwanaku shows a notable expansion in field building during this phase of the Upper Formative (John Janusek, personal communication 1994; Kolata 1986, 1996). This increased intensive farming is also suggested in the expanding local economic base seen at Lukurmata (Bermann 1994; Graffam 1990). The botanical evidence at Lukurmata includes the important local domestic food crops, tubers, and *Chenopodium* (Lennstrom et al. n.d.). Where we have evidence, herding also seems to remain important. This is seen indirectly in the Pukara ceramic iconography where tethered llamas are being held by a front-faced female fecundity deity (S. Chávez 1992). The overall expansion of settlements into the valleys suggests a gradual increasing focus on pampa farming during this time. At Pukara, there might have been craft specialists, especially for ceramic production of decorated liquid holding vessels and trumpets (S. Chávez 1992).

The only excavated evidence for domestic houses comes from Lukurmata. The ovoid, somewhat irregular houses that Bermann (1994) uncovered seem to have packed clay floors and were approximately 3.0 x 5.0 m in size. These houses have indoor hearths, providing us with a sense that people lived and processed food in small family units. Experimental production and harvesting of the agricultural fields suggests there were permanent habitation near the high-yielding fields (Erickson 1988a, 1996; Janusek 2001). From the layout of the individual fields in evidence across the pampas, we do not know if there was lineage land ownership, if herds were owned and inherited by individuals, or if all productive resources were overseen by ayllus (larger groups).

RITUAL ARCHITECTURE

A new architectural feature constructed in this phase was the stepped platform, seen most clearly at Pukara (Figure 5.8), with smaller versions at Sillumocco-Huaquina and Titimani.

These architectural developments speak clearly to the political and economic changes of the time. Similar to the related buildings on the north coast, there is a strong and increasing sense of restriction and eliteness in these structures (Moore 1996b). Control over access is hinted at in these buildings, suggesting that political life has become more forceful in the ritual arena.

The larger size of the alliance that participated in the Pukara ritual-political sphere is reflected by the massive stone platforms built on the cliff, topped by six large enclosures. These well-constructed enclosures are almost 50 m across (including the joined encircling rooms), and open toward the river and eastern mountains, forming a U-shaped plan. This same shift in scale has been seen to the north and west of the Titicaca Basin in the ceremonial traditions from Huaynuná, Cardal, Ica, and Chavín de Huantar. The Pukara enclosures differ from the earlier Chiripa ones in that the Classic Pukara architecture is built of cut, trimmed, and polished stone. As at Chiripa and Ch'isi, carved stone stelae were found in these enclosures, although they were primarily of anthropomorphic figures at the elaborate end of the Pa'Ajano/ Yayamama tradition and into the Tiwanaku type styles.

Karen Chávez (1988:24, Figure 9) provides a plan of Enclosure 2 at Pukara, which was excavated by Kidder. In that, we see the clear stylistic ties with the Chiripa Upper Houses. The floors are plastered red. The walls are not cobble-mudbrick as at Chiripa but are stone lined. There are also interior building compartments (bins), albeit larger than at Chiripa, found in these enclosures. These compartments comprise 35% of the floor area of each building (K. Chávez 1988:22). Very ritualized burials are located within these inner enclosures, suggestive of an ancestor cult, also elaborated on the Chiripa sensibilities. The major difference, besides scale, between the Chiripa and Pukara buildings is the greater ease of entry into the wall bins at Pukara. These have doors with sills instead of the smaller bin windows. Some bins were wider than 1 m across, suggesting that individuals could enter the bin easily to get what was within. Another elaboration at Pukara on the

FIGURE 5.8. Stepped platform at the site of Pukara

Chiripa architectural forms is the presence of small stone enclosures (niches) along the four sides of the central sunken enclosure. Some of these niches in the semisubterranean enclosures had evidence of burials (Wheeler and Mujica 1981). These burial chambers had the same elaborate door jambs typical of Chiripa building entrances.

The semisubterranean "temple" built during this phase at Tiwanaku is the largest known of this type of structure and is more elaborate in style than other such structures (Ponce Sanginés 1990). Numerous excavators have worked in the temple, but the final excavation and restoration was done by Ponce Sanginés in the 1960s. It is approximately 26 x 28.5 m (Ponce Sanginés 1990:82) and has elaborate stone-faced stonework. There is evidence of a stone-lined drainage canal below the floor, also following from the Chiripa tradition. It has well-carved standing stones, as at Pukara, but carved human tendon heads are inserted among the flat stone-faced walls. These suggest a human body resonance with the burial chambers and the mandible Kidder excavated at Pukara, the power emanating from the dead ancestors, with special significance of their heads (S. Chávez 1992). Also, like the trophy head imagery on pottery and textiles

of later times, there is a sense of power in having conopas of the ancestor's heads, or in this case, stone heads. The number is so high that these ancestors might be from many groups from the surrounding area. Placing these images on the walls would have been an effective way of bringing everyone together in one enclosure spiritually. Other carved stones found in the soil include curving snakes (Ponce Sanginés 1990: 171). This enclosure at Tiwanaku, however, does not have evidence of either surrounding bins or small chambers. There was some clear reworking of the enclosure during the later Tiwanaku times with added Classic style stelae placed next to the earlier standing stones, perhaps deleting any bins, or perhaps just recreating the past nostalgically if not correctly (Bennett 1936).

This semisubterranean enclosure is located next to the Qalasasaya whose construction might have been initiated at this time. This slightly raised enclosed court is much larger than any other of this time and possibly could have held the entire populace. The series of small (5 x 5 m) buildings inside the Qalasasaya makes that part of the edifice structurally like the Upper House level at Chiripa, with its encircling structures that surround an enclosure. These structures could have functioned like

Chiripa's small buildings, holding the most sacred items, including the ancestors themselves for a series of different groups brought together in one place. Much like the Inca, the Tiwanaku might have brought in the most sacred ancestors of conquered or allied peoples in order to unify the spirits and therefore their ideologies. The larger scale of this enclosure at Tiwanaku, like the six enclosures at Pukara, is larger than the one mound plus the three or so sunken enclosures at Chiripa, providing us with a solid trajectory of increasing ritual-political materiality. Although the rituals could have still been kinship-based, they became much more elaborate, with more fancy (and more labor intensive) buildings and a larger space in which to congregate.

The Qalasasaya structure suggests political ritual influence well beyond a single Chiripa polity, as it would have incorporated a population that spanned many villages. The change in ceremonial scale parallels the change seen on the coast at about 1500 BC (Moore 1996b), although in the Titicaca Basin this shift occurs around 200 BC. Exclusion in ritual space is another feature shared with coastal residents. It is as if the ceremonies were not accessible to all as only a select portion of the populace could see the event. What was transpiring in the smaller communities as they were incorporated into this new level of commitment and interaction?

It is likely that the rural residents continued to have smaller versions of these feasting, drinking, musical, ancestor-worshiping, fertility-requesting rituals in ceremonial spaces and on hilltops. With time, such locations eventually were built up into platforms or built down into the earth. Certain kin groups and settlements gained local prestige and therefore access to labor for such construction. While each community contributed in its own way, they also probably made periodic visits to the extant centers to gain spiritual inspiration and cultural identity, returning home to reproduce at least portions of the increasingly elaborate ritual complex.

ICONOGRAPHY

At Pukara, mica and sand-tempered cream-on-red ceramics persist, while accompanying new polychrome, incised wares (S. Chávez 1992). The Pukara styles, however, became more geometric and stylized than previous forms (Franquemont 1986). More supernatural imagery was added, with lines emanating out of split vertical eyes. Felines became common on the Pukara decorated pottery, as seen in the common feline man theme (S. Chávez 1992; Conklin 1983; Franquemont 1986; Mujica 1978; Rowe and Brandel 1969). The mythical front-facing camelid/woman is a second dominant image. The camelid/woman is surrounded by growth and fertility imagery, while the feline male images allude to death. Preserved weavings from the Pacific coast stress the male image with many accompanying severed heads. When looking at the Pukara artifacts, their designs provide a more elaborate visual experience than previous imagery.

Accompanying the elaborately incised and polychrome painted ceramics and the stone carvings are ritual paraphernalia that have modeled feline figures on ceramic trumpets and ceremonial burners. Stone carved stelae were found by Kidder inside the Pukara enclosures, most likely standing in these courtyards. Although few stelae are found in the northern basin during this phase, one important stone has been located at Taraco. The stone carvings evolved out of the Pa'Ajano style, with human-like images on both sides having their hands placed asymmetrically on their torsos (the classic Yayamama form) or kneeling, holding something like a head (the later style). Shared canons exist and are seen in the large eyes, head bands, belts, and trophy heads of the carvings. Snakes and frogs sometimes still accompany these images, although the life-death power images evoked by the heads increased through this phase. These kneeling figures eventually became standing and then evolved into the figures that dominated the Classic Tiwanaku and Wari and on into the Inca, when the imagery of ritual power transferred to statecraft. If this sequence is correct, then we can begin to see this more aggressive power imagery begin at this time when heads became ubiquitous in the iconography.

Along with the increased numbers of anthropomorphic images on the pottery and weavings, we see the entry of the staff deity, a person holding something in each hand. These, like other new images, resonate with the coastal Chavín tradition in the Nasca area (Figure 5.1), but there the staff deities always hold a trophy head in the right hand and a knife or staff in the left. At Pukara, the items held are fertility oriented. This can perhaps be linked in some way to the Karwa female deities of the coast (Cordy-Collins 1978; Lyon 1979), but more likely these images reflect the continuation of the Titicaca Basin Chiripa evidence, whereby female fertility activities were placed in a central position. Female fertility, linking to the earth and agriculture as well as to herd fertility, is a long-term theme in the southern Andes.

A theme that ascends in the Pukara style is the severed head. In the Late Upper Formative, floating head profiles were used as decoration around bowl and jar rims, as were running or winged flying figures (Franquemont 1986:Figures 18–20; S. Chávez 1992). Entering from the north or west and manifest for the first time in the region, this head imagery suggests growing inter-group tensions with a sense of threatening force entering the sacred realms of power (S. Chávez 1992). Mandibles have been found in caches at Pukara (Wheeler and Mujica 1981). These could have been a manifestation of shamanistic powers or fertility rites. They could be a familial cache of ancestral power. But they also suggest that *tinku* (ritual warfare) had developed by this time, with the image of political competition and power localized especially in the head.

These battles not only link humans to the chthonic powers of the earth, but they also reflect a type of political power and leadership structure that could be tied to personal or group gain. They are the clearest sign of an acephalous regional political system. Sergio Chávez (1992) notes that such fearful imagery of severed heads was probably present in the Andes when there was not an overarching panregional leadership. Chávez makes an important point about this first evidence for the morbid, deathly side of ritual in his discussion of feline/male severed head imagery, joining the pantheon with the fertility female images at the same time that there were increased efforts to coalesce people into larger, more closely interwoven entities. Periodic force must have been part of political and even

ritual activities as these polities formed and spread their influence. These images were probably just an amplification of these pressures within the larger society. In the end, the existence of local ritual battles suggest that there was no overarching political force above the opposing communities or alliances that provided sanctions to manage intercommunity disagreements. Even though many were involved in a strong basin-wide cultural sphere, there is still a sense of local political autonomy.

These images, like the central female, become a long-term attribute in the highlands. The heads, as Paul and Turpin (1986) note in the Paracas textiles, are linked to shamanistic power. They evoke a suggestion of ancestral control in the life and death cycle. The dead seem to command a presence and figure prominently in the daily life of the living. The images promote the head as a center of power in ritual events. The shaman's image also has an aggressive fighting connotation. The representation of an aggressive and powerful shaman is clear in flying shamans with long hair holding flutes, fans, and heads (Paul and Turpin 1986). It is as if these representations of people or deities have the capability to manipulate human spirits and control both the life and the death of a group.

Shamans might also be depicted on drug induced flights—flights to contact spirits, to help others, or perhaps even to harm others. With the drug taking, the shaman transforms, travels to the spirits, learns from them or fights them, then returns to bring help to the group. These images seem to be linked to hallucinogenic substances, although except for one snuff tablet found at Pukara by Kidder (S. Chávez 1992), there is little evidence for drug paraphernalia in the Titicaca Basin during this phase. However, it might not be too far of a stretch to consider that ceramics with head imagery were used in rituals that included shamanistic flight.

The early ceramics associated with Tiwanaku Qalasasaya phase are incised, stamped, modeled, post-fire painted, flat-based bowls with pedestals. Felines are important from the beginning of this tradition, and there is a strong similarity in the designs between Pukara and Tiwanaku. In fact, the Tiwanaku I phase was first defined at the site by burnished yellow ware with red or yellow decoration and black or white incisions (Ponce Sanginés 1990). These ceramics are thought to have been influenced by Ocucaje 9 and 10 and Nazca 13 styles from the coast, as seen in the bowls, the horizontal handles, and the human figures (Mathews 1995; John Rowe, personal communication 1999).

Furthermore, as the population spread throughout the Titicaca landscape and increasingly turned to more intensive farming along the west lakeshore, ritual warfare must have increased to maintain inter (and intra) group social relations. Such *tinkus* not only regulated the hostilities between independent (acephalous) groups, but they were also part of the fertility ritual cycle (Platt 1986). Stanish (1994b, 2003) reports an early historic example of the power of the head in local politics along the western Titicaca shore. As in modern ritual battles, some blood must be spilled on the ground to aid in the production and fertility for the coming year. Heads taken from killed warfare victims are still used in female fertility rituals in Bolivia (Denise Arnold, personal communication 1999). The ancestors and the earth are fed with the blood and bodies in order to reproduce the living. In these *tinku* rituals today, we can still see the merging of these two Pukara Late Upper Formative phase images: fertility and death.

POLITICS

The Late Upper Formative is the time of Pukara's influence, though Pukara was a less strongly organized urban civic center than what is surmised for the Tiwanaku settlement (Janusek 2003). The Pukara ideology was prominent across the northern basin, although its regulatory powers at the settlements is still unclear and probably was never strongly centralized. Outside of Pukara's sphere to the south, we see a series of developing centers with associated villages, which some call ranked (Stanish et al. 1997). Overall, there is political cross-pollination present in the bigger ritual centers, which have larger populations and more kin groups involved. These centers include Incatunuhuiri, Sarapa/Asiruni, Sillumocco, Ckackachipata, Moachi, Kala Uyuni, and Tiwanaku.

Enclosed mound ceremonies continued to grow in scale. The political developments, as interpreted from the architecture, were more in size than in structure. Rather than having much larger plazas that suggest a larger single population, as we see in the north Peruvian coast ceremonial developments of this time, at Pukara there were more numerous enclosures of the same size. The earlier Chiripa enclosures ranged from 11 x 13 m to 26 x 26 m (Bandy 1999b; Browman 1978a; Hastorf et al. 1997). At Pukara during this subphase, the measured enclosures were 15 x 16 m, but were more numerous (K. Chávez 1988:22). This suggests continuities in the size and type of group rituals. From the single mound enclosing a sunken plaza with several sunken enclosures at Chiripa, there was a Chiripa mound structure repeated six times along the hillside at Pukara. Such spatial centralization of regional rituals informs us of a new intensity of interest in nested group identities and influence spanning more communities. The evidence suggests that the Pukara organization did not bring the entire society together in one unifying urban center. Rather, we have a sense that there were separate periodic rituals in one sacred precinct. This redundancy provides a clue to the number of alliances congregating at Pukara and also confirms that the groups across the northern basin retained a considerable amount of autonomy, which is most clearly expressed in their ceramic diversity.

In the southern basin, Tello (1935), Franquemont (1986), and Kidder (1948) saw the Pukara pottery styles and shapes infiltrating into the Chiripa and Tiwanaku imagery. These southern styles were also impacted by the Alto Ramírez phase of the Chilean coast and the coastal Chavín images from the Ocucaje 10 and Nasca I phase sites. These long-distance influences and interactions during the Early Intermediate times suggest exotic interests within the basin. The earlier Chiripeño interest in external relations seems to have been expressed also on a larger scale in the north, although it is premature to specify exactly how it was implemented. While the imagery clearly suggests interaction, there is no evidence for vast quantities of goods moving between these areas (although again, wood, hallucinogens, spices, pelts, and weavings might be the missing invisible links due to current archaeological methods of recovery). These results are not completely compatible with the earlier trade models that Núñez and Dillehay (1979) and Browman (1978b, 1981) proposed for early Tiwanaku political expansion, where an increasing reliance on trade economics through long- distance llama caravans formed the economic engine of the society. While we can all agree that interaction increased through time at both Pukara and Tiwanaku, I do not think it comprised their main economic base. Instead, I think that trade participated more in the development of the new ideologies, building upon, among other things, the display and consumption of exotic goods and practices that provided symbolic and political ascendance for certain ayllus, or families (Helms 1993). These symbolic webs of meaning were accepted by an ever-larger populace, and with this ritual-political worldview construction, the potential for channeling local resources and labor correspondingly increased as well.

The Terminal Upper Formative, AD 200 to 400

This is a short but curious moment in the Titicaca Basin. This last Formative subphase has been called the Qeya or Tiwanaku III phase in the southern basin and the late Pukara phase in the north. There is a strong sense of cultural continuity during this time, as many sites continue through this subphase (Figure 5.5). Many settlements from the previous subphase continued to be occupied, especially along the western shore of the lake. Whereas at the beginning of this phase Pukara was important, its importance waned by AD 400, and this is in many ways the most important result of this two-hundred-year period. Whilst Tiwanaku existed at the beginning of this phase, there is increasing evidence that its activities had not begun to expand outside of its neighboring valleys until after this phase. Tiwanaku seemed to start slowly, managing to gain influence over its local rivals during this phase (Bandy 2001a). In the southern basin, sites that had once had their own styles were, in the Terminal Upper Formative, full of Tiwanaku-influenced pottery. This story became muddled when some archaeologists working in the region recently suggested that the Qalasasaya (Tiwanaku I) and the Qeya (Tiwanaku III) phases are, in fact, contemporaneous, and that these were arti-

ficially separated by Bennett and then Ponce Sanginés based on different ceramic types (Albarracin-Jordan 1992; Bermann 1994; Mathews 1992b, 1995). Site excavation has not yet clarified this issue, but Janusek's recent analysis of Wila Jawira's excavations at Tiwanaku does suggest that Tiwanaku in fact did not really begin its supra-regional expansion until AD 400–500. On the other hand, our work at Chiripa and the Taraco Peninsula supports the idea that Tiwanaku's influence was expanding throughout the Peninsula during these years, as seen in the abandonment of the central site of Kala Uyuni as well as the Tiwanakoid remodeling of the Chiripa mound. This subphase therefore seems to represent the final days of the long-term existence of the Formative cultural tradition in the Titicaca Basin, consisting of acephalous but interacting village communities with fairly regularly spaced ritual centers. Some of these centers became more prominent and show evidence of having attracted population and therefore having increased production. No large centers like Pukara or Tiwanaku developed in the central east and west side of the Titicaca Basin, although smaller centers continued. The overall pattern for this subphase is one of increasing influence from the Tiwanaku area into the southeastern and southwestern areas, with sites increasingly being pulled into an emerging Tiwanaku orbit (see Steadman 1995; Stanish 2003). In general, however, there is a sense of long-term continuity throughout the basin.

MAJOR SITES

There is little pure Tiwanaku III evidence in the southern basin. The new hilltop site of Qeya Qolla Chico on the Island of the Sun, excavated by Bandelier (1910), provides some evidence of this early religious and political expansion. Like other island sanctuaries such as Suriti and Pariti, this centrally located Island of the Sun was definitely one of the sacred places in the lake region during these early Tiwanaku expansive days. We know that by the Middle Horizon times, this island was a sacred location (Seddon 1998). Qalasana and Kantapa (Portugal Ortíz 1991) at Kallamarka in the upper Tiwanaku Valley are thought to be Tiwanaku III sites based on ceramic styles and the presence of raised platforms

(Albarracin-Jordan et al. 1993; Girault 1977; Portugal Ortíz and Portugal Zamora 1975, 1977). So, while the overall settlement pattern for the Tiwanaku Valley shows aggregation at the center, there were still people moving around the valley.

Along the western shore, these were the final days of the substantial polity centers of Sillumocco-Huaquina, Palermo, Tumatumani, Incatunuhuiri, and Ckackachipata (Stanish et al. 1997). After 900 years of peer-polity interaction, competition, and nested identities in the north, Pukara was abandoned, and the northern basin's political web faded. The causes of this demise are almost unstudied at this point, if we assume that it was not Tiwanaku's hegemony that initiated the fading of the multi-group ritual center. Is this demise linked to the AD 100 drought? Is it linked to political shifts on the west coast and to the north in the greater Cusco region, or to new pressures from the east? Were trade routes for important ritual paraphernalia cut off, influencing both the economics and the rituals? This seems to be an important period of study for the future.

ECONOMICS

On the brink of expansion, with all ingredients present, Tiwanaku's religious cult, like Pukara's before, was integrating the nested supra-ayllu's expandable local economic base (evident in raised-field farming by the lake, herding in the dried southern pampas, and the agricultural terraces along the hillsides). Fishing in the lake, along with caravan trading (marine shells were carried into the region), also took place during this subphase (Kolata 1986). This diverse subsistence base was not only productive, but could provide surpluses and therefore specialization. Long-distance trade probably became more regular during this phase, with trade networks extending to the coast, the north, the east, and the south, and involving such items as iconography, ritual esoterica, copper, gold, silver, obsidian, semiprecious stones (malachite, turquoise, and lapis lazuli), tropical wood, marine shells (Browman 1980), coca, hallucinogenic drugs, and probably spices (such as chile peppers, although we have no material evidence for this yet).

The ceramic traits associated with the Qeya phase include a lack of complete burnishing and the increasing use of geometric designs, designs that replaced the earlier naturalistic designs. These changes in design suggest a broader spread of trade wares with more expedient production. The ceramic assemblage is more diverse not only in shape but also in level of execution, representing a broader range of uses as well as more elaboration in ritual activities. The overall style of the Qeya phase ceramics, however, is more standardized, as if many of the more elaborate ceramics were being made in workshops by specialists (Rivera Casanovas 1994).

RITUAL EVIDENCE

As the evidence shows, group rituals, feasting, sacrifice, and the storage of sacred items in the ceremonial precincts continued during this subphase. The centers seem to have continued with a network of ceremonies and regular exchanges, linking different language groups throughout the whole basin. Rituals focused in the sunken enclosures, located often on platforms, increasingly removed ritual leaders from their community. The sculpted stone images provided a sense of more fearful life-and-death power and less beneficent fertility. These stelae grew in size such that they became much larger than human size, whereas previously they were shorter than those who were viewing them and more rounded. New ritual complexes could have been brought in by the burgeoning elite at Tiwanaku as they actively tried to make their mark throughout the south. This is seen inside the moat at Tiwanaku, where at the AD 395 palace of Putuni we have our first well-dated evidence of maize in the southern basin (Couture 2002). I suggest that maize came into Tiwanaku as part of a ritual package of maize beer and *keros* (drinking vessels) that would allow ritual leaders to bring together larger groups of people, uniting them through transformative rituals. This would have occurred in the ritual core of the site. Its scale is variable, such that not all inhabitants would have participated in this central ritual area, which was, in fact, bounded off by a water canal. There is a sense at the site that family (secular) houses still had importance, being substantially constructed with their own periodic rituals within their patio walls (Janusek 1994, 2003). There probably were multiple levels of rituals in many communities, but especially so at Tiwanaku.

The Chiripa rites and religious importance that so prominently foregrounded agriculture and fertility were eclipsed, went underground, or remained only in household rituals, as the deeply rooted fertility images disappeared from ceremonial precincts, having been replaced by images cut in stone of scary and distant ritual leaders holding sacred hallucinogenic bundles and drinking vessels. The smaller rituals probably persisted in the familial world, in homes, on mountaintops, and in the fields. While these same themes might have remained within the larger elaborated state religion, the evidence at Tiwanaku in sacred precincts is less clearly focused on fertility. More overt power and codified imagery dominated, with elaborate gods and supernatural attendants coming in from afar, much like shamanistic travel.

ICONOGRAPHY

Traits that were seen so prominently in Chiripa and Pukara, like the Pa'Ajano/Yayamama style stelae, were no longer produced. The semisubterranean enclosures, common for over 1,000 years as sacred ceremonial spaces, stopped being constructed. Other traits like the modeled felines and incense burners increased and became more common. Tiwanaku, with its own combination of selectively transformed Formative traits mixed with foreign aesthetics, which were important in local political dynamics and ritual practices, finally became the political religious complex that overpowered all others in the basin. While the kneeling feline anthropomorphic *chachapuma* (who is depicted as holding human heads in its hands in front of its chest [Valcárcel 1932, 1935]) continued in this phase, we see other blocky styles of stone carving that also elaborate the suggestion of power over others. These images and styles lead into the Bennett and Ponce stelae style of the next phase.

POLITICS

Leadership surely was becoming codified. Tiwanaku seemed to function at a scale not seen in the basin before, with many different groups living in this central city (see Janusek, Chapter 10, this volume; Janusek 2003). Each group would have had different interactions with the political machine. There seem to have been elites, merchants, workers, and craftsmen—as well as the local farmers, herders, and fisherfolk—in residence. In the end, because of previous links and aggressive central pressures, the local alliances throughout the basin slowly coalesced. The elite families began to build palaces within the moat at Tiwanaku, palaces with elaborate plumbing and cut stone architecture (Kolata 2003). The iconography displayed the power of mythic ancestors and powerful priesthoods, an ideological power linking together kin groups as well as larger regional groups and ethnicities. Despite the continuing sense of autonomy at settlements in the basin, the inter-site relationships reflected increasing stratification, if not specialization, during this phase. The basin was perched to be a unified political entity at AD 400.

CONCLUSIONS

This 1000-year phase saw the evolution of a mix of indigenous political-religious structures that were interwoven within a religious world infused with external exotic beliefs and images among local ancestral rituals. These beliefs united people with their landscape while increasingly making them feel similar. These dynamics worked to bring people together, yet fueled them with potential competing power nexus emanating from the local families as well as from the ritual enclosures, the sites of periodic group gatherings, and renewal of group community. This pattern around the lake created an ebb and flow of alliances that allowed loose (acephalous) polities to develop throughout the basin. While redundant at many levels, the symbolic and political geography allowed some communities to expand their influence through ritual events at certain critical times. In many parts of the basin, the communal feasts in small chambers (feasts meant to communicate with and placate the ancestors) changed to larger feasts, intensifying the potential for stratification through group cohesion while developing visual cues to power in larger enclosures. As Pauketat (2000) notes for southeastern North America, some people join in these building endeavors because of their belief in and desire for these social bonds between the living and the dead. These activities can lead to rules that go beyond the ritual manifestations that initiated the process.

By the end of this phase, a shift could be seen from communality and consumption in the creation and use of public works and collective rituals to individuals and specialists guiding the rituals of surplus from an inner core. Part of this escalatory cycle was developed from increased food yields and labor to build and maintain more ritual centers. The place of warfare and threats associated with this must have been ever present, only becoming evident in the later Pukara ceramic and stone carving imagery. These on-the-ground activities probably expanded throughout this Upper Formative period, along with the acquisition of long-distance goods and practices that aided the ascendance of certain centers around the lakeshore, perhaps as Stanish (2003) and Bandy (2001b) propose, and as seen in the settlement locations along these trade routes. Was it the agricultural base, the many herds and grasslands, the fish and birding resources of the lake, the plant resources, the access to trade or traders, or the links to the most sacred mountains that allowed some communities to elaborate their ritual activities? Ritual authority grew at some centers, building on certain family lineages and moieties, and shifting the role of the shaman and the power of dead ancestors over life. This became manifest in the architecture and its expansion and elaboration at key centers around the lake. We know that the larger Formative centers were associated with agricultural intensification, pockets of raised fields, canals, and agricultural terraces. Control over production was not strong until the scale was large, as at Pukara and Tiwanaku, yet there are patches of raised fields associated with some of these enclosure sites that suggest a cohesion of not only architectural construction and ritual but also of production and trade in these earlier Formative times. Perhaps the organizational leaders were the same as the local ritual leaders and the shamans. Centralization was not the way, however. Rather, an overlapping culture of different family and activity groups developed. A regularization of site architecture developed and eventually site hierarchy also developed. The Upper Formative was a time of growth and elaboration throughout the basin, not just of population but also of ritual practices and political connectedness. It exemplifies the onset of an Andean state.

ACKNOWLEDGMENTS

Many scholars have contributed to this compilation, most prominently all of the members of the Taraco Archaeological Project, Matt Bandy, José Luis Paz, Amanda Cohen, Lee Steadman, Bill Whitehead, and Charles Stanish, who provided much of the western and northern data. Much of the specific archaeological knowledge is still in the process of being collected and thus receiving information from all my colleagues who work around the Titicaca Basin was crucial. The excavations at Chiripa were in part supported by The National Science Foundation, the National Geographic Society, and the Stahl Foundation. I also want to thank the Archaeology Institute in La Paz and the community of Chiripa, which enabled and enlivened our work there. I would like to dedicate this chapter to Karen Mohr Chávez, who completed so much fundamental research on this time period to the benefit of us all. We hope her memory will live on in these sites and works, like those whom we study who are gone.

NOTES

1. Some label the first 400 years the Middle Formative, focusing this phase only on the rise and decline of Pukara.
2. We are unable to locate each individual place name on a map given the very large number of site and place names included in this chapter. We have instead identified on the maps the area where the sites are found (e.g., Huata Peninsula, lower Tiwanaku Valley, etc.) and recommend that readers consult the appropriate cited works for more detailed locations [the editors].
3. There are two Huata (or Huatta) Peninsulas: one in the north in Peru and one in the southeast in Bolivia.
4. The Cero Cupe referred to here is different from the one reported on in Stanish et al. (Chapter 17, this volume).

6.

Pukara Influence on Isla Soto, Lake Titicaca, Peru

Joel Myres and Rolando Paredes

INTRODUCTION

ARCHAEOLOGICAL RUINS significant to the prehistoric cultural development of the altiplano are located on Isla Soto in the northern part of Lake Titicaca, Peru. We refer to these ruins as the "Isla Soto Archaeological Complex." Characteristics that define the Soto complex include paired sunken courts oriented along an east-west axis and surrounding terraces that architecturally enhance the courts. In association with the sunken courts was a partial monolithic sculpture in the Pukara style. These features, coupled with its prominent location overlooking the island and lake, make this an ideal location for a ritual site.

Assigning a date to the Isla Soto archaeological complex is possible through a comparison of the architectural features and other artifacts on the surface. Similar sunken courts used as temples or shrines for ceremonial purposes are found throughout the Andean zone, and particularly the Titicaca Basin. We propose that the archaeological structures on the island comprise a limited use location built primarily for ceremonial purposes. In addition to the sunken court complex, the northern edge of the island retains cleared plazas situated on a bluff overlooking the lake. In this chapter, the existence and placement of other ruins located on other Titicaca islands are noted, and the relationship with Isla Soto of these other island sites is considered.

Based on these observations, we propose that the Isla Soto complex as a ceremonial center was established during the Early Intermediate period, during Pukara times. Although eventually abandoned, the site was presumably recognized as an ancestral *huaca* during the Late Horizon. The nature and location of these ruins contribute an added spatial and temporal dimension to a model of an Early Intermediate period cultural expansion originating from Pukara and extending southward. Subsequent work on the Titicaca islands should provide additional data to establish the extent and relationship of these unique island complexes.

ISLA SOTO

Isla Soto is located in the northeastern margin of the lake near Conima on the mainland. The current population of the island numbers about 100 inhabitants. It is divided into two communities—Cabrauyo and Cijatane—and together these comprise the residences of the entire population of the island. Both Quechua and Aymara speakers inhabit the island. The island is relatively bare, and due to the scarcity of resources some of the inhabitants practice seasonal migrations to other areas, particularly to San Juan del Oro to the north. The dynamics of such migrations have been previously studied (Collins 1988) and are important to understanding the population demographics of the current residents.

The island entered the scientific literature in the nineteenth century. While writing from the sacred Inka Island of the Sun, Ephraim Squier (1877a) commented on Isla Soto, the island visible in the distance to the north. Squier notes that Isla Soto contained the remains of ancient architecture (Squier 1877a:333), but curiously does not elaborate or provide any description of the remains. Such a vague commentary does little to elucidate the purpose or origin of the remains on the island. However, in a region with such an abundance of ancient architectural ruins, this mere mention does beg the question of what the significance of these buildings was to Squier's indigenous informants. It is possible that their descriptions of the site did not convey a sense of grandeur, and as a result Squier felt his limited remark was sufficient. Nevertheless, the mention by Squier of a rather obscure island (some maps do not even depict the island) and the ruins located there reinforce the island's importance in the prehistory of the Titicaca region.

The Lake Titicaca archipelago of islands is central to Andean ideology and cosmology. Venerated by indigenous residents of the altiplano, early reports of the area noted the importance of islands in folklore and mythology. Today, these islands constitute pockets of isolated communities whose livelihoods and identities are intimately connected with the island of their residence (Frame 1989). Because there are so many small islands in Lake Titicaca, Isla Soto has received relatively little attention. Located on the periphery of the Lake within the district of Moho (Figures 1.3 and 6.1), this island contains ancient remains that, in light of altiplano development, are significant and informative.

Having a long and prominent position in Andean cultural development, the Lake Titicaca Basin is fundamental in a larger sense not only to the altiplano basin but also to the creation and maintenance of later Inka institutions (Rowe 1960). Lake Titicaca itself held a central role in Inka cosmology, and ancestral mythical origins were traced to islands located on the lake (Guaman Poma de Ayala 1980; Murúa 1946 [1590]). Remains and structures throughout the region attest to the Inka interest and occupation in the area (Hyslop 1990; Julien 1983), and ethnohistorical accounts support this conclusion (Murra 1968). Long before the Inka, however, this inland ocean nestled in an altiplano basin at 3,800 m.a.s.l., together with the surrounding area, provided unique environmental and ecological conditions that supported growing population centers. The exploitation of the abundant natural resources made this area one of the most pro-

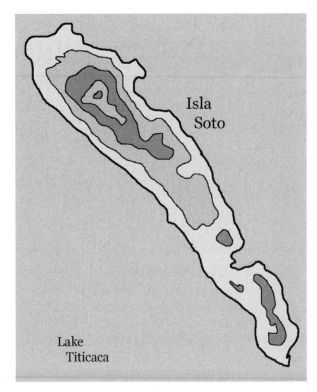

FIGURE 6.1. Plan of Isla Soto

ductive in Pre-Columbian times, as seen in the evolution of such regional centers as Pukara, Chiripa, and Tiwanaku. Sharing a similar history and derived from an established southern sierra tradition, these sites constitute shifting foci of importance in altiplano and Andean cultural history (Conklin and Moseley 1988). Early efforts to document the scope and nature of this cultural expansion in the region identified stylistic elements and architectural features characteristic of the Titicaca region (Kidder 1943).

ARCHAEOLOGY

The principal site, like the others on the island, is attributed by the locals to a giant, *puka calson*, who came across the waters from the south. This site is strategically located on a leveled mound atop a small plateau adjacent to Cabrauyo (Figure 6.2). Offset and surrounded by a series of terraces modified from the natural terrain, this site provides a vantage to view the entire island and the encompassing lake and mainland shoreline in all directions. These three levels of terraces surround an elevated mound and create a type

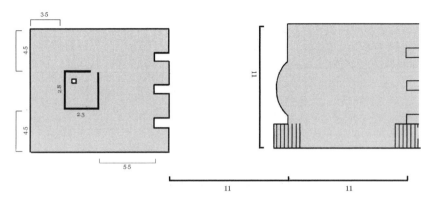

FIGURE 6.2. Sunken plazas Ispallauyu and Maranuyu

of platform which contains two sunken plazas. Both plazas are square and of equal dimensions of approximately 11.0 x 11.0 m. They differ in depth, however, varying from 1.5 m to up to 3 m. The outermost, or eastern, plaza is referred to by local residents as Ispallauyu. Adjacent to Ispallauyu is an another sunken plaza known as Maranuyu. These plazas are oriented in an east-west direction and are separated by a distance of 14 m. Visible remains of small walls originate on the northwest and southwest corners of Ispallauyu and effectively partition the plateau into two separate areas, each containing one of the sunken plazas. A small lip or wall is also evident around the peripheral edge of the plateau. Many of the stones associated with this site have been removed by residents of the island such that the true extent and possible height of these walls cannot be determined.

Ispallauyu—the outermost, or exterior, plaza—is 1.5 m in depth. Lined with stones, this semisubterranean structure is nearly square except for a slight concave recess in the rear wall protruding outward and toward the adjacent plaza to the west. Three distinct niches were built into the eastern wall. Stairs descending into the interior were built into the wall on the southeast corner, and similar stairs are symmetrically located on the opposite or southwest side.

The second sunken court, Maranuyu, shares the same construction style and features of the first. However, the level of the floor, in relation to the ground level of the entire plaza area, is lower, measuring over 2.8 m in depth on the eastern wall. Due to the poor preservation of the structure, this depth is offset by the sloping wall and fallen rubble on the south and east sides. In part, the height and contour of the walls follow a downward slope in the plateau. This allows this court to be lower than the other. There is evidence on the eastern wall of at least four recessed niches, each measuring approximately 1.0 x 1.0 m. It is possible that one or more of these niches served as a stairway into and out of the plaza. However, the overgrowth and dilapidation of the ruin did not permit extensive reconstruction. Nevertheless, the features and characteristics of these niches were not consistent with the stairway in the accompanying plaza, and the severity of the drop is much greater than would be expected for functional stairs. As these niches did not evidently serve the purpose of entry or exit to this plaza, there is no obvious access via stairs from the eastern side. Presently, an entrance is located on the northern side where the sloping walls reach a minimum. It is not known whether this present entrance is truly the original one or a later modification. Just outside this entrance on the north was a fragment of a stone sculptured monolith. Broken at the neck and waist, the remaining fragment exhibited characteristics consistent with Pukara stonework.

Located off-center within Maranuyu are the remains of a small rectangular structure defined by four sets of foundation stones (Figure 6.3). The placement and spacing of several foundation stones indicates an entryway in the southwest

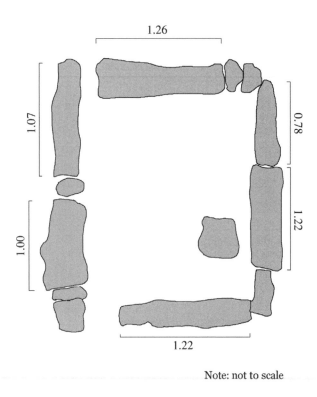

1.26

1.07

0.78

1.00

1.22

1.22

Note: not to scale

FIGURE 6.3. Plan of the enclosure within the Maranuyu

corner. Inside this space, near the northwestern corner, was a carved stone pedestal. Both plazas are and have been used by people today and in the recent past for various ceremonies; however, this second plaza (Maranuyu) is more important to people today than is the other. In particular, the inner structure shows a greater degree of usage and continued veneration, as it is adorned with objects denoting the apparent sanctity of this spot. Serving as a huaca, this location is of particular importance to the residents of the island and retains a place in their cosmology and as a tie to their ancestral past.

A plastic bottle for *chicha* located on the pedestal was left over from the *pagapu*, or yearly ritual payment to the earth for which this site is regularly used. Similar to its present purpose, the artifacts and remains found in this location support the notion that this area serves as a huaca. We may surmise that this also reflects its function in antiquity. Consistent with contemporary sources, this huaca embodies a sacred space and is revered as the founding spirit or protector-spirit materialized in hills, water, caves,

stones, and ancestor spirits (Harrison 1989:46). Similarly, Garcilaso de la Vega (1987) notes that some of the many possible manifestations of a huaca include temples, graves, or places where offerings were preformed. The use of the site by modern people today has seriously altered the site area, but has not obliterated the most important features. These conditions have not interfered with its ritual importance or discouraged the modern people from revering this location.

A reconnaissance of the island did not discover other ancient structures, except some problematic ones associated with a small group of *andenes* (terraces). These terraces are present in at least one location on the eastern slope of the island. While these andenes are relatively few and are not used today, they do suggest past agricultural activity on the island. No other andenes were noted by us or referred to by the local inhabitants. If this is the extent of Pre-Columbian agricultural activities on the island, then the land did not support a large population; at most it could have supported only a few families. Present residents have agricultural plots on the beach and subsist by growing a limited number of crops and exploiting the lake resources. Overall, the island does not provide a fertile setting, and in recent times many immigrants have abandoned attempts at cultivation and subsequently deserted the island.

As mentioned above, evidence for a Pukara occupation included the recovery and identification of a broken sculpture (Figure 6.4). Although the carved sculpture had been severely damaged, leaving only the center thoracic portion intact, distinctive Pukara characteristics were preserved. This sculpture measured 0.31 m across the base by 0.27 m high, with a thickness of 0.14 m. Manufactured of pinkish stone, the completed sculpture would obviously have been a small anthropomorphic statue. The condition of the statue was lamentable, as Colonial efforts to deface or destroy indigenous objects considered pagan by the Spaniards were common in the Lake Titicaca region. This is possibly a fate suffered by this sculpture (e.g., see Rowe 1960). The head and leg portions of the figure had been broken off and all that remained was the torso. Across the shoulders on the back was a band. Another similar band or belt was evident at the

Front view   Side views

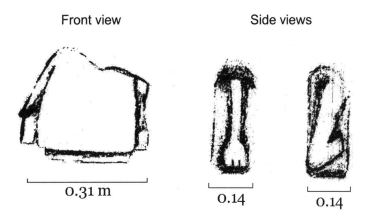

0.31 m   0.14   0.14

FIGURE 6.4. Monolithic sculpture

position of the waist on the front side. The arms are well defined and carved in relief on the side of the figure. The left arm was extended straight down with carved fingers visible, while the right arm was bent at the elbow toward the front. No hand was present on the right arm, this arm having been broken off at the wrist. These features are typical of Pukara sculpture and have been found throughout the Lake Titicaca Basin (S. Chávez and K. Chávez 1975; Kidder 1943).

The source of this stone is unknown, as no stone of similar type or quality was identified on the island. It is likely an import, associated with the ritual or ceremonial use of this location. It is also likely that the small statue was associated with the sunken courts and upon abandonment or destruction was removed and intentionally defaced. While the stratigraphic context of this object is uncertain, its significance in this location provides an additional indication of Pukara influence. Ironically, the statue fragment had not been utilized by island residents.

The northernmost end of the island is a checkerboard of cleared plazas arranged in a slightly terraced fashion according to the topography of the terrain. The plazas average 50 m long and 20 m wide in dimension. Some are much larger. Stones cleared to make the plazas were deposited along its edges to delineate plaza boundaries. This network of plazas covers a rise facing north and following the island shoreline around to the west, and extends inland tracing the contour of the hill. They do not appear to have been used for agricultural purposes, as they show few similarities with known agricultural terraces in the area. They do, however, resemble terraced platforms reminiscent of other altiplano sites, including Pukara and Tiwanaku. A structure was located between two plazas on the principle level. This structure consisted of two compartments and was enclosed by rocks. The contents of these units had been removed. It is not possible to determine whether this structure was built at the same time as the plazas or represents a later addition. However, it does appear that these units served as small burial towers, or *chullpas* (Hyslop 1977a).

At the top of the hill overlooking the cleared plaza was a circle of stone placed in the ground with a break or opening to the south. The circle measured 2.0 m in diameter. It was not possible to determine the function of this circle. It is likely that these remains are recent and not associated with the plazas that the site overlooks.

We found virtually no datable ceramic fragments on the surface. Because of this, our dating of the Isla Soto Pre-Columbian presence on the island is limited and based on the isolated sculpture fragment and the described architectural features.

DISCUSSION

Sunken courts are not unique to the Titicaca Basin. They are found in the sierra and coastal areas of the central Andes. Although the earliest examples from central and northern Peru are circular, rectangular versions appear in the sierra during ceramic times at Chavín de Huantar (Moseley 1992). In the altiplano, the long tradition of rectangular sunken plazas has been established (K. Chávez 1988; Hastorf, Chapter 5, this volume). The importance of the sunken court throughout the region and through time can be seen at the site of Chiripa in Bolivia (Hastorf et al. 1999b) and later at the regional centers of Pukara, in the northwestern Lake Titicaca region, and at Tiwanaku to the south. While the design and features of the sunken court were modified through time, the importance and prominence of the sunken court among altiplano sites remained intact. The architecture of the sunken court at Chiripa follows a similar pattern of niches inset into the walls, a single centralized location situated among surrounding structures, and a deliberate distinction between levels above- and below-ground. Such utilization of opposing space fits the architectural canon of sunken courts of the altiplano by restricting the size of the ceremonial area. The example from Isla Soto does vary somewhat from the elements of the Chiripa model by incorporating features such as dual courts, terraces, and stone constructions. These features are more reminiscent of later Pukara architecture. Despite the absence of associated enclosing structures, the platform is circumscribed by a small wall defining the topographic limits of the level in the form of a U. The significance of the U hilltop orientation to present-day Aymara has been considered. Moseley states that sanctuaries of the type seen at Soto serve a powerful mountain spirit that influences meteorological phenomena and that the shrine is employed for rain-bringing rites to benefit crops (Moseley 1992:137). Other U-shaped structures in the Titicaca Basin include one found at Tumatumani near Juli (Stanish and Steadman 1994) and the site of Huajje near Isla Esteves (Stanish et al., Chapter 17, this volume).

The visual impact of the placement of this site on the central and most prominent flat area of the island is enhanced by a series of terraces. The plateau has been modified and is sectioned along a roughly north-south axis creating east and west halves. The symmetry of this configuration implies an underlying ideology consistent with Andean concepts of duality, as seen in the dual courts, the division of platform ground space into halves, and the partitioning of space, both above and below ground.

Niches set into the wall are well defined but poorly preserved and confined to a single side. No evidence of storage was found in conjunction with the niches, but their presence within the sunken court is consistent with the above noted features. It is possible, however, that these niches served important functions in ceremonial observances and possibly contained offerings or other such effigy statues or sculpture.

The orientation of the plazas and the placement of the stairs would indicate that both sunken courts were utilized simultaneously. Likewise, the spatial relationship and structural features of these plazas suggest that together they served a combined and/or dual purpose. Separated from each other by the fallen wall, access to each subdivided segment of the platform was directed only via the southwest stairway leading in and out of Ispullauyu. Depending upon the original height of the wall, this barrier could have been symbolic without actually serving as a physical barrier, or it could have prevented access to the court by funneling people through the entrance and exit of the respective courts. Space affiliated with each plaza is demarcated by the low-lying wall running from the northwest and southwest corners of the outer plaza to the periphery wall, which defines the platform. One could enter through the eastern or western stairs, descend into the court, and ascend out through the opposing stairs, which exit into the area adjacent to the court. Still, however, the placement of the original entrance to the second court remains inconclusive. The shared features and similar configuration of the plazas suggests that the courts were contemporary. There was no evidence to suggest that either of the two courts were modified or expanded. Similarity in design, layout, and the visual vantage of this site compared to others in the altiplano suggests this complex functioned as a ceremonial center.

The relationship of two plazas created an interesting architectural effect. The altering of the "traditional" layout of the early single sunken court theme through the inclusion of a second may reflect a shift in ideology that emphasized duality. These features appear more consistent as a Pukara influence. This juxtaposition of courts has been described previously at Pukara

(Paredes 1985) and its appearance here may support its utility as a satellite ritual installation founded during an expansion southeastward from this regional center. Moreover, similarly constructed compounds have been recorded across the lake on Isla Amantaní (Niles 1987a). The combined results of the site layout and the architectural feature found on the island in terms of dual courts, orientation, and a circumscribed platform enclosure support a Pukara influence from the northwest as opposed to strong influences from the south. It is very likely that investigations in the Moho region may identify the existence of comparable structures. Based on the resemblance between the Isla Soto sunken court complexes and those of similar arrangements at Pukara, we would date this complex to late Early Intermediate times circa AD 200–400.

The archaeological remains of Isla Soto provide a glimpse into the place of this island within the framework of the cultural development in the Titicaca Basin. Reports of ancient ruins on the major islands of the lake provide an intriguing picture of their importance and placement within the cultural history of the region as well as their continued significance to the modern population. This is especially true in an unproductive island such as Soto (Bandelier 1910). Of interest are the similarities between ruins reported on Amantaní (Niles 1987b) and those described on Soto. Their importance is emphasized by the effort invested in these locations and reflected in the significance of their structural features and configurations. While little work has been done to examine the extent of these finds, Isla Soto is just one of the islands on the lake that contains significant archaeological remains.

ADDITIONAL CONSIDERATIONS

The Titicaca islands are of considerable importance in Andean history. The most renowned of the Lake Titicaca islands are Titicaca and Coati, or the Islands of the Sun and Moon, respectively. In one of the earliest recorded explorations of the Titicaca Basin, Ephraim Squier (1877a) devoted considerable attention to these most venerated islands of the lake, which together constituted sacred centers and held particular prominence in Inka mythology (and see more re-

cently Bauer and Stanish 2001; Seddon, Chapter 9, this volume). Archaeological ruins have been located and attributed to an Inka occupation. Because of their relationship to and importance in Inka cosmology, these ruins have generated considerable interest. Nevertheless, not much is known concerning the pre-Inka occupation of the islands. Work on Isla Soto may provide some insight into the relationships of Titicaca islands to archaeology of the altiplano in general. In particular, the work discussed here is relevant to the pre-Inka archaeology of the region.

Squier (1877a:333) records that for the Inka, Isla Soto was the Isle of Penitence and served as a place for fasting and reflection. It is not clear whether the ancient architecture on the island was involved in these observances, and while Squier does not provide any details concerning the architecture on Soto, this mention that Soto was recognized and evidently was frequented by the Inka is important. As noted previously, no evidence of Inka occupation was observed, and the remains described show no modification or structural elements characteristically Inka in style. Soto, as we have seen, emerged as a propitious location in pre-Inka times as part of the altiplano cultural landscape, but is reported by Squier in the nineteenth century as being of interest to pilgrims in Inka times. Because many of the pre-Inka ruins were acknowledged and incorporated during Inka imperial expansion, Soto may have fit well into this scheme, possibly attaining a degree of significance in the pantheon of Inka sacred sites. Our survey of the island supports an interpretation of a pre-Inka presence on the island. The lack of structural features or modifications, together with an absence of identifiable surface artifacts, may indicate that any Inka occupation here was only temporary and transitory.

After the collapse of Late Horizon cultures and the arrival of the Spanish presence, Andean settlements and demography were substantially altered. During the Colonial period, when community resettlement occurred and when *reducciones* were established, Lake Titicaca islands were granted as *encomiendas* to Spanish arrivals (Espinoza 1983). Soto, however, did not experience a population increase as did other islands such as Taquile and Amantaní. While islands such as Taquile were utilized and settled during the Colonial period, efforts to colonize Soto did not flourish. At one point during the eighteenth century, precisely because of its inhospitable environment, Soto served as a penitentiary for banished political prisoners. It was later reoccupied at the end of the nineteenth century when families from Amantaní Island and the lakeside town of Conima established residences on Soto (personal communication with island residents). Most recently, additional settlers from Moho and Huancané have added to the already small population. Today the island population represents a mix of altiplano peoples from throughout the lake region.

SUMMARY AND CONCLUSION

The site on Isla Soto provides the most informative data for establishing not only the origins of this archaeological complex, but also the function of the island and its relationship to altiplano history. Architectural features support the conclusion that Isla Soto was a ceremonial center constructed sometime during the Late Pukara era (AD 200–400). Also, the recovery of the partial sculpture indicates a Pukara affiliation. Considering the absence of dwellings, few people inhabited the island, and if a permanent settlement did exist, no record of it was found. Since the island is believed to have been visited primarily for ritual and ceremonial purposes, its location is significant and should raise the level of interest in the Titicaca islands in altiplano cultural history. The cleared plazas on the north end of the island provide no surface evidence to indicate their function. It is possible that this location served as a landing spot for arrivals from the mainland (although other preferable locations exist), or possibly as a site for ceremonial plazas or clearings for assemblies. The location of the plazas on the north end of the island and their orientation to the north and west toward Pukara, as opposed to some other location or direction, may demonstrate a connection or relationship to the Pukara heartland.

At some point in time, as importance in the northern regional center of Pukara declined, Isla Soto most likely suffered eventual neglect. Nevertheless, in spite of its abandonment and probable disuse, the island evidently retained some religious status in the collective memories of altiplano residents, as attested by its veneration in modern times. If present conditions are any indication of past circumstance, the barrenness of the island may have discouraged permanent settlement. For this reason, the island may have been a good setting for later Inka-period pilgrims, perhaps as a place of penitence. As a result, the island was never entirely forgotten. During Late Horizon times, this location, we believe, regained a place of significance and was again recognized and visited as a huaca revered by the Inka.

Lake Titicaca holds an important ideological place in the Andean world and continues to intrigue and spark the curiosity of scholars and tourists alike. Continued research and exploration is revealing a region alive with history and tradition. While the Isla Soto has experienced dramatic change throughout the centuries of human occupation, its significance endures in the minds and memories of the resident population of the Titicaca Basin. Today the inhabitants consider the huaca a link to the past as well as a vibrant part of their ritual life.

As our understanding of the cultural prehistory of this region grows, it is becoming increasingly clear that ancient cultural activities associated with the Titicaca islands reflected this ideological underpinning, and no doubt contribute to its preservation. Having received little attention, the ruins located and described on Soto consist of just one piece of the complex picture of Andean cultural history. They likewise represent a living link to the past. It is anticipated that future research in the altiplano will further our understanding of this phenomenon.

Translated by C. Stanish

7.

Tiwanaku Expansion into the Western Titicaca Basin, Peru

Charles Stanish, Kirk Lawrence Frye,
Edmundo de la Vega, and Matthew T. Seddon

THE TIWANAKU STATE was the largest autochthonous polity to develop in the Andes south of Cuzco before the Spanish conquest (Figure 1.3). Sometime in the first millennium AD, the Tiwanaku state extended its influence over a vast territory covering parts of four modern nations and a variety of ecological zones. Tiwanaku artifacts have been found over an area of approximately 400,000 km², an area the size of modern California.

Defining the processes of state formation and territorial expansion of the Tiwanaku polity outside of its core territory stands as one of the most important and intriguing problems in Andean prehistory. Tiwanaku expansion involves a number of related questions. What was the nature of the Tiwanaku political economy? Was Tiwanaku an expansionist state at all, or was its influence in areas outside of the Tiwanaku Valley a result of social, religious, or other nonpolitical factors? Was Tiwanaku a conquest state structurally similar to the later Inca empire, or did it expand through more subtle political and economic strategies by establishing exchange relationships and colonies in targeted provincial areas? If it was indeed an expansionist state, when did Tiwanaku expand? Was its expansion early, during, or before its Tiwanaku III or Qeya period, or did its major expansion occur later? These questions are central in understanding the processes of the Tiwanaku expansion throughout the vast south central Andean region. In this chapter, we present settlement data from the

western Titicaca basin area that serve to answer some of these questions.

Our knowledge of the Tiwanaku polity in its core region (the Tiwanaku, Catari, and Desaguadero River Basins) is based upon several decades of research on the Peruvian and Bolivian sides of the lake. The archaeological research of Arturo Posnansky (1945), Wendell Bennett (1934a, 1934b), Stig Rydén (1947), and Carlos Ponce Sanginés (1981) has served to define a broad cultural chronological framework for the region. This chronology, which we refer to as the "Bennett-Ponce" chronology (Bermann 1990:55; Stanish 2003), is based upon two relatively good stratigraphic cuts by Bennett (out of ten excavated) and other excavations by Ponce Sanginés and Gregorio Cordero at the site of Tiwanaku. It is also based upon a stylistic typology of Tiwanaku materials collected from these and other sites from around the area.

In the Tiwanaku core territory, definable Tiwanaku I pottery manufacture is reported to have begun around 300 BC. Subsequent Tiwanaku pottery styles (Tiwanaku III–IV) were manufactured up to around AD 1100. Recent excavation and survey data reported by Sonia Alconini Mujica (1995) and Paul Goldstein (1989) in Moquegua; Marc Bermann (1990) at Lukurmata; and Juan Albarracin-Jordan and James Mathews (1990), as well as John Janusek (2003; Chapter 10, this volume) in the Tiwanaku Valley, have refined this chronology, although problems still remain with the Bennett-Ponce chronology. In spite of these problems, it is still the only viable framework we have, and we will continue to utilize it for interpreting the archaeological data from the western Titicaca region.

Early archaeological research outside of the core Tiwanaku area established the fact that Tiwanaku materials were widely distributed over the south central Andes. Alfred Kidder (1943) reconnoitered the northern Titicaca region. He described several Tiwanaku sites in the region, including Incatunuhuiri (1943:13), Asiruni, and Sarapa (1943:10). Incatunuhuiri is located near Ichu, directly northwest of Chucuito. Asiruni and Sarapa are located in the Ilave Pampa. Incatunuhuiri is a large, terraced hill that has Pukara and Tiwanaku occupations. It also has a semi-subterranean sunken court with carved stone stelae. Kidder inferred that there was complex architecture from the sites of Asiruni and Sarapa as well. Both of these sites had Tiwanaku occupations. Kidder described Tiwanaku pottery at these sites and is therefore one of the first archaeologists to document a Tiwanaku presence in the Ilave region. A few years later, Marion Tschopik described three late Tiwanaku vessels that she purchased in Chucuito (M. Tschopik 1946:41), confirming a Tiwanaku presence in that immediate area as well. The exact nature of this presence, however, remained poorly understood.

John Rowe (1956) published a brief report on the site of Huayna Roque in Juliaca. This site sits on one of the large mountains in the area near the modern town of Juliaca. The habitation area is located along the edges of the hill. Unfortunately, the site has been badly disturbed. Tiwanaku pottery is located throughout the site area, however, and there is little doubt that Huayna Roque was a major Tiwanaku settlement (Lisa Cipolla and Rolando Paredes, personal communication 2001).

John Hyslop conducted the first systematic reconnaissance of the area located between Puno and Desaguadero. Based upon these data, he proposed the "Tiwanaku and Antecedents Macropattern." The Tiwanaku and Formative period patterns were similar, as the name of the settlement macropattern implies. He observed that Tiwanaku sites in the Lupaqa area were concentrated near the lakeshore, that these sites

may have been associated with raised fields, and that the nature of the Tiwanaku occupation may have been similar to that of the later Lupaqa "Kingdom" (Hyslop 1976:92–98).

Hyslop's work confirmed the suggestion of earlier researchers that there were indeed a number of Tiwanaku sites in the region. However, many questions remain. The precise date of Tiwanaku expansion, for instance, remains a subject of debate. Several archaeologists have suggested a Tiwanaku IV date for the expansion of Tiwanaku outside of its core territory. Ponce Sanginés (1981:78–79) argued that Tiwanaku enclaves were established in Ayacucho and Arica during Tiwanaku IV times. Kolata (1983:252–253) recognizes the Tiwanaku IV period as the time in which Tiwanaku "achieved true imperial status," establishing colonies in lowland Bolivia and the Pacific coast. These observations are supported by Goldstein's data from Moquegua. In the upper reaches of this coastal valley, the earliest occupation by Tiwanaku was during the Omo phase, a time that corresponds to the "middle or later part of Phase IV of the Bolivian Tiwanaku sequence" (Goldstein 1989:61). Finally, Browman (1984) suggests a date of AD 300–400 for "an ever-quickening series of expanding economic networks" by the Tiwanaku state, dates consistent with other archaeologists who see Tiwanaku expansion in the early Tiwanaku IV period. In sum, previous research had clearly indicated that Tiwanaku sites were located in the western Titicaca area. The nature, date, and intensity of that occupation were unknown.

It is in this research context that we report on our research in this chapter. The data reported here are based upon survey and reconnaissance in several areas. In the Juli-Pomata region we conducted a full regional coverage pedestrian survey of an area measuring 360 km^2. A similar survey was conducted in the Chucuito region (Frye and de la Vega, Chapter 11, this volume). Systematic, intensive reconnaissance was carried out in the Ccapia and Desaguadero River areas, and nonsystematic reconnaissance was carried out in the rest of the area up to Paucarcolla (Figure 7.1). Subsequent work was conducted by Carol Schultze (2000) in the Puno Bay. Amanda Cohen (2000, 2001) surveyed the Pukara Valley, and various members of Programa Collasuyu

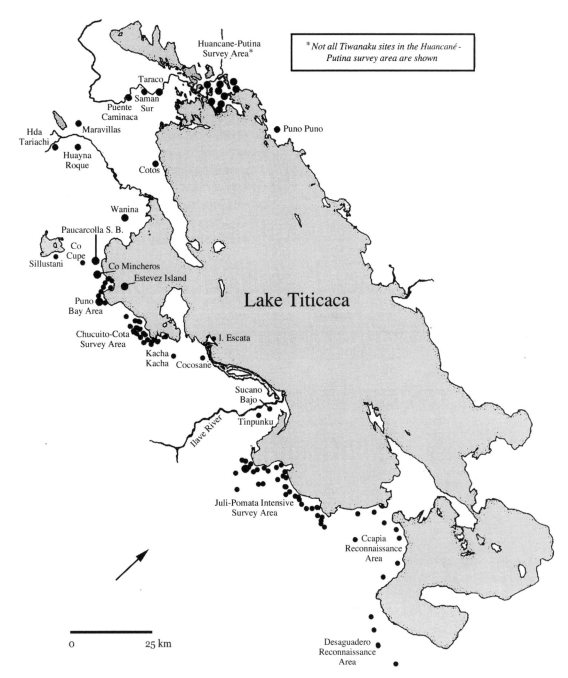

FIGURE 7.1. Survey and reconnaissance areas discussed in the chapter

have completed survey in the Huancané-Putina area, as well as in the perimeter of Lake Arapa.

THE TIWANAKU OCCUPATION OF THE WESTERN TITICACA BASIN

Tiwanaku sites are easily identified by the presence of a high density of decorated Tiwanaku pottery on the settlements and, in some cases, architectural modifications using Tiwanaku canons. Tiwanaku pottery in the region is recognized by very distinctive shapes and design motifs. Certain Tiwanaku fineware pastes are also distinctive and represent imports into the region. The best Tiwanaku marker, however, is pottery in the form of *kero*, *tazón* (flaring sided bowl), and incense burner shapes. In most cases, the pottery was locally made, but a number of nonlocal imports were also found on these sites. We argue that the existence of substantial quantities of Tiwanaku pottery on a site indicates a strong relationship to the Tiwanaku state. Where other iconographic traditions are not present, and where there is architectural modification using Tiwanaku canons, we can argue that the site was in the Tiwanaku political orbit. In the case of Tumatumani near Juli (Figure 7.2), for instance, the work of Steadman (in Stanish and Steadman 1994) nicely illustrates how the pre-Tiwanaku assemblage contained iconographic and vessel form elements from both the north and south Titicaca Basin, along with a local ceramic tradition. During the Tiwanaku occupation, in contrast, all iconographic canons were from the southern basin, specifically from the Tiwanaku state.

The Tiwanaku occupation of the western region is represented by a number of diverse site types in the area. Our survey work allows us to define a number of site types for Tiwanaku period occupations:

- Large, artificial mounds, which are greater than 50 x 50 m at the base, represent the first type of site. These mounds are built with artificial fill that was used to construct non-domestic architectural features. This site type represents a considerable labor investment and is a kind of elite/ceremonial construction. The mounds are not just collapsed structures, but rather represent considerable quantities of fill intentionally used to create architectural features.

- Small, artificial habitation mounds represent a second type of Tiwanaku site in the region. These artificial mounds are small, generally measuring less than 20 x 20 m at the base, and represent individual collapsed houses. The distinction between large and small

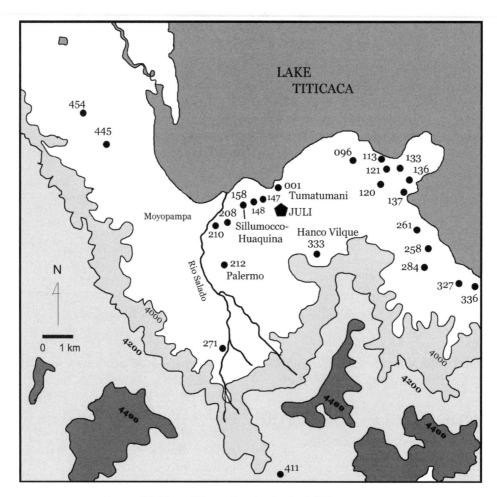

FIGURE 7.2. Map of Tiwanaku sites in the Juli-Pomata region

mounds is greater than merely a difference in size. Unlike the large mounds, the fill found in this second site type was not intentionally moved to build corporate constructions. Rather, small mounded sites represent collapsed domestic structures that then turned into a mound after abandonment. It is not unusual for small mounds to have intrusive tombs placed on top. These sites are generally found in the pampas near the lake.

- Sites built on low, generally nondefensible, natural hills with domestic terraces represent the third major site type in the study area. These sites often have sunken courts on the hilltop and represent an architectural representation of the Akapana-Kalasasaya sunken court tradition—a tradition that reached its fullest and most dramatic expression at the site of Tiwanaku itself (see Hastorf, Chapter 5, this volume).

- The domestic terrace settlement is the most common Tiwanaku site type. The domestic terrace type accounts for a significant percentage of the habitation sites and housed a majority of the total population in the intensively studied areas. Many of the hillsides in the region are terraced and used today for agricultural purposes. Our research clearly indicates that a substantial number of these agricultural terraces may have originally been built for domestic purposes and were later plowed under for agriculture land use. The agricultural and domestic terraces are almost always faced with fieldstones. Today, one can observe house compounds built on the hillside terraces in a pattern that appears to go back millennia.

- Tiwanaku artifact scatters that lack any evidence of domestic terracing or other constructions are occasionally found. These are usually dispersed sites built on flat land, generally near the lake or in the puna regions. These sites could represent small destroyed mounds or very light or transient occupations. Dispersed sites are rare in the region, accounting for a small percentage of the habitation sites found in our work throughout the region.

- "Conical mounds" are a seemingly rare site type in the Ilave River area on the Ilave Pampa. They are also found in the Ramis River area as well. These are earthen mounds that are small at the base (10 m in diameter, for instance) but quite high (5–8 m). These appear to be habitation and/or ceremonial constructions of unknown origin and distribution.

- Tiwanaku cemeteries are found throughout the western Titicaca basin area as well, and are almost always associated with nearby habitation areas. There are no above-ground Tiwanaku tombs, such as *chulpas* (burial towers) or slab-cist tombs. All Tiwanaku tombs discovered so far are below-ground cists without any surface features.

TIWANAKU SETTLEMENTS IN THE WESTERN TITICACA REGION

The Northwestern Titicaca Region

The northwestern Titicaca region is the area of the sixteenth century Aymara *señorío* of the Colla. The Colla polity extended approximately from the bay of Puno in the south to the Canas polity in the north and the Canchis polity to the east. There has been no systematic survey in this area to date. Mario Núñez (1994) has published a review of the known Tiwanaku sites in the Puno area. A number of sites have since been destroyed or are now covered by modern constructions. They were identified by the presence of Tiwanaku diagnostics recovered from rescue work or as a byproduct of construction activities. Núñez lists a number of such sites, including one found in the present site of the Colegio Nacional en Puno located in Barrio José Antonio Encinas; the site of Huajjsapata, located 300 m from the Plaza de Armas; the site of Molloqo Mata, located near the lake off the main highway south of Puno (Molloqo Mata was also visited by Hyslop [1976]); and Punanave, located above the military base south of Puno. Núñez also notes that Tiwanaku artifacts were located on Isla Salinas and, of course, Isla Esteves (Figure 7.1). Isla Esteves was at least 15 ha in size, with evidence of corporate architecture.

We also located several additional sites in the Puno area. For example, a small unnamed site was located approximately 500 m from Isla Esteves on the side of the hill. The site had a few terraces that measure about 75 x 50 m total. The occupation appeared to be purely domestic, with no evidence of Tiwanaku finewares. At the eastern side of the Punanave hill is a major domestic terrace site with Tiwanaku Expansive occupations. The site is composed of at least four terraces. Unfortunately, the site is being mined for gravel and will be lost in the next few years.

Another site, Chuchuparqui, is located on the road north from Isla Esteves along the hill adjacent to the railroad tracks and lake edge. It is located on the larger southern hill between Viscachane and Chullune. It is a modest-sized domestic terraced hill site, approximately 3 to 4 ha in area. There are four to six domestic terraces on all sides up to a flat area that probably had a sunken court and/or a ceremonial area. The site of Toclomara is located at the curve on the same road as Chuchuparqui. It is a substantial domestic terrace site with abundant Upper Formative, Tiwanaku, Late Intermediate period, and Inca period occupations. This site is at least 3 ha in size, possibly more, and it is associated with the raised fields below. A series of broad domestic terraces are located above and below the curve on the road. Although the Tiwanaku occupation appears to be restricted to the lower terraces, it is still considered large anyway (greater than 1.0 ha). There is no evidence of corporate architecture on this site.

Several Tiwanaku sites have been reported between Puno and Paucarcolla. Revilla Becerra and Uriarte Paniagua (1985:86–95) report finding Tiwanaku levels in their excavations at the site of Sillustani. They also note the presence of Tiwanaku ceramics on a site called Patas, 2 km north of Sillustani (Revilla Becerra and Uriarte Paniagua 1985:46). Likewise, they found "miscellaneous" fragments at the site of Cerro Ale, 3 km north of Sillustani (Revilla Becerra and Uriarte Paniagua 1985:46). Similarly, L. Steadman (1995) notes a significant Tiwanaku occupation at the site of Paucarcolla. Recently, Carol Schultze completed a full regional coverage of the Puno Bay. Her work confirms the existence of a major Tiwanaku enclave in the Puno Bay.

The Chucuito Region

The Chucuito-Cutimbo region was intensively surveyed using a full coverage methodology. All extant archaeological sites were recovered in an area of approximately 200 km² (Figure 7.1). Twenty-seven Tiwanaku sites were located. All of these sites are concentrated near the lakeshore, with only one site located in the higher-altitude puna zone. Two of the sites within the study region were reported by Hyslop (1976), one located on the lower slopes of Cerro Ccota and another at Camata. Tiwanaku sites were found in two main topographic zones: in flat pampa areas near the lakeshore and on the surrounding hill slopes. The majority of sites in the pampa are small habitation mounds associated with relict raised-field systems, while larger sites, of which Camata is an example, are located on natural hills rising above the lakeside plain. Hill slopes sites were situated on small domestic terraces located along the base of the surrounding hills. The majority of the sites are small and include five cemeteries, seven hamlets, ten small villages, and four large villages. One site is a temple construction with no apparent occupation. The total combined occupation size of all Tiwanaku sites in the survey is not large, at 12.93 ha.

Tiwanaku sites in the Chucuito-Cutimbo survey occur in clusters in four specific areas: Pampa Huataraque, Pampa Pirape, Ichu Pampa and near the modern town of Chucuito. The Pampa Huataraque group includes the unnamed habitation sites of CC-47, CC-66, and CC-197, and a small cemetery identified as CC-65. Site CC-47 is one of the sites reported by Hyslop and is the largest site in the Huataraque group, measuring 1.2 ha in size. The second cluster of sites, found in the Pampa Pirape area, is the most clearly associated with relict raised-field agricultural systems. Two canals, one on the north side and another on the south side of the pampa, were recorded and mapped. Site CC-54 is located near the northern canal, while CC-25 and CC-38 are found along the southern one. Sites CC-57, CC-53, CC-45, CC-58, CC-60, and CC-48 are situated along a road that was in use during the Late Horizon (Hyslop 1984:130). The largest site in the group is Camata (CC-52), first described by Hyslop (1976:381) and intensively excavated by L. Steadman (1995). Steadman noted a concentration of slipped Tiwanaku ceramics associated with what may have been a Tiwanaku period plaza structure at Camata (Steadman 1995:8–9), but a modern house compound occupies the area where a structure may have been, making detailed observation there difficult. Although Camata may have included some formal architecture, the Tiwanaku occupation is approximately 2.0 ha in size, much reduced from the 3.5 ha reported by L. Steadman (1995:9) for the Late Formative occupation. The settlement pattern in the Pampa Pirape is therefore two tiered, with smaller sites located between larger ones within the small-sized raised-field system.

A third area of Tiwanaku sites is situated south of the modern town of Chucuito. Two Tiwanaku sites, CC-92 and CC-94, are located on the slopes of a *quebrada* along the southern flank of Cerro Atoja. These are associated with a canal that may have extended into the Chinchira Pampa. CC-92 is 0.5 ha in size, and is defined by dispersed ceramic artifacts across several domestic terraces and an associated cemetery further up the slope.

The fourth and final grouping of Tiwanaku sites in this region is found in the Ichu pampa. Three Tiwanaku sites were found in this area, including Incatunuhuiri, an important Formative period site. Mapping and intensive surface collections at Incatunuhuiri indicate a small Tiwanaku occupation restricted to an area of 0.5 ha along the sides of a canalized quebrada at the base of the Incatunuhuiri hill on the northeast side. Only a few Tiwanaku fragments were found on the slopes of Incatunuhuiri, and none were found at the Formative period temple complex at the summit. Other sites in the Ichu area include CC-102, a low mound measuring 0.04 ha and located in the pampa above the Panamerican highway. CC-103 is a site along the modern road that was disturbed when the road was reconstructed. Like the sites found in the Pirape Pampa, the sites in the Ichu Pampa area represent small-scale agricultural settlements associated with lakeside raised fields.

Site CC-215 deserves special mention. Located on the island of Quipata, CC-215 is an impressive although modest (1.0 ha) truncated

pyramid structure which, given its architectural style, suggests a civic ceremonial function. Enigmatically, however, no decorated ceramics were found at the site, and with the exception of a few Tiwanaku plainwares there were almost no surface ceramics at the site at all.

The Tiwanaku settlement data from the Chucuito-Cutimbo survey area provide important comparisons with settlement data from other areas in the western Titicaca Basin. Similar to other studied areas, the Tiwanaku settlement pattern in the Chucuito-Cutimbo is associated with raised-field agricultural systems. The area of highest site density, the Pampa Pirape, is also the area with the greatest potential for raised fields. In contrast to the Juli-Pomata and Ccapia areas (this chapter), no large Tiwanaku civic-ceremonial centers (sites over 4 ha) were found in the survey area. Although two sites were documented in the survey area that may have been used as Tiwanaku civic-ceremonial sites, the largest, Camata, does not appear to have functioned as an important political center in Tiwanaku times. While the Formative occupation in the Chucuito-Cutimbo is characterized by a clear site size hierarchy and the occupation of several densely settled ceremonial centers, with Incatunuhuiri being by far the most important, the Tiwanaku occupation of the region is very different. None of the Formative period ceremonial sites in the Chucuito-Cutimbo area were reoccupied during Tiwanaku times, suggesting that the Late Formative political system had declined prior to the expansion of Tiwanaku influence in the region.

The Juli-Pomata Region

The Juli-Pomata area was intensively surveyed using a full regional coverage methodology (Stanish et al. 1997). All extant archaeological sites were recovered in an area of approximately 350 km². We discovered about forty Tiwanaku sites in the area from the southern Ilave pampa to the pampa just south of Pomata (Figure 7.1). The preferred site types for the Tiwanaku period were the low, terraced hill and the hillside domestic terraces, respectively. Of the eight terraced hill sites identified, at least three of them have cut stone blocks and evidence of semisubterranean sunken courts at the top of the hill.

Hyslop (1976:84–85) refers to these constructions as "Kalasasayas" after the famous construction at the site of Tiwanaku itself. Such constructions are typical at other major Tiwanaku sites in the region as exhaustively discussed by Hastorf in this volume, in Chapter 5. The sites with sunken courts are most certainly the principal ceremonial-elite centers of the Upper Formative Late Sillumocco and Tiwanaku period occupations in the Juli-Pomata area.

The Tiwanaku settlement pattern in the Juli-Pomata area is characterized by a lakeside settlement focus and the absence of fortified settlements. The most common type of Tiwanaku site is the domestic hillside terrace. These sites are found in the lower sections of hills adjacent to the pampas, the raised fields, and the lake. Domestic terrace sites lack any evidence of ceremonial architecture and are almost certainly nonelite domestic residences. They are indistinguishable from agricultural terraces today and can only be found by pedestrian survey.

Six Tiwanaku sites are classified as artificial mounds. Three of these are quite substantial in size: Tumatumani, Huaquina, and Huarahuarani. Tumatumani, in fact, is composed of two large mounds, one of which is characterized by a pyramid-like structure with artificial terraces, while the second one was built in an extended U-shape (Stanish and Steadman 1994). Tumatumani may represent the southernmost U-shaped structures in the Andes (Stanish 2001a). The sites of Huaquina and Huarahuarani represent smaller mounds on the periphery of the Moyopampa zone. Huaquina is approximately 100 x 175 m in dimension and rises several meters above the pampa. The mound is obviously artificial, but without excavation it is impossible to determine the nature of its architecture. The unnamed site number 444 is located in the north of our survey area. It is approximately 100 x 100 m at the base and rises several meters above the pampa. Three smaller artificial mounds also had Tiwanaku occupations: Kalatirawi, Ankoake, and an unnamed site (number 284). Two of the three sites, Kalatirawi and Ankoake, are located in the Moyopampa near the Salado River in the northern part of the survey area (see de la Vega, Chapter 8, this volume). This area is a major raised-field zone. Site 284 is located in the El Molino sector. All three of these smaller mounds are low, small, and have post-Tiwanaku intrusive tombs.

Small Tiwanaku mounds are rare in the area, and both Ankoake and site number 284 did not have earlier occupations. Only Kalatirawi, the site on the periphery of the Moyopampa raised-field area, had an earlier occupation. It is therefore most likely that the small mounded Tiwanaku sites represent a late Tiwanaku occupation in the region.

Two other sites are characterized by a flat topography with a dispersed settlement. Flat land anywhere in the study area is found only in a few areas such as the lakeside pampas, a thin strip along the lake itself, and in some flat areas in the puna. The site of Hanco Vilque and unnamed site number 349 are found in the puna and on the lakeshore, respectively. Hanco Vilque, along with unnamed site number 411, represents sites typical of the high puna that most likely had pastoral functions. One atypical site is unnamed site number 500, a rock shelter with Upper Formative, Tiwanaku, and post-Tiwanaku occupations.

Another atypical site is Altarani-Bebedero, located at the base of the uplifted geological formation known as Bebedero. Altarani-Bebedero was first discovered by Hyslop (1976:352; 1977a:161). The site has a large, squarish platform at the southern base of the uplifted strata. Hyslop's description matches our survey observations except that we have included the entire Bebedero rock outcrop with the platform and a carved niche as one site. The carving is an inverted trapezoidal or T-shaped niche inside of an upside-down square U-shape carved in one of the uplifted natural walls. The carving stands about 7 m high and about 14 m wide. Hyslop noted that the "doorway has a T-shape reminiscent of a Tiwanaku sculptural motif" (Hyslop 1977a:161–162), although he felt that it was more likely a chulpa facade built in the Altiplano or Late Intermediate period. We feel that the carving is most likely Inca in date, but this remains to be tested with further stylistic analysis of other similar motifs in the region (compare to Arkush, Chapter 14, this volume).

Test excavations at three sites in the region indicate that Tiwanaku consistently occupied and substantially modified previous Upper Formative period sites such as Tumatumani. The earlier terraces were rebuilt into larger ones with the same architectural pattern (Stanish and Steadman 1994). Testing at the site of Palermo also indicated that Tiwanaku substantially modified this site as well. Clear Upper Formative period levels were separated from Tiwanaku levels by a burning event, which may have been associated with the arrival of Tiwanaku in the area (Stanish et al. 1992). The site was constructed into an Akapana/Kalasasaya/semisubterranean temple complex typical of core Tiwanaku sites as well as external ones (Goldstein 1993b), indicating a strong Tiwanaku interest in establishing site layouts similar to those of the homeland. Testing at the site of Sillumocco-Huaquina indicates a similar pattern (see de la Vega, Chapter 8, this volume). Here, again, Tiwanaku modified a previous Upper Formative period occupation at the site. In this case, the entire top terrace of a terraced hill was added during the Tiwanaku period.

It is significant that there is no evidence of Tiwanaku settlement in its earlier or pre-Tiwanaku IV phases. The lack of Qeya and earlier sites in the region is significant. The occupation of the region occurred only after Tiwanaku had coalesced into a powerful polity in its core territory in the Pacajes region. The Tiwanaku state expanded into the Lupaqa region at a time when the area was controlled by complex Upper Formative polities.

The Ccapia Region

The Ccapia Reconnaissance Area includes the edge of the lake around the large Ccapia Mountain that dominates the southern Titicaca Basin (Figure 7.1). The Desaguadero Reconnaissance area was restricted to the Peruvian side of the river, from the town of Desaguadero to a distance several kilometers south. We discovered a number of important Tiwanaku sites in both of these areas. The results from this reconnaissance are consistent with those from the Intensive Survey Area. That is, we found the full range of sites and site types in the Ccapia and Desaguadero areas, as we did in the Juli-Pomata area.

A number of major Tiwanaku sites are located along the lake edge along the Checca-Yunguyu highway. The sites of Acero Phatjata, Imicate, and Qeñuani (Fortina Vinto), plus the site complex of Tintinpujopata-Ticamaya, Chatumapata, Morocollo, Pukara Chatuma, and Kcusill-Chacca in the Chatuma Pampa represent major Tiwanaku occupations along this productive lakeshore area (Figure 7.1). The site of Llaquepa Mancja, located inland away from the lake on the southern edge of the Chatuma Pampa, is a major site as well. Many of these sites are between 4 and 6 ha in size and have some evidence of corporate architecture.

Along the southern edge of the lake on the road is a large beach and pasture area called the Misavi Pampa. We surveyed a section of the beach about 100–200 m from the lake. This area exhibits a settlement pattern distinct from any in the Juli-Pomata Intensive Survey Area. The entire area surveyed, approximately 3 km^2, has at least a light concentration of pottery with occasional heavier concentrations of artifacts in restricted areas. In other words, the entire beach constitutes a habitation area with some concentrations of now-destroyed structures. Pre-Hispanic diagnostics included substantial but small concentrations of Tiwanaku sherds all along the lake edge. There is also a substantial Tiwanaku occupation along the edge of the small lake (Huiñamarka) on the Peruvian side. In particular, the sites of Amaizama China, Kanamarca, Yanapata, and Caninsaya represent major Tiwanaku sites along this side of the lake. All of these sites are larger than 3 ha in area.

Desaguadero River Reconnaissance Area

We discovered several major Tiwanaku sites in the Desaguadero River area on the Peruvian side. The Tiwanaku sites of Callanga and Linquinchira were discovered and reported by Hyslop (1976:290). Linquinchira is at least 2 ha in size, and probably much larger. The site of La Casilla is located at the crest of the road that separates the Desaguadero area pampa from the Challaquenta area, which is a pasture zone today. An important aspect of La Casilla is that there is abundant raw copper ore on the surface. The residents of the site were therefore almost certainly exploiting the copper source near the site of Chicane less than 1 km away. The settlement location of this site could therefore represent a compromise between access to the raised-field area near the river, access to the copper source, and a suitable location for habitation on the hillside.

The reconnaissance of the Desaguadero River indicates a substantial Tiwanaku presence in association with the extensive raised-field areas on the river bottoms. Furthermore, Posnansky (1938) reported the site of Simillake in the Desaguadero River, a site with stelae and a probable sunken court and/or Kalasasaya construction. The area across the river on the Bolivian side has not been surveyed, but there is a strong probability of substantial Tiwanaku settlement there as well, given the substantial agricultural terracing and raised-field construction in the area.

The North: Arapa-Huancané-Putina

The northern Titicaca Basin region was surveyed from 1999 through 2003, and we are still compiling these data. We discovered over 1200 new sites, including several dozen major Formative and Tiwanaku period ones. The pattern from the northern lake area is unequivocal: Tiwanaku sites abound along the lake edge and along the modern Taraco-Huancané road, but are virtually nonexistent up-valley from the lake. There are no Tiwanaku sites north of Huatasane, a town about midway between Huancané and Putina (see Figure 4.3 for a map of this area). There are likewise very few sites between that town and Huancané. The same pattern holds for the Arapa area.

INTERPRETATIONS

Our understanding of the nature of the Tiwanaku presence in the Titicaca Basin outside of the Tiwanaku heartland continues to change as we acquire new data. Our research demonstrates that the Tiwanaku presence along the western lake edge was substantial. Wherever we have done reconnaissance and survey south of the Ilave River, we find large Tiwanaku sites. In areas where we carry out systematic, 100% full-regional coverage survey south of the Ilave River, we find very dense clusters of Tiwanaku sites. Settlements are heavily concentrated along the lake edge and rivers, and dramatically decrease in density into the puna. We have isolated more than 100 sites in the western Titicaca region,

from Juliaca to the Desaguadero River region. Dozens of other Tiwanaku sites have been located in the Puno Bay area (Schultze 2000) and in the northern Huancané-Arapa zone.

The survey and reconnaissance data therefore strongly suggest that the Tiwanaku state maintained political control of the southwestern region during its expansive periods circa AD 500–1000 as a typical expansive state—that is, the entire territory and people were incorporated into the political orbit of the Tiwanaku polity. There is no Tiwanaku-controlled settlement prior to this time, although the existence of an occasional trade ware suggests contact between the Upper Formative cultures of the region with the pre-Tiwanaku IV Pacajes-area cultures. North of the Ilave and probably Escoma Rivers, in contrast, Tiwanaku selectively controlled enclaves and areas near raised fields, roads, and the lake edge. These data confirm the model proposed in Stanish (2002, 2003) that Tiwanaku expansion was selective north of its core territory, and was based upon an economic and political logic that we as yet do not completely understand. Certain empirical patterns, however, point to factors that were important in that logic.

First, the settlement data indicate that the Tiwanaku population maintained a mixed economy of intensive and extensive agriculture, pastoralism, lake resource exploitation, and regional exchange in all areas that they controlled. Intensive agriculture is represented by the raised fields (Ortloff 1996; Kolata et al. 1996). These fields date at least to the Tiwanaku period, as evidenced by the location of major Tiwanaku sites adjacent to aqueducts, canals, and the fields themselves (Stanish 1994a, 2001c, 2002). Extensive agriculture is represented by terraced agriculture, typical of the area today. A number of Tiwanaku sites are found away from the raised-field areas and are geographically associated with agricultural terraces. In short, both raised-field and non-raised-field areas were used by Tiwanaku sites occupants.

The lakeside focus is indicative of the exploitation of the lake resources, although this proposition needs to be refined with excavation data. A few Tiwanaku sites are also found in the high puna area above 4000 m above sea level, a settlement pattern that suggests a control of camelid grazing lands. The number of Tiwanaku sites in the puna is small, however, compared to the number of sites from the later Altiplano and Late Horizon periods (Stanish 1994a).

Furthermore, the coexistence of a locally manufactured Tiwanaku imitation pottery along with imported polychromes indicates the existence of a trade network of as yet unknown intensity or characteristics. It is not known whether the locally produced ceramic type is chronologically later, as in Moquegua (Bermann et al. 1989; Stanish 1991:9–10), or simply represents a local imitation of the genuine Tiwanaku ceremonial pottery. The existence of the nonlocal finewares is suggestive of a complex exchange relationship between a centralized state and local populations. Likewise, the difference in site types may represent a resident Tiwanaku administrative elite among a local support population. In this instance, it is fairly obvious that the large mounds and terraced hill sites represent elite centers, given the existence of semisubterranean constructions. We can hypothesize that the other site types represent the local population, a proposition that remains to be tested in the future.

It is instructive to compare these survey and reconnaissance data with those from the Tiwanaku valley collected by Albarracin-Jordan and Mathews (1990). In the first instance, there is a substantial pre-Tiwanaku IV settlement in the Tiwanaku Valley. This is to be expected in the ancestral homeland of the Tiwanaku state. At Tiwanaku, there is an unbroken evolution of Tiwanaku settlement from the earliest Upper Formative period (Tiwanaku I or Kalasasaya) to the dramatic expansion of Tiwanaku in its later phases.

In the Juli-Pomata region, the Upper Formative-Tiwanaku period transition is very different. Here, Tiwanaku replaced two already complex polities that had formed in the Upper Formative period—Late Sillumocco and Late Ckackachipata (Stanish et al. 1997). Curiously, the settlement patterns of both the Upper Formative and the Tiwanaku periods are very similar. Also like the earlier Upper Formative pattern, sites are clearly associated with raised-field areas, canals, and aqueducts. It is significant that all major Upper Formative elite/ceremonial sites continued to be occupied in the Tiwanaku period. As mentioned above, excava-

tions at three of these elite/ceremonial sites in the Juli area (Tumatumani, Palermo, and Sillumocco-Huaquina) indicate that they were architecturally enhanced in the Tiwanaku period. Similar patterns of a very strong Tiwanaku occupation built over earlier ones is evident in the Desaguadero and Ccapia areas. There is a substantial Tiwanaku presence in the region, and the intensity of occupation is quite strong.

The number of sites in the Tiwanaku Valley is an order of magnitude larger than those in the Juli-Pomata area. In a total survey of approximately 400 km^2, Albarracin-Jordan and Mathews discovered 100 Tiwanaku IV sites and 339 Tiwanaku V sites (Albarracin-Jordan and Mathews 1990:7, 89, 130). The methodologies of the Tiwanaku Valley Project and the Lupaqa Project were similar. Likewise, the definition of a site is comparable in both projects. Therefore, the difference in settlement density between the Pacajes and Lupaqa areas is empirically valid. Clearly, the core territory of Tiwanaku has a radically different and more intensely occupied history than did the Lupaqa zone.

In contrast to the strong Tiwanaku presence in the southwestern and southern Titicaca area outside of the core territory, the Tiwanaku occupation in the Chucuito area is far less intense. The Chucuito-Cota survey did not discover a pattern of Tiwanaku sites overlaying earlier Upper Formative ones. In fact, the intensity of Tiwanaku occupation in the region, in spite of the fact that the area near the lake was agriculturally rich, was considerably lower than that in the areas south of the Ilave River. Likewise, Tiwanaku settlement in the northern basin was much lighter than it was in the south or west.

The intensity of Tiwanaku in any area curiously does not seem to be strictly a function of distance. The Puno Bay area, unlike that in Chucuito, appears to have been heavily occupied by the Tiwanaku state. Sites were located all along the bay area from south of modern Puno to the southern edge of the Huatta Pampa. This area also had a number of raised-field areas and intensive terrace agriculture. In short, the Puno area was a major Tiwanaku enclave. The factors responsible for these different patterns in adjacent zones remain as central problems for future research.

SUMMARY AND CONCLUSIONS

The nature of the Tiwanaku political economy during its Tiwanaku IV and Tiwanaku V (Expansive) phases remains a subject of considerable debate. On one side, some have suggested that Tiwanaku was not an expansive polity. Proponents of this view suggest that such interpretations derive from contemporary political ideologies associated with Bolivian nationalism (Stanish 2002). This critique represents a type of deconstructionist attack that we find unsatisfying. Instead of offering an alternative, empirically based model to explain the archaeological record, it merely attempts to associate a theory with an existing and completely unrelated hegemonic ideology.

For this class of model, the Tiwanaku phenomenon represents the voluntary or noncoercive spread of an art style and its concomitant ideology among the various peoples of the south central Andes. The integration of the Tiwanaku polity, according to these models, was achieved through nonmilitaristic, noncoercive means integrated at an *ayllu* or even family level. There exist no historical or ethnographic analogies for such models, and they fail to explain the profound and substantial changes in art, architecture, settlement patterning, and economy concomitant with the appearance of Tiwanaku materials in any particular region. They fail to explain why virtually all local art traditions were replaced by Tiwanaku styles, and in fact, they utterly ignore the empirical fact that the changes in the archaeological record in the pre-Tiwanaku/Tiwanaku transition are actually more profound than that for the pre-Inca/Inca transition in the same region.

On the other side, scholars such as Ponce Sanginés (1981) and Kolata (1993) have argued for what we can call the "miniature Inca model" of Tiwanaku statecraft: that the Tiwanaku polity was built on the same militaristic and expansionist principles as the Inca, but on a smaller scale. These scholars argue that Tiwanaku was a conquest state, employing coercive material and ideological power to bring groups within the Tiwanaku orbit.

Between these two polar extremes of Tiwanaku polity economy exist a series of alternative models that vary according to the degree of economic and political hierarchy in the Tiwanaku core, and the degree to which coercive means were or were not used to bring together different ethnic groups and polities into a Tiwanaku sphere of influence. Most importantly, the model proposed by Albarracin-Jordan (1996b) argues for a segmentary organization of the Tiwanaku state. In this model, the Tiwanaku polity was built on Andean sociological organizations of ayllu and *marka*.

Our research reported on here helps to redefine the nature of Tiwanaku expansion and geopolitical control. Tiwanaku was not a small version of the Inca state. It was a first-generation state with very different, and less complex political and economic institutions. Tiwanaku control was highly selective in nature, expanding along roads and creating enclaves or colonies outside of its core territory. Our data do support the models of a centralized political organization, suggesting that Tiwanaku coerced populations along the western edge of lake Titicaca south of the Ilave into their polity. In this sense, Tiwanaku is best conceived of as a expansive polity with a restricted core south of the Ilave and Escoma areas, and a selective control of roads and enclaves outside of this zone. In short, our current data are quite compelling that Tiwanaku was indeed an expansive polity of some complexity, similar to Wari and Moche, but one that did not create the same kind of administrative organizations as the later Andean empires.

ACKNOWLEDGMENTS

The authors thank members of the Programa Collasuyu, our friends in the town of Juli, Fresia Sardón, Percy Calisaya, and Rolando Paredes. We gratefully acknowledge the support of the National Science Foundation, the Cotsen Institute of Archaeology at UCLA, the Wenner-Gren Foundation for Anthropological Research, the John Heinz III Foundation, the Field Museum of Natural History, and the Dean of Social Sciences, UCLA.

8.

Excavations at Sillumocco-Huaquina

Edmundo de la Vega

SILLUMOCCO-HUAQUINA IS LOCATED on the southwestern margin of Lake Titicaca, in the circum-lacustrine region of the south-central Andes in the community of Huaquina-Sapiji-cani.[1] The site area is divided into small land-holding parcels as well as community land. Most of the landowners live in the community of Huaquina-Sapijicani, but at least three families from the town of Juli own the site property and at the time of our field study (1995) used it for residential and agricultural purposes. Identified as Site 158 during the survey conducted by the Proyecto Lupaqa (Stanish et al. 1997), Sillumocco-Huaquina lies approximately 1 km west of Juli, at 16°12'22" latitude south and 69°28'32" longitude west, with an elevation of 3,850 m above sea level (Figures 3.1 and 8.1).

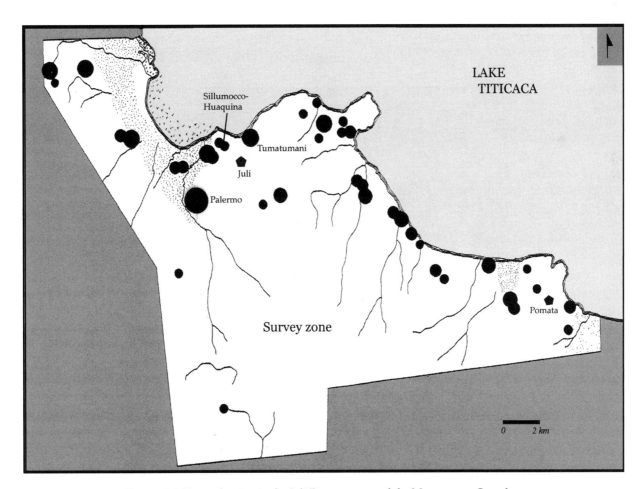

FIGURE 8.1. Tiwanaku sites in the Juli-Pomata area and the Moyopampa Complex

115

THE MOYOPAMPA COMPLEX

Although our work was concentrated on Sillu-mocco-Huaquina itself, the study area that encompasses it is known as the "Moyopampa Complex." This complex is comprised of at least thirteen sites with Sillumocco (Formative period) or Tiwanaku occupations, which are part of a sophisticated agricultural system of *waru warus* (raised fields) and irrigation canals that capture and redirect the water from the Río Salado in the lower reaches of the watershed.

The complex lies west of the city of Juli, extending throughout the range of the pampa below 4,000 m, bounded naturally by the Zapacollo, Caracollo, Chocorasi, Chila-Pukara, Caspa, and Suankata Hills and the lakeshore. The northeastern boundary is defined by the absence of Sillumocco and Tiwanaku settlements, with an arbitrary line running from the base of Suankata to the lakeshore. The Río Salado crosses the pampa, running from south to north (Figure 8.2).

The two principal sites in the Moyopampa Complex are Palermo (Site 212) and Sillumocco-Huaquina (Site 158), which appear to be local administrative centers (see Hastorf, Chapter 5, this volume). According to the Proyecto Lupaqa's classification system, these sites fall into the category of Type 3 sites, characterized as ones on low hills with domestic terraces and a sunken court complex at the top (Stanish et al. 1997). All other Moyopampa Complex sites are either Type 1 (Site 210, which has a possible semisubterranean structure); Type 2, or small mound sites (Sites 208, 228, and 271); Type 4, or domestic terrace sites (Sites 147, 148, 157, 160, 179, and 236, some of which have yielded possible post-Tiwanaku burial remains); or Type 12, or miscellaneous sites (Site 220).

WARU WARUS (RAISED FIELDS)

The Moyopampa region had previously been identified as an area of raised-field agricultural activity (Erickson 1988b; Smith et al. 1968). This

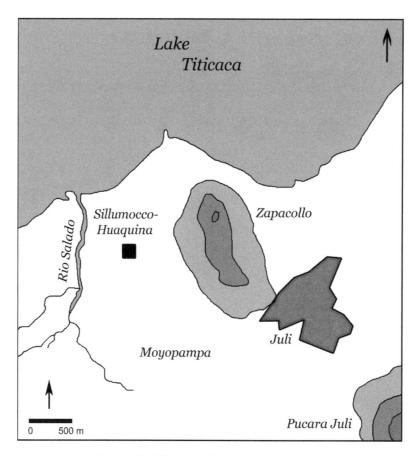

FIGURE 8.2. Sillumocco-Huaquina site location

was again confirmed by the Proyecto Lupaqa survey, which calculated that waru warus extend over an area of at least 10 km², and further confirmed the association of waru warus with structures that reflect hydraulic engineering, such as small canals to catch water from *puquios* (springs) and *bofedales* (swamps) at Palermo and Sillumocco-Huaquina, and canals that altered the natural flow of the Río Salado (Stanish 1994a; Stanish and de la Vega 1991; Stanish et al. 1997). Examination of aerial photographs and maps, and subsequent field visits, further confirmed the existence of very extensive and sophisticated hydraulic systems.

The remains of one of the most interesting hydraulic systems lies approximately 500 m southeast of Sillumocco-Huaquina, on the course of the Río Salado. This hydraulic system is a canal that would have deviated the natural course of the river. This detour was made for two purposes: (1) to capture water by means of a network of canals extending several kilometers south of Sillumocco-Huaquina, and (2) to direct part of the captured water toward a canal that runs across a network of waru warus at the edge of Sillumocco-Huaquina before finally draining into the lake. This canal also merges with a smaller canal that runs in a broken line from the *bofedal*, at the base of Zapacollo, to some 150 m north of the site.

The canal network consists of two main canals. The first collects water from the *quebradas* between the hills of Zapacollo and Pukara Juli. The second canal captures water from the Río Salado, which it then redirects to run parallel to the river. In its final stretch, this canal cuts a zigzag pattern with sharp 90° angles. The course of this canal is associated with the large site of Palermo.

The canal system was of such magnitude that it undoubtedly required significant manpower. It is very important to chronologically place the construction of this hydraulic system. If it pertains to the Sillumocco period, this would imply that the Formative social organization was very evolved and complex. On the other hand, if it represents a Tiwanaku development, this canal system would have required special attention and control from the Tiwanaku seat of power.

The presence of the diverse site types associated with the extensive waru warus and hydraulic system suggests that these sites were articulated within a local agricultural system. The differences between sites reveal the distinct role each site played within the settlement system.

SITE DESCRIPTION

Sillumocco-Huaquina is found on the western end of the Pampa de Moyo (Moyopampa), at the foot of the western slope of the Zapacollo Hill. The site is on a small natural knoll that has been extensively terraced along its slopes and top. The surface bears an abundant scatter of sherds and lithics spanning several occupational periods from the Formative period to the present. Several post-Tiwanaku funerary structures are also found on the south slopes (*chullpas* and collared tombs). The site covers an area of approximately 3.5 ha, and rises up to 16 m above the pampa. The general orientation of the site is southeast to northwest, with its main access probably at the southeast. Raised fields and remains of canals are found in the pampa surrounding the site, as well as terraces along the western slopes of Zapacollo. Although the terraces have no architectural features, there are at least four small sites associated with them, identified by surface finds as Tiwanaku.

Terraces

The site consists of five levels of irregular terraces, which correspond to the irregularity of the natural terrain (Figure 8.3). At the southeastern end, where the height of the knoll is only 5 m from base to top, only three terraces can be identified, T1 being the thickest, at 2 m. On the other hand, at the northeastern end, where the knoll height reaches 16 to 17 m, all five terraces can be recognized, varying in thickness between 2 m (T1, T3b, T4c, and T4d) and 4 m (T2 and T4b).

A striking feature that is observed is the way the terrace retaining wall follows a broken line with angles up to 90°. This can best be observed in the T2 terrace where, at the northern and southern extremes, they form a segment of the Andean cross, or squared cross, with three angles pointing out and two pointing in. A similar pattern with an irregular squared cross is revealed in a floor plan of T1. Both the site dimensions and the terrace configurations are very similar to those of the pyramid of Akapana, in the urban ceremonial center of Tiwanaku (Manzanilla et al. 1990:84). Another significant aspect is the presence of inclined earthworks on three of the T1 corners that seem to have functioned as entries to the uppermost terrace. The average size of the earthworks is 6 x 3 m, spanning an average depth of 2 m.

The lower terraces have been seriously damaged by the modern homesteads on the western portion of the knoll, as well as by the heavy machinery that stripped the site for fill in the construction of the Pan-American highway. Members of the community report that a chullpa was looted and destroyed at that time and that numerous "gold and silver objects" and a mummy with a deformed cranium were removed. The destruction occurred in the late 1980s when the owner of the property used a

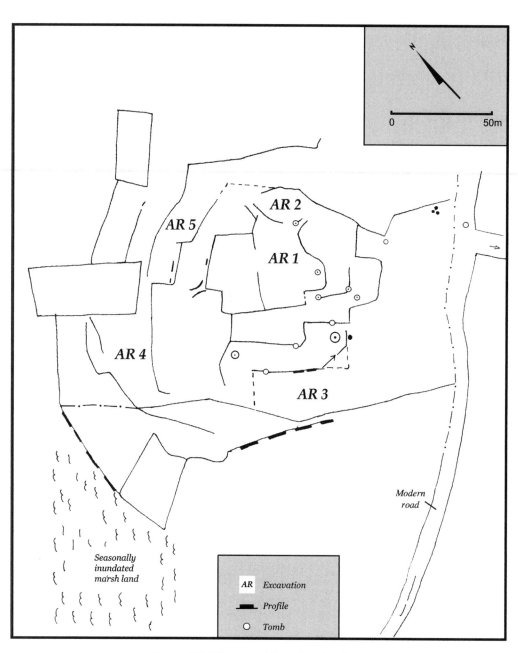

FIGURE 8.3. Sillumocco-Huaquina site plan

Caterpillar tractor to level the terrain. A great part of T4a (where the destroyed chullpa was reported to have been), the southern corner of T3a, the surface and the southeastern sector of T3c, and the wall and surface of T2 were most severely impacted. Currently, the entire site is utilized for cultivation and for grazing animals.

Funerary Structures

A variety of funerary structures are concentrated on top of the knoll and on the south and southeastern sectors. These include chullpas, collared tombs, and subterranean tombs. A total of four chullpas were identified (Tombs 2, 3, 4, and 8) on the T3a terrace. The largest of these was Tomb 8, with an external dia7 of approximately 4.5 m (although the tomb wall is almost completely destroyed) and with large stone blocks (up to 1.1 m long) strewn around it. Tomb 3 shows a double-ring rock base. The exterior ring (3.1 m in diameter) consists of fragments of worked stone, while the interior ring consists of field stones (2.3 m in diameter). Some cranial fragments and human long bones were seen inside this structure.

Tombs 1 and 2, atop the knoll, are seemingly the most important, not only because of their prominent location on the site, but because they are the only ones to have been built on a large platform (8.6 x 6.5 x 1.7 m). Tomb 1 is a collared tomb with an external diameter of 2.4 m, delimited by seven large stone blocks embedded vertically. Tomb 2, on the other hand, is a chullpa, recognized only by the remains of its foundation, which measures 3.8 m in its external diameter. Cists of subterranean tombs have been found on T2 and T3c. Cist openings range between 1 and 1.5 m in width, and the average depth is 0.7 m.

The remaining funerary structures are collared tombs, formed by vertically arranged stone blocks of various sizes and enclosing a circular area with internal diameter between 1.5 and 2 m. These funerary components of the site all seem to correspond to the post-Tiwanaku period.

SITE EXCAVATION

The excavation strategy theoretically was to entail two stages of excavation. Initially, the excavation of test units was planned with the objective of evaluating the terrace architecture and internal structures (if any were to exist), as well as to identify the various occupations of the site. The testing results confirmed the need to expand the excavations, and in a second stage, excavation of at least 50% of the terrace was planned. However, the unfortunate denial of permission to excavate by the landowners made it impossible to realize the second stage.

Testing was completed throughout the site (Figure 8.3), either by means of test units or by cleaning a terrace profile. Detailed descriptions of the test results of areas 2, 3, 4, and 5 are presented below. Area 1, however, was tested by another person, and will not be included in this report.

Excavation Area 2

This area is located on the northeastern arm of T1, and lies 5 m from the northern corner of the terrace (Figure 8.3). Three test units were excavated in this area: one 2 x 2 m square and two 1-m extensions of the north and east wall profiles. A sequence of three levels of occupation was represented in a depth of 2.2 m: two Formative levels and one Tiwanaku level. Above these were post-Tiwanaku fill and a cap of recent deposit.

The Formative occupation was partially exposed in the northern profile and was deposited directly over bedrock. A wall made of large stone blocks was seen to run east-west, parallel to the T1 wall, which is thought to be the base of the first retaining wall of the terrace. Formative ceramics consist of fiber-tempered wares. Superimposed on this, the second Formative occupation was also revealed in the north profile. Several disturbed burials were associated with this level.

The remains of a circular structure, associated with the Tiwanaku occupation and approximately 3.0 m in diameter, was evidenced by a fieldstone block foundation that was arranged in two rows. The structure's interior showed a red compacted clay floor. To the west of the structure, a thick layer (50–60 cm deep) of guano was found, leading to the interpretation that the area had been a corral relating to the habitations. This hypothesis is reinforced by the analysis of faunal remains, which demonstrates large quantities of both adult and young camelids and a full range of skeletal parts (skull, vertebrae, ribs, scapula, pelvis, and long bones). Since all body parts are represented, it can be concluded that the animals were killed and butchered close to the residential area (Elkin 1994). These data conflict with the interpretation that Sillumocco-Huaquina was a ceremonial site, but they do not eliminate the possibility that the animals were used for sacrificial purposes as part of ritual activities. The Tiwanaku occupation was covered by a 0.35-m fill layer either at the end of the period or in post-Tiwanaku times.

PROFILE 1

This test area is located on the eastern wall, along the northeastern arm of the upper T1 terrace. Three test units were excavated with the in-

tent of defining the construction of the retaining wall. Test Unit 1 was placed on the talus, toward the interior of the terrace, behind the wall. Test Units 2 and 3 were located at the foot of the wall, outside the terrace.

Test Unit 1. Test Unit 1 was excavated with the objective of defining the characteristics of the terrace fill, as well as the occupational or construction levels. The unit measured 1.9 x 1.5 m, and had an average depth of 1 m. Nine levels were excavated, resulting in the definition of the following strata: (1) the modern surface, (2) terrace fill, (3) possible wall foundation, and (4) natural deposits (Figures 8.4 and 8.5).

Stratum A (Level 1) is the modern surface, consisting of an accumulation of agricultural soil

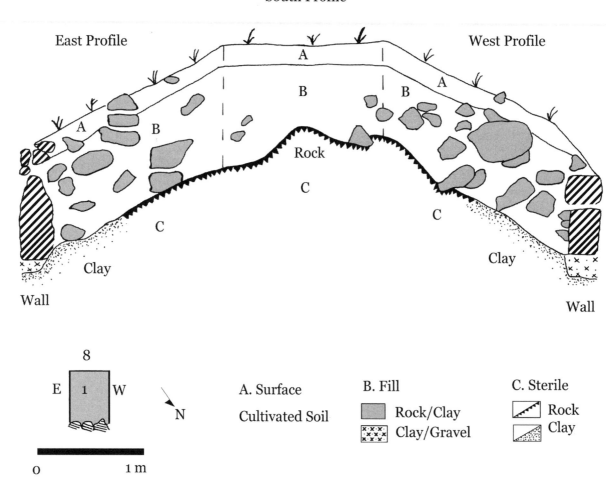

FIGURE 8.4. Stratigraphic profile of Area 2, Unit 1

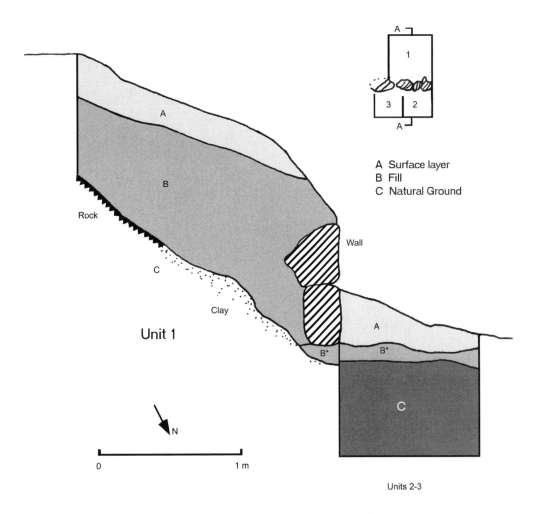

FIGURE 8.5. Profile of Area 2, Units 1, 2, and 3

atop the terrace. It is a dark brown (10YR4/3), semicompacted sandy clay, containing 1- to 3-cm pebbles, and having an average depth of 0.2 m. Artifacts recovered from this level include a mixture of Formative, Tiwanaku, and Altiplano ceramics, lithic debris, andesite hoe fragments, and some sandstone pebbles, as well as an abundance of camelid faunal remains (carpals, ribs, scapulae, etc.).

Stratum B (Levels 2–9) is composed of terrace fill. The soil is a sandy clay with stone blocks, which range in size from large (60 x 40 x 20 cm to 40 x 30 x 18 cm), medium (30 x 25 x 20 cm to 20 x 15 x 12 cm), small (10 x 8 x 6 cm to 15 x 12 x 8 cm), to very small (8 to 10 cm). Despite the complex nature of the fill, it was still possible to distinguish two distinct features. Feature 1 is found immediately behind the wall, occupying more than half the test unit floor. It consists of numerous stone blocks of variable sizes, loosely arranged and mixed with a dark brown (7.5YR4/2) sandy clay soil with a granular structure, the matrix being loosely compacted, with air bubbles and inclusions of reddish clay. It is interesting to note that grinding stones (*manos* and *batanes*) were used for the fill, broken down to the medium and small block sizes, and sometimes fractured at right angles.

Feature 2 primarily consists of reddish brown (5YR5/3) semicompacted sandy clay soil with abundant air pockets. It also contains small and very small stone blocks. Its average thickness is 1 m. This fill rests directly atop the natural deposit (Stratum C).

The cultural content consists of ceramic fragments from the Formative and Tiwanaku periods

(Figure 8.6) in all levels, although in the upper-most levels (2 and 3) there are also fragments of what appears to be Altiplano style ceramics. This is a significant find, as it helps to place the terrace construction into a chronological framework. The presence of Tiwanaku and Altiplano ceramics in the fill eliminate the possibility that the construction date from the Formative period. The absence of Altiplano ceramics in the lower level (where only Formative and Tiwanaku sherds are found) leads us to conclude that the terrace was built during the Tiwanaku period. The fill content includes an abundance of lithic materials (primarily hoe fragments and lithic debris, consisting primarily of andesite and, less frequently, basalt, as well as quartzite, red jasper, and chalcedony) and sandstone and rhyolite pebbles. The faunal remains reflect a heavy reliance on camelids (99% of the bone recovered is camelid bone), and include vertebrae, ribs, scapulae, and phalanges. These faunal remains represent individuals ranging in age from neonate to juvenile and adults. The bones had been cleaned and burned; some exhibit butchery marks. The remaining 1% of the faunal assemblage is unidentifiable, but could possibly be rodent or bird.

Stratum B′ is a thin, compacted lens of brown (7.5YR5/2) sandy clay, mixed with gravel and slivers of charcoal. It is found beneath the rock wall and functions as a foundation for the wall. It was not excavated. Stratum C is a culturally sterile level of natural soil that corresponds to bedrock. It consists of a red clay (2.5YR5/6) that is compacted and homogeneous.

Test Units 2 and 3. Both Units 2 and 3 were 1 x 1 m squares that were placed in front of the wall, with the objective of defining the characteristics of the wall construction, as well as seeking evidence for ritual offerings. Three strata were identified (Figure 8.5).

Stratum A is the modern ground surface, featuring rubble from the wall and fill. The soil is a dark brown (10YR4/3), semicompact, sandy clay with 1- to 3-cm pebbles. The crumbled wall reveals only medium-sized (20 x 20 x 14 cm to 20 x 15 x 10 cm) and small (10 x 8 x 6 cm) stone blocks. The average depth of this stratum is 0.20 m, although in the area adjacent to the wall it is almost double that.

In Stratum B, Formative, Tiwanaku, and Altiplano ceramic fragments are mixed in the deposit, the most notable of which is a *kero* (drinking cup) base retrieved from the wall base. Additionally, hoe fragments, andesite, quartzite, and basalt debris, and fragmentary camelid remains were found in this stratum.

Stratum B′ is defined as terrace fill. It consists of a brown (7.5YR5/2), compact, sandy clay, with 1- to 5-cm pebbles, and contains charcoal fragments and ceramics. Its average depth is 0.1 m. The T1 retaining wall rests directly upon this level. Although infrequent, Formative and Tiwanaku sherds are present. Andesite flakes continue to be present. However, other raw material types (quartz, jasper, and rhyolite) are also represented.

Stratum C is again the natural sterile deposit. Compact and homogeneous red clay (2.5YR5/6) predominates, although there are a few whitish inclusions. The excavation of this level was abandoned at a depth of 0.7 m.

Retaining Wall East of the T1 Terrace. The orientation of this wall runs southeast to northwest, with a length of 22.5 m and a width between 0.4 and 0.5 m, depending on the dimensions of the stone blocks. Based on the current terrace height (0.8 to 1 m), it is calculated that the original wall height was 2 m. The terrace construction seems to have been done over the red clay natural deposit by first digging a trench to use as a foundation. A clay mixture was placed at the bottom of the trench before arranging the stone blocks over it.

The wall consists of a single row of masonry comprised of irregular blocks of various sizes: large blocks (1 x 1 m, 90 x 50 cm, and 60 x 40 cm), medium-sized blocks (25 x 12 cm, 40 x 20 cm, and 20 x 12 cm), and small blocks (15 x 8 cm and 10 x 5 cm). The small blocks seem to have been used as shunts to plug the empty spaces left between larger blocks. The stone blocks seem to have been paired randomly and are cemented with clay. Irregular blocks were primarily used, although some appear to have been lightly shaped and others have worked or cut surfaces.

Preliminary interpretations of these data enable us to define two important things: (1) construction of the uppermost terrace took place during the Tiwanaku period, and (2) fill material

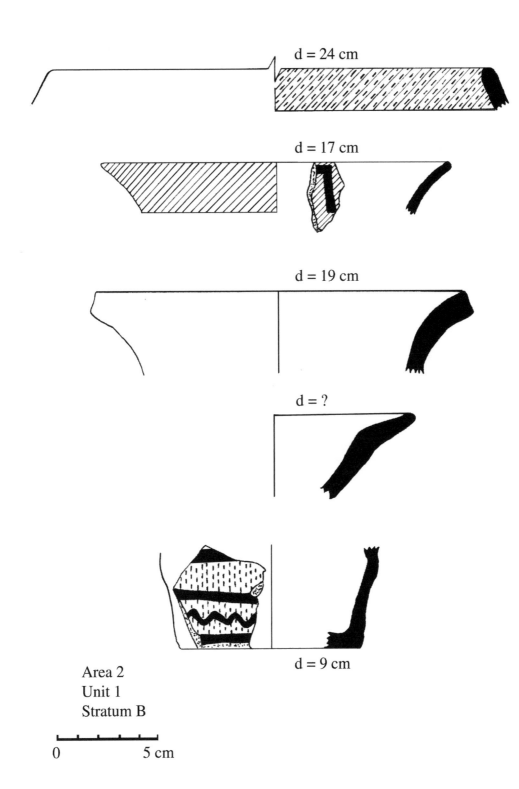

FIGURE 8.6. Test Unit 1, Formative and Tiwanaku period pottery fragments

used for terrace construction was derived from previous occupations, probably from residential contexts. It would thus appear that Sillumocco-Huaquina had two episodes of Tiwanaku occupation. The first of these features a residential component, while the second reveals the expansion of the T1 terrace, using fill from prior occupations, including the those from Formative period. It is quite likely that part of the destruction of residential Tiwanaku sites occurred toward the end of the Tiwanaku period itself.

Excavation Area 3

PROFILE 2

Excavation Area 3 is situated by the wall of the T3 terrace at the corner where heavy machinery may have truncated the retaining wall and dragged the fill some 2 to 3 m toward the interior of the terrace (Figure 8.3). A highly impacted area was selected to be cleaned, excavating a 1.6 x 1.1 m (at surface), 0.3 m (at base) trench. Several levels were distinguished within five strata (Figure 8.7).

Stratum A (Level 1) consists of an agricultural surface. The soil is a homogeneous, semicompact, brown (10YR4/3) sandy clay with gravel (1–3 cm), pebble (6–10 cm), and rock (> 10 cm) inclusions and many roots. The average depth is 0.25 m, and ceramic fragments reflect the Formative, Tiwanaku, and Altiplano periods.

In Stratum B (Levels 2 and 3), Fill 3 consists of at least three pockets of sandy clay, distinguished by color and compactness: B1 is a compact, dark brown (10YR3/3) soil with air pockets; B2 is a semicompact to loose brown (7.5YR5/4) soil with air pockets, and B3 is a compact, homogeneous brown (7.5YR5/2) soil with carbon flecks, gravel, and pebble inclusions. The average depth of Stratum B is 0.65 m, and the ceramics consist of Formative, Tiwanaku, and possibly Altiplano styles in the uppermost portion.

In Stratum C (Level 4), Fill 2 has small and medium (1–6 cm) rolled cobbles, as well as some large (10–20 cm) cobbles mixed in with homogeneous, semicompact brown (10YR4/3) sandy clay. This stratum has an average depth of 0.4 m. It is practically a single layer of rocks that, because of their abundance and homogeneity in size, would appear to have been the result of a natural deposition. However, the presence of ceramics, lithics, hoes, and some bone splinters suggests that the rock layer had been mixed to form the terrace fill. Plain wares that cannot be positively classified were recovered, as were a few fragments that have Tiwanaku-like pastes.

Stratum D (Level 5) Fill 1 consists of homogeneous, compact, dark brown (7.5YR4/2) sandy clay, mixed with gravel inclusions (1–2 cm) and a quantity of small rocks (15–20 cm).

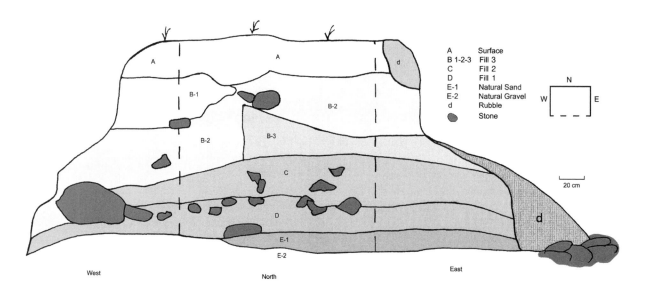

A   Surface
B 1-2-3   Fill 3
C   Fill 2
D   Fill 1
E-1   Natural Sand
E-2   Natural Gravel
d   Rubble
●   Stone

20 cm

FIGURE 8.7. Profile of area 3

Resting directly atop a natural deposit, its average thickness is 0.2 m. Because of its stratigraphic position, no evidence of walls or floors was found, although this stratum seems to correspond to the earliest occupation of this sector of the site. It is interesting to note that the surface of this level is so flat and even that it appears to have been leveled. Fragments of Formative ceramics were recovered, but the majority of ceramics recovered are plain and nonclassifiable. Nonetheless, the fiber and mica tempering in the ceramics recovered is suggestive of the Formative period. It seems that the content of this level is randomly mixed.

For Stratum E (Level 6), the natural deposit yields two well-defined and distinct superimposed levels. The uppermost, E1, is a coarse sand (1–5 mm grain size), generally compact and homogeneous, reddish gray in color (5YR5/2), and including some small (1–3 cm) cobbles. The lower level, E2, consists of compact gravel and rolled cobbles that could possibly have been the source for the cobbles in Stratum C. Neither of these layers yielded any evidence of human occupation.

The data from Profile 2 confirm two observations made from the excavation of Profile 1: (1) that overall, the terrace construction occurred during the Tiwanaku period, and (2) that construction materials consisted of recycled earlier deposits. At the same time, two new observations can be made: (1) it is possible that the terrace was constructed directly over previous occupations (Stratum D), which were leveled prior to construction, and (2) natural rocky deposits were utilized for construction materials (Stratum C).

Excavation Area 4

This excavation area is situated along the western slope of the knoll (Figure 8.3). The excavation units were placed on the T4b terrace with the objective of finding evidence of an occupational component on the lower terraces. Although two test units were excavated, no significant discoveries were made. On the basis of the relative frequency of Formative ceramics in the lower levels, it can be postulated that a significant Formative occupation would likely be found in this area, either because of the great intensity of use of the area or because the area had not been affected by later reconstructions.

Test Unit 1

The excavation of Test Unit 1, a 2 x 2 m square, enabled us to evaluate the terrace fill (Figure 8.8). This fill averages 0.5 m in thickness and consists of rock and soil. It is estimated that more than half of the fill has been removed recently, during the course of modern agricultural activities. The deepest and least disturbed levels (Levels 6 and 7) demonstrated an irregular north-south alignment of debris, which was originally thought to be wall remnants. On closer inspection, it was determined that this debris was merely scattered fill. There was no evidence of architectural structures, nor evidence of any form of habitation. The deepest levels (Levels 5, 6, and 7) yielded an abundance of Formative ceramics.

The stratigraphy of Test Unit 1 revealed only three strata. Stratum A (Levels 1–4) consists of terrace fill. The uppermost 0.3 m can be considered a plow zone, disturbed by agricultural activities. The soil in the plow zone is a brown (10YR4/3) sandy clay matrix with 1- to 3-cm gravel and 3- to 5-cm pebbles, as well as 10- to 12-cm rocks. The plow zone soil is relatively loose, but is semicompact throughout the rest of the stratum, which ranges in depth between 0.4 and 0.5 m. This entire stratum has been churned recently, as evidenced by the recovery of glass, metal, and modern wares in Level 4, which is approximately 0.4 m below the ground surface. The ceramics from Stratum A are diverse, ranging in style from Formative trumpets to modern materials such as glass tempered wares and china. There is an abundance of very small fragments (< 1 cm) that have been heavily eroded, which again confirms the extent of churning of artifacts coupled with erosion. Lithics and hoe fragments made from andesite, basalt, and quartzite are numerous, and camelid and rodent remains are also common.

Stratum B (Levels 5–7) consists of more terrace fill. Similar to Stratum A, it features sandy clay soil mixed with abundant mid-sized (15–20 cm long) fieldstone blocks. This fill is primarily concentrated on the upper part of the east profile of the terrace and was initially mistaken for

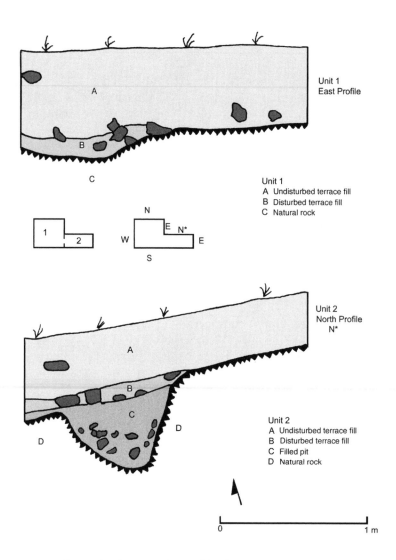

FIGURE 8.8. Stratigraphic profile of Area 4, Units 1 and 2

wall fragments. The thickness of this varies between 0.1 and 0.15 m. For the most part, the ceramic assemblage reflects the Formative period, although various Tiwanaku elements are also present. Faunal remains and lithic materials decrease sharply in this stratum compared to the concentration of these found in Stratum A. Stratum C is a sterile, natural rocky deposit of a light brown (2.5YR6/2) color.

TEST UNIT 2
In Area 4, the 1 x 2 m extension of the eastern wall of Test Unit 1 was designated as Test Unit 2 and excavated to follow a rock concentration that had appeared in Test Unit 1 and was thought to be a collapsed wall. The content of

both test units is essentially similar, with only a few variations as described below.

The stratigraphy shows four well-defined strata. The content and composition of Stratum A differs in the two test pits only inasmuch as Test Unit 2 is slightly shallower (0.35 to 0.4 m) and yields a slightly greater proportion of Formative ceramics. Similar to Stratum B in Unit 1, Stratum B in Unit 2 also contains medium-sized fieldstone blocks, but includes slightly smaller stones as well (10–20 cm). Similarly, Formative ceramics were recovered from this stratum.

Stratum C reveals an attempt to fill a depression with a mixture of soil, rocks, and artifacts. The full extension of the depression was not excavated, but the excavated sample had a 0.8 m diameter at the top and a 0.3 m diameter at its base with a seemingly elongated shape, oriented north to south. The ceramic assemblage from both test units was predominantly Formative, although some Tiwanaku fragments were also recovered. Among the lithic artifacts collected were some ground stone fragments and a sandstone rock with a polished surface. Faunal remains consisted primarily of camelid bones with a few fish and/or rodent bone fragments.

Stratum D is a rocky natural deposit, similar to that of Test Unit 1.

Excavation Area 5

Excavation Area 5 is situated on the northern sector of T2 below Area 1 (Figure 8.3). This location was selected for comparative purposes, in order to contrast T1 with T2 and to define the functional or occupational differences that might exist be-

tween them. Two units were excavated: TU 1, a 2 x 2 m square, and TU 2, a 2 x 1 m extension of the TU 1 northern wall. Because both units are so similar and represent a single depositional process, they will be described simultaneously.

Two levels of fill, each yielding Formative artifacts, are associated with the construction of the terrace. Fill B is superimposed over Fill C, and appears to have been built to raise the height of the knoll, as well as to increase its size. Both fills primarily yield Formative sherds, although an occasional Tiwanaku sherd is found in the upper levels of Fill B.

The stratigraphy consists of five levels (Figures 8.9 and 8.10). Stratum A (Levels 1 and 2) consists of the modern terrace surface. It is a light brown (7.5YR5/4), loose, sandy clay, with gravel inclusions (1–3 cm) and some pebbles (6–10 cm). Its average depth is 0.20 m, with roots

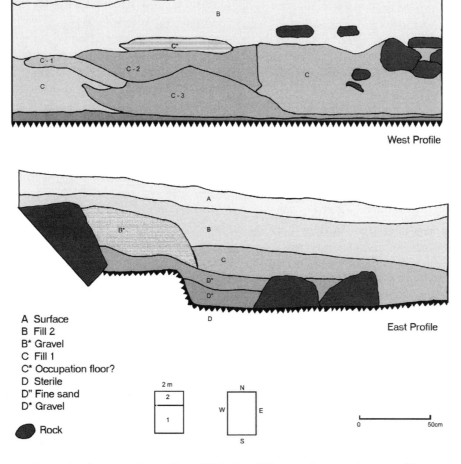

A Surface
B Fill 2
B* Gravel
C Fill 1
C* Occupation floor?
D Sterile
D" Fine sand
D* Gravel

Rock

West Profile

East Profile

FIGURE 8.9. Stratigraphic profiles of Units 1 and 2 in Area 5, east and west profiles

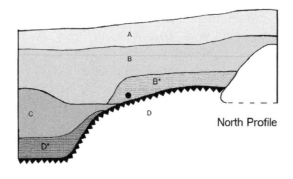

North Profile

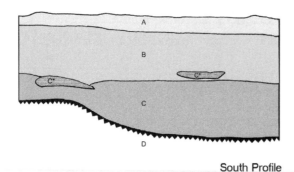

South Profile

A Surface layer
B Fill 1
B* Gravel
C Fill 2
C* Occupation floor?
D Sterile
D* Gravel

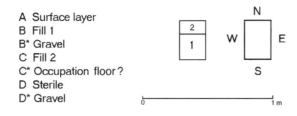

FIGURE 8.10 Stratigraphic profiles of Units 1 and 2 in Area 5, north and south profiles

that penetrate into the next level. The cultural content includes Formative and Tiwanaku ceramics, as well as material from later periods. Andesite, basalt, quartzite, and sandstone flakes were recovered. While this portion of the site is currently not cultivated, it is apparent that previous cultivation has mixed the archaeological deposit.

Stratum B (Levels 3–5) corresponds to Fill B. It is primarily formed by a dark brown (7.5YR3/2), very loose, sandy clay, with large air bubbles, and sits directly atop a rocky bedrock. Its average depth is 0.6 m and it is fairly homogeneous in its horizontal distribution. Artifact recovery was higher in this stratum than in the upper stratum, with Formative ceramics having the highest relative frequency (Figure 8.11). In Level

3 and part of Level 4, however, fragments of Tiwanaku-like wares (in terms of paste and finish) or Late Intermediate wares were also found (Figure 8.11). The lithic collection includes andesite, basalt, and quartzite debris, as well as stone hoes and adzes. An abundance of camelid and fish remains was also recovered.

Stratum B' is a gravel stratum mixed in with Stratum B that blends into the underlying bedrock. With a depth between 15 and 30 cm, it is dark grayish-brown (10YR4/4) color. A collapsed human cranium was found on the rock surface, covered by this gravel, and encrusted in the northern profile. It is possible that the skull is associated with a disturbed burial from Stratum C.

Stratum C' is an occupational level wedged between Strata B and C. A semicircular stone configuration contained the partial remains of a looted burial; only three vertebrae, a pelvis, the left leg and the articulated bones of the left foot, and fragments of the right leg were present. The cranium and other disarticulated bones were strewn outside the tomb. Formative ceramics were found in association with the burial, including a clay mask. A compact gray (7.5YR6/4) clay lens, thought to be a floor, was found in this level. Clearly seen in the south and west profiles, it showed a variable thickness between 5 and 20 cm. Slightly below this, but still in association with the clay lens, was a 10-cm (average) lens of ash (Stratum C') containing Formative ceramics. This level lies directly over the Stratum C fill and is directly associated with it. The first fill that was used for terrace construction for this occupation seems to have been severely disturbed and totally covered by the second fill (Stratum B).

Stratum C (Levels 6 or 7–11) shows that the first terrace construction phase consists of Fill 1, a light brown (7.5YR5/2) compact, sandy clay, with some air bubbles. The matrix has intrusive pockets of clayey soil, mixed with ash (C-1, C-2, C-3, and C-4) and it is covered by large stone blocks. This fill lies over the natural soil of Stratum D. The material associated with this consists of Formative ceramics and a large quantity of andesite, basalt, and quartzite lithic debris, as well as fragments of stone hoes. Abundant camelid bones, as well as fish scales, constitute the faunal assemblage.

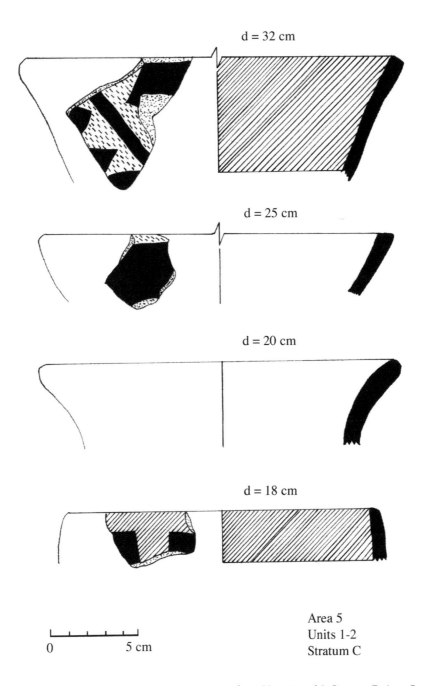

d = 32 cm

d = 25 cm

d = 20 cm

d = 18 cm

0   5 cm

Area 5
Units 1-2
Stratum C

FIGURE 8.11. Formative and Tiwanaku pottery from Units 1 and 2, Stratum B, Area 5

Stratum D consists of the natural deposit—a rocky foundation with a steep slope at the western end. The highest point is 0.17 m below the actual ground surface (visible in the east profile), and the lowest point is 1 m below, seen in the west profile. Gravel deposits (D') are intermittent.

The excavation results of this area were especially significant, enabling the identification of the Formative period for the terrace construction (Strata C and C'). It is still unclear whether the later Fill B, which raised the level of the terrace, pertains to the Late Formative or the Tiwanaku occupation of the site. In identifying Formative residential occupations in the T1 and T2 terraces on the northeastern slopes, we can conclude that (1) the occupation during this time period was concentrated in this area and (2) the first phase of terrace construction took place during the Formative.

THE SILLUMOCCO OCCUPATION

With these test results, the Sillumocco settlement system begins to take shape, enabling an evaluation of the changes and continuities that transpired into the Tiwanaku occupation of the site. The Sillumocco occupation can best be described as a residential occupation, since no ceremonial architecture has been discovered at the site. Sillumocco remains have been found across the site, indicating that the entire site was utilized. The terrace complex on the western portion of the site, in Area 4, has the most extensive residential use, which undoubtedly also is responsible for the terrace construction. The north and northeastern upper slopes (Area 5) are very similar, where there is an almost exclusive Sillumocco presence that is associated with funerary and residential contexts.

A Formative occupation with at least two construction phases has been documented on the upper terrace (T1). These data are currently being analyzed to describe their characteristics and functions.

THE TIWANAKU OCCUPATION

Tiwanaku influences are superimposed upon the Sillumocco tradition in a manner very similar to that seen at the nearby site of Tumatumani (Stanish and Steadman 1994). Using the preexisting architectural features, the Tiwanaku period peoples were able to reconstruct the upper terraces (T1 and T3) and reproduce a pyramid very similar to the Akapana pyramid at the site of Tiwanaku itself. In changing the morphology of Sillumocco-Huaquina, its function was also modified, resulting in a site of ceremonial or administrative importance. Residential structures found within this context imply that the site housed individuals who performed some administrative or ceremonial function.

Distribution of Tiwanaku artifacts and features suggests that the northern slopes of the upper terraces were primarily occupied; the Tiwanaku occupation was not very extensive on the southern slopes, perhaps reflecting the elite nature of the occupation. Another important aspect of the Tiwanaku presence is the fact that there were at least two phases of occupation. No in situ remains of the first have been identified, although it is clear that the remains were used for extending the T1 and T3 terraces. The second phase is recognized by a reconstruction of the terrace complex. It has not yet been possible to establish the chronology of these events.

Additionally, the association of terrace complexes for cultivation with the raised fields and canal irrigation systems further confirms that the ceremonial function of Sillumocco-Huaquina would have necessitated administration and control of the agricultural production. This helps to better delineate and explain the Tiwanaku presence at the site and Tiwanaku expansion in the region.

Two models have been proposed. One sees Tiwanaku as a unified state, while the other perceives it as a fragmented state. In order to address these two models we must look to the similarities between the architecture at Sillumocco-Huaquina and the Akapana pyramid at Tiwanaku.

MODEL OF TIWANAKU AS A UNIFIED STATE

This model defines Tiwanaku as a state that expanded its domination and control over a vast territory with minor political entities, and then governed its subordinates with strict control under a central bureaucracy (Kolata 1983, 1985; Mathews 1992a; Ponce Sanginés 1981, 1991, 1992; and see Stanish 1992, 2002, 2003; Stanish and Steadman 1994; and this volume, Chapter 7).

Taking this perspective, the replication of sacred symbols, as in the case of the Akapana pyramid, must have been done under the direct orders of the state bureaucracy. In the study of states such as Tiwanaku, the public architecture built for civic, military, or religious functions is an indicator of the degree to which the social organization has evolved. The large-scale ceremonial architecture is interpreted as the manifestation of the economic and political power of the state, inasmuch as it reflects the ability to organize and control an immense work force, and it also reflects the hierarchical class structure as well as the ideological framework of the state. When these kinds of structures are found outside the nuclear centers, it demonstrates the extent of dominance and expansion, the degree of political integration, and the mechanisms of social control (Goldstein 1993a).

In the study of Andean state expansion, "typical" architectural features of public structures (such as *ushnu*, or sunken courtyards) seen outside the nuclear area are an expression of control over that political entity. In the case of the Inkas, sites like Hatun Xauxa (D'Altroy 1981), Huánuco Pampa (Morris 1982; Morris and Thompson 1985), Huancay Alto (Dillehay 1977), and Hatuncolla (Julien 1983) functioned as provincial centers or capitals, administering for the region. For the Wari time period, Pikillacta, Wiracochapampa, and Jinkamocco had a similar function (Isbell 1985, 1987; Isbell and Schreiber 1978; McEwan 1990; Schreiber 1992).

Two main monumental construction styles have been recognized for the Tiwanaku period: (1) pyramids (Akapana, Pumapuncu, Wila Pukara), and (2) walled enclosures (Kalasasaya, Putuni, semisubterranean temple) (Manzanilla et al. 1990:83). To these we must also add the important architectural features of doorways and ramps that give access to the important spaces (Goldstein 1993b:24).

Two expansion spheres with provincial centers have been attributed to Tiwanaku on the basis of ceremonial architecture featuring sunken courtyards similar to the semisubterranean temple found in Tiwanaku proper. The first is in one of the Pacific valleys, represented by the central site, Omo, in Moquegua (Goldstein 1989, 1993b). The second sphere is in the circum-lacustrine region, represented by Pajchiri (Bennett 1936), Pokotia (Lumbreras 1974b), Chiripa (Browman 1978a, b), Pachatata (Niles 1988), Lukurmata and mounds PK-5 and PK-6 (Kolata 1985), and Tumuku (Stanish et al. 1997).

The only known replication of the Akapana pyramid is at Sillumocco-Huaquina. The only possible exception is the highest hill on Esteves Island that may have also been modeled after the Akapana (see Stanish et al., Chapter 7, this volume). The Akapana pyramid is the principal urban structure in the Tiwanaku complex (Mesa and Gisbert 1957; Ponce Sanginés 1981; Posnansky 1957). Its central location, the associated ceramic offerings, and the animal and human sacrifices reflect its importance in Tiwanaku (Alconini Mújica 1995; Manzanilla et al. 1990). The excellent quality of the masonry, the complex architecture, and the sophisticated internal and external canal systems of Akapana underscore its importance among Tiwanaku structures for its pivotal point in ideological organization (Manzanilla et al. 1990:102).

The association that may exist between the very common stepped motif in Tiwanaku iconography and the profile of the Akapana pyramid with its superimposed terraces is an interesting concern (Goldstein 1993a:24). One would only need to add another horizontal extension to make it resemble a segment of the Andean cross, much like the one reported by Linda Manzanilla and her crew. It has also been suggested that Akapana is a representation of the sacred mountains of the western cordilleras (Goldstein 1993a; Kolata and Ponce Sanginés 1992; Reinhard 1991), which would reinforce the sacred importance attributed to this structure.

With this perspective, the reproduction of such important traits at Sillumocco-Huaquina suggests that the Tiwanaku state directly influenced the local population. In addition to its ceremonial importance, Sillumocco-Huaquina's association with agricultural and irrigation systems implies that its function extended to control over the agricultural production for the area. Both facts unquestionably support the assumption that Sillumocco-Huaquina was under Tiwanaku state control.

NESTED HIERARCHY MODEL

The model put forth by Albarracin-Jordan (1992, 1996a) is known as the nested hierarchy model. It is indirectly substantiated by the work of Erickson (1982, 1988b), Graffam (1992), and Platt (1987b). This model suggests that Tiwanaku constituted a fragmented state, composed of different minor socio-political entities that maintained a local control over populations and territories and simultaneously participated in a larger socio-political Tiwanaku infrastructure.

Social cohesion of the different entities was achieved by a shared ideology that was continuously reinforced and revitalized by public ceremony and ritual. These rituals responded to "a specific hierarchy; some carried out at the level of the most basic social segments, others at the level of the territorial nodes, and others at the regional or multi-regional level" (Albarracin-Jordan 1996a:218).[2]

That is to say, the most important rituals were conducted at Tiwanaku itself, while the lesser rituals were relegated to sites of lesser importance within a hierarchic order. This division of ritual hierarchy was also expressed in a hierarchy of settlements. In the case of Sillumocco-Huaquina, the arguments that favor this model are derived from an analysis of the construction traits and contextual associations, rather than from a general perception of the architectural features or the associated production systems.

The replication of the most important Tiwanaku ceremonial structure provides a series of details that are absent when contrasted to the sacred prototype, the Akapana at Tiwanaku itself. For example, the quality of masonry is rustic at Sillumocco-Huaquina and lacks the fine finish characteristic of the Akapana blocks. The general outline of terrace size and corner angles lacks the uniformity featured at Akapana. That is, the overall structure does not appear to have a predetermined orientation. A second important divergence is the absence of canals or water-collection systems built into the architectural design. Sacrificial offerings are also absent.

These features indicate that if Sillumocco-Huaquina was modeled after the Akapana, it was not constructed as an exact replica. This, in turn, can be interpreted to mean that Sillumocco-Huaquina was not charged with a major role in implementing state control. Rather, it was simply a local development, built by local workers who had neither the technical knowledge nor experience to build a perfect replica, or perhaps enjoyed a greater autonomy and could modify these state designs, sacred symbols, and ideology.

The differences between the Akapana and Sillumocco-Huaquina can also be attributed to chronological differences. The Akapana was built during Stage III (Manzanilla et al. 1990; Ponce Sanginés 1981), with reconstructions taking place in later periods until the structure was abandoned at the end of Tiwanaku V (Alconini Mújica 1995). The Sillumocco-Huaquina ceramics suggest construction during Stage V, which would correspond to the time when the Akapana proper was in a state of decline. In acknowledging this possibility, the local elite could mobilize a workforce to construct such projects with a margin of independence, reinterpreting and modifying the expression of the important sacred symbols. This conclusion fits well. There is a cohesion of sociopolitical entities based on a shared, common ideology, with a hierarchical system of ceremonial and ritual expression. In summary, the data from Sillumocco-Huaquina help to explain the Tiwanaku expansion into the region, although the information is as yet insufficient for definitive conclusions to be drawn about the mechanisms of social integration or the degree of Tiwanaku control over local populations during its expansion.

SUMMARY

In conclusion, the following assertions can be made about Sillumocco-Huaquina:

- The pre-Hispanic occupation of Sillumocco-Huaquina is a multicomponent occupation, spanning the local Formative period (Sillumocco) to the Inka period.

- The terrace construction represents two separate episodes of construction and use, one during the Formative and the other during the Tiwanaku period.

- The Tiwanaku occupation reflects changes of terrace size, shape, distribution, and use.

- The Tiwanaku occupation at Sillumocco-Huaquina has at least two distinct phases.

- The architectural similarities to the Akapana pyramid suggest that Sillumocco-Huaquina had primarily a ceremonial function and the residential component of the site was reserved for the elite. This, however, does not rule out the possibility that it may also have served an administrative function for control of the agricultural production on the raised fields associated with the site.

- While the terraces were not significantly altered by post-Tiwanaku occupations, their function did change. During the Late Intermediate period, they were used for funerary purposes and during the Inka and Colonial periods, they were used for agricultural purposes.

Translated by Karen Doehner

NOTES

1. Politically, the site is located in the Department of Puno, Province of Chucuito, District of Juli.

2. Translated by the editors: "una jerarquía específica; algunos realizados al nivel de los segmentos más simples, otros al nivel de los nódulos territoriales, y otros a nivel regional o multiregional" (Albarracin-Jordan 1996a:218).

9.

The Tiwanaku Period Occupation on the Island of the Sun

Matthew T. Seddon

THE ISLAND OF THE SUN is located at the southern end of Lake Titicaca (Figures 1.3 and 9.1). The island is approximately 2 km wide and 12 km long. The topography of the island is very steep, with five peaks that rise 200 m above the lake. The island also sits in a unique ecological zone within the Titicaca Basin. Due to the lake and other local climatic factors, ambient temperatures are higher for the island than the average for the region, permitting the cultivation of maize (*Zea mays*) in quantities not possible elsewhere in the Titicaca Basin. These ecological characteristics, along with other factors, may account for the long pre-Hispanic occupation of the island, which spans from the Late Archaic (ca. 3000–2000 BC) through the Inka period (AD 1400–1532) (Figure 1.4).

During the Inka period, the island served as an important shrine/pilgrimage area, one of the three most important in the Inka empire (Bauer et al. 1996; Bauer and Stanish 2001; Betanzos 1987 [1551]; Calancha 1981 [1638]; Cieza de Leon 1959 [1532]; Cobo 1990 [1653]; Dearborn, et al. 1998; Ramos Gavilán 1988 [1621]; Stanish and Bauer 2004). The focus of Inka religious activity was a large sandstone outcrop at the northern end of the island known as the Titikala (Figure 9.2). An elaborate sacred ritual complex was erected by the Inka in this area (Dearborn et al. 1998).

A number of chronicles suggest that the island was an important ritual area for polities in the Titicaca Basin prior to the arrival of the Inka (Cobo 1990 [1653]:92-93; Ramos Gavilán 1988 [1621]:39). This chapter focuses on the Tiwanaku occupation of the island. Research indicates that the occupation of the island during the Tiwanaku period was substantial. Additionally, a number of lines of evidence suggest that the Tiwanaku state may have exploited the island as a sacred area in ways similar to the Inka use of the island, though there are significant differences in the organization of the island between the two periods.

HISTORY OF ARCHAEOLOGICAL RESEARCH ON THE ISLAND OF THE SUN

After the initial visits of the Spanish priests and the chroniclers Alonso Ramos Gavilán (in the late 1500s; Ramos Gavilán 1988 [1621]) and Bernabé Cobo in 1616 (Cobo 1990 [1653]), the island escaped the historic record until visits in the nineteenth century by naturalists such as Ephraim Squier (1877b). At the end of the nineteenth century, Adolph Bandelier (1910) conducted the first survey of the island. This survey was not systematic, consisting primarily of asking the local occupants the locations of archaeological sites. Bandelier assigned most of the occupations he recorded to the Inka period, although he did acknowledge the presence of a pre-Inka component, which he called "Chullpa" (Bandelier 1910:165). He also unknowingly provided the first published account of one of the major Tiwanaku sites on the island, Chucaripupata (Bandelier 1910:225).

The archaeologist Alberto Perrin Pando (1954) carried out excavations at the site of Wac'uyo (Wakuyu) in the early 1950s. Wac'uyo is located at the south end of the island in the community of

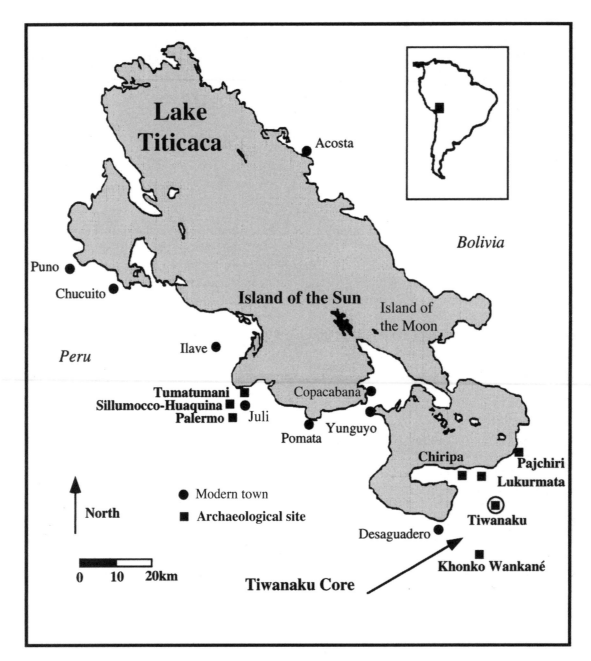

FIGURE 9.1. Map of southern Lake Titicaca

Yumani. Perrin Pando excavated eight subterranean tombs, all with Tiwanaku artifacts. The results will be discussed in greater detail below.

In the late 1980s and early 1990s, a project led by Johan Reinhard of the Woodlands Mountain Institute and Carlos Ponce Sanginés of the Bolivian Archaeology Institute conducted underwater explorations on a shallow reef located off the northern tip of the island (near the island of Khoa) (Ponce Sanginés et al. 1992). In their ex-

plorations, they encountered a number of sunken offerings placed in stone boxes on the reef (Ponce Sanginés et al. 1992). These included offerings from both the Inka and Tiwanaku periods. The Tiwanaku offerings included a number of large puma *incensarios* (incense burners), as well as a hammered gold disk with an image of the front-face, or staff god (best known from the Puerta del Sol at Tiwanaku itself) (Ponce Sanginés et al. 1992).

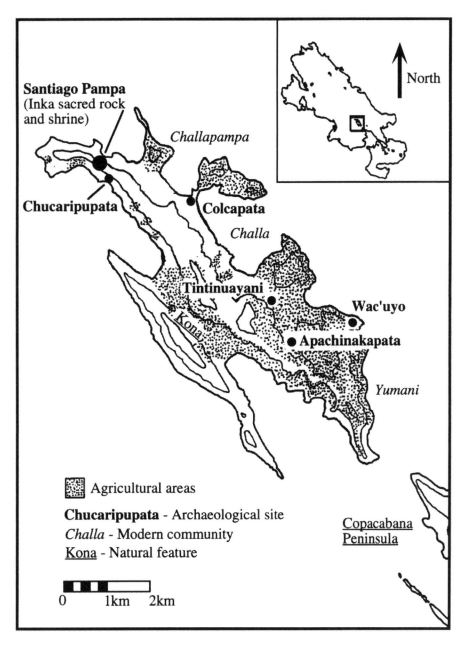

FIGURE 9.2. The Island of the Sun and major Tiwanaku period sites

In 1994, Proyecto Tiksi Kjarka began intensive archaeological work on the island (Bauer and Stanish 2001). The project began with an intensive, total coverage, pedestrian survey of the entire island, which recorded approximately 180 sites, including a substantial Tiwanaku occupation. To date, two of the Tiwanaku sites recorded in this survey (Chucaripupata and Titinhuayani) have been excavated. The combined survey and excavation data provide us with our best body of information thus far on the relationship of the island to the Tiwanaku heartland during the height of the Tiwanaku period.

SURVEY RESULTS

The survey recorded thirty-five sites with surface evidence of Tiwanaku period occupation (Figure 9.3). Virtually all of these sites were identified through the presence of Tiwanaku IV/V *kero* (drinking cup) and incensario fragments on the surface. Direct evidence of Tiwanaku III or

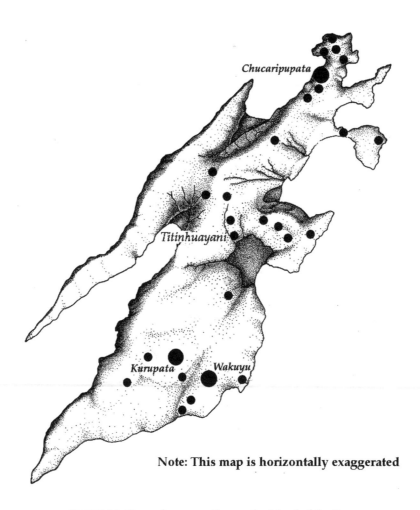

FIGURE 9.3. Tiwanaku occupation on the Island of the Sun

Qeya-style ceramics is virtually absent, these ceramics being present only at the site of Qeya Kollu (upon which the Tiwanaku III style is based). Thus, for the moment, the first clear and extensive Tiwanaku period occupations can only be defined for the Tiwanaku IV and V periods.

Tiwanaku sites on the island range from 0.01 ha to over 4.0 ha in size. Fifteen are 0.1–1.0 ha, seven are 1.0–2.0 ha, two are 2.0–3.0 ha, and four are 3.0 ha and over in total occupation size. Smaller sites (0.1–1.0 ha) generally consist of 50 m² to 1 ha of light ceramic scatter, with occasional Tiwanaku diagnostics, over a series of terraces. The larger sites (over 3 ha) generally consist of denser scatters of ceramics over large, usually modified, hilltops or ridges with many descending terraces (type III sites in the survey of the Juli-Pomata region of Peru [Stanish et al. 1997:108]). The majority of these sites cluster in the areas of high agricultural production on the

island, with the exception of a cluster of eight sites, one over 4 ha in size, located at the extreme northern tip of the island, in the area of the later Inka sacred precinct. This is actually one of the most barren parts of the island, with the least potential for agricultural production. Interestingly, the Tiwanaku period is one of only three periods when occupation of this desolate area was high. The others are the Inka period and the Middle Formative (or Middle Chiripa) period. All three of these periods evidence increased political complexity in the Titicaca Basin. The evidence of a major occupation of this area during the Tiwanaku period (particularly when combined with the data from the underwater explorations) suggests the possibility that the area may also have been a locus of intense nonagricultural ritual activity during the Tiwanaku period, as it was during the Inka period.

A second major aspect of the Tiwanaku settlement pattern is the presence of a line of sites along the southwestern ridge of the island (Figure 9.3). This line runs from the major site of Apachinacapata to the northern, and possibly ritual, area. This line certainly indicates the presence of a Tiwanaku period road connecting the southern to the northern ends of the island. This southwestern side of the island is not occupied today, and shows little occupation in other periods. Given this, occupation along the road during the Tiwanaku period indicates that travel along the road was heavy during the Tiwanaku period. This suggests the possibility of processes akin to a pilgrimage route at this time.

In summary, these settlement data indicate an intense occupation of the island during the Tiwanaku period. Sites range from small (less than 1 ha) hamlets to a number of large settlements. A heavily traveled road led from the southern end of the island to the area of the later Inka "sacred" precinct. Occupation was also high in the area of the later Inka precinct, suggesting that the area may have had a similar function in the Tiwanaku period as well. The major Tiwanaku period occupations bear further description.

MAJOR TIWANAKU PERIOD SITES ON THE ISLAND

There are five sites over 3 ha in size with Tiwanaku diagnostics present on the surface. These are roughly evenly spaced (about thirty minutes' to one hour's walk apart) from the southern to the northern ends of the island (Figure 9.2).

Site Number 142—Wac'uyo

The site of Wac'uyo is located in the modern community of Yumani at the southern end of the island. The site consists of approximately 4 ha of total occupation, 1 ha of which is a large flat area that presently serves as Yumani's soccer field. Adjacent to this field is a low, flat-topped hill that rises approximately 30 m above the soccer field. The entire area is located on a ridge between high peaks, approximately 200 m above the lake. The site commands a view of Qeya Kollu, the site of Titinhuayani, and the Island of Koati. Bedrock outcrops are extensive on the hilltop adjacent to the field as well as the sides of the hill. Between

eight and ten irregular terraces descend from the hill, all with a low to medium density of scattered ceramics. Ceramic density is actually highest in the area of the soccer field and the terraces adjacent to it. There are very few ceramics on the hilltop. Tiwanaku diagnostics include kero and *tazon* (large cup) fragments, though surface density of Tiwanaku period diagnostics is low. Formative and Inka period ceramics are present as well. There is a very high density of chert debitage present on the surface, raising the possibility that the site may, at least in part, have served as a lithic production center during one or more of its periods of occupation. Overall, the site fits nicely into Stanish's Type III category—a large hill with descending terraces. As mentioned above, Perrin Pando (1954) placed a test trench into the site and found eight clustered subterranean tombs. These were stone-lined shaft tombs, each containing the remains of one individual. Six of the tombs contained vessel offerings. These included three keros, two *olla* (jar) bases, and one rough bowl. This indicates at the very least that the area also served as a Tiwanaku cemetery.

Site Number 109—Apachinacapata

The site of Apachinacapata is located in the southern sector of the present community of Ch'alla, between the two peaks of Cerro Santa Barbara and Cerro Palla Khasa. The site lies on a natural saddle, and the western side of this saddle descends sharply to a small bay on the lake 175 m below. The site commands views of Qeya Kollu, Titinhuayani, the western side of the island, the Peruvian shore, and the modern town of Copacabana. The site consists of a 10- to 15-m rise above the floor of the saddle. This rise forms an oblong ridge 100 m long by 50 m wide, which may have been artificially modified to form the present shape. On the eastern side of this ridge, ten to fifteen terraces descend to a natural spring. All of these terraces have a medium to high density of surface ceramics. The western side is steeper, with only two terraces present, both having surface ceramics. There is some chert debitage present, although the density of lithic debris is much lower than that at the site of Wac'uyo. The surface ceramic scatter covers an area of about 3 to 4 ha. It is lighter on the lowest terraces and becomes very high on the top platform. Formative and Inka ceramics are present. Tiwanaku diagnostics include kero bases and rims. The highest density of Tiwanaku diagnostics is present at the ridge or platform at the top of the site. This site forms the beginning or southern edge of the line of sites running along the Western ridge of the island toward the northern tip. As it also sits directly above a natural bay, there is the possibility that the site served as an occupation above a landing point.

Site Number 92—Titinhuayani

Titinhuayani is one of the largest sites on the island in terms of total occupied surface area and density of surface ceramic scatter. It is located in the center of the community of Ch'alla, almost directly in the center of the island. It sits below the modern cemetery for the community of Ch'alla. The site commands a view of Qeya Kollu, Qeya Kollu Chico, Apachinacapata, Wac'uyo, the Bay of Koa, and the modern community of Ch'allapampa. The site consists of a large flat-topped hill, with fifteen to twenty narrow terraces descending from this hill. The top is 1 ha in area, and the total site size is up to 4 ha of formal structures, with possibly additional habitations on the periphery. The ceramic density on the surface is high over all areas of the site, and all pre-Hispanic periods are represented. At the top of the site there is a raised platform, approximately 10 m^2 in size. Profiles of modern pits in this platform indicate that a dense black midden fill was used to construct the upper platform. Tiwanaku diagnostics on the site include kero and tazon bases and rims. However, the density of clear Tiwanaku diagnostic fragments is low on the upper portion of the site and higher on the lower terraces. Furthermore, the overall quality of Tiwanaku diagnostics is much lower than at Apachinacapata or Chucaripupata (discussed below). Testing by Esteban Quelima and Charles Stanish in 1995 and 1996 on the upper portion of the site indicated a very thin and ephemeral Tiwanaku occupation in this area, with a very dense stratified Formative and Archaic occupation below. While the site is very large and impressive, the Tiwanaku period occupation may be a light domestic occupation confined primarily to the lower terraces. Clearly, more testing of the site is needed.

Sites Numbers 1 and 2—Colcapata

Colcapata is a large, flat-topped hill that rises approximately 50 m above the modern community of Ch'allapampa at the northern end of the island. The hill is bordered by the lake to the north and south, the beach and population concentration of Ch'allapampa to the west, and the peninsula of Collawaya to the east. The north, south, and west sides of the hill are very steep, and more terraces are present on the east side of the hill than on any of the other sides. At the top is a flat area measuring roughly 30 by 50 m, with occasional bedrock outcrops. Toward the northern end of this area is a roughly 10 m^2 depression that may indicate the remains of a semisubterranean temple. Terraces descending from this area have a high density of ceramics. Formative and Inka sherds as well as Tiwanaku diagnostics are represented. To the north, on the side of a steep cliff, are a large number of rough slab tombs. Tiwanaku diagnostics are also found in the beach area of the modern town of Ch'allapampa below the site, indicating that the occupation may have extended into this area. A conservative estimate of site size places the Tiwanaku period occupation at around one to 1.5 ha. The site is intriguing, with a possible sunken temple and cemetery area. Further testing is needed to clarify the extent and nature of the Tiwanaku versus the Formative and Inka occupations.

Site Number 22—Chucaripupata

Chucaripupata is a 4.2-ha site located 100 m to the southwest of the Titikala rock in the northern area of the island and in the modern community of Ch'allapampa (Seddon 1998). The site is located on a ridge running approximately due west toward the lake. It is comprised of a walled upper area (called the upper platform) with nine to ten terraces descending from each side of the platform. The lake-facing edge of the site, below the front walls of the upper platform, is a very steep cliff that drops 150 m down to the lake. A dense surface scatter of artifacts covers the entire site. These artifacts include large quantities of diagnostic Tiwanaku IV/V kero bases and rims. Middle Formative fiber-tempered sherds are present as well. An intensive systematic surface collection in 1996 also revealed a few Inka sherds, which is not surprising given the site's proximity to the Inka sacred area. Excavations were carried out by the author in 1995 and 1996, and the site is the only major Tiwanaku period site on the island to have been extensively excavated. The data indicate an intensive occupation from the early Tiwanaku IV through the Tiwanaku V period (Seddon 1998).

The site contained domestic occupations (houses) on the lower terraces, and the upper platform contained a temple structure that was built within a walled enclosure during the site's final Tiwanaku occupation (Klarich and Seddon 1997; Seddon 1998). Evidence from excavations indicates that a major activity at the site during the later Tiwanaku IV period and the Tiwanaku V period included rituals (Seddon 1998). However, there is little evidence as yet to suggest that Tiwanaku period rituals focused on the later Inka sacred rock, the Titikala. The focus of the Tiwanaku period activities appears to have been the site itself, or the major rock outcrop known as Murokato, from which the site descends. This evidence is tantalizing, because it suggests that the island may have been an important ritual center during the Tiwanaku period, although the focus and nature of this ritual would have been very different from that of the later Inka shrine.

TIWANAKU PERIOD CERAMICS ON THE ISLAND OF THE SUN

Tiwanaku period sites on the island were identified primarily on the basis of Tiwanaku IV/V kero and incensario bases and rims found on the surface. Classic Tiwanaku III, or Qeya, is found nearly exclusively on the site of Qeya Kollu and nowhere else on the island. Thus, our identification of Tiwanaku ceramics indicates that the Tiwanaku occupation of the island was predominantly in the Tiwanaku IV and V periods. These phases are difficult to separate on the basis of only a few sherds, particularly highly eroded surface sherds (Janusek and Alconini Mújica 1994). As stated by Janusek:

> There is no Tiwanaku IV style and no Tiwanaku V style…. While there are diagnostics, these are limited to specific types of contexts (e.g. ritual, elite, domestic). For the most part a sherd will not tell us whether a context dates to the Tiwanaku

IV or V periods, or to a subdivision therein. It has to be examined within an entire ceramic assemblage associated with broader ceramic and social contexts [Janusek 1994:93].

This caveat rules out an easy phasing of the sites, particularly one based on surface assemblages. However, the ceramics do merit further description. Because Chucaripupata is the only excavated site to date yielding substantial quantities of Tiwanaku-style artifacts, these artifacts will be used for a preliminary discussion of the Tiwanaku ceramics from the Island of the Sun.

Following the major Tiwanaku ceramic types as presented by Alconini Mújica (1995:51–60) and Janusek (1994:Figure 5.3), the full range of Tiwanaku vessel types is present at least at the site of Chucaripupata. Ollas, *tinajas* (small jars), keros, tazones, *escudillas* (serving bowls), *fuentes* (basins), *cuencos* (bowls), restricted bowls, incensarios, *sahumadores*, recurved bowls, and *wako retratos* are all represented. Several forms are present only in low or infrequent quantities, notably escudillas, restricted bowls, and basins. Very high quantities of keros were recovered, and they are thick compared to keros found at Tiwanaku (John Janusek, personal communication, 1996). Interestingly, a fairly significant proportion of blackware keros are present (see Goldstein 1989). The majority of the Tiwanaku-style artifacts are locally made copies of Tiwanaku forms. Some are very crude copies with rough slip and little or no decoration. But a significant portion are so carefully executed and are so similar to Tiwanaku forms (with classic Tiwanaku designs) that, on the basis of paste alone, they are indistinguishable from forms found at Tiwanaku itself. These may well be considered "imperial" style forms, that is, pieces that are locally made, but made in a manner that closely follows the norms for ceramic manufacture found in the heartland. Decorative motifs on the artifacts include incision on the blackware, and almost the full range of Tiwanaku iconography, including common geometric, wavy line, and interlocking motifs, as well as anthropomorphic and zoomorphic designs with a very high quantity of puma motifs (Figure 9.4).

These data indicate very close ties to Tiwanaku symbolized by ceramic use, even if many of

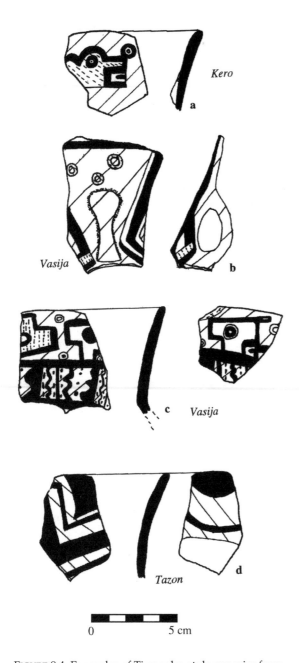

Kero

Vasija

Vasija

Tazon

0   5 cm

FIGURE 9.4. Examples of Tiwanaku-style ceramics from the Island of the Sun

the ceramics were locally manufactured. The exact nature of the relationship of the site to the Tiwanaku center is discussed in Seddon (1998). It is clear that very strong affiliations with Tiwanaku are reflected in the adoption of the Tiwanaku canon for both the forms and decorative motifs of ceramics manufactured on the island.

CONCLUSIONS

The results of surveys and test excavations on the Island of the Sun to date indicate a major and intense occupation of the island during the Tiwanaku period. Twenty-eight sites in a rough hierarchy are present, including five that are 3 ha or larger in size. Ceramics recovered from both test and substantial excavations suggest very close ties to the Tiwanaku state, if not outright control of the island by the state during the later Tiwanaku periods. Precise understanding of exactly how the island was related to the state (for example, whether the island was administered through local elites, whether it was the subject of a direct takeover, etc.) will require further testing of a wider range of sites than has been possible to date.

The intensive occupation of what was to become the Inka sacred area, combined with a probable temple at the site of Chucaripupata (Seddon 1998) and Tiwanaku offerings offshore (Ponce Sanginés et al. 1992), indicates that this area may have been ritually important during the Tiwanaku period as well. However, there is little evidence to indicate that the focus of Tiwanaku offerings and other ritual activities was on the Titikala rock. Testing by Bauer et al. (Bauer and Stanish 2001; Bauer et al. 1996; Stanish and Bauer 2004) in front of the Titikala turned up no evidence of Tiwanaku ritual activity directly in front of the Inka sacred rock. Analysis of the excavation results from Chucaripupata, the largest Tiwanaku site in this area, indicated no orientation to, or focus on, the site of the Titikala, although evidence of ritual activity was present (Seddon 1998). This may indicate that the Inka took a previously sacred area and changed the precise locale, focus, and nature of the ritual activities to suit the demands of the state religion.

Generally, the data from the island conform to patterns that we are now seeing emerge from other parts of the Titicaca Basin. By at least the Tiwanaku IV period, what was previously an independent polity or series of occupations (on the island as elsewhere) became closely associated with the Tiwanaku state.

10.

Residential Diversity and the Rise of Complexity in Tiwanaku

John W. Janusek

ALTHOUGH TIWANAKU WAS for over six hundred years (AD 500–1150) one of the most influential centers in the pre-Hispanic Andes, the site has remained a great mystery. Early travelers and archaeologists noted Tiwanaku's extant monumental edifices and exquisite stone sculptures (Posnansky 1945; Squier 1877a; Stübel and Uhle 1892), but the apparent isolation of these ruins fueled the notion that Tiwanaku was an uninhabited ceremonial center. Nowhere were there clear surface indications for associated habitations, and what is more, the ruins appeared incongruously in what was considered a barren, windswept environment. Ephraim Squier remarked over a century ago, after traveling through the region:

> We can hardly conceive of remains so extensive as those of Tiahuanaco, except as indications of a large population, and as evidences of the previous existence on or near the spot of a considerable city. But we find nowhere in the city any decided traces of ancient habitations, such as abound elsewhere in Peru, in connection with most public edifices. Again, the region around is cold, and for the most part arid and barren.... This is not, prima facie, a region for nurturing or sustaining a large population, and certainly not one wherein we should expect to find a capital. Tiahuanaco may have been a sacred spot or shrine, the position of which was determined by an accident, an augury, or a dream, but I can hardly believe that it was a seat of dominion [Squier 1877a:300].

Over fifty years later, even after conducting the first systematic excavations in Tiwanaku, Wendell Bennett (1934:480b) reached a similar conclusion. The best of his ten narrow test pits revealed dense layers of midden rather than conclusive evidence for habitation. "For lack of definite information," Bennett decided that "Tiwanaku is distinctly a ceremonial site, composed of an aggregation of temples." Bennett's conclusion remained the last word on Tiwanaku for decades and still draws considerable support. Many scholars support the proposition that Tiwanaku was a cult center or pilgrimage site, but not the center of a major polity (Lumbreras 1974b:143, 1981; Menzel 1964; Schaedel 1988; Wallace 1957, 1980). By the 1960s, evidence was emerging in support of an alternative model of the Tiwanaku site. A brief survey conducted by Parsons (1968) revealed a dense scatter of surface artifacts surrounding the visible ruins. However, it was a group of Bolivian archaeologists headed by Ponce Sanginés who most effectively argued that Tiwanaku was a permanently inhabited settlement. Although the group never recorded having excavated a domestic context dating to the periods of Tiwanaku florescence, their work in and under visible monumental structures clearly established evidence for a long history of occupation (Ponce Sanginés 1969, 1971, 1981, 1991). Ponce Sanginés proposed that Tiwanaku incorporated hundreds of houses, but argued that they were built largely of earth bricks that had eroded onto the landscape. Tiwanaku, he argued, developed into an urban center of 4.2 km², and housed a dense population differentiated by class and occupation.

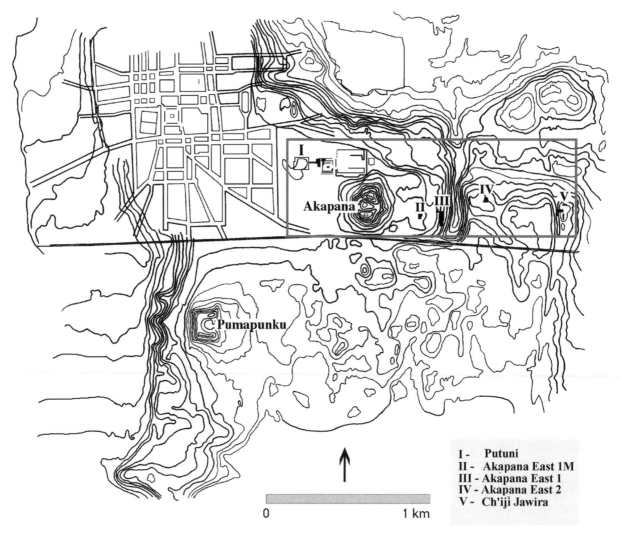

FIGURE 10.1. Plan of the Tiwanaku site

Recent reconnaissance by the Proyecto Wila Jawira indicates that the center reached at least 6.5 km² (Figure 10.1). At this size, Tiwanaku was a true city, with a projected resident population ranging between 10,000 and 30,000 individuals. Until recently, however, no household contexts or residential sectors had been systematically excavated at the site. In this chapter, I summarize the results of extensive excavations in residential contexts and offer an interpretation of the social character and spatial organization of Tiwanaku's residential populations. I focus on household contexts in Akapana East 1 and 2, east of the site's monumental core, and compare these contexts with residential areas in the Putuni and Ch'iji Jawira sectors. Residential patterns demonstrate that Tiwanaku was a socially diverse,

densely populated city with a long and complex history. More broadly, this research invites a critical examination of the concepts of social complexity and urbanism.

SOCIAL COMPLEXITY AND URBANISM

Archaeologists have traditionally invoked complexity to refer to social relations and institutions that manifest a high degree of both order and difference. Order usually implies a relatively high degree of integration that is usually identified with the centralized sociopolitical structures of chiefdoms and states (Carneiro 1981; Claessen 1984; Cohen 1978; Earle 1987, 1997; Fried 1967; Kirch 1984; Service 1962, 1975; Wright 1977). A state is a particularly complex and developed form of society that is rooted in urbanism and incorporates an institutionalized political structure (Cohen 1981; Wright and Johnson 1975). Complexity also refers to a high degree of social differentiation, or heterogeneity (Blau 1977; McGuire 1983; Smith 1994:144). Social differences may take numerous forms, but archaeologists tend to focus on hierarchy and role. Hierarchy, an expression of inequality (Fried 1967; compare to McGuire 1983), is grounded in institutionalized differences of wealth, status, or power (Brumfiel and Earle 1987; Weber 1947:152–153). Role, an expression of specialized livelihoods, is grounded in complementary differences that ultimately foster social integration. Hierarchy itself is considered a form of integration to the extent that leadership and bureaucracies provide specialized services for society (see, for example, Service 1975; Wright and Johnson 1975). Following this traditional view, complex societies are considered highly ordered systems in which other potential forms of heterogeneity, such as faction, lineage, ethnicity, or gender either are not considered or are considered primitive and potentially disruptive survivals.

Urbanism is the concrete expression of state organization and social complexity. Archaeologists have not yet articulated a comparative definition of the preindustrial city that is much more systematic than Childe's (1936, 1950). Central to Childe's vision is the idea that the city, though an extensive and densely populated focus of diversity, is a social community sui generis. The reasons behind urban development may be manifold, but urban societies are held together by two processes: first, by "organic solidarity," through which "Peasants, craftsmen, priests and rulers form a community..." largely "...because each performs mutually complementary functions, needed for the well-being of the whole" (Childe 1950:16); and second, by "ideological devices" that mask or render natural the appropriation of "social surplus" by a "tiny ruling class" (Childe 1950:16). As a diagnostic expression of complex society, the city incorporates occupational specialization and class differentiation, but remains an integrated community with a shared sense of well-being. According to Childe (1950:16), in ancient cities there is simply "no room for skeptics and sectaries."

The idea that Tiwanaku was a complex society characterized by urbanism is an intriguing hypothesis, but one that has not yet been fully explored at the principal site itself. Until recently, no household contexts had been systematically excavated. In this chapter, I seek to examine the nature of Andean social complexity and urbanism at Tiwanaku. As mentioned, complexity refers in part to the development of social relations and institutions such as status differences, which manifest relations of inequality, and craft specialization, which manifest functional differences. Here I compare excavated residential areas in Tiwanaku in order to determine the extent to which social inequality and specialized production characterized the urban settlement, and to clarify the spatial configuration of such forms of heterogeneity.

Nevertheless, an examination of Tiwanaku urbanism may demand a deeper examination of the nature of social complexity. Archaeological research around the world indicates that hierarchy and specialization are not the only constituents of preindustrial social complexity (see, for example, Brumfiel 1994a; Crumley 1995; McGuire 1983; Smith 1994; Stein 1994). Ethnic identity, lineage divisions, factional differences, and other forms of heterogeneity may be endemic features of an entire social order and its centralizing institutions. For example, the ruling classes of the Aztec and Inka empires maintained and even celebrated kinship and lineage principles traditionally thought to be characteristic of primitive societies (Brumfiel 1994a; Conrad and Demarest 1984; Zuidema 1990). In many polities of Asia, Africa, and Mesoamerica (Demarest 1992; Fox 1987; Geertz 1980; Southall 1988; Smith 1994; Tambiah 1977), lineage segments and rival factions formed the basis of both socioeconomic differentiation and political centralization. The very centralizing institutions of such polities were rooted in kinship ties and factional competition.

Responding to the implications of such interpretations, some archaeologists have attempted to develop alternative theoretical approaches to social complexity. One of the most intriguing ideas is the concept of *heterarchy*. Crumley (1987, 1995) and others (Brumfiel 1994a; King and Potter 1994; White 1995) have developed the concept to criticize the usual equation of order and complexity with hierarchy. Archaeologists often construct models of social complexity based on differences in the degree of hierarchy and political centralization. But complex societies always incorporate organizations that are unranked, or that "possess the *potential* for being ranked in a number of ways" (Crumley and Marquardt 1987: 163), and ranking itself is often one among other elements of social differentiation. Heterarchy "reminds us that forms of order exist that are not exclusively hierarchical, and that interactive elements in complex systems need not be permanently ranked relative to one another" (Crumley 1995:3). As King and Potter (1994:84) remark, the concept of "heterarchy does not negate hierarchy, it subsumes it."

I examine evidence for characteristics of complexity in Tiwanaku that, not being overtly functional, may have differentiated urban populations as discrete social groups. I explore group affiliation and identity as a potential heterarchical dimension of complexity in Tiwanaku. Local identity may be based in kin-based groups (see, for example, King and Potter 1994) or in interest groups and factions cross-cutting kinship or class ties (Brumfiel 1994a). In either case, social identity may be an important dimension of such differences. Through time, groups may shift in relative status or power, or an entire social order may become hierarchical as an elite class crystallizes, but rifts of status or class may well follow or coexist alongside ethnic, clan, kin, and other "totemic" boundaries (see, for example, Brumfiel 1994a; Conrad and Demarest 1984; Fox 1987; Zuidema 1990). Thus, a hierarchical order may come to subsume a heterarchical social order, but even as ranked relations shift through time, and as states rise and fall, perduring social boundaries may continue to form part of a society's basic organizing principles.

CHRONOLOGY AND TIWANAKU CERAMIC ASSEMBLAGES

Addressing such theoretical problems requires a firm grasp on chronology. The foundation for a rigorous chronology, based in an examination of changing material culture in relation to solid stratigraphic excavations and an extensive suite of radiocarbon measurements, has been established for Tiwanaku and its surroundings (Janusek 2001). This chronology builds on the chronology originally proposed by Carlos Ponce Sanginés (1981), with certain significant alterations based on a series of critiques that have been raised over the past ten years (Albarracin-Jordan and Mathews 1990; Janusek and Alconini 1994; Mathews 1995). Ponce Sanginés argued that Tiwanaku developed over three evolutionary stages—village, urban, and imperial—that he divided into five major periods (I–V). In this paper, the time span (AD 500–1150) coeval with Tiwanaku urban expansion and regional influence is termed the Tiwanaku period, which includes two principal phases: Tiwanaku IV and V. This chapter focuses on the Tiwanaku IV phase (AD 500–800), when Tiwanaku emerged as a major urban and ceremonial center at the center of a pan-regional polity. In many contexts we can distinguish distinct early (AD 500–600) and late Tiwanaku IV (AD 600–800) subphases. In general, though, domestic occupations and artifact types demonstrate great continuity over these 300 years.

The beginning of Tiwanaku IV was marked by the abrupt appearance of an entire range of red-slipped (and to a lesser degree black-slipped) serving and ceremonial forms (Figure 10.2). Although diverse, these vessels demonstrated a relatively high degree of standardization in certain canons of form, treatment, and iconography. Most common were *keros, tazones,* and *vasijas,* but a number of special serving types, including *escudillas, cuencos,* and *fuentes,* were more selectively distributed across contexts and throughout society. Tiwanaku-style iconography depicted themes that developed out of earlier (Kalasasaya and Qeya) decorative styles, but it was strikingly different in execution and meaning. In Early Tiwanaku IV, Tiwanaku remained a relatively small settlement (most likely < 2 km^2), and the range of specific ceramic types and variants remained relatively low. After AD 600, in the Late IV period, Tiwanaku expanded into a major urban settlement, and ceramic forms and iconography demonstrated greater stylistic diversity. Certain forms and motifs became more standardized, marking the crystallization of a Tiwanaku corporate style.

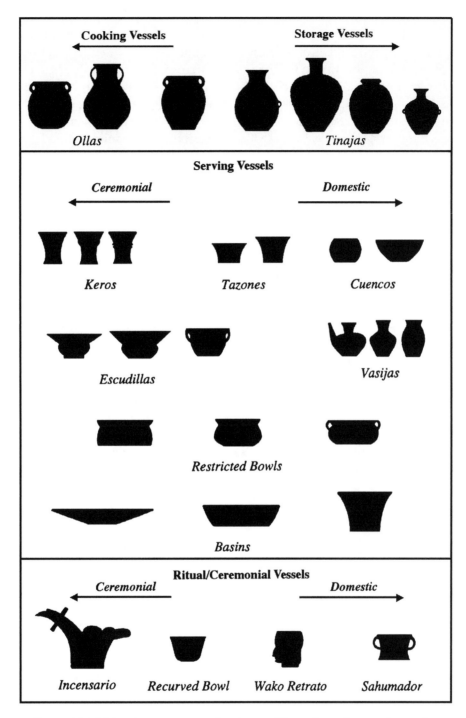

FIGURE 10.2. Major classes, types, and variants of Tiwanaku-style ceramic vessels

For example, most escudillas had wide rims decorated with stylized mythical imagery (Figure 10.13), while *sahumadores* tended to display stylized condor wings and feathers (Figure 10.8). Nevertheless, almost every major vessel type multiplied into a variety of forms, treatments, and iconographic repertoire. Meanwhile, nonlo-

cal vessels formed a small but significant component of many Late Tiwanaku IV residential assemblages. Foreign and foreign-inspired serving vessels at Tiwanaku included the Omereque style, most common in the Cochabamba Valley region to the southeast (Ibarra and Querejazu 1986); the Yampara style, characteristic of the

Chuquisaca Valley south of Cochabamba (Janusek et al. 1997); and the Yura style, most characteristic of the highlands and valleys of the Potosí region south of Tiwanaku (Ibarra and Querejazu 1986). In most cases, nonlocal characteristics of form, treatment, and iconography corresponded with distinctive pastes and tempers (Janusek 1994:126–128; Rivera Casanovas 1994).

RESIDENTIAL ARCHAEOLOGY AT TIWANAKU

This project was originally conceived as an exploration in "household archaeology," and one fundamental objective was to define the material constitution of the household unit, what I define as a minimal coresidential social group with corporate roles (Janusek 1994:81). To this end, I sought to encounter the "the smallest artifactual and architectural assemblage repeated over a settlement" (Stanish 1989a:11). A great deal of research has demonstrated the promise that household archaeology holds for investigating economic, social, and even religious organizations in the past (Ashmore and Wilk 1988; Bermann 1994, 1997; Manzanilla 1996; Palka 1997; Smith 1987; Stanish 1989a; Wilk 1983; Wilk and Netting 1984; Wilk and Rathje 1982).

However, this research highlighted several problems in doing household archaeology at a major pre-Hispanic settlement such as Tiwanaku. First, contrary to traditional wisdom in the Andes (for example, Bolton and Mayer 1977; Custred 1977; Orlove and Custred 1980), the household was not necessarily the primary or primordial corporate unit in the past (Collins 1986; Harris 1981). Today's Andean households are indigenous responses to five hundred years of Western administration, markets, and cultural values (Stanish 1992:19–20), during which time more inclusive corporate organizations, such as *ayllus* (Isbell 1977:91) and lineages (Abercrombie 1986; Collins 1986), have eroded. Second, and related to this point, although household archaeology is often considered to be primarily concerned with reconstructing past domestic life, in Tiwanaku (just as in major pre-Columbian centers such as Teotihuacan) the conventional divisions between domestic, ritual, and specialized spaces and activities break down

(Ames 1995; Feinman and Nicholas 1995; Janusek 1999). Much of Tiwanaku was devoted to activities not explicitly domestic, and residences often incorporated ritual practices and specialized economic activities into domestic life. Places where people slept, ate, and raised children often were the same places they conducted periodic ceremonies or plied a particular trade.

Finally, depositional complexity at Tiwanaku further complicated the prospect of conducting an effective project of household archaeology. Repeated cycles of building, disposal, abandonment, and reconstruction had continuously disturbed previous archaeological contexts. Tiwanaku was an extraordinarily dynamic site. At least 40% of excavated occupations consisted of middens and refuse pits, many several meters in cross-section and 0.5 to 1.0 m deep. On the positive side, the sheer volume of refuse and the extent of space devoted to depositing refuse point to Tiwanaku's significance as a major center. The patterns indicate that through time, household life was increasingly linked to the role of the settlement as a center of social and ceremonial convergence.

The theoretical and practical complications of doing household archaeology in Tiwanaku invite a more encompassing research focus. Beyond uncovering repetitive household units, we revealed significant diversity across the settlement, and exposed in each residential area the remains of a wide spectrum of life spanning domestic, specialized, and ritual activities. Thus, rather than attempting to elucidate an arbitrarily defined group of "domestic activities," I seek to illuminate certain "concrete rhythms of daily life" (see Ensor 2000). This perspective promises to illuminate some of Tiwanaku's internal dynamics and the complexities inherent in its social organizations and interactions.

Residential Patterns in Akapana East during the Tiwanaku IV Phase

Arthur Posnansky (1945:121–122) hypothesized that water once surrounded much of Tiwanaku, an argument taken up more recently by Kolata (1993). A massive ditch or "moat" some 20 to 40 m wide and several meters deep "surrounds and separates like an island the most important and sacred part of Tihuanacu" (Posnansky 1945:121), the site's monumental core. From the air, the moat outlines a roughly rectangular area measuring 0.9 km^2 and oriented several degrees east of the cardinal directions. On the ground, it is visible in most areas as a deep, wide, swampy channel partially filled with sediment. The form and coherent orientation of the moat indicate that it is at least in part anthropogenic. Most likely, it served as a soil quarry or "borrow pit" to provide fill for some of the major edifices that it encircled. However, we have no idea when or over what period of time it was excavated. Inside of the moat, excavations under the Kalasasaya (Ponce Sanginés 1969, 1971) have established that Tiwanaku was first settled at the beginning of Tiwanaku I (or Late Formative I, 200 BC). By the end of Tiwanaku III (Late Formative II, AD 500) the site extended to the limits of

and slightly beyond the moat, encompassing an area of approximately 1 km^2.

The research methodology emphasized extensive horizontal blocks in a few strategically chosen areas. The bulk of this research focused on Akapana East, which includes Akapana East 1 (or AkE 1) and Akapana East 2 (or AkE 2) (Figure 10.3). I compare these two residential areas to occupations under the Putuni, located within Tiwanaku's monumental core, and in Ch'iji Jawira, on the site's eastern boundary. Surface collections throughout Akapana East pointed to the existence of dense Tiwanaku IV–V period occupations (Sutherland 1991), and mapping revealed subtle topographic regularities, including a low rectangular mound of approximately 40 x 40 m, termed Akapana East 1M. Two excavation blocks in AkE 1M exposed 170 m^2 of surface area

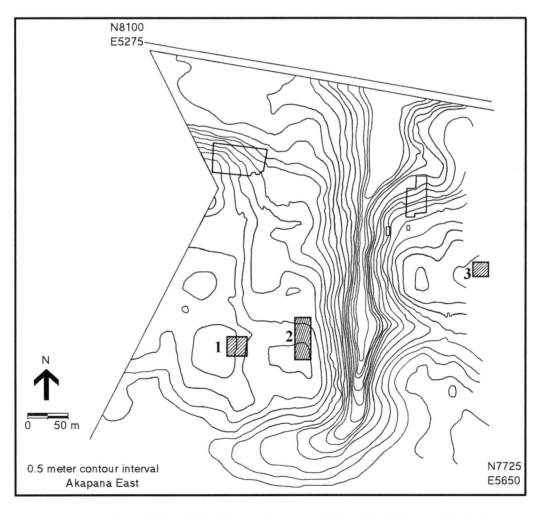

FIGURE 10.3. General plan of the Akapana East sector in Tiwanaku: *(1)* Akapana East 1M, *(2)* Akapana East 1, and *(3)* Akapana East 2

and revealed the east edge of a large residential compound with two small structures, each with activity areas and refuse middens dating to the Tiwanaku IV and V phases. Some 70 m to the east, in Akapana East 1, extensive excavations along the west bank of the moat revealed a long history of occupation spanning Tiwanaku III–V. In Akapana East 2, on the other side of the moat, excavations on another low mound exposed a sequence of occupations dating from Late Tiwanaku IV through Tiwanaku V.

AKAPANA EAST 1M

In AkE 1M, a large, roughly north-south cobble foundation crossed both excavation blocks (Figure 10.4). This foundation clearly supported a massive wall that bordered the east side of the rectangular mound. An east-west foundation of similar size followed the south edge of the mound, indicating that the structure represented an architecturally bounded compound. Structure 1, in the southern block, measured 5.5 x 2.4 m, and consisted of two rooms attached to a small outdoor patio (Figure 10.5). The structure's foundation and walls were built principally of earth brick, which consisted of a durable, fine clay loam. Each of the primary activity areas contained several superimposed surfaces of compacted sandy clay (5YR 4/3). The small room in the north side of the structure served as a kitchen with a corner hearth. The hearth consisted of a deep ash-filled pit (10YR 6/1) outlined with baked adobe bricks and large vessel fragments. Like many Aymara hearths today, a small opening, reinforced with a broken cooking vessel, faced into the room. The superimposed surfaces of this room were covered with a thin lens of greenish-gray ash (2.5Y 7/2), carbonized camelid dung (taquia), cooking ware (olla) sherds, and fragmented camelid and guinea pig (cuy) bones.

The second room probably served primarily as sleeping quarters. A shallow rectangular bin outlined with adobe bricks and filled with ash and taquia bordered the west wall of the room. Like similar features in contemporary Aymara houses (Loza Balsa 1971:73), this bin may have served to store taquia, a combustible fuel. Between the bin and the north wall of the room was a small adobe platform about 30 cm high,

similar to small adobe seats (patillas) in traditional Aymara houses. On the earliest surface, two basalt cobbles with pounding scars were found directly in front of the platform, suggesting that generalized lithic production was one activity carried out here. Although the room contained no obvious sleeping platforms, its north quarter was compact and free of ash, suggesting that simple beds of textile or ichu grass were laid along the warm wall next to the hearth.

An outdoor patio with ten superimposed surfaces occupied the west side of the structure. Charcoal from the second surface provided a calibrated radiocarbon date of AD 540 ± 100 (Beta-5549, Stuiver and Pearson 1993), which corresponds to the Early Tiwanaku IV period. Changes in ceramic assemblages on the subsequent eight surfaces indicated that occupation continued through Late Tiwanaku IV. The surfaces revealed artifacts representing a wide range of activities, indicating that this was a key locus of domestic activity. The first three floors were associated with the opening for a deep pit, the restricted globular shape of which suggests that it served as a storage chamber. Like contemporary Aymara subterranean bins, this chamber would have served to store dry consumable goods, such as tubers and quinoa. During the packing of the fourth occupation surface, the chamber was converted into a refuse pit.

An outdoor midden and refuse zone occupied the area north of Structure 1. Layers of greenish-gray ash with taquia and domestic refuse alternated with more compact layers of laminated silty clay (5YR4/3), the latter most likely from seasonally eroding adobe walls. The area along the north wall of the kitchen contained chunks of burnt adobe and broken ollas, where inhabitants discarded hearth cleanings. A great deal of the artifactual material was burned, as in many secondary contexts at Tiwanaku, indicating that trash was burned periodically to discourage scavengers.

The north excavation block in Akapana East 1M revealed a second domestic structure. The foundation wall of the compound continued through this area, broken by a staggered section that appears to have been an entrance. Structure 2 was not as well preserved as Structure 1, and

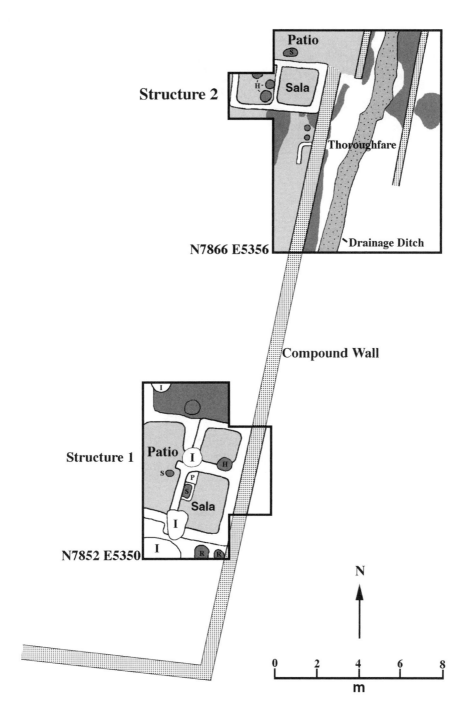

FIGURE 10.4. Plan of Tiwanaku IV phase occupations in Akapana East 1M

lacked clear floor sequences. Like Structure 1, its foundations consisted principally of adobe brick, reinforced in places with field cobbles. A kitchen with three hearths occupied the west end of the structure. A deep hearth or oven, sim-

ilar to that in Structure 1, occupied its southeast corner. The hearth consisted of a pit outlined with baked adobe bricks, and contained a small opening plugged with a cut sandstone block. As in the kitchen of Structure 1, green ash, taquia,

A

B

FIGURE 10.5. Views of areas associated with Structure 1, Akapana East 1M: *(a)* small kitchen area with corner hearth, and *(b)* early surface of outdoor patio showing artifact distributions

olla sherds, and burnt camelid and rodent bone fragments were strewn over the surface of the room.

A room with a compact floor occupied the area between the kitchen and the eastern compound wall. In this room, a nearly complete cooking vessel sat upright in a small subterranean basin. A poorly preserved patio containing a boot-shaped subterranean storage pit was located north of the room. Like the storage pit outside of Structure 1, this pit was converted into a refuse pit once it fell into disuse. South of the structure, a trampled surface served as an auxiliary outdoor activity zone and midden. Three shallow pits and an L-shaped structure along the west side of the compound wall probably served as storage bins. About 4 m east of the large compound wall was a parallel wall foundation, most likely the west edge of a second compound. The area between the two compounds consisted of compact soil covered with superimposed lenses of refuse midden. Down the middle ran a long, irregular band of laminated sandy clay loam containing gravel and artifactual refuse. This feature clearly represented a drainage ditch that received waste from the domestic compounds, much like the ditches that run through the roads of highland towns today. Like the pre-Hispanic feature, these ditches gradually fill with laminated, gravely loam.

The area between the compounds apparently was an unpaved street facilitating travel through the residential sectors of the settlement. In the Tiwanaku V period, a small drainage canal carried waste and water from the east compound into the street. The image of walled residential compounds separated by narrow streets, with water trickling into open drainage ditches, is strikingly reminiscent of contemporary Andean towns.

Akapana East 1M included two mortuary contexts. One was a human infant buried in a small pit in the foundation of the large wall that bounded the east side of the compound (Feature 1, N7866 E5356). The second burial was located at the south end of the parallel compound wall to the east, and it may have actually intruded into the foundation. The poorly preserved remains represented a young adult female who was buried in a flexed position, facing east (Feature 1, N7868 E5362). Several of the bones (including many vertebrae, hand bones, and feet bones) were missing, suggesting either secondary interment or that the burial had been disturbed by later activity.

AKAPANA EAST 1

By the Late Tiwanaku IV phase (AD 600–800), the area along the west bank of the moat was the "backyard" for a nearby residential compound or group of compounds (Figure 10.3). Excavations in Akapana East 1 revealed a deep well, several ephemeral hearths, and over twenty deep amorphous pits filled with immense quantities of ash, taquia, and refuse. Such pits were common throughout Tiwanaku, and they typically tore into huge sections of prior occupations. The refuse in the pits reflected an incredibly diverse range of domestic activities. The energy that went into the excavation of these pits, and the amount of materials deposited in them, suggest that they served two purposes. The pits functioned as adobe quarries that provided the clay loam necessary to form adobe and *tapia* bricks for wall construction. Once excavated, the pits served as refuse deposits for ash and refuse generated at the growing settlement.

The pits yielded large quantities of olla, *tinaja*, and serving ware sherds, fragmented and butchered camelid bone, broken ground stone tools, food remains such as quinoa seeds and maize kernels, ash, and camelid dung (taquia) fuel. The growing center generated immense amounts of material, including elaborate crafted objects, domestic implements, and waste. Still, the pits represented more than simply domestic garbage pits. Adobe quarries in contemporary Tiwanaku often take years to fill with ash and refuse. Most of the pits in Akapana East 1 presented 1–3 strata of ash, indicating that they were filled relatively quickly. Also, remains of partially reconstructible tinajas and elaborate serving wares were often strewn about a single pit. In these massive pits the type and sheer abundance of refuse, as well as its manner of its disposal, indicate that they held more than the waste generated during everyday domestic activities. They also contained the abundant refuse generated during periodic ceremonies and feasts.

AKAPANA EAST 2

Excavations outside of the moat revealed substantial evidence for occupation during the Late Tiwanaku IV and Early Tiwanaku V periods (Figure 10.6). One excavation unit in Akapana East 2 reached precultural red clay directly under Late Tiwanaku IV occupations, indicating that this area was first occupied later than the first occupations in AkE 1M. Much of the occupation had been disturbed by post-abandonment quarrying, deflation, and plowing. What remained consisted of a single domestic structure surrounded by several features, occupation surfaces, and wall foundations. All of the visible foundations were oriented—6 to 8 degrees east of north, following the orientation of the monumental complex and the AkE 1 residential complex.

Two large foundations, supporting compound walls similar to those in AkE 1M, surrounded a single structure. Only the northeast corner of a structure with three superimposed occupation surfaces remained intact. The foundations consisted of adobe blocks on cobble foundations, and a doorway opened to the east. The earliest floor consisted of red clay (5YR 5/4), and it rested on a thick (30 cm) layer of ash and refuse. The upper two surfaces consisted of sand (5YR 4/3), like those in AkE 1M. The final surface was covered with a thin lens of carbonized ichu grass, the remains of the collapsed roof. The structure measured at least 4 x 5 m, but poor preservation prevents a more precise determination of its dimensions.

East of the structure was an outdoor patio consisting of two superimposed, compact surfaces (5YR 4/3). As in the case of Akapana East 1M, this patio revealed a great diversity of activity. Associated with the patio were a deep cylindrical pit and a cluster of three small circular pits, possibly subterranean storage bins. At the north edge of the patio was a massive refuse pit that appeared to date to Early Tiwanaku V, perhaps relating to the abandonment of the structure. A cooking area littered with olla sherds occupied the space south of the structure. A nearby platform of red clay, similar to the patilla found in AkE 1M, may have served as a seat.

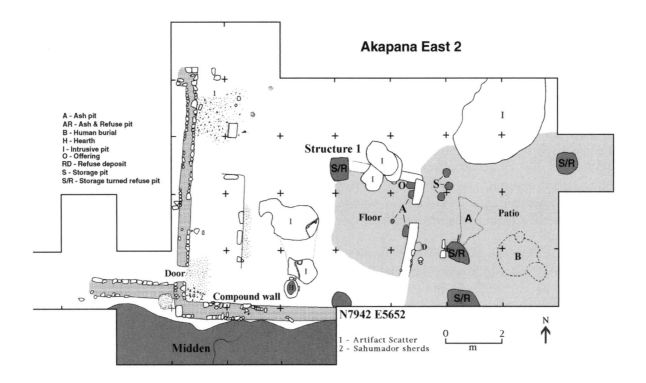

Figure 10.6 Plan of occupations in Akapana East 2

Further west, the west compound wall and a parallel foundation framed a narrow corridor. At its north end was a dense cluster of large artifact fragments, including high proportions of elaborate serving vessel sherds, exhausted grinding stones, and lithic debitage. The cluster most likely represented an interior toss zone, where broken or obsolete implements were discarded from the principal activity zones. We exposed a small area south of the compound wall, which revealed high densities of ash and domestic refuse and indicated that this area was an exterior midden.

Akapana East 2 yielded two clear ritual contexts, a camelid offering, and a complex burial (Figure 10.6). The camelid was fetal and had been placed under the northeast corner of the structure. Under the patio, and marked by a stone protruding above the patio surface, was a human burial consisting of three separate chambers, each with an individual. The main chamber was an adobe-lined shaft 1.9 m deep that contained the poorly preserved remains of an adult male, 35–45 years old at death, and accompanied by two decorated ceramic vessels. A smaller unlined chamber to the southeast contained the remains of a child interred with a wide assortment of goods, including basketry, textiles, and three elaborate vessels. To the north, a small adobe-lined chamber contained yet another child, this one with two vessels.

HOUSEHOLD ACTIVITIES IN AKAPANA EAST 1 AND 2

The Akapana East zones presented a wide range of domestic activities. As expected, refuse left on outdoor patios and deposited in secondary middens represented the greatest range of activities. Patios were the principal focus of day-to-day social and domestic life for household members. Domestic activities served both the material reproduction and social well-being of resident social groups. Not surprisingly, the acquisition, preparation, and consumption of food were principal household activities. Food preparation was consistently represented by certain types of ground stone implements, including flat *batánes* with a concave working surface at one end, convex *moleadores* for grinding grains such as maize and quinoa (Figure 10.7), and

rounded pestle-like crushers for processing peppers, dried meat (*charqui*), and seeds. Butchering also was conducted in residential compounds, as represented by the substantial quantities of ad hoc, unretouched, or quickly retouched lithic scrapers and knives, and by butchering marks on the bones of camelids, guinea pig (cuy), *vizcacha*, and birds. Dry foods were stored in bins and in underground pits with small openings, and liquids were fermented and stored in jars and large tinajas. Cooking was represented by hearths, deep ovens, and enclosed kitchens of varied sizes, and also by great quantities of cooking vessel sherds, taquia fuel, and ash. Other common domestic activities included the production of bone and stone tools, which was represented by significant quantities of lithic debitage and cut and splintered bone. Surprisingly, while spindle whorls were prevalent, evidence for weaving was uncommon in Akapana East.

Two common implements served specific activities that remain unclear (Figure 10.7). Mandible tools consisted of the ascending ramus and posterior body of a camelid mandible, which was broken off just behind the last molar and intentionally polished (Bermann 1994:Figure 12.10; Janusek 1994:Figure 7.7). Several examples from the Moquegua Valley of Peru were hafted to a wooden handle (Goldstein 1989:Figure 50). The production of these bone implements was a general domestic activity in Tiwanaku. They apparently were used as cleaning or burnishing tools, perhaps for camelid hides in the production of leather goods. Conical stone or fired clay objects, known locally as "*trompos*," were also common in Tiwanaku domestic contexts, and they often appear in small caches. They may have served as plugs for small container openings, or as weights in the exchange of foodstuffs or other goods.

Domestic life in Tiwanaku also included a wide range of activities not restricted to the material reproduction of the household. Ceramic sahumadores were used to burn some substance with high lipid content (Michael Marchbanks, personal communication 1991), which may have been resin or camelid fat (Tschopik 1950:208) (Figure 10.8). Most likely, sahumadores served both quotidian and ritual ends. Like similar

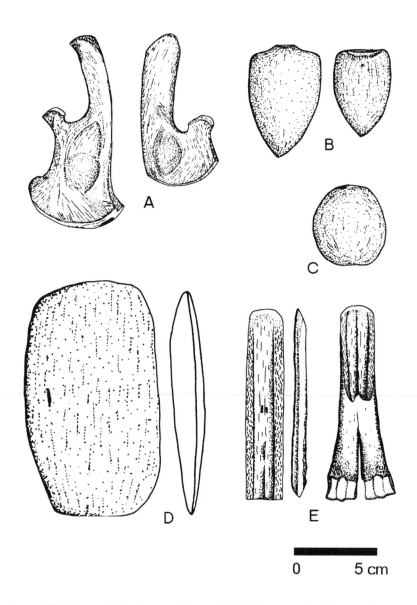

FIGURE 10.7. Domestic implements from residential contexts in Akapana East: *(a)* mandible tools, *(b)* conical objects *(trompos)*, *(c)* a spheroid, *(d)* a grinding *moleador (urqo)*, and *(e)* wichuñas

vessels in contemporary Aymara communities, they probably served both as domestic lamps to provide light and warmth and as ceremonial burners in intimate domestic rituals.

Burying fetal camelids and humans under the floors and walls of residential areas was a common ritual practice (Bermann 1994; Janusek 1994). Contemporary Aymara still practice rituals in which the burial of a human placenta and fetal camelid are elements in a broader context of offerings conducted during the construction or renewal of a house compound (Arnold 1992:51). Fetal burials in Tiwanaku, like those today, were undoubtedly offerings dedicated to the well-being of a house's inhabitants. Placing a human infant under a compound wall (Akapana East 1M) and a llama under the corner of an individual house (Akapana East 2) accords well with the different scales of social grouping. While the fetal llama was likely dedicated to a house and its inhabitants, the human baby, under the compound wall, may have been dedicated by and for the entire social group living in the compound.

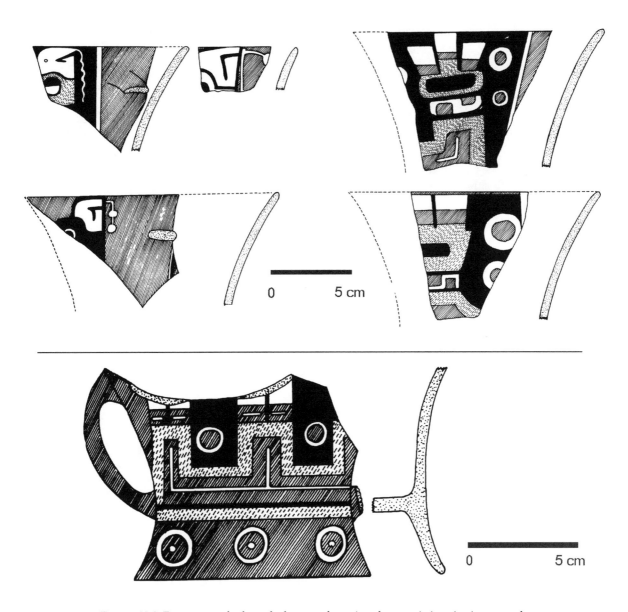

FIGURE 10.8. Fragments of *sahumador* burners featuring characteristic avian iconography

Sherds of elaborate serving vessels, found in especially high proportions on patios and in middens, indicate that social gatherings and life-cycle rituals were important events in each residential compound. The most common serving vessels were bowls (tazones), chalices (keros), and small pitchers (vasijas), but rarer special forms included flaring bowls (escudillas) and large basins (fuentes). Serving vessel sherds comprised 19.5% of Akapana East 1 assemblages and 19% of Akapana East 2 assemblages. Most of these vessels were finely made, and most displayed key elements of Tiwanaku corporate style: red or black slip, hyperboloid form, and elaborate polychrome iconography. The vessels, along with clothing and other valued goods, became important vehicles for the affirmation and negotiation of social status and identity during periodic feasts.

The Putuni Area and Ch'iji Jawira

Excavations in other sectors of the site confirmed that household patterns in Akapana East were, at least in many respects, characteristic of Tiwanaku residential life as a whole. Excavations in Mollo Kontu (Couture 1992, 2003), La Karaña (Escalante 2003), Putuni (Couture 2002; Couture and Sampeck 2003), and Ch'iji Jawira

(Rivera Casanovas 1994, 2003) demonstrated that minimal households, each represented by dwellings associated with patios, middens, and ancillary buildings, were incorporated into larger, architecturally bounded compounds. As in Akapana East, material reproduction, mortuary practice, ritual offerings, and local feasting characterized these residential areas. All yielded substantial proportions of ceramic vessels and lower proportions of other objects (for example, engraved bone) displaying elements of Tiwanaku corporate style. Residential patterns in the Putuni area and in Ch'iji Jawira, however, varied in certain key respects from those in Akapana East, demonstrating the variability of Tiwanaku residential activity.

RESIDENTIAL ACTIVITY UNDER THE PUTUNI

Within Tiwanaku's moated core stands the Putuni (Couture and Sampeck 2003; Janusek and Earnest 1990; Kolata 1993:149–164; Sampeck 1991), a late monumental complex built over two early occupation surfaces, the first dating to Late Tiwanaku III–Early Tiwanaku IV and the second to Late Tiwanaku IV. Excavations in the Late Tiwanaku IV occupation revealed part of an extensive residential complex bounded to the south by a large east-west compound wall that extended at least 30 m to the west, toward the Kherikala. Following the alignment of the Kalasasaya, and diverging slightly from that of the Akapana, all architecture in the complex followed an orientation 8 degrees east of the cardinal directions. One of the larger structures appears to have served as a specialized kitchen for preparing and cooking food (Figure 10.9). In and around it were several hearths, refuse pits, and abundant artifactual evidence for cooking and food preparation. The structure's walls rested on foundations composed in part of cut stones and faced with plaster.

This occupation differed significantly from those in Akapana East in its proximity to an elaborate mortuary complex located in the compound south of the residential complex (Couture and Sampeck 2003; Sampeck 1991). Interments contained fine sumptuary offerings, including elaborate ceramic vessels, turquoise beads, and adornments of gold lamina. Some burials contained literally hundreds of sherds

FIGURE 10.9. View of food preparation structure in the Late Tiwanaku IV occupation, Putuni area

from partially reconstructible serving vessels, including particularly high quantities of elaborate escudilla sherds.

The Late Tiwanaku IV occupation also differed from that in Akapana East in its association with an elaborate, stone-lined drainage network (Figure 10.10). First encountered by a French expedition around the turn of the century (Créqui-Monfort 1906), a primary canal of carved ashlars sealed with clay, measuring 1 m high and 0.9 m across, descended gently from south to north about 1 m below the occupation surface (Janusek and Earnest 1990; Ponce Sanginés 1961:22). The canal followed an alignment 6 degrees east of north, similar to that of the wall foundations. Numerous feeder canals, one of which originated in an ad hoc basin set into a Late Tiwanaku IV residential surface, drained into the primary canal.

FIGURE 10.10. Views of the primary subterranean drainage canal under the Putuni complex

TABLE 10.1. Percentages of serving vessel types in distinct Tiwanaku residential sectors

Form	Putuni		AkE 1M		AkE 2		C. J.	
	#	%	#	%	#	%	#	%
Kero	36	4%	203	17%	108	19%	1628	33%
Tazon	88	11%	556	47%	305	53%	2505	50%
Vasija	275	34%	210	18%	86	15%	566	11%
Escudilla	284	35%	159	13%	22	4%	0	0
Fuente	102	13%	9	1%	10	2%	115	2%
Cuenco	18	2%	15	1%	26	4%	148	3%
Other	11	1%	35	3%	21	4%	0	0
Total Count	814	100%	1999	100%	578	100%	4962	100%

TABLE 10.2. Percentages of sahumador sherds in different Tiwanaku sectors (as a proportion of combined serving and ritual vessels)

Form	Putuni		AkE 1M		AkE 2		C. J.	
Sahumador	64	7%	190	14%	124	17%	5	0%

RESIDENCE AND CERAMIC PRODUCTION IN CH'IJI JAWIRA

Located on the far east edge of Tiwanaku, well outside of the principal moat, Ch'iji Jawira differed from Akapana East in manners very distinct from those in the Putuni area (Figure 10.11). Here, on a low mound of about 1.2 ha, Rivera Casanovas (1994, 2003), and others (Alconini Mújica 1995; Franke 1995) located residential contexts and middens dating to the Late Tiwanaku IV and Tiwanaku V periods. Many patterns of residence and domestic activity reproduced those found elsewhere. A channel 10 m wide separated Ch'iji Jawira from the rest of the site, and its isolation was emphasized by a large cobblestone compound wall foundation. The compound incorporated several incompletely preserved building foundations oriented 8 degrees east of north, associated with storage pits, refuse middens, human burials, and a ceramic offering. Occupations and middens yielded cooking, storage, and serving vessel sherds (Table 10.1), as well as weaving tools, lithic debitage, and ground stone batanes and moleadores.

Despite these general similarities, Ch'iji Jawira differed from Akapana East in numerous ways. Dwelling foundations consisted purely of adobe, and residential contexts were surrounded by immense quantities of refuse (Figure 10.12). Sahumadors, common in all other residential areas, were exceedingly rare here (comprising only 0.01% of combined serving and ceremonial wares; see Table 10.2). Also, small baked clay figurines, representing humans and various other animals, were common throughout the mound. These were relatively uncommon in other residential areas, and were clearly made at Ch'iji Jawira. Rivera Casanovas (1994) suggests, drawing on the significance of miniature representations in the contemporary ceremonies (La Barre 1948:195–196; Tschopik 1950:208), that the figurines served in household rituals stressing reproduction and abundance.

More notable, the inhabitants of Ch'iji Jawira specialized in producing certain types of ceramic vessels (Rivera Casanovas 1994, 2003; Janusek 1999). Implements and by-products of ceramic manufacture, absent in other excavated sectors of the site, appeared throughout the mound. Implements and raw materials included fragments of plaster molds, burnishing tools, and a range of mineral pigments, while by-products included high quantities of partially baked

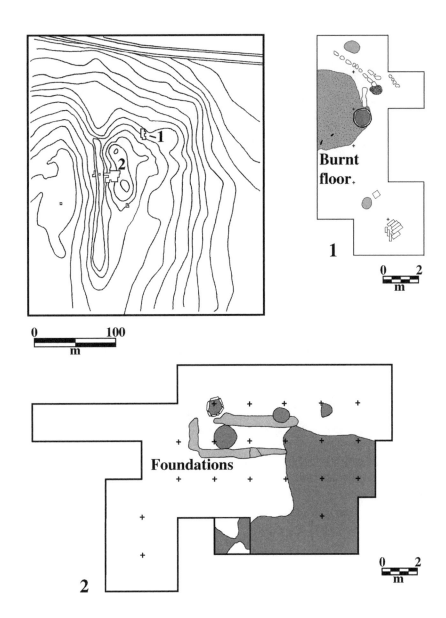

FIGURE 10.11. Map and plans of excavation blocks in Ch'iji Jawira, including *(1)* northeast block with burnt surface and pit kiln (Area A), and *(2)* north block with remnant adobe foundations. After Rivera Casanovas 1994:Figures 8.1, 8.12, and 8.27.

clay nodules, misfired wasters, and slumped vessels. Regarding primary firing contexts, excavations revealed only baked open enclosures and small pit kilns (Franke 1995; Rivera Casanovas 1994), indicating that firing procedures were relatively informal, as they were in other pre-Hispanic complex societies (Balkansky et al. 1997; Janusek 1999). Archaeobotanical analysis revealed that the remains of fuels preferred by ce-

ramic specialists in many Andean communities today were far denser in Ch'iji Jawira middens than anywhere else in Tiwanaku (Wright et al. 2003). Also, being near a semipermanent water supply and down from the prevailing northwest winds, the area was ideally located for ceramic production. Thus, a conjunction of evidence suggests that Ch'iji Jawira was inhabited by people performing both domestic and craft activities.

FIGURE 10.12. View of excavation block in Ch'iji Jawira (facing the urban core), showing adobe building foundations. Photo by Wolfgang Schuler, courtesy of Alan Kolata.

The Tiwanaku IV Period in Tiwanaku: Urban Growth, State Culture, and Social Diversity

RESIDENTIAL PATTERNS AND URBAN GROWTH

Excavations in AkE 1M, AkE 1, and Putuni (all inside of the moat) and in Akapana East 2 and Ch'iji Jawira (outside of it) demonstrate that by AD 500 Tiwanaku incorporated substantial residential occupations. Our excavations consistently exposed relatively small structures associated with outdoor activity areas, middens, and a wide range of domestic activities. In Akapana East, features and activities associated with the structures leave little doubt that most buildings were dwellings. Evidence for long-term occupation, represented in multiple superimposed floors in AkE 1M, AkE 2, and Putuni, indicates that Tiwanaku was permanently inhabited.

Spatial order, especially in Akapana East, reveals much about residential patterns in Tiwan-aku and about the nature of Tiwanaku urban society. Tiwanaku was not settled in a disorganized way through the random accretion of individual household units. Rather, the city grew systematically, through the planned construction and occupation of large, uniformly aligned compounds. Each dwelling and its associated activity areas represented the smallest repeating artifactual and architectural unit, or the household group. Individual households were encompassed within larger residential compounds, a repetitive archaeological unit that housed a larger social group. In Akapana East 1M and Ch'iji Jawira, the large size of the mounds raises the possibility that each represented an entire barrio, or neighborhood. Streets and canals ran between some of these planned compounds, providing arteries of movement for people and drainage.

Urban residence and residential activity increased dramatically during the Tiwanaku IV period, as demonstrated by two key patterns. First, it is represented in the chronology of residential occupation across the site. The settlement core was occupied well before AD 500, but there is no evidence for substantial occupation outside of the moat before AD 600, the beginning of the Late Tiwanaku IV phase. Until this time, residential occupation in Tiwanaku was concentrated mainly in the area bounded by the moat, an area just under 1 km². Over the next two hundred years, urban settlement expanded well beyond this early boundary. Akapana East 2 and Ch'iji Jawira were first occupied during the Late Tiwanaku IV phase, as were Mollo Kontu and La Karaña. Clearly, the urban population of Tiwanaku increased dramatically during Late Tiwanaku IV. One residential sector after another was inhabited, until the moat, which bounded Tiwanaku during the Late Formative and Early Tiwanaku IV periods, was now inside of the settlement. If the moat originally encompassed the entire city, by Late Tiwanaku IV it began to mark differences between the city's inhabitants. The moat remained an exclusionary boundary, but its significance shifted through time.

Urban growth was reflected in increasing volumes of waste produced throughout the Tiwanaku IV period. As the settlement expanded, so did the amount of waste generated by its inhabitants, as indexed by the high numbers of refuse pits and middens in Akapana East 1. Borrow pits provided the adobe required for continual construction and upkeep of the residences, and many of these pits were quickly filled with ash and refuse. Refuse was discarded outside of houses, in streets, and into old wells; it was always nearby.

CONFORMITY IN RESIDENTIAL LIFE: THE EMERGENCE OF TIWANAKU STATE CULTURE

Two intersecting patterns characterized residential life as Tiwanaku expanded into an urban center: conformity and heterogeneity. Material patterns in any residential sector presented a unique conjunction of these larger patterns of urban life. In all areas, most material patterns emphasized conformity with the overarching "state culture," the suite of ideologies, styles, and technologies promoted by ruling elites at any given time. Notably, material evidence indicates that state culture was highly conservative from Early Tiwanaku IV through Late Tiwanaku V, a period of over 600 years (Janusek 2001). First, all architecture replicated a common directional orientation approximately 8 degrees east of north. This orientation was reproduced over the settlement and through time, in local cycles of construction, abandonment, and urban renewal. The orientation attests to the existence of a grand urban design keyed to a total spatial cosmology. The proximity of the orientation to the cardinal directions suggests that it was grounded in the movement of astronomical bodies (Kolata 1993:96–98). In addition, it approximates the lines of vision marked by the Pumapunku and Akapana eastward toward the sacred mountain (achachila) of Illimani. Thus, it is likely that this spatial cosmology was tied to both celestial and terrestrial sacred elements.

Ceramics, because of their importance in Tiwanaku culture and their durability in the altiplano environment, are critical for gauging stylistic patterning at Tiwanaku. In particular, serving and ceremonial vessels—those visible in feasts, ceremonies, and other social gatherings—would have been most significant in this regard (Smith 1987). As in the Andes today, feasts would have been the principal contexts for social competition and for the negotiation of prestige and status. Compared with simultaneous cultural developments in the eastern valleys (Janusek et al. 1997), ceramic style in Tiwanaku presented great uniformity. Throughout Akapana East, forms comprised a well-defined range of types. Most serving vessels had red, orange, or black surfaces, and iconography presented a repeating range of mythical, anthropomorphic, and stylized designs (Janusek 2001). The widespread use of Tiwanaku ceramic style is striking and, I argue, significant. It points to a thorough dissemination and acceptance of many aspects of Tiwanaku state ideology. In any residential sector, most ceramic serving vessels, including keros and tazones, displayed elements of this corporate style. The broad distribution of Tiwanaku-style vessels also points to an operating system of redistribution, in which goods were obtained as reciprocal compensation for participation in the emerging political economy. Some groups, such as the residents of Ch'iji Jawira, produced specialized goods, while others may have participated in public projects as court functionaries, camelid herders, farmers, or rotating laborers. Local urban residents clearly desired vessels with great display value that, like elaborately decorated clothing, would have been employed in contexts of high social visibility, when groups gathered in lively feasts involving music, dancing, and drinking.

SOCIAL RANKING IN RESIDENTIAL LIFE

Within broader patterns of uniformity, material patterns revealed a roughly concentric gradient of status differentiation accentuated by the moat. By AD 600, inhabitants of the Late Tiwanaku IV phase sub-Putuni occupations distinguished themselves from other groups in several key ways (Janusek and Earnest 1990; Sampeck 1991). They incorporated ashlar masonry in their wall foundations and enjoyed access to an intricate subterranean drainage network with both instrumental and symbolic significance. Sumptuary ornamentation was common in burials in the south compound.

The proportion of serving wares in occupation contexts, at 25%, was significantly higher than it was in the Akapana East occupations (Table 10.1). More notably, the range of ceramic serving vessel types and variants used in both mortuary and occupation contexts was remarkably diverse (Couture and Sampeck 2003; Janusek 2001). Serving wares included high proportions of elegantly wrought escudillas (34% of serving ware sherds), a special form that was much lower in frequency in other areas (Figure 10.13; Janusek 1994, 2001; Janusek and Alconini 1994). Other special forms recovered from the Putuni included fuentes (12%), recurved tazones (1%), and elaborate modeled figurines. Keros and tazones composed only 14% of serving assemblages.

By contrast, in Akapana East 1M, architectural foundations consisted purely of unmodified field stones and adobe, and residents had no access to formal sanitation systems. Waste and excess water were guided toward an open drainage ditch running down a street just outside of the residential compound. On the other hand, all serving wares presented corporate Tiwanaku style, and most were finely formed and deco-

rated. Unlike assemblages in the Putuni complex, assemblages here were dominated by tazones and keros (64% of serving ware sherds), while elaborate escudillas were much less frequent (13% of serving ware sherds).

Residential sectors beyond the principal moat differed from those inside as one moved east across Tiwanaku. In Akapana East 2 during Late Tiwanaku IV, as in Mollo Kontu South and La Karaña, domestic architecture was similar in construction and organization to that in Akapana East 1. Waste and water drained into ad hoc canals leading to outdoor streets. Most serving wares in Akapana East 2 displayed Tiwanaku-style elements, but 70% of them consisted of keros and tazones, while escudillas were uncommon (4% of serving ware sherds). Further, in Akapana East 2 approximately 25% of the serving wares were more roughly formed and decorated than those in Akapana East 1. They included a consistent proportion (5%) of nonlocal wares from valleys southeast of the altiplano (Janusek 1994), which were absent in Akapana East 1M and Akapana ceremonial contexts (Alconini Mújica 1995).

Material patterns in Ch'iji Jawira in Late Tiwanaku IV diverged most significantly from those inside of the moat. Here, structures rested on pure adobe foundations, and domestic contexts were surrounded by dense refuse. More than 80% of serving wares were cruder in manufacture and less elaborate than those in Putuni or Akapana East 1. Keros and tazones made up 83% of serving wares, and escudillas were rare. Red slip, a hallmark of Tiwanaku ceramic style, was present on only a small portion (approximately 20%) of serving and ceremonial wares. Nonlocal vessels and vessels with nonlocal influence were common (Rivera Casanovas 1994, 2003).

Differences in architecture, serving wares, and sanitation defined a roughly concentric gradation of social status within the emerging city. High status residential groups concentrated around the monumental structures of the urban core (Kolata 1993). The moat, an ancient and highly visible boundary, emphasized status differences as the settlement expanded. By the end of Late Tiwanaku IV, the moat demarcated the civic-ceremonial core from what was now a sprawling residential periphery. The moat came

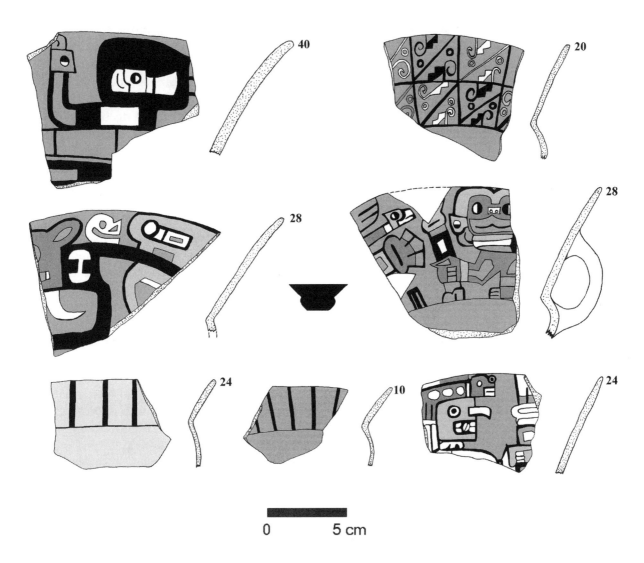

0   5 cm

FIGURE 10.13. Elaborate *escudillas* from residential and mortuary contexts in Late Tiwanaku IV occupations
in the Putuni area

to differentiate previous inhabitants and their nearby temples from inhabitants of newly established residential subdivisions. These newer inhabitants shared many elements of domestic activity and corporate style, the material expressions of Tiwanaku state culture, with those living near the center. However, they simultaneously maintained distinct patterns of material culture, marked in part as differences in the quality of valued objects and in the proportions of elaborate goods they possessed and consumed.

CRAFT SPECIALIZATION IN RESIDENTIAL CONTEXTS

Some residential groups engaged in specialized productive activities. The direct evidence for ce-

ramic production in Ch'iji Jawira is the clearest example, as is evidence for the production of musical instruments in a residential barrio in Lukurmata (Janusek 1993, 1999). The evidence for relatively informal firing technologies at Ch'iji Jawira is not surprising. Few permanent kilns have been reported in contemporary Andean ceramic-producing communities (Sillar 1988; Tschopik 1950; but see Rice 1987:159), and fewer still in archaeological contexts (see, for example, Russell 1994). Recent research into pre-Hispanic Mesoamerican ceramic firing practices (Balkansky et al. 1997) indicates that archaeologists, in the search for permanent kilns, have overlooked evidence for informal firing, which may have been most common in the past. Such firing may leave only a conjunction of patterns, which, individually, would be nondiagnostic: carbon, fire pits, middens filled with ash, high quantities of sherds, wasters, and clay nodules. All of these, in addition to implements, were abundant in Ch'iji Jawira.

The informal nature of firing practices in Ch'iji Jawira, in conjunction with the peripheral location of the barrio and its unique ceramic assemblages (see below), strongly suggests that production was not directly controlled by or conducted for ruling elites (Janusek 1999; Rivera Casanovas 1994). In addition, the ceramic variants produced here were not found in the settlement core. Production therefore was not directly "attached" to Tiwanaku elites. Rather, it appears to have been run locally as the enterprise of a group of coresident households. Although production contributed to the overarching political economy, it was conducted and managed in a local residential context.

URBAN SEGMENTATION AND SOCIAL DIVERSITY

Spatial and Architectural Segmentation. Interwoven with patterns of conformity, status differentiation, and craft production were significant patterns of spatial segmentation and material diversity. These patterns highlight the heterarchical dimensions of Tiwanaku society. If architectural orientation was uniform, it also served as the principal means by which a group separated its daily living spaces from others. Bounded compounds, or barrios, formed the most salient unit of social differentiation. Each compound consisted of a large perimeter wall enclosing one or more domestic structures and various activity areas, including patios, middens, and storage pits. Such a unit, apparently, incorporated several households, each represented by a dwelling and its associated activity zones. Still, even though this basic pattern was repeated across the urban center, compounds differed greatly in size, spatial organization, and activities, suggesting that the nature of resident social groups also varied.

Ceramic Diversity. Spatial segmentation corresponded with significant distinctions between ceramic assemblages. Within compounds, ceramic assemblages maintained surprising spatial and historical continuity. Between them, stylistic patterns varied significantly. For example, ceramic assemblages from Akapana East 1M and 2 revealed subtle but significant differences. All serving vessels from AkE 1M adhered to Tiwanaku canons of form and decoration (Figure 10.14a–c). Apparently, the inhabitants used only vessels with stylistic affinities to the Tiwanaku nuclear area. Keros and tazones maintained red, orange, or reddish-brown slip, and escudillas, with elaborate mythical imagery, were common on early household surfaces. The designs on keros and escudillas tended to become more stylized and abstract through time. Notable here, though, was the absence of tazones decorated with continuous volutes.

Ceramic assemblages from AkE 2 differed in subtle ways (Figure 10.14, d–e). Most contexts yielded Tiwanaku serving vessels (keros, tazones, escudillas, and vasijas) decorated with mythical, anthropomorphic, or geometric figures, collectively similar to those from later occupational surfaces in AkE 1M. Nevertheless, special serving wares like escudillas were much less common than they were in Putuni and Akapana East 1. Nonlocal vessels, representing the eastern valley complexes of Omereque and Yampara (see Janusek et al. 1997), composed 5% of serving wares (over 10% of combined tazones, vasijas, and cuencos). The high proportion of nonlocal tinaja (9%) sherds also was significant relative to their frequencies in Putuni and Akapana East 1 (less than 1% in each). Another distinctive stylistic pattern was the frequency of tazones decorated with continuous volute motifs (10% of tazones), a variant absent on such vessels in Akapana East 1M but common in other areas of Tiwanaku. Other variants rare or absent inside of the moat were keros with wide toruses, redware keros with rough incised zoning, "coca-cola glass" keros, and small, carinated fuentes.

Ceramic assemblages in Ch'iji Jawira were by far the most distinct from those inside of the moat, in both technology and style (Figure 10.15). Although residents produced various types of vessels, many of these were not distributed to groups residing in or near the monumental core (Janusek 1999; Rivera Casanovas 2003). As mentioned above, escudillas were extremely

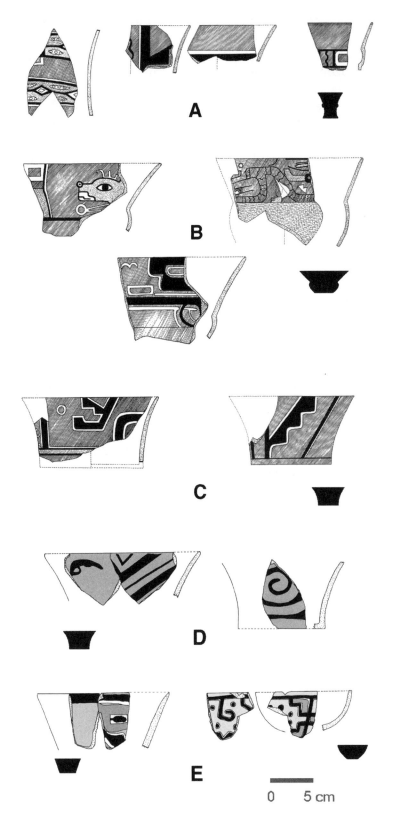

Figure 10.14. Typical serving wares from Akapana East 1M (a–c) and
Akapana East 2 (d–e). Sherds from Akapana East 2 include *tazones* decorated
with continuous volutes (d) and nonlocal Omereque-style bowls (e).

rare, and red slip decoration, the hallmark of Tiwanaku ceramic style, was present on less than 20% of serving and ceremonial wares. Llama motifs were common on tazones and ceremonial vessels from local offerings, and they appear on slumped vessels (Rivera Casanovas 1994:163; also Alconini Mújica 1995:198–199). These representations appeared on approximately 23% of vessels without geometric iconography, and were extremely uncommon, far less than 1% of such vessels, in any other residential or ceremonial context. Nonlocal vessels and vessels with nonlocal influence were present at Ch'iji Jawira in even higher proportions than in Akapana East 2. Most common were vessels in the "derived" Tiwanaku style (Bennett 1936:402; Ponce Sanginés 1981; Rydén 1959) typical of the Cochabamba valleys 200 km to the southeast. These Cochabamba-style vessels composed about 19% of all serving wares, and included a range of distinctive forms such as *challadores*, or kero variants with a tapering body and narrow base, and small bowls, or cuencos. Cuencos composed 3% of the assemblages, higher than in any other residential area.

Therefore, while all residents obtained and used Tiwanaku-style vessels, each compound simultaneously revealed a distinct assemblage of serving forms and styles. Key differences included the predominance of escudillas and a variety of other special serving wares in Putuni, the prevalence of tazones with continuous volutes and nonlocal wares in Akapana East 2, and the popularity of camelid motifs and Cochabamba-style vessels in Ch'iji Jawira. Certain domestic rituals also varied between compounds. The sahumador, a ritual burner common to domestic life in all other residential areas, was virtually absent in Ch'iji Jawira, where small figurines of humans and animals were common. Possibly household rituals stressing abundance were performed to the near exclusion of an otherwise ubiquitous ritual complex involving sahumadores.

Archaeobotanical Diversity. Evidence for spatial segmentation and ceramic diversity between residential compounds is corroborated by archaeobotanical analysis. Wright et al. (2003) have determined that the proportions of tubers, chenopodium, and maize varied significantly between distinct contemporaneous occupations of Tiwanaku. Chenopodium, or quinoa seeds, were most frequent (highest density) and best distributed (greatest ubiquity) throughout the site, followed by tubers and maize. Maize, a crop not widely cultivated in the altiplano, should have greater density and ubiquity measures among high status groups, because it was highly valued in the Andean highlands (Murra 1980:8–14) but could be obtained in quantity only through long-distance relations of trade or vertical complementarity (Goldstein 1989; Kolata 1992). In Tiwanaku, however, maize density and ubiquity measures were highest in Akapana East 2, and its ubiquity measure was also high in Ch'iji Jawira. Therefore, it appears that this crop was not strictly associated with high-status groups. Maize was most abundant among groups in the settlement periphery, who also used relatively high quantities of vessels from the lower, more temperate, valleys in which maize grows.

Local Mortuary Practices. The presence of human burials inside of residential compounds—in the Putuni area, Akapana East 1M, Akapana East 2, and Ch'iji Jawira—indicates that mortuary activity was not entirely relegated to discrete cemeteries. In Tiwanaku, mortuary ritual was closely linked to domestic life, and appears to have been variable in practice. In the Putuni area, for example, some burial chambers contained scores of broken, partially reconstructible escudillas, possibly representing a unique mortuary tradition common to this high-status group. The desire to inter certain individuals near living spaces shared by intimate kindred suggests some type of local ancestor cult, analogous to mortuary rituals practiced at the time of European contact (Cobo 1956 [1653]:73, 163–165; Rowe 1946:286, 298; Zuidema 1978). In Akapana East 2, the placement of a stone marker in the patio above the complex burial supports this idea. Household or residential compound members remembered, made offerings to, and perhaps celebrated with deceased relatives at auspicious times, reaffirming in ritually charged contexts group solidarity and identity.

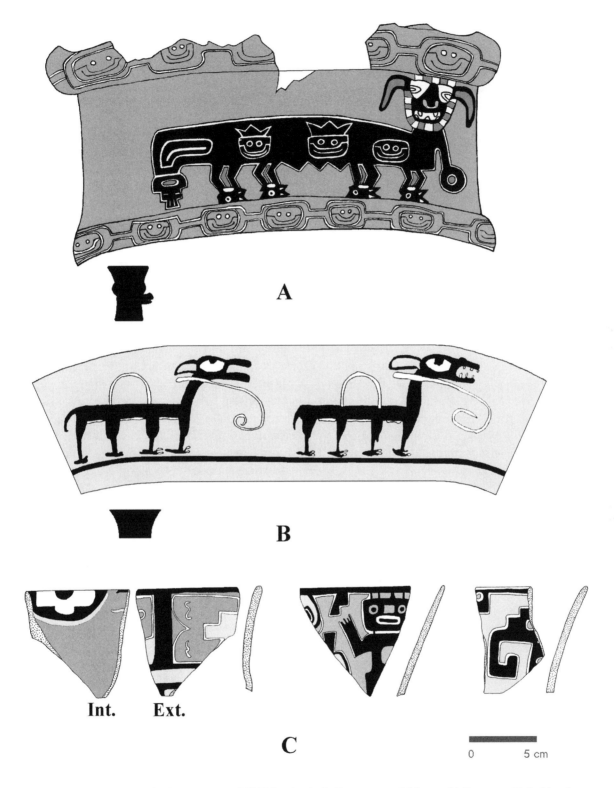

FIGURE 10.15. Serving vessels characteristic of Ch'iji Jawira, including ceremonial *keros* with llama motifs *(a, b)* and Derived-style vessel sherds *(c)*. After Alconini Mújica 1995:Figure 74, and Rivera 1994:Figures 12.1–12.2.

Summary. Tiwanaku urban growth correlated with the popular acceptance of a dominant state culture and clear status differences, and it correlated with other social differences as well. Combined patterns of segmentation and diversity suggest that as the urban center expanded, many compound groups, in particular those settled outside of the moat, maintained distinct social networks and social identities. These most likely represented kin groups or lineages, perhaps related by common ancestry and focused ritually around individuals buried under compound floors. Compound groups maintained enduring identities, local resource networks, distinct diets, specialized trades, and intimate domestic and mortuary rituals. I argue that they were kin-based groups ancestral to the micro-ayllus so prevalent until recently in the southern Andes (see, for example, Abercrombie 1986:24–101; Platt 1982:50, 1987b; Rasnake 1988:49–64). Some social groups, like the inhabitants of Ch'iji Jawira, may have immigrated from the eastern valleys and most likely maintained interaction with their homelands for several hundred years. Local social affiliations and identities, grounded in kin-based principles, index the heterarchical dimensions of Tiwanaku society.

Apparently, ceramic serving wares were significant in the negotiation of status and identity during periodic social gatherings and festivals. On the one hand, these festivals would have affirmed the emerging Tiwanaku order of things, as promoted by ruling elites and expressed in the conspicuous display of corporate style. The influx of groups to Tiwanaku, and their participation in Tiwanaku's social hierarchy and political economy, would have enhanced the demographic strength and political legitimacy of the emerging state. On the other hand, many of these same groups maintained their social identities and means of production, fortified by their access to Tiwanaku-style goods and their participation in Tiwanaku's prestigious religious, economic, and social spheres. Thus, evidence points to a simultaneous invigoration of both state and local avenues to power by AD 800, the beginning of the Tiwanaku V phase.

CONCLUSIONS: SOCIAL COMPLEXITY IN TIWANAKU

This research demonstrates conclusively that Tiwanaku incorporated extensive residential occupations. During the Tiwanaku IV phase, the settlement expanded into a sprawling urban center of at least 6.5 km^2, the largest in the Titicaca Basin and one of the largest in the pre-Hispanic Andes. Nonetheless, by no means was Tiwanaku limited to residential activity. In and around the monumental core were numerous temples and courtyards dedicated to various forms of public and private ceremony (Alconini Mújica 1995; Janusek 1994:103–123; Kolata 1993: 103–149; Manzanilla 1992; Ticlla and Vranich 1997). Not unlike many other political centers in the New World, Tiwanaku was important both as a religious place of ceremony and as a permanently and densely populated urban center. Bennett came close to understanding Tiwanaku, but ultimately fell slightly short of the mark. Tiwanaku consists of extensive refuse pits and middens, to some extent the product of large-scale ceremonial activities, as he suggested. But these lively feasts and social gatherings both involved and were sponsored by people living within the settlement. As in other major Andean settlements (Cobo 1990 [1653]; Kolata 1993; Moore 1996b; Morris 1982; Shimada 1991), ceremony and urbanism went hand in hand.

This research has begun to illuminate the nature of urbanism and complexity in Tiwanaku. First, a wide range of evidence demonstrates clearly that during the Tiwanaku IV period, Tiwanaku incorporated social groups that were differentiated in social status and in occupation. Differences in status followed a broadly concentric grade, in which many elite groups resided inside of the moated core, near the monumental constructions, while groups of lesser status resided in compounds toward the edge of and outside of the moat. At the edges of the settlement were groups of lower status, in one case with strong ties to a distant region. If status was roughly concentric, it was also marked by a gradient of identity separating Tiwanaku elites from groups with strong foreign ties. It also was tied to the history of settlement in the sense that those outside of the moat were also the most recently settled.

Some commoner groups were also craft specialists. At both Tiwanaku and Lukurmata, specialist groups used significant proportions of display goods associated with the eastern valley regions. Native craft specialists in South America often traveled far to obtain raw materials or to exchange their goods (Gutierrez Condori 1991; Helms 1993:39; Mohr-Chávez 1992), and so evidence for relations with distant, exotic regions is not too surprising. In the case of Ch'iji Jawira, the proportions of such goods were truly substantial, suggesting that the groups may have emigrated from the Cochabamba region. The location of Tiwanaku's specialists on the edges of urban settlements may have been related to their relative status and foreign ties. To the extent that the artisans traveled widely, they mediated cultures and lived "between" societies (see Helms 1993). Their location on the urban fringe may reflect their association with more distant foreign lands, in contrast to the emerging hierarchy focused around the Tiwanaku elite.

Tiwanaku, therefore, was a complex urban society in the ways outlined by Childe and Service. The expansion of the settlement corresponded with the emergence of clear inequality and functional differentiation, as manifested in differences of social status and craft specialization. It also corresponded with the emergence of a prestigious state culture, represented in a widely disseminated corporate style. But these characteristics merely scratch the surface of the basic social dynamics involved in the emergence of the Tiwanaku state. Throughout the Tiwanaku IV period, Tiwanaku incorporated an increasing number of bounded residential compounds, each housing a social group that consisted of a number of constituent households. Each of these larger groups shared similar resources, practiced local domestic and mortuary rituals, and maintained a common identity, suggesting strongly that they formed kin-based groups analogous to later micro-ayllus. Status and occupation were inherently tied to social boundaries that were expressed in social identity and everyday practice. Urban complexity in Tiwanaku, as in many pre-Hispanic societies of the New World, developed out of segmentary social differences that had profoundly "horizontal" dimensions.

This examination joins many others in questioning the traditional concept of social complexity (see, for example, Crumley 1995; Joyce and Winter 1996; Smith 1994; Stein 1994). Relations of inequality and institutions of integration became increasingly developed as Tiwanaku expanded during the Tiwanaku IV phase, but these materialized in specific types of social relations and activities. More fundamental historically was the social segmentation out of which state institutions developed. The state developed out of social inequalities and political institutions already embedded in preexisting kin groups and communities, and over the course of the next six centuries state rulers promoted, consolidated, and expanded the roles of social difference and political integration. We return to Childe, who argued that in preindustrial cities there is simply "no room for skeptics and sectaries" (1950:16), or as Max Weber (1958:65–120) put it, for the kin-based "totemistic" ties characteristic of "primitive" societies. A growing corpus of research shows that sectarian and totemistic ties were often the very ground on which chiefly and state institutions were built.

11.

The Altiplano Period in the Titicaca Basin

Kirk L. Frye and Edmundo de la Vega

THIS CHAPTER PRESENTS data from several seasons of systematic archaeological research conducted in the western Titicaca Basin. It focuses on the development of the Lupaqa Kingdom, one of several groups that occupied the Lake Titicaca Basin during the Late Intermediate, or Altiplano period (circa AD 1100 to AD 1450). Historically, the Lupaqa have figured prominently in Andean archaeology because they are portrayed in ethnohistorical accounts as a powerful pre-Inca polity whose economy included the control of ecological zones well outside the core area of the Altiplano (Murra 1968). These ethnohistorical documents provide a graphic account of the development of a complex and unified pre-Inca highland polity (Cieza de León 1984 [1553]; Cobo 1956; Diez de San Miguel 1964 [1567]). However, until recently, many of the claims concerning Lupaqa political complexity have not been tested against rigorously collected empirical data. In this chapter, we show that the collapse of the Tiwanaku state and changing climatic conditions within the Titicaca Basin created a political landscape characterized by chronic conflict and competition between separate Lupaqa subgroups. Rather than leading to centralized leadership, chronic warfare and factional competition prevented the Lupaqa from becoming politically unified during the Altiplano period. The archaeological perspective, then, contrasts with the general picture of Lupaqa complexity portrayed in ethnohistorical documents.

HISTORY OF RESEARCH

Early research in the Lupaqa area consisted of site reports that included descriptions of the large fortified sites (*pukaras*) and *chullpa* burial towers (Franco and González 1936; Vásquez 1939). One of the earliest descriptions of Lupaqa sites and ceramics comes from the work of Marion Tschopik (1946). As part of Harvard University's research program, Tschopik lived in the Lupaqa town of Chucuito between 1940 and 1942. Working in and around Chucuito, she excavated a number of cist and slab-cist tombs, she excavated at the Late Horizon building of Inca Uyu, and she located Lupaqa sites with chullpas located inland from the lake. On the basis of burial excavations and surface collections, Tschopik defined a number of ceramic styles, including the Allita Amaya pre-Inca ware, the Chucuito Polychrome, and the Sillustani Plain and Polychrome styles, the latter dating to the Late Horizon (M. Tschopik 1946).

John Hyslop's (1976) reconnaissance of the southwestern Titicaca Basin provided important new data concerning the archaeological features found at Lupaqa sites. Hyslop's survey, extending over much of Lupaqa territory, located 25 sites containing Lupaqa artifacts and defined these sites as part of the "Altiplano Macro Pattern" within the Altiplano period (AD 1100–1450). Hyslop's work includes descriptions of architectural features and ceramic assemblages from the most prominent sites (the hilltop fortified towns) throughout the Lupaqa area.

Our understanding of the Altiplano period has been broadened by several recent studies focusing on Lupaqa sites in the western Titicaca Basin. These studies sought to define Altiplano period settlement patterns, architectural styles, burial practices, and ceramics complexes within a regional context. Beginning in 1988, a multi-year research project, the Proyecto Lupaqa, was initiated in the heart of Lupaqa territory by Charles Stanish and colleagues (Stanish et al. 1992, 1997). One of Proyecto Lupaqa's research goals was to gather systematic data to test different models associated with the political development of the Lupaqa polity. As a project member, Edmundo de la Vega (1990) conducted one of the first excavations of an Altiplano period fortified site at Pukara Juli. The site includes four separate habitation areas, of which the 5-ha area of Tuntachawi was selected for excavation and mapping. From these excavations a new ceramic style, Pukarani, was defined, a style that bears similarities to ceramic assemblages from other Altiplano period sites studied by Hyslop (1976) and M. Tschopik (1946). In addition, de la Vega (1990) identified specific architectural features at Pukara Juli and artifact categories associated with one domestic terrace unit. The minimal depth of the cultural deposit unit suggested that Pukara Juli was either occupied briefly or was only used on a temporary basis. Additional research on Altiplano period fortified sites was carried out at the sites of Pukara Juli, Huichajaja, Llequepa, and Tanapaca by Frye (1997a) and focused on intersite comparisons of architecture and ceramic styles.

During the 1990 and 1991 field seasons, Proyecto Lupaqa conducted a systematic pedestrian survey covering approximately 360 km^2 between the modern towns of Juli and Pomata (Figure 11.1). Over 500 occupations dating to six different time periods were located during the survey and are the basis for defining a settlement sequence from the Preceramic through the Colonial periods. Twelve site types were defined from the survey, falling into four size categories (see Stanish et al. 1992). Sites with areas less than 0.2 ha are designated as hamlets, sites measuring between 0.2 and 1.0 ha are small villages, those with areas between 1.0 and 4.0 ha represent large villages, and sites with areas over 4.0 ha are designated as centers (Stanish et al. 1992:74–75).

Using the same methodology developed for the Juli-Pomata survey (Stanish et al. 1997:17–33), the Chucuito-Cutimbo survey was carried out by Frye in 1994–1995 (Figure 11.1). The survey was located in and around the modern town of Chucuito and covered an area of approxi-

mately 200 km^2, incorporating three specific ecological zones: (1) a lakeside (3808–3825 m above sea level) and hillside terrace (3825–4100 m above sea level) agricultural zone, (2) an inland agro-pastoral zone, defined by its distance from the lake, and (3) a higher-elevation mountain zone (> 4100 m above sea level) dominated by Cerro Atoja. Because most of the important cultural developments in the western Titicaca Basin have taken place within the agricultural zone near the lake edge, researchers have tended to focus their investigations there. The Chucuito-Cutimbo survey was specifically designed to include a large area of agro-pastoral land away from the lake edge. Although the inhabitants of the area today practice some agriculture, the primary economic focus of contemporary inhabitants of this area is animal husbandry. Higher-elevation mountain areas are used primarily for herding animals. This zone is characterized by some permanent prehistoric and modern occupations, and in higher altitudes, seasonal occupations. The Chucuito-Cutimbo survey shows that political developments in the agro-pastoral zone are key for interpreting Lupaqa political history.

ALTIPLANO PERIOD CLIMATE

The role of climatic shifts in the cultural development of the Titicaca Basin cannot be underestimated. In the case of the Lupaqa, there appears to be a strong correlation between drought conditions and culture change in the region (but see Erickson 1993, 1994, 1999, and 2000). In 1992, Ortloff and Kolata, using data from Thompson's Quelcaya ice cap research (Thompson et al. 1988), presented a strong case for the idea that variations in ice core thickness can be used as a general proxy for prehistoric rainfall levels (Ortloff and Kolata 1992). They noted that during wet periods the ice cap averaged a thickness of about 1.5 m, while lower average thicknesses indicated drier periods. During the Altiplano period, ice core thicknesses fell below the 1 m mark several times, indicating peak dry periods at approximately AD 1100 and AD 1200, and again during an extended drought episode between AD 1245 and AD 1310. Oxygen isotope measurements from the cores indicate that for much of the Altiplano period average air temperatures in

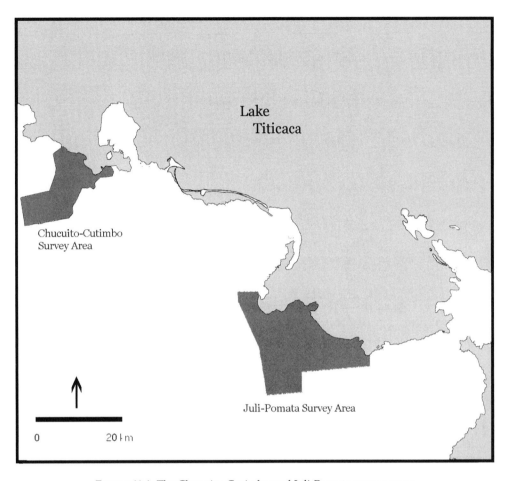

FIGURE 11.1. The Chucuito-Cutimbo and Juli-Pomata survey areas

the Titicaca Basin increased by between 0.5 and 1.0° C, a factor which would have increased the evapo-transpiration rate. Extended drought periods, as documented by the ice core data, would have been accompanied by a drop in the lake level. During a six-year drought in the 1940s, when the ice core thickness averaged 1.27 m, the lake level dropped by nearly 4 m. It is not unreasonable to expect that during the Altiplano period, when ice cores were less than 1 m thick, lake levels could easily have dropped 10 m or more and could have stayed at low levels for long periods of time. Even a 5-m decrease in lake level would mean that much of the land bordering the lake in the Chucuito area—today some of the most productive land in the region—would have been dry and covered with a salty layer. Soils along the lake edge in the Pampa Huataraque in the Chucuito-Cutimbo area today become encrusted with a white salt layer as the lake recedes, and no crops are grown in this

area. Although the agricultural productivity of land exposed by a receding shoreline is unknown, given modern examples, it is expected that without significant fresh water entering into the hydrological cycle, the lakeside agricultural success during periods of drought would be low. During the Altiplano period then, extended drought episodes would have significantly altered agricultural productivity and animal husbandry in the basin. Even in good years, the basin is characterized by unevenly distributed rainfall and unpredictable crop-killing frosts, such that closely adjacent areas may experience radically different crop yields and herd growths. All together, fluctuations in rainfall during much of the Altiplano period would have created highly unstable living conditions characterized by periods of frequent crop failures and food shortages.

During the Formative period and through the Middle Horizon, settlement patterns in the

Titicaca Basin were characterized by continuity; that is, sites that were occupied early had a tendency to be occupied for a long time. These settlements eventually included small civic-ceremonial sites whose populations became increasingly aggregated into ever-larger political centers. It was during the Altiplano period that the long-standing pattern of cultural development abruptly changed in the Titicaca Basin. In the western Titicaca Basin, settlement data from both the Juli-Pomata and Chucuito-Cutimbo survey zones provide dramatic testimony of changing adaptive and political strategies associated with the period of climate deterioration that began during the terminal Middle Horizon and lasted throughout much of the Altiplano period. The collapse of Tiwanaku influence, at least in the western basin, is reflected in changes in settlement patterns, architectural and ceramic styles, and burial traditions. Throughout the Lupaqa territory, Tiwanaku ceramic forms and iconographic styles were discontinued, so that the early Altiplano wares (such as the Allita Amaya and Pukarani from the Juli area and ceramic assemblages from other Altiplano period sites) bear little resemblance to Tiwanaku ceramics (Figure 11.2). In fact, the Altiplano period is characterized by a great deal of stylistic diver-

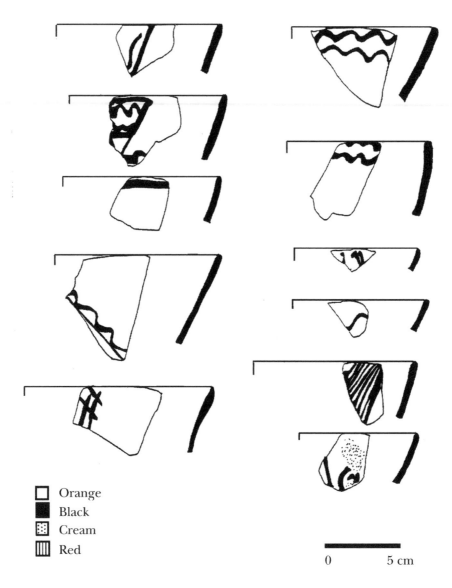

□ Orange
■ Black
▦ Cream
⦀ Red

0   5 cm

FIGURE 11.2. Late Intermediate, or Altiplano period, ceramics

sity. Although much more detailed analysis remains to be done, at least three general groupings of ceramics in the Lupaqa area are evident so far: (1) the ceramics from the Ccapia area to the south, whose style is related to the Pacajes style, (2) ceramics found in the Taraco Peninsula, and (3) ceramics from the Tiwanaku valley. Pukarani ceramics occur mostly around the Juli area, and the Altiplano period ceramics from the Chucuito-Cutimbo area are more closely related to Colla-style ceramics than they are to the ceramic assemblages from the Juli or Ccapia areas.

ALTIPLANO SETTLEMENT PATTERN

The Altiplano period settlement pattern in the Juli-Pomata survey zone is characterized by the abandonment of many Tiwanaku political centers and habitation sites in raised-field areas. This pattern is also seen in the Chucuito-Cutimbo survey region. It was also during the Altiplano period that many more sites than in previous periods were found in the agro-pastoral zone (Table 11.1). This trend toward increased settlement of the agro-pastoral resource zone is very pronounced in the Chucuito-Cutimbo survey area. Other than evidence of

Archaic period cave sites, no Formative or Tiwanaku period sites were found in this ecological zone. Although the agro-pastoral resource zone was occupied in the Juli-Pomata survey zone in both Formative and Tiwanaku times, it was more densely settled during the Altiplano period.

The population shift from lakeside areas into agro-pastoral zones during the Altiplano period likely represents an increased focus on animal husbandry as an important economic pursuit. This is consistent with the drought conditions documented for the Altiplano period from the ice core data. One of the most interesting questions concerning the Lupaqa political development is the relationship between inland pastoral and lakeside agricultural groups. It is not clear whether these new settlements in the inland agro-pastoral zone represent a movement of the population from abandoned Tiwanaku centers and raised field systems, or whether they represent the movement of people into this area from the western interior region. One possible scenario is that as lakeside economic systems failed during drought cycles, the populations there adopted a mixed agriculture and herding lifestyle or abandoned agriculture altogether for full-time herding. Alternatively, populations

TABLE 11.1. Altiplano and Tiwanaku period site distributions by production zone

	Altiplano Period	Late Horizon
Number of habitation sites	52	110
Total site area (ha)	26.93	83.56
Mean size of all sites	0.52	0.79
LAKESIDE AGRICULTURAL ZONE		
Total habitation sites	3	16
Total site area (ha)	0.63	6.85
Mean size of all sites	0.21	0.63
TERRACED AGRICULTURAL ZONE		
Total habitation sites	31	64
Total site area (ha)	15.45	61.23
Mean size of all sites	0.50	0.95
AGRO-PASTORAL ZONE		
Total habitation sites	18	30
Total site area (ha)	10.85	15.48
Mean size of all sites	0.60	0.59

from regions further inland, for whom pastoralism was a primary economic focus, may have moved into new areas as a result of the Tiwanaku collapse, population pressure, and resource scarcity, or as result of military action to increase landholdings in warmer micro-climates nearer the lake. What is clear is that the largest and most complex Altiplano period fortified sites—for example, Cutimbo in the northern Lupaqa area and Tanka Tanka in the southern Lupaqa area—lie within the agro-pastoral ecological zone. Hyslop (1976) speculated that these two sites might have been two separate capitals for two Lupaqa subgroups. That these sites are situated in prime grazing areas suggests that a herding economy was important, an observation consistent with the ethnohistorical documentation of huge camelid herds under the control of Lupaqa elites during the Late Horizon (Diez de San Miguel 1964 [1567]).

The Altiplano period settlement patterns indicate a relatively fluid political landscape, characterized by alliance building and warfare between ever-changing corporate groups (Figure 11.3). Political instability likely created a situation where people moved their habitations from one area to another and back again through time. Along the lake, the typical Altiplano period settlement system consisted of habitation sites, likely used by individual or extended family households, and located within terraced agricultural fields. Forming small corporate groups, probably on the basis of lineage affiliation, several individual habitation sites represented the basic social unit. A defining feature of the Altiplano period settlement pattern and political landscape is the use of both local refuge sites and large fortified sites (Figure 11.4). Local refuge sites are located primarily on hilltops and, in comparison to large fortified sites, are much smaller, have few structures other than site containment walls, and have few surface artifacts. However, although local refuge sites are much less complex architecturally than large fortified sites, they are found near almost all Altiplano period settlement clusters and are especially dense throughout the agro-pastoral zone. Fortified sites (pukaras) are mountaintop sites surrounded by walls, which in some cases reach

10 m in height, often contain ramparts, towers, and doorways, and can extend for many kilometers around the site. Site walls enclose clearly visible architectural remains, including dividing walls, passageways, terrace constructions, domestic structures, and ceramic and lithic artifacts. Major fortified sites studied to date range in altitude from 4500 m above sea level (Huichajaja), to 4000 m above sea level (Cutimbo). An analysis of the architectural layouts of fortified sites shows that social space was characterized by separate habitation areas, which most likely were associated with individual lineages and/or extra-familial corporate groups (Frye 1997a). At Pukara Juli (a steeply sided, walled, mountaintop site), four separate habitation areas are contained within the walls. One of these habitation areas, Inca-Tuntachawi, was internally subdivided by the placement of walls running up, down, and across the site. The architectural layouts of sites located on flat mesas in the agro-pastoral zone of the Chucuito-Cutimbo survey area also show evidence of spatial segregation, such that domestic structures are grouped around several separate, large, circular structures and/or chullpas, or are separated from each other by internal walls (Figure 11.5). Although the chronology of the development and use of fortified sites in the basin requires more attention, an accelerator mass spectrometry (AMS) date from the lowest level of a domestic context at Cutimbo shows that this fortified site was occupied as early as AD 1320.

Excavations and architectural studies at major fortified sites have provided insights into their use. Nearly all of the structures in Altiplano period fortified sites are either oval or circular. The range of structure sizes within sites varies considerably, with the largest measuring from 7 to 8 m in diameter. Although surface artifacts do not make clear the function of the large circular structures within large fortified sites, they may have been meeting places or possibly elite residences. Hyslop cites Cobo, who observed large circular structures, some up to 7 m in diameter, which were used as residences for high-status individuals (Hyslop 1976:106). In general, however, the majority of structures at fortified sites are small (Frye 1997a), and initially many were interpreted

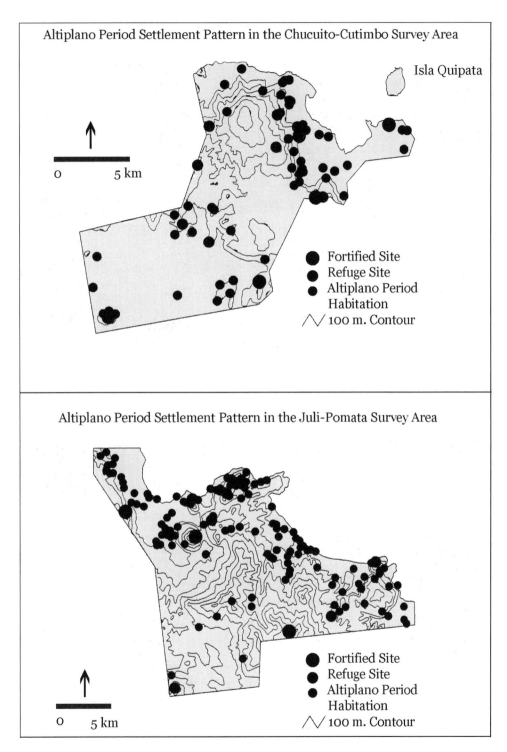

FIGURE 11.3. Altiplano period settlement patterns in the Chucuito-Cutimbo and
Juli-Pomata survey areas

as slab-cist tombs. At Pukara Juli and Cutimbo, excavations of the smallest structures—those measuring between less than 1 m and 2 m in diameter—were not tombs and had no artifacts associated with them. De la Vega suggests that these small structures may have served as storage facilities at Pukara Juli and may have looked like small silos with a stone base and *totora* siding (de la Vega 1990). On the other hand, medium-sized structures—those measuring 2 to 4

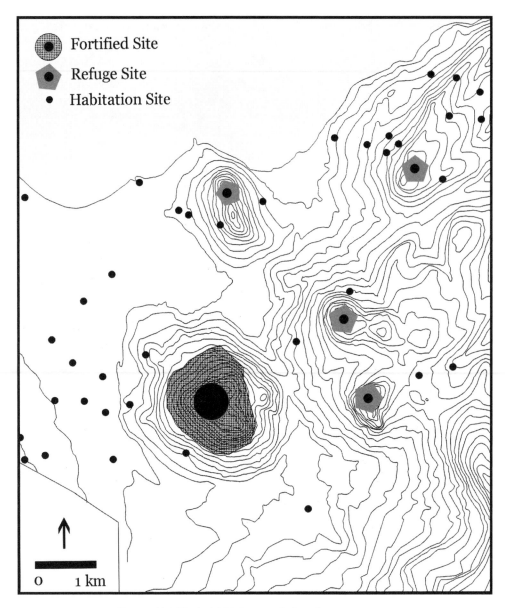

FIGURE 11.4. Typical Altiplano period settlement pattern

m in diameter—show evidence that some were used to prepare food while others were probably used as sleeping areas. While it is not always possible to identify specific corral areas as such, areas within all fortified sites could also have served to protect animals during times of conflict or raids. Although status differences in individual habitation areas is suggested by variations in structure sizes, major fortified sites lack clearly defined corporate architecture, as would be expected if they had been controlled by well-established leaders. In general, fortified sites do not exhibit a great deal of ranking between the individual habitation areas. Rather, the different communities that occupied them appear to have operated under a fairly informal political system.

Burial Patterns

The Altiplano period burial traditions in the western basin differ from those of earlier periods. Formative and Tiwanaku period burials in the Lupaqa area usually contain only one individual and are below ground. Altiplano period burials, in contrast, form three basic categories: (1) cave and grotto burials (see Chapter 12, this volume), (2) subterranean cist and slab-cist

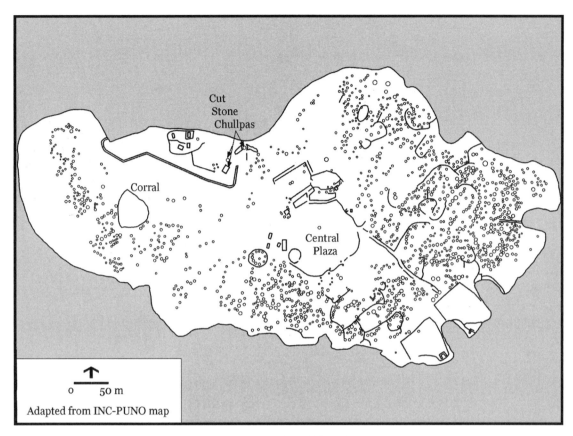

FIGURE 11.5. Site of Cutimbo

tombs, and (3) chullpas. Cist tombs generally contain single individuals, while slab-cist, cave, and chullpa burials frequently contain multiple interments. Although the chronology of Titicaca Basin tomb types needs further refinement, cave burials in the Chucuito-Cutimbo survey region contain predominately Altiplano period artifacts. Some cave burials are little more than individuals placed within naturally occurring holes or grottoes along cliff faces, rock outcrops, or mountaintops whose openings are covered with rocks. While some cave burials are large and contain multiple burials, even these are covered up and hard to see. For reasons as yet unclear, during the Altiplano period, people were buried in the more visible above-ground slab-cist and igloo-style chullpa tombs. While the linkage between *allyu* formation, territory, and burials has a long history in the Titicaca Basin (Steadman and Hastorf 2001) and elsewhere throughout the Andes (Isbell 1997), during the Altiplano period, investment in burials became much more widespread. Rather than being confined to important

ceremonial sites, as in previous periods, tomb building occurred in all Lupaqa communities. We attribute the use of above-ground tombs to the development of newly formed corporate groups comprised of individuals who banded together for mutual protection against raiding from neighboring groups. Over time, as alliances became more established, ever-larger tombs were used to signal the status of emerging elites and to demarcate territorial limits. However, if large above-ground tombs were associated with individual leaders, then their wide distribution across the Lupaqa territory argues for the presence of many, rather than fewer, competing leaders (Figure 11.6).

Elizabeth Brumfiel (1994b) has shown the importance of factions for understanding the development of political complexity and the emergence of stratified political systems in the New World. Factions are defined as "structurally and functionally similar groups which, by virtue of their similarity, compete for resources and positions of power and prestige" (Brumfiel 1994b:4-

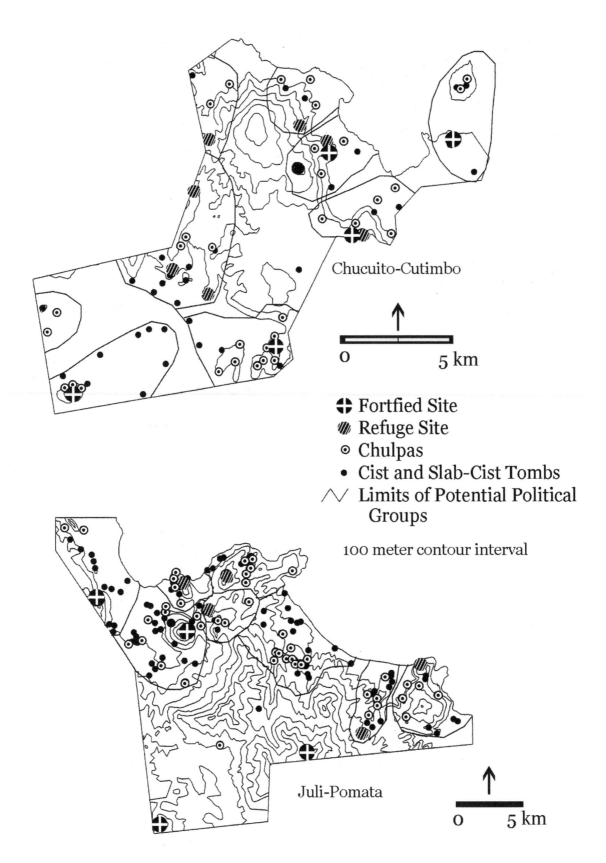

FIGURE 11.6. Distribution of Altiplano period above-ground tombs in the Chucuito-Cutimbo and Juli-Pomata survey areas

6). We think that Altiplano period burial practices support the interpretation that Lupaqa political development was characterized by factional competition. It is expected that if the Lupaqa had been politically unified, then chullpa burial towers would have been restricted to either a royal cemetery or used by a limited number of ruling lineages. Instead, even though specific groups of chullpas differ in number, size, and labor cost, and though they tend to cluster in higher numbers near fortified sites, they are found throughout the Lupaqa territory. Judging from the masonry techniques used to construct fancy chullpas, and the ceramics associated with these chullpas, many of the largest examples were built during the Late Horizon, and some are what Stanish calls redressed chullpas—igloo-shaped chullpas initially constructed in the Altiplano period that were rebuilt and faced with cut stones after the Inca conquest (Stanish 2003).

If chullpas are the material expression of the economic power and the level of political prestige of their builders, then the wide distribution and high number of chullpas documented throughout the western lake region indicates that chullpa building was not restricted to only a few elite groups. That the majority of large chullpas constructed with cut stones likely date to the Late Horizon suggests that political prestige and power afforded to local leaders during the Altiplano period was more difficult to achieve and maintain than previously. Mortuary remains at Altiplano period sites that do not have a Late Horizon component consist of poorly constructed igloo chullpas and/or a series of slab-cist or cist tombs—types which do not appear to convey major status differences between the individuals or groups of individuals contained in them. It was only later, perhaps as the result of Inca incursions into the region or ameliorating climatic conditions, that status differences became more pronounced, and the Lupaqa took on the level of political centralization indicated in the ethnohistorical documents.

CONCLUSIONS

We offer several important observations in our conclusion. First, climatic conditions beginning in the terminal Middle Horizon and lasting well into the Altiplano period led to a landscape characterized by social and political instability. Responses to the deterioration of the Tiwanaku state and climatic downturn that occurred in this period included the abandonment of Tiwanaku political centers and agricultural systems, a dispersal of the population from large centers across the landscape, competition over available resources, and increased economic focus on animal husbandry. We see the increased settlement density, and the fact that the largest and most architecturally complex fortified sites developed within the agro-pastoral zone, as an indication that animal husbandry played a critical role in the Altiplano period political economy. A shift to an increased focus on animal husbandry would be consistent with variable climate conditions because animals can be moved to wherever water is available, and it is fairly easy to collect water in ponds. Likewise, many fortified sites have permanent or semipermanent springs where water can be drawn.

The social and political landscape reflected in the Altiplano period settlement pattern, both in the Juli-Pomata and Chucuito survey areas and elsewhere (Arkush, Chapter 14, this volume; Arkush 2001) is a fluid one, characterized by constantly shifting alliances, competition, and warfare between small-scale political groups. The intensity of warfare and conflict between different groups was probably varied. During some periods, warfare might have been characterized by hit-and-run raids, which do not require much organizational complexity to initiate or to defend against. As a response to this kind of threat, people built and used local refuge sites for protection. When threatened by larger groups, the populations living near local refuge sites would band together for protection in the larger fortified sites. Although the construction and use of major fortified sites implies a higher organizational complexity than does the use of local refuge sites, architectural layouts in major fortified sites suggests their use by heterogeneous groups rather than groups with a well-developed social hierarchy (Frye 1997a).

Although there are differences in the size and number of structures at major fortified sites, within the Lupaqa territory as a whole no one site can be considered a political capital. Instead, as the systematic survey and reconnaissance data show, the pattern of small habitation sites located near fortified sites is one that is repeated throughout the Lupaqa territory. The high number of similar fortified and refuge sites, the nature and wide distribution of chullpa burials, and the pattern of locally developed ceramic assemblages in the western Lake Titicaca area indicate the existence of many small-scale polities. At least during most of the Altiplano period, these polities, though they may have been periodically aligned with their immediate neighbors, do not appear to have been under the direction of a centralized leader. However, by the end of the Altiplano period, major fortified sites had become the focus of ritual feasting and political activity going beyond their initial function as refuge centers. For instance, Altiplano period decorated ceramics are found in the highest concentrations in major fortified sites, sometimes in burials, and almost never in unfortified habitation sites. The ceramic component at these major fortified sites is composed of a high frequency of crudely decorated bowl forms, large serving pots, and liquid containers that probably were part of local feasting ceremonies. Although we consider fortified sites to have been important political centers, accession to leadership roles in these peer polities does not appear to have been institutionalized. By the end of the Altiplano period, large fortified sites probably became the centers of political and economic activity, most likely headed by an emerging elite group, which expanded its political and economic influence through feasting ceremonies and political alliances.

Despite the appearance of large fortified sites across the Lupaqa landscape, the complexity attributed to the Lupaqa in several ethnohistorical documents appears to be due more to the effects of Inca imperial expansion into the region than to internal political development during the Altiplano period. At present there are no archaeological indicators to suggest the existence of a Lupaqa king, a Lupaqa capital, or a unified Lupaqa confederation during the Altiplano period. These findings differ from the view contained in ethnohistorical documents, which suggest a politically unified Lupaqa. Instead, the Altiplano period Lupaqa appeared to have been comprised of a series of small-scale peer polities who competed among themselves.

12.

The Cave Burial from Molino-Chilacachi

Edmundo de la Vega, Kirk L. Frye, and Tiffiny Tung

THIS CHAPTER PRESENTS the preliminary results of a rescue operation conducted at the cave burial site of Molino-Chilacachi. Pertaining to the Late Intermediate or Altiplano period (AD 1100–1450), the Molino-Chilacachi site, along with other recently discovered cave burials, enables us to define a new burial tradition within the western Lake Titicaca region. The study of funerary traditions continues to provide archaeologists with valuable information about ethnic identity and ideological systems and is traditionally used to define the level of social ranking within and between different social groups.

Three basic tomb types are defined for the western Titicaca Basin: subterranean cist tombs, below-ground or partially above-ground slab-cist tombs, and *chullpa* burial towers (Hyslop 1977a; M. Tschopik 1946). While multiple burials may be found in all types, in general cist tombs are primarily associated with individual interments, with slab-cist and chullpas more frequently containing multiple burials (Cieza de León 1984 [1553], 1985 [1553]; Cobo 1964 [1653]; Hyslop 1976, 1977a; Ponce Sanginés 1993; Rydén 1947; M. Tschopik 1946). Hyslop (1977a) suggested a chronological dimension to the appearance and use of different burial traditions, with below-ground burials preceding above-ground ones. He speculated that the use of a particular tomb type may have served to delimit territorial boundaries as well as to signal the relative status of those interred, such that larger above-ground tombs may have served as a visual repertoire for displaying relative status position. The appearance of chullpas, which show greater labor costs than in earlier periods for burials during the Altiplano and (especially) Late Horizon, bears out this observation. Our understanding of the social and political importance of different burial traditions within the circum-Titicaca region is substantially enhanced by the recent study of several cave burials. Additionally, material from the Molino-Chilacachi cave burial helps clarify enigmatic references to burial practices contained in the Aymara dictionary of Ludovico Bertonio (1956 [1612]).

Located approximately 50 km southeast of the city of Puno, the site of Molino-Chilacachi is part of a topographic feature of Tertiary period age comprised of the Puno, Maure, and Tacaza geologic groups. Characterized by a combination of rounded and flat-topped peaks, this mountain chain forms the southeastern edge of the Río Grande Basin, the Río Grande being one of the principal rivers of the Río Ilave drainage system (Figure 12.1). The basin floor contains an extensive pampa bordered to the west by the mountains rising along the western edge of Lake Titicaca. Although the ecology of the region is complex, characterized by warmer microclimates in selected sheltered areas, in general, agriculture in the region is limited in scope. The primary economic activity pursued in the region today is a form of transhumant animal husbandry. During the wet season, animals are grazed throughout the pampa, becoming increasingly concentrated in river channels and in natural and artificial depressions until the dry season, when herds are moved to higher drainage basins and *bofedales* (swamps) in the surrounding mountains.

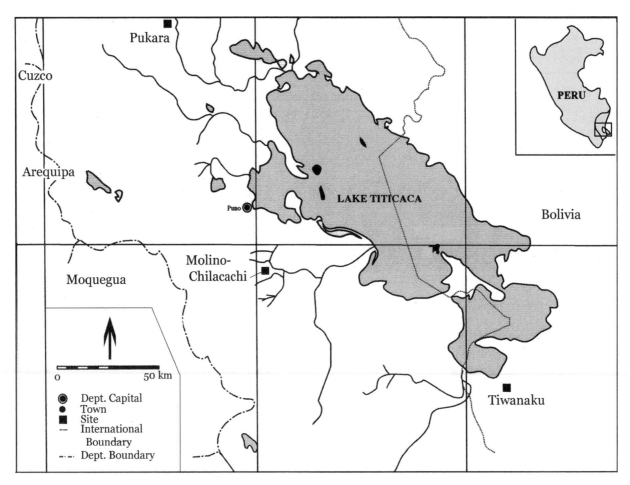

Figure 12.1 Map of the Lake Titicaca Basin with Molino-Chilacachi indicated

THE LOCATION AND SPATIAL LAYOUT OF THE CAVE

The cave is situated at an elevation of 4045 m above sea level on the northeastern side of a flat-topped mountain named Cerro Pukara, whose uppermost geological layer is a horizontal volcanic tuff measuring between 5 and 10 m in thickness. Similar to other mountains in the immediate area, the top of Cerro Pukara forms a flat mesa containing typical Altiplano period architectural remains. Architectural features at the site include boundary walls and circular stone foundations (similar to those found at other local fortified or refuge sites containing well-built circular chullpa burial towers), located along its southern base. Compared to other nearby Altiplano period sites—including Nunumaraca, Cutimbo, and Chaata, all of which are large ma-

jor fortified sites (see Frye and de la Vega, Chapter 11, this volume)—Cerro Pukara is a small refuge area, characterized by sparsely distributed architectural remains. Because the cave is located below the mesa top at the junction of the hill slope and the volcanic layer, which is away from standing architecture, the temporal relationship between the two areas is unclear.

The cave was entered through a small opening measuring 90 x 40 cm, but the original entrance is oriented to the northeast and measures 2.2 m in width. The original entrance remains closed and is concealed by a large and possibly intentional rock fall. The volcanic tuff forming the cave walls is an excellent insulator, moderating the high diurnal temperature extremes of the region. During the month of May, when readings were taken, the relative humidity inside the cave was between 83 and 88%, with an interior temperature of 9.8° Celsius. Measuring 14.5 m in overall length, the cave varies between 1.5 and 4 m in width, with variations in elevation between 1 m in the entrance area and 5 m in the main vault. The burial chamber is divided into three basic areas: Area I is a small space that includes the original opening; Area II corresponds to the central and largest part of the cave; and Area III, a narrow and constricted space, extends approximately 3 m beyond Area II to the end of the cave (Figures 12.2 and 12.3). A study of the distribution of grave goods and mummies inside the cave resulted in the definition of three separate burial contexts designated A, B, and C.

Context A, a surface level extending from the back end of the cave to near the opening, is made up of a mixture of mummy bundles, unwrapped bodies, crania, and whole and fragmented ceramics. Although it was clear that looting activities had substantially altered the original positioning of the surface materials, Context A units (especially Units 8 through 11), were the most intact of all surface material. Context B is defined from material recovered from Units 4, 5, 6, and 7. Specifically, it contained the jumbled remains of unarticulated crania, vertebral elements, and long bones mixed together with broken pottery and fragmented basket and textile pieces. The extremely mixed nature of the majority of materials within Context B suggests that it is a secondary burial feature, partially overlaid by Context A. Although in some areas it was difficult to distinguish a clear boundary between Context C and those overlaying it, Context C corresponds to a subsurface level below Contexts A and B. Context C may correspond to an earlier burial event, with additional mummies and artifacts embedded in a soft matrix comprised of a mixture of dried grass, animal dung, and dust.

A small test excavation into Context C was initiated, but due to logistical constraints, we were unable to determine the depth of the deposit. Based on a test probe we made along the edge of the cave, however, we estimate that Context C, especially in the Area 2 units, may be between 70 cm to 1 m thick. A more thorough investigation of this layer remains a top priority for future research.

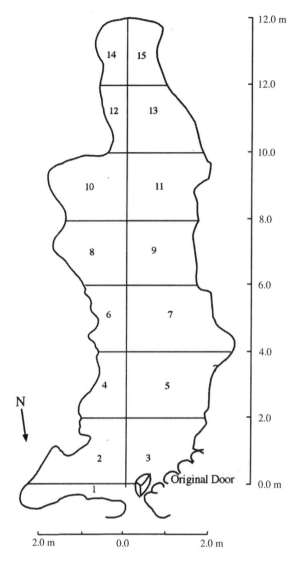

FIGURE 12.2. Cave layout with unit numbers

MUMMY BUNDLES

Although lithics, ceramics, wooden tools, and basketry were recovered, mummy bundles represent the single most impressive artifact category recovered from the site. Bundles contain individuals flexed in a fetal position, fully encased by *Stipa ichu* cords of variable thickness, intertwined around the body to form a cocoon-like bag. A total of sixty-two mummy bundles were recovered. Of these, forty-eight contained human remains, while others were cut open by looters, and still others remained only as fragments.

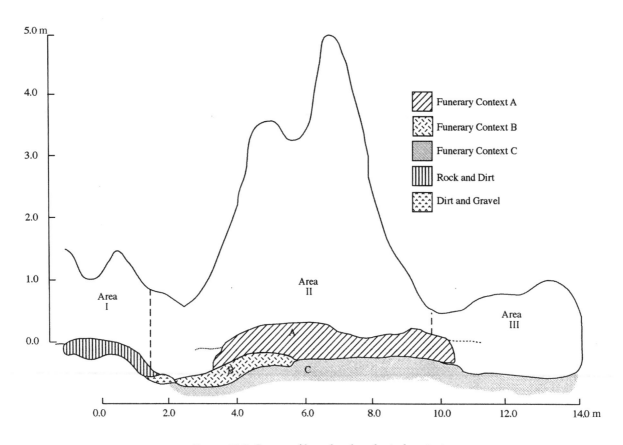

FIGURE 12.3. Cave profile and archaeological contexts

Concentration of mummy bundles was highest in Areas II and III. It is possible that the examples found in Area I were displaced during looting episodes (Figure 12.4). Reports by community members, who first saw the cave when it was opened, stated that the mummies had been placed in an upright position and that Area III had been filled with upright bundles. There is some independent indication that the bundles may have originally been placed in a vertical position. The position of mummies in units 8 and 9 suggests that the bundles there were upright but fell over, either because of their own weight, because of the addition of additional bundles over time, or from animal disturbances. Although some areas in the cave appeared to be more intact than others, in general the mixed spatial relationship between mummies and other artifacts made it very difficult to associate specific grave goods with individual bodies.

Casement Material and Braiding Types

Locally referred to as *Chiiwah*, *Stipa ichu* is a common grass native to the Altiplano, which, when rubbed together and intertwined, produces strong and durable cords that are used today for a variety of household purposes. Two basic encasing techniques were used to enclose the cadavers at Molino-Chilacachi. Type 1 consists of a thick horizontal element, coiled from a tightly wound base upward around the body. Between twenty and sixty thinner cords were attached to the base, with a hitch forming two cords that were used as the vertical element. One of the cords ran along the exterior of the body, looping at every other horizontal row binding the interior cord, which ran straight up the inside (Figure 12.5). Differentiated by the space between horizontal and vertical elements, Type 1 includes both a tight and loose variant. Consisting of a simple over-under interlacing of

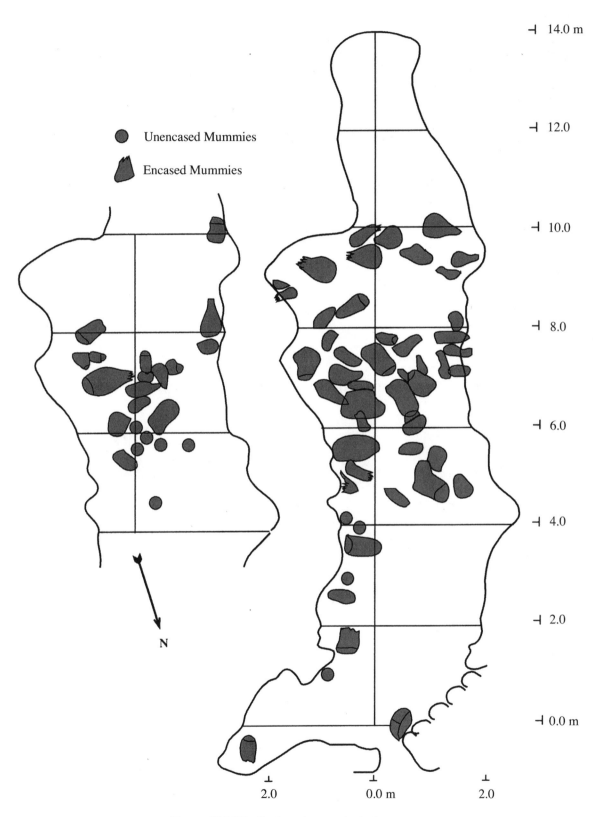

FIGURE 12.4. Distribution of mummies in the cave

horizontal and vertical cords, the Type 2 technique is less complex and more variable in quality than the Type 1 technique (Figure 12.5). Braiding quality was variable; some bodies were tightly encased with very closely spaced cords, while others were loosely enclosed with large gaps between the cords. Future research may indicate if casement quality can be correlated with gender, age, and/or social status categories. The term *chullpa*—referred to by Bertonio (1956 [1612]:93) in his Aymara dictionary as an "[e]ntiero o serón donde se metían sus difuntos…"—likely represents these *Stipa inchu* casements and not the burial towers so prevalent on the Altiplano landscape.

THE HUMAN POPULATION

The human remains from Molino-Chilacachi represent one of the best preserved and complete skeletal populations in existence from the Peruvian Altiplano. Skeletal data were collected in 1995 to document demographic profiles, developmental health status, evidence of trauma, and cranial deformation practices. At least 166 individuals were recovered from the surface of the cave. Of these, 143 were removed, including sixty-two individuals either within or associated with ichu casings and another eighty-one individuals represented by partially commingled skeletal elements. Of the eighty-one crania studied, fifty-nine were

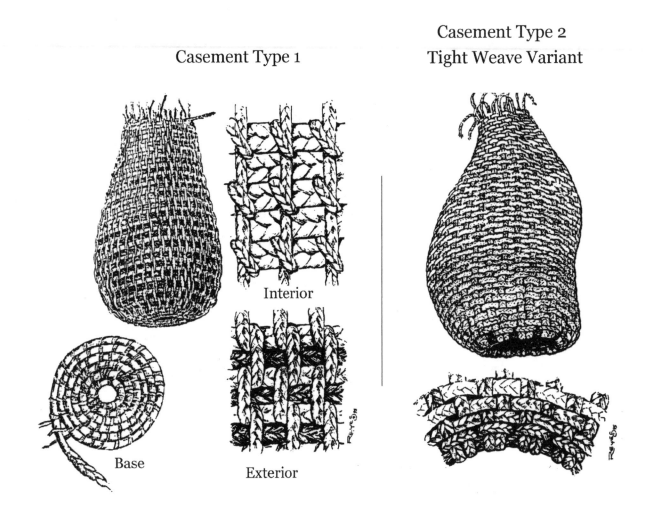

FIGURE 12.5. Casement types

complete or partially complete, ten were still covered in soft tissue and articulated with postcranial remains, and twelve were fragmented.

The age-at-death profile of the skeletal population shows that more than a third died between birth and seven years of age (Table 12.1). This frequency is similar to that of contemporaneous (Late Intermediate period) populations from the nearby Osmore-Moquegua drainage, where infants and children (individuals 0–10 years of age) comprise 36% of the skeletal population at both the sites of Estuquiña in Moquegua (Williams 1990) and San Geronimo in the Osmore Valley (Burgess 1999). In contrast, the contemporaneous Osmore Valley sites of Chiribaya Alta and El Yaral have a higher rate of infant and child deaths (deaths of individuals aged 0–10 years), ranging from 43 to 47%, respectively (Burgess 1999). The latter age-at-death distributions appear to be more characteristic of prehistoric populations, leading Burgess (1999) to suggest that there may be a sampling bias at San Geronimo whereby infants and children are underrepresented. Perhaps a sampling bias is also present among the Molino-Chilacachi sample, resulting from differential preservation, mortuary practices that limited infant/child burials in the cave, or recovery bias. Conversely, the age-at-death profile could be representative of the once-living population, which would suggest that Molina-Chilacachi and Estuquiña populations shared similar population structures, both of which differed from those at Chiribaya Alta and El Yaral.

Skeletal sex was assigned based on the morphology of partial and complete pelvic bones. Among the thirty adults whose sex could be determined, fourteen (47%) were male and sixteen (53%) were female/possible female, indicating a roughly equal sex distribution among the cave burial population (Table 12.2). There were four adults whose sex could not be determined.

The presence of *criba orbitalia* and porotic hyperostosis suggests that some of the population suffered from iron deficiency anemia during childhood (see Stuart-Macadam 1987). The anemia may have developed as a result of malnutrition, intestinal parasites that led to diarrheal disease, or, what is most likely, a combination of both.

Fifteen percent of the adult population displayed cranial wounds, all of which were located on the frontal parietal bones. The anteriorly placed wounds suggest that they were sustained in face-to-face combat. Several head wounds were healed, indicating that the victims did not die as a result of the head injury. In contrast, two adults displayed perimortem cranial trauma, suggesting that a blow to the skull may have resulted in death.

Based on an extensive analysis of cranial deformation styles from cemeteries on the south central coast, Lisa Hoshower, Jane Buikstra, Paul Goldstein, and Anne Webster (Hoshower et al. 1995) concluded that models correlating deformation styles with broad geographic regions (altiplano-coast) are too simplistic. Their study found that "…the patterns

TABLE 12.1. Sex of individuals from Molino-Chilacachi

Sex	Number of Individuals	%
Male	14	27
Possible male	0	0
Female	14	27
Possible female	2	4
Prepubescent	13	25
Sex undetermined	9	17
Total	52	100

TABLE 12.2. Age range of individuals from Molino-Chilacachi

Age Group	Number of Individuals	%
Infant (0–2 years)	18	22
Child (2–7 years)	10	12
Adolescent (8–14)	5	6
Subadult (15–21 years)	4	5
Adults (22–40)	32	40
Elderly (> 41 years)	12	15
Total	81	100

of cranial deformation within the Omo M10 cemetery complex clearly emphasize homogeneity within individual cemeteries and heterogeneity across cemeteries" (Hoshower et al. 1995:145). In contrast, the Molino-Chilacachi cave burials exhibit at least two, possibly three, deformation styles within a single cemetery context. Of the eighty-one crania examined, sixty display cranial deformation. The most common is the tabular oblique style (39 cases), which is a type of fronto-occipital deformation (Buikstra and Ubelaker 1994) and is associated with both males and females. The second deformation style is also a fronto-occipital modification, but of the tabular erect form (10 cases). This type is primarily observed on infant crania, suggesting that the deformations could have been accidental (i.e., from cradle boards), rather than intentional. A third type, designated simply as "other," is characterized by nearly normal skulls exhibiting pressure marks on the frontal bone and parietal bosses (11 cases). Although still encased, a detailed study of the remaining mummies might help explain whether the deformation categories can be correlated with age, sex, social status, and ethnicity, or whether they pertain to changes in deformation style through time.

The skeletal data suggest that the Molino-Chilacachi population suffered from childhood iron deficiency anemia as well as skeletal trauma that may have been linked to interpersonal violence. This pattern may partially be explained by economic and social instability arising from long-term periodic drought episodes documented for the Altiplano period throughout the Titicaca Basin (Ortloff and Kolata 1992; Thompson et al. 1988; and see Chapter 11, this volume).

MATERIAL REMAINS FROM THE SITE

Several whole ceramic vessels were recovered from the cave, including large double- and smaller single-handled pitchers, cooking pots, and serving bowls. The majority of the ceramics were poorly made utilitarian wares characterized by highly friable pastes and surface finishes of variable quality. Decorative styles were more common on bowl forms and were similar to those found on the Sillustani brown-on-cream and black-on-red wares, the Collao black-on-red ware, and the Allita Amaya wares described by M. Tschopik (1946:23, 26, 34). Interestingly, the ceramic component bears little resemblance to the Pukarani styles defined in the Lupaqa region farther to the south (de la Vega 1990; Frye 1994, 1997a). Three radiocarbon dates from the site were processed. Two samples were carbonized material from ceramics and are derived from Units 5 and 7. One sample is a textile fragment from Unit 8. The two radiocarbon dates from the ceramic scrapings both date to approximately AD 1300 ± 18 and the date from the textile is AD 1350 ± 55. These dates place the use of the cave firmly in the Altiplano period.

The presence of a hallucinogenic kit in the cave, similar in style to those defined from the Bolivian site of Niño Korin (Wassén 1972) and those defined from burial contexts from the Northern Chilean coastal region (Torres 1985), represents an extraordinary find. Unfortunately, none of the recovered items was directly associated with any specific individual or came from any one collection unit. Hallucinogenic paraphernalia included cane tubes closed at one end that contained leather-tipped sticks and/or spines. One tube contained the residue of an unidentified, white powder. Wassén (1972:43-44) reports similar tubes from the Niño Korin site, which he suggests may have been used as part of a kit for administering enemas. Other specimens from the complex included leather containers, a bone spoon, quills, and a small wooden mortar. Also recovered were an incised wooden snuff tablet bearing the central figure of a raptorial bird, as well as snuff tubes, one with polychrome incised designs portraying a bird figure and geometric motifs (Figure 12.6). Taken as a whole, the materials probably formed one complete hallucinogenic ingestion kit. Stylistically, the snuff tablet and incised tube are derived from Tiwanaku motifs and were likely produced during the Middle Horizon. However, their association with Altiplano period ceramics suggests that the tray and tubes were curated for use over a long period of time.

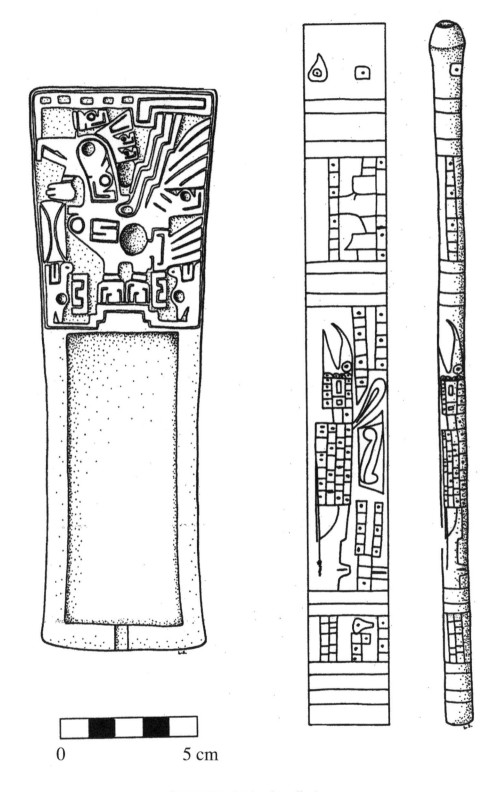

0   5 cm

FIGURE 12.6. *Rapé* and snuff tube

SPATIAL DISTRIBUTION OF CAVE BURIALS

At present, the distribution of cave burials in the south central Andes is not well documented. There are, however, several references to multiple burials in natural openings, including caves, niches, grottoes, and rock shelters throughout the region. In the northern area of Omasuyu, Erland Nordenskiöld (1953), Heath MacBain (1959), and Stig Rydén (1947) describe burials in rock openings, while in the Callaway sector to the southeast, sites including Niño Korin have been studied by Enrique Oblitas (cited by Wassén 1972). Several publications refer to burials in rock cavities in the Mallku territory to the south (Arellano López and Berberián 1981; Arellano López and Kuljis 1986; Berberián and Arellano López 1980). Oscar Ayca (1995) reports the presence of funerary grottoes from the Colla site of Sillustani. Limited almost exclusively to the agro-pastoral zone located well inland from the lake shore, at least thirty cave burials have been located in the Lupaqa territory. Nine cave burials were found in the Chucuito-Cutimbo survey zone and southward into the Río Ilave and Río Huenque Basins, and Mark Aldenderfer (personal communication) located another twenty cave burials, some associated with presumably Archaic period cave art. Significantly, no cave burials have yet been found within the Juli-Pomata survey area farther to the south.

DISCUSSION

We offer important observations concerning cave burials in the circum-Titicaca Basin region. The presence of burials in natural cavities from Archaic period contexts (Aldenderfer 1990) and the association of cave burials with cave art support the interpretation that burying the dead in natural cavities and caves has a long, if not well-documented, history in the region. Oblitas's (cited by Wassén 1972:14) mention of a cave with multiple burials containing funerary material similar to that from Niño Korin may indicate that a cave burial tradition continued through Tiwanaku III times; but at present, there is no clear evidence that the practice was maintained in Tiwanaku IV–V times. Although habitation

sites spanning the early Archaic through the Late Horizon have been documented in the Ilave drainage basin and in the Chucuito region, as yet few burials from the pre-Altiplano period have been found. The only exceptions are the Tiwanaku-related materials from the Molino-Chilacachi site and a cave burial with Tiwanaku-style sherds found in the Ilave River drainage (Cynthia Klink, personal communication 1996). An overwhelming association between cave burial sites and Altiplano period ceramics indicates that it was during this time period that cave burials were most common. At present, there is no evidence that cave burials were used in the Late Horizon or in the Colonial period, although de la Vega believes that the secondary burial context from Molino-Chilacachi may have resulted from the movement of burials from other sites to Molino-Chilacachi during the Colonial period destruction of indigenous burial and ritual centers by Spanish missionary zealots.

In the Lupaqa territory, with the exception of one cave burial in view of the lake, cave burials are primarily found in the agro-pastoral zone located away from the lakeshore. Although this geographic zone contains diverse and highly variable microclimates, it is primarily inhabited by groups whose economic livelihood centers on pastoralism. Based on the distribution of cave burials within this zone, there appears to be a strong correlation between cave burials and these pastoral groups. It remains to be seen whether the practice of cave burials can be used as an ethnic marker for a pastoral lifestyle, and whether the practice was continuously used through time.

The collapse of a state level political system is often coupled with radical realignments of political power, characterized by a shift from centralized bureaucratic structures to ones centered at the local level. We speculate that a resurgence of cave burials and the use of collective burials in discrete cemeteries during the Altiplano period are tied to the collapse of the Tiwanaku state and to the need for diverse and newly established corporate and political groups to express their identities in territorially defined geographic boundaries. Group burials, then, are a tangible expression of a shift throughout the Titicaca Basin from more complex and centralized political systems, whose burial practices emphasized individuals, to smaller scale and localized political groups. These group burials may signal the emergence of pastoral groups as important political entities.

The practice of preserving the bodies of community members in a central locale, as in the case of the Molino-Chilacachi cave burial, represents a social mechanism for strengthening ethnic or corporate identity through time. The fact that many cave burial sites are difficult to find and are not easily visible on the landscape suggests that their use may be independent of tradi-

tional territorial demarcation behavior. Rather, their use may reflect internally focused ritual behavior of the pastoral groups in the region. We suggest that cave burials represent an early form of collective burial, a system that was replaced through time by the more visible forms of above-ground slab-cist tombs and chullpa burial towers. These burial forms developed as authority became more centralized and the need to express political power and define territorial boundaries intensified between increasingly competitive Altiplano period groups.

13.

The Inca Occupation of the Lake Titicaca Region

Kirk L. Frye

THIS CHAPTER DESCRIBES the effect of the Inca expansion into the Lake Titicaca region, focusing on the Colla, Lupaqa, and Pacajes ethnic groups. I review the available archaeological data from these regions and discuss the relevant ethnohistorical information about the Inca administration. The Titicaca Basin was considered an important area to the expanding Inca Empire for several reasons. First, it was important from the standpoint of labor availability because it possessed one of the more densely settled populations of the central Andes at the time (Cieza de Léon 1984:353 [1553:Ch. 99]). Second, the economic resources of the Titicaca Basin were considerable. In good years, the agricultural productivity of the region was quite high, and the region was considered the "breadbasket" of the Altiplano during the Colonial period. The wealth represented by animal herds was one of the assets that impressed colonial tax assessors the most. Perhaps more importantly, the Titicaca Basin was important to the Inca from an ideological perspective, figuring prominently in the origin myths of the Inca royal lineage, with the Islands of the Sun and the Moon representing important pilgrimage sites for the Inca elite (Arkush, Chapter 14, this volume; Arkush 2000; Bauer and Stanish 2001; Stanish and Bauer 2004).

As elsewhere in the empire, Inca political organizers took into account military, economic, and ideological factors while incorporating a subject region. The Lake Titicaca region is part of Collasuyu, the southern quarter of Tawantinsuyu. Catherine Julien (1983:28), using ethnohistorical documents, demonstrates that during the late Inca period the Lake Titicaca area of Colla-suyu was comprised of at least four provinces: Colla, Lupaqa, Pacajes, and the Copacabana sanctuary. Of these, the Colla, Lupaqa, and Pacajes were incorporated into, and administered by, the Inca Empire as separate ethnic and political entities. Because of historical circumstances and the level of pre-Inca political complexity, each of these regions experienced the effects of Inca administration differently. This chapter discusses these differences and demonstrates that Inca influence in the Lake Titicaca region was complex and intensive, and reached far into the local cultures. For the Colla region in the north basin, military concerns affected Inca administrative decisions. For the Lupaqa area, economic and religious factors were paramount, while in the Pacajes area to the south, at least near the lake, the Inca administrative system appears to have been less intrusive than in the west and north.

Early written documents, detailed accounts of which are reviewed excellently by Catherine Julien (1983) and John Hyslop (1976), provide a basic account of the political landscape encountered by the Inca when they expanded into the Lake Titicaca region sometime around AD 1450. The most cited early accounts are those compiled by Bernabé Cobo (1979:140 [1653:Bk. 12 Chapter 13]), and Pedro Cieza de León (1959 [1553]:Bk. 2 Chs. 41–43). According to these accounts, at the time of Inca expansion into the Titicaca Basin, the Colla region was occupied by a hereditary ruler named Zapana who ruled from a regional capital at Hatuncolla and who was engaged in a bitter rivalry with Cari, his Lupaqa counterpart from the Lupaqa capital at

Chucuito. The documents portray a region with hereditary rulers in control of large territories and armies, features which suggest a relatively high level of political complexity. Archaeological research, however, demonstrates the inaccuracies contained in these documents, showing in fact that the Inca encountered a region where the political landscape was extremely fragmented, a condition that characterized the area for much of the Late Intermediate period (AD 1100–1450) (see Arkush 2000, Arkush, Chapter 14, this volume; Frye and de la Vega, Chapter 11, this volume; Frye 1997a; and Stanish et al. 1997). With the possible exception of the Pacajes region, where there is less evidence of warfare, most of the western and northern basin was characterized by endemic conflict between small-scale polities. These groups may have managed at times to coalesce into larger political and military entities, but they never seem to have developed the level of complexity portrayed in early ethnohistorical documents. What, then, did the Inca find and how did they organize the Titicaca Basin groups during their imperial occupation of the region?

THE COLLAS

Much of what is known about the Collas is the result of Julien's (1982, 1983, 1993) excellent research at Hatuncolla and from important ethnohistorical documents (especially Cieza de León 1959 [1553] and Cobo 1979 [1653]). Arkush shows that the Colla at the time of Inca contact were probably comprised of a series of small-scale competing groups that were engaged in constant warfare. Oscar Ayca's (1995) work at the Sillustani provides insight into the site's history and burial traditions. Although there are many gaps in our knowledge of the Colla region, it is possible to glean from the available resources a basic understanding of how the region changed in the Late Horizon.

In general, it appears that Inca administration of the Colla region was influenced by military concerns. Cobo outlines a relatively straightforward account of the Inca expansion into the Titicaca Basin. He places this expansion during the reign of Pachacuti Inca, who wanted to include the Titicaca Basin into his realm:

...he sent a brave captain named Apu Condemayata, and the Inca ordered him to stop and wait in Luuacache, which is on the border of the provinces of Collao; the cacique of these provinces was very powerful...[extending]...up to the town of Hatuncolla, where he resided [Cobo 1979 (1653):139].

This document describes how the head of the Colla, hearing of the Inca's intention to expand into his territory, raised his forces to do battle but was beaten by the Lupaqa. Perhaps because the Colla resisted Inca expansion, the Inca radically reorganized the region by establishing many administrative provinces, setting up a militarily oriented capital, resettling the population, and reorganizing Colla access to coastal valley resources. Following the Inca road system through the region, the Colla province was comprised of Urosuyu and Umasuyo divisions, which were further delineated into eight smaller territorial provinces. These included Azángaro, which was organized as an Inca estate, and others, such as the Chiquicache province, which may have been a royal estate holding the state religion (Julien 1993). Julien (1983:246, 1993) notes that the resettlement policies were instituted by moving people away from fortified sites and by moving some of the population out of the area, some to Arequipa, and others to the eastern lowlands. Part of the population was also settled in new towns such as Cupi in order to produce durable goods.

Another effect of Inca administration of the Colla was to reduce the Colla economic ties to coastal valley resources. While there is evidence—in the form of Colla-derived ceramic types (Stanish 1991, 1992:158)—of a Colla presence in Pacific watershed valleys during the Late Intermediate period (LIP), this access appears to have ended during the Late Horizon. Coastal valley areas that had an LIP Colla presence appear to have come under the control of the Lupaqa during the Late Horizon, a change signaled by the appearance and wide distribution of Lupaqa and Chuquito polychrome style ceramics at important Late Horizon coastal sites (Stanish 1992; van Buren et al. 1993). Because the Colla initially resisted the Inca expansion and later rebelled against its authority, the Colla region was organized and administered to reflect military concerns, more so than were other regions in the Lake Titicaca Basin. We see the many territorial divisions, the forced resettlement policies whereby people were moved from hilltop areas either to more easily controlled areas or out of the region altogether, the establishment of Hatuncolla as a military center, and the stripping of Colla elites from control of coastal resources. In general, the Inca occupation of the Colla region contrasted starkly with the Inca occupation of the Lupaqa zone.

THE LUPAQA

More is known about the Lupaqa area during the Late Horizon than any other province in the Lake Titicaca region. The Lupaqa area has a long history of archeological research, in part because there are many important references to the area in ethnohistorical documents. Both Pedro Cieza de León and Bernabé Cobo provide excellent early accounts of the Lupaqa. Garci Diez de San Miguel's (1964 [1567]) *Visita* gives invaluable insights into the Lupaqa political and economic organization in the early Colonial period. The richness of ethnohistorical documents that describe the Lupaqa has inspired many important theoretical discussions concerning zonal complementarity (Murra 1968, 1972; Stanish 1992), the nature of the Inca decimal system (Julien 1982), and labor organization under the Inca state (Murra 1985; Stanish 1997).

The Lupaqa region also has a rich history of archaeological research. Early site reports were published for important Lupaqa sites by José María Franco Inojosa and Alejandro González (1936) and by Emilio Vásquez (1939). In the 1940s, Marion Tschopik (1946) defined early Lupaqa ceramic types and burial styles from around Chucuito. In the 1970s, John Hyslop (1976, 1977b) conducted an unsystematic survey of sites located in Lupaqa territory, defined burial types, and documented where the Inca road passed through the region (Hyslop 1984). Beginning in 1988, the Project Lupaqa, under the direction of Charles Stanish, began systematic research near the town of Juli, including excavations at the Lupaqa site of Pukara Juli (de la Vega 1990). Beginning in 1990, the Proyecto Lu-

paqa initiated a systematic full coverage survey covering an area measuring 360 km^2 in the heart of Lupaqa territory (Stanish et al. 1997). Subsequently, in 1995, the author conducted another full coverage survey, covering an area measuring approximately 200 km^2 and centered on Chucuito, the Late Horizon Lupaqa capital. The wealth of systematic survey data from the Lupaqa zone provides a very clear picture of Inca occupation of the region.

In contrast to the Colla region, ethnohistorical documents portray the Lupaqa as more receptive to Inca domination of the region. Cieza de León (1959) details a history whereby Cari, a hereditary Lupaqa ruler, defeats his Colla rival, Zapana, and unites a series of Lupaqa towns under his control prior to the arrival of the Inca. Cobo's (1979 [1653]) account differs somewhat from that of Cieza de León. Although he indicates that a peace was brokered with Cari by the Inca, he also suggests that the Lupaqa were not a unified group. Cobo describes how Pachacuti went to Chucuito, where the:

> …cacique of the nation of the Lupaqa Indians, who resided in Chucuito, was just as powerful as the cacique of Collao, but he took to sounder advice, because he received the Inca in peace and turned over his state to him…. [O]n his expedition the Inca subjected all the towns and nations surrounding the great Lake Titicaca, which on the one side includes the provinces of Lupaqa and Pacasa Indians…along with the Islands of the aforesaid lake which was densely populated at the time [Cobo 1979 (1653):140].

Cobo includes in his description what seems to be an account of battles that took place between Pachacuti and other tribes that he encountered along the shores of Lake Titicaca:

> Some of the towns defended themselves bravely, and they had many clashes with the Inca before they were subjugated. The Inca subjugated many of them to a relentless siege, and they built forts in order to defend themselves such as those at Caquingora and the one we see on a high hill near the town of Juli, which has five dry stone walls, one inside the other,

where the natives took refuge and fought for a long time in defending themselves . . . [Cobo 1979 (1653):140].

These accounts show that the Inca advance into the Lupaqa territory may have been contested, although there is no mention of conflict in the Chucuito area, a factor which might account for why Chucuito became the regional administrative center. The Lupaqa were administrated as a single territorial unit (with Chucuito as its capital), along with six other regional centers established along the Inca road. Important economic and political changes in the Chucuito region during the Late Horizon are demonstrated by

the analysis of settlement data derived from the Chucuito-Cutimbo survey. The survey was designed to include a cross-section of the three ecological zones in the region (Figure 13.1), and in order to allow direct comparison with the Juli-Pomata survey, the Chucuito-Cutimbo survey followed the same methodology as that developed in the Juli-Pomata survey (Stanish et al. 1997) (Figure 13.2). Inca changes to the Lupaqa political landscape included an influx of people from others area, the resettlement of the local population toward lakeside sites, the abandonment of the majority of Altiplano period political centers, the founding of Chucuito as the seat of

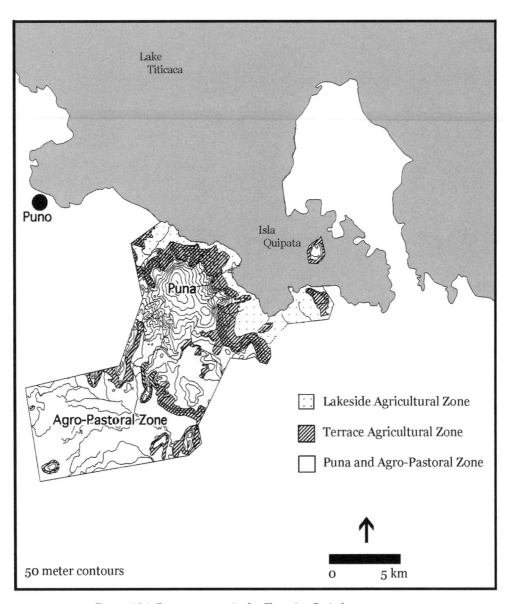

FIGURE 13.1. Resource zones in the Chucuito-Cutimbo survey area

regional administration, and the appearance of second-tier civil/ceremonial, administrative, and ritual sites. Evidence of Late Horizon economic reorganization of the Chucuito area includes the establishment of labor into specialized production towns, the building of roads, and the intensification of agricultural and pastoral systems.

A total of 110 Late Horizon habitation sites, occupying a total of 83.56 ha, comprise the Late Horizon settlement in the Chucuito-Cutimbo survey area (Figure 13.3). The number of Late Horizon habitations in the survey zone represents a 100% increase over the number in the preceding Altiplano period, with the overall area of habitation more than three times that of the preceding period (Table 13.1). Notably, a comparable pattern of site number and habitation area increase between the Late Horizon and

Altiplano period is reported from the Juli-Pomata region (Stanish et al. 1997:Table 3; Stanish 1997:205). The most profound changes indicated by these data are the dramatic increase in population, as represented by the change in site occupation area, and the increase in settlements on the lakeshore and in the terrace agricultural zones.

One of the most notable changes in the settlement pattern between the two periods was the abandonment of Altiplano period fortified sites. The survey located ten fortified sites, of which four are categorized as major fortified sites. They contained standing architecture, fortification walls, and abundant surface artifacts. Six minor or temporary refuge sites were also found, characterized by their small size, lack of standing architecture, and few surface artifacts

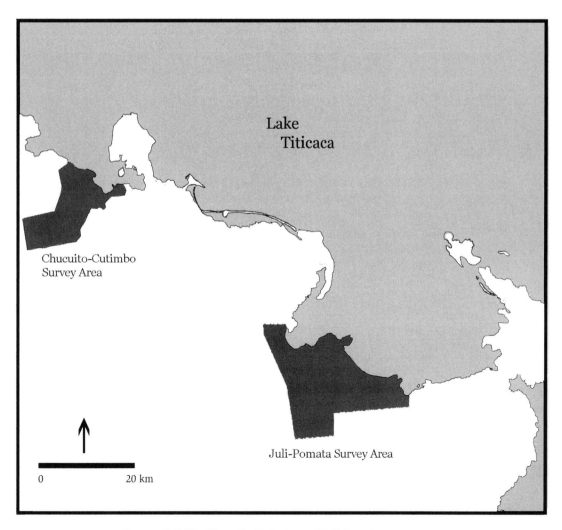

FIGURE 13.2. The Chucuito-Cutimbo and Juli-Pomata survey areas

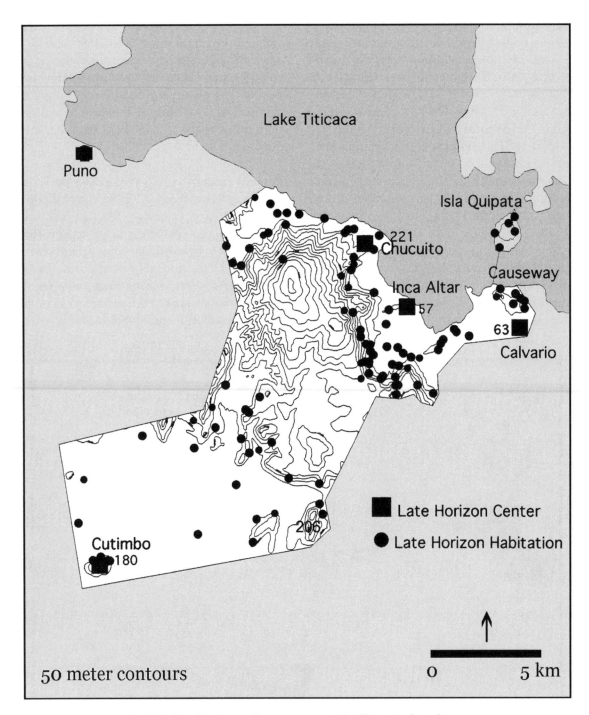

FIGURE 13.3. The Late Horizon settlement pattern in the Chucuito-Cutimbo survey area

(see Chapter 11, this volume). Most fortified sites in the survey area were abandoned during the Late Horizon.

Two previously reported lakeside fortified sites fell within the survey limits. Initially described by Hyslop (1976), Pukara Chucuito and Pukara Coata were abandoned as Altiplano period political centers, although the construction of cut-stone *chullpas* (burial towers) at the sites and their association with Late Horizon ceramics indicate continued use as ritual areas during the Inca period. Another major fortified site, Chaata (site number 206 in Figure 13.3), which is located in the agro-pastoral economic zone outside of Cutimbo, was also important during the Altiplano period, but was completely abandoned in

TABLE 13.1. Settlement pattern data from the Chucuito-Cutimbo and Juli-Pomata surveys

| | Chucuito-Cutimbo Area | | Juli-Pomata Area |
	Tiwanaku Period	Altiplano Period	Altiplano Period
Number of habitation sites	22	52	140
Total site area (ha)	11.85	26.93	74.16
Mean size of all sites (ha)	0.49	0.52	0.53
Mean elevation of all sites	3851	3931	3905
LAKESIDE AGRICULTURAL ZONE			
Total habitation sites	16	3	44
Total site area (ha)	8.67	0.63	21.04
Mean size of all sites (ha)	0.54	0.21	0.48
Percentage of total	72.58%	2.30%	28.00%
TERRACED AGRICULTURAL ZONE			
Total habitation sites	8	31	75
Total site area (ha)	3.25	15.45	42.64
Mean size of all sites (ha)	0.41	0.50	0.57
Percentage of total	27.42%	57.30%	57.00%
AGRO-PASTORAL ZONE/PUNA			
Total habitation sites	0	18	21
Total site area (ha)	0	10.85	10.48
Mean size of all sites (ha)	0	0.60	0.50
Percentage of total	0	40.4%	14.0%
REFUGE SITES	0	9	7
Approximate site area (ha)	0	14.98	6.82
FORTIFIED SITES	0	4	3
Approximate site area (ha)	0	43.0	> 50.0

the Late Horizon. An exception to the pattern of fortified site abandonment is Cutimbo (site number 180 in Figure 13.3), one of the largest fortified sites in the Lupaqa territory. Surface features—including Inca-style cut-stone chullpas, rectangular buildings, a central plaza, a large corral, and an abundance of decorated ceremonial Late Horizon ceramics—indicate that Cutimbo was an important site during the Inca period. Recent work at the site by the National Institute of Culture in Puno uncovered elaborate offerings associated with the construction of the largest chullpas there (Rolando Paredes, personal communication 2002). Because the large chullpas at Cutimbo are made with impressive examples of Inca-style masonry, Hyslop (1976:124) speculated that Cutimbo may have originally been the home of the Cari lineage during the Altiplano period and continued to

function during the Late Horizon as a burial ground for the Chucuito elite. Systematic surface collections at Cutimbo indicate a heavy predominance of Late Horizon decorated ceramics near the largest chullpas, which are in association with rectangular buildings and a central plaza area (Figure 11.5). The sheer size of the finely cut stone chullpas and the presence of highly stylized ceramics must have influenced Hyslop when he proposed his cemetery hypothesis (Hyslop 1976). Alternatively, I suggest that Cutimbo, in addition to its role as one of many Lupaqa elite cemeteries, functioned as a central place for organizing the considerable wealth represented by animals in the agro-pastoral zone. Since little is known about how pastoral groups were incorporated into the Inca Empire, it remains an important topic for future research.

Three important sites were founded during the Late Horizon in the Chucuito-Cutimbo survey zone. Chucuito (site number 221 in Figure 13.3) is by far the largest and most complex Late Horizon settlement in the Lupaqa territory. Containing two plazas, Chucuito was laid out in an orthogonal pattern, incorporating a radial plan (Hyslop 1990:196–197). One of the plazas contains the remains of an Inca structure known as Inca Uyu (M. Tschopik 1946). Inca Uyu is the only example of Inca civic/ceremonial architecture from any Lupaqa *cabecera*. Chucuito covered more than 20 ha and is characterized by a very high density of finely decorated Late Horizon ceramics, including Chucuito polychrome ceramics and Taraco and Urcusuyu wares (M. Tschopik 1946). Although Hyslop (1976) initially suggested that Chucuito was occupied during the Altiplano period, thereby supporting ethnohistorical accounts of a pre-Inca origin of the town, he later stated that Chucuito was, in fact, built during the Late Horizon (Hyslop 1990:196). The data from the detailed surface collections of the town confirm this later interpretation. No Altiplano period ceramics or architectural features are represented at the site.

Leaving Chucuito to the south, the Inca road passes through the Chincera Pampa and cuts through a small hill bordering the lake. As the road enters into Pirpe Pampa one finds the site of Calahuata or Inca Altar. The site had a modest Tiwanaku occupation, but was significantly expanded in the Late Horizon to include several rectangular buildings and a deeply pitted stone covering an area of about 1 ha. An altar-like worked stone slab is associated with a deeply pitted rock jutting over the road, which, when struck, gives off a distinct metallic ringing noise. The slab measures 2.4 x 1.4 m and contains depressions connected by a small chiseled channel such that liquid poured into the top depression flows downward, filling each successive depression and finally spilling over the edge of the rock (Figure 13.4). Small holes were drilled through the thinnest part of the rock at one end of the altar. Above this rock is a small patio area that contains what appear to be tether rocks with holes bored through them. Today, animals are tethered to these stones. It is possible that the small holes in the altar rock were used to tie sacrificial ani-

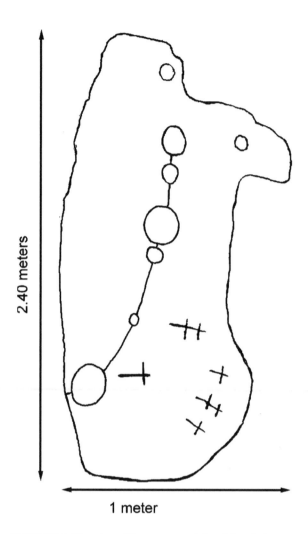

FIGURE 13.4. Drawing of Inca ceremonial rock located near Chucuito

mals so that their blood filled the depressions, perhaps as part of a fertility ceremony or other ritual. This complex consists of the pitted rock, slab, two associated patio areas, several rectangular structures, and highly stylized Inca ceramics. Given the presence of Tiwanaku and Altiplano period settlements near the site, it is possible that the worked stone was used before the Late Horizon. It is likely that Calahuata is an important stop on the pilgrimage route from Cuzco to the Island of the Sun.

Site 63, Calvario, is located near the modern town of Coata. It is near the Altiplano period fortified site of the same name. It covers 4 ha and contains a high density of Chucuito polychrome ceramics, including bottles and highly polished and decorated bowl forms. A ceremonial function is suggested for Calvario by a plaza area containing a simple upright stone (possibly a *huanca*) and many fine ceramics. Its size and surface ceramic assemblage indicate the importance of Calvario as a second order civil/ceremonial site.

On the northwest side of Cerro Ccota, a raised causeway connects the mainland with Quipata Island (Julien 1988:53), which was intensively settled in Inca times. Isla Quipata is one of a few areas around Chucuito where maize is grown. Inca labor organization is demonstrated at the two other Late Horizon towns of Pilag Patag and Pallalla. Both towns are mentioned in the Garci Diez Visita (Diez de San Miguel 1964 [1567]:14, 27), with Pilag Patag being comprised of an *ayllu* of metal workers while Pallalla was a ceramic-producing town (Hyslop 1976).

In addition to resettling the local population into new centers, investing in the road infrastructure, and establishing specialized production towns, Inca reorganization of the Chucuito area included intensification of agricultural systems. Throughout the Chucuito-Cutimbo survey area, one can see "big block" terrace constructions, a terrace style that is different from those of other time periods, and, occasionally similar to those near Cuzco. Although it is very difficult to attribute specific terrace building episodes to any one time period, the presence of Late Horizon ceramics in big block terraces supports an interpretation for Late Horizon use and, possibly, Late Horizon construction. Most of these terraces with the large blocks are no longer used. They tend to be found at the upper-altitude limits of agricultural production, a fact that might coincide with the Inca introduction of engineered species and/or the wetter and warmer climate shift that has been documented for the years after AD 1400 (Ortloff and Kolata 1992). Other terrace styles in the survey zone are more easily attributable to the Late Horizon, terraces such as the concentric terraces found in the Ichu community near Chucuito, which resemble the terraces near Pisac in the Sacred Valley. Similar terrace constructions have yet to be associated with other Lupaqa towns.

As shown in Table 13.1, the most dramatic increase in settlement between the Altiplano period and the Late Horizon occurred in or near the terraced agricultural zone. This change, and the significance of agricultural intensification of the Chucuito area in general, may be attributable to a micro-climate created by the Chucuito Bay—a shallow body of water sheltered from the main body of the lake by the peninsula extending to the north from Palmasita Bay. The Chucuito microclimate permits double-cropping in many areas bordering the lake, but, more importantly, local climatic conditions support maize cultivation. During the survey, maize was observed to grow at an altitude as high as 4050 m above sea level in unprotected terraces near Chucuito. Because maize figures prominently as a high-status good in the ethnohistorical accounts of the Lupaqa economy (Diez de San Miguel 1964 [1567]) and as an important component in the Inca imperial redistributive system, its growth in very restricted areas of the basin makes it a highly symbolic and valuable resource. Local informants state that maize also grows well on Isla Quipata, which may account for the construction of the Inca causeway from Ccota to the island and the increased Late Horizon settlement there.

The most striking difference between the Chucuito area and other Late Horizon Lupaqa centers is the evidence for ritual and religious activity. Chucuito is laid out in a radial pattern (Hyslop 1990:206) and contains Inca Uyu, arguably the only known example of Inca well-dressed masonry from any Lupaqa administrative site. Inca Uyu is set in one of two large plaza areas in the town and contains a high concentration of Late Horizon ceramic styles, including Chucuito Polychrome and some Taraco and Urcusuyu wares, which were first identified by M. Tschopik (1946) and later discussed by Julien (1993:190). Julien suggests that the Urcusuyu and Taraco styles originated in the basin and are associated with Inca estates and religious sites. The heavy concentration of bottles, large containers, and finely decorated plates associated with the Inca Uyu plaza suggest that a principal Chucuito function was the sponsorship of ritual events involving consumption of large quantities of food and *chicha*. As at other important Inca centers, a key form of political control revolved around periodic festivals during which the reciprocal nature of imperial administration was structurally reaffirmed when different social segments of the local population participated in the feasting and drinking at state-sponsored ceremonies.

Given the presence of Inca-style terraces, the finely cut masonry of Inca Uyu, and the high density of ceremonial ceramics at Chucuito, it is likely that the area had special religious significance to the Inca. Elsewhere, I have suggested that Chucuito was founded as the Lupaqa administrative center, not because of a high population density or overall agricultural potential, but because significant quantities of maize could be grown nearby (Frye 1997b). The role of maize in the Inca economy is well known, but its cultivation in the Titicaca Basin must have had special significance. Ethnohistorical documents mention a connection between Chucuito and the sacred sites at Copacabana and the Island of the Sun. It may be that maize was included in the goods that Ramos Gavilán (1988 [1621]:120) refers to when he describes lands near Chucuito being obligated to produce food for the Copacabana sanctuary. It is not simply coincidence that many areas favorable for maize cultivation in the Titicaca Basin are also important Inca habitation or ceremonial sites.

Although ethnohistorical documents concerning the Lupaqa make it clear that local leaders were used to administer the region, archaeological evidence indicates that the Lupaqa population and economy was radically restructured to meet imperial needs. The substantial reorganization of the population, the intensification of the economy, and the organization of the imperial infrastructure documented in the Chucuito area imply a direct Inca role in restructuring the region. However, these changes appear to have been carried out using local administrators. Along with its ability to produce maize, the Chucuito area may have been chosen as the Late Horizon administrative center because the local population allied themselves with the Inca occupiers.

THE LUPAQA IN THE JULI-POMATA AREA

Stanish's (1997) discussion of the Inca administrative policies in the Lake Titicaca region demonstrates that in nonmarket economies labor control is an important focus of imperial administration. Settlement data from the Juli-Pomata

survey area demonstrate that the Inca policy of relocating subject populations in different ecological zones was part of a strategy for enhancing wealth production. Inca strategies for increasing wealth production in the Juli-Pomata area included attempts to increase the population in optimal agricultural and pastoral resource zones, and to process goods in newly created towns. The Juli-Pomata survey area contains the Inca administrative centers of Juli and Pomata, both founded during the Late Horizon. In addition to these large towns, several other newly occupied, second-tier centers were founded in the Late Horizon. Altogether, 242 Inca period sites occupying 178.43 ha were located in the Juli-Pomata survey boundaries. As in the Chucuito area, fortified sites were abandoned, and existing populations were resettled along the Inca road near the lakeshore. In fact, nearly 40% of the Inca period population was settled into newly formed towns.

As in other areas of the Inca Empire, the Inca utilized ideological tools in its incorporation of the Juli-Pomata region. Several sites in the area were likely linked to the pilgrimage trail leading through the Lupaqa territory toward the Copacabana peninsula and the Island of the Sun. These include the sites of Bebedero and Altarani, located along the southern boundary of the survey zone (Stanish et al. 1997; see also Arkush, Chapter 14, this volume; and Arkush 2000). Likewise, sites in the Chucusuyo Peninsula may have been connected to the pilgrimage route or may have functioned as an Inca residence, as indicated by the terrace constructions and site layouts. The Lupaqa area was significantly reorganized during the Late Horizon to meet the needs of the Inca. In contrast to the Colla region, the maximization of economic systems, possibly in support of the Sanctuary at Copacabana and the Island of the Sun, characterized Inca reorganization and administration of the Lupaqa.

THE PACAJES

Like the Colla and Lupaqa groups, the Pacajes were reorganized by the Inca conquerors, with the region divided into two large territorial blocks separated by the Inca road (Julien 1993). There are only a few ethnohistorical references of Pacajes assimilation into the Inca Empire, although Cobo mentions the Pacajes Indians in his recounting of the Inca conquest of the Titicaca Basin. He states that "...for a few days the Pacasa Indians defended the bridge over the outlet [Desaguadero] of Lake Titicaca or Chucuito, and in order to win it from them, the Inca sent part of his army to look for a ford eight leagues downstream" (Cobo 1979 [1653]:140–141). After crossing the outlet, Pachacuti continued on to Tiwanaku, where he was so impressed by the structures there that he commanded that they be studied so that the architectural techniques could be incorporated into Inca building practices (Cobo 1979 [1653]:141). Although the site of Tiwanaku figures prominently in the cultural history of the region and as such has received a great amount of study, the nature of the Inca occupation there is less well documented than are earlier periods of Tiwanaku history.

Our understanding of the Late Horizon in the Titicaca area of the Pacajes zone comes from three systematic surveys conducted in the Tiwanaku core area—that of Juan Albarracin-Jordan and James Mathews (1990) in the Tiwanaku Valley, a survey in the Catari Basin area (Janusek and Kolata 2003), and the Taraco survey along the Taraco Peninsula (Bandy 2001b). Other evidence of Inca influence in the region comes from the many chullpas, some with cut stones, dating to the Late Horizon that are found throughout the Pacajes area (Bellido 1993).

Survey data from the Pacajes region demonstrate that the Inca population resettlement policies in this region mirrored those seen in other areas in the basin. Local populations were moved into newly created settlements, especially to areas with the greatest agricultural potential near the lake. A large proportion of the Tiwanaku Valley population previously living in dispersed hamlets and small villages appears to have been relocated to the lakeshore along the Taraco Peninsula. No clear site size hierarchy describes the Late Horizon settlement pattern in the Tiwanaku Valley. As reported by Albarracin-Jordan and Mathews (1990:161) and by Mathews (1992b), there were 202 sites with Inca Pacajes or Late Horizon material, in contrast to 526 sites dated to the previous Early Pacajes or Altiplano period. There are no large Inca period sites in the

valley. Guaqui is the possible exception, which Albarracin-Jordan and Mathews mention as occupying about 6 ha. In contrast to the settlement pattern in the Tiwanaku Valley, the Taraco Peninsula shows increased settlement characterized by a site size hierarchy during the Late Horizon. Of the 125 Late Horizon sites in the Taraco Peninsula survey area, eight are larger than 2.0 ha. Of these, three could be called large population centers, with sizes ranging from 4.2 to 6.5 ha (Bandy 2001b).

The general pattern of resettlement in the Pacajes region near the lake during the Late Horizon is a movement of population toward the lakeshore. Resettlement policies appear similar to those seen in the Lupaqa region, where larger population centers were established during the Late Horizon. As in the Chucuito area, this pattern may be tied to agricultural intensification of local maize, a product used for state-sponsored feasts in administrative centers and for consumption at the Island of the Sun (Bauer and Stanish 2001). That no large administrative sites were established in the Pacajes region near the lake may be a reflection of a lack of political preexisting complexity. It is also possible that as a group the Pacajes were compliant in their assimilation into the Inca realm.

CONCLUSION

The Titicaca Basin was one of the first regions incorporated into the Inca Empire. The diverse nature of its inhabitants, the distribution of resources in the region, and the existing levels of political complexity were all factors in how the Inca state administrated the region. In some areas, military concerns were paramount. In these cases, a region was divided into many administrative territories. In other areas like the Lupaqa and Pacajes, economic goals appear to have been important. The available survey data from the Lupaqa and Pacajes regions show that the Inca pursued a maximization strategy designed to increase the productive resources available in the Titicaca Basin. The strategy involved moving people from less productive areas into those with the greatest agricultural potential near the lakeshore. The surplus production of foodstuffs was used in state-sponsored festivals and to support sacred sites along a pilgrimage route leading through the Titicaca Basin to the Island of the Sun. Inca resettlement policies were designed to both minimize military resistance and to maximize agricultural production. In other cases, towns were established that housed specialized workers involved in the production of goods. Examples of such towns include Cupi in the Colla area, and Pilag Patag and Pallalla near Chucuito. Part of the strategy to control the local populations included alliance-building with local elites, such as in the Lupaqa case, or the imposition of military administrative centers in areas were resistance was demonstrated, as seen in the case of Hatuncolla. The fact that the Colla region contains many more territorial divisions than either the Lupaqa or the Pacajes zones suggests that this strategy was a means of establishing a tighter military control of the region. The Lupaqa were organized into only one territory but had many individual administrative centers.

Of these, Chucuito appears to have been chosen as the administrative capital because local leaders allied themselves with the Inca conquerors and because maize could be grown there. The Pacajes populations, at least those in the richer lakeside zone, were not reorganized in the same way. Rather, the town of Pucarani was established away from the lake. The Pacajes area population was most likely concentrated on the pampas along the road to the south. The lakeside area does not appear to have warranted the establishment of large administrative centers, and the Inca appear to have been content to move people out of the Tiwanaku Valley and onto the Taraco Peninsula and farther inland in order to increase agricultural and possibly camelid production. When looking at the Inca administration of the Lake Titicaca area, one sees that the Inca chose different strategies based on the political, historical, and economic factors specific to each region.

14.

Inca Ceremonial Sites in the Southwest Titicaca Basin

Elizabeth Arkush

TAWANTINSUYU, as the Incas called their empire, grew in perhaps a hundred years (ca. AD 1430–1532) to encompass a huge territory of numerous ecological zones and peoples with diverse customs, languages, economies, and political institutions. The Incas relied on religious ideology as one important element of imperial control over this vast and varied area. Ethnohistoric documents describe a concerted Inca policy of religious incorporation of the provinces (e.g., Cobo 1979:191 [1653: Bk. 12 Ch. 23], 1990 [1653]; MacCormack 1991:98–118; Rowe 1946:293–314, 1982; Valera 1950:145). The subject people's local divinities, or *huacas,* were assimilated into Inca state control, and subjects were gathered to engage in Inca rituals at pilgrimage centers or state festivals at Cuzco. Inca state ritual was also brought to the provinces and was performed in sun temples built at provincial centers, at local festivals, and at special state ceremonies (such as the *capacocha,* or sacrifice ceremony) that were performed away from the center. Nevertheless, the ethnohistoric record gives us an incomplete and Cuzco-centric view of the way religion worked on the ground in the empire. A close examination of the archaeological record can illuminate the ways in which religious ideology in Tawantinsuyu interacted with, rather than supplanted or ignored, the preexisting cosmologies, ritual practices, and shrines of its new provinces.

This chapter looks at the archaeological manifestations of religion, ideology, and ritual in an Inca province by compiling the results of surface survey and incorporating previous research on Inca period ceremonial sites in the southwestern Lake Titicaca Basin of Peru. This region was important to the Incas, both politically as the home of the rich, populous, and powerful Lupaca and Colla ethnic groups, and religiously, because it was the doorway to the famous Inca pilgrimage center on the Islands of the Sun and Moon. Analysis of the style, size, and placement of ceremonial sites in the Lupaca region suggests that Inca administrators did not mandate ceremonial site construction merely as a wholesale imposition of Inca ideology, but took many other factors into account, including previous non-Inca traditions of worship. Furthermore, it is likely that some sites were constructed and modified at least partly by local workers without Inca supervision. This general picture of inclusion and accommodation contrasts with more rigid class exclusion at the sanctuary on the Island of the Sun itself. These little-known sites and their relation to the Island of the Sun sanctuary give us a window into the inner mechanisms of outwardly monolithic, legitimizing ideologies. In practice, in the Titicaca Basin, as perhaps everywhere, ideology was shaped and contested by countless agents of greater and lesser power.

RELIGION IN THE INCA EMPIRE

The question of the degree of Inca religious control may be viewed as a subset of a more general debate on the impact of Inca conquest on local populations. To some scholars, the Inca policies of indirect rule meant that little changed at the local level after the Inca conquest (Murra 1980 [1956]). Others have emphasized the intrusive policy of labor extraction used by the Incas (for example, Julien 1988; Stanish 1997). In fact, the impact of Inca conquest in Tawantinsuyu ranged from complete reorganization of some subject provinces to the loosest control of others (Bauer 1992; D'Altroy 1992; Dillehay 1977; González 1983; LeVine 1985; Menzel 1959; Netherly 1978; Pease 1982; Salomon 1986a, 1986b; Stanish 2001b). The amount of control exerted in any one place was affected by the length of time the Incas controlled it, the desirability or use of the region in question, the sociopolitical complexity of polities already present in the region, the threat that these polities posed to Inca rule, and strategic considerations.

For religion, the question is whether Inca religious ideology was imposed wholesale in an attempt to communicate Inca dominance to conquered peoples or, rather, evolved to accommodate the practices and needs of new subject populations. Both possibilities are supported by different lines of evidence, and it is certainly possible that different religious policies were utilized in different regions or time periods by the state.

Most contact period documentary sources on Inca religion tend to portray a uniform imposition of official Inca religion everywhere in the empire, although some accounts of the extirpation of idolatry emphasize the importance of local nonelite shrines and portable huacas in the daily lives of ordinary folk (e.g., Arriaga 1968 [1621]). The Huarochiri manuscript documents a remarkably detailed and, from a Cuzco perspective, unorthodox provincial mythology that must have incorporated many pre-Inca elements (Avila 1991 [ca. 1598]). The Huarochiri manuscript also vividly attests to the expedient Inca policy of incorporating regionally important shrines into their origin mythology: "In the highlands, they say, the Incas worshiped the sun as the object of their adoration from Titi Caca, saying, 'It is he who made us Inca!' From the lowlands, they worshiped Pacha Camac, saying, 'It is he who made us Inca!'" (Avila 1991:111, sec. 276 [ca. 1598:Ch. 22]). According to the chroniclers, the major portable huacas of conquered *naciones* were brought to Cuzco and tended to by rotating colonists from the huacas' homelands, kept by the Incas both as hostages and as potentially powerful guests (Cobo 1979:191 [1653: Bk.

12 Ch. 23]; Valera 1950:145). The Incas also frequently enhanced aboriginal religious sites and consulted important local huacas (Rowe 1946: 302; MacCormack 1991:141–159).

Our archaeological knowledge of Late Horizon ceremonial sites outside the Inca heartland is incomplete (see, for instance, Van de Guchte 1990:406, illustration 2). Some provincial ceremonial sites, such as Sayhuite in Apurímac and Vilcashuamán in Ayacucho, are intrusive and pure Inca in style; others, like Pachacamac or Wari Wilka (Shea 1969), are Inca additions to important pre-Inca shrines, built with significant adaptations of local, non-Inca styles and materials. Rarely, there was actual destruction of indigenous huacas (Nielsen and Walker 1999). In addition, numerous modest, rural ceremonial sites exist—a few will be described below—but they are little known, giving the erroneous impression that where ceremonial sites were built in the provinces, they were major sanctuaries directly designed and controlled by the Inca elite.

It is debatable whether intrusive Inca ceremonial installations were placed strictly to influence the conquered masses. For instance, a proliferation of high-altitude mountain shrines in Argentina and Chile, a region where the Incas invested comparatively little in economic or political infrastructure, shows considerable effort and expense poured into ceremonial sites that were not very visible or accessible to local populations (Beorchia Nigris 1973, 1985; McEwan and Van de Guchte 1992; Reinhard 1992; Schobinger and Constanza Ceruti 2001). Class exclusivity is clearly apparent in Inca religious practices in general and at the Island of the Sun sanctuary in particular. Elaborate regulations controlling access to the island sanctuary reproduced and reflected social divisions. Overall, Inca religious sites did more, and sometimes less, than signal Inca dominance.

Factors affecting Inca ideological strategy may have included the political and economic investment in the region, local religious practice and the prestige of local religious sites, and, apparently, military considerations (Hyslop 1990:189). The ideological incorporation of the provinces was not an event, but an ongoing process, as Cobo noted:

...from the beginning of their empire the Incas were not always steadfast in their religion, nor did they maintain the same opinions and worship the same gods....They were prompted to make such changes because they realized that this way they improved their control over the kingdom and kept it more subservient [Cobo 1990:5 (1653:Bk. 13 Ch. 1)].

THE TITICACA BASIN UNDER INCA RULE

The traditional date for the expansion of the Incas into the Titicaca Basin is AD 1450 (Rowe 1944:65). The conquest of the Titicaca Basin was recounted by Cieza de León (1985:130–136 [1553: Bk. 2 Chs. 41–43]) and Cobo (1979:140 [1653:Bk. 12 Ch. 13]). While they differ in some details, both accounts state that the Lupacas and the Collas were engaged in a war at the time of Inca contact. The Collas were eventually vanquished, and the Lupacas welcomed the Incas as allies. The Collas later rebelled several times under the yoke of the Incas (Cobo 1979:143, 153 [1653:Bk. 12 Chs. 14, 16]).

The Inca incorporation of the Titicaca Basin caused dramatic changes on almost every level. The most obvious change that is visible archaeologically is the massive resettlement of the Titicaca Basin and the introduction of large numbers of *mitimas*, or colonists from other subject areas (Stanish 1997). The hilltop forts, or *pukaras*, were abandoned, along with those habitation areas situated to take advantage of non-residential pukaras. Most of the inhabitants of the region were resettled in intrusive, nucleated centers along two main Inca roads, one on each side of the lake (Hyslop 1984).

These new settlements served both as *cabeceras*, or administrative centers (Diez de San Miguel 1964 [1567]; Toledo 1975 [1575]), and as *tambos*, or way stations along the road. Among them, the most important were the new capitals of the Lupacas and Collas: Chucuito and Hatuncolla, respectively. The cabeceras were administered by local lords (*kurakas*) in a hierarchical system. It is likely, although not certain, that these kurakas were descended from the pre-Inca chiefs of the region (Julien 1983:36–38). *Chulpa* burial towers continued to be built. Monumental examples with beautifully finished stone masonry in the Late Horizon may have signaled the strength and security of a hereditary elite newly confirmed in its position of power within the Inca hierarchy.

Along with the resettlement of native people, a distinct demographic spike is observable in the Late Horizon from Stanish et al.'s (1997) survey of the southwest basin, best explained as the movement of large numbers of mitima colonists into the Titicaca Basin. Ample textual evidence also exists for mitimas in the region, destined for service at the Island of the Sun or for specialized production workshops (Ramos Gavilán 1988:84 [1621:Bk. 1 Ch. 12]; Murra 1978: 418; Julien 1983:75; Espinoza Soriano 1987: 248, 253; Stanish 1997:204).

The most extraordinary act of Inca control in the Titicaca Basin was the establishment of an elaborate sanctuary complex and pilgrimage center on the Islands of the Sun and Moon (Titicaca and Coati Islands).[1] Here, according to Inca mythology, the sun first arose, and here the Incas were created by the god Viracocha. Titicaca Island appears to have been used as a religious center in the Tiwanaku period (Bauer and Stanish 2001; Seddon, Chapter 9, this volume), and Tiwanaku-style archaisms at the Inca sanctuary, in both ceramics and architecture, attest to an Inca attempt to link their control of the island to ancient tradition (Gasparini and Margolies 1980: 13, 262; Julien 1993). Inca emperors regularly visited the sanctuary, reaffirming its importance in imperial religious ideology (Cobo 1979:141, 144, 154 [1653:Bk. 12 Chs. 13, 14, 16]).

While hosting the highest echelons of Inca society, the island sanctuary was also a pilgrimage center, and sources state that pilgrims came to it from every corner of the empire (Cobo 1990:95–96 [1653:Bk. 13 Ch. 18]; Ramos Gavilán 1988:41, 164 [1621:Bk.1 Ch. 4, 26]). After passing through a number of checkpoints and purifications, pilgrims arrived at the Sacred Rock on the Island of the Sun, where they participated in seasonal festivals, obtained oracles, gave rich offerings of gold, silver, shells, feathers, and fine *cumbi* cloth, and observed sacrifices of children, llamas, and guinea pigs (Ramos Gavilán 1988

[1621]). Pilgrims then passed on to a temple on the Island of the Moon.

Regulations at the sanctuary compartmentalized people into distinct groups by geographical or ethnic origin and by social status (Ramos Gavilán 1988:153 [1621:Bk. 1 Ch. 24]). Access to the Sacred Rock itself was highly restricted. A wall and a series of three gates about 250 m away from the Sacred Rock marked the closest point to which non-Inca pilgrims could come. There, they were permitted to watch rituals at the Rock and left their offerings at the gate (Cobo 1990:96 [1653:Bk. 13 Ch.18]; Ramos Gavilán 1988:87, 94 [1621:Bk. 1 Chs. 12, 13]). Some local, nonelite groups were not permitted to visit the island at all (Lizarraga 1987:187 [1605:Ch. 86], Ramos Gavilán 1988:150, 176 [1621:Bk. 1 Chs. 24, 29]). In brief, the picture from the documents and from the archaeological evidence is one of a highly structured environment in which each pilgrim's position was precisely assigned based on geography and social status.

Brian Bauer and Charles Stanish's (2001) work on the Inca pilgrimage center at the Island of the Sun and Moon, as well as my reconnaissance project in 1998 on the southwest margins of the lake, attest to a spurt of activity in the construction of new ceremonial sites in the Inca period in the southern and western Titicaca Basin. This remodeling of the religious landscape of the region went hand in hand with the massive alteration of the demographic, political, and economic landscape.

Despite these Inca measures of control, or perhaps because of them, the inhabitants of Collasuyu developed a reputation for rebelliousness (Molina "el Almagrista" 1968 [1552]:75). The Collas rebelled at least once under the Inca yoke and were harshly punished for it (Cobo 1979:143,153 [1653:Bk. 12 Chs. 14, 16]). Catherine Julien notes that one of the insubordinate Colla lords named himself "Pachacuti Inca" (Julien 1983:258).

In contrast to the fractious Collas, the Lupacas followed a pattern of negotiation with Inca power. Although the kuraka of the Lupacas declared himself the son of the Sun and rebelled under Spanish rule in 1538 (Sitio del Cuzco 1934 [1539]:121), the Lupacas are not clearly reported

to have been as troublesome as the Collas under Inca rule (but see Cieza 1985:155 [1553:Bk 2 Ch. 53]). Stanish (2000) argues that in practice they held an apparently privileged position in the Titicaca Basin in the Late Horizon, perhaps deriving from their initial negotiation of the peace with the Inca emperor (Cieza de León 1985:135–136 [1553:Bk. 2 Ch. 43]). According to Cobo, the Lupacas were favored for their loyalty by Topa Inca and his son Guayna Capac (Cobo 1979:144, 154 [1653:Bk. 12 Chs. 14, 16]), and the Lupacas were considered "Incaized" relative to other subject peoples (Hyslop 1977a:160).

In fact, both the Collas and the Lupacas, as well as the other naciones of the Titicaca Basin, were remarkably "Incaized" in their material culture. Locally produced ceramics from the Late Horizon, including nonelite ware, drew heavily on Cuzco-Inca ceramic forms and designs, and the local ware was technologically and stylistically closer to Cuzco-Inca ware than it was to indigenous Late Intermediate period pottery (Stanish 1991; Julien 1983). Houses, generally circular in the Late Intermediate period, became rectangular in the Late Horizon, following Inca tradition. Inca-style cut-stone masonry was occasionally adopted for edifices that do not seem to have been executed under Inca supervision, and were therefore probably constructed under local initiative; examples include the Inca Uyu in Chucuito, capital of the Lupacas (treated below), and chulpas with a square footprint or faced in fine Cuzco-style masonry, which were probably constructed and used by the local kurakas rather than by Inca administrators residing in the Collao (Hyslop 1977b:160; Julien 1983:254). It seems that the local non-Inca elite, whether Colla or Lupaca, adopted an Inca architectural style for their most symbolic constructions, and even reworked the tombs of their ancestors to fit a new era in which Inca style was synonymous with prestige and dominance.

The interpretation of stylistic adoption is always problematic, and never more so than in the context of political domination. However, it is worth noting that stylistic emulation in material culture need not be seen as signifying political allegiance. Among the many Inca-style ceremonial sites discussed in this paper, at least three appear to be local emulations of Inca ceremonial forms. It is difficult to conclude exactly how these sites functioned in the context of local adaptation to, co-option by, and resistance to Inca rule. However, we must remember that they may not have signified wholesale participation in the Inca cosmology or in Inca imperial ideology.

THE RESEARCH QUESTION

How are we to interpret subsidiary ceremonial sites in the southwest Titicaca Basin and their relationship to the Island of the Sun pilgrimage center? I argue that overall patterns in their style, placement, and accessibility should tell us something about the way religion, as expressed in religious sites, was used and negotiated between Incas and local inhabitants. The style of carving at a ceremonial site indicates whether it was built under Inca supervision and at the order of Inca administrators, or by workers (presumably local) with a hazy idea of Inca ceremonial style. Inca ceremonial sites are classically distinguished by carved rocks, in particular carved bedrock (as opposed to monoliths or portable stones), as well as by uncarved boulders enclosed by masonry walls or incorporated into larger sites (Bauer 1998; Hyslop 1990:Ch. 4; Van de Guchte 1990). They may also include fountains, nonutilitarian canals, and carved channels for the manipulation of liquid offerings, as well as structures with exceptionally fine stone masonry. Local religious forms and styles were different from those executed under Inca artistic canons. Tiwanaku and pre-Tiwanaku ceremonial constructions include sunken courts, monoliths, and artificial mounds. It is clear from the documents (Arriaga 1968 [1621]:79; Ramos Gavilán 1988:196–197 [1621: Bk. 1 Ch. 32]) that many Tiwanaku or Formative carved stelae were revered in the early Colonial period and probably the Late Horizon. They may also have been held sacred in the Late Intermediate period (LIP). In the LIP, huge chulpa cemeteries such as Sillustani probably constituted the major ceremonial centers (Hyslop 1977a:153). This stylistic distinction between Inca-built and locally built sites is also suggestive of who may have used the sites. Contact period textual references occasionally identify the groups who used a particular site.

The placement of sites is also telling. Sites near the Inca road[2] and near major towns and administrative centers could in theory have been accessible to all, including local residents (elite and nonelite), Inca administrators, and pilgrims traveling the Inca road from the Cuzco region to the Island of the Sun. Sites far away from the road and from major towns are less likely to have been visited by pilgrims and Incas. Sites near Copacabana, the stopping-point for pilgrims before embarking for the Island of the Sun and a major religious center in itself, were presumably tied to the island cult. Highly visible, large, and accessible sites could have served the additional purpose of signaling ideology or imperial control to a wide audience. Less visible, small, or out-of-the-way sites would not have been well suited to this propagandistic function.

Given that there were many new ceremonial sites built in the Late Horizon and that Inca administrators were clearly interested in the region's religious landscape, I propose to use the above criteria of style and placement to distinguish between two possible models of Inca religious policy. In the first model, the Incas used ceremonial sites to disseminate imperial ideology and mark the landscape as Inca territory. They attempted to incorporate the region's population into Inca state religion, but did not accommodate preexisting sacred sites or ceremonial styles and practices. For example, Bauer and Stanish (2001) interpret ideology and its manifestations in ceremonial construction at the Island of the Sun as a tool for supporting or legitimizing the rule of the Incas over subject peoples. Smaller Inca ceremonial sites could have functioned in the same way, indoctrinating local participants into an imposed religious ideology in which the dominance of the Incas was naturalized. Maarten Van de Guchte uses this interpretation in his analysis of Inca carved rock sites: "By carving rocks, the Incas effectively molded their world. The patterns on the rocks succinctly and directly helped to replicate icons of Inca ideology. As such the carved rocks served a purpose, similar to textiles in Andean society, as vehicles for the dissemination of an Andean catechism" (Van de Guchte 1990:50). Likewise, DeMarrais et al. (1996:29) propose that Inca roads, tambos, fortresses, and storehouses were symbolic as well as functional, constituting "a landscape and architecture of power." Most of the small ceremonial sites in the southwest Titicaca Basin feature rocks carved in more-or-less typical Inca style. Such rocks would have indicated an Inca presence as clearly to the local inhabitants of the Titicaca Basin in the Late Horizon as they do to the modern observer. Thus, the subsidiary ceremonial sites in the Collao could have been designed primarily to mark the landscape with symbols of Inca rule.

Such a policy should have resulted in impressive, intrusive sites close to major towns and roads, for the best visibility and the widest audience. These sites would have been mandated and designed by Inca administrators and constructed under close Inca supervision, and thus the style of these sites should be similar to that of sites in the Cuzco area, following the Inca stylistic canons outlined above. The sites could have been visited by Inca, pilgrim, Aymara elite, and nonelite alike, but the Incas might have wished to retain some control over their use, in keeping with a religious policy of imposition, rather than accommodation. Therefore, finding evidence of associated elite habitation areas, and even of access restriction, similar to the pattern on the Island of the Sun, would not be surprising. However, these last indices should not be considered essential to the model, especially as access could have been restricted to sites while leaving no observable trace on the landscape.

In the second model, imperial ideology might have been promoted through ceremonial sites, but with significant accommodation to local traditions and participation by local actors. Ceremonial sites could have been part of an ongoing process of negotiation and accommodation between local and imperial actors, in which imperial ideology was expanded and altered to fit local needs. Here, more varied characteristics would be expected than in the other models. Some sites could have been built by local workers on Inca orders but without direct Inca supervision. Thus, some sites might be stylistically "Inca," while others could be hybrid Inca-local creations. In the latter category, we might also see later additions by local workers to Inca ceremonial sites, and vice versa. Some sites might be situated at pre-Inca huacas. Not all sites would be located close to major towns and administra-

tive centers, especially those that took advantage of preexisting sacred places. Those sites, likewise, might not be particularly visible or accessible.

A subsidiary question is whether Inca-style sites in the region were intended or used as ritual stations on the pilgrimage route from Cuzco to the Island of the Sun. If they were, they should have been on the road or near tambos (way stations), and either Inca in style or related to the pilgrimage cult in other ways. In either scenario, huacas that were locally built and used could also have served the religious needs of the population.

LATE HORIZON CEREMONIAL SITES

In July and August of 1998, I completed a reconnaissance of the southwest lake region under the aegis of Programa Collasuyu, a multi-year collaborative research project in the Titicaca Basin directed by Charles Stanish (UCLA) and Edmundo de la Vega (Universidad Nacional Técnica del Altiplano, Puno). My goal was to document several inadequately published Inca period ceremonial sites in the southwest lake region and to find new ones. Because of the dispersed and highly visible nature of Inca ceremonial sites, and the enormous size of the potential study area, I chose a nonsystematic reconnaissance methodology. This permitted me to cover the largest possible geographical area, target the known sites, sample areas of high probability, and therefore optimize data recovery from a relatively short season. The area of study was the approach to the Island of the Sun on the southwest side of the lake, from Chucuito south, including the peninsula of Copacabana (Figure 14.1). No attempt at full coverage of this large area was made. Rather, the aim was to characterize the general nature of the Inca religious landscape in that area. Thus, the list of sites given here is in no way exhaustive.

The reconnaissance methodology was based on a combination of strategies: (1) the survey of selected places, such as large rock outcrops and hilltops, that were deemed likely candidates for Inca ceremonial sites, (2) the use of local informants, and (3) the investigation of places with toponyms in Quechua or names that indicated

FIGURE 14.1. The Lake Titicaca Basin, with Late Horizon towns, ceremonial sites, and the road

the presence of sites (e.g., "Inca Pukara"). The reconnaissance was not restricted to sites along the probable Inca road, but an inevitable bias toward that strip of land arose from the simple fact that the modern road lies close to the probable Inca road in most places (Hyslop 1984). In about two and one-half weeks of on-the-ground reconnaissance, three new ceremonial sites were found, and one large site—Kenko (Tres Ventanas), previously thought to be pre-Inca—was shown to be an important Inca ceremonial center. In addition, all previously known Late Horizon ceremonial sites in the region as well as several known chulpa sites were visited, and

many previously unrecorded features of these known sites were recorded. Chulpa sites that lacked other Late Horizon ceremonial features are excluded from the catalogue below.

Sites or site sectors were considered to be "ceremonial" based on the presence of carved rocks, ritual canals, or other clearly nonutilitarian constructions. Sites were considered Late Horizon if they showed stylistic similarities in carving or masonry to known Inca sites (preferably in the Inca heartland) or were associated with single-component habitation sites datable with Late Horizon pottery. The ceramic sequence used for the analysis was refined by

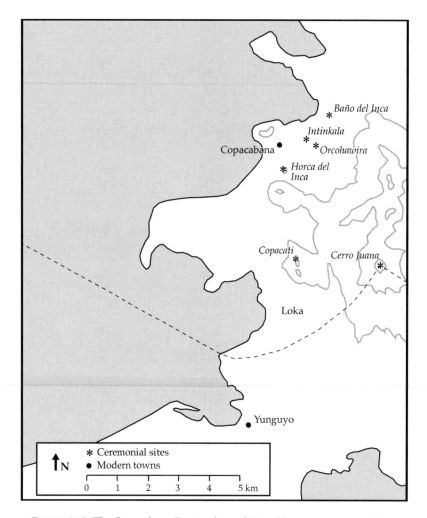

FIGURE 14.2. The Copacabana Peninsula, with Late Horizon ceremonial sites

Stanish et al. (1997:40–49) for the survey of the Juli-Pomata region. Late Horizon pottery in the study area includes bowl and aryballoid forms in Cuzco Inca, Local Inca, Chucuito, Sillustani, and Pacajes types (for Cuzco Inca, see Rowe 1944; for the region, see Julien 1993; for Local Inca, see Julien 1983; for Chucuito, see M. Tschopik 1946; for Sillustani, see M. Tschopik 1946, Revilla Becerra and Uriarte Paniagua 1985, and Stanish 1991; for Pacajes, see Rydén 1957, Albarracin-Jordan and Mathews 1990, and Mathews 1992a).

The catalogue of sites lists all known Late Horizon ceremonial sites from the study area, excluding the Islands of the Sun and Moon. Detailed descriptions of the new sites from the reconnaissance are included, as are somewhat briefer treatments of previously published sites.

Two known sites outside of the reconnaissance area, Pucara and Amantaní, are briefly mentioned in the catalogue because of their relevance to the topic. The sites are listed in order of their location, moving away from the Island of the Sun through the Copacabana Peninsula and northward along the west side of the lake, in reverse pilgrimage order (Figures 14.1 and 14.2).

Intinkala and Orcohawira

"Intinkala" ("stone of the sun") lends its name to the collection of carved boulders in which it is found. These boulders are located about 300 m east of the modern town of Copacabana. The rocks are carved with flat altars, niches, and canals, with a quality of carving comparable to Cuzco work (Figure 14.3). The site and its most prominent rock, called the "Seat of the Inca" or

FIGURE 14.3. Intinkala

"Seat of the Sun," have been noted by numerous travelers and archaeologists (for example, Bandelier 1910; Hyslop 1990; Mantilla 1972; Rivera Sundt 1978a; Squier 1877a; Trimborn 1967; and Wiener 1880). Hermann Trimborn (1967:19–23) gives a precise map of the Seat of the Inca. Cleaning and excavation by INAR (Instituto Nacional de Arqueología) in 1975 uncovered walls built directly into the rocks, traces of a paved floor, and a system of drainage canals (Rivera Sundt 1978a:76). Orcohawira (also called Río Macho or Río Fuerte), first documented in 1968 (Mantilla 1972), consists of three stones finely carved with "seats" and lies 200 m to the east of Intinkala (Figure 14.4). These "seats" are oriented in the general direction of Intinkala and are of the same quality and style. INAR reported very fine, decorated Late Horizon ceramics on the surface at both Intinkala and Orcohawira (Rivera Sundt 1978:75–6). Indeed, the whole area between the sites and for about 100 m on all sides has a dense scatter of fine Inca ceramics. The Copacabana Peninsula was the stopping point for pilgrims just before they embarked for the Island of the Sun. This is the only ceremonial sector in Late Horizon Copacabana that survives, and the rites related to the pilgrimage at Copacabana that are mentioned in the documents (e.g., Ramos Gavilán 1988:171 [1621:Ch. 28]) may well have taken place at Intinkala and Orcohawira.

Both carved-rock sites are so consistent with Inca stylistic canons that there can be no doubt they were executed on Inca orders and under Inca supervision. However, early Colonial documents suggest that an important local huaca, the idol of Copacabana, may have been found at Intinkala or Orcohawira (Sanz 1886). Ramos Gavilán gives a detailed account of where it was found:

> Among the Idols that were found in this place, the principal and most famous among the Yunguyos was the Copacabana Idol. In the time of the priests of my order, certain Spaniards, looking for some treasure, had the place dug out where the Idol was reputed to be located, and found it, and nearby, also found two huge rocks. One had the name Ticonipa, and the other Guacocho. They were worshiped by the Yunguyos, who,

FIGURE 14.4. Orcohawira

being poor, had no riches in this, their principal sanctuary. Their continual offerings were of livestock, chicha, and other things, because the silver and gold which they managed to find, they offerred to the principal temples of the Sun and the Moon. This Copacabana Idol was in the same town [of Copacabana], as you go to Tiquina. It was of fine blue stone, and it had nothing more than a human face, disembodied of feet or hands...this Idol faced towards the temple of the Sun, as if to signify that from there came its well-being...[Ramos Gavilán 1988:191 (1621:Ch 32), author's translation].

Ramos Gavilán's account places the idol on the route east out of Copacabana toward Tiquina, which corresponds well to the location of Intinkala and Orcohawira. The two great sacred rocks near the idol may well have been the rocks at Intinkala.[3] The descriptions of the idol are far from detailed—according to Calancha (1972:1.139 [1639:Bk. 1 Ch. 3]), it had the head of a man and the body of a fish—but it was most likely a Formative or Tiwanaku monolith (see,

for example, K. Chávez 1988; S. Chávez and K. Chávez 1975). Stone sculptures of human figures are practically unknown from the Late Horizon, while the continued worship of Formative or Tiwanaku monoliths in the early Colonial era is well documented for the Lake Titicaca area (e.g., Arriaga 1968 [1621]:79).

Horca del Inca

On the hill of Kesanani just south of Copacabana is the misnamed "Horca del Inca," which, according to the findings of Rivera Sundt (1984), functioned as an astronomical device rather than a gallows. A stone cross-beam is set between two crags, and two small holes are drilled in outcrops nearby (Figure 14.5). On the June solstice the rising sun casts its light through the northern hole onto the cross-beam. On the September equinox, a crag casts a shadow on the cross-beam (Rivera Sundt 1984). The Island of the Sun can be seen from the Horca, and taking into account its proximity to Copacabana, it is likely that rituals in connection with the Island of the Sun pilgrimage cult were performed here. While Rivera Sundt (1984:98) offers the possibility that the Horca was a pre-Inca construction, the ob-

FIGURE 14.5. The Horca del Inka

servatory can be safely assigned to the Late Horizon based on its association with nearby Inca-style stairs and walls. One trace of a wall, with some blocks still in place, cuts across the space directly in front of the Horca (Figure 14.6). Although this wall could not have been very high or it would have blocked the trajectory of the sun's rays on the solstice, it probably served as a boundary separating sacred from profane space, and may have indicated a social division as well, such as that between officiators and the public (Rivera Sundt 1984:98).

The Baño del Inca

The "Baño del Inca" ("bath of the Inca") is located in the former hacienda Kusijata, 2 km northeast of Copacabana. Noted and drawn by Squier in 1877 (1877a:325), it is a large open cylinder (the cavity measures 1.2 x 0.6 m) carved out of a single piece of rock, highly polished on the surface, and sunk into a stone-paved platform. Two semicircular gaps in its edge served to fill it with water from canals extending out from the bath.

FIGURE 14.6. Traces of a wall at the Horca del Inka

Copacati

Copacati is a carved-rock site on top of a steep, rocky hill about 4 km south of Copacabana, first described by Maks Portugal Zamora (1977:299, see also Rivera Sundt 1978:81). The bedrock is finely carved in flat stepped shelves ("seats" and "altars") at several points along the ridge-top in unmistakable Cuzco-Inca style (Figure 14.7). On the northwest flank of the ridge (a steep slope makes the main carvings almost inaccessible) are two additional worked areas first noted in this reconnaissance. One is a triangular "seat" carved in a rock far down on the side of the hill; the other consists of two rectangular "seats" in the steep rock higher up the hill (Figure 14.8). As will be shown, a pattern of carved rocks scattered away from the main ceremonial sector is rather common for the small Inca sites described here. No Late Horizon habitation site was found in the immediate area.

As at Intinkala, the Inca carvings at Copacati were apparently associated with a pre-Inca idol. According to Ramos Gavilán:

Besides this Copacabana Idol, the Yunguyos had another which they called Copacati. The hill where it was located took its name from this same Idol, which was on the way out of the town. It was made of stone, an evil figure completely curled round with snakes; the people would resort to it in times of drought, asking it for water for their crops. Padre Almeyda, who had charge of the curacy before the missionaries of my sacred order came into it, heard of this Idol and had it brought to the town, and when it was placed in the plaza in the presence of many people, a snake was seen to detach itself from the Idol and go around it. The priest seeing this gave them to understand that it was the devil, and that they should be ashamed to have held such a vile creature for a god....The master of the chapel, Don Gerónimo Carvacochachi, seventy-eight years of age, told us he had seen the snake uncoil itself from the discarded Idol, which was

FIGURE 14.7. Carved rocks at Copacati

FIGURE 14.8. Carved rocks on the northwest flank of Copacati

thrown in the lake, and the snake was beaten and stoned to death [1988:196–197 (1621:Bk. 1 Ch. 32), author's translation].

Portugal Zamora (1977:301) notes correctly that the description of the idol corresponds to Formative and Tiwanaku period stone monoliths. (A Formative date is most likely, considering the snake iconography.) At Copacati, as at Intinkala, an elaborate, Cuzco-style Inca cut-stone site, probably connected with the island cult in some way, seems to have featured an ancient stone monolith still revered by the local people of Yunguyu in the early Colonial period. The Incas may have placed their carvings at Copacati to take advantage of a preexisting huaca, or they may have moved the huaca here, which fits with the pattern of Inca reuse of pre-Inca sacred sites such as Pucara, Tiwanaku, and the sanctuary itself on the Island of the Sun. Alternatively, the idol's local worshippers may have moved it to this Inca cut-stone site. Either possibility suggests a striking degree of accommodation between the two religious traditions.

One interesting aspect of Ramos Gavilán's account is that in both cases, the monoliths, rather than the Inca carved rocks, were the main focus of worship by local inhabitants in the early Colonial period (and the focus of destruction by the Spanish clerics). Pre-Inca monoliths may have proved to have more enduring symbolic significance for the inhabitants of the southern basin, although Ramos Gavilán's account may simply reflect the Spanish concern over the worship of representative (especially anthropomorphic) idols, as opposed to the abstract, geometric carvings of the Incas. Another intriguing element of the account is that the idols were apparently worshipped by the nonelite. The Yunguyus held them sacred, and in the case of the Copacabana idol, these included Yunguyus too poor to make valuable offerings.[4] This post-Conquest reality may not have reflected Inca period conditions, of course, but it raises the question of for whom these explicitly Inca-style stone carvings were intended. The scenario of local nonelite worshipping at Inca sites contrasts markedly with elite restriction at the Island of the Sun.

Copacati is close to the modern road from Yunguyu to Copacabana, and probably was near the Inca road as well. The site could easily have been visited by pilgrims en route from Yunguyu to Copacabana, or alternatively it could have been visited as a short subsidiary pilgrimage from Copacabana (like the Horca del Inca). The walking time from Copacabana to the top of Copacati is about one hour using the modern road. Although it does not take long to reach Copacati, the trip does involve making a detour up a rather steep hill and knowing where the site is located—in other words, taking a miniature pilgrimage in itself. The Island of the Sun is not visible from Copacati. Clearly, placing the site on top of the hill, or near an already sacred site, was more important to the Incas than making it highly visible and accessible.

Carved Stone at Cerro Juana

On the mountain of Cerro Juana (Koana), located southeast of Copacabana and northeast from Copacati, is an unusual carved block, which was also described by Portugal Zamora (1977:307, 323, Fig. 16). The block is 4.3 x 3.3 m in size, and its top surface is covered with rectangular depressions and canals. While the block probably dates to the Late Horizon, it is stylistically much less "Inca" than the other ceremonial sites on the Copacabana Peninsula, and displays very atypical features, including several short canals arranged in a radiating pattern. In view of its relatively inaccessible location and style, it is unlikely that this site was an "official" ritual station. It may have been a local imitation of Inca ceremonial expression.

Playa Chatuma and Nearby Sites

Playa Chatuma is located on the flank of a low ridge at the lakeshore, about 10 km southeast of Pomata. It consists of carvings on a stretch of soft, sloping limestone exposed above the beach and is about 400 m wide and 100 m from top to bottom. The rock is carved extensively with thin vertical channels and other carvings (Figure 14.9). A network of more deeply carved channels is located on the western edge of the site, toward the top of the exposed bedrock. There is a short, shallowly carved "staircase" next to this network of channels. This staircase, which is similar to the Inca stairs at Kenko (Tres Ventanas) and at the

FIGURE 14.9. Playa Chatuma

"Inca's Chair" at Bebedero, securely dates the site to the Late Horizon on stylistic grounds (Figure 14.10). The rock nearby displays sets of shallow transverse cuts, a repetition of the stair motif too tiny for any human climber. The western portion of the site also has eight vertical channels running straight down the rock face toward the shore, each one dotted with shallow hollows, some converging or diverging on their course. On the east side of the site, beyond a natural fault, plain channels without hollows predominate. The most recognizable elements of Inca ceremonial style—geometric planes and niches—are absent at Playa Chatuma.

On the beach below are two identical stone blocks, lying about 50 m apart, and finely carved with an unusual step-motif (Figure 14.11). An undecorated, but finely made block, about 1.0 x 0.5 m in dimension, is also found on the beach to the east. The exposed beach below the canals yielded a total of only four diagnostic sherds, all dating to the Late Horizon. However, abundant ground stones and grinding surfaces of hard sandstone and granite are present. These were polished to a surface suggestive of plant processing.

The site of Ckackachipata, recorded by Stanish et al. (1997:90), was probably the closest associated habitation area to the Playa Chatuma blocks. Ckackachipata is found on the peninsula just next to Playa Chatuma (Figure 14.12) and has a Late Horizon component with fairly modest local ceramics (Stanish et al. 1997). The Island of the Sun is visible from Ckackachipata, though not from Playa Chatuma itself.

Other nearby Inca features may be related to Playa Chatuma (Figure 14.12). In the bay to the east of the Ckackachipata Peninsula, a large, square block of stone with a straight groove carved into one side rests in the water just off the beach. This is almost certainly from the Late Horizon, but its relationship to Playa Chatuma cannot be determined. Pukara Chatuma is a hill with a Late Intermediate period and Late Horizon presence, as evidenced by pukara walls and an Inca-style square chulpa with fine Inca sherds, respectively (Stanish et al. 1997:95). On top of the hill, Stanish et al. noted several carved rocks (1997:95–96). These include an Inca-style carved rock with a rectangular depression, a large, finely shaped ashlar block near what may be a slab-cist tomb, a rock with a single straight groove about

Figure 14.10. Close-up of Playa Chatuma

Figure 14.11. Carved rock on the beach at Playa Chatuma

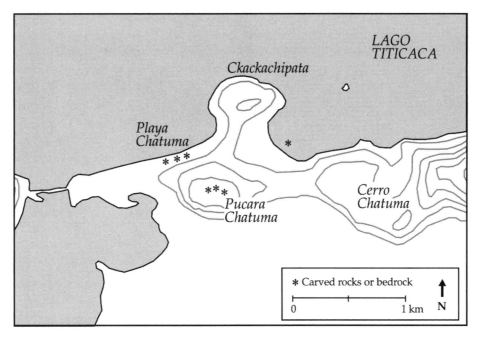

FIGURE 14.12. Playa Chatuma and surrounding area. After Stanish et al. 1997:86

10 cm long, and another rock carved with an un-usual concentric circle design (Figure 14.13). This last motif is characteristic of neither Inca nor lo-cal carving, but the rock may be Late Horizon in view of its location near the other rocks at this site.[5] These dispersed ceremonial features scat-tered across the landscape near Playa Chatuma, and the relatively disorganized, asymmetrical layout of the channels (compare, for instance, Sa-maipata in Bolivia, near the eastern edge of the Inca Empire), suggest that the site may not have been organized by a master plan.

Hyslop (1984) was unable to find the Inca road south of Pomata, but it is unlikely that it passed closer to Playa Chatuma than the mod-ern road does because of the hilly topography of this area and the swamp land just to the west. The site is accessible by foot and requires only about a half-hour's walk to reach it from the modern road leading to Yunguyu. It probably required no more effort to reach it in the Inca pe-riod. The site could easily have been along a route from Pomata to Yunguyu and the Copaca-bana Peninsula beyond.

The canals at Playa Chatuma and Chinchin Jalave (described below) relate these sites to nu-merous others across Tawantinsuyu that used

water or liquid ritually. Canals and basins are features of most of the Inca ceremonial sites in the study area.[6] The forking canals at Playa Cha-tuma (for instance, the network of canals at the "stair") are particularly interesting because, like other cases of Inca diverging channels, they may have been used for divination. Forking-channel *pacchas* are found at some of the most important Inca ceremonial carved-rock sites: Kenko (near Cuzco), Samaipata, Sayhuite, Ingapirca, Santa Apolonia (Cajamarca), and Vilcashuamán (Van de Guchte 1990:146). The forking channels at Playa Chatuma are far more crudely carved than those listed above, but may have fulfilled the same role.

Playa Chinchin Jalave

Playa Chinchin Jalave is located on the lake-shore north of San Bartolomé Hill, just west of the Choquesuyo Peninsula, about 5 km north-east of the Inca (and modern) town of Juli. Al-though the site is not on the Inca road surveyed by Hyslop (1984), it is close enough to Juli to have been easily reachable by residents. The site is on a thin strip of beach at the foot of a steep cliff, about 100 m from the lake edge. It consists of several boulders of chalky white limestone,

FIGURE 14.13. Carved rocks at Pukara Chatuma

carved with short canals and basins, which are now heavily eroded (Figures 14.14 and 14.15). One boulder displays seven channels, but most have two or three. As at Playa Chatuma, the geometric shapes most typical of the Inca carving style are absent. These boulders are close to the level of the lake and would have been inundated since they were carved, contributing to their surface degradation. Not surprisingly, no pottery is present in this area. The north end of the Island of the Sun is visible from the site.

On a point just west of the beach on the cliff above the lake is the small Late Horizon habitation site of Chinchin Jalave, noted by Stanish et al. (1997:63). Plainwares abound, and there are several collapsed circular structures that may be fallen chulpas. Those who lived at this site may have been able to control access to the boulders

on the beach, which can be reached by a ravine and a footpath, but is otherwise difficult to access.

Playa Chinchin Jalave displays obvious similarities with Playa Chatuma, including the lakeside location of both sites, the carved channels present at both sites, and the limestone used at both sites. Although the lack of ceramics and the atypical carving style would make this site difficult to date in isolation, it can be reasonably placed in the Late Horizon based on its parallels to Playa Chatuma, its association with the nearby Late Horizon site of Chinchin Jalave, and its connection to water ritual.

The carving here and at Playa Chatuma does not follow the typical Inca stylistic canon evoked at other sites in the region, despite the fact that both sites are relatively close to the Island of the Sun and conveniently located for the pilgrim.

FIGURE 14.14. Carved rocks at Playa Chinchin Jalave

Unlike Intinkala or Copacati, these sites do not have landscapes that have been stamped with clear statements of Inca power. They may have been fashioned without direct supervision from Cuzco, either as a secondhand directive or a locally motivated imitation.

CUT STONE NEAR SILLUMOCCO-HUAQUINA

This isolated stone is located on the northeast flank of Mt. Sapacollo near Juli, not far from the important Upper Formative and Tiwanaku period site of Sillumocco-Huaquina (de la Vega, Chapter 8, this volume). A branch of the Inca road surveyed by Hyslop (1984:123) runs near it. It is a large (1.5 m wide) boulder that has been smoothed and carved in an abstract, gently curved shape. It is perhaps significant that this rock is found on the east branch of the Inca road, on the lakeside branch, rather than on the more direct branch into Juli to the west side of Mt. Sapaqollo.

CARVINGS AT BEBEDERO

Two examples of Inca ceremonial rock carving are found at the Bebedero sandstone outcrop, which is located about 8 km north of Juli and just west of the modern road. Here the modern road is probably very close to the Inca road and may overlie it (Hyslop 1984:123). "The Inca's Chair," first described by Squier in 1877 (1877a: 350), is a set of carvings in classic Cuzco-Inca style on a section of the outcrop near the road (Figure 14.16). The carvings consist of several shallow planes or "seats," a stairway leading to the top of the rock, and the thin vertical channel after which the outcrop is named (*bebedero*, or drinking-trough). The rock has been capped with a tower in recent times.

The vertical channel on the front of the Inca's Chair tie this site, along with others in the area, to a typical Inca pattern of libation. The quality of work at this site and the similarity of its carving to that in the Cuzco heartland make the site stand out among more modest ceremonial

FIGURE 14.15. Carved stone at Playa Chinchin Jalave

FIGURE 14.16. The "Inka's Chair" at Bebedero

FIGURE 14.17. Altarani

installations in the area. The location of the site near the probable Inca road makes it highly likely that it was associated with a pilgrimage to the Island of the Sun.[7] In other words, it is exactly what we would expect to see in a pilgrimage station symbolizing Inca power on the provincial landscape.

The impressive carving of Altarani (Figure 14.17), about 2 km away, was first published by Alberto Cuentas (1928) and more fully described by Hyslop (1976:352) and Stanish et al. (1997:61). It consists of a rock outcrop into which a 7.0-m tall and 8.0-m wide vertical plane has been carved. This central section is outlined by two grooves on the sides and an unfinished "lintel" on top. In the middle of it is carved a blind doorway (1.9 x 1.1 m) in a rough T-shape. Two smaller planes flank this central section, bringing the total width of the carving to 14 m. The 1998 reconnaissance found one previously unpublished feature at Altarani: a low rock outcrop to the east (with a good view of the Altarani carving) displays two abstract designs of small holes, or cupules (Figure 14.18), similar to the cupules at Kenko (Tres Ventanas). As at Copacati and Playa Chatuma, Altarani shows a pattern of

impressive ceremonial carving with more modest elaboration nearby.

While the carving style of the "Inca's Chair" is unmistakably Inca, the Altarani carving is more difficult to date. The terraces and plain at Bebedero yield artifacts and ceramics of all periods from Late Archaic to Inca (Stanish et al. 1997:61). Stanish and colleagues argue that the Altarani carving is Late Horizon, based on its association with the Inca's Chair (1977: 62). Hyslop (1976) attributed the site to the Altiplano (Late Intermediate) period, calling the T-shaped carving a "chulpa façade." This hypothesis is difficult to support, given that no comparable examples of Altiplano rock carving are known to exist. Hyslop's alternative suggestion that the carving is Tiwanaku, based on the niche's T-shape (Hyslop 1977a:162), is possible. While T-shapes are not unknown in Inca carving and architecture, they are uncommon.[8] The cupules nearby are analogous to scatters of cupules noted by Trimborn at known Inca carved rock sites such as Samaipata and Lacatambo, near Cochabamba in Bolivia (Trimborn 1967:26). In sum, a Late Horizon date is most likely.

FIGURE 14.18. Cupules at Altarani

Kenko (Tres Ventanas)

Local residents call the site Kenko. Here I add the name "Tres Ventanas" to distinguish it from the site of Kenko near Cuzco.[9] It was briefly described by M. Tschopik (1946:8) and Hyslop (1976:348). As one of the more impressive and unusual Inca ceremonial sites in the province, it deserves further attention. This large (4 to 6 ha) site is located about 1 km from the lakeshore, on the eastern edge of a range of hills east of the plains between Acora and Ilave. The site includes a ceremonial sector, consisting of thin walkways and niches constructed on a cliff face, and three distinct Inca period habitation sectors: one behind, a second in the fields in front, and a third near the entrance to the walkways (Figures 14.19, 14.20, and 14.21). The cliff is part of a geological formation consisting of a series of sheer sandstone ridges running northwest to southeast, enfolding thin strips of steep terraced land between them. The cliff face holding the walkways is the most northeastern of these ridges and has an unimpeded view of the lake.

The walkways (Figure 14.22) are formed and retained by walls of fine, Inca-style coursed masonry clinging to the cliff face, about 10 m above the level of the plains. The masonry is extremely fine for the region and very regular. Individual blocks vary little in size, ranging from 35 to 45 cm across, and most are square or nearly square (Figure 14.21). The walkways are reached by passing through the fields behind the front ridge. Here, a series of four rectangular depressions are carved into the bedrock. About 11 m north of this carving, a set of Inca steps carved in the rock leads through a gap in the ridge to its northeast face, where the main walkway begins. Another flight of steps is carved on the face of the cliff at this point, but does not lead anywhere (Figure 14.23). These steps could have been intended to connect with a higher walkway, which stops some 45 m from this stair. The walkways are inaccessible except by this route.

There are four distinct walkways, the largest being about 150 m long and 7 m wide at its widest point. This main walkway has three raised sections or platforms, each progressively increasing in length. The last platform is reached by ascending a series of four small rises, each 0.5 to 1 m in height. Three large rectangular niches are carved into the rock face at various points along the walkways. One of

FIGURE 14.19. Kenko (Tres Ventanas)

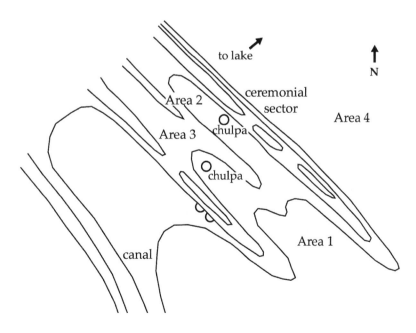

FIGURE 14.20. Sketch map of Kenko (Tres Ventanas) (Map and contour lines are not to scale.)

FIGURE 14.21. Kenko (Tres Ventanas) ceremonial sector

them is in an incomplete stage of carving, and in addition, two groups of hollows on the rock face indicate the beginning stage of two more unfinished niches (Figure 14.24). No ceramic or lithic artifacts were found on the walkways.

Locally produced ceramics from domestic occupations and stone agricultural tools are found on the surface of several sectors close to the niches and walkways (Figure 14.20). Area 1 consists of about 1.5 ha of fields behind the ridge and to the east of the ceremonial sector, just beyond the stair leading to the walkways. This area displays a dense scatter of fine Inca ceramics. Areas 2 and 3 consist of the thin terraced strips of land lying between ridges to the south of the site. Areas 2 and 3 feature a slab-cist tomb and a modest chulpa, respectively. Areas 2 and 3 have a light scatter of mostly undecorated Late Horizon ceramics and possible Late Intermediate period ceramics. Area 4 is located in the fields that lie below the cliff face to the north, where a moderate scatter of Inca and early Colonial ceramics can be found in a 2- to 3-ha area (Chokasuyu types as defined in Stanish et al. 1997:49; Pakajes Tardío in Albarracin-Jordan and Mathews 1990). All four areas have stone agricultural tools, and these tools are particularly common in Area 4.

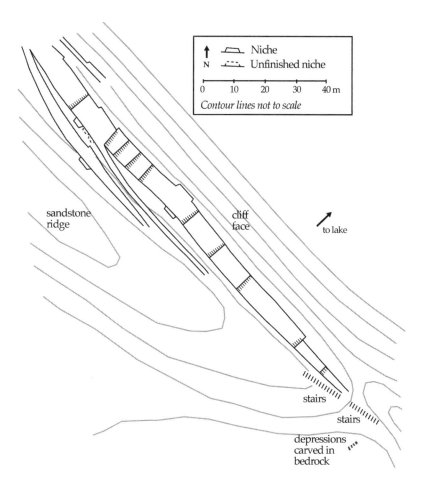

FIGURE 14.22. Masonry retaining the walkways at Kenko (Tres Ventanas)

FIGURE 14.23. Carved stairs on the cliff face at Kenko (Tres Ventanas)

FIGURE 14.24. Niches at Kenko (Tres Ventanas), in varying stages of completion

Although Kenko is far more impressive and more stylistically "Inca" than some of the other sites listed here, Kenko, like the other sites, has a pattern of modest subsidiary carvings dispersed around the site. A natural gap in the rock ridge behind Area 3 allows access to a much wider trough in the landscape. At this gap, on the south side of the ridge, are ten small depressions, or cupules, pecked in a pattern on the rock (Figure 14.25). On the opposite side of the trough, against the ridge that rises to the south, a thin, straight groove or canal carved into the rock is almost certainly Late Horizon in date. It might have carried water from a spring uphill to the east. Finally, a shallow semicircular "seat" has been carved in a boulder about 2 km northwest of Kenko, at the base of the cliffs facing the lake (Figure 14.26).

It may be significant that the main ceremonial sector has only one entrance: the stairway from Area 1. Decorated fineware is common in Area 1. It is possible that this was an elite area and that access to the site was restricted, or at least monitored, by the elite. Though it no longer

exists, a stone gateway is reported to have stood at the gap where the Inca stairs give access to the ceremonial sector.[10] It may have marked a point at which access was restricted, as well as demarcating the border between sacred and profane space.

In the overall pattern of Inca ceremonial sites in the region, Kenko uniquely juxtaposes a significant labor investment and Inca stylistic canons with a very remote location. It currently requires a detour of about 15 km from the modern road running from Acora to Ilave, although the location of the corresponding section of the Inca road is difficult to ascertain.[11] Why was this location chosen? The rock ridges on which the site was constructed are spectacular and unusual, and geologically similar to the Bebedero outcrop, which constitutes another sacred site. This may explain why the area, if not the site itself, is still ritually important to local residents. Although the Island of the Sun is not visible from the cliff at Kenko, the site does have a magnificent view of the lake from a fairly easy-to-reach setting. Given that many of the ceremonial

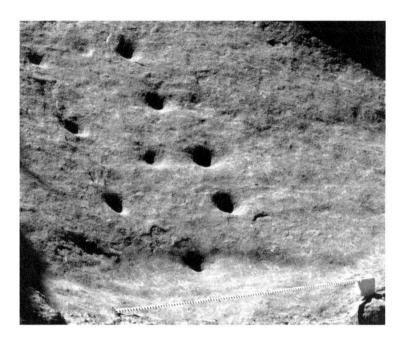

FIGURE 14.25. Cupules at Kenko (Tres Ventanas)

FIGURE 14.26. Carved stone to the west of Kenko

sites in the area are on the lakeside, this may have been a factor in the decision to build at Kenko. Perhaps more importantly, the cliff face and any activities that may have taken place on it are clearly visible from the fields below. Kenko is the perfect location for ritual performed publicly, but with restricted participation—a pattern identical to what the historical documents indicate occurred at the Island of the Sun.

The Inca Uyu at Chucuito

Late Horizon Chucuito is a very large, intrusive site under and to the east of the present-day town of Chucuito (Hyslop 1976:415; Stanish 2001b; M. Tschopik 1946). It is known from ethnohistoric accounts to have been the cabecera, or administrative center, of the Lupacas. It was also a tambo on the Inca road from Cuzco (Diez de San Miguel 1964 [1567]; Vaca de Castro 1908 [1543]:437) and, at around 80 ha in size, was the largest known Inca settlement in the Titicaca Basin (Stanish 2003).

An intriguing structure in the plaza, known as the Inca Uyu, probably fulfilled a ceremonial function. The Inca Uyu is a walled enclosure measuring about 10 x 10 m and consisting of two courses of massive stonework (Figure 14.27). Although the masonry was clearly modeled on Cuzco-style polygonal stonework, curved rather than right-angle joinings betray it as a poor imitation.[12] The shape of other stones uncovered in the plaza indicate that either this or an associ-ated structure had windows (Stanish 2001b). The structure was therefore not an *ushnu*, or ceremonial platform.

Marion Tschopik excavated the structure in the 1940s, finding Colonial era fieldstone walls, ceramics, and faunal remains, but no prehistoric stratigraphy (Hyslop 1984:129–130). Hyslop relates that she was told of another structure called the Kurinuyu to the east of the Inca Uyu, but she did not see it, and there is no observable trace of this structure today. The upper row of stones at the Inca Uyu were found and replaced by Orompelio Vidal in the 1960s, who continued excavations at the site.

Although Chucuito was probably a rest stop on the pilgrimage to the Island of the Sun from Cuzco, it would be premature to assume that the Inca Uyu's primary function was tied to the pilgrimage. Its location in the center of the Lupaca cabecera of Chucuito and its quasi-Inca stonework suggest that it is the construction of local lords unsupervised by architects from Cuzco. Its role in ritual may have had more to do with the expression of the authority of the Lupaca kurakas than with Inca-Lupaca relations.

SITES OUTSIDE THE SURVEY AREA

Hatuncolla

Hatuncolla was the provincial administrative center corresponding to the Colla ethnic group, just as Chucuito was the administrative center

FIGURE 14.27. The Inka Uyu at Chucuito

FIGURE 14.28. The Pachatata sunken court on Amantaní Island. The upper wall is a recent addition.

for the Lupacas. As at Chucuito, it is likely there was at one time an Inca religious or ceremonial center of some kind at Hatuncolla. Cieza de León (1984:361 [1553:Ch. 102]) mentions a sun temple at Hatuncolla, among other Inca edifices. No whole structure remains, but Julien (1983:90) suggests that the fine Cuzco masonry reused in more recent buildings—masonry including one whole doorway—may be from this temple.

Amantaní Island

Amantaní Island's two major ceremonial constructions, Pachamama and Pachatata, are problematic, but the site is too important to leave out of this discussion. Both constructions are sunken courts on low mountains. Pachatata (also called Aylicancha) is rectangular and Pachamama is circular, making it very unusual within the Titicaca Basin (Figure 14.28).[13] Both have been restored and modified to an unknown extent in recent times, and continue to be used for rituals and offerings (Niles 1987b, 1988; Spahni 1971; see also Kidder 1943:116 Stanish 2003:188, and Vásquez 1940). The courts appear to have been in use in the early Colonial period, for Martín de Murúa reports a famous huaca at Amantaní (Murúa 1946:216–7 [1590:Bk. 3 Ch. 21]).

The date of the ceremonial constructions at Amantaní is difficult to determine. Although rectangular sunken courts are common to Formative and Tiwanaku period ceremonial sites, Pachatata's atypical fieldstone masonry, triple stair, and noncardinal orientation make assigning it to the Tiwanaku period with certainty difficult (Stanish 2003). The inclusion of two large (uncarved) boulders in the circular temple of Pachamama (see Spahni 1971:222, pl. 3) suggests an Inca period date. There is little to no surface Tiwanaku pottery on the island, although Niles (1987b, 1988) reports some pottery looted from a grave on the island, pottery that included a fragment of an incense-burner that is almost certainly Tiwanaku. Formative pottery, including Pucara polychrome incised, is apparent on the surface, though in small quantities (see also Kidder 1943:16; Spahni 1971:15). On the other hand, Inca ceramics litter the island, and the terraces near the ceremonial structures have dense scatters of fine Inca ware. The Pachatata sunken court may therefore be a Formative or Tiwanaku court restored and modified in Inca times. Although such a construction would be unusual, it would have fit with a program of Tiwanaku stylistic references apparent in the sanctuaries on the Islands of the Sun and Moon. Jean-Christian Spahni (1971:219) also reports carved seats or shelves on the southwest shore of the island (facing the peninsula of Capachica) that may possibly be Inca period in date. If the ceremonial structures and carvings at Amantaní were in use in the Inca period, the inaccessibility of the island makes it very unlikely that they were directly related to the pilgrimage.

Pucara

While Pucara is far to the north of the study area, it deserves to be mentioned for its ceremonial role in the Late Horizon. An important Formative center, it was restored and modified in Inca times. A terrace wall was remodeled with trapezoidal niches, and a stairway with finely dressed corner stones was built into Pucara walls (Wheeler and Mujica 1981:58–9). Fine Inca pottery of both local and Cuzco manufacture can be found at the site (Wheeler and Mujica 1981:58–70), and Pucara is listed as a tambo in early Spanish colonial documents (Guaman Poma de Ayala 1980 [1613]:1006 [1091/1101]; Vaca de Castro 1908 [1543]:437). Pucara appears in Inca mythology as a site at which Viracocha, in his voyage of creation, turned disobedient subjects to stone or called down a rain of fire upon them (Molina of Cuzco 1947 [1584]):26). The association of Pucara with Viracocha's journey outward from the sacred center of Titicaca makes the site a good candidate for a ceremonial station on the pilgrimage, which traced Viracocha's course in reverse back to the Islands of the Sun and Moon.

Other Shrines in the Northern Titicaca Basin

In a more recent survey of Colla fortified sites (pukaras) in the northwest basin, I found a number of modest Inca administrative or ceremonial structures located on hilltops that had formerly been used by the Collas as defended settlements. While these data will be described elsewhere, it is worth noting that at least one of these Inca complexes displayed unusually elaborate architecture, including double-jambed niches (which are very rare in the Titicaca Basin), and probably had ceremonial functions. This and similar Inca structures were located in relatively inaccessible places far from the Inca roads,

and rather than being placed for maximum visibility and use in the Late Horizon, their placement may have been intended as architectural statements of Inca control over formerly important political centers (Arkush 2001).

Vilcanota and Beyond

At the La Raya Pass, the entrance to the Titicaca Basin from the Cuzco region was marked by the Inca temple and tambo of Vilcanota (Reinhard 1995). Placed as it was directly on the road, this facility may well have been designed as a pilgrimage station for high-ranking travelers. To the north of the pass, another series of shrines both large and small traced the route from Cuzco. This series includes Raqchi, Urcos, Tipon, and huacas along the *ceque* lines of Collasuyu, the southeast quarter of the empire (Bauer 1998).

CONCLUSIONS

The proliferation of small ceremonial sites along the southwest shores of Lake Titicaca—as well as the justly more famous Island of the Sun sanctuary—amounted to something of a religious florescence in the Late Horizon. While the region does not have nearly the density of ceremonial sites as the area near Cuzco, the region displays a surprising variety of small sites available for ritual. These are mostly carved rock sites, and they clearly refer to Inca, rather than indigenous, ceremonial styles, yet they are highly varied in location, size, level of labor investment, and technical skill.

The most obvious pattern that emerges from this group of subsidiary sites is the very lack of a pattern. Out of fifteen sites,[14] six would have required a minor detour from the probable Inca road, and four sites (Cerro Juana, Kenko and the carved stone to the west of it, and Amantaní Island) would have required a major detour. Nine sites are on the lakeshore or within view of the lake, even though the Island of the Sun is not visible from most of them. However, the pattern may simply reflect the predominance of lakeside settlement in the Late Horizon. A cluster of Cuzco-style sites around Copacabana contrasts with sites outside the Copacabana Peninsula, which vary widely in style. Size and labor investment do not obviously correlate with Cuzco-style sites or decorated pottery. Several sites have a "dispersed" site plan including minor elaborations or additions, and two (Altarani and Kenko) show clearly unfinished carving. Two of the most stylistically "authentic" Inca religious sites, Intinkala-Orcohawira and Copacati, are associated with indigenous and possibly nonelite huacas. The Inca use of Amantaní and Pucara also took advantage of preexisting ceremonial structures that may well have held religious significance for local inhabitants in the LIP. Meanwhile, in the Late Horizon, the massive chulpa cemeteries probably provided the main ceremonial sites that were not associated with the Inca state in the minds of local residents.

While it is difficult to determine exactly what was going on in the region in the Late Horizon to produce this heterogeneous mix of sites, comparison with the expectations of the models of Inca policy outlined above can rule out some possibilities.

The first model, in which Inca administrators used Cuzco-style ceremonial sites to mark the region as Inca territory and impose imperial ideology on the Aymara-speaking peoples without accommodation, is untenable in the face of the data. The styles, locations, and overall pattern of the sites all argue against this scenario. Several sites feature a mix of styles. Playa Chatuma, for instance, has a Cuzco-Inca style "stair" carving, canals which refer to but do not reproduce Cuzco-Inca canons, and the nearby carved rocks on Pukara Chatuma, whose styles range from typical Inca to highly unusual and innovative. Kenko (Tres Ventanas) displays Cuzco-Inca style stairs, masonry, and niches, but an innovative site plan. Furthermore, the locations of the ceremonial sites are not what would be expected from a propagandistic building program. Several sites, such as Playa Chinchin Jalave and even Copacati, are not very visible or accessible. Many are not close to areas of dense population, and in consequence are ill-suited as vehicles for the dissemination of imperial ideology to local people. Kenko, in particular, has only a small associated habitation sector. Furthermore, there are no large towns nearby comparable to the cabeceras on the Urcosuyu road. In fact, the Late Horizon pattern of ceremonial sites in the study

area is perhaps notable for the lack of an overall "master plan." Unfinished features and additions at some sites imply that there may have been an ongoing process of site construction and modification, rather than a single monumental building program. I suggest that these sites were not all conceived and constructed at one time by one group. They were not part of an imperial program designed to stamp the landscape with symbols of Inca power in the most visible and accessible way.

The second scenario, in which Inca religious policy allowed input from local traditions and participation by local actors, is best supported by the reconnaissance data. Most telling in this regard are those sites that appear to have been placed to take advantage of pre-Inca huacas, indicating a mutual accommodation between Inca and local religious traditions. These instances of reuse fit with the revival of a Tiwanaku sacred center on the Island of the Sun and the reuse of Tiwanaku itself as a sacred site (Vranich et al. 2002). They also fit with the Inca reuse of other sacred sites such as Pachacamac. However, reuse of sacred sites on the small scale represented here is surprising, and points to finer-grained religious policies that integrated smaller, less elite communities and their sites of worship into the Inca cosmology.

The location and style of these sites also indicate a surprising degree of local participation in their construction and use. Four sites (Cerro Juana, Playa Chatuma, Playa Chinchin Jalave, and the Inca Uyu) are so stylistically atypical that they appear to have been constructed as local imitations, or at least fashioned without Inca design or supervision. It is interesting that such modest, unsupervised sites had a place in the pattern of lakeside religious installations. Stylistic innovation and elaboration at certain Inca-style sites also point to a construction process that may have been open to local input. Clearly, there was considerable room for innovation and local participation in the fashioning and use of Inca-style ceremonial sites, suggesting a greater role for Aymara residents than was permitted, according to the ethnohistorical documents, at the island sanctuary. Although access may have been restricted without leaving visible traces on the ground, we may guess that small, remote sites such as Cerro Juana and the carved rock west of Kenko were probably not visited primarily by the elite.

The sites described here constitute a marked contrast with the Island of the Sun. Tight controls on access to the island sanctuary served to institutionalize a highly stratified social hierarchy, one that placed Incas at the top. In the southwest basin outside of the island, there was apparently a far looser control over the sacred. Here, a range of larger and smaller sites, sites that appear more and less "Inca," and more and less controlled sites extended the cline of the sacred achieved by the island sanctuary, allowing the incorporation and participation of small local communities in the rituals and beliefs of the Late Horizon.

This picture of Inca religious policy exemplifies an interesting gradation of control over ideology and religious sites from the center to the periphery. The spectrum of ideological control bears similarities to the continuum from territorial (direct) to hegemonic (indirect) political and economic control argued for the Inca by D'Altroy (1992). Inca political control was, of course, centered at Cuzco, while major administrative centers in the provinces such as Huánuco Pampa served as nodes in the political hierarchy. Outside of these centers and away from the major roads and forts (especially on the coast), Inca political control was looser and more flexible, accommodating local hierarchies and sometimes leaving few traces on the landscape (D'Altroy 1992; Hyslop 1990; Morris and Thompson 1985). Inca ideological power may well have followed a similar pattern of a highly controlled center (Cuzco), subsidiary centers in the provinces (e.g., the Island of the Sun), and a hinterland in which significant compromises were made with local actors and local tradition. The result was a flexible approach to ideological governance, one that would have been more economical to the rulers while being more palatable to the ruled.

A balance between local and imperial needs in religious practice could only have been achieved if it provided acceptable benefits to both sides. Aymara people were given, or demanded, license to participate in a prestigious religion whose value was defined by the exclusive, ancient island sanctuary, all the while retaining their local huacas and a degree of religious autonomy. Meanwhile, their participation in this religious framework helped to reinforce conceptions of social hierarchy in which the dominance of the Incas was naturalized. The cosmology of the Incas readily adopted local beliefs, embraced locally sacred places, and accommodated local innovation, while retaining its essential tenet, the divine solar origin of the conquering Incas. A recursive relationship for ideological influence resulted. Inca ideology, religious practices, and sacred sites were continually altered and reshaped by non-Incas and the nonelite, as well as by their rulers.

Inca religious accommodation contrasts sharply with the forcible and exclusive imposition of Spanish Catholicism that was to succeed it (MacCormack 1991). Was there a downside to an imperial policy of toleration of existing local or regional huacas? While Inca religious accommodation probably helped to reconcile subject populations to Inca rule, it may also have weakened the empire by allowing subjects to continue a strong tradition of identification with smaller ethnic or regional groups. By the LIP, Andean ethnic consciousness was anchored in huacas and *pacarinas* (mythologized ancestors and origin places fixed in the landscape), providing a concrete and inalienable sense of ethnicity or grouphood. There is evidence that the Inca rulers were attempting to weaken regional/ethnic identification with many of their other policies. These policies, enumerated by Rowe (1982), include the imposition of forcible resettlement or temporary labor service, the standardization of the arts and technologies, and the spread of Quechua and some elements of Inca religion. Yet the Incas themselves arose out of a traditional Andean conceptualization of self and grouphood and participated fully in it, as evidenced by their own landscape-based sense of ethnicity (involving descent from a handful of ancestors originating at Pacariqtambo; see Urton 1990). They could hardly have done otherwise; but this existing ideological base may have hindered rather than helped them in the task of consolidation and unification. The historical documents show that at the time of Spanish contact the empire was still thought of as a collection of ethnic units, anchored to place and genealogy by their respective pacarinas and local huacas. When these groups splintered off, as they did in the Huascar-Atahualpa civil war and at the time of the Spanish conquest, they did so as whole units. The parts of which the body politic was composed, tenuously connected by a few empire-wide institutions, came apart easily as soon as the head fell.

NOTES

1. Bauer and Stanish (2001) and Stanish and Bauer (2004) provide a detailed treatment of the archaeology and history of the islands, and Adolph Bandelier (1910), the first archaeologist to systematically work on the islands, remains an excellent source. Also, Ephraim Squier (1877a) and other nineteenth-century naturalists wrote a number of useful descriptions of the remains on the Islands of the Sun and Moon.

2. The Inca road from Cuzco split into two at the northern end of Lake Titicaca at Ayaviri, with one road tracing each side of the lake. They rejoined to the south at Caracollo. Access to Copacabana and the Island of the Sun was from the western or Urcosuyu branch. As the Urcosuyu road continued south, a side road passed through Yunguyu and on to Copacabana (Hyslop 1984; see also Cieza de León 1984:361, 364–5 [1553:Bk. 1 Chs. 102, 104]; Guaman Poma de Ayala (1980 [1613]); Lizarraga 1987:185 [1605:Bk. 1 Ch. 85], and Vaca de Castro (1908 [1543]).

3. Such was the opinion of Fray Rafael Sanz (1886), compiler of an early edition of Ramos Gavilán, who associated the idol of Copacabana with the "restos de graderias" at Copacabana, as he did the idol of Copacati with the Inca site of the same name.

4. Ramos Gavilán recounts that the aboriginal inhabitants of Copacabana and the Island of the Sun were relocated to Yunguyo by the Incas, and replaced by mitima colonists who enjoyed a special prestige as attendants to the temples (1988:84 [1621:Bk. 1 Ch. 12]). He uses the term *Yunguyo* to refer to non-mitima inhabitants of the Copacabana Peninsula.

5. One possible analogy is found in the description of priest José Mario Blanco in 1834 of a rock he calls "Qqenco" or "Ccasana," near Cuzco's plaza (it is apparently not the Kenko now known to us): "una piedra que tiene labrados dos circulos concentricos" (J. M. Blanco 1974 [1834]:181, cited in Van de Guchte 1990:150, note 14).

6. Liquid offerings of water, *chicha*, or blood, constituted an important feature of worship at the Island of the Sun, according to contact period texts (Cobo 1990:97 [1653:Bk. 13 Ch. 18]; Ramos Gavilán 1988:116, 149 [1621:Bk. 1 Chs. 17, 24]), and ritual canals on the islands attest to them (Bandelier 1910:198, 221; Bauer and Stanish 2001).

7. Squier (1877a:350) gives the "tradition" that the Inca's Chair "was the 'resting-place of the Inca,' in his journeys or pilgrimages, where the people came to do him homage, bringing chicha for his delectation and that of his attendants." Dubious as his ethnohistoric information may be, it is worth noting that the site was specifically connected with the pilgrimages of the Inca even at this late date. Alberto Cuentas (1928) noted that some informants believed this was where the Incas and Lupacas first celebrated their alliance by libating chicha. Thus, in its name and in legends surrounding it, Bebedero was strongly associated with Incas, libation, and chicha.

8. Examples are found on the southeast side of Suchuna (Rodadero) Hill by Sacsayhuaman and north of Suchuna near a large circular depression, at the carved-rock complex known as Kusilluchayoc or the "Templo de los Monos" near Kenko (Cuzco), and in Tiwanaku-style niches at the cave site of Choquequilla. It is worth noting also that the Incas deliberately used Tiwanaku stylistic canons in the architecture of the temple on the Island of the Moon nearby, as well as in ceramics used on the Island of the Sun (Julien 1993).

9. In both Quechua and Aymara, *kenko* means twisting, sinuous, or zigzag (Bertonio 1956 [1612]:295). At Kenko near Cuzco, the term refers to the zigzag paccha. Here, it may refer to the zigzag walkways on the cliffside.

10. A local informant gives this report, which matches M. Tschopik's (1946:8) observation: "A well dressed stone wall and doorway have been erected across a break in the escarpment."

11. Hyslop (1984) found no trace of the Inca road between Kacha Kacha B, a chulpa site 3 km southeast of Acora, and the town of Juli. The location of the Inca town of Ilave, listed as a tambo in early colonial records (Vaca de Castro 1908 [1543]), is similarly ambiguous (Hyslop 1984:123; Stanish 2003).

12. One unusual stylistic feature of the masonry at the Inca Uyu, a pattern of "tails" from the upper course that fit into the curved join of blocks on the lower course, has an intriguing parallel at Ollantaytambo. Although much less accentuated, masonry on the Wall of the Unfinished Gate and on some terrace walls at Ollantaytambo has a similar tailed form, termed "scutiform" masonry by Harthe-Terré (1965: 158; see also Protzen 1993:82, Figure 3.13). There may be a possible connection between these two isolated instances, for according to Sarmiento de Gamboa, Colla captives were brought to build Ollantaytambo by Pachacuti (Sarmiento de Gamboa 1988:112 [1572:Ch. 40]). A Colla ayllu at Ollantaytambo is also attested in a land dispute document from 1560 (Protzen 1993:269, note 1).

13. One circular structure at Sillustani may be viewed as somewhat similar to the one at Pachamama.

14 The difficulty of determining what to call a distinct "site" is considerable, since so many of the sites described here show a pattern of small, widely dispersed ceremonial features. For the purposes of this tally, features within an arbitrary radius of 1 km are considered a single ritual area or "site." For instance, Intinkala and Orcohawira are grouped as one site, while the "Inca's Chair" and Altarani are considered separate. Sites on the Islands of the Sun and Moon are not included in the tally; neither is the Inca occupation at Tiwanaku. The statistical limitations of this sample of fifteen are obvious.

The fifteen sites considered here are Intinkala and Orcohawira; the Baño del Inca; the Horca del Inca; Copacati; the Cerro Juana stone; Playa Chatuma and associated features; Playa Chinchin Jalave; the Sillumocco stone; Altarani; the "Inca's Chair"; Kenko; the carved stone west of Kenko; the Inca Uyu at Chucuito; Amantaní Island's sunken courts; and Inca additions at Pucara.

15.

Archaeological Reconnaissance in the Carabaya Region, Peru

Lawrence S. Coben and Charles Stanish

THE REGION OF CARABAYA is located in the northern and eastern portions of the modern Peruvian department of Puno (Figure 15.1). One of the least-studied geographical areas in the Andes, it encompasses the vast eastern slopes that lead to the Amazonian drainage to the northeast of Lake Titicaca. While Carabaya is located outside of the hydrological limits of the Titicaca Basin proper, ethnohistorical documents indicate that this area was part of the circum-Titicaca Basin cultural sphere in the post-Tiwanaku periods. Tiwanaku and post-Tiwanaku polities also likely exploited these eastern slopes, as they did those of the Larecaja region (e.g., especially see Faldín Arancibia 1990, 1991; Ponce Sanginés 1977). The Mollo culture of Larecaja and the eastern Omasuyus in Bolivia, for example, were post-Tiwanaku phenomena that are little understood today. However, the settlements of this cultural area are impressive in their size and architectural complexity. Similarly, the iconographic linkages on pottery to Churajón in the Peruvian valley of Majes (Lumbreras 1974a) raise fascinating questions about the place of the eastern slopes in the overall cultural history of the south central Andes.

Ethnohistoric documents indicate that the Carabaya region contained many gold mines exploited by the Inka. Jean Berthelot (1986) has located numerous references to these mines. Such documents describe two systems of mining, one controlled by the Inka and the other by local caciques. The former system was subject to direct imperial control, and gold from these mines was transported to Cusco alone. Likewise, the Toledo *Tasa* indicates that virtually all of the Titicaca Ba-

sin towns that were required to provide gold as tribute to the Spanish state, and presumably to the Inka as well, were located on the eastern and northern shores of Lake Titicaca (Stanish 2003). This suggests that these towns had some kind of access to the mines of the eastern slopes in the Colonial period. Such access was limited to this region and contrasts with that of other polities from the west and south of the lake that did not pay tribute in gold. From this, we can deduce that Inka period groups, and possibly pre-Inka polities, maintained economic and/or cultural connections to the Carabaya region and its mines.

In 1999, we spent approximately one week conducting reconnaissance in the Ollachea Valley. Based upon this admittedly brief work, we believe that the Ollachea Valley (Figure 15.2) was a likely access route to the gold mines for the northern and eastern Lake Titicaca polities that inhabited the region in later prehistory, as well as a direct route to the Carabaya resources for the state officials in the Inka capital of Cusco. The valley is a combination of steep hills and numerous streams, rivers, and waterfalls that feed the Ollachea River (Figure 15.3). The altitude of the valley ranges from about 2800 m above sea level to the east (where the land plateaus and the high forest begins) to over 5000 m above sea level in the high mountains to the west. The steepness of the valley and the excellent supply of water have led the Peruvian government to select this area as the site of the new San Gabán hydroelectric facility. This new plant replaced the one destroyed at Machu Picchu and supplies power to Juliaca, Puno, and the rest of southern Peru.

243

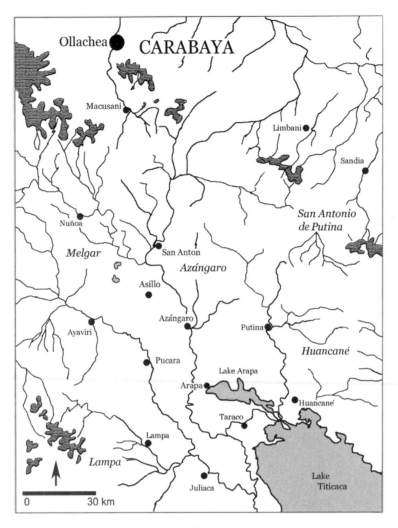

FIGURE 15.1. Map of the Carabaya region

The principal access to the Ollachea Valley from the northern Titicaca region is via a road that runs from Pucara through Asillo and Macusani, and then down into the eastern slopes. The valley contains an extensive prehistoric settlement and road system, and is replete with agricultural terraces and many habitation areas with square, rectangular, and round structures with low walls. The pre-Hispanic road (Figure 15.4) parallels the modern one and runs on the first plateau above the river on the north side of the valley. It connects the larger habitation and farming sites described below. Scores, if not hundreds, of sites are found along the sides of the river valley. *Chulpas*, habitation sites, roads, modified rock outcrops, and terraces all indicate an extensive and very dense prehistoric occupa-

tion of the region. In the following paragraphs, we describe a few of these sites and then assess the significance of these data for understanding the use of the region by the Inka state.

A RECONNAISSANCE OF LATE SITES IN THE OLLACHEA REGION

Our reconnaissance was nonsystematic and nonintensive, as described in Stanish (2001b) as the first stage in a regional research design in an unknown area. The intent of this work was to document the nature and range of settlement types in an area that had virtually no published or accessible previous research. The methodology consisted of simply examining sites encountered along the road, as well as walking to sites

FIGURE 15.2. View of the Upper Ollachea Valley

FIGURE 15.3. View of the mid Ollachea Valley

FIGURE 15.4. Pre-Hispanic road, Ollachea Valley

described by informants. As such, our data are not representative of the settlements in the region. Likewise, we did no subsurface testing and our surface collections were kept to an absolute minimum.

We discovered scores of sites from the beginning of the hydrological drainage of the Ollachea to a few kilometers below the town of the same name. In our reconnaissance, we discovered only Late Intermediate period (LIP) and Inka period sites. These sites generally fell into two categories. Lower-altitude settlements (Figure 15.5) consist primarily of houses, terraces, and possibly corrals, and are normally found on the first plateau above the river on the pre-Hispanic road. Higher-altitude sites lack the corral-like structures but contain more structures that we believe are of a ritual nature.

A substantial number of sites in the reconnaissance area show evidence of Inka construction and manipulation of space on what are essentially pre-Inka settlements. The surface artifacts at these locations indicate strong stylistic links with Collao LIP pottery from the Lake Titicaca region, along with what are most certainly

local Late Horizon pottery assemblages. We also found a few pieces, possibly trade wares, that were Chucuito in style. Our interpretation is that most of the settlements in the region were constructed in the LIP. A number of them that were located along or near the road were co-opted by the Inka state. We furthermore assume that most of the sites with both LIP and Inka occupations were continuously occupied in both periods, given the short time span of the latter.

Unplanned, aggregated household compounds built on terraces characterize the domestic architecture of almost all of the settlements. The walls are of *pirka* masonry. Domestic debris—including eroding middens, bone, burnt pottery sherds, carbon, and ash—are found on the sites. On a number of sites, one can detect architectural areas that are clearly distinct in orientation, size, and style from the rest of the site. These areas are hypothesized to be Inka period additions to the settlements, and are interpreted to represent attempts by the Inka state to co-opt this important road system and impose some degree of political ideology on the population of the area. As discussed below, we conclude that

FIGURE 15.5. Low-altitude site, Ollachea Valley

these modifications are the result of an Inka-imposed plan for the exercise of political authority within this region (Low 1995). Evidence of such manipulation is present at almost all sites where sufficient standing architecture remains to make such a determination. Such evidence includes platforms (Figure 15.6), plazas (Figure 15.7), and specially placed worked and unworked stones (Figure 15.8).

The habitation area of the lower-altitude site of Kille Kille (Figure 15.9), for example, is about 4.0 ha in area and is located on the main pre-Hispanic road on the first plateau above the river. Two types of terracing are clearly present—a finer construction utilizing larger stones and well-made terraces in the central area of the site, flanked on both sides by structures using a cruder construction technique. Structures on the central terraces are primarily square or rectangular, while those on the sides are primarily round. A cursory analysis of the surface pottery distribution reveals a similar division, with local LIP Collao styles found principally on the flanks and locally produced Inka ceramics in the central zone. Rock tombs were found immediately adjacent to non-Inka style habitations or terraces.

While the terraces on the flanks continue to the end of the plateau overlooking the river, the lower section of the central zone contains ceremonial architecture evocative of the Inka. The primary feature is a large trapezoidal plaza 55 m long and 10–20 m wide (Figure 15.10). Abutting the plaza is a natural stone mound with benches or terraces carved into it (Figure 15.11). On the opposite side of the plaza is a series of constructed terraces. The lowest terrace or bench on both sides is significantly wider than those above it, as if designed for spectators or passage (Figure 15.12). To the west of the terraced mound is a multi-room structure with an impressive doorway (Figure 15.13). Immediately

FIGURE 15.6. Platform at the site of Illingaya

FIGURE 15.7. Plaza at the site of Kille Kille

FIGURE 15.8. Large carved stone, Pitumarka

FIGURE 15.9. Overview of Kille Kille

east of the plaza is a room measuring about 12 x 18 m (Figure 15.14), followed by a second smaller plaza with a large and small stone at its center. In the northeast corner of this plaza is a small, roundish structure with a large, worked rectangular stone placed into one of its walls (Figure 15.15).

The plaza area is entered from the east by a walled-off pathway that cuts through a portion of the earlier-period terraces. This pathway is aligned with, and appears to continue onto, the lowest wide bench or terrace on one side of this large plaza. The entrance to the plaza from the west is narrow and not distinguished in any way.

We believe that this entire central plaza area (Figure 15.16), the terracing, and the structures are a later, Inka period construction. While the rest of the site consists merely of habitations and terraces, this set of plazas, mounds, and stones appears to have been dropped directly on the site from above, without regard for the preexisting spatial arrangement or use. While the Inka-style terraces above this zone may have reused the gradings of earlier periods, they are clearly

integrated with the plaza structures, while the remaining terraces are not. This interpretation is further supported by the entry road described above, which slices through the earlier terraces to integrate itself with this center complex that we believe to have had ritual connotations.

About 2 km northwest of Kille Kille on the pre-Hispanic road are other lower-altitude, unnamed sites (Figures 15.17–15.19). The site seen in Figure 15.17 is a lower habitation and terrace complex of about 3.0 ha. This site is also located on the first plateau above a river bend. Reversing the pattern of Kille Kille, the multiple round and square structures are on the lower portion of the site, with multiple terraces above them (Figure 15.18). There are also several large rectangular rooms with walls ranging from 10 to over 10 m in length. A platform is situated just above these structures (Figure 15.19). Another plaza has two stones that are still upright and resemble the contour of the double mountain behind them (Figure 15.20). Between the two mountains is a waterfall (Figure 15.21). At the base of the site, close to the river, is the foundation of a structure, consisting of four 1.0 x 4.0 m

FIGURE 15.10. Central plaza, Kille Kille

FIGURE 15.11. Rock with levels, Kille Kille

FIGURE 15.12. Wide lower level on plaza, Kille Kille

FIGURE 15.13. Doorway, Kille Kille

FIGURE 15.14. Room adjacent to plaza, Kille Kille

Figure 15.15. Well-made stone in room, Kille Kille

Figure 15.16. Central plaza, Kille Kille

FIGURE 15.17. Lower-altitude site, Ollachea Valley

FIGURE 15.18. House foundations on lower-altitude site

FIGURE 15.19. Platform, lower-altitude site

rectangular units (Figures 15.22 and 15.23), of a type (though on the small end of the size range) that at other Inka sites has been interpreted as a type of storage building or *colca* (D'Altroy 1992, Levine 1992; Morris 1982).

A number of other sites are found on the mountain sides and tops in areas such as those seen in Figure 15.24. Located just west of Ollachea is the 1.5-ha hilltop site of Pitumarka. The fields below this hilltop are farmed and are covered with large scatters of LIP ceramics and one or two round houses of uncertain age. On the hilltop, the site is surrounded by an exterior low 1.5-m wall and a higher 1.8-m interior wall On the north side, a canal runs between these walls. The entrance within the walled area is reached by passing through a doorway in the outer wall, followed by passing through a second doorway at a right angle to the first within the inner wall. This form of entrance is reminiscent of the one associated with the zigzag walled structure on the hilltop of the site of Inkallakta, Bolivia (Coben i.p.). Near the walls

are several small structures, most of which are circular. In the center of this interior space is a raised area on which are multiple square (2.0 x 2.0 m) and rectangular (2.0 x 3.0 m) structures. At the end of this elevated platform-like zone is a doorway flanked by a wall of large stones and a stone shaped like a mountain leading to the lower part of the site.

The site appears to have been originally an LIP fortified site, suggested by its hilltop location, surrounding walls, and round structures all overlooking agricultural fields and habitations. The surface pottery confirms this date. The central platform appears jammed into the center of this enclosure, and is clearly of a different shape and likely a different style than the other constructions. We suggest that this is a later Inka period addition, serving as an elite residence, a ritual area, or both.

The spectacular 3-ha site of Illingaya exhibits characteristics that are similar to those of Pitumarka and other hilltop higher-altitude sites (Figure 15.25). Located high on a promontory

Figure 15.20. Mountains behind platform, lower-altitude site

overlooking the confluence of the Ollachea with two side rivers, Illingaya—in conjunction with the surrounding terraces, house remains (Figure 15.26), and rock tombs— appears at first to be a classic LIP fortified site. Two walls run the length of this promontory (Figure 15.27), while another crosses this ridge at its north end. However, examination of the site's construction and layout are again suggestive of the imposition of Inka ritual structures. Two construction episodes, one of a finer stone and form (Niles 1987a), are visible on some of the walls (Figure 15.28). The interior area consists of a plaza and a series of paired rectangular rooms of various sizes, with those on the western side higher and larger than those on the eastern. A single

FIGURE 15.21. Waterfall between mountains, lower-altitude site

platform is found in one of the larger rectangular rooms in the plaza (Figure 15.29), and two platforms are found in another (Figure 15.30). At the northern end of the site, overlooking the river, is a large multi-roomed structure. An Inka midden, filled with ceramics that include the Late Horizon Titicaca Basin Chucuito style as well as locally produced Inka forms, lies just outside of this structure. A few LIP sherds are also present. The ground drops several meters abruptly behind this wall to agricultural terraces. A well-made staircase (Figure 15.31) leads down toward a hot spring at the base of the promontory.

FIGURE 15.22. Foundation of storage structure-like building, lower-altitude site

FIGURE 15.23. Foundation of storage structure-like building, lower-altitude site

FIGURE 15.24. Location of other high-altitude sites

FIGURE 15.25. Illingaya

FIGURE 15.26. House, likely modern, on approach to Illingaya

FIGURE 15.27. Illingaya, long wall to point

FIGURE 15.28. Two building episodes at Illingaya

FIGURE 15.29. Platform, Illingaya

FIGURE 15.30. Double platform, Illingaya

FIGURE 15.31. Stairway, Illingaya

Slightly above the site of Illingaya was a rock tomb with several skulls (Figure 15.32). In the large rock formation above this tomb is a rock petroglyph of a red dot within a red circle (Figure 15.33). This glyph is best viewed from the central axis of the site.

Not every site we identified in the valley contained evidence of Inka construction. Several smaller habitation sites consist only of LIP round structures and terracing, with only ceramics of that period present. While many of the sites manifesting Inka construction were associated with rock tombs, the only burial towers or chulpas we located within the valley had no Inka stylistic elements (Figure 15.34), although the possibility of Late Horizon chulpas in the region is by no means discounted.

CONCLUSION

Imperial control may be exercised and manifested in a number of ways. While such control requires military force or the threat thereof, empires throughout history have constructed and

FIGURE 15.32. Skulls in tomb, Illingaya

FIGURE 15.33. Red petroglyph dot on hill above tomb, Illingaya

FIGURE 15.34. Burial tower, Ollachea Valley

manipulated architectural space as an important additional strategy for exercising dominion (Godelier 1977:69; Schaedel 1978:289). We propose that the Inka controlled the Ollachea region of Peru in this manner. Ollachea lies on a likely access route to the gold mines in the eastern end of the empire. Control over this route would have been critical, both to ensure an adequate supply of this metal as well as to transport military forces to the east to meet any threats to the mines. Dominion over this major valley in the Carabaya region is indicated by the presence of Inka roads, settlements, and ritual centers along this major river. The imposition of Inka ideology is also demonstrated by the placement of Inka ritual structures such as platforms, plazas, and large worked stones in the center of previous, non-Inka settlements. Through such placement atop and among the residential constructions of the region's residents, the Inka exercised control and provided a continuous reminder of their political authority. This hypothesis will be evaluated utilizing the data from our reconnaissance.

Based on our preliminary survey, we conclude that the Inka constructed and manipulated architectural space at many of the significant sites and locations throughout the Ollachea Valley. Inka architecture is placed within and upon the preexisting Late Intermediate layout, often wedged or jammed therein without regard to, and often destroying, the preexisting architectural pattern in order to create Inka-type spaces. We believe that the repeated and extensive nature of this spatial imposition may result from the importance of this valley as part of the access route from Cusco to the gold mines to the east. Berthelot (1986) notes that the Inka took special precautions to count and secure this gold, and to send it directly to Cusco. Unlike many other areas of Inka governance, the Inka relied on direct control and oversight of the mining and transportation process rather than governing through local leaders. It is logical to assume, therefore, that these precautions would include the safeguarding of and assurance of control over the transport routes, and our data support this assumption.

The imposition of Inka architecture in central areas of non-Inka sites plays an integral role in this strategy of control. It serves, like a flag, as a distinct and repeated reminder of Inka political authority over the region. Construction of new structures in the military installations represents a particularly arrogant demonstration of the Inka's power and the impotence of the local populace's military forces, while Inka structures in the centers of other sites reflects the ability to exercise ideological and political hegemony over the local region. The repeated and physical reminders of such power and hegemony, reflected undoubtedly both in the architecture and the performance of ritual within it, would serve as a powerful deterrent to any uprising or attempt to interfere with the gold trade. Such reminders would of course be strengthened by the geographic proximity of Cusco to this region and by the placement of some of these ritual sites within plain view of the roads on which the Inka army and the gold trade would pass. By impressing the local populace with architecture and creating a powerful link between military, ritual, and political control, the Inka reduced the need to maintain a strong physical presence in the area while reinforcing the incorporation of this region and its peoples into the empire.

We have noted the placement of Inka ritual structures in two distinct regions. (See Heffernan [1996] for an analysis of the Limatambo Valley showing a similar placement.) On the pre-Hispanic road, in lower-altitude sites, the imposed ritual structures were open platforms or plazas, visible by the sites' inhabitants from almost anywhere within its boundaries, as well as by travelers on the road. The very public nature of these spaces would allow for the selection and performance of particular rituals to send or reinforce any desired messages (Moore 1996a:797), and would provide additional security to those Inka involved in the transport of gold. Other structures were placed in more private, less accessible, fortified sites. The more private nature of these rituals may suggest that they were for the Inka and local elites only, reinforcing identity with the empire while excluding others and mystifying the source of the power which propelled the Inka military.

In conclusion, we have demonstrated the presence of a significant LIP and Late Horizon period occupation for this portion of the Carabaya region. A very extensive pre-Inka occupation continued into the Late Horizon, when it was joined by a powerful Inka presence manifested throughout the region. Utilizing the construction and manipulation of architecture, and no doubt ritual, the Inka secured authority over this area and thus the access route between the gold mines to the east and Cusco to the west. The Inka thereby ensured that they, and not the preexisting residents of the valleys, would control this important resource.

ACKNOWLEDGMENTS

The authors wish to thank Rolando Paredes and José Núñez, who accompanied us on this trip. We likewise thank the anonymous reviewers for their useful comments.

16.

Settlement Patterns, Administrative Boundaries, and Internal Migration in the Early Colonial Period

Matthew S. Bandy and John W. Janusek

THE PERIOD OF SPANISH imperial domination in the Andean region is generally considered to have been demographically catastrophic. The decline of the indigenous populations has been widely discussed (Dobyns 1983; Kubler 1946; Ramenofsky 1987; Sánchez-Albornoz 1979; Zubrow 1990), and is often considered to have resulted from the "grim triumvirate of overwork, insufficient food, and disease" (Spalding 1984:174). The Early Colonial period was a difficult time for indigenous populations, exposed as they were to excessive labor demands not only from the colonial state but also from administrative officials, priests, and often their own leaders. Proximity to the Potosí mines could only exacerbate the severity of these stresses for the inhabitants of the south-central Andes. In the sixteenth century especially, the predations resulting from the "plunder economy" (Spalding 1984:109) amplified the effects of exotic disease, malnutrition, and overwork, tipping the demographic balance to the negative.

Early Colonial period demographic changes observed archaeologically are often understood in this light. Juan Albarracin-Jordan, for example, attributes a sharp Early Colonial demographic decline evident in his Lower Tiwanaku Valley study area to the incorporation of the area into the colonial *mit'a*—or labor tax—system.

> ...no se puede ignorar la depresión demográfica que se presenta hacia comienzos del siglo XVII. La minera de plata, en Potosí, se convirtió en principal factor de desequilibrio poblacional en la región. El Valle Bajo de Tiwanaku fue incorporado a la *mit'a*. Un gran número de tributarios fueron reclutados para trabajar las minas de Potosí....La versión española de la mit'a hizo que de 868 tributarios, enlistados en el Repartimiento de Tiwanaku en 1583, solamente resten nueve, en 1658.... [Albarracin-Jordan 1996a:313][1]

Of course, historians have long recognized that the steady decline in size of the native population evident in colonial census records is a result of more complex processes than simply increasing mortality and decreasing fertility. George Kubler made the early suggestion that the decline might be less an actual demographic phenomenon than a historiographic one. He proposed that a large part of the apparent decline was caused by people escaping from Spanish colonial control by fleeing to remote and inaccessible areas, especially the *yungas,* or rugged eastern valleys of the Andean chain. In his view, high mortality was certainly one component of the Early Colonial population decline, but "...the factor of massive dispersals away from the area held by the Spaniards must also be reckoned with" (Kubler 1946:339; also see Saignes 1987).

Nicolás Sánchez-Albornoz (1978, 1979) later took up Kubler's observation and expanded it. He noted that the organization of the labor tax, or mit'a, early in the Colonial period was such that a contribution was required only from persons born into their community of residence. These persons were known as *originarios*. However, displaced persons residing in foreign communities—termed *forasteros*—were exempted from the mit'a. An incentive structure was therefore established that encouraged internal migration, since to move to a foreign community allowed one to evade taxation. Sánchez-Albornoz then asked the obvious question: "¿contracción demográfica o disminución de la masa tributaria?" (Sánchez-Albornoz 1978:19–34). Was the apparent decline in population in the Colonial period a true demographic contraction, or did it simply represent a reduction in the number of tribute payers (*tributarios*) resulting from massive internal migration and tax evasion?

Sánchez-Albornoz observed that most calculations of Colonial period population used a tally of tributarios as a proxy measure for overall population. This is because counts of tribute payers are considerably more common in colonial archives than are true population counts.[2] To answer his question, he then compared counts of tributarios with total population counts from ten separate *repartimientos* in La Paz and La Plata in both 1573 and 1683. His analysis strongly indicated three things:

- Overall population did decline in this 110-year period. The number of "adult Indians" in his sample fell overall by 22%.

- The number of tributarios declined much more dramatically than did the population as a whole, by 57%.

- The discrepancy between these figures can be explained by internal migration. Forasteros had come to represent 45% of adult males in his area by 1683.

Sánchez-Albornoz concluded that the demographic contraction does appear to have been a reality, but that it was not as pronounced as had previously been believed. The dramatic decline in the number of tributarios that is documented in so many colonial records can be attributed to an administrative distinction drawn by the colonial government between originarios and forasteros, the former subject to taxation and the latter exempt.

In his admirable study of indigenous communities in the Early Colonial period of Ayacucho, Steve Stern documents in more depth the linked processes of tax collection and evasion. He describes instances in which communities in Huamanga faked deaths, left births unreported and children unbaptized, and hid substantial numbers of people in remote and inaccessible regions of their territory in order to reduce the number of tributarios on official rolls and therefore their collective mit'a contribution. He also confirms the existence of widespread population displacement and the increasing numerical significance of forasteros, as suggested by Sánchez-Albornoz. He likens the census process to a protracted campaign of subterfuge and litigation between indigenous communities and representatives of the colonial administration. He characterizes it as "[a game of] hide-and-seek played with documents, witnesses, payoffs or political alliances, and elusive settlement patterns" (Stern 1982:124).

Some archaeological observations seem to support this reconstruction. For example, Albarracin-Jordan notes that the very high, inaccessible intermontane zone to the south of the Tiwanaku Valley was first inhabited in the Early Colonial period. He interprets this fact as indicating "an extreme recourse to evade Spanish imposition" (Albarracin-Jordan 1992:329). In another case, Stanish and his colleagues note a settlement pattern shift in the Early Colonial period away from the shores of Lake Titicaca and into the less-accessible interior regions of the Juli-Pomata area (Stanish et al. 1997:59). Stanish et al. interpret the change as indicating the increased importance of camelid pastoralism rather than indicating the existence of hidden population elements. However, these two explanations are in no way contradictory. Hidden populations in areas not well suited to agricultural production would naturally turn to pastoralism for their subsistence. In this way, the social dynamics of taxation and tax evasion could produce economic shifts on a regional scale, an interesting example of the intimate relationship that always pertains between the political, economic, and social domains.

When we understand the political and economic significance of the colonial *revisitas*, and the extent to which population counts were consequently contested and actively manipulated (not only by indigenous communities but also by colonial functionaries), the use of administrative documents to estimate actual rates of population growth or decline becomes extremely problematic. "The results of the recounts," Stern concludes, "reflected the relative skills, advantages, and luck of the interested parties as much as they did demography" (Stern 1982:125). In other words, there was so much at stake in the process of generating population measures that the actual documents are very unlikely to be accurate.

If we cannot trust population estimates in colonial documents, how then can we evaluate the question of the Early Colonial period demographic catastrophe? How can we begin to evaluate the relative contributions of population movement, demographic decline, and intentional deception in the Early Colonial period? Settlement archaeology may help to provide an answer. Though the archaeological measurement of population growth and decline is a difficult and controversial process (Cook and Heizer 1968; Fish and Kowalewski 1990; Hassan 1981; Naroll 1962; Parsons 1976; Tolstoy and Fish 1975), the archaeological record at least is free of the intentional, politically motivated distortion we have just been discussing. Archaeologists estimate population directly from human occupation debris. Archaeological data can therefore provide an independent means of addressing these questions.

THE STUDY AREA

As other chapters in this volume have made clear, the Titicaca Basin was the demographic and cultural core of Collasuyu, the southern quarter of the Inka Empire. Inka rule came to an end in the Titicaca Basin in 1532, when the invading Spaniards toppled the imperial dynasty and bureaucracy. However, the first decades after the Spanish arrival were very chaotic ones. The first Spanish visit to the Titicaca Basin was in 1534, when a small scouting party sent by Pizarro arrived at the lake. Actual Spanish control, however, was not established for some time. As late as 1538 the Lupaqa mounted armed resistance to Pizarro's army at Desaguadero (Bouysse-Cassagne 1987:27). Colonial rule was therefore established in the Titicaca Basin by around 1540.

The present study attempts to reconstruct an Early Colonial period population history for a portion of the southern Titicaca Basin. The dataset we employ is the result of three separate settlement survey projects (indicated on Figures 16.5 and 16.8). The first of these was a survey of the Lower Tiwanaku Valley by Juan Albarracin-Jordan (Albarracin-Jordan and Mathews 1990; Albarracin-Jordan 1992; Albarracin-Jordan 1996a), completed between 1988 and 1990. This survey covered an area measuring approximately 200 km^2. Albarracin-Jordan located 342 sites with Early Colonial period occupations in his study area. His project was part of a larger survey of the Tiwanaku Valley, which also included James Mathews's study of the Middle Tiwanaku Valley (Albarracin-Jordan 1996a; Mathews 1992a). Mathews's data were not reported in such a way as to allow detailed demographic reconstruction, however. For this reason the Middle Tiwanaku Valley has not been included in this analysis. A major contribution of the Tiwanaku Valley surveys was the creation of a three-phase ceramic chronology for the period AD 1100–1600. We use this chronology in the current study. It is described in considerable detail in the following section.

The second project was a survey of a 102-km^2 section of the southern Katari Basin by Janusek (Janusek 2001; Janusek and Kolata 2003). Like the Tiwanaku Valley surveys, this project was affiliated with the Wila Jawira project (Kolata 1996), and was intended to address questions relating to Tiwanaku state emergence and the functioning of the Tiwanaku political economy. One hundred and five sites with Early Colonial period occupations were identified by this project.

The third project was a survey of approximately 98 km^2 on the Taraco Peninsula. This project was directed by Bandy in 1998–99 (Bandy 2001b). The survey was associated with the Taraco Archaeological Project (Hastorf 1999a), and was oriented primarily to elucidating the evolution of village life in the region. However, 326 sites with Early Colonial period occupations were recorded in the course of the research. The area of this survey was intentionally chosen in order to connect it with the boundaries of both of the earlier survey areas and therefore to create a contiguous 560-km^2 survey block in the southern Titicaca Basin. In addition, Bandy's work centered on a detailed study of population growth, decline, and migration over time. The measures and techniques for addressing population dynamics employed in this chapter are the same as those developed for that study.

The present study unites the archaeological settlement evidence produced by these three projects in order to examine demographic decline and internal migration in the Early Colonial period. To calculate population growth rates and identify population movements, however, it is necessary to employ the settlement data for the preceding Pacajes-Inka phase (the period of Inka domination) as a baseline for comparison. This study will therefore be concerned with two phases: (1) Pacajes-Inka (Late Horizon, approximately AD 1450–1540), and (2) Late Pacajes (Early Colonial period, approximately AD 1540–1600). We will therefore describe these two phases in detail.

DEFINING THE PHASES

The post-Middle Horizon ceramic sequence for the southern Titicaca Basin was first defined by Albarracin-Jordan (1992) and Mathews (1992a) in their survey of the Tiwanaku Valley. They defined three phases: Early Pacajes, Pacajes-Inka, and Late Pacajes. We have found their chronology to be correct and, almost as importantly, easy to apply to mixed surface assemblages. It is therefore very suitable for use in archaeological settlement surveys.

We will be concerned here only with the later two phases of their sequence, or those corresponding to the period of Inka occupation—(the Late Horizon) and the Early Colonial period, respectively. We will extend their phase definitions only slightly to include features and decorative motifs that they did not report. In particular, we will expand the decorative repertoire of the Late Pacajes phase, of which we ap-

pear to have a much larger and more varied sample than did the authors of the original ceramic phase description. The identification of the later Pacajes phases relies mainly on decorated wares. However, diagnostic ceramics—defined by distinctive painted or modeled decoration—are abundant on the surface of Late Horizon and Early Colonial sites in the study area, so the reliance on decorated wares presented no practical difficulties.

The Pacajes-Inka Phase

We have identified four distinct Late Horizon ceramic styles in our survey areas. These are, in order of descending frequency of occurrence:

- Saxamar (Pacajes-Inka),
- Chucuito Black-on-Red (and Chucuito Polychrome),
- Inka Imperial, and
- Taraco Polychrome.

We have identified no Urcusuyu Polychrome (M. Tschopik 1946:32–33) in our collections. This is rather surprising, given this style's predominantly southern distribution and possible association with the Inka sanctuaries at Copacabana and the Island of the Sun (Julien 1993: 192–199).

By far the most common of the four styles identified was a local Late Horizon style associated with the Pacajes polity and/or ethnicity. The style has variously been termed "Pacajes-Inka" (Albarracin-Jordan 1992; Albarracin-Jordan and Mathews 1990; Mathews 1992a), Saxamar (Browman 1985; Daulsberg H. 1960), and "llamita ware" (Graffam 1990). We prefer Saxamar. Examples are illustrated in Figure 16.1p–ae. Saxamar ceramics consist exclusively of shallow bowls, plates, or basins. These are typically covered with a deep red slip and polished to a high burnish on both the interior and exterior. The paste is very fine, dense, and well fired. Bowl or plate rims are usually direct and rounded, but often have a slight interior bevel. Saxamar bowl rims are only very rarely flared, and are never tapered. Therefore, slip color and rim form alone are normally enough to distin-

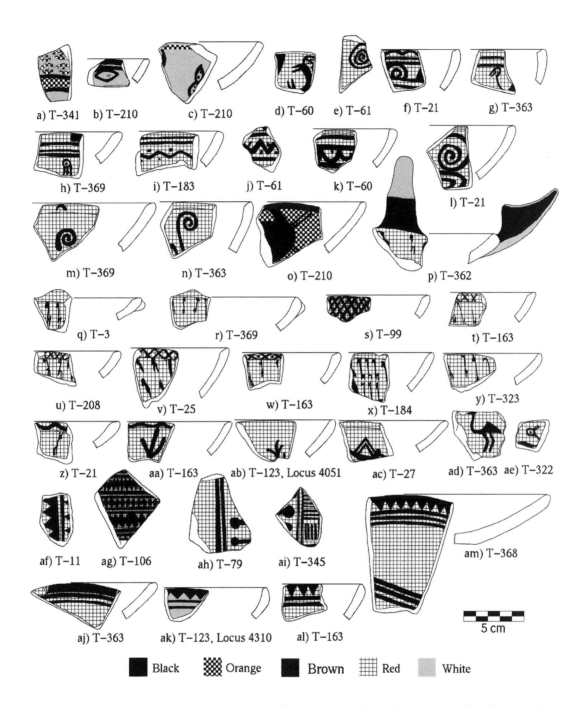

FIGURE 16.1. Late Horizon ceramics from the Taraco Peninsula: *(a–c)* Taraco Polychrome, *(d–n)* Chucuito Black-on-Red, *(o)* Chucuito Polychrome, *(p–ae)* Saxamar (Pacajes-Inka), *(af–am)* Inka Imperial

guish Saxamar from Early Pacajes (Late Intermediate period) unrestricted vessels.[3]

Saxamar modeled decorative motifs include what appears to be a duck head (Figure 16.1p) or more commonly single or double nubs (Figure 16.1q–r) protruding from the rim. Painted decoration is always applied using a black pigment. We found only a single example of a Saxamar polychrome (Figure 16.1p). This example used a white pigment to color the beak and neck of a stylized duck head. Cross-hatching on an interior rim bevel is very diagnostic of this style (Figure 16.1s–w), and an undulating line occupying the same position is not uncommon

(Figure 16.1z–aa). Also extremely diagnostic are arrays of what appear to be stylized camelids rendered with very delicate brush strokes (Figure 16.1p–r, t–z). These are clearly distinguishable from their thicker and coarser Early Pacajes precursors (Bandy 2001b:Figure 9.1r–u).

While the stylized camelid motif is the most common element in Saxamar decorative painting, other objects and animals are also represented, though infrequently. These include lake birds (possibly flamingos; see Figure 16.1ad–ae), what appears to be a grasshopper (Figure 16.1ac), and a dendritic design, possibly representing a tree or other plant (Figure 16.1aa–ab). This last motif is particularly interesting, since it becomes much more common in the subsequent Late Pacajes phase. All three of these noncamelid motifs are quite rare in the Saxamar style.

The second-most common Late Horizon style in the southern Titicaca Basin is the Inka Imperial style (Figure 16.1af–am), related to the imperial Cuzco A and B styles (D'Altroy and Bishop 1990; D'Altroy 1992; Rowe 1944; M. Tschopik 1946:36–39). Ceramics of this general style are found throughout the former territory of the Inka Empire and are the principal markers of the Late Horizon in the Andean region. These vessels are of two main types: shallow bowls or plates, clearly the inspiration for the Saxamar examples, and large restricted-neck jars generally known as aryballoid vessels, or *arybalos*. Both are normally fine, dense, and well fired, and are covered with a deep red slip (although exceptions exist, such as Figure 16.1ak, which has a white slip). In fact, the Saxamar style's technology and slip color clearly imitate attributes of the Inka Imperial style. Inka Imperial plates also frequently have modeled decoration, in the form of bird heads or nubs, on the rim. In addition, a typical arybalos sports a highly stylized modeled animal head on its body. This head, known as an *adorno*, is usually thought to have served to attach a tumpline. Inka Imperial bowls often are decorated with chains of triangles pendant from the rim (Figure 16.1ak–am). Arybalos are often decorated with chains of triangles or diamonds (Figure 16.1af–ag), or with a highly distinctive motif probably representing some kind of plant (Figure 16.1ah–ai). Ceramics

of the Inka Imperial style seem to have been produced by state specialists and distributed as part of the functioning of the administrative apparatus (Costin and Earle 1989; Costin and Hagstrum 1995).

The third most common Late Horizon style is the Chucuito style. Its center of distribution seems to be the western Titicaca Basin, south of Puno, and north of Yunguyu. This was the territory of the Lupaqa "kingdom" (Hyslop 1976; Murra 1968, 1970; Stanish 1989a). A small number of trade pieces are present in the southern Titicaca Basin. The Chucuito styles were originally described by Tschopik, and her analysis is still the definitive source (M. Tschopik 1946).

Chucuito polychromes (M. Tschopik 1946: 27–29) are very rare in the southern Titicaca Basin. Only one example was recovered from the Taraco Peninsula survey; it seems to represent a catfish (Figure 16.1o). More common is Chucuito Black-on-Red (M. Tschopik 1946:29–31). These ceramics are very similar to the Saxamar style in terms of their basic technology. They also are fine and dense, and are decorated with a glossy black pigment over a deep red slip. Diagnostic— that is, painted—examples are exclusively open bowls. Tschopik documents a wide variety of decorative motifs for this style. In our area, very few of these motifs are represented. Some figurative elements are present (Figure 16.1d, g–h), but most examples present some combination of spirals, undulating lines, and pendant loops (Figure 16.1e–f, i–l). In this, at least, our sample resembles that of Stanish et al. (1997:47–48, 55) from the Juli area of Peru.

The fourth Late Horizon ceramic style is Taraco Polychrome, also defined by M. Tschopik (Julien 1993:190–191). The distribution of this style seems to be centered in the Peruvian town of Taraco, on the northern side of the lake. It is exceedingly rare in the southern Titicaca Basin. Only four examples were recovered by the Taraco Peninsula survey, three of which are illustrated in Figure 16.1a–c. Tschopik described the style as follows:

> . . . a fine, compact ware with a white or cream-colored paste, containing a very fine temper and occasional reddish-

brown inclusions. The surface is also cream-colored, carefully smoothed on both sides so as to be quite lustrous. There is no slip; designs are painted directly on the surface in orange, red, and a dark color which is usually black but which may appear olive green when thinly applied. With few exceptions the shapes represented are bowls. (M. Tschopik 1946:31)

The black/green paint is immediately recognizable in the field, as are the cream surface color and the apparently common "eye" motif.

The Late Pacajes Phase

Ceramically, the Late Pacajes phase seems to be quite homogeneous. Only a single style of decorated ceramics has been identified that pertains to this phase. Late Pacajes decorated ceramics are almost always bowl forms, with the occasional plate (plates are illustrated in Figure 16.2m–n). With a few exceptions (like the example shown in Figure 16.2c) they are unslipped, with a surface color that sometimes approaches purple—normally in the 10R 3/6–4/7 Munsell range. The rare slipped bowl may be burnished, but the vast majority have a wet wiped surface finish that is highly distinctive. Virtually all Late Pacajes bowls have everted rims (exceptions are illustrated in Figure 16.2j, s), and a rare subtype has a very widely flared rim (Figure 16.2a–c), which sometimes approaches a shelf rim. Late Pacajes everted rims have a clearly defined interior corner point, and in this way may be distinguished from Early Pacajes rims, which are typically characterized by vague inflection. Thus, a combination of surface treatment, surface color, and rim form is usually sufficient to identify a Late Pacajes bowl even in the absence of any painted or modeled decoration.

Two kinds of modeled decoration are known to occur on Late Pacajes decorated ceramics, both of which are derived from Late Horizon ceramics. First, some plates have cylindrical stems protruding from the rim, similar to the Late Horizon "duck plates" (Figure 16.2m–n). The only intact example we have observed has an "X" incised on the end of the cylinder (Figure 16.2n). More common are a series of nubs or small protrusions modeled on the rim of bowls (Figure 16.2o–p), occurring in groups of two or three spaced regularly around the circumference. These nubs are occasionally perforated (Figure 16.2p).

Late Pacajes painted decoration is frequently polychrome, and three pigments are employed. The first appears to be an organic pigment, which produces a black or occasionally dark gray color over the red surface. The color area is normally quite diffuse, and its edges poorly defined. The principal parts of any design are usually rendered using this pigment (but see Figure 16.2j for an exception). The second type of painted decoration is a white pigment, which is applied positively. It is normally used to embellish a design with the addition of white dots (Figure 16.2a–d, g, l–m).[4] The third and rarest type of painted decoration consists of a yellow pigment that is applied positively. It is used in exactly the same manner as the white paint just described. The yellow pigment is often somewhat runny (Figure 16.2r, u), suggesting that it was either sloppily applied or that it has melted and run during firing. It may be some kind of glaze, though we are uncertain on this point.

The white and yellow pigments never occur on the same vessel, which may suggest that the yellow is simply a result of overfiring the white paint. Whatever the case, Late Pacajes decorated ceramics are always either a monochrome Black-on-Red, or a bichrome Black-and-White-on-Red or Black-and-Yellow-on-Red.

The most common decorative motif consists of a series of short parallel lines pendant from the interior rim of bowls (Figure 16.2o–t). These may be black, white, or alternating black and white. Also fairly common is a branching motif (Figure 16.2i–m), probably representing a tree or other plant and clearly derived from a similar Pacajes-Inka (Saxamar) motif (Bandy 2001b:Figure 10.1 aa–ab), though it is also present in the Late Horizon Chucuito Black-on-Red style (M. Tschopik 1946:31). Less common decorative motifs include avian profile figures (Figure 16.2c–d), geometric designs (Figure 16.2g–h), a possible quadruped (Figure 16.2f) and biped (Figure 16.2e), and other figures that are not immediately identifiable (Figure 16.2a–b). The Late Pacajes ceramic decorative repertoire is apparently considerably more varied than has previously been appreciated.[5]

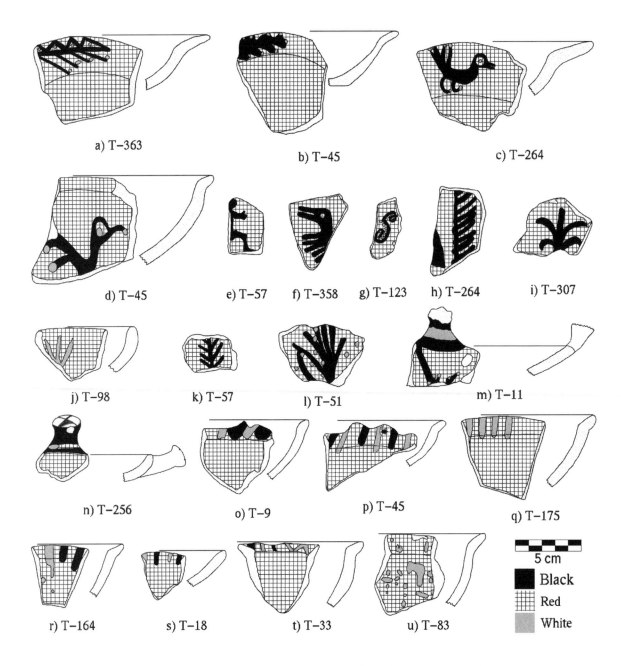

FIGURE 16.2. Early Colonial period ceramics from the Taraco Peninsula

ARE THE PACAJES PHASES TEMPORALLY DISCRETE?

In discussing the Pacajes ceramic phases, we are compelled to address an issue that was raised by the original formulators of the Pacajes ceramic sequence. In their original survey report, Albarracin-Jordan and Mathews (1990:Figure 14) suggested that the Pacajes-Inka phase may in fact have overlapped temporally with both the Early Pacajes and Late Pacajes phases. In this view, Pacajes-Inka phase ceramics represented a foreign stylistic intrusion into the southern basin, which coexisted with both late Early Pacajes ceramics and early Late Pacajes ceramics. Mathews argues that certain ceramic attributes, such as disk bases and everted rims, are present in both Early and Late Pacajes ceramics, but not in Pacajes-Inka ceramics.

> In essence, this argument requires the assumption of the contemporaneous manufacture of two distinct ceramic types, emerging from two separate cultural traditions, in the Tiwanaku Valley. Specifically, we need to posit that the Inka ceramic material represented a tradition that was superimposed over the existing cultural matrix, rather than one which replaced it completely. Inka-Pacajaes could have represented an elite or sumptuary class of ceramic which was available only to certain elements of the indigenous Pacajaes society, possibly determined by position within the Inka administrative hierarchy of indirect rule. At the same time, commoners continued to produce the diagnostic Early Pacajes wares described above, for everyday domestic consumption. [Mathews 1992a: 194]

Testing this hypothesis is straightforward. If Mathews's suggestion is correct, then a high percentage of sites with Pacajes-Inka ceramics will also have Early Pacajes ceramics on the surface. On the other hand, if Pacajes-Inka ceramics are partially contemporary with Late Pacajes ceramics, then a high percentage of sites with Pacajes-Inka ceramics will also have Late Pacajes ceramics on the surface. If neither one of these is true, then no such relationships will be observed.

Table 16.1 displays these data for the Taraco Peninsula, for the Lower and Middle Tiwanaku Valley,[6] and for the Katari Basin. The Tiwanaku Valley data were derived from the dissertations of the Tiwanaku Valley researchers (Albarracin-Jordan 1992; Mathews 1992a), the Taraco Peninsula data were culled from Bandy's dissertation (Bandy 2001b), and the Katari Basin data were collected by Janusek and Kolata (Janusek and Kolata 2003).

It is easy to see how Mathews could think that Early Pacajes and Pacajes-Inka ceramics were partially contemporaneous. In his sample (the Middle Tiwanaku Valley), 94% of Pacajes-Inka sites also have Early Pacajes ceramics on the surface, and 88% have Late Pacajes ceramics. The Lower Tiwanaku Valley data are similar, though the relationships are somewhat weaker.

However, the Taraco Peninsula data present a very different picture. Only 25% of Pacajes-Inka sites on the Taraco Peninsula have Early Pacajes ceramics on the surface, and only 57% of Pacajes-Inka sites on the Taraco Peninsula have Late Pacajes ceramics. The Taraco data therefore support the conclusion that the Early Pacajes, Pacajes-Inka, and Late Pacajes ceramic phases are sequential and not contemporaneous. The association between Early Pacajes and Pacajes-Inka occupations in the Tiwanaku Valley (and in the Katari Basin, though more weakly) must be due to some other factor. We suggest that the sheer number of Early Pacajes sites in the Middle Tiwanaku Valley (more than 500) implies that there is an Early Pacajes phase occupation on the vast majority of the sites of any phase. For example, 92% of Tiwanaku phase sites in the Middle Tiwanaku Valley also have Early Pacajes occupations, as do 91% of Middle Formative (Late Chiripa) and 89% of Late Pacajes sites. It therefore seems that there is an Early Pacajes site in

TABLE 16.1. Percent of Pacajes-Inka sites containing other Pacajes occupations

	Taraco Peninsula (T)	Lower Tiwanaku Valley (TLV)	Middle Tiwanaku Valley (TMV)	Katari Basin (CK)
Early Pacajes	25	88	94	73
Late Pacajes	57	74	88	55

T: Taraco Peninsula (Bandy 2001b)
TLV: Lower Tiwanaku Valley (Albarracin-Jordan 1992)
TMV: Middle Tiwanaku Valley (Mathews 1992a)
CK: Katari Basin (Janusek and Kolata 2003)

virtually every habitable location of the Middle Tiwanaku Valley, and that these associations are therefore fortuitous. The results of this exercise refute Mathews' argument and support the view that the three Pacajes phases are in fact sequential and have no appreciable temporal overlap.

MONITORING POPULATION GROWTH, DECLINE, AND MOVEMENT

The present study will track changes in the density and distribution of population during the Early Colonial period. It will do so by comparing Late Pacajes phase settlement data with Pacajes-Inka phase settlement data. Differences between the two settlement patterns will be taken to indicate demographic and migratory processes operating during the Early Colonial period. It is important to emphasize here, however, that it is impossible for us to discuss population directly given the state of knowledge concerning prehistoric settlement configurations in the region. We will therefore speak not of population values, but rather of population index values. We believe the population index, as derived below, to be proportional to actual population, and therefore useful as a proxy measure.

The process by which we derive population index values for sites is described in Bandy's dissertation (Bandy 2001b:Chapter 4). The method is critical to our argument, however, and for this reason we review it here in some detail. Our population index depends upon an ethnographically derived model of southern Titicaca Basin settlement behavior. At present, local habitations are arranged in a manner similar to that seen in most Aymara communities in the Bolivian highlands. A single family group— a married couple together with unmarried children and frequently with elderly relatives—inhabits a small compound of structures (perhaps three to five rooms altogether) that is often enclosed by an adobe wall and separated from other such compounds by cultivated fields (Arnold 1988:Chapter 9).[7] Figure 16.3 is a schematic representation of a typical residential compound. Each of these compounds is adjacent to outdoor areas—much of the daily work of the household is done out-of-doors—where activities such as threshing, *chuño* processing, weav-

ing, and other daily tasks take place. There are no well-defined middens, and this entire inhabited area contains a sufficient density of cultural material to qualify as a "site."

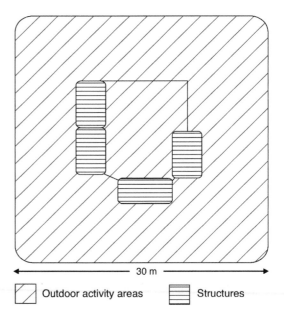

FIGURE 16.3. Schematic representation of a contemporary Aymara residential compound

To date, very few pre-Hispanic household units have been excavated in the southern Titicaca Basin. Those that have been excavated seem to indicate a residential pattern broadly similar to that of the present day. The Late Intermediate period structures excavated at the North Point sector of the extensive site of Lukurmata are tentatively interpreted by the excavator as forming a "compound containing a number of houses and enclosed by a large wall" (Wise 1993:111). A Late Horizon residential compound was excavated at the same site, which was comprised of at least two fieldstone structures and a fieldstone corral, all enclosed by a compound wall (Wise 1993:109).[8] The limited information at our disposal therefore seems to indicate that the post-Tiwanaku household form has remained relatively stable, and has been broadly similar to that observed among the modern inhabitants of the area.

We are considering a household compound to be composed of a small number of adobe structures together with associated outdoor activity areas. In the present, these activity areas include places for storing food, tools, agricultural by-products, and firewood, as well as places for tethering animals, for threshing and winnowing cereals, and for other domestic tasks. The human activities in these structures and activity areas generate debris, some of which is durable, like ceramics. This debris is the source of the artifact scatters by which we identify archaeological sites.

However, the correlation between the extent of the artifact scatter and the extent of the habitation area (structures and unenclosed activity areas) is not direct. This is so for two reasons. First, deposition of refuse is not restricted to habitation areas, though it is certainly concentrated in habitation zones. Second, debris is subject to post-depositional processes that tend to disperse what may initially have been a relatively discrete concentration. These processes include displacement due to trampling and kicking by livestock and humans (Nielsen 1991) and, perhaps most important for our study area, displacement due to the plowing of agricultural fields (see Roper 1976 for a general treatment). The result is that an artifact scatter (archaeological sites) will include both a habitation area and its associated "splash zone," a corona of displaced and peripheral artifacts deriving from the habitation area. This area could also reasonably be called a "toss zone," but we prefer the former term since its creation is due largely to natural site formation processes. This is illustrated in Figure 16.4. The first area (the habitation area) directly represents human occupation; the second (the splash zone) does not. To arrive at a population estimate, we must therefore subtract the splash zone from the total area of the sherd scatter order to derive the habitation area.

The simplest case is that illustrated in Figure 16.4a. This is the isolated household compound, surrounded by cultivated fields. Bandy personally observed a number of such cases in the field—house compounds of the present-day Aymara inhabitants of the region—and took informal measurements (pacing) of the habitation area and the area of the artifact scatter. His observations indicated that the average habitation area was no less than 30 x 30 m (0.09 ha) in area. This seems to be broadly consistent with what

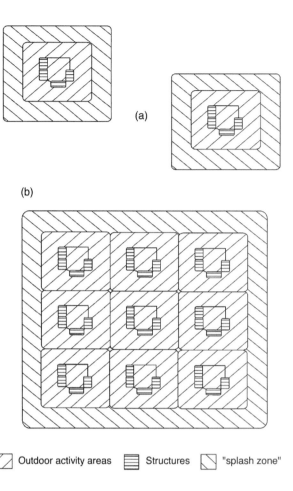

Outdoor activity areas   Structures   "splash zone"

FIGURE 16.4. Habitation area and "splash zone": (a) dispersed, and (b) nucleated residential patterns

we know of pre-Hispanic household compounds. For example, the Pacajes-Inka compound partially excavated by Karen Wise at Lukurmata consisted of at least three rooms and seems to have been enclosed by a stone wall (Wise 1993). It is therefore very similar to modern compounds. The compound at Lukurmata measures 16 m on one side, though the other dimension could not be determined. Assuming it was square, the architectural compound alone covered 0.03 ha. Since this was an isolated household ("dispersed habitation"), many of the activity areas would have been located outside of the architectural compound itself, as is the case with modern houses.

A habitation area of 30 x 30 m is, in Bandy's small sample of modern household compounds, associated with an artifact scatter of approximately 50 x 50 m (0.25 ha). That is, the splash zone extended for approximately 10 m beyond each side of the habitation zone. He consistently found this figure to be a good descriptor of the splash zones surrounding modern houses, so we will use this figure in this chapter.[9]

If we measure area in hectares and model the plan of the artifact scatter as a square, then:

$$H = \frac{\sqrt{100000(A-20)^2}}{10000}$$

Where A = artifact scatter area
H = habitation area

Figure 16.4b shows the more complicated case of nucleated habitation in towns and villages. In this case, we have densely packed habitation areas (residential compounds) with overlapping splash zones in all but the outer edges of the habitation area. Almost all of the interior of the settlement is habitation area, with a rim of uninhabited splash zone around the edge.[10] If we view a village in this way, then we can apply exactly the same correction equation to it that we applied to the isolated household compound. Therefore, there is no need to distinguish between different residential patterns in order to correct for the splash zone.

In practice, of course, things are often not this simple. Habitation density (persons per hectare) may vary in contexts of nucleated or dispersed habitation, so that the relation between population and habitation area is not direct. Other factors can affect the relation, as well. For example, habitation density will typically be higher in walled settlements than in nonwalled ones (Wenke 1975), as people exchange living space for a reduction in collective labor investment. However, to derive a useful relation empirically would require very extensive horizontal excavations or excellent surface visibility and architectural preservation (see de Montmollin 1987 for a Mesoamerican example). This has been accomplished in some contexts (see Milner and Oliver 1999:90–93 for an example from Cahokia) with excellent results, but we are very far from this point in Titicaca Basin archaeology. Mississippian or Mesoamerican data

clearly cannot be directly applied to the Titicaca Basin case. Such measures are specific to particular historical contexts. The method outlined above for calculating habitation area is dramatically simplified, but is consistent with what we know of contemporary and prehistoric habitation in the region.

As discussed above, modern Aymara households seem to occupy on average approximately 0.09 ha of habitation area. An estimated number of households per site may therefore be calculated as follows:

$$H = \frac{A_s}{A_h}$$

Where H = number of households
A_s = corrected site area
A_h = average household compound area (0.09 ha)

A population index value for the site is obtained by multiplying the site's estimated number of households by an average number of persons per household. The same set of informal observations used to establish an average residential compound area also yielded an average of six persons per household compound. This concurs approximately with ethnohistoric information. For example, at the time of Viceroy Toledo's visit to Tiwanaku in 1574, a total population of 4329 was recorded for the repartimiento (Choque Canqui 1993:81). Among these were 868 *tributarios* (heads of household). This yields an approximate ratio of 4.99 persons/household.

Therefore:

$$P_s = HPh$$

Where P_s = population index value of site
H = estimated number of households in site
P_h = persons per household (6)

This sequence of steps eventually returns a population index value of 42.67 persons for a 1-ha sherd scatter, and a value of 66.67 persons for 1 ha of occupied area. These numbers are on the low end of the range of numbers typically used to derive population estimates from site area. Robert McC. Adams (1965), for example, used a figure of 200 persons/ha in his study of Meso-potamian settlement. This was based on modern population densities from the old quarters of Baghdad and from other local examples. Carol Kramer's ethnoarchaeological study of modern settlements in Southwest Asia yielded an average of 120 persons/ha (Hassan 1981:66–67). Similarly, the classical city of Melos has been estimated to have contained between 130 and 200 persons/ha within its walls (Whitelaw and Davis 1991:280). While our numbers therefore seem low compared to figures employed in the analysis of Mediterranean and Near Eastern urban settlements, they fall within the 25–50 persons/ha range of the Basin of Mexico's "High Density Compact Villages" (Parsons 1976: 72). Our numbers are also considerably lower than the 100 persons/ha used by Parsons to estimate the population of Tiwanaku (Parsons 1968). Finally, 43–67 persons/ha falls into the middle of the range of Robert Drennan's (1986: Table 13.1) "compact settlement" category of Mesoamerican archaeological sites.

Once the population index value has been calculated, analyzing population change through time is simply a matter of tracking the increases and decreases of this quantity. The most convenient way to do this is by calculating an annual rate of population growth relative to the previous phase. This is done using the following equation (Hassan 1981:139):

$$r = \frac{1}{T}\ln\left\langle\frac{P_f}{P_i}\right\rangle$$

where r = annual rate of population change
T = number of elapsed years
P_i = initial population index value (at $T = 0$)
P_f = final population index value

Multiplying the derived value of r by 100 yields an annual percentage rate of population growth. This is the figure that we will use in this study to measure rates of population growth or decline, since growth rates seem often to be reported in terms of annual percentage rates (Hassan 1981:140). Population growth rates can in this way be calculated for individual sites, groups of sites, or entire regions.

We should also emphasize, again, that our population index is not really a population measure. Rather, it is a corrected site area measure, which we have argued to be proportional to population. It does not take into account varying densities, intensities, or durations of occupation. The population index as utilized here is directly proportional to the corrected site area. Therefore, all of the results would be identical if expressed in corrected hectares rather than in population index units.

The correction method described here has the salutary effect of reducing the relative importance of small sites at a regional scale. When this correction is applied to a regional settlement dataset, the cumulative habitation area ("corrected area") of small sites is reduced relative to that of larger sites. This corrects an error that is common in settlement archaeology. In analyses that do not correct for the "splash zone" (or the nonoccupation area of small sites), that part of the ceramic scatter produced by post-depositional processes comprises a much greater percentage of the overall site size in small sites than is the case for larger sites. This has the effect of analytically inflating the significance of small sites and of time periods in which sites were small and impermanent. The correction method we have adopted here avoids, at least to some degree, this major analytical bias.

We are prepared to acknowledge the shortcomings of our method. These problems are shared with most archaeological attempts to address demographic processes from a settlement perspective. Any refinement of this method, however, must await significant advances in our knowledge of Titicaca Basin households and domestic units through time. For the moment, our figures represent the best estimates possible of prehistoric population levels in the region.

PACAJES-INKA SETTLEMENT PATTERNS

Figure 16.5 displays the Pacajes-Inka phase settlement pattern within the study area. The total population index value for this phase is 15,306, of which 6439 (42%) is accounted for by sites with a population index value of less than 100 (area ≤ 2.0 ha). Altogether, 496 sites were recorded with Pacajes-Inka phase occupations, of which 470 (95%)

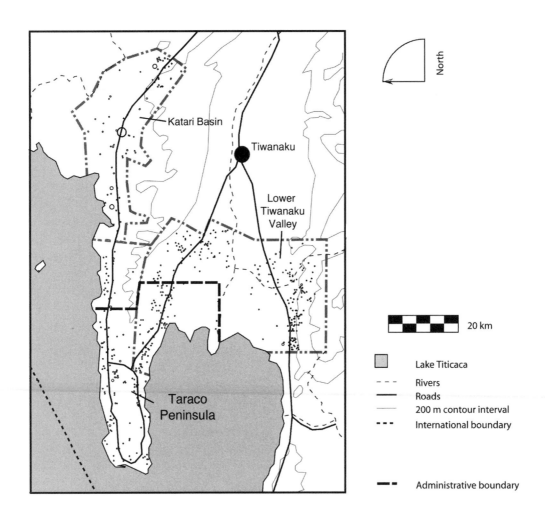

FIGURE 16.5. Pacajes-Inka phase settlement pattern

have a population index value of less than 100. The great majority of sites from this time period are therefore small, isolated household compounds, and the overall settlement pattern is one of dispersed habitation. However, a significant number of large sites also existed during this phase, which actually account for more than 50% of the total phase population.

Figure 16.6a shows the distribution of total population (as measured by the population index) by site size intervals for the Pacajes-Inka phase. A brief inspection of this site size histogram reveals a tri-modal distribution. The smallest group of sites is the group whose population index values are less than 400. These are predominantly individual isolated farmsteads, but the category also includes a number of small towns and villages. The second size mode has popula-

tion index values ranging from 500 to 900 (10–15 ha in area). This category contains only four sites, all of which are located in the Katari Basin. These sites are Wakullani (CK-114), Lukurmata (CK-125), Chojasivi (CK-132), and Tumuyu (CK-186).

The largest Pacajes-Inka phase site in the study area is Chukara Pata (CK-12). This site covers 33.5 ha, and has a population index value of 2081. It is by far the largest Late Horizon site in the study area. The site was archaeologically unknown prior to its discovery by Janusek during his Katari Basin survey. It must be considered one of the principal Inka administrative centers in the Titicaca Basin, comparable to Chucuito (M. Tschopik 1946) and Hatuncolla (Julien 1983). The rank-size diagram of the Pacajes-Inka phase settlement system (Figure 16.7a) closely conforms to a log-normal distribution (Johnson

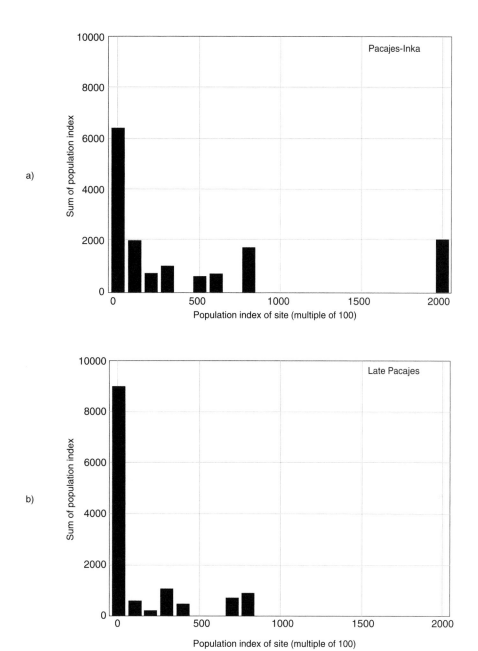

FIGURE 16.6. Distribution of population by site size: *(a)* Pacajes-Inka, and *(b)* Late Pacajes

1977). Together, the log-normal rank size distribution and the three-level site size hierarchy suggest that the study area was a closely administered and tightly integrated province of the Inka Empire.

When the different survey areas are considered individually, however, it becomes apparent that the Pacajes-Inka phase settlement patterns vary dramatically. Table 16.2 displays a series of settlement statistics by survey area. First, settle-

ment is much more dense and nucleated in the Katari Basin than in the Lower Tiwanaku Valley or on the Taraco Peninsula. The population density (population index/km²) of the Katari Basin is also much higher than that of the other two survey areas. The population density of the Katari Basin is calculated to be 2.1 times that of the Taraco Peninsula and 4.1 times that of the Lower Tiwanaku Valley. At the same time, the site density (sites/km²) in the Katari Basin is much

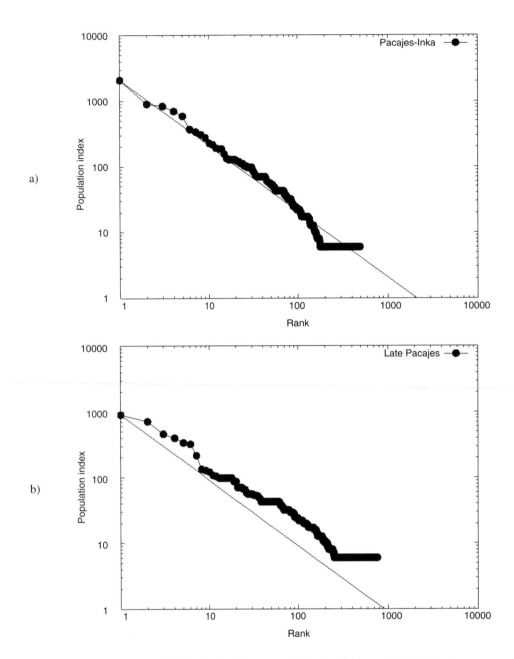

FIGURE 16.7. Rank-size diagrams: *(a)* Pacajes-Inka, and *(b)* Late Pacajes

TABLE 16.2. Pacajes-Inka settlement system statistics by area

	Lower Tiwanaku Valley	Taraco Peninsula	Katari Basin
Number of sites	292	125	79
Total pop. index	3761	3676	7868
Average site pop. index	12.9	29.4	99.6
Sites/km²	1.46	1.28	0.77
Pop. index/km²	18.8	37.5	77.1

lower than the site densities in the other two areas. This means that the Katari Basin contains fewer but much larger sites than the other two areas. The Katari Basin has an average site population index value of 99.6, 3.4 times that of the Taraco Peninsula and 7.7 times that of the Lower Tiwanaku Valley. The Katari Basin was the demographic and political core of Pacajes-Inka phase settlement within the study area. The other two areas were peripheral and subsidiary. Settlement within the Katari Basin seems to have been tightly controlled and nucleated, while in the other areas it was more fluid and dispersed.

LATE PACAJES SETTLEMENT PATTERNS

In some respects, the Early Colonial period settlement system represents a radical departure from the Pacajes-Inka phase. Figure 16.8 displays the Late Pacajes phase settlement pattern within the study area. The total population index value for this phase is 12,969, down from 15,306 in the Pacajes-Inka phase. This represents an overall population growth rate of –0.28% annually. Of the 12,969 population index for the

Late Pacajes phase, 9032 (70%) is accounted for by sites with a population index value of less than 100 (area ≤ 2.0 ha). A total of 773 sites were recorded with Late Pacajes phase occupations, of which 761 (98%) have a population index value of less than 100. Overall, the Late Pacajes settlement system was more dispersed—characterized by a greater number of smaller sites—than was the Pacajes-Inka phase system. While the average population index value of Pacajes-Inka phase sites was 30.9, the same figure for the Late Pacajes phase is only 16.8.

Further, as Figure 16.6b shows, the Pacajes-Inka phase three-level site size hierarchy was replaced by a two-level hierarchy. The sites that had occupied the upper tiers of the Pacajes-Inka phase site size hierarchy were all either abandoned or greatly reduced in size in the Late Pacajes phase. Chukara Pata (CK-12), which had a population index value of over 2000 in the Pacajes-Inka phase, is reduced to a value of 710 in the Late Pacajes phase. Together with Lacaya (CK-32, population index value of 899), it comes to form the upper of the two tiers of the Late Pacajes site size hierarchy. The remainder of the

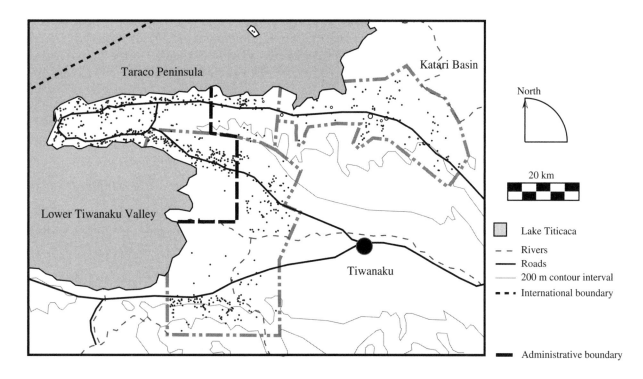

FIGURE 16.8. Late Pacajes phase settlement pattern

TABLE 16.3. Late Pacajes settlement system statistics by area

	Lower Tiwanaku Valley	Taraco Peninsula	Katari Basin
Number of sites	342	326	105
Total pop. index	2793	5021	5155
Average site pop. index	8.2	15.4	49.1
Sites/km^2	1.71	3.33	1.03
Pop. index/km^2	14.0	51.2	50.5
Annual pop. growth rate	–0.50%	0.52%	–0.70%

Late Pacajes sites have population index values of less than 500.

When the survey areas are considered separately, however, some continuity is evident. Table 16.3 shows that although settlement became more dispersed in all three areas, the Katari Basin settlement continued to be more nucleated than the settlement in the other two areas. The Katari Basin average site population index value remained over three times that of the Taraco Peninsula or the Lower Tiwanaku Valley, and its site density (sites/km^2) remained well below that of the other two areas. The general properties of the settlement system of each area relative to that of the other two areas remained more or less constant. The Katari Basin continued to be characterized primarily by nucleated settlement, and the Taraco Peninsula and Lower Tiwanaku Valley by dispersed settlement. What changed, however, was the percentage of the total population that resided in each area.

In the Pacajes-Inka phase, the Katari Basin contained 51% of the population of the study area, the Taraco Peninsula 24%, and the Lower Tiwanaku Valley 25%. In the Late Pacajes phase these percentages changed radically. The Katari Basin contained only 40% of the total population of the study area, while the Taraco Peninsula increased to 39%, and the Lower Tiwanaku Valley decreased to 21%. Despite the fact that the Taraco Peninsula continued to be characterized by dispersed habitation, its overall population density (population index/km^2) came to be nearly equal to that of the Katari Basin. This reflects a dramatic difference in the population growth rates of the three areas. As Table 16.3 indicates, the Late Pacajes annual population growth rate for the Taraco Peninsula was 0.52%, while those

of the Katari Basin and Lower Tiwanaku Valley areas were –0.70% and –0.50%, respectively.

As dramatic as these figures are, they disguise an even more remarkable pattern. The study area is divided among a number of modern political units. Most of the Taraco Peninsula survey area, and a portion of the Lower Tiwanaku Valley survey area, pertains to the modern Cantón Taraco. Cantón Taraco at present contains sixteen indigenous communities. Most of these communities are the modern political descendants of pre-Hispanic and Colonial period *ayllu*, or corporate landholding groups. In the mid-seventeenth century, Taraco was a *marka* (Albarracin-Jordan 1996a; Albarracin-Jordan 1996b, for detailed discussion of the concept), or a town with eight ayllu under its jurisdiction. In the Lower Tiwanaku Valley it (the Taraco marka) included the ayllu of Iwawe, Chivo, Pillapi, and Jawira Pampa (Mamani Condori 1991:22). All of these are still communities today. Assuming their borders have remained relatively constant, this allows us to locate the seventeenth-century borders of Taraco as follows:

- on the South near the Tiwanaku River, or approximately 8172000 N, and

- on the East near the modern town of Pillapi, or approximately 524000 E.

Its border on the northern side of the Taraco Hills is somewhat more obscure, but we can with some reason locate it near the boundary between the modern cantons of Taraco and Huacullani. This boundary is:

- between the modern communities of Pequery and Cala Cala, or approximately 521000 E.

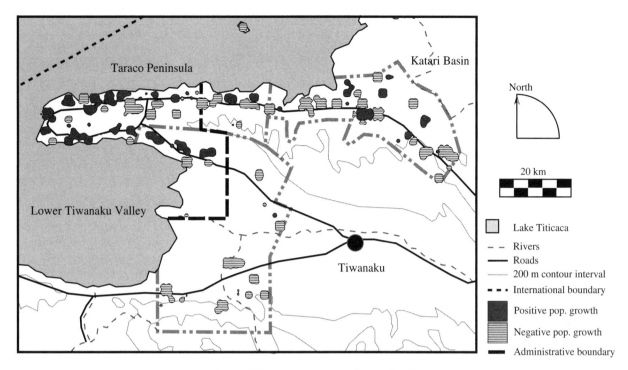

FIGURE 16.9. Change in population density

The seventeenth-century boundaries of Taraco, as determined above, are shown on Figures 16.5, 16.8, and 16.9. Figure 16.9 displays areas of positive and negative population growth in the Late Pacajes phase. This map was generated by calculating total population index values for 0.25 km^2 areas for each of the Pacajes-Inka and Late Pacajes phases. For each square, we subtracted the Pacajes-Inka population index value from the Late Pacajes population index value. Areas that lost population in the Late Pacajes phase are indicated by hatching, while areas that gained population are indicated by a solid color. The map clearly shows a preponderance of population growth within the boundaries of seventeenth-century Taraco, and of population decline beyond these boundaries.

Figure 16.10 shows a west-to-east profile of population growth or decline for the entire study area. The chart clearly shows a preponderance of population increase inside the boundaries of Taraco, and a preponderance of population decrease beyond those boundaries.

Table 16.4 shows the Late Pacajes population index values and annual population growth rates for Taraco (including most of the Taraco Peninsula survey area and part of the Lower Tiwanaku Valley survey area), non-Taraco north (including part of the Taraco Peninsula survey area and all of the Katari Basin survey area), and non-Taraco south (including most of the Lower Tiwanaku Valley survey area). The differences in the population growth rates are even more pronounced than those between the survey areas themselves. In the Late Pacajes phase, Taraco experienced population growth at the very rapid annual rate of 0.76%. At the same time, adjacent areas experienced population decline, at rates varying between –0.66% and –1.29% annually.

The baseline population growth rate for the southern Titicaca Basin throughout prehistory was on the order of 0.10% annually (Bandy 2001b). This being the case, the very high rate of Late Pacajes population growth for Taraco— seven times the baseline rate—certainly indicates an influx of population into the area. Such a dramatic growth rate cannot be accounted for by internal growth alone. The negative rates in the adjacent Katari Basin and Lower Tiwanaku Valley reveal the source of this influx. Very clearly, people were abandoning their homes in the Katari Basin and Tiwanaku Valley and were moving onto the Taraco Peninsula during the

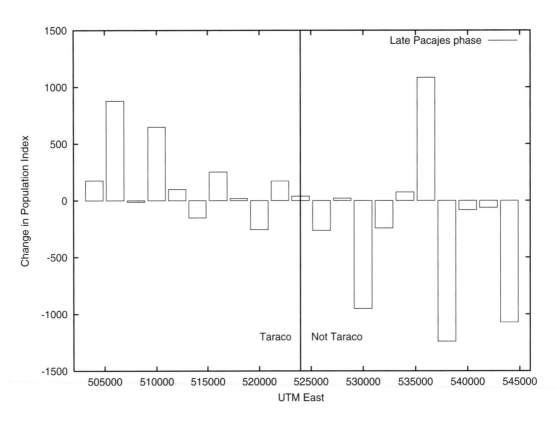

FIGURE 16.10. Profile of population index density change: west to east

TABLE 16.4. Growth rates by area and phase

	Taraco		Non-Taraco (North)		Non-Taraco (South)	
	Pop. Index	Growth	Pop. Index	Growth	Pop. Index	Growth
Pacajes-Inka	3677	—	8919	—	2711	—
Late Pacajes	5800	+0.76%	5917	–0.66%	1251	–1.29%

Late Pacajes phase. What could account for this kind of population displacement?

Spanish administration of the Titicaca Basin was regularized around the same time as the discovery of the Potosí silver deposits in southern Bolivia in 1545. At this time, the Titicaca Basin became essentially a sustaining area of the Potosí mines. Its population was reorganized in order to provide food, coca, other supplies, and, critically, manpower to the mining operations. The founding of the city of La Paz in 1548—early in the Late Pacajes phase—was part of this process.

Titicaca Basin groups were subjected to various administrative devices—*encomienda, repartimiento, corregimiento*—which served to enrich their conquerors and to impoverish themselves.

In the Early Colonial period, the Lower Tiwanaku Valley contained territory pertaining to both the encomiendas (later repartimientos) of Tiwanaku and Guaqui.[11] Huacullani, in the Katari Basin was also administered as an encomienda. Taraco, however, was *tierra de la corona*, crown territory (Waldemar Espinoza Soriano, personal communication 1999), and was ruled directly by the viceregal government. As Roberto Choque Canqui puts it, "[l]os pueblos de Waki y Tiwanaku estaban tan despoblados y perdidos sin gente por la mita porque muchos indios tributarios se han huido . . . " ["The pueblos of Waki and Tiwanaku were so depopulated and left without people to serve in the mita that many tribute-paying indians fled . . . "] (Choque Canqui 1993:83). If they were fleeing from Tiwanaku and Guaqui, some at least were escaping to Taraco. The anomalously high Late Pacajes population growth rate may therefore be explained by a historical anomaly: Taraco was ruled by the Crown, and surrounding areas by encomenderos. The settlement dynamics of the Late Pacajes phase conclusively demonstrate that the inhabitants of the southern Titicaca Basin preferred the crown.

CONCLUSIONS

What then of the Early Colonial period demographic catastrophe? Using the tools of settlement archaeology, we have identified several trends that bear on this issue.

First, the Early Colonial period in the southern Titicaca Basin was in fact characterized by a demographic downturn. The Late Pacajes phase population growth rate in our study area was –0.28% annually. Thus, whether through disease, warfare, or outmigration, population did decline during this period. The rate of decline, however, was not nearly as severe as previous researchers (Albarracin-Jordan and Mathews 1990; Albarracin-Jordan 1992; Mathews 1992a) have suggested.

Second, we have identified a general shift toward more dispersed patterns of settlement throughout the study area. In each of the three survey areas, the Early Colonial period was characterized by an increase in the number of sites and a decrease in the average population of sites. This fact would seem to contradict a general ethnohistoric emphasis on *reducciónes*, the forced concentration and resettlement of populations that were supposed to have accompanied the Toledan reforms. If our evidence is at all representative, the reducción may be more a documentary phenomenon than an empirical one. Dispersal of population would certainly facilitate the manipulation of census figures and tribute

levies in the manner described by Stern (1982), and may provide circumstantial evidence for such behavior.

Finally, we have documented large-scale population movements in the Early Colonial period. Within our study area population growth rates are strongly associated with administrative boundaries. Archaeological settlement patterns demonstrate a clear preference for residence within the boundaries of Taraco, a Crown territory. The massive movement of population out of the encomiendas of the Lower Tiwanaku Valley and the Katari Basin testify to the importance of population mobility in Early Colonial period demographic reconstructions. Our evidence provides strong support for Sánchez-Albornoz's contention that the Early Colonial period was characterized by extensive internal migration.

Demographic processes in the Early Colonial period were extremely local. This study has documented simultaneous population growth and decline within an area as small as 400 km^2. It may be that no generalizations are possible at a larger scale. What is certain, though, is that any treatment of Colonial period demography must take internal migration into account. The imposition of Spanish rule was uneven and heterogeneous. It created a mosaic of administrative practices. Mobility and migration within this variegated social landscape was perhaps the primary mechanism by which persons and households could situate themselves with respect to the colonial administration.

ACKNOWLEDGMENTS

The authors would like to acknowledge the assistance of Christine Hastorf, Alan Kolata, Amanda Cohen, Matthew Seddon, Erika Simborth, Robin Beck, Eduardo Pareja, Felipe Choque, and Facundo Llusco. The lower Tiwanaku Valley data we are using were, of course, collected and published by Juan Albarracin-Jordan.

NOTES

1. ". . . it is impossible to ignore the demographic decline that is evident toward the beginning of the seventeenth century, Silver mining in Po-

tosi became the principal factor in regional population disequilibrium, The Lower Tiwanaku Valley was incorporated into the *mit'a* system. A large number of tribute-payers were carried off to the mines in Potosi. . . . The Spanish version of the mit'a had such an effect that of the 868 tribute-payers listed in the *Repartimiento* of Tiwanaku in 1583, only nine remained in 1658 . . . " [Albarracin-Jordan 1996a: 313].

2. The passage quoted above from Albarracin-Jordan is typical in this regard. He notes that in 1583 there were 868 tributarios in Tiwanaku, and in 1658 only nine. He takes this discrepancy to indicate a massive depopulation resulting from the *mit'a*.

3. Bandy's dissertation contains a description of Early Pacajes ceramics (Bandy 2001b:229–232), as do the earlier studies of Albarracin-Jordan and Mathews (1990), Albarracin-Jordan (1992, 1996a), and Mathews (1992a).

4. This is similar to a common decorative technique of the Sillustani Black-and-White-on-Red style from the northern Titicaca Basin (M. Tschopik 1946:27), though this is apparently the only point of similarity between these two styles.

5. Albarracin-Jordan (1992:327), for example, characterized Late Pacajes ceramics as "essentially a debilitated extension of the previous local Pacajes-Inka style." Also, "[el] decorado se limita a puntos negros y blancos, y en reducidos casos a líneas paralelas" ["the decoration is limited to black and white points, and in a few cases to parallel lines"] (Albarracin-Jordan and Mathews 1990:175).

6. Note that the data in this table supersede those presented in Table 10.1 of Bandy's dissertation (Bandy 2001b:258). The data in the Late Pacajes row of that table have been revised.

7. "The Aymara household, although variable, typically consists of a nuclear or extended family living together in an architecturally defined compound, or at least near one another in a nucleated compound cluster. Household members...ideally share a common patio and other outdoor spaces ... " (Janusek 1994:35).

8. The record from the Juli-Pomata area for this time period is somewhat better understood (Stanish et al. 1993; Stanish et al. 1997). However, the sites from the western basin may not be directly compared to the southern case. This is so because the basic organizational unit of Late Intermediate period domestic groups in the western basin is the domestic terrace, and terracing is conspicuously absent in the south.

9. It should be noted that Bandy's sample is small and informal. The results are impressionistic and should be considered provisional. A systematic ethnoarchaeological study of the scale and spatial structure of modern Aymara residential areas would be very useful. No such study has been carried out in the southern Titicaca Basin.

10. Excepting nonhabitation space occupied, for example, by public architecture, plaza space, and so on. For present purposes this complication will be ignored, though we acknowledge the difficulty of identifying habitation versus nonhabitation space in sites without preserved surface architecture.

11. In fact, the first *encomendero* of both Tiwanaku and Guaqui (AD 1538–1541) was none other than Francisco Pizarro, the conqueror of Peru (Choque Canqui 1993:60).

17.

Archaeological Reconnaissance in the Northern Titicaca Basin

Charles Stanish, Amanda B. Cohen, Edmundo de la Vega,
Elizabeth Arkush, Cecilia Chávez, Aimée Plourde, and
Carol Schultze

MEMBERS OF PROGRAMA COLLASUYU have conducted archaeological reconnaissance throughout the Lake Titicaca Basin in the last several years. The intent of this work was to assess the nature and variety of archaeological settlement in a number of areas in order to formulate future research designs. As a result, many sites have been recorded that do not fall into the area of any ongoing, systematic study. In this chapter, we provide data from a number of important sites in the northern and western basin area discovered on such reconnaissance fieldwork.

We make the distinction between intensive survey, systematic reconnaissance, and reconnaissance (Stanish 2001b). A reconnaissance refers to nonsystematic surface survey with the intent of finding and recording archaeological sites. Reconnaissance is particularly useful in areas where we have little knowledge of the range and nature of the archaeological remains. This research strategy assists archaeologists in defining broad patterns of settlement and style distribution, and serves to generate hypotheses for future testing. It is in this context that these sites were discovered. The data generated from this work helped us define new projects in several areas of the region, including the Pukara Valley (Cohen 2000, 2001), the Huancané-Putina Valley (Stanish and Plourde 2000), and in the Puno Bay area (Schultze 2000).

The first modern reconnaissances in the Titicaca region were conducted by José María Franco Inojosa and Alberto González (1936), Emilio Vásquez (1937, 1939), Alfred Kidder II (1943), Máximo Neira (1967), and Marion Tschopik (1946) in the 1930s through the 1960s. Vásquez (1940:143–150) described a number of important sites in the Peruvian Titicaca Basin, such as Sillustani, Cutimbo, Kacha Kacha, Tanka Tanka, Siraya, Maukallajta, Cheka, Wilakolla, and Taraco. At Cheka, he described the cut stones known as "El Baño del Inca," and described monoliths in the north near Huancané and Pukara. M. Tschopik published an article in 1946 that served to define a number of pottery types, including the Sillustani Series, Chucuito, and local Inca types. Kidder, likewise, reconnoitered the northern Basin, concentrating on earlier sites. He documented a number of Pukara, Pukara-related, and Tiwanaku sites throughout the region. Neira's (1967) report stands as one of the most important sources of information for the northern and northeastern sides of the lake. Likewise, Manuel Chávez Ballón, Elías Mujica, John Rowe, Sergio Chávez, and Mario Núñez discovered a number of sites throughout the northern area and beyond.

In the mid-1970s, John Hyslop (1976, 1977a) conducted a more systematic reconnaissance throughout the western Titicaca region in the area of the Lupaqa kingdom. His work included surveys in part of the area covered in this chapter. The bulk of his research was conducted in an area to the south that was covered by a systematic, full-coverage regional survey in the early 1990s and reported on in Stanish et al. (1997).

The work reported on here is neither systematic nor intensive. It is a large-site reconnaissance methodology that comprises the first stage of a multi-stage research design in the northern Titicaca Basin. This chapter reports on newly discovered or under-reported sites in this region. A few of these sites were discovered and described by earlier scholars. In cases where sites were already reported, we sought to confirm the observations of these earlier scholars and/or elaborate on the existing descriptions. We have attempted to provide a schematic description of each of the sites, briefly mention their significance, and provide graphics of the artifacts and landscapes associated with these settlements.

THE NORTHERN TITICACA BASIN

Lake Titicaca is actually oriented northwest to southeast (Figure 17.1) but it is common among researchers in the region to casually use cardinal directions as if the lake were oriented directly north-south. The northern Titicaca Basin is defined here as the area north-northwest of the Ilave River in the west, and north-northwest of the Río Suches near Escoma in the east. The southern boundary of the northern Titicaca Basin is therefore defined by two of the largest rivers that flow out of the lake near its midsection in the east and west.

The geographical areas separated by the two rivers appear to be more than an artificial distinction. Based upon a systematic survey in the Juli-Pomata area (Stanish et al. 1997), previous research by other archaeologists (in particular K. Chávez 1988; Hyslop 1976; and Kidder 1943), and the work reported on here, we propose that the Ilave and Suches Rivers divided two culturally distinct areas since the time of the earliest agricultural populations in the region. Fiber-tempered pottery, for instance, is rarely found north of these rivers. Likewise, the southernmost limit of the Pukara settlement distribution

is found near Acora, and the nature of Tiwanaku settlement appears to have been qualitatively different in the north compared to the south (Stanish 1999, 2003).[1] Lisa Cipolla (Chapter 4, this volume) makes the compelling case that this cultural distinction goes back to the Archaic.

SURVEYS

In the last decade or so, our program has intensively surveyed or reconnoitered a large number of areas in the Titicaca Basin (Figure 17.1). The Juli-Pomata survey covered an area measuring approximately 360 km[2]. The reconnaissance associated with this latter project extended from Pomata to Yunguyu to the east, and southeast to Desaguadero. These data have been published in several publications (e.g., Stanish 1994b, 1997; Stanish et al. 1997). The Island of the Sun was intensively surveyed by one of us (C. Stanish) and Brian Bauer in 1994, 1995, and 1996, and the final results have been published (Bauer and Stanish 2001, Stanish and Bauer 2004). Amanda Cohen surveyed the Pukara Valley in 1998 and 1999 (Cohen 2000, 2001). The Huancané-Putina Valley was surveyed in 1999 and 2000 by Stanish and Plourde (Stanish and Plourde 2000). Carol Shultze has conducted a survey in the Puno Bay area. All of the regions outside of these areas are the subject of this chapter, although selected sites from within these regions have been included as well.

CERAMIC CHRONOLOGY

Numerous seasons of excavations, systematic survey, and reconnaissance have provided a corpus of discrete ceramic types that were manufactured and used for restricted periods of time in the region. In the north and northeast Titicaca Basin, the following pottery types have been used to date sites discovered on the proposed survey.

Inca (Late Horizon), Circa AD 1450–1532

Late Horizon pottery is very easily distinguished by its paste, decoration, surface treatment, and form. Many plainware forms, surface treatments, and pastes are distinct from all previous pottery manufactured in the region. As such, there is no difficulty in dating an Inca site. The best work on Inca pottery in the region to date is Julien's (1983). Her work defined Hatuncolla area Inca pottery. Likewise, Tschopik defined the Taraco Polychrome "ware" and Sillustani "series" that are commonly found in the region (M. Tschopik 1946:22, 25–27, 31–32).

Examples of chronologically useful Inca types that we have used to date sites in the region include those illustrated in the following sources: Julien (1983:Appendix 1), Stanish et al. (1997: Appendix 1), and M. Tschopik (1946:Figures 17j; 18a–c, e; 22a–i; 23a–h; 24c, g; 25d–i; 26e). In 1998, we discovered what appears to be the

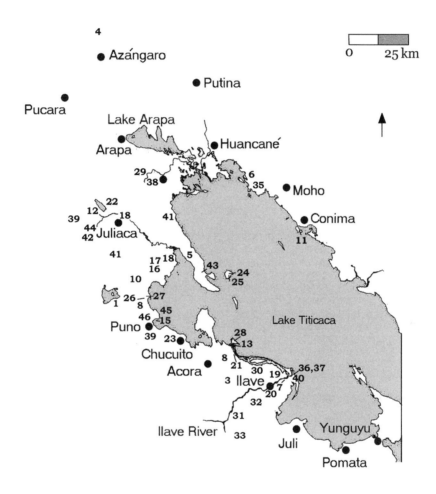

1: Sillustani; 2: Cutimbo; 3: Kacha Kacha; 4: Cancha Cancha Asiruni; 5: Capachica; 6: Carpa; 7: Cebaduyu; 8: Cerro Ccaca; 9: Chincheros; 10: Cupe; 11: Chacchune; 12: Chimpajara; 13: Cocosane; 14: Cotos; 15: Huajje; 16: Huata clay source; 17: Huata area; 18: Huayna Roque; 19: Huimpuco; 20: I-1; 21: Isla Escata; 22: Maravillas; 23: Orejani; 24, 25: Amantaní; 26: Paucarcolla; 27: Paucarcolla-Santa Barbara; 28: Peninsula Socca; 29: Caminaca; 30: Kapalla; 31: Pukara San Francisco; 32: Checca; 33: Pukara Totorani; 34: Punanave; 35: Puno Puno; 36, 37: Ilave mound sites; 38: Saman Sur; 39: Santisima Cruz del Rancho; 40: Sucano Bajo; 41: Taparachi; 42: Tariachi; 43: Tunuphara; 44: Unocolla; 45: Viscachani; 46: Wanina.

FIGURE 17.1. Map of Titicaca Basin with sites discussed in text

manufacturing center of the Sillustani kaolin paste pottery defined by Tschopik. This center is the Inca and modern town of Huatasani, located in the upper Huancané River Valley. The area around Huatasani has huge quantities of black-on-white and red-on-white pottery. This pottery is virtually identical to the Sillustani white paste type found in Sillustani (Figure 17.2). These data will be presented in future publications on the systematic surveys from the northern Titicaca Basin.

Altiplano period (Late Intermediate or Colla Period), Circa AD 1100–1450

The Altiplano period corresponds to the time in which the pre-Inca polity, known as the Colla, dominated the northern Titicaca Basin. There are several distinctive pottery types that occur only in this period. These types are distinguished largely by their paste and surface decoration. M. Tschopik's pioneering work (1946) defined the "Collao Series." Most of her period attributions are correct, although the "Allita Amaya" type is not valid as a chronological marker, and the Sillustani Black-on-red type may be both pre-Inca and early Inca in date. Hernán Amat has identified another pottery type called Quequerana, named after the site of the same name near Moho (Amat 1977:5). The pottery has a cream paste decorated with brown (or oxidized) paint with distinctive plastic and incised decorations.

Collao pottery is found throughout the northern Titicaca Basin region. Paste colors vary from a light red to a light gray of 2.5YR 6/6, 2.5YR 6/8, 5YR 7/4, 5YR 7/6, 5YR 7/8, and 5YR 6/8. Heavy calcareous inclusions are common.

Late Huaña

There are huge areas in the northern Titicaca Basin that do not have Tiwanaku occupations. These areas are replete with sites in productive zones that have all other pottery types. Some sites, in fact, have a small scatter of finely made Tiwanaku pieces, but not in sufficient quantities or varieties to indicate an occupation dating to approximately AD 600–1100. We hypothesize the existence of a local Tiwanaku-contemporary pottery style that we call Late Huaña. (Early Huaña pottery is described below). Late Huaña has some *kero*-like forms that are poorly executed in local pastes. It is also likely that some pottery types with "Collao paste" are earlier than the traditional dates for the LIP, and instead represent Late Huaña types.

Tiwanaku Expansive, Circa AD 600–1100

The Tiwanaku Expansive period corresponds to the time in which the Tiwanaku state exercised

FIGURE 17.2. Example of Late Horizon period pottery in the Huatasani style

some type of control or influence in the northern Titicaca Basin. Tiwanaku finewares are highly distinctive based on form and surface decoration. Certain plainware types, based upon their shapes and pastes, are also chronologically useful. Our research to date indicates that once an area was incorporated by, or came under the political influence of, the Tiwanaku state, all decorated pottery followed Tiwanaku canons (e.g., Stanish and Steadman 1994). Domestic plainwares remained largely the same as those that had been in use prior to Tiwanaku contact, with the occasional addition of some Tiwanaku plainware types. In other words, a provincial Tiwanaku site is characterized by the replacement of earlier fineware types with Tiwanaku ones, and the addition of some new plainware types.

Tiwanaku finewares from the southern Titicaca Basin have been ably described in a variety of publications (Alconini Mújica 1995; Bennett 1934a; Ponce Sanginés 1981). Provincial finewares are faithful copies of core territory ones, though the former are usually executed in a local paste (see Steadman 1994:61). This appears to be the case with most Tiwanaku sites, as it was with the Inca sites. Examples of chronologically useful Tiwanaku period decorated types include those illustrated in the following sources: Kidder (1943:Figure 3, Numbers 31, 33–38); Steadman (1994:Figures 156–165); Steadman (1995), and M. Tschopik (1946:Figure 27a–f). Examples of chronologically diagnostic Tiwanaku plainware types in the northern Titicaca Basin are illustrated in Steadman (1994:Figures 79–80).

The "Hiatus" problem

The Terminal Upper Formative period (circa AD 200–400) in the northern basin was a period of substantial settlement and political shifts. As early as 1974, Lumbreras pointed out that there was a hiatus between the cessation of Pukara pottery and the beginning of Tiwanaku pottery in the Puno area. Our reconnaissance and systematic survey in the northern Titicaca Basin has discovered dozens of large sites in the area that substantiates Lumbreras' observation about an absence of Tiwanaku IV (or Classic Tiwanaku) pottery in the region. We do find some later Tiwanaku pottery on a number of sites in what is a restricted geographical area. We also find Pukara

pottery or Pukara-affiliated styles around the region. However, virtually no sites north of Pukara toward Ayaviri have Tiwanaku pottery in any quantity to qualify as a bona fide Tiwanaku-affiliated settlement. The Juliaca area is full of Tiwanaku sites, and the northernmost Tiwanaku site known to date in this region is that of Maravillas (see below). Other late Tiwanaku sites are found up the Ayabacas River Valley. Around Lampa, one of us (C. Stanish) noted some dense Tiwanaku artifact scatters but did not have permission to work in the area. Toward the northeast, our most recent surveys have found substantial numbers of Tiwanaku sites along the main lake edge, along the road, and along the edge of Lake Arapa. However, there are no Tiwanaku sites away from the roads or lake edge, and there are none in the Putina area.

In short, there are presently no known Tiwanaku III (Qeya) sites in the area (with the possible exceptions of Isla Estéves and Cerro Chincheros). Tiwanaku Expansive (very late Tiwanaku IV and Tiwanaku V) settlements are restricted to enclaves in a few areas along the two roads on the sides of the lake, and along the road to Cuzco. Outside of these areas, there are no known Tiwanaku sites.

We find numerous sites that have Middle Formative pottery, Pukara or Pukara-related pottery, Altiplano period pottery, and occasionally Inca pottery. It is certainly possible that there was a major abandonment of sites in the area with the cessation of Pukara pottery production and the dispersal of settlement, with a subsequent reoccupation of these large sites with the advent of the Altiplano period.

Can this apparent "hiatus" be explained with another model that incorporates these observations? The more parsimonious explanation is that our ceramic chronology is not accurate, and that Tiwanaku III (or Qeya) pottery is not a diagnostic for this time period in the extreme north between the collapse of Pukara (circa AD 300–400) and the expansion of Tiwanaku (circa AD 600). In other words, it is more likely that many sites located in rich agricultural and pasture lands away from the major road system were continuously occupied and that our ceramic chronology is unable to distinguish the Tiwanaku III- and Tiwanaku IV-contemporary occupations.

One of us (Stanish 2003) has hypothesized a fluid political landscape for this period, in which small, Pukara-derived polities focused on intensive agro-pastoral economies prior to the Tiwanaku expansion. Raised fields continued to be worked next to sites such as Maravillas and along the Ramis River, but generally receded in areas where fields could not be watered with canals. With the collapse of the Pukara political economy, stelae production also ceased, as did most of the manufacture of decorated pottery in the Pukara tradition. The culture that developed is hypothesized to be one that responded to the drought conditions by concentrating on the riverine areas and lake edges and by utilizing the pampas for pasture. We call this the Early Huaña culture and date it from the end of Pukara influence to the expansion of Tiwanaku influence into the area. At the time of this publication, our best estimate of the date for this period is AD 400–650. This is based upon liberal terminal dates for Pukara pottery manufacture cessation and unreported 14C (calibrated) dates of circa AD 700 from putative initial Tiwanaku occupations on Isla Estéves.[2]

The Early Huaña occupations are, by and large, on the same sites as the preceding Pukara ones. Such a fact emphasizes the continuity of settlements in well-watered areas. The sites are commonly located on the hills near the rivers, as well as on the low mounds lining the rivers in the north. The pottery of the Early Huaña culture is poorly known at the present time because we do not as yet have good excavation data. Our initial reconnaissance indicates that the pottery assemblage is at least represented by a distinct style derived from Pukara plainwares. Thickened rimmed and flat-bottomed bowl fragments appear to be one diagnostic. The red slip on a sand and mica-tempered paste that Kidder called "Pukara Red" also is found on these sites. There is no obvious decorated pottery style associated with this assemblage, and this may reflect the collapse of the centralized polities during this time.

Upper Formative, circa 400 BC–AD 600

The Upper Formative was a politically dynamic time in which several complex polities existed in the region prior to the emergence of Tiwanaku

as a regional power (see Hastorf, Chapter 5, this volume). Upper Formative diagnostic types in the northern Titicaca Basin area are recognized by their decoration, by their form, and, in two cases, by both their surface treatment and form. The most easily recognized type of this period is the Pukara polychrome incised. This polished, incised type with red, black, and/or yellow paints is illustrated in a number of sources, including S. Chávez (1992), Kidder (1943:Figure 2, Numbers 1–18, 21–29, 31–36, 42–43), Franquemont (1986), and Rowe and Brandel (1969). Another diagnostic type is the ceramic trumpet decorated in the Pukara polychrome incised style. What makes this form so easily recognizable is the grass molding tracks in the interior of the tube. Illustrated examples of Upper Formative period trumpets include those shown by Kidder (1943:Figure 2, Number 14/15). Several plainware types are restricted to the Upper Formative period as well and can be used to date the sites. These Pukara or Pukara-related plainwares are illustrated in Stanish et al. (1997) and Steadman (1995).

Middle Formative, circa 1100–400 BC

Diagnostics for this period include the Qaluyu types, both plain and decorated, identified by Rowe and Brandel (1969) and later by Steadman (1995). The chronologically useful types have very distinct rims. Neckless *ollas* are particularly useful plainware diagnostics found on many sites. The incised *incensario* recognized by K. Chávez (1985) and Steadman (1994) is useful for settlement archaeology. This very distinctive type, found occasionally with post-firing pigments in the incisions, is illustrated in Steadman (1994:Figures 137–146) and K. Chávez (1985).

RECONNAISSANCE DATA

Project Site Numbers

We use a simple designation for sites found in the Titicaca Basin for the purposes of our general reconnaissance. An identifying letter or letters that represent a geographical area is followed by a number. This identification system is intended to be temporary—until such time that the sites are incorporated into individual research projects and input into the database of the Instituto Nacional de Cultura, Puno. The letters have little meaning apart from a general area identification. The numbers are assigned as the sites are recorded into the Programa Collasuyu master site register, and are therefore analytically meaningless. The list of letter designations and their corresponding geographical area is as follows:

P=Puno area; H=Huata area; T=Taraco area; Hu=Huancané area; Pc=Pukara Valley; C=Chucuito area; S=Sillustani area; Ch=Capachica Peninsula; I=Ilave River area; M=Moho area; J=Juliaca area; Az=Azangaro area.

The time period designations are as follows:

MF=Middle Formative; UF=Upper Formative; E. Huaña=Early Huaña; L. Huaña=Late Huaña; Tiw=Tiwanaku; Alt=Altiplano; LH=Late Horizon.

ARCHAEOLOGICAL SITES IN THE RECONNAISSANCE AREA

Explanatory Notes

The sites are listed in alphabetical order. Site names in parentheses indicate alternative names provided by informants or alternative names in the literature. UTM coordinates and other more precise location information have been intentionally omitted from this public publication.[3]

Many of these sites have been classified as being consistent with a "type" of site. These site types were defined during the Juli-Pomata survey. Types are based on the size of the site, along with their structural characteristics. For a full description of the types, see Stanish et al. (1997: 17–33).

Canchacancha-Asiruni (Tintiri)

The site of Cancha Cancha-Asiruni was first systematically reported and renamed by S. Chávez and K. Chávez (1970). They noted, as with so many previously reported sites in the northern Titicaca Basin, that the original scientific discoverer was Manuel Chávez Ballón. It is located northeast of Azángaro and across the river from the hacienda of Tintiri. Tintiri was apparently the name that Chávez Ballón used for the site (e.g.,

see reference in Rowe 1963:7). The site is huge, covering at least 12 ha and probably an even larger area (Figure 17.3). Canchacancha-Asiruni is composed of a series of compounds with probable sunken courts and stelae in the centers of these courts. The compounds are not planned, but represent a series of what appear to be architecturally similar units that aggregated over time. The compounds are visible on the surface. Similar structures can be found at Qaluyu and at the site of Cachichupa near Putina (Plourde 2004). Structure walls are noted as double-brick constructions, and many modern walls follow the outline of the older walls. This type of compound, in fact, appears to be the normative type of household construction in large sites for at least the latter part of the Formative period in the northern Basin. Pottery from the surface of the site also indicates a Formative date.

Perhaps the most notable aspect of the site is the presence of fine stelae on the surface that were first reported by S. Chávez and K. Chávez (1970:28–30) (Figures 17.4–17.5). The finely carved stelae depicted in these figures are all Formative period in date. Most fit into the broadly defined traditions of Yaya-Mama and other pre-Tiwanaku, pre-Pukara sculpture. Of additional interest are the numerous stones that have some evidence of having been worked, but that contain no carved motifs. S. Chávez and K. Chávez (1970:30) depict many stones that we consider to have been "stelae" as well, but stelae that were perhaps painted or decorated in other ways. It is particularly interesting that the form of some of these undecorated stelae are similar in overall shape to later, decorated Pukara stelae in that the former have a blocky, massive appearance. The full significance of these pieces remains to be established, but we hypothesize that each of the compounds housed at least one stela, decorated or otherwise.

Canchacancha-Asiruni is one of the most important sites in the northern Titicaca Basin. It is possibly twice the size of Qaluyu and appears to have dominated this section of the Tintiri River Valley. The site is one of the largest pre-Pukara primary regional centers in the northern Basin. Apart from Pukara itself, it is the largest known Pukara period settlement in the northern Titicaca region.

FIGURE 17.3. Stone compounds on the surface of Canchacancha-Asiruni

FIGURE 17.4. Carved stela located on the surface of Canchacancha-Asiruni

FIGURE 17.5. Partially carved stela located on the surface of Canchacancha-Asiruni

Size: at least 12 ha
Periods: MF, UF, E. Huaña (?), L. Huaña,
    Alt, LH
Programa Collasuyu ID: Az-1
Additional references: Rowe (1963:7),
    S. Chávez and K. Chávez (1970)

Capachica

Capachica is today a small town on the peninsula of the same name. In the Toledo Tasa, the town is listed as having a total of 5360 persons, of which 1303 were tribute-payers. Of the tribute payers, almost 40% were Urus (515 "Huros or Uros"), making Capachica one of the towns of the Titicaca Basin with the highest percentage of Uru people.

We did not have much time to work in the town, and in fact were only able to spend an hour or two passing through. However, a quick walking tour indicated that there is a substantial number of Inca potsherds incorporated into the adobe bricks. Likewise, we did not note any pre-Inca pottery in the bricks in two exposed middens along the road. While this is hardly an exhaustive study, such evidence fits the pattern seen elsewhere, where a major Inca and Early Colonial town was newly founded in the Late Horizon (Stanish 1997).

     Size: unknown
     Periods: LH
     Programa Collasuyu ID: Ch-3

Carpa

Carpa was first mentioned by M. Tschopik in her 1946 publication. Likewise, Neira (1967) mentions it in his reconnaissance report. The site is a beautifully preserved Inca administrative center located directly adjacent to the modern road from Huancané to Moho (Figures 17.6–17.7). It is located at the neck of the Wilasalto Peninsula. The modern village is built on the Inca site and follows the Inca grid pattern. The streets in the village are in fact original, and there are many Inca walls still being used. The pottery on the site is overwhelmingly characterized by well-made local Inca wares. This site is an important Inca administrative center on the Omasuyus highway. It is small by western basin standards, but is a significant secondary urban center on this side of the lake.

     Size: at least 3 ha
     Periods: LH
     Programa Collasuyu ID: Hu-2

Cebaduyu (Tinpunku)

This site is located along the south bank of the Ilave River, about 150 to 200 m from the present course of the river. It is on a low hill with domestic terraces, a kind of site that we have referred to as "type 4" in previous publications (Stanish et al. 1997; Stanish 2003). Type 4 sites are basically low terraces on hills used as surfaces to build structures. They may also originally have been built as agricultural terraces and then later used as a building site. Conversely, terraces used for construction are routinely converted to agricultural planting surfaces.

     There is a very high density of pottery on this site, including Upper Formative, Tiwanaku, Late Intermediate, and Late Horizon diagnos-

tics. The site is approximately 1.5 ha in size. There is no evidence of corporate architecture. It therefore is most likely a modest domestic site whose inhabitants farmed the river area. There is no evidence of raised fields in the area.

     Size: 1.5 ha
     Periods: MF, UF, Tiw, Alt, LH
     Programa Collasuyu ID: I-3

Cerro Ccacca

This is a small Tiwanaku hamlet on the northwest side of Cerro Ccacca. It is located on the low hill that juts into the pampa off of the main hill. It is a type 4 domestic terrace site about 50 x 50 m in size. The pottery is not very fine. Above the site to the south is Pukara Ccacca. This latter site has a substantial Altiplano period component with Inca and pre-Inca *chulpas*, at least on the west side.

     Size: approximately 1 ha
     Periods: Tiw
     Programa Collasuyu ID: C-3

Cerro Chincheros

This is one of the most important sites in the western Titicaca region. This huge type 3 settlement is characterized by one of the best-preserved sunken courts in the area. Type 3 sites are low hills with terraced sides that lead up to an artificially flat area with some kind of court or other corporate constructions. They served as primary and secondary regional centers in the Titicaca Basin from the early Formative period to Tiwanaku times. A description of the site types is found in Chapter 7 of this volume.

     Cerro Chincheros is situated just outside of Puno, along the Puno-Cuzco highway. The sunken court is approximately 20 x 30 m in size, making it the largest such construction outside of the Pukara and Tiwanaku areas. Surrounding the sunken court on Chincheros is between 15 and 20 ha of domestic terracing. The existing walls of the court are up to 3 m high and they appear to be virtually intact. Likewise, there are large slabs around the court area, suggesting that it was faced with cut stone blocks. The pottery on the surface includes Qaluyu or Qaluyu-like fragments, Pukara, Tiwanaku III, Tiwanaku IV/V, and Middle Formative neckless ollas. Some Altiplano period and Inca fragments are

FIGURE 17.6. Stone wall at Carpa

FIGURE 17.7. Close-up of stone wall at Carpa

associated with a number of chulpas at the top of the site, which is a typical pattern in this region. Most of the chulpas are round, fieldstone types. The diameters of the chulpas ranged from 3.0 to 5.0 m.

The domestic terraces are very wide and broad and were constructed up all sides of the site. Some of the terraces are 3 m high, and would have been higher in antiquity. There is no doubt that these were domestic habitation sites.

The terraces are covered with domestic debris, and various exposed cuts indicate very thick deposits of midden fill. The terraces are also covered with a high density of agricultural implements, particularly hoes. These implements were most likely used on the rain-fed terraces and on the extensive raised fields in the pampa below. There are also many other kinds of lithic tools on the surface, including debris from all stages of manufacture.

Along with Paucarcolla-Santa Barbara, Cerro Chincheros was one of the largest primary regional centers in the western Titicaca Basin during Formative and Tiwanaku times.

Size: at least 15 ha
Periods: MF, UF, Tiw, Alt, LH
Programa Collasuyu ID: P-13

Cerro Cupe

On the road to Hatuncolla is this major Middle Formative through Altiplano period site. This type 3 site has a very high quantity of debris, including decorated pottery, bone, and many agricultural implements. There is a substantial quantity of well-made Tiwanaku pottery, as well as a few fragments of Pukara incised. At the top of the site is an area that could have been the location of corporate architecture. There is a chulpa at the top. It is a large, round, fieldstone chulpa about 7.0 m in diameter. There are about six major domestic terraces along the side of the hill facing the pampa.

The name "Cupe" or "Cupi" is mentioned in documents as a village of craft specialists in the Titicaca Basin during Inca times (e.g., see Julien 1993:189). Julien locates two such toponyms, one between Chucuito and Acora and a second near Ayaviri. This site does not seem to be related to these documentary accounts, and the lack of Late Horizon materials on the surface confirms this.

Size: approximately 2.0 ha
Periods: MF, UF, Tiw, Alt
Programa Collasuyu ID: H-2

Cerro Marenza

Cerro Marenza is an Altiplano period site on a hill of the same name overlooking the Huata Pampa. There are many slab-cist tombs and possible chulpa bases all along the ridge. It is likely that M. Tschopik visited this site during her reconnaissance (see M. Tschopik 1946). Virtually all of the diagnostic pottery is Altiplano period in date. The pottery includes the very diagnostic Collao black-on-red and plainwares with identical pastes. Such Altiplano period cemetery sites are common in the region. The existence of this site confirms the large post-Tiwanaku occupation in the area. Some of these sherds could date to the Late Huaña period as well.

Size: large cemetery area
Periods: Alt
Programa Collasuyu ID: H-5

Chacchune

We believe that this site was briefly referred to by Kidder and Neira in their respective reports (Kidder 1946; Neira 1967), but the descriptions are too incomplete to be certain. The site is located on the northeast side of the isthmus that faces the Huata Peninsula.[4] It is a small but major *pukara* on this side of the lake dating to the Altiplano period, as indicated by surface collections (Figure 17.1), site plan, and architecture. There are a number terraces that also seemed to function as defensive walls up the sides of the hill. These terraces are very well preserved. In fact, on the side toward the main access road are a series of domestic terraces that still preserve aboriginal houses. The site was densely populated. It is at least 4 ha in size, and probably includes 2 ha more.

The top of this pukara is very important. There is a plaza-like area on what appears to be small structures that are best interpreted as storage rooms on either end. We counted about five structures on each side. Each one was about 2 m^2. Behind the storage structures are other buildings that are most likely residential in nature. This site would make an excellent case study for the analysis of Altiplano period architecture.

Size: > 4 ha
Periods: Alt
Programa Collasuyu ID: M-1

Checca A

This site was discovered by John Hyslop (1976). We confirmed that this type 4 site has a moderate occupation of about 1.5 ha in extent. The site also has a number of chulpas, as Hyslop originally noted. The lower terraces (at the base of the hill) are largely Upper Formative and Tiwanaku occupations, and some Altiplano and Late Horizon settlements are present above. There is no evidence of corporate architecture. The chulpa is square and has two carvings of snakes.

Size: 1.5 ha
Periods: UF, Tiw, Alt, LH
Programa Collasuyu ID: none

Chimpajara

This site is a small mound on an old oxbow terrace near the Ayabacas River. Today, there is a house compound built over a raised-mound area. There is no evidence of corporate architecture. We found two obsidian points, Pukara diagnostic pottery, and a number of plainwares suggestive of post-Tiwanaku types. The lithics on the surface include agricultural tools and debris. There are no evident Altiplano period diagnostics or any Tiwanaku pottery.

This is a good example of a small Pukara village. This is significant because it establishes the fact that small villages with relatively high quantities of Pukara pottery exist in this area. This contrasts substantially with the regional data south of the Ilave River, where no such Pukara villages are found. In the south, all diagnostic Pukara pottery (or perhaps varieties of Tiwanaku I or Sillumocco Polychrome Incised—see Steadman 1994) are found in small quantities on large sites. Such data serve to reinforce our methodological principles of distinguishing between bona fide settlements linked to larger regional polities and settlements with trade wares.

Size: approximately 1.0 ha
Periods: Pukara, E. Huaña (?), L. Huaña (?), LH
Programa Collasuyu ID: J-5

Cocosane

This small Upper Formative site is located on the small road west of Isla Escata. The road cuts through some middens and an area with a number of stone blocks. In 1995, there were a number of uncut, but shaped, blocks on the surface. When we returned in 1998, part of the area had been leveled for construction. Since then, we have returned several times, and the site has been 80% obliterated by new house construction and the widening of the road. Unfortunately, we did not take photographs in 1995 because it was too late in the day. The site most likely was a modest type 1 mound that has since been bulldozed. The result is a very heavily disturbed site. The east side, however, has a small house compound on it. We were unable to gain access to this compound, but it is possible that this area has some preserved portion of the mound left on it.

This site is largely Upper Formative in date with a small Tiwanaku occupation measuring perhaps 30 x 50 m. There is also some Altiplano period material on the surface. A few of the cut stone blocks are tapered on one end, suggesting that they were Formative period stelae. None of the blocks had any evidence of carving on the surface.

Size: difficult to determine. (The site in 1995 was perhaps about 1.0 ha in size, based upon the distribution of what appeared to be intact archaeological deposits.)
Periods: UF, Tiw, Alt
Programa Collasuyu ID: I-9

Cotos

This site is located on a natural geological rise near the lake, south of Taraco and north of Pusi. It is a type 4 site with well-made, broad terraces up the saddle of the hill. At the crest of this hill are a number of sharp rock outcrops. From here there is an exceptional view of the cordillera and lake. Below this crest and toward the lake is a flat, marshy area that may have had raised fields. There is an impressive density of artifacts on the surface, including pottery, agricultural implements, and midden remains. There are a number of Tiwanaku diagnostics. We also found a small piece of a carved slab, which is typical of Upper Formative settlements.

Size: 1–2 ha
Periods: UF, Tiw, LIP, LH
Programa Collasuyu ID: T-1

Huajje

Huajje is a huge, U-shaped artificial mound opposite Estéves Island. The interior of the "U" faces Estéves Island. The mound is located on the road that passes along the edge of the hill and that ultimately curves around and heads north to the Paucarcolla Pampa. The northeast side of the mound has a double platform. We were unable to examine the top of the site. The road to Estéves Island cuts directly through the mound on the north and northeast sides. In this cut there is evidence of at least 2 m of construction fill, including a small canal or sewer that is exposed in the profile. The fill is composed of midden material and quarried soil.

The entire south face of the mound, which faces Estéves Island, measures about 450 m in length. The southeast side of the mound is badly damaged, but it is clearly part of a single architectural complex. This side of the mound appears to be natural and was probably even flattened to obtain the desired shape. There is an internal terrace wall that connects the two arms of the "U" and faces a low rise. This mound is very similar to, though much larger than, the mound at Tumatumani, near Juli (Stanish and Steadman 1994). It is worth noting that at Tumatumani the U-shaped mound also was partially constructed from an excavated hill, and the fill was used to build up the other side of the mound in order to obtain the desired shape of the mound.

The surface artifacts include abundant lithic debris and pottery sherds, including numerous Middle Formative, Upper Formative, Tiwanaku, and later diagnostics. There are numerous agricultural implements. This site is extremely important, as it was clearly part of the Tiwanaku complex associated with Estéves (Schultze 2000). However, unlike Estéves, this mound was very large in the pre-Tiwanaku periods. We can, therefore, provisionally suggest that Huajje was a major Upper Formative period center in the Puno Bay prior to the Tiwanaku occupation of the area. Coincident with the incorporation of the bay area by Tiwanaku, Huajje continued in importance, as evidenced by the Tiwanaku occupation of the site. Huajje, along with Estéves, constitutes an ideal database for modeling the interaction between the Tiwanaku state and local elites.

Size: at least 5 ha
Periods: MF, UF, Tiw, LH
Programa Collasuyu ID: P-5

Huata Pampa Clay Source

We discovered a mica source as well as a likely clay source in the pampa. The people today are still mining the site. Mica tempering is used in pottery throughout the sequence in the area, but it is particularly common in Pukara pottery. The closest large Pukara site is Wanina. The only other known mica source in the region is described by Plourde (1999) at the site of Hu-14 in the Putina Valley.

Size: < 0.25 ha
Periods: ?
Programa Collasuyu ID: H-8

Huata Area, Unnamed Site

In the hillsides above the clay source is a small site with some very good Collao ceramics. This is a typical type 4 domestic terrace with some very fine decorated pottery fragments in the Collao tradition. One of the pieces is a kero-like base and others are very straight-sided bowls. The significance of this pottery is that it is a candidate for Late Huaña.

Size: < 0.5 ha
Periods: Alt, LH
Programa Collasuyu ID: H-3

Huayna Roque

The hill of Huayna Roque dominates one of the largest hills in the Juliaca area. It was first reported by John Rowe in the 1960s. The site superficially looks like a classic type 3 site with many, broad domestic terraces around the hill (Stanish et al. 1997). There is abundant pottery and other domestic debris on the surface. Agricultural implements and other lithic artifacts abound on the site. Unfortunately, the site is so badly disturbed that it is very difficult to determine its extent.

Size: > 5.0 ha
Periods: MF (?), UF, Tiw, Alt, LH
Programa Collasuyu ID: J-2

Huimpuco

This is one of the Río Ilave mound sites. It consists of two mounds, each about 4 to 5 m high and approximately 15 to 20 m in diameter. The small diameter makes for a conical-shaped mound that we had never before seen in the Titicaca Basin. The site is largely Upper Formative, with some possible Altiplano material. There is no Tiwanaku or Inca pottery on the site. It is possibly a walled compound as well, with a high hilly rise and exterior wall enclosing these two principal mounds.

These mounds represent a settlement type not previously defined in the Juli-Pomata region. These mounds are found on the Ramis River in the north, suggesting that this is a kind of site that is typically found on river floodplains.

Size: approximately 1.0 ha
Periods: UF, Alt
Programa Collasuyu ID: I-10

Ilave, Unnamed Late Site

This is a small Inca and Early Colonial period site located across the Ilave River near the bridge on the main Puno-Desaguadero road. The site is located on a natural river terrace, very close the river itself. The site is relatively unimportant given the large numbers of similar small, Late Horizon and Early Colonial sites throughout the region (for example, see Stanish et al. 1997). However, given our lack of information on the Ilave region, and given the fact that Hyslop (1976) could not identify the Ilave Inca occupation, the fact that we identified a small hamlet on the Ilave River away from the lake is an important observation.

Size: 0.25 ha
Periods: LH
Programa Collasuyu ID: I-1

Isla Escata

A small Tiwanaku site was located on the south center of the former island. It is now a peninsula and one can drive to the town that is on the island. The site appears to be very small, perhaps 50 x 50 m at most, although we could not survey the area very effectively. The site is located partially in a modern house compound and we could not find the owner to gain permission to enter. Tiwanaku sherds are found on the edges of what would have been a type 4 domestic terrace site.

Size: approximately 0.25 ha
Periods: Tiw
Programa Collasuyu ID: I-11

Kacha Kacha A

Kacha Kacha A is a site named by Hyslop in his dissertation (1976). This site includes the famous chulpas south of Acora on the hill first published by Ephraim Squier in 1877 and mentioned by naturalists, travelers, and scholars ever since.

Above the chulpa area is a large, classic, type 3 site that has evidence of occupations from the Middle Formative through the Inca period. The site covers about 4 ha of area. Although there is no visible corporate architecture, it is possible that a small court exists at the top. The artifact density is particularly high on the top of the hill and on the domestic terraces along the sides of the site.

Size: approximately 4 ha
Periods: MF, UF, Tiw, Alt, LH
Programa Collasuyu ID: I-8

Maravillas

Maravillas is located just north of the bridge outside of Juliaca that crosses the Río Ayabacas on the highway to Pukara. The entire hill flank to the west of the road is covered with raised fields and terraces. The terraces are both agricultural and domestic. On the northern part of the site is a large, type 1 mound about 1 ha in size. This is a gross estimate, however, because there is a modern building on the mound at present, and there has been substantial damage to the mound. Behind the mound and to the north and south are domestic terraces with Middle Formative, Upper Formative, Tiwanaku, Late Intermediate, and Late Horizon materials on the surface. Furthermore, on the flats between the raised fields and terraces are large domestic compounds, reminiscent of Formative and possibly Tiwanaku period constructions in other sites in the region. One of the better-preserved compounds measures 30 x 42 m. The walls are made with very small stones.

Between these compounds, one can detect some very well-preserved canals, similar to those discovered in excavations at the site of Lukurmata in Bolivia. There are interior divisions inside of the compounds demarcated by either linear lines of earth or very ephemeral lines of stone. These are most certainly internal walls for rooms. The raised-field area is quite large.

Size: > 5 ha
Periods: MF, UF, Tiw, LIP, LH
Programa Collasuyu ID: J-1

Ojerani

This is a site area north of Chucuito that Hyslop (1976) described as a possible Tiwanaku site. We were able to walk on the south and west sides of the valley, as well as walk through the center of the pampa where the most intensive agriculture is found. We found no Tiwanaku materials, but we did find some late diagnostics, particularly Inca period pottery.

This valley is very rich. It has its own springs with canals, and some deep wells at the base of the valley with a fair amount of fresh water. Maize grows here in abundance. At first analysis, it looks like a nice little Late Horizon pocket that took advantage of the maize and other agricultural potential.

Size: dispersed
Periods: LH
Programa Collasuyu ID: C-5

Pachamama Amantaní

Pachamama Amantaní is the circular structure several meters in diameter with five concentric walls inside that is located on the hill of the same name. There is some resemblance to the circular structures as Sillustani. There are no sherds associated with the immediate area of this site. However, the north face of the hill, the side on which the structure lies, is full of Inca pottery and some Altiplano materials. We found no pre-Altiplano materials in this area. The relationship between the habitation areas and this structure remain problematic.

Size: < 1.0 ha
Periods: Alt, LH
Programa Collasuyu ID: Ch-4

Pachatata Amantaní

Niles (1988) has written an article describing the Pachatata Amantaní, a high hill with a sunken court at the top. The sunken court is built with fieldstones and measures about 14 x 14 m in size. The overall style of the sunken court is Tiwanaku or Upper Formative, albeit with some differences from sunken courts elsewhere. Features that are typically Tiwanaku and/or Upper Formative on this site include the court's semisubterranean construction, the court's size, a corner doorway in the court that is virtually identical to that found at Lukurmata, and a stairway similar to that at Tiwanaku itself. On the other hand, the second stairway is not typical of Tiwanaku canons, nor is the fieldstone construction of the court. The outside wall, that today is an obvious modern construction, appears to be built on pre-Hispanic foundation stones. If this outer foundation wall is indeed pre-Hispanic, then it is not a typical Tiwanaku construction. Finally, there is no evidence of a Tiwanaku period or earlier occupation on the hillside below Pachatata, although Niles reports finding some Tiwanaku pottery in the region (Niles 1988:Figures 6–7). Without intensive excavations, it is difficult to know the precise architectural history of the temple construction. At the present time, the best estimate is that the temple was originally built as a Tiwanaku construction, with a rebuilding of the area by the Inca or later peoples.

Size: total site > 2.0 ha
Periods: LH
Programa Collasuyu ID: Ch-2

Paucarcolla

Paucarcolla is a fairly large modern village located directly on the Puno-Juliaca highway. Paucarcolla was a moderately large Early Colonial settlement as attested to by the Toledo Tasa. The site had 1003 taxpayers and more than 4500 individuals (Toledo 1975:59). The town was divided into Aymaras and Uros, with the latter constituting about nine percent of the total population. In the Tasa, it is interesting to note that apart from the usual tribute items such as meat and wool, the people of Paucarcolla also contributed dried fish and salt (Toledo 1975:60). The area therefore was most likely an important area for salt production in the Inca period as well, although we have no direct evidence of this.

The site of Paucarcolla has a substantial Inca occupation, as confirmed by our observations and that of Julien (1983:144). Julien notes that the surface materials on the site are similar to her first four phases defined at Hatuncolla. In other words, these data suggest that Paucarcolla was contemporary with Hatuncolla in its entire pre-Colonial phase. The modern town is built in a grid pattern, and this appears to have been originally the Inca layout. This conclusion is based upon similarities to other sites in the region with grid patterns. The Inca occupation of the site, based upon the distribution of pottery in the streets and adobe walls, is approximately 25 ha. This figure is merely an approximation, and should be understood as such. There are thick middens throughout the site with very high densities of Late Horizon pottery, among other debris (i.e., bone, carbon, and lithics). Cut stone blocks in unmistakably Inca style are found in the town as well. Of considerable significance is an area of raw copper ore found on the southern side of the site.

There is no evidence of a pre-Inca occupation on the western side of the modern road. On the eastern side is the site of Paucarcolla-Santa Barbara, composed of the large hill and adjacent flanks. This pre-Inca site is discussed below.

Size: approximately 25 ha
Periods: Inca
Programa Collasuyu ID: H-1

Paucarcolla-Santa Barbara

Paucarcolla-Santa Barbara was first excavated by Lee Steadman (1995). Her work demonstrated that there was a substantial time-depth to the site, beginning in the earliest Formative periods and continuing on to the Tiwanaku period. Ilana Johnson (2003) conducted work at the site confirming these dates. The site is composed of a series of very large and wide terraces that encircle the Santa Barbara Hill outside of Paucarcolla. The terraces are littered with domestic debris on the surface, including high densities of pottery sherds, agricultural implements, and other lithic debris. The terraces and associated habitation area cover as much as 15 ha, making

this and Cerro Chincheros the two largest sites in the area during the Tiwanaku and pre-Tiwanaku periods.

Our unsystematic survey of this site suggests that it was one of the largest Tiwanaku primary regional centers outside of the core territory. The Tiwanaku pottery fragments found on the surface are of exceptional quality.

The site is associated with a large raised-field complex in the pampa below. We have not located any obvious corporate architecture on the site, but there may be some sunken courts on terraces high up on the hill. There is a substantial Middle Formative occupation at the site of Paucarcolla-Santa Barbara as well. Diagnostics on the surface include Qaluyu or Qaluyu-related incised wares. The total area of the Middle Formative appears to be at least 4 ha, and possibly this component is even larger. More intensive work at this site could demonstrate that it was comparable to Chiripa or Ckackachipata in size during the Middle Formative.

Size: 15 ha
Periods: MF, UF, Tiw, Alt, LH
Programa Collasuyu ID: H-6

Peninsula Socca (Auquipadja)

This is a stunningly beautiful area of uplifted sandstones. It has good terrace agriculture and excellent potential for raised fields. However, we did not find much evidence for a prehistoric use of the area except for a very light Altiplano period occupation. The modern town and the hill above the town appeared to be an ideal area for a significant Inca occupation, based upon the criteria that we had developed for other areas of the region. However, we found only a few Late Horizon sherds and one fiber-tempered fragment that dates to the Middle Formative period. The whole area appears to be a very light concentration of Altiplano period pottery with some Inca sprinkled in. There is no pre-Altiplano period occupation in this area, with the maddening exception of one Middle Formative sherd found on the hilltop. Of course, this could be a case of a unique geomorphological environment in which the archaeological deposits are covered. The lack of a substantial occupation in this rich area remains a curious problem for future research.

Size: small, dispersed
Periods: Alt
Programa Collasuyu ID: C-4

Puente Caminaca

The Puente Caminaca site is located adjacent to the river on the southern side of the Río Ramis. The river at this point is deeply entrenched, and there is a high and broad river terrace to the south. The site is located on this natural terrace. The site limit is about 300 to 500 m away from the river, a distance that shifts along the northern limit of the site area as the river twists. A series of low mounds and some retaining walls comprise the site. These mounds are scattered along a length of the river terrace measuring approximately 250 m and are oriented more or less parallel to the river along the terrace. This site type is different from what we see in the Juli-Pomata area and is more typical of the Ilave River mounds. In this case, the site appears to be a series of type 2 mounds that were built in an unplanned fashion on an ancient river terrace. There is abundant midden material on the surface, as well as looted tombs and exposed walls. All indications are that this is a domestic site. There is no evidence of corporate architecture. There is a dense scatter of pottery, lithic flakes (including basalt), bone, and carbon. There is

abundant Pukara pottery on the site, as well as Middle Formative plainwares (neckless ollas in particular), some Late Intermediate Collao decorated types, and local Late Horizon pottery, including Sillustani koalin paste wares.

Size: at least 3 ha
Periods: MF, UF, Huaña (?), Alt, LH
Programa Collasuyu ID: T-4

Pukara Kapalla

This site is located a few kilometers south of Acora on the main highway (Figure 17.8). It was first reported by Tschopik in her 1946 report (M. Tschopik 1946:8, 16). It is a huge mesa formation with a number of well-preserved, igloo chulpas leading up a ridge to the major pukara. The site has several large defensive walls with doors, and at least 2 ha (probably more) of habitation area. It is reminiscent of Tanka Tanka. There are only igloo chulpas on this site and no other chulpa style. There are also slab-cist tombs. Furthermore, the sherds appear to be early, including several that are kero-like on the base. It is safe to conclude that this site is early in date. We made several collections of the site. The only Late Horizon sherds are found at the very top, near a well-maintained *apacheta*.

One of the igloo chulpas is unusual because it is on a rectangular base about 7.0 x 8.0 m in

FIGURE 17.8. View of Pukara Kapalla from the north

size. The chulpa itself is about 2.5 to 3.0 m in diameter and sits on top of the base. There are other clusters of chulpas on the site outside of the habitation area. These are between 3.0 and 5.0 m in diameter. The pottery in this area is mainly Altiplano period in date, but there are some Tiwanaku-like pieces and some Inca pottery, as mentioned above.

The top of Pukara Kapalla has several walls that were built across the ridge to fully protect the top of the habitation area. Behind the site on the opposite side is a very high, natural cliff. This site is significant for a several reasons. First, it appears to be one of the rare early Altiplano period occupations without a later Altiplano period occupation. Pukara Kapalla is therefore good evidence for the transition from Tiwanaku to Early Altiplano period. Also, there are some different post-Tiwanaku period sherds with a kaolin paste and red slip. There are also many straight-sided bowls that could be derivatives of keros. Therefore, this site is evidence for an early post-Tiwanaku fortified settlement type. Unlike other pukaras in the region (with the exception of Huichajaja), this site has good evidence for transitional Tiwanaku/Altiplano period pottery. This is evidence for population continuity between these two periods and argues against the Aymara migration hypothesis.

Size: approximately 2.0 ha
Periods: Alt, scattered LH
Programa Collasuyu ID: I-2

Pukara San Francisco

Pukara San Francisco is a small but major pukara in the puna on the road to Totorani. (The distinction between major and minor pukaras is defined in Stanish et al. 1997.) This pukara has a major concentration of Altiplano period pottery, including some nicely decorated jars and bowls. The walls are well made, and there is solid evidence of domestic activity inside and immediately adjacent to the walls. The importance of this site, like the site of Pukara Totorani, is that it demonstrates that typically Altiplano pukaras were located well away from the lake edge. In fact, the lead author has visited these kinds of pukaras as far west as Mazo Cruz.

Size: < 2.0 ha

Periods: Alt, LH (at base)
Programa Collasuyu ID: I-5

Pukara Totorani

This minor pukara (see Stanish et al. 1997 for a definition of major and minor pukaras) is located near the town of Totorani in the upper Ilave River area. This is a small pukara, consisting of two and three walls encircling the hill. Along the base of the hill are the remains of looted Altiplano period tombs, Altiplano period pottery fragments, and a few raised canals that extend into the marshy area near the river. We found no obvious habitation area, but we only reconnoitered a small area on the roadside about halfway up the mountain. This pukara is typical of the hundreds found in the puna away from the lake. Small, and probably designed to round up camelids and serve as a defensive refuge in raids, this site was not permanently inhabited.

Size: total complex < 3.0 ha
Periods: Alt
Programa Collasuyu ID: I-12

Punanave

Punanave was first discovered and reported by Mario Nuñez in his reconnaissance of the Puno Bay (1994). The site is located on a crest high above Puno near the pass to Moquegua. It is composed of a series of broad, rectangular terraces with considerable quantities of debris on the surface. These terraces comprise the normative domestic compound on the site and are usually associated with pre-Altiplano or Late Intermediate period settlements. One typical terrace, for instance, measures 23 x 33 m. It most likely housed an extended family or larger social unit. Disturbed areas on the site indicate that these terraces were domestic, with large quantities of midden material eroding out of road cuts and other exposures. The terraces on this site are particularly broad due to the low, undulating, natural topography onto which they were built. The site is huge, possibly containing as many as fifteen contiguous hectares of domestic residences. Curiously, there is no evidence of corporate architecture on the site. There are no obvious sunken court areas, nor are there any cut or shaped stone blocks on the surface. This is noteworthy because of the fact that most sites over 4 or 5 ha have indications of some kind of nondomestic construction. Punanave, in contrast, appears to be one large residential site.

There is a substantial amount of lithic debris on the site. This debris represents a broad range of raw material types and, most significantly, a broad range of manufacturing stages. Used and broken andesite and basalt hoes are abundant, indicating agricultural uses. Furthermore, there is a large quantity of scoria on the surface. It is impossible to accurately date the scoria of course, and it is possible that it dates to the Colonial or Republican periods.

The major occupations indicated by the surface of this site are Formative and Tiwanaku in date. At this time and without excavation, it appears that Punanave was a major Tiwanaku and/or pre-Tiwanaku lithic manufacturing center in the region, and it may have been a place where metal was forged.

Size: > 12 ha
Periods: MF (?), UF, Tiw, LIP, LH
Programa Collasuyu ID: P-9

Puno Puno

Puno Puno is located directly on the road on the eastern side of the lake, near the gate to the Moho province. In fact, the road runs along the lowest occupational areas of the site on the western side. Puno Puno is a very fine type 3 site located near the lake and the possible raised-field areas. This, of course, would be significant, because there are few known raised-field areas on this side of Lake Titicaca. The hill on which the site sits has about three to four terraces on the east, and about five terraces on the west. We did not have permission to go very far to the south, so the estimate of the site size assumes that the domestic areas ended where the flat land begins, as it does in rest of the site.

We found a fair amount of red-slipped pottery fragments that were probably Pukara plainwares. We also found a fair amount of Pukara incised pieces. Apart from that, there were few other diagnostics on the surface, in spite of the fact that there were fairly dense concentrations of pottery on the surface. This site is a significant secondary regional center in at least the Upper

Formative period. At the top of the hill is an area that is very likely to house a sunken court. This is reinforced by the fact that there is an Altiplano period chulpa built out of shaped blocks, which were most likely quarried from an earlier court construction.

There is most likely a Middle Formative period occupation as well, as suggested by the presence of a few plainware diagnostics. There is a very wide variety of lithic tools on the surface. In particular, there are abundant agricultural implements, including the ubiquitous hoes so common on these sites. A Formative period quartz projectile point was also recovered from the surface. Obsidian was found on the site as well.

Size: 3–4 ha
Periods: MF, UF
Programa Collasuyu ID: Hu-1

Río Ilave, Flagpole Mound

Along the Río Ilave is a mound with a flagpole right in the middle. The mound measures 17 x 28 m at the base, is about 3.0 m high, and has a very heavy concentration of sherds. This type of conical mound is common along this river area, but is nonexistent in the Juli-Pomata region.

Size: < 0.5 ha
Periods: MF, LF, Tiw, Alt (?)
Programa Collasuyu ID: I-6

Río Ilave, Unnamed Small Mound

This is a late mound that stands 3 to 4 m high. It is a rectangular mound that measures about 17 x 20 m at the base. All of the pottery is post-Tiwanaku. This is therefore a rarity, in that this site appears to be either an intentionally built platform (a type 1 site) or a very large collapsed structure (a type 2 site). In either case, such a site type is rare in the post-Tiwanaku periods.

Size: 0.1 ha
Periods: post-Tiwanaku
Programa Collasuyu ID: I-7

Saman Sur

This is a modest type 4 village located near the Ramis River. The artifact scatter is light, but it has good diagnostic Tiwanaku and Upper Formative pottery. There are only a few (perhaps three or four) low terraces that were habitation areas on the ancient river ridge. The significance of this site is that there are Tiwanaku materials this far north on a small village site.

Size: approximately 1.0 ha
Periods: Tiw, LH
Programa Collasuyu ID: T-3

Santisima Cruz del Rancho (Kunkapata)

This very important Inca site is located at the base of the Unocolla Hill (Figure 17.9). It is geographically adjacent to an earlier Altiplano site in that the Inca occupation extends partially up the base of the hill, merging with Altiplano period terraces. However, this site is low (adjacent to and level with the road) and distinct from Unocolla in that it is a purely Inca period occupation. The site area consists of undulating, low mounds and very broad terraces. It is about 500 m from the river. The site area has many double-stone wall foundations exposed on the surface. There is also a small segment of a road that leads from the site to the modern road. The site is a possible *tambo*. It is located in an excellent location between the river and a very large pampa area. There is abundant water on this site, and today continues to provide water from a well.

Size: > 5.0 ha
Periods: LH
Programa Collasuyu ID: J-7

Sillustani

Sillustani is one of the most famous sites in the altiplano. Today, it is a national park and major tourist destination. The chulpas are well known, and work by Revilla Becerra and Uriarte Paniagua (1985) indicates that Sillustani is not just a cemetery, but has a substantial habitation component that goes back at least to Tiwanaku times. Our own observations indicate that the domestic habitation component is substantial, covering well over 2 ha. For instance, in front of the main chulpa area, near the road in front of the parking lot, is a substantial midden. Part of the road is on, and part cuts through, this midden that is associated with the domestic terraces. This midden has burnt bone, many basalt flakes, other lithics, evidence of hearths, and other materials. There are at least 50 to 100 cm of midden material in some areas.

Below the parking lot toward Lake Umayo is a Late Horizon midden that covers at least 0.5 ha. To the south, at the ticket booth, is a low ridge with some walls on the surface and a lot of pottery. This area is about 1 ha in size.

Size: > 5.0 ha
Periods: Tiw, Alt, LH
Programa Collasuyu ID: S-1.

Sucano Bajo

This is another small mound located on the ancient river ridge. The ridge more or less parallels the Ilave River, and the site is located about 1 km to the north of the river. This site is one of dozens of such large and high mounds on this ridge. The mound is about 2.0 to 3.0 m high. It is in essence a well-preserved type 2 mound that has a slightly conical shape.

Figure 17.9. View of Santisima Cruz del Rancho (Kunkapata)

Size: about 0.1 ha
Periods: MF, UF, Tiw (?)
Programa Collasuyu ID: I-4

Taparachi

This site is located in the edge of the pampa south of Juliaca, west of Caracoto. By the standards of the Juli-Pomata survey, this is not an exceptional site. It is a type 4 Altiplano and Inca domestic terrace site at the edge of the pampa. However, since this area is so poorly known, it is important to note this site in this particular publication. The terraces are broad and low, and are situated along the hillside. On the hilltop, there are a series of looted tombs, all of a late date, and all with few fancy objects. Most of the Altiplano period materials seem to be concentrated in this higher area, and it is possible that the terraces are purely Inca period in date. The site also has a number of lithic artifacts, including agricultural tools.

Size: approximately 2.0 ha
Periods: Alt, LH
Programa Collasuyu ID: J-4

Tariachi[5]

Tariachi is the name of the hacienda where this site is found. The hill is similar to Huayna Roque or Incatunuhuiri in overall appearance. From the bottom, near the hacienda house looking southwest toward the hill, there is a series of low and relatively broad domestic terraces that cut across the base (Figure 17.10). These terraces are filled with eroding midden material, including substantial diagnostic pottery. The terraces continue around the base of the hill in the direction of Juliaca.

On the south side, there are more terraces that are a bit narrower but better preserved. Several images below show one of these terraces that had been recently disturbed, exposing the fill used to construct the domestic terraces. On the side of the hill, close to the top, is a flat area with an eroded sandstone monolith. The monolith is worn, and there is no evidence of carving on the observable sides. This large monolith is 3.80 m long and about 40 to 65 cm wide. Being eroded and with worn edges, it is difficult to get a precise measurement. We were not able to identify any sunken courts either near the monolith or above on the hilltop. Another small monolith is found on one of the terraces, but it is badly eroded, as seen in Figure 17.11.

The site appears to have a 2-ha Tiwanaku, Altiplano, and Late Horizon occupation on the lower terraces near the ground where the modern hacienda buildings are now located. At the northern side of the site, the terraces at the base of the hill are largely Upper Formative (Pukara), Altiplano, and Inca in date. The terraces up to

FIGURE 17.10. View of Tariachi

FIGURE 17.11. Terrace on Tariachi with stela

FIGURE 17.12. Carved stone head from Tariachi

the top are largely Upper Formative and possibly Middle Formative. This therefore gives a Tiwanaku occupation of around 2 ha at most, with a larger Pukara occupation of at least 8 ha. There is, of course, a modest Inca occupation as well at the base of the site. It is curious that one Archaic point was also discovered on the surface. Unfortunately, we did not have the permission to check the northwest side of the site. There may be additional domestic terraces on that side as well.

We also were kindly given access to a private collection of some artifacts that had been collected from the site, as seen in the figure below. Of particular interest is a small feline carving and a carved head (Figure 17.12). The figure is most likely Pukara in style. The owner said that it came from the area of the site.

Size: at least 8 ha
Periods: Late Archaic (?), MF (?), UF, Tiw, Alt, LH
Programa Collasuyu ID: J-3

Tunuphara

This site was first reported by Luperio Onofre during a reconnaissance of the Capachica Peninsula that he conducted with several students from the Universidad Nacional Técnica del Altiplano. Tunuphara is a type 4 site with domestic terraces alongside a hill facing the lake. The hill is quite steep, and the terraces are narrow in many places. To the north, the topography is much less steep. Here, a few of the terraces are much broader. There is no evidence of corporate architecture. Unlike many similar sites in the region, there are also no post-Tiwanaku chulpas on the surface. The hilltop itself is too narrow to have supported any significant corporate constructions.

The artifact densities on this site are extremely high. In many cases, this is due to heavy erosion that has concentrated the contents of eroded middens in a number of areas. This site is significant for a number of reasons. In particular, there are Middle Formative through Early Colonial sherds on the surface. Yet, we recovered no Tiwanaku diagnostics. This site, therefore, is very likely an example of an Early and Late Huaña period site—that is, a local post-Pukara and Middle Horizon site that was outside of the political orbit of Tiwanaku between approximately AD 600 and AD 900 (Stanish 1999). The existence, for example, of Upper Formative plainwares indicates a Pukara-contemporary occupation. However, no Pukara sherds were recovered. Likewise, the presence of a substantial amount of Collao pottery that may date to the Middle Horizon suggests that the site had an occupation contemporary with Tiwanaku, but without any evidence of the use or exchange of Tiwanaku pottery.

> Size: 2–4 ha
> Periods: MF, UF, Alt, LH
> Programa Collasuyu ID: Ch-1

Unocolla

This site at first appears to be a type 3 site by its location on a low hill with terraces, but in reality is a type 4 site with a series of domestic terraces built around a large hill. The site is located directly off of the road. The Río Aybacas is directly behind the site. There is not a large quantity of decorated pottery on this site. There are a few Tiwanaku fragments, but the quantity is too sparse to call this a Tiwanaku occupation. There are also a few Pukara fragments, as well as many Middle and Upper Formative plainware diagnostics. On the hilltop there is no evidence of corporate architecture, nor any evidence of depressions or sunken courts. The site has a number of agricultural tools and a variety of raw materials. Obsidian seems to be rare. The top of the site has a few post-Tiwanaku period tombs.

In short, this is a fairly large nonelite domestic habitation site located in very good agricultural land. We did not get to survey the opposite side of the site. However, from across the river, we could see a number of wide and well-built terraces. If these are habitation areas, then the site could be two to three times larger than our estimate.

> Size: > 5.0 ha
> Periods: MF, UF, Alt
> Programa Collasuyu ID: J-6

Viscachune (Mirador) (Huacaparki)

This is a small site and is otherwise insignificant except for the presence of a long, transverse wall across a ridge and the existence of a platform mound. It is situated on the ridge known as Viscachune, on the hills above the pampa between Estéves and Paucarcolla. There is a low wall across the site with a platform to the east. This platform is about 10 x 11 m in dimension. The site is no more than 1.0 ha in size. The diagnostic surface artifacts are Formative in date. Inca diagnostics are found to the west, on the other side of the wall. There is a fair amount of obsidian on the surface of this site.

> Size: 0.5–1.0 ha
> Periods: MF (?), UF, LH
> Programa Collasuyu ID: P-7

Wanina

This is a very important Pukara site located a few kilometers from Huata on the road to the southeast. It is a large site on the last two hills that jut into the pampa on the southeast side (Figure 17.13). Wanina is a type 3 site. There are a number of moderate to narrow terraces up the sides of the hill, some with stone walls (Figures 17.14–17.15). The area that we defined as habitational was estimated to be about 200 x 600 m. There is abundant Pukara and other Upper Formative pottery (Figures 17.16–17.17). An Inca occupation is noted at the base of the hill. However, there is no Tiwanaku pottery evident on the surface.

The site has a recently looted burial that had been placed below a wall on the upper part of the site. This is suggestive of a ceremonial offering like that found at Tumatumani (Stanish and Steadman 1994). The wall leads to a natural hole several meters in length and width, and about 2 meters deep. There is no evidence of any sunken court or other corporate architecture, but the site is badly disturbed. It is possible that certain areas at the top of the site housed sunken courts. Some of the lower terraces could have had courts as well. Excavations are needed to determine if such courts existed. The site has a number of lithic artifacts throughout the site, including agricultural implements.

This site was a very significant regional center during Pukara times in the Upper Formative. It is obviously located in the Huata Pampa, where there are a number of raised fields (see Erickson 1988a). This site is similar in importance

FIGURE 17.13. View of Wanina

FIGURE 17.14. View of terraces at Wanina. Looted burial with wall leading to natural hole visible in foreground

FIGURE 17.15. Domestic terrace at Wanina

FIGURE 17.16. Pukara pottery from Wanina

FIGURE 17.17. Incised and painted pottery from Wanina

to Incatunuhuiri for understanding Pukara distribution.

    Size: about 12 ha
    Periods: MF, UF, E. Huaña (?), L. Huaña (?),
        LH
    Programa Collasuyu ID: H-5

Unnamed Site above Vilquechico

This is a small, unfortified Altiplano period site with chulpas and a small habitation area. The chulpas are early in date, based upon the typology utilized on the west side of the lake. These are fieldstone constructions, round in size, and around 2 m in diameter. There are a number of domestic terraces with a good scatter of pottery as well. The site has a large concentration of Altiplano period diagnostic pottery.

    Size: < 1.0 ha
    Periods: Alt
    Programa Collasuyu ID: Hu-5

CONCLUSION

This paper has presented sites from various regions around the Lake Titicaca Basin. Some sites are published here for the first time, while others are revisits of previously identified sites in the basin. As noted, all of the authors implement full-coverage survey strategies in their own research. Yet, the reader will note that the majority of these sites have been identified through large site reconnaissance strategies. We are not suggesting a return to this somewhat outdated method of survey. Rather, the aim of the authors is to communicate, through this chapter, the large number of regions around the Lake Titicaca Basin that remain to be studied through systematic survey. Reconnaissance, whether through the use of aerial photographs or "roadside survey" techniques, can be a highly effective means of identifying regions on which to focus one's survey efforts.

ACKNOWLEDGMENTS

The authors thank members of the Programa Collasuyu, our friends in the towns of Juli, Puno, Taraco, and Pukara, Fresia Sardón, Percy Calisaya, and Rolando Paredes. We gratefully acknowledge the support of the National Science Foundation, the Cotsen Institute of Archaeology at UCLA, the Wenner-Gren Foundation for Anthropological Research, the John Heinz III Foundation, the Field Museum of Natural History, and the Dean of Social Sciences, UCLA.

NOTES

1. We make the distinction between a bona fide settlement that can be linked to a political entity versus the occurrence of pottery that could be the result of a variety of mechanisms. A broader discussion of this methodological problem is found in Stanish and Steadman (1994) and Stanish (2003).

2. Dates for initial Tiwanaku occupation of Estéves island, obtained by two of us (de la Vega and Chávez), cluster around AD 650–700.

3. Scholars who want these location data can obtain them by requesting them from any of the authors.

4. Note that this is the Huata Peninsula on the east side of the lake, not to be confused with the Huata area in the northwest or the Huata or Huatta Peninsula in the south in Bolivia.

5. We express our gratitude to Ing. Hermogenes Pilco for permission to survey on his land and permission to photograph his collections.

18.

Future Directions in Titicaca Basin Research

Amanda B. Cohen

THE PUBLICATION OF THIS volume comes at a particularly exciting time for research in the Titicaca Basin. While archaeological research in this region has been ongoing since the 1930s, we have seen a great increase in scientific investigations beginning with the 1970s. Indeed, the year 2003 saw the publication by Charles Stanish of the first comprehensive synthesis of archaeological research of the entire Titicaca Basin in both Peru and Bolivia (Stanish 2003). At present, there are a large number of doctoral and post-doctoral research projects being conducted by a new generation of scholars. We are looking forward to an impressive quantity of data and publications on Titicaca Basin archaeology in the next decade that will change our perspectives on many aspects of social complexity and the culture history of this region. This volume represents a modest contribution to this exciting future.

REGIONAL APPROACHES TO TITICACA BASIN PREHISTORY

Perhaps the most impressive contribution to archaeology in recent years has been the introduction of regional approaches embedded in anthropological theory. Beginning in the 1990s, survey archaeologists began to focus on the southern and western Titicaca Basin. In particular, the studies of Juan Albarracin-Jordan (1992) and James Mathews (1992a, 1992b) focused on the Tiwanaku core area, with one of the main goals being to document the presence of raised fields in the region (Albarracin-Jordan and Mathews 1990). John Janusek and Alan Kolata's (2003) survey in the Pampa Koani expanded on this earlier survey and clarified the use of raised fields through selective excavations. These ar-

chaeologists implemented full-coverage systematic survey strategies and documented all time periods from the Archaic to the Early Colonial to the level of chronological limitations. More recent survey work has been completed by Matthew Bandy (2001b) on the Taraco Peninsula in Bolivia.

Surveys in the Juli-Pomata area of the western basin were conducted by Charles Stanish and his colleagues in 1990–1992 and published in 1997. Since then, Stanish and his students have surveyed a broad range of areas in the western basin. Kirk Frye surveyed the area around Chucuito. Carol Schultze has conducted surveys and test excavations in Puno Bay. Cynthia Klink and Mark Aldenderfer surveyed the Ilave River area. In the northern basin, Stanish and Aimée Plourde have surveyed the area around Huancané and Putina (Plourde 2004; Stanish and Plourde 2000). I have surveyed the Pukara River Valley (Cohen 2000, 2001). Finally, Programa Collasuyu teams have completed a survey of the Ramis River from Taraco to Arapa.

Future survey work will be moving in two directions. One, quite literally, is the expansion of survey areas to the north and to the east. The first systematic survey in the eastern side of the lake was completed by Carlos Lémuz (2001) around Santiago de Huata. Research is currently planned by Sonia Alconini and Jose Luis Paz Soría for additional surveys along the eastern side of the lake.

An admirable example for survey archaeologists can be seen in the current project directed by Matthew Bandy, working in cooperation with Lémuz, in the Tiwanaku Valley. Bandy and Lémuz are revisiting the survey areas of Albarracin-Jordan and Mathews in order to standardize site records and to apply the more recent ceramic chronology that has been developed by Lee Steadman (Hastorf et al. 2001; L. Steadman 1997). Once completed, this project will yield a body of survey data covering an area approximately 600 km^2, allowing for comparisons with survey regions in other parts of the world such as the Valley of Oaxaca (Kowalewski et al. 1989) and the Basin of Mexico (Parsons 1971; Parsons and Whalen 1982). The advantages of combining survey areas for more powerful analyses of datasets can be seen in Bandy and Janusek's work in Chapter 16 as well as in Stanish et al.'s contribution in Chapter 7.

CHRONOLOGICAL APPROACHES TO THE TITICACA BASIN

The Archaic Period

One of the more exciting directions taken by survey archaeologists in this volume is exemplified in the work of Cindy Klink for the Archaic period (Chapter 2). Indeed, Klink's work is representative of one of the most recent directions for research in the Titicaca Basin—that of Archaic period research. Klink notes that systematic studies of the Archaic did not begin until as recently as 1996 with Mark Aldenderfer's Proyecto Ch'mak Pacha in the Ilave River Valley. Klink's rigorous survey with selective sampling strategy of areas covered by 5-m transects illustrates the challenges presented to archaeologists as they attempt to effectively identify and record Archaic period sites.

Indeed, the work of Klink and Aldenderfer (Chapters 2 and 3) represent some of the first publications of Archaic period research in the Titicaca Basin. As indicated by Klink in Chapter 2, the earliest evidence for the human occupation of the Titicaca Basin is during the Early Archaic, with sites dating to between 8000 and 6000 BC. The difficulty with Archaic sites has always been their dating. Chapter 3 is particularly promising in that it presents a projectile point chronology that can now be used for the dating of Archaic period sites around the Titicaca Basin.

Lisa Cipolla's work (Chapter 4) represents the first publication of research utilizing Klink and Aldenderfer's Archaic projectile point chro-

nology. Cipolla effectively uses this chronology to analyze Archaic period settlement data recovered by Stanish and Plourde's (2000) Huancané-Putina survey. Cipolla is able to identify riverine adaptations during the Early and Middle Archaic periods. Interestingly, she is able to identify a shift toward lakeside river valley sites in the Late Archaic. She further states that "a number of sites were also found on hillsides and hilltops, perhaps indicating the diversification of subsistence strategies" (Cipolla, Chapter 4, this volume). Another significant contribution of Cipolla's work is the recognition that cultural differences that have long been identified between the North and South basin during the ceramic periods (Bennett 1950) seem to have roots in the Late Archaic.

Cipolla's article introduces the problem of the Terminal Archaic period, where a reduction in the number of sites may be a reaction to increasing rainfall, an artifact of site formation processes, or an indication of the beginnings of sedentism and settlement aggregation that are the hallmarks of the Formative period. This is an important aspect of the Titicaca Basin that still remains understudied.

The Formative Period

The Formative period has certainly been one of the areas of study to benefit most from systematic settlement pattern studies. Since these sites tend to be small, they are unlikely to be identified in the absence of pedestrian surveys, but are virtually certain to be identified by surveys utilizing 25–30 m transect spacing. The increase in systematic survey has resulted in significant changes in the way we think about the Formative period cultures of the Titicaca Basin.

The Formative period is one of the topics that we will be learning much more about in the near future. Christine Hastorf, in Chapter 5, does a superb job of introducing the Titicaca Basin Formative research that has taken place as well as many of the ongoing projects. In particular, her discussion of the Formative period indicates the many aspects of Formative lifeways that are in need of research.

Not mentioned in Hastorf's chapter is the full extent of her own extensive research contributions in the area of Formative period studies.

Hastorf and Bandy are currently directing the Taraco Archaeological Project (TAP) in a multi-year project that combines the efforts of specialists to address problems in Formative period domestic and ritual spheres (and see Hastorf 2003). The project focuses on distinctions between ritual and domestic space in the Middle and Late Formative periods and looks at variations in architecture, nutrition, and subsistence, among other topics. This project integrates the work of specialists to more roundly address these questions. Lee Steadman is studying the ceramics; Katherine Moore is analyzing the fauna; Susan de France, the fish; David Steadman the birds; Maria Bruno is focusing on the paleoethnobotanical remains; Matthew Bandy is studying the lithic materials. Deborah Blom will analyze the human remains. Melissa Goodman has introduced the new technique of soil micromorphology to Titicaca Basin archaeology. Deborah Pearsall will be looking at the phytoliths. Through the work of these specialists, TAP has been able to address broad theoretical questions regarding the origins of complexity and the role of trade and ritual in that process.

Another significant advance in Formative period studies has been in the area of ceramic technology and chronology. In particular, Lee Steadman has made great contributions with her detailed ceramic studies, and continues to tackle the problem of Formative chronology. Steadman's (1995) dissertation is the text to which all refer when investigating Formative pottery, and her studies at Chiripa (Hastorf et al. 2001; L. Steadman 1997) have been particularly effective. Indeed, it is this research that has allowed Bandy (2001b) to subdivide the Formative period settlement pattern in order to identify subtle changes in population size through time. However, variations between regions in the basin reduce the effectiveness of Steadman's work as a basin-wide chronology. For example, Cohen (2000) has documented the high surface erosion of Formative sherds in the Pukara Valley and the difficulties this produces for phase identification when conducting surveys. For this reason, more detailed, local ceramic studies, and in particular paste chronologies, are sorely needed.

Another area of study that has not been sufficiently addressed is the archaeology of the domestic household. A combination of poor preservation and impermanent prehistoric construction techniques and materials has made the identification of Formative period households very difficult. Cohen (2000) has located two Formative period domestic structures in the Pukara Valley, one likely dating to the Early Formative and the other to the Terminal Archaic. Elizabeth Klarich has identified Late Formative elite household activities at the site of Pukara (2004). In the northern basin, Aimée Plourde (2004) has mapped and excavated probable habitation structures at the site of Cachichupa in the Putina area. On the whole, however, the recovery of domestic architectural remains from the Formative period remains difficult and irregular.

Much more is known about Formative period public or ritual architecture than is known about domestic architecture. Hastorf gives a full summary of sunken court research in Chapter 5. Her research on ritual structures at the site of Chiripa, along with the excavations of sunken courts on the Copacabana Peninsula by K. Chávez and S. Chávez, have been instrumental in the current focus on Formative period ritual structures. Three dissertations are in process on related topics. Robin Beck (2004) has excavated two Middle Formative ritual structures at the site of Alto Pukara on the Taraco Peninsula. Plourde (1999, 2004) has excavated a massive Early Formative terrace and has cleared a stone structure, both of which she interprets as being ritual in function. Cohen (2003a, 2003b) has excavated a sequence of superimposed Middle–Late Formative sunken courts in the Pukara Valley. In addition, John Janusek is currently conducting research at the site of Khonko Wankane in the nearby Desaguadero Valley, investigating the ritual architecture of the Tiwanaku Formative and beyond (Janusek et al. 2003). He has recently excavated an impressive sunken court from the Late Formative. His research also includes a settlement survey of the surrounding area. Similarly, Myres and Paredes record a series of ritual structures on Isla Soto in Chapter 6. These research projects are beginning to elucidate some of the issues surrounding ritual activities in the Formative period, in particular the origins of the sunken court complex and its associated ritual paraphernalia and rites, and the association of this complex with the origins of sociopolitical complexity. Hastorf's recent article (2003) addressing the significance of ancestor worship to the formation of Formative period religious traditions is a significant advance in this regard.

Other advances are being made in the area of Formative period subsistence patterns. William Whitehead (Hastorf 1999b) is analyzing the paleoethnobotanical material from the site of Chiripa. Maria Bruno will be analyzing the same dataset for the site of Kala Uyuni. Together, they have recently written an article that addresses the origins of quinoa agriculture in the region (Bruno and Whitehead 2003). Their research has shown that the transition to agriculture may have been more drawn out than previously thought. As noted, Moore has been analyzing the faunal data from Chiripa and Kala Uyuni and is integrating in this work the analysis done by de France and D. Steadman for the fish and fowl (Hastorf 1999b; Hastorf et al. 2001). The research of Moore, de France, and D. Steadman has shown that Chiripeños were relying heavily on fish as a foodstuff even though the site would have been located at a great distance from the lake due to low lake levels at that time (Hastorf 1999b; Hastorf et al. 2001).

One dissertation project of interest that is focused on the Early Formative period is the project of Cynthia Herhahn (2004), located at the site of San Bartolomé Wiscachani in the west basin near the town of Juli. Herhahn has identified what appears to be a homestead, with one or more possible domestic structures present at the site. This is clearly an important study for our understanding of early village adaptations in the basin.

Tiwanaku

More research has been devoted to Tiwanaku than to any of the other Titicaca Basin cultures. As mentioned above, surveys in the core Tiwanaku area (Albarracin-Jordan and Mathews 1990; Bandy 2001b; Janusek and Kolata 2003; Kolata 2003), as well as in the western basin, have focused on the origins and development of the Tiwanaku state. Settlement pattern studies are particularly effective in monitoring shifts that took place between the Formative period and

the Tiwanaku expansion. This shift was addressed in Chapter 7 by Stanish et al. for the western Titicaca Basin. Through this type of analysis, they are able to target Tiwanaku subsistence strategies as well as understand modes of expansion. In particular, they identify a focus by Tiwanaku peoples on lakeside resources, even in areas that would have been appropriate for raised-field agriculture. A similar survey focus has been applied by Carol Schultze for her dissertation project in Puno Bay.

The settlement surveys in the western basin have also been followed up with excavations at a number of sites with Tiwanaku occupations. In Chapter 8, de la Vega reports on one such site, Sillumocco-Huaquina, with occupations spanning the Formative through the Late Intermediate periods. The excavations identify terrace construction that dates to both the Formative period and the later Tiwanaku occupation. Additionally, de la Vega identifies the construction of ritual and elite residential sectors of the site during the Tiwanaku period. Carol Schultze has also conducted test excavations in several sites in Puno Bay that contain both Formative and Tiwanaku occupations. Her dissertation will shed light on changes in ritual and subsistence after the Tiwanaku expansion.

Brian Bauer and Charles Stanish conducted a full-coverage survey on the Island of the Sun, the results of which have recently been published (Bauer and Stanish 2001; Stanish and Bauer 2004). In Chapter 9, Seddon reports on the Tiwanaku sites identified in the course of this survey in combination with his own excavations at one of the sites, Chucaripupata. He finds evidence suggesting a pilgrimage route on the site, as indicated in the layout of the site, as well as clear ritual activities at the site of Chucaripupata.

These studies in the Tiwanaku "periphery" could not have been nearly as effective without all of the work that has been accomplished in the Tiwanaku core territories, and in particular at the site of Tiwanaku. One of the most influential figures has been the Bolivian archaeologist Carlos Ponce Sanginés, who has been actively researching and publishing about Tiwanaku since the 1950s (i.e., 1961, 1971, 1981, 1990). He has been joined by many others who have published their research about the Tiwanaku capital, including Linda Manzanilla (1992) and Javier Escalante (2003). Special notice should also be given to the work of Alan Kolata (see, e.g., Kolata 1986, 1993, 1996b, 2003), who directed a multicomponent research project at Tiwanaku and has recently published two superb volumes summarizing these investigations. Kolata and his students and colleagues focused on many varied topics as part of their research, topics including issues of chronology (Janusek 2003), elite residential architecture (Couture and Sampeck 2003), ceremonial and public architecture (Couture 2003), diet (Wright et al. 2003), and human remains (Blom et al. 2003).

Janusek has published on various aspects of Tiwanaku residential life, including articles about urbanism and ethnicity (2001b, 2002), and workshop production (1999). In Chapter 10, he compares distinct residential sectors at Tiwanaku and identifies variations in ethnicity, introducing a more complex and rich view of the Tiwanaku urban center.

Other scholars continue to study issues concerning various aspects of the Tiwanaku state. Following up on her research on the Mollo Kontu sector of the Tiwanaku capitol, Nicole Couture has recently completed her dissertation on elite residences at Tiwanaku's Putuni palace (Couture 2002, 2003; Couture and Sampeck 2003). Deborah Blom's research focuses, in part, on the intriguing question of ethnicity in the state capitol of Tiwanaku and its environs (Blom 2001; Blom and Janusek 2004; Blom et al. 1998, 2003). Blom has analyzed human skeletal material from Tiwanaku as well as collections from the Moquequa Valley of southern Peru, where Tiwanaku colonies have been identified, and from Lukurmata, a Tiwanaku regional center in the Katari Valley (Blom 1999; Goldstein 1989). Based on cranial shape modification and other stylistic archaeological correlates, Blom identified distinct ethnic groups from these areas. Interestingly, each of these ethnic groups seems to have been represented at the capitol city of Tiwanaku (Blom et al. 2003). Couture and Blom are directing ongoing investigations on residential and mortuary patterns at Tiwanaku designed to further explore issues of diversity in the capitol. Alexei Vranich (1999), in his disserta-

tion, addressed the architecture of the Pumapunku, and he continues to investigate ceremonial architecture with ongoing research at the Akapana (Vranich 2001; Vranich et al. 2002). Vranich's research has been done in collaboration with other archaeologists, most notably Jason Yaeger.

Research has also been undertaken at other Tiwanaku centers within the Titicaca Basin. In the 1980s, Kolata directed a multicomponent research project on the shores of the lake at the other Tiwanaku heartland city of Lukurmata. Several dissertation projects came out of this research, including Marc Bermann's (1990b, 1994) study of Formative and Tiwanaku households. Janusek's (1994) dissertation compared excavations at the two core cities (Tiwanaku and Lukurmata), focusing on patterns of urban residence through the trajectory of the Tiwanaku florescence.

The Late Intermediate Period

While Late Intermediate period sites have long been of interest to travelers and scholars alike, our knowledge of the settlement pattern during this time period was generally skewed by the focus on the hilltop fortresses known as pukaras. The investigation of these sites tended to be descriptive and did not elucidate the nature of the role of these sites in the settlement pattern or the larger social system. John Hyslop (1976), for example, conducted a reconnaissance of Lupaqa hilltop fortresses. In 1998, Stanish began Proyecto Lupaqa, a multi-year project aimed at testing models for the political development of the Lupaqa polity. Using the same survey methodologies, Kirk Frye conducted the Chucuito-Cutimbo survey to the north. In Chapter 11, Frye and de la Vega combine the results of the Juli-Pomata survey and the Chucuito-Cutimbo survey to address the Lupaqa settlement pattern. This chapter reports on fortresses, but also identifies many other types of sites, such as hamlets, that were occupied during this time period. Frye and de la Vega note a shift in the settlement pattern from lakeside adaptations to inland agropastoral zones, indicating a changing focus on pastoralism, possibly due to drought conditions. The introduction of hilltop fortresses is a result of increasing conflict at this time.

As part of Stanish's Proyecto Lupaqa, a number of more in-depth studies were undertaken at Lupaqa hilltop fortresses. One of these involved the excavation of Pukara-Juli by Edmundo de la Vega (1990), which identified short-term occupations. Kirk Frye (1997a) conducted an analysis of the architecture and ceramics at the hilltop sites Pukara-Juli, Huichajaja, Llequepa, and Tanapaca.

Elizabeth Arkush (2004a, 2004b) returns to the question of the hilltop fortresses in her dissertation, but applies a systematic approach, investigating aerial photos for evidence of such sites across the Colla territory of the western basin. She incorporates survey methods with test excavations and extensive radiocarbon testing to investigate the role of warfare in the Late Intermediate period.

An interesting find has been that of the cave burial site of Molino Chilacachi, which is described in Chapter 12. De la Vega, Frye, and Tiffiny Tung report on the burials and grave goods from this site, which represents unusually well-preserved textile and basketry remains from the altiplano.

The Late Horizon and Early Colonial Periods

The Late Horizon marks the incorporation of the Titicaca Basin into the Inca Empire and the dissolution of the Late Intermediate period kingdoms. Frye, in Chapter 13, discusses the various tactics employed by the Inca in dealing with the Colla, Pacajes, and Lupaqa kingdoms. These strategies were wide ranging. For the Colla, who were notoriously rebellious and had resisted the Inca occupation, for example, the Inca implemented a number of different tactics, including economic sanctions and relocation of communities, often to distant locations. For the Pacajes, the tactics seem to have been less extreme, as is indicated by the lack of an administrative center in their territories, with the possible exception of the town of Pucarani. This may have been due to a lower level of integration among the Pacajes. However, the Inca did relocate some Pacajes populations, as is demonstrated in Cohen's (2000) Pukara Valley survey, which identified Pacajes pottery in the northern basin on a site

called "Pampa Pacajes." The Lupaqa had formed an alliance with the Inca against their foes, the Colla. Perhaps for this reason, the Inca established their regional administrative center in Chucuito. Frye identifies a number of different strategies, in addition to those already listed for the Colla and Pacajes, including economic intensification (in the form of establishing specialized towns for production) and road building.

Bauer and Stanish (2001) and Stanish and Bauer (2004) address the Inca control of the basin through their survey of the Island of the Sun. They remark on the predominance of very small sites on the island, similar to the pattern in the Juli-Pomata survey by Stanish et al. (1997). They suggest that this pattern of small sites was evidence of another form of Inca control, that of using few large administrative centers and limiting the size of other occupations. This settlement pattern leads them to believe that Copacabana had been the local administrative center. They also remark on the continuous use of the island as an Inca pilgrimage center.

In Chapter 14, Arkush publishes the results of her reconnaissance of Inca ritual sites in the western basin. She contrasts the types of ritual sites found in the Lupaqa and Colla terrains with those found on the Island of the Sun by Bauer and Stanish. Arkush makes a very convincing argument that the Inca employed dual strategies of welcome and incorporation for most ritual sites, with strategies of hierarchy and exclusion for the sites on the Island of the Sun.

The ritual architecture of the Inca is a topic that has also been addressed by Jason Yaeger, whose research at the Pumapunku structure in Tiwanaku is ongoing (Vranich et al. 2002). Yaeger has identified a number of Inca period structures and evidence of ritual activity at the Pumapunku.

SUMMARY AND CALL FOR RESEARCH

The articles included in this volume comprise an exciting collection of research incorporating new geographical areas, strategies, and theoretical foci. The most extreme advances have been made in the area of full-coverage surveys. However, these advances indicate just how much more work remains to be done. In particular, Chapter 17, which presents data from an old-fashioned reconnaissance approach, conveys the wide expanses of territory still archaeologically unknown. Large parts of the northern and eastern basin remain unstudied. In the absence of these surveys, studying the processes behind the origins of social complexity in the basin, among other important questions, remains difficult.

With regard to regional approaches to Titicaca Basin archaeology, another promising advance seen in this volume (see Chapters 7, 11, 13, and 16) and in a number of ongoing projects is the combination of results from distinct surveys in order to create larger and more powerful sets of data. This approach is a research tactic that will surely improve our understanding of prehistoric settlement systems in the basin.

One particularly promising advance has been in the area of Archaic period research. Klink and Aldenderfer's (Chapter 3) projectile point chronology is sure to lead to many more exciting studies of Archaic settlements. Cipolla's research in the Huancané-Putina region (Chapter 4) is just one such study. Because research focused on the Archaic period requires such fine-grained survey strategies, these advances are sure to come along slowly. Yet, more work like that of Aldenderfer, Klink, and Cipolla is desperately needed if we are to understand the early adaptations of the first Titicaca Basin inhabitants.

With regard to excavation strategies, one important aim toward which we can work in the next ten to fifteen years is the implementation of collaborative projects. While this is a tradition that has been firmly established with the work of, for example, Kolata at Tiwanaku, and Hastorf at Chiripa, this is clearly an area where improvement is possible. Of course, this type of research can be costly and is usually out of reach for most doctoral students embarking on dissertation re-

search projects. Still, we must keep in mind the benefits of specialized analyses for addressing larger theoretical issues. In particular, it is through the work of faunal, botanical, soil, and human remains specialists that we will be able to answer questions about long-distance trade, household activities, ritual and feasting events, as well as broader issues of social evolution.

One final point to be made concerns the Titicaca Basin ceramic chronology. As we have already mentioned, Lee Steadman's fine and detailed work on Formative period pottery in the western and southern basins, and in particular on the Taraco Peninsula, has permitted advancements in archaeological studies that previously were not possible. At Chiripa, and now at Kala Uyuni, Steadman (1999) has been able to identify Early, Middle, and Late Chiripa pottery assemblages, and is now working on the pottery from the Formative Tiwanaku period. Steadman has been focusing on technological as well as stylistic attributes and, through this time-consuming approach, has been able to identify more subtle chronological indicators that are not visible through type-variety analysis alone. As a result, the Taraco Archaeological Project has been able to address more sophisticated questions (see, e.g., Bandy 2001b, 2004) than would otherwise have been possible. A detailed study such as Steadman's is sorely needed in other parts of the Titicaca Basin—in particular, in the northern basin—if we are to make similar advances in settlement pattern and other diachronic studies.

I would like to stress that a continuation of research that incorporates the testing of models is the only way to broaden our theoretical knowledge. We look forward to the publication of Volume 2 of *Advances* in order to continue to report on the exciting developments in Titicaca Basin research.

References

Abbott, M., M. Binford, M. Brenner, and K. Kelts. 1997. A 3500 14C yr high-resolution record of water-level changes in Lake Titicaca, Bolivia-Peru. *Quaternary Research* 47:169–180.

Abbott, M., G. Seltzer, K. Kelts, and J. Southon. 1997. Holocene paleohydrology of the tropical Andes from lake records. *Quaternary Research* 47:70–80.

Abercrombie, T. 1986. *The Politics of Sacrifice: An Aymara Cosmology in Action.* Ph.D. dissertation, Department of Anthropology, University of Chicago.

Adams, R. McC. 1965. *Land Behind Baghdad: A History of Settlement on the Diyala Plain.* University of Chicago Press, Chicago.

Albarracin-Jordan, J. 1990. Prehispanic dynamics of settlement in the lower Tiwanaku Valley, Bolivia. In A. Kolata and O. Rivera, editors, *Tiwanaku and Its Hinterland: Third Preliminary Report of the Proyecto Wila Jawira,* pp. 276–296. La Paz.

Albarracin-Jordan, J. 1992. *Prehispanic and Early Settlement Patterns in the Lower Tiwanaku Valley, Bolivia.* Ph.D. dissertation, Department of Anthropology, Southern Methodist University, Dallas.

Albarracin-Jordan, J. 1996a. *Tiwanaku: Arqueología regional y dinámica segmentaria.* Editores Plural, La Paz.

Albarracin-Jordan, J. 1996b. Tiwanaku settlement system: The integration of nested hierarchies in the lower Tiwanaku Valley. *Latin American Antiquity* 7(3):183–210.

Albarracin-Jordan, J., C. Lemúz, and J. Paz. 1993. Investigaciones en Kallamarca: Primer informe de prospección. *Textos Antropológicos* 6:11–123.

Albarracin-Jordan, J., and J. Mathews. 1990. *Asentamientos prehispánicos del Valle de Tiwanaku,* Vol. 1. Producciones CIMA, La Paz.

Alconini Mújica, S. 1995. *Rito, símbolo e historia en la pirámide de Akapana, Tiwanaku: Un análisis de cerámica ceremonial prehispánica.* Editorial Acción, La Paz.

Alconini Mújica, S., and C. Rivera Casanovas. 1993. Proyecto arqueológico Taraco: Excavaciones en Chiripa. *Boletín de Actividades* 5:25–31. Instituto Nacional de Arqueología, La Paz.

Aldenderfer, M. 1985. Archaic Period archaeology in southern Peru. Preliminary report of the 1984 field season of NUAP. Northwestern University Archaeological Reports 6. Evanston, Illinois.

Aldenderfer, M. 1989. The Archaic period in the south-central Andes. *Journal of World Prehistory* 3(2):117–158.

Aldenderfer, M. 1990. Informe preliminar de las excavaciones de Quelcatani, Puno. Report submitted to the Instituto Nacional de Cultura, Lima.

Aldenderfer, M. 1993. Cronología y definición de fases arcaicas en Asana, sur del Perú. *Chungará* 24/25:13–35.

Aldenderfer, M. 1996. Reconocimiento arqueológico de la cuenca del Río Ilave. Report submitted to the Instituto Nacional de Cultura, Lima, Peru.

Aldenderfer, M. 1997. Jiskairumoko: An early sedentary settlement in the southwestern Lake Titicaca basin. Paper presented at the 37th Annual Meeting of the Institute for Andean Studies, Berkeley.

Aldenderfer, M. 1998. *Montane Foragers: Asana and the South-Central Andean Archaic.* University of Iowa Press, Iowa City.

Aldenderfer, M., editor. In press. *Quelcatani and the Evolution of Pastoral Societies in the Titicaca Basin.* Smithsonian Institution Press, Washington, DC.

Aldenderfer, M., and C. Klink. 1996. Archaic Period settlement in the Lake Titicaca basin: Results of a recent survey. Paper presented at the 36th Annual Meeting of the Institute for Andean Studies, Berkeley.

Amat O. H. 1977. Los reinos altiplánicos del Titicaca. *Rumi* 8:1–8.

Ames, K. 1995. Chiefly power and household production on the Northwest coast. In T. Price and G. Feinman, editors, *Foundations of Social Inequality*, pp. 155–187. Plenum Press, New York.

Angelo Zelada, D., and J. Capriles Flores. 2000. La importancia del uso de plantas psicotrópicas para la economía de intercambio y las relaciones de interacción en el altiplano sur andino. *Complutus* 11:275–284.

Arellano López, J. C. 1975. *La ciudadela prehispánica de Iskanwaya*. Publicación 6, n.s. Centro de Investigaciones Arqueológicas, La Paz.

Arellano López, J., and E. Berberían. 1981. Mallku: El señorío post-Tiwanaku del Altiplano sur de Bolivia. *Bulletin de l'Institut Français d'Études Andines* 10(1–2):51–84.

Arellano López, J., and D. Kuljis. 1986. Antecedentes preliminares de las investigaciones arqueológicas en la zona circumtiticaca de Bolivia sector (occidental sur). *Prehistoricas: Revista de la Carrera de Antropología y Arqueología de la Universidad Mayor de San Andrés* 1:9–28. La Paz.

Arkush, E. 2000. *Small Inca Ceremonial Sites in the Southwest Lake Titicaca Basin, Peru and Bolivia*. Master's thesis, Department of Anthropology, University of California, Los Angeles.

Arkush, E. 2001. Colla forts: The face of war in the south-central Andes. Paper presented at the 66th Annual Meeting of the Society for American Archaeology, New Orleans.

Arkush, E. 2004. Colla pukaras and the chronology of warfare in the northwest Titicaca Basin. Paper presented at the Annual Meetings of the Institute of Andean Studies, Berkeley.

Arnold, D. 1992. La casa de adobes y piedras del Inka: Genero, memoria, y cosmos en Qaqachaka. In D. Arnold, coordinator, *Hacia un orden Andino de las cosas: Tres pistas de los Andes meridonales*, pp. 31–108. Talleres Gráficos Hisbol, La Paz.

Arnold, D. 1988. *Matrilineal Practice in a Patrilineal Setting: Rituals and Metaphors of Kinship in an Andean Ayllu*. Ph.D. dissertation, Department of Anthropology, University of London.

Arriaga, P. 1968 [1621]. *The Extirpation of Idolatry in Peru*. Facsimile edition. University of Kentucky Press, Lexington.

Aschero, C. 1984. El sitio ICC-4: Un asentamiento precerámico en la Quebrada de Inca Cueva (Jujuy, Argentina). *Estudios Atacameños* 7:62–72.

Ashmore, W., and R. Wilk. 1988. House and household in the Mesoamerican past. In R. Wilk and W. Ashmore, editors, *Household and Community in the Mesoamerican Past*, pp. 1–28. University of New Mexico Press, Albuquerque.

Avila, F. 1991 [ca. 1598]. *Dioses y hombres de Huarochirí: Narración Quechua recogida por Francisco de Avila*. Edicion bilingüe. Translated by José María Arguedas. Facsimile edition. Estudio Bibliográfico Pierre Duviols, Lima.

Ayca, O. 1995. *Sillustani*. Instituto de Arqueología del Sur, Tacna, Peru.

Baied, C., and J. Wheeler. 1993. Evolution of high Andean puna ecosystems: Environment, climate, and culture change over the last 12,000 years in the Central Andes. *Mountain Research and Development* 13:145–156.

Baker, P., G. Seltzer, S. Fritz, R. Dunbar, M. Grove, M. Tapia, S. Cross, H. Rowe, and J. Broda. 2001. The history of South American tropical precipitation for the past 25,000 years. *Science* 291:640–643.

Balkansky, A., G. Feinman, and L. Nichols. 1997. Pottery kilns of ancient Ejutla, Oaxaca, Mexico. *Journal of Field Archaeology* 24:139–160.

Bandelier, A. 1910. *The Islands of Titicaca and Koati*. The Hispanic Society of America, New York.

Bandy, M. 1999a. The montículo excavations. In C. Hastorf, editor, *Early Settlement at Chiripa Bolivia*, Contributions of the University of California Archaeological Research Facility, number 57, pp. 43–50. Archaeological Research Facility, Berkeley.

Bandy, M. 1999b. Systematic surface collection. In C. Hastorf, editor, *Early Settlement at Chiripa Bolivia*, Contributions of the University of California Archaeological Research Facility, number 57, pp. 23–28. Archaeological Research Facility, Berkeley.

Bandy, M. 2001a. Environmental and political change in the Formative period Titicaca Basin. Paper presented at the 66th Annual Meeting of the Society for American Archaeology, New Orleans.

Bandy, M. 2001b. *Population and History in the Ancient Titicaca Basin*. Ph.D. dissertation, Department of Anthropology, University of California, Berkeley.

Bandy, M. 2004. Fissioning, scalar stress, and social evolution in early village societies. *American Anthropologist* 106(2):322–333.

Bastien, J. 1995. The mountain/body metaphor expressed in a Kaatan funeral. In T. Dillehay, editor, *Tombs for the Living: Andean Mortuary Practices,* pp. 355–378. Dumbarton Oaks, Washington, DC.

Baucom, P., and C. Rigsby. 1999. Climate and lake-level history of the northern altiplano, Bolivia, as recorded in Holocene sediments of the Río Desaguadero. *Journal of Sedimentary Research* 69(3):597–611.

Bauer, B. 1992. *The Development of the Inca State.* University of Texas Press, Austin.

Bauer, B. 1998. *The Sacred Landscape of the Inca: The Cusco Ceque System.* University of Texas Press, Austin.

Bauer, B., L. Cipolla, and J. Terry. 1996. Excavations at the Sacred Rock area. In C. Stanish, B. Bauer, O. Rivera, J. Escalante, and M. Seddon, editors, Report of Proyecto Tiksi Kjarka on the Island of the Sun, Bolivia, 1994–1995, pp. 25–36. Report submitted to the Instituto Nacional de Arqueología, La Paz.

Bauer, B., and C. Stanish. 2001. *Ritual and Pilgrimage in the Ancient Andes: The Islands of the Sun and the Moon.* University of Texas Press, Austin.

Beaton, J. 1991. Colonizing continents: Some problems from Australia and the Americas. In T. Dillehay and D. Meltzer, editors, *The First Americans: Search and Research,* pp. 209–230. CRC Press, Boca Raton, Florida.

Beck Jr, R. n.d. Architecture and polity in the Formative Lake Titicaca basin, Bolivia. Manuscript in possession of C. Hastorf.

Beck Jr, R. 2004. *Platforms of Power: House, Community and Social Change in the Prehispanic Lake Titicaca Basin.* Ph.D. dissertation, Department of Anthropology, Northwestern University, Evanston, Illinois.

Bellido, J. 1993. Arqueología funerario del señorío Pakasa (post-Tiwanaku). *Pumapunku (nueva época)* 2:5–6. Producciones CIMA, La Paz.

Bennett, W. 1933. Archaeological hikes in the Andes: An introduction to two of the four great pre-Spanish cultures. *Natural History* 33 (2):163–174.

Bennett, W. 1934a. Lake Titicaca: An archaeologist explores the high lake which lies between Peru and Bolivia. *Natural History* 34:713–724.

Bennett, W. 1934b. *Excavations at Tiahuanaco.* Volume 34 of *Anthropological Papers of the American Museum of Natural History.* American Museum of Natural History, New York.

Bennett, W. 1936. *Excavations in Bolivia.* Volume 35 of *Anthropological Papers of the American Museum of Natural History.* American Museum of Natural History, New York.

Bennett, W. 1948. A revised sequence for the south Titicaca basin. *American Antiquity* 13:90–92.

Bennett, W. 1950. Cultural unity and disunity in the Titicaca basin. *American Antiquity* 15:88–89.

Beorchia Nigris, A. 1973. *La arqueología de Alta Montaña en la Provincia de San Juan.* C.I.A.D.A.M. (Centro de Investigaciones Arqueológicas de Alta Montaña), San Juan, Argentina.

Beorchia Nigris, A. 1985. *El enigma de los santuarios indígenas de Alta Montaña.* C.I.A.D.A.M. (Centro de Investigaciones Arqueológicas de Alta Montaña) 5, San Juan, Argentina.

Berberían, E., and J. Arellano López. 1980. Desarrollo cultural prehispánico en el Altiplano Sur de Bolivia. *Revista Museu Paulista,* nova série 27:259–281. Sao Paulo, Brazil.

Bermann, M. 1990. *Prehispanic Household and Empire at Lukurmata, Bolivia.* Ph.D. dissertation, Department of Anthropology, University of Michigan, Ann Arbor.

Bermann, M. 1994. *Lukurmata: Household Archaeology in Prehispanic Bolivia.* Princeton University Press, Princeton.

Bermann, M. 1997. Domestic life and vertical integration in the Tiwanaku heartland. *Latin American Antiquity* 8(2):93–112.

Bermann, M., P. Goldstein, C. Stanish, and L. Watanabe. 1989. The collapse of the Tiwanaku state: A view from the Osmore drainage. In D. Rice, C. Stanish, and P. Scarr, editors, *Ecology, Settlement and History in the Osmore Drainage, Peru,* pp. 269–286. British Archaeological Reports International Series, No. 545(ii). Oxford.

Berthelot, J. 1986. The extraction of precious metals at the time of the Inka. In J. Murra, N. Wachtel, and J. Revel, editors, *Anthropological History of Andean Polities,* pp. 63–90. Cambridge University Press, Cambridge.

Bertonio, L. 1956 [1612]. *Vocabulario de la lengua Ay-mará,* Centro de Estudios de la Realidad Económica y Social, Cochabamba, Bolivia.

Betanzos, J. 1987 [1551]. *Suma y narración de los Inca.* Facsimile edition. Ediciones Atlas, Madrid.

Bills, B. G., S. de Silva, D. Currey, R. Emenger, K. Lillquist, A. Donnellan, and B. Worden. 1994. Hydro-isostatic deflections and tectonic tilting in the central Andes: Initial results of a GPS survey of Lake Minchin shorelines. *Geophysical Research Letters* 21(4):293–296.

Binford, L. 1980. Willow smoke and dogs' tails: Hunter-gatherer settlement systems and archaeological site formation. *American Antiquity* 45(1):4–20.

Binford, M., and A. Kolata. 1996. The natural and human setting. In A. Kolata, editor, *Tiwanaku and Its Hinterland: Archaeology and Paleoecology of an Andean Civilization,* pp. 23–56. Smithsonian Institution Press, Washington, DC.

Blau, P. 1977. *Inequality and Heterogeneity.* The Free Press, New York.

Blom, D. 1999. *Tiwanaku Regional Interaction and Social Identity: A Bioarchaeological Approach.* Ph.D. dissertation, Department of Anthropology, University of Chicago.

Blom, D.E. 2001. Two distinct patterns of cutmarks as evidence for human sacrifice and ancestor worship in Tiwanaku, Bolivia. *American Journal of Physical Anthropology,* Supplement 32:40.

Blom, D., B. Hallgrímsson, L. Keng, M. C. Lozada C., and J. E. Buikstra. 1998. Tiwanaku "colonization": Bioarchaeological implications for migration in the Moquegua Valley. *World Archaeology* 30(2):238–261.

Blom, D. E., and J. Janusek. 2004. Making place: Humans as dedications in Tiwanaku. *World Archaeology* 36(1):123–141.

Blom, D., J. Janusek, and J. Buikstra. 2003. A Reevaluation of human remains from Tiwanaku. In A. Kolata, editor, *Archaeology and Paleoecology in the Tiwanaku Heartland: Vol. II, Rural and Urban Archaeology,* pp. 435–448. Smithsonian Institution Press, Washington, DC.

Bouysse-Cassagne, T. 1987. *La identidad Aymara: Aproximación histórica (siglo XV, siglo XVI).* Hisbol-IFEA, La Paz.

Bouysse-Cassagne, T. 1991. Poblaciones humanas antiquas y actuales. In C. DeJoux and A. Iltis, editors, *El Lago Titicaca: Síntesis del conocimi-ento limnológico actual,* pp. 481–498. ORSTOM/HISBOL, La Paz.

Bolton, R., and E. Mayer. 1977. *Andean Kinship and Marriage.* American Anthropological Association, Washington, DC.

Browman, D. 1972. Asiruni, Pukara-Pokotia and Pajano: Pre-Tiahuanaco south Andean monolithic stone styles. Manuscript in possession of C. Hastorf.

Browman, D. 1978a. The temple of Chiripa (Lake Titicaca, Bolivia). In R. Matos Mendieta, editor, *El hombre y la cultura Andina, III Congreso Peruano,* pp. 807–813. Editorial Lasontay, Lima.

Browman, D. 1978b. Toward the development of the Tiahuanaco (Tiwanaku) state. In D. Browman, editor, *Advances in Andean Archaeology,* pp. 327–349. Mouton, The Hague.

Browman, D. 1980. Tiwanaku expansion and altiplano economic patterns. *Estudios arqueológicos* 5:107–120.

Browman, D. 1981. New light on Andean Tiwanaku. *American Scientist* 69(4):408–419.

Browman, D. 1984 Tiwanaku: Development of interzonal trade and economic expansion in the Altiplano. In D. L. Browman, R. L. Burger, and M. A. Rivera, editors, *Social and Economic Organization in the Prehispanic Andes,* pp. 117–142. British Archaeological Reports International Series No. 194. Oxford.

Browman, D. 1985. Cultural primacy of Tiwanaku in the development of later Peruvian states. *Diálogo Andino* 4:59–71.

Browman, D. 1986. Chenopod cultivation, lacustrine resources and fuel use at Chiripa, Bolivia. *Missouri Archaeologist* 47:137–172.

Browman, D. 1995. Pa-Ajanu: Formative Titicaca regional stela tradition. Paper presented at the 60th Annual Meeting of the Society for American Archaeology, Minneapolis.

Brumfiel, E. 1994a. Ethnic groups and political development in ancient Mexico. In E.Brumfiel and J. Fox, editors, *Factional Competition and Political Development in the New World,* pp. 89–102. Cambridge University Press, Cambridge.

Brumfiel, E. 1994b. Factional competition and political development in the New World: An introduction. In E.Brumfiel and J. Fox, editors, *Factional Competition and Political Development in the New World,* pp. 3–13. Cambridge University Press, Cambridge.

Brumfiel, E., and T. Earle. 1987. Specialization, exchange, and complex societies: An introduction. In E. Brumfiel and T. Earle, editors, *Specialization, Exchange, and Complex Societies,* pp. 1–9. Cambridge University Press, Cambridge.

Bruno, M. C., and W. Whitehead. 2003. *Chenopodium* cultivation and Formative Period agriculture at Chiripa, Bolivia. *Latin American Antiquity* 14(3):339–355.

Brush, S. 1982. The natural and human environment of the Central Andes. *Mountain Research and Development* 2:19–38.

Bueno Mendoza, A. 1982. Arquitectura y sociedad pre-Chavin en los Andes centrales. *Boletín de antropología Americana* 6:119–140.

Buikstra, J. E., and D. H. Ubelaker. 1994. *Standards for Data Collection from Human Skeletal Remains.* Arkansas Archaeological Survey, Fayetteville.

Burger, R., F. Asaro, F. Stross, and G. Salas. 1998a. The Chivay obsidian source and the geological origin of Titicaca basin type obsidian artifacts. *Andean Past* 5:203–224.

Burger, R., F. Asaro, P. Trawick, and F. Stross. 1998b. The Alca obsidian source: The origin of raw material for Cuzco type obsidian artifacts. *Andean Past* 5:185–202.

Burger, R., K. Chávez, and S. Chávez. 2000. Through the glass darkly: Prehispanic obsidian procurement and exchange in southern Peru and northern Bolivia. *Journal of World Prehistory* 14(3):267–362.

Burgess, S. D. 1999. *Chiribayan Skeletal Pathology on the South Coast of Peru: Patterns of Production and Consumption.* Ph.D. dissertation, Department of Anthropology, University of Chicago.

Calancha, A. 1972 [1639]. Crónica moralizada del Orden de San Augustín. In M. Merino, editor, *Crónicas Agustinas del Perú. Biblioteca missionalia Hispánica XVII.* Facsimile edition. Consejo Superior de Investigaciones Científicas, Instituto Enrique Flores, Madrid.

Calancha, A. 1981 [1638]. *Crónica moralizada del orden de San Augustín en el Perú.* Facsimile edition. I. Prado Pastor, Lima.

Cardich, A. 1958. *Los yacimientos de Lauricocha.* Centro Argentino de Estudios Prehistóricos, Buenos Aires.

Carneiro, R. 1981. The chiefdom: Precursor of the state. In G. Jones and R. Kautz, editors, *The Transition to Statehood in the New World,* pp. 37–79. Cambridge University Press, Cambridge.

Casanova, E. 1942. Dos yacimientos arqueológicos en la Peninsula de Copacabana (Bolivia). *Antropología, etnografía y arqueología* 82:333–407.

Chávez, K. 1977. *Marcavalle: The Ceramics from an Early Horizon Site in the Valley of Cuzco, Peru, and Implications for South Highland Socio-economic Interaction.* Master's thesis, Department of Anthropology, University of Pennsylvania, Philadelphia.

Chávez, K. 1985. Early Tiahuanaco-related ceremonial burners from Cuzco, Peru. *Diálogo Andino* 4:137–178.

Chávez, K. 1988. The significance of Chiripa in Lake Titicaca basin developments. *Expedition* 30(3):17–26.

Chávez, K. 1997. Excavations in Copacabana. Paper presented at the 62nd Annual Meeting of the Society for American Archaeology, Nashville.

Chávez, K., and S. Chávez. 1997. Remarks on "The Yayamama Project." Symposium organized at the 62nd Annual Meeting of the Society for American Archaeology, Nashville.

Chávez, S. 1975. The Arapa and Thunderbolt stelae: A case of stylistic identity with implications for Pucara influences in the area of Tiahuanaco. *Ñawpa Pacha* 13:3–26.

Chávez, S. 1988. Archaeological reconnaissance in the Province of Chumbivilcas, south highland Peru. *Expedition* 30(3):27–38.

Chávez, S. 1992. *The Conventionalized Rules in Pucara Pottery Technology and Iconography: Implications for Socio-Political Development in the Northern Lake Titicaca Basin.* Ph.D. dissertation, Department of Anthropology, Michigan State University, East Lansing.

Chávez, S., and K. Chávez. 1970. Newly discovered monoliths from the highlands of Puno, Peru. *Expedition* 12(4):25–39.

Chávez, S., and K. Chávez. 1975. A carved stela from Taraco, Puno, Peru, and the definition of an early style of stone sculpture from the Altiplano of Peru and Bolivia. *Ñawpa Pacha* 13:45–83.

Childe, V. 1936. *Man Makes Himself.* The Thinker's Library, No. 87. Watts and Company, London.

Childe, V. 1950. The urban revolution. *Town Planning Review* 21(1):3–17.

Choque Canqui, R. 1993. *Sociedad y economía Colonial en el sur andino.* Hisbol, La Paz.

Cieza de Léon, P. 1959 [1553]. *The Incas of Pedro de Cieza de León.* Translated by H. de Onis. Facsimile edition. University of Oklahoma Press, Norman.

Cieza de León, P. 1984 [1553]. *La crónica del Perú.* Facsimile edition. Historia 16, Madrid.

Cieza de León, P. 1985 [1553]. *El señorío de los Incas (part 2 of the crónica).* Facsimile edition. Historia 16, Madrid.

Claessen, H. 1984. The internal dynamics of the early state. *Current Anthropology* 25:365–379.

Clapperton, C. 1993. *Quaternary Geology and Geomorphology of South America.* Elsevier Science Publishers B.V., Amsterdam.

Coben, L. In press. Other Cuzcos: Replicated theaters of Inka power. In T. Inomata and L. Coben, editors, *Theaters of Power and Community: An Archaeology of Politics and Performance.* Altamira Press, Lanham, MD.

Cobo, B. 1956 [1653]. *Historia del Nuevo Mundo,* Vol. II. Facsimile edition. Ediciones Atlas, Madrid.

Cobo, B. 1964 [1653]. *Historia del Nuevo Mundo.* Facsimile edition. Biblioteca de Autores Españoles, Madrid.

Cobo, B. 1979 [1653]. *History of the Inca Empire.* Translated and edited by Roland Hamilton. University of Texas Press, Austin.

Cobo, B. 1990 [1653]. *Inca Religion and Customs.* Translated and edited by Roland Hamilton. University of Texas Press, Austin.

Cohen, A. 2000. The Pukara Valley Survey, 1999 season. Report submitted to the Instituto Nacional de Cultura, Lima.

Cohen, A. 2001. Results of a settlement pattern survey in the Pukara Valley, northern Lake Titicaca basin, Peru. Paper presented at the 66th Annual Meeting of the Society for American Archaeology, New Orleans.

Cohen, A. 2003a. Domestic and ritual architecture of the Pukara Valley Formative Period. Paper presented at the Society for American Archaeology, 66th Annual Meeting, Milwaukee.

Cohen, A. 2003b. Formative period domestic and ritual architecture of the Pukara Valley, Peru.

Paper presented at the Institute for Andean Studies, 43rd Annual Meeting, January 8, 2003, Berkeley.

Cohen, A. 2004. Ritual architecture of the Titicaca Basin Formative period. Paper presented at the Society for American Archaeology, 67th Annual Meeting, Montreal, Canada.

Cohen, R. 1978. Introduction. In R. Cohen and E. Service, editors, *Origins of the State: The Anthropology of Political Evolution,* pp. 1–20. Institute for the Study of Human Issues, Philadelphia.

Cohen, R. 1981. Evolution, fission, and the early state. In H. Claessen and P. Skalnik, editors, *The Study of the State,* pp. 637–650. Mouton, The Hague.

Collins, J. 1986. The household and relations of production in southern Peru. *Comparative Studies in Society and History* 28(4):651–671.

Collins, J. 1988. *Unseasonal Migrations.* Princeton University Press, Princeton.

Conklin, W. 1983. Pucara and Tiahuanaco tapestry: Time and style in a Sierra weaving tradition. *Ñawpa Pacha* 21:1–44.

Conklin, W., and M. Moseley. 1988. The patterns of art and power in the Early Intermediate Period. In R. Keatinge, editor, *Peruvian Prehistory,* pp. 145–163. Cambridge University Press, Cambridge.

Conrad, G., and A. Demarest. 1984. *Religion and Empire.* Cambridge University Press, Cambridge.

Cook, S., and R. Heizer. 1968. Relationships among houses, settlement areas, and population in aboriginal California. In K. Chang, editor, *Settlement Archaeology,* pp. 79–116. National Press Books, Palo Alto, California.

Cordy-Collins, A. 1978. The dual divinity in Chavin art. *El Dorado* 3(2):1–31.

Costin, C., and T. Earle. 1989. Status distinction and legitimation of power as reflected in changing patterns of consumption in late Prehispanic Peru. *American Antiquity* 54(4):691–714.

Costin, C., and M. Hagstrum. 1995. Standardization, labor investment, skill, and the organization of ceramic production in late prehistoric highland Peru. *American Antiquity* 60(4):619–639.

Couture, N. 1992. *Excavations at Mollo Kontu, Tiwanaku.* Master's thesis, Department of Anthropology, University of Chicago.

Couture, N. 2002. *The Construction of Power: Monumental Space and Elite Residence at Tiwanaku, Bolivia.* Ph.D. dissertation, Department of Anthropology, University of Chicago.

Couture, N. 2003. Ritual, monumentalism, and residence at Mollo Kontu, Tiwanaku. In A. Kolata, editor, *Tiwanaku and Its Hinterland: Archaeology and Paleoecology of an Andean Civilization,* Vol. II, pp. 202–225. Smithsonian Institution Press, Washington, DC.

Couture, N., and K. Sampeck. 2003. Putuni: A history of palace architecture at Tiwanaku. In A. Kolata, editor, *Tiwanaku and Its Hinterland: Archaeology and Paleoecology of an Andean Civilization,* Vol. II, pp. 226–263. Smithsonian Institution Press, Washington, DC.

Créqui-Montfort, G. 1906. Fouilles de la mission scientifique Française à Tiahuanaco: Ses recherches archéologiques et ethnographiques en Bolivie, au Chile et dans la République Argentine. *Internationaler Amerikanisten Kongress* 2:531–550. Stuttgart.

Crumley, C. 1987. A dialectical critique of hierarchy. In T. Patterson and C. Gailey, editors, *Power Relations and State Formation,* pp. 155–159. American Anthropological Association, Arlington, Virginia.

Crumley, C. 1995. Heterarchy and the analysis of complex societies. In R. Ehrenreich, C. Crumley, and J. Levy, editors, *Heterarchy and the Analysis of Complex Societies,* pp. 1–4. American Anthropological Association, Arlington, Virginia.

Crumley, C., and W. Marquardt. 1987. *Regional Dynamics: Burgundian Landscapes in Historical Perspective.* Academic Press, New York.

Cuentas, Alberto. 1928. *Chucuito, álbum gráfico e histórico. Centenario de la ciudad de Juli. Como capital de la provincia de Chucuito, 1828–1928.* Juli, Puno.

Custred, G. 1977. Peasant kinship, subsistence and economics in a high altitude Andean environment. In R. Bolton and E. Mayer, editors, *Andean Kinship and Marriage,* pp. 117–135. American Anthropological Association, Washington, DC.

D'Altroy, T. 1981. *Empire Growth and Consolidation: The Xauxa Region of Peru under the Incas.* Ph.D. dissertation, Department of Anthropology, University of California, Los Angeles.

D'Altroy, T. 1992. *Provincial Power in the Inka Empire.* Smithsonian Institution Press, Washington, DC.

D'Altroy, T., and R. Bishop. 1990. The provincial organization of Inka ceramic production. *American Antiquity* 55(1):120–138.

Daulsberg H., P. 1960. Contribución al estudio de la arqueología del Valle de Azapa. In R. Matos M., editor, *Antiguo Perú: Espacio y tiempo,* pp. 273–296. Mejia Baca, Lima.

Daulsberg H., P. 1983. Tojo-Tojone: Un paradero de cazadores arcaicos (características y secuencias). *Chungará* 11:11–30.

de France, S. 1997. Vertebrate faunal use at Yaya-Mama religious tradition sites on the Copacabana Peninsula, Bolivia. Paper presented at the 62nd Annual Meeting of the Society for American Archaeology, Nashville.

de la Vega M., E. 1990. *Estudio arqueológico de Pucaras o poblados amurallados de cumbre en territorio Lupaqa: El caso de Pucara-Juli.* Bachelor's thesis, Universidad Católica Santa María, Arequipa, Peru.

de la Vega, E., K. Frye, C. Chávez, M. Núñez, F. Sosa, B. Antesana, J. Nuñés, D. Maldonado, N. Cornejo, A. Mamani, and J. Chalcha. 1995. Proyecto de rescate del sitio arqueológico de Molino-Chilacachi (Acora). Proyecto Lupaqa, Universidad Nacional del Altiplano, Instituto Nacional de Cultura-Puno. Manuscript in possession of authors.

de Montmollin, O. 1987. Forced settlement and political centralization in a Classic Maya polity. *Journal of Anthropological Archaeology* 6:220–262.

Dearborn, D., M. Seddon, and B. Bauer. 1998. The sanctuary of Titicaca: Where the sun returns to earth. *Latin American Antiquity* 9:240–258.

Demarest, A. 1992. Ideology in ancient Maya cultural evolution. In A. Demarest and G. Conrad, editors, *Ideology and Pre-Columbian Civilizations,* pp. 135–157. School of American Research, Santa Fe.

DeMarrais, E., L. Castillo, and T. Earle. 1996. Ideology, materialization and power strategies. *Current Anthropology* 37(1):15–31.

Diez de San Miguel, G. 1964 [1567]. *Visita hecha a la Provincia de Chucuito*. Facsimile edition. Ediciones de la Casa de la Cultura de Perú, Lima.

Dillehay, T. 1977. Tawantinsuyo integration of the Chillón Valley, Peru: A case of Inca geo-political mastery. *Journal of Field Archaeology* 4:397–405.

Dillehay, T. 1997. *Monte Verde*, Vol. 2: *The Archaeological Context and Interpretation*. Smithsonian Institution Press, Washington, DC.

Dobyns, H. 1983. *Their Number Became Thinned*. University of Tennessee Press, Knoxville.

Drennan, R. 1986. Household location and compact versus dispersed settlement in prehispanic Mesoamerica. In R. Wilk and W. Ashmore, editors, *House and Household in the Mesoamerican Past*, pp. 273–293. University of New Mexico Press, Albuquerque.

Earle, T. 1987. Chiefdoms in archaeological and ethnohistorical perspective. *Annual Review of Anthropology* 16:279–308.

Earle, T. 1997. *How Chiefs Come to Power: The Political Economy in Prehistory*. Stanford University Press, Stanford.

Earle, T., T. D'Altroy, C. Hastorf, C. Scott, C. Costin, G. Russell and E. Sandefur. 1987. *Archaeological Field Research in the Upper Mantaro, Peru, 1982-1983: Investigations of Inka Expansion and Exchange*, Monograph 28, Institute of Archaeology, University of California, Los Angeles.

Elkin, D. 1994. Análisis del material óseo del sitio de Sillumocco-Huaquina. Preliminary report of the Proyecto Lupaqa. Manuscript in possession of author.

Ensor, B. 2000. Social formations, modo de vida, and conflict in archaeology. *American Antiquity* 65:15–42.

Erickson, C. 1982. *Experiments in Raised Field Agriculture, Huatta, Peru 1981–2*. University of Illinois.

Erickson, C. 1988a. *An Archaeological Investigation of Raised Field Agriculture in the Lake Titicaca Basin of Peru*. Ph.D dissertation, Department of Anthropology, University of Illinois at Urbana-Champaign.

Erickson, C. 1988b. Raised field agriculture in the Lake Titicaca Basin. *Expedition* 30(3):8–16.

Erickson, C. 1993. The social organization of prehispanic raised field agriculture in the Lake Titicaca Basin. In V. Scarborough and B. Isaac, editors, *Prehispanic Water Management Systems*, Supplement 7, Research in Economic Anthropology, pp. 369–426. JAI Press, Greenwich, Conn.

Erickson, C. 1994. Methodological considerations in the study of ancient Andean field systems. In N. Miller and K. Gleason, editors, *The Archaeology of Garden and Field*, pp. 111–152. University of Pennsylvania Press, Philadelphia.

Erickson, C. 1996. *Investigación arqueológica del sistema agricola de los camellones en la cuenca del Lago Titicaca del Peru*. PIWA, La Paz.

Erickson, C. 1999. Neo-environmental determinism and agrarian "collapse" in Andean prehistory. *Antiquity* 73:634–642.

Erickson, C. 2000. The Lake Titicaca Basin: A Pre-Columbian built landscape. In D. Lentz, editor, *Imperfect Balance: Landscape Transformations in the PreColumbian Americas*, pp. 311–356. Columbia University Press, New York.

Escalante, J. 2003. Residential architecture in La K'araña. In A. Kolata, editor, *Tiwanaku and Its Hinterland: Archaeology and Paleoecology of an Andean Civilization*, Vol. II, pp. 316–326. Smithsonian Institution Press, Washington, DC.

Espinoza, J. 1983. *Taquile: Historia-economía-artesania*. Instituto de Investigaciones para el Desarrollo Social del Altiplano, Puno, Peru.

Espinoza Soriano, W. 1987. *Los Incas: Economía sociedad y estado en la era del Tahuantinsuyu*. Amaru, Cuzco.

Faldín Arancibia, J. 1985. La arqueología de las provincias de Larecaja y Muñecas y su sistema precolombino. *Arqueología Boliviana* 2:53–74.

Faldín Arancibia, J. 1990. La provincia Larecaja y el sistema precolombino del Norte de La Paz. In *Larecaja, ayer, hoy y mañana* (no editor), pp. 73–90. Comité de Cultura, La Paz.

Faldín Arancibia, J. 1991. La cerámica de Chiripa en los valles de Larecaja y Muñecas. *Puma Punku* 1 (nueva época):119–132.

Feinman, G., and L. Nicholas. 1995. Household craft specialization and shell ornament manufacture in Ejutla, Mexico. *Expedition* 37:14–25.

Fish, S., and S. Kowalewski. 1990. Introduction. In S. Fish and S. Kowalewski, editors, *The Archaeology of Regions: A Case for Full-Coverage Survey*, pp. 1–5. Smithsonian Institution Press, Washington, DC.

Flores Ochoa, J. 1987. Evidence for the cultivation of *qochas* in the Peruvian altiplano. In W. Denevan, K. Mathewson, and G. Knapp, editors, *Pre-Hispanic Agricultural Fields in the Andean Region: Proceedings of the 45th Congreso Internacional de Americanistas*, pp. 399–402. British Archaeological Reports International Series No. 359. Oxford.

Forgey, K. 2001. The Nasca trophy heads: Warfare trophies or revered ancestors. Paper presented at the 66th Annual Meeting of the Society for American Archaeology, New Orleans.

Fox, J. 1987. *Maya Postclassic State Formation.* Cambridge University Press, Cambridge.

Frame, M. 1989. *A Family Affair: Making Cloth in Taquile, Peru.* University of British Columbia, Vancouver.

Franco Inojosa, J., and A. Gonzalez. 1936. Exploraciones arqueológicas en el Peru, Departamento de Puno. *Revista del Museo Nacional* 5(2):157–183.

Franke, E. 1995. Ceramic craft specialization at Ch'iji Jawira, Tiwanaku: Organization and technology. *Journal of the Steward Anthropological Society, Current Research in Andean Antiquity* 23(1/2):111–120.

Franquemont, E. 1986. The ancient pottery from Pucara, Peru. *Ñawpa Pacha* 24:1–30.

Fried, M. 1967. *The Evolution of Political Society.* Random House, New York.

Frye, K. 1994. *Modelling the process of political unification: The Lupaqa in the Titicaca Basin, Peru.* Master's thesis, Department of Anthropology, University of California, Santa Barbara.

Frye, K. 1997a. Political centralization in the Altiplano Period in the southwestern Titicaca Basin. In C. Stanish, E. de la Vega, L. Steadman, C. Chávez Justo, K. Frye, L. Onofre Mamani, M. Seddon, and P. Calisaya Chuquimia, *Archaeological Survey in the Juli-Desaguadero Region of Lake Titicaca Basin, Southern Peru*, Volume 29 of *Fieldiana Anthropology*, Appendix 2, pp. 129–141. Field Museum of Natural History, Chicago.

Frye, K. 1997b. Of maize and men. Paper presented at the 62nd Annual Meeting of the Society for American Archaeology, Nashville.

Frye, K., and L. Steadman. 2001. Incatunuhuiri: A case for early socio-political complexity in the Titicaca Basin. Paper presented at the 66th Annual Meeting of the Society for American Archaeology, New Orleans.

Garcilaso de la Vega, E. 1987 [1617]. *Royal Commentaries of the Incas and General History of Peru.* Facsimile edition. University of Texas Press, Austin.

Gasparini, G., and L. Margolies. 1980. *Inca Architecture.* Indiana University Press, Bloomington.

Geertz, C. 1980. *Negara: The Theatre State in Nineteenth Century Bali.* Princeton University Press, Princeton.

Girault, L. 1977. Las ruinas de Chullpa Pata de la comunidad de Kallamarka. *Arqueología en Bolivia y Peru*, II:191–210.

Godelier, M. 1977. *Perspectives in Marxist Anthropology.* Cambridge University Press, Cambridge.

Goldstein, P. 1989. *Omo: A Tiwanaku Provincial Center in Moquegua, Peru.* Ph.D. dissertation, Department of Anthropology, University of Chicago.

Goldstein, P. 1993a. House, community, and state in the earliest Tiwanaku colony. In M. Aldenderfer, editor, *Domestic Architecture, Ethnicity and Complementarity in the South-Central Andes*, pp. 25–41. University of Iowa Press, Iowa City.

Goldstein, P. 1993b. Tiwanaku temples and state expansion: A Tiwanaku sunken-court temple in Moquegua, Peru. *Latin American Antiquity* 4(1):22–47.

González, A. 1983. Inca settlement patterns in a marginal province of the empire: Sociocultural implications. In E. Vogt and R. Leventhal, editors, *Prehistoric Settlement Patterns: Essays in Honor of Gordon R. Willey*, pp. 337–360. University of New Mexico Press, Albuquerque, and Peabody Museum of Archaeology and Ethnology, Harvard University, Cambridge, Massachusetts.

Graf, K. 1981. Palynological investigations of two post-glacial peat bogs near the boundary of Bolivia and Peru. *Journal of Biogeography* 8:353–368.

Graffam, G. 1990. *Raised Fields without Bureaucracy: An Archaeological Examination of Intensive Wetland Cultivation in the Pampa Koani Zone, Lake Titicaca, Bolivia.* Ph.D. dissertation, Department of Anthropology, University of Toronto.

Graffam, G. 1992. Beyond state collapse: Rural history, raised fields, and pastoralism in the

South Andes. *American Anthropologist* 94(4): 882–904.

Grieder, T., and A. Bueno Mendoza. 1985. Ceremonial Architecture at La Galgada. In C. Donnan, editor, *Early Ceremonial Architecture in the Andes*, pp. 93–110. Dumbarton Oaks, Washington, DC.

Guaman Poma de Ayala, F. 1980 [1613]. *El primer nueva crónica y buen gobierno*. Facsimile edition. Siglo Veintiuno Editores, SA, Bogotá.

Gutiérrez Condori, R. 1991. Instrumentos musicales tradicionales en la comunidad artesanal Walata Grande, Bolivia. *Latin American Musical Review* 12:124–159.

Harris, O. 1981. Households as natural units. In K. Young and C. Wolkowitz, editors, *Of Marriage and the Market*. Committee of Socialist Economists Books, London.

Harrison, R. 1989. *Signs, Songs and Memory in the Andes*. University of Texas Press, Austin.

Harthe-Terré, E. 1965. Técnica y arte de la cantería Incaica. *Revista Universitaria* 51–52(122–132, 1224–125):152–168. Cuzco, Peru.

Hassan, F. 1981. *Demographic Archaeology*. Academic Press, New York.

Hastorf, C. A. 1999a. An introduction to Chiripa and the site area. In C. Hastorf, editor, *Early Settlement at Chiripa Bolivia*, Contributions of the University of California Archaeological Research Facility, number 57, pp. 1–6. Archaeological Research Facility, Berkeley.

Hastorf, C. A., editor, 1999b. *Early Settlement at Chiripa, Bolivia*. Contributions of the University of California Archaeological Research Facility, number 57. Archaeological Research Facility, Berkeley.

Hastorf, C. A. 2003. Community with the ancestors: Ceremonies and social memory in the Middle Formative at Chiripa, Bolivia. *Journal of Anthropological Archaeology* 22(4):305–332.

Hastorf, C. A., S. Alconini, S. Arnott, M. Bandy, R. Burke, L. Butler, N. Jackson, C. Nordstrom, C. Rivera, and L. Steadman. 1992. Reporte preliminar de las excavaciones de 1992 en Chiripa, Bolivia por el Proyecto Arqueológico Taraco. Report submitted to the Instituto Nacional de Arqueología, La Paz.

Hastorf, C. A., M. Bandy, D. Blom, E. Dean, M. Goodman, D. Kojan, M. Montaño Aragón, J.

Luis Paz, D. Steadman, L. Steadman, and W. Whitehead. 1997. Proyecto Arqueológico Taraco: Excavaciones de 1996 en Chiripa, Bolivia. Report submitted to the Instituto Nacional de Arqueología, La Paz.

Hastorf, C. A., M. Bandy, W. Whitehead, and L. Steadman. 2001. El periodo Formativo en Chiripa, Bolivia. In C. Rivera Casanovas, M. R. Michel Lopez, and J. M. Capriles Flores, editors, *El periodo Formativo en Bolivia: Regiones y sociedades. Textos Antropológicos*, Vol. 13(1–2): 17–91. La Paz.

Heffernan, K. 1996. *Limatambo: Archaeology, History and the Regional Societies of Inca Cusco*. British Archaeological Reports International Series No. 644. Oxford.

Helms, M. 1979. *Ancient Panama: Chiefs in Search of Power*. University of Texas Press, Austin.

Helms, M. 1993. *Craft and the Kingly Ideal: Art, Trade, and Power*. University of Texas Press, Austin.

Helms, M. 1998. *Ulysses' Sail: An Ethnographic Odyssey of Power, Knowledge, and Geographical Distance*. University of Utah Press, Salt Lake City.

Herhahn, C. 2001. Investigations into Early to Middle Formative domestic economy in the southwestern Titicaca Basin, Peru. Paper presented at the 66th Annual Meeting of the Society for American Archaeology, New Orleans.

Herhahn, C. 2004. Moving to live: A pastoral mobility model from the South-Central Andes, Peru. Manuscript in possession of author, Department of Anthropology, University of California, Santa Barbara.

Hodder, I. 1982. The identification and interpretation of ranking in prehistory: A contextual perspective. In S. Shennen, editor, *Ranking, Resource, and European Exchange: Aspects of the Archaeology of Early European Society*, pp. 150–155. Cambridge University Press, Cambridge.

Hoshower, L., J. Buikstra, P. Goldstein, and A. Webster. 1995. Artificial cranial deformation at the Omo M-10 Site: A Tiwanaku complex from the Moquegua Valley, Peru. *Latin American Antiquity* 6(2):145–164.

Hyslop, J. 1976. *An Archaeological Investigation of the Lupaqan Kingdom and Its Origins*. Ph.D dissertation, Department of Anthropology, Columbia University, New York.

Hyslop, J. 1977a. Chulpas of the Lupaca zone of the Peruvian high plateau. *Journal of Field Archaeology* 4:149–170.

Hyslop, J. 1977b. Hilltop cities in Peru. *Archaeology* 30:218–225.

Hyslop, J. 1984. *The Inka Road System.* Academic Press, New York.

Hyslop, J. 1990. *Inka Settlement Planning.* University of Texas Press, Austin.

Ibarra Grasso, D. E., and R. Querejazu L. 1986. *30.000 Años de prehistoria en Bolivia.* Los Amigos del Libro, La Paz.

Isbell, B. 1977. "Those who love me": An analysis of Andean kinship and reciprocity within a ritual context. In R. Bolton and E. Mayer, editors, *Andean Kinship and Marriage,* American Anthropological Association Special Publications Number 7, pp. 81–105. American Anthropological Association, Washington, DC.

Isbell, W. 1985. El origen del estado en el valle de Ayacucho. *Revista Andina* 3(1):57–106.

Isbell, W. 1987. State origins in the Ayacucho Valley, central highlands, Peru. In J. Haas, S. Pozorski, and T. Pozorski, editors, *The Origins and Development of the Andean State,* pp. 83–90. Cambridge University Press, Cambridge.

Isbell, W. 1997. *Mummies and Mortuary Monuments: A Postprocessual Prehistory of Central Andean Social Organization.* University of Texas Press, Austin.

Isbell, W., and K. Schreiber. 1978. Was Huari a state? *American Antiquity* 43:372–389.

Janusek, J. 1993. Nuevos datos sobre el significado de la producción y uso de instrumentos musicales en el estado de Tiwanaku. *Puma Punku* 2(4):9–47.

Janusek, J. 1994. *State and Local Power in a Prehispanic Andean Polity: Changing Patterns of Urban Residence in Tiwanaku and Lukurmata.* Ph.D. dissertation, Department of Anthropology, University of Chicago.

Janusek, J. 1999. Craft and local power: Embedded specialization in Tiwanaku cities. *Latin American Antiquity* 10:107–131.

Janusek, J. 2001a. Asentamiento rural y campos elevados de cultivo en el Río Katari durante el período Formativo Tardío. *Textos Antropológicos* 13(1–2):111–134.

Janusek, J. 2001b. Diversidad residencial y el surgimiento de la complejidad en Tiwanaku.

In P. Kaulicke, editor, *Huari y Tiwanaku: Modelos vs. evidencias (Segunda parte).* Boletín de Arqueología PUCP 5:251–294. Pontificia Universidad Católica del Perú, Lima.

Janusek, J. 2002. Out of many, one: Style and social boundaries in Tiwanaku. *Latin American Antiquity* 13(1):35–61.

Janusek, J. 2003. Vessels, time, and society: Toward a chronology of ceramic style in the Tiwanaku heartland. In A. Kolata, editor, *Tiwanaku and Its Hinterland: Archaeology and Paleoecology of an Andean Civilization,* Vol. II, pp. 30–94. Smithsonian Institution Press, Washington, DC.

Janusek, J., and S. Alconini. 1994. Social diversity and historical change in Tiwanaku ceramics: Steps toward a Tiwanaku IV–V chronology. Paper presented at the 59th Annual Meeting of the Society for American Archaeology, Anaheim, California.

Janusek, J., and H. Earnest. 1990. Excavations at Putuni: The 1988 Season. Informe preliminar. Manuscript in possession of J. Janusek.

Janusek, J., and A. Kolata. 2003. Prehispanic rural history in the Katari Valley. In A. Kolata, editor, *Tiwanaku and Its Hinterland II: Urban and Rural Archaeology,* pp. 129–174. Smithsonian Institution Press, Washington, DC.

Janusek, J., S. Alconini M., D. Angelo, and P. Lima. 1997. Asentamiento prehispánico en la region de Icla, Chuquisaca, Bolivia. Final report of the Proyecto Icla, 1993–1996, submitted to the Universidad Mayor de San Andrés and the Instituto Nacional de Arqueología de Bolivia. La Paz.

Janusek, J., A. T. Ohnstad, and A. P. Roddick. 2003. Khonko Huancane and the rise of Tiwanaku. *Antiquity* 77(296). *http://antiquity.ac.uk/ProjGall/janusek/janusek.html.*

Johnson, G. 1977. Aspects of regional analysis in archaeology. *Annual Review of Anthropology* 6:479–508.

Johnson, I. 2003. *The Changing Nature of Political Power in the Titicaca Basin: The View from Paucarcolla.* Master's thesis, Department of Anthropology, UCLA.

Joyce, A., and M. Winter. 1996. Ideology, power, and urban society in pre-Hispanic Oaxaca. *Current Anthropology* 37:33–86.

Julien, C. 1982. Inca decimal administration in the Lake Titicaca region. In G. Collier, R. Rosaldo, and J. Wirth, editors, *The Inca and Aztec States: 1400–1800,* pp. 119–152. Academic Press, New York.

Julien, C. 1983. *Hatunqolla: A View of Inca Rule from the Lake Titicaca Region.* University of California Press, Berkeley.

Julien, C. 1988. How Inca decimal administration worked. *Ethnohistory* 35(3):258–279.

Julien, C. 1993. Finding a fit: Archaeology and ethnohistory of the Incas. In M. Malpass, editor, *Provincial Inca: Archaeological and Ethnohistorical Assessment of the Impact of the Inca State,* pp. 177–233. University of Iowa Press, Iowa City.

Keefer, D., S. de France, M. Moseley, J. Richardson III, D. Satterlee, and A. Day-Lewis. 1998. Early maritime economy and El Niño events at Quebrada Tacahuay, Peru. *Science* 281:1833–1835.

Kelly, R. 1995. *The Foraging Spectrum: Diversity in Hunter-Gatherer Lifeways.* Smithsonian Institution Press, Washington, DC.

Kent, J. 1982. *The Domestication and Exploitation of the South American Camelids: Methods of Analysis and Their Application to Circumlacustrine Archaeological Sites in Bolivia and Peru.* Ph.D. dissertation, Department of Anthropology, Washington University, St. Louis.

Kidder, A. 1943. Some early sites in the northern Lake Titicaca Basin. *American Archaeology and Ethnology* 27(1). Peabody Museum, Harvard University, Cambridge, Massachusetts.

Kidder, A. 1948. The position of Pucara in Titicaca Basin archaeology. *American Antiquity* 13(4): 87–89.

Kidder, A. 1956. Digging in the Lake Titicaca Basin. *University Museum Bulletin* 20(3):16–29.

King, J. and D. Potter. 1994. Small sites in prehistoric Maya socioeconomic organization: A perspective from Colha, Belize. In G. Schwartz and S. Falconer, editors, *Archaeological Views from the Countryside: Village Communities in Early Complex Societies,* pp. 64–90. Smithsonian Institution Press, Washington, DC.

Kirch, P. 1984. *The Evolution of the Polynesian Chiefdoms.* Cambridge University Press, Cambridge.

Klarich, E. n.d. From the Monumental to the Mundane: Defining Early Leadership Strategies at Late Formative Pukara, Peru. Manuscript in possession of author, Department of Anthropology, University of California, Santa Barbara.

Klarich, E., and M. Seddon. 1997. A Tiwanaku domestic occupation on the Island of the Sun, Bolivia. Paper presented at the 62nd Annual Meeting of the Society for American Archaeology, Nashville.

Klink, C. 1998. Proyecto Arcaico del altiplano 1997: Prospección arqueológica en el valle del Río Huenque. Report submitted to the Instituto Nacional de Cultura, Lima, Peru.

Klink, C. 1999. On the edge: Prehistoric trends on the Peruvian Altiplano rim. Paper presented at the 64th Annual Meeting of the Society for American Archaeology, Chicago.

Klink, C., and M. Aldenderfer. 1996. Archaic Period settlement on the Altiplano: Comparison of two recent surveys in the southwestern Lake Titicaca basin. Paper presented at the 24th Annual Midwest Conference of Andean and Amazonian Archaeology, Beloit, Wisconsin.

Kolata, A. 1983. The South Andes. In J. Jennings, editor, *Ancient South Americans,* pp. 241–285. W. H. Freeman, San Francisco.

Kolata, A. 1985. El papel de la agricultura intensiva en la economía política del estado de Tiwanaku. *Diálogo Andino* 4:11–38.

Kolata, A. 1986. The agricultural foundations of the Tiwanaku state: A view from the heartland. *American Antiquity* 51(4):13–28.

Kolata, A. 1992. Economy, ideology, and imperialism in the south-central Andes. In A. Demarest and G. Conrad, editors, *Ideology,* pp. 65–86. School of American Research, Santa Fe.

Kolata, A. 1993. *The Tiwanaku.* Blackwell, Cambridge.

Kolata, A. 1996a. Proyecto Wila Jawira: An introduction to the history, problems, and strategies of research. In A. Kolata, editor, *Tiwanaku and Its Hinterland: Archaeology and Paleoecology of an Andean Civilization,* pp. 1–22. Smithsonian Institution Press, Washington, DC.

Kolata, A., editor. 1996b. *Tiwanaku and Its Hinterland: Archaeology and Paleoecology of an Andean Civilization.* Smithsonian Institution Press, Washington, DC.

Kolata, A., editor. 2003. *Tiwanaku and Its Hinterland: Archaeology and Paleoecology of an Andean Civi-*

lization, Vol II. Smithsonian Institution Press, Washington, DC.

Kolata, A., and C. Ponce Sanginés. 1992. Tiwanaku: The city at the center. In R. Townsend, editor, *Ancient Americas: Art from Sacred Landscapes*, pp. 317–335. Art Institute of Chicago.

Kolata, A., O. Rivera, J. Ramírez, and E. Gemio. 1996. Rehabilitating raised-field agriculture in the southern Lake Titicaca Basin of Bolivia: Theory, practice, and results. In A. Kolata, editor, *Tiwanaku and Its Hinterland: Archaeology and Paleoecology of an Andean Civilization*, pp. 203–230. Smithsonian Institution Press, Washington, DC.

Kowalewski, S., G. Feinman, L. Finsten, R. Blanton, and L. Nicholas. 1989. *Monte Alban's Hinterland, Part II*. Memoirs of the Museum of Anthropology, University of Michigan Number 23, Ann Arbor.

Kubler, G. 1946. The Quechua in the colonial world. In J. Steward, editor, *Handbook of South American Indians*, Vol. 2: *The Andean Civilizations*, pp. 331–410. Bureau of American Ethnology, Washington, DC.

La Barre, W. 1948. *The Aymara Indians of the Lake Titicaca Plateau, Bolivia*. Volume 68 of *Memoirs of the American Anthropological Association*. American Anthropological Association. Menasha, Wisconsin.

Lavallée, D. 1985. The prehistoric occupation of the Andean highlands. *Anthropologie* 89(3):409–430.

Lavallée, D., M. Julien, and J. Wheeler. 1982. Telarmachay: Niveles precerámicos de ocupación. *Revista del Museo Nacional* 46:55–127.

Lavallée, D., M. Julien, J. Wheeler, and C. Karlin. 1985. *Telarmachay: Chasseurs et Pateurs Préhistoriques des Andes*. Institut Français d'Études Andines, Paris.

Lee, M. 1997. Paleoethnobotanical evidence from the Yayamama excavations. Paper presented at the 62nd Annual Meeting of the Society for American Archaeology, Nashville.

Lémuz, Carlos. 2001. *Patrones de asentamiento arqueológico en la peninsula de Santiago de Huatta, Bolivia*. Licenciatura de Arqueología, Universidad Mayor de San Andrés, La Paz.

Lennstrom, H., C. Hastorf, and M. Wright. n.d. *Informe: Lukurmata*. In C. Hastorf, editor, Papers of the University of California Berkeley Paleoethnobotany Lab.

LeVine, T. 1985. *Inka Administration in the Central Highlands: A Comparative Study*. Ph.D. dissertation, Department of Anthropology, University of California, Los Angeles.

Lizarraga, R. de. 1987 [1605]. *Descripción del Perú, Tucumán, Río de la Plata y Chile*, edited by I. Ballesteros. Facsimile edition. Historia 16, Madrid.

Low, S. M. 1995. Indigenous architecture and the Spanish-American plaza in Meosamerica and the Caribbean. *American Anthropologist* 97:748.

Loza Balsa, G. 1971. La vivienda Aymara. *Pumapunku* 3:68–73.

Lumbreras, L. 1981. *Arqueología de la América Andina*. Milla Batres, Lima.

Lumbreras, L. 1974a. Los reinos post-Tiwanaku en el área altiplánica. *Revista del Museo Nacional* 40:55–85.

Lumbreras, L. 1974b. *Peoples and Cultures of Ancient Peru*. Smithsonian Institution Press, Washington, DC.

Lumbreras, L., and H. Amat. 1968. Secuencia arqueológica del altiplano occidental del Titicaca. *37th International Congress of Americanists. Buenos Aires, 1968. Actas y memorias*, Vol. II:75–106.

Lyon, P. 1979. Female supernaturals in ancient Peru. *Ñawpa Pacha* 16:95–140.

MacCormack, S. 1991. *Religion in the Andes: Vision and Imagination in Early Colonial Peru*. Princeton University Press, Princeton.

Mamani Condori, C. 1991. *Taraqu 1866–1935: Masacre, guerra, y "renovación" en la Biografía de Eduardo L. Nina Qhispi*. Ediciones Aruwiyiri, Taller de Historia Oral Andina, La Paz.

Mantilla, R. 1972. *Arquitectura rupestre en Copacabana*. Arte y Arqueología 2 (supplement). Instituto de Estudios Bolivianos de la Universidad Mayor de San Andrés, La Paz.

Manzanilla, L. 1992. *Akapana: Una pirámide en el centro del mundo*. UNAM: Instituto de Investigaciones Antropológicas, Mexico City.

Manzanilla, L. 1996. Corporate groups and domestic activities at Teotihuacan. *Latin American Antiquity* 7(3):228–246.

Manzanilla, L., L. Barba, and M. Boudoin. 1990. Investigaciónes en la pirámide de Akapana, Tiwanaku, Bolivia. *Gaceta Arqueológica Andina* 5(20):81–107.

Mathews, J. 1992a. *Prehispanic Settlement and Agriculture in the Middle Tiwanaku Valley, Bolivia.* Ph.D. dissertation, Department of Anthropology, University of Chicago.

Mathews, J. 1992b. Some notes on the early development of the Tiwanaku State. Paper presented at the 20th Annual Midwest Conference on Andean and Amazonian Archaeology and Ethnohistory.

Mathews, J. 1995. A re-evaluation of the Formative period in the southeast Titicaca Basin, Bolivia. *Journal of the Steward Anthropological Society* 23:83–110.

McBain Chapin, H. 1959. The Adolph Bandelier archaeological collection from Pelechuco and Charassani, Bolivia. *Revista del Instituto de Antropología* I:9–80.

McEwan, G. 1990. Some formal correspondences between the imperial architecture of the Wari and Chimu cultures of ancient Peru. *Latin American Antiquity* 1(2):97–116.

McEwan, C., and M. Van de Guchte. 1992. Ancestral time and sacred space in Inca state ritual. In R. Townsend, editor, *The Ancient Americas: Art from Sacred Landscapes,* pp. 347–358. The Art Institute of Chicago.

McGuire, R. 1983. Breaking down cultural complexity: Inequality and heterogeneity. *Advances in Archaeological Method and Theory* 6:91–142.

Menghin, O., and G. Schroeder. 1957. Un yacimiento en Ichuña (Departamento de Puno, Perú) y las industrias Precerámicas de los Andes centrales y septentrionales. *Acta Prehistórica,* pp. 41–54.

Menzel, D. 1959. The Inca conquest of the South Coast of Peru. *Southwestern Journal of Anthropology* 15:125–142.

Menzel, D. 1964. Style and time in the Middle Horizon. *Ñawpa Pacha* 2:1–107.

Mesa, J., and T. Gisbert. 1957. Akapana: La pirámide de Tiwanacu. In C. Ponce Sanginés, editor, *Arqueología Boliviana (Primera Mesa Redonda),* pp. 141–161. Alcaldía Municipal, La Paz.

Milner, G., and J. Oliver. 1999. Late prehistoric settlements and wetlands in the central Mississippi Valley. In B. Billman and G. Feinman, editors, *Settlement Pattern Studies in the Ameri-*

cas: Fifty Years since Virú, pp. 79–95. Smithsonian Institution Press, Washington, DC.

Mohr, K. 1966. *An Analysis of the Pottery of Chiripa, Bolivia: A Problem in Archaeological Classification and Inference.* Master's thesis, Department of Anthropology, University of Pennsylvania, Philadelphia.

Mohr-Chávez, K. 1992. The organization of production and distribution of traditional pottery in south highland Peru. In G. Bey and C. Pool, editors, *Ceramic Production and Distribution: An Integrated Approach,* pp. 49–92. Westview Press, Boulder.

Molina "el Almagrista," C. de. 1968 [1552]. Relación de muchas cosas acaescidas en el Perú. In F. Esteve Barba, editor, *Crónicas peruanas de interés indígena,* pp. 57–95. Facsimile edition. Biblioteca de Autores Españoles 209. Ediciones Atlas, Madrid.

Molina de Cuzco, C. de. 1947 [1584]. *Relación de los fábulas y ritos de los Incas.* Editorial Futuro, Buenos Aires.

Molina, E., and A. Little. 1981. Geoecology of the Andes and the natural science basis for research planning. *Mountain Research and Development* 1(2):115–144.

Moore, J. 1996a. The archaeology of plazas and the proxemics of ritual. *American Anthropologist* 98(4):789–802.

Moore, J. 1996b. *Architecture and Power in the Ancient Andes: The Archaeology of Public Buildings.* Cambridge University Press, Cambridge.

Moore, K. 1999. Chiripa worked bone and bone tools. In C. Hastorf, editor, *Early Settlement at Chiripa, Bolivia,* Contributions of the University of California Archaeological Research Facility, number 57, pp. 73–94. Archaeological Research Facility, Berkeley.

Moore, K., D. Steadman, and S. de France. 1999. Herds, fish, and fowl in the domestic and ritual economy of Formative Chiripa. In C. Hastorf, editor, *Early Settlement at Chiripa Bolivia,* Contributions of the University of California Archaeological Research Facility, number 57, pp. 105–116. Archaeological Research Facility, Berkeley.

Morris, C. 1982. The infrastructure of Inka control in the Peruvian central highlands. In G. Collier, R. Rosaldo, and J. Wirth, editors, *The Inca and Aztec States 1400–1800,* pp. 153–171. Academic Press, New York.

Morris, C., and D. Thompson, 1985. *Huánuco Pampa: An Inca City and Its Hinterland.* Thames and Hudson, London.

Moseley, M. 1992. *The Incas and Their Ancestors.* Thames and Hudson, New York.

Mujica, E. 1978. Nueva hipótesis sobre el desarrollo temprano del altiplano del Titicaca y de sus áreas de interracción. *Arte y Arqueología* 5–6:285–308.

Mujica, E. 1985. Altiplano-coast relationships in the South-Central Andes: From indirect to direct complementarity. In S. Masuda, I. Shimada, and C. Morris, editors, *Andean Ecology and Civilization,* pp. 103–140. University of Tokyo Press, Tokyo.

Mujica, E. 1987. Cusipata: Una fase pre-Pukara en la cuenca norte de Titicaca. *Gaceta Arqueológica Andina* 13:22–28.

Mujica, E. 1988. Peculiaridades del proceso histórico temprano en la cuenca del norte del Titicaca: Una propuesta inicial. *Boletín del Laboratorio de Arqueología,* pp. 75–124. Escuela de Arqueología e Historia, Universidad Nacional San Cristobal de Huamanga, Ayacucho.

Muñoz Ovalle, I., B. Arriaza, and A. Auferheide, editors. 1993. *Acha-2 y los orígenes del poblamiento humano en Arica.* Ediciones Universidad de Tarapacá, Arica, Chile.

Murra, J. V. 1964. Una apreciación etnología de la Visita. In *Visita hecha a la Provincia de Chucuito por Garci Diez de San Miguel en el Año 1567. Documentos Regionales para el Etnología y Etnohistoria Andinas (Lima, Peru)* 1: 419–444.

Murra, J. 1968. An Aymara kingdom in 1567. *Ethnohistory* 15:115–151.

Murra, J. 1970. Información etnológica e histórica adicional sobre el reino Lupaqa. *Historia y Cultura* 4:49–61.

Murra, J. 1972. El "control vertical" de un máximo de piscos ecológicos en la economía de las sociedades andinas. In J. Murra, editor, *Visita de la Provincia de León de Huánuco en 1562,* Vol. 2, pp. 429–76. Universidad Nacional Hermilio Valdizán, Huánuco, Peru.

Murra, J. 1978. Aymara lords and their European agents at Potosí. *Nova Americana* 1:231–243. Giulio Einaudi, Torino.

Murra, J. 1980 [1956]. *The Economic Organization of the Inka State.* Research in Economic Anthropology Supplement 1. JAI Press, Inc., Greenwich, Conn.

Murra, J. 1985. "El archipielago vertical" revisited. In S. Masuda, I. Shimada, and C. Morris, editors, *Andean Ecology and Civilization,* pp. 3–14. University of Tokyo Press, Tokyo.

Murúa, M. 1946 [1590]. *Los orígenes de los Inkas.* Facsimile edition. Los Pequeños Grandes Libros de Historia Americana, First Series, Vol II. Imprenta Miranda, Lima.

Naroll, R. 1962. Floor area and settlement population. *American Antiquity* 27(4):587–589.

Neira, M. 1967. Informe preliminar de las Investigaciones arqueológicas en el Departamento de Puno. *Anales del Instituto de Estudios Socio Económicos* 1(1):107–161.

Neira, M. 1990. Arequipa prehispánica. In M. Neira A., G. Galdos R., A. Malaga M., E. Quiroz P.S., and J. G. Carpio M., editors, *Historia general de Arequipa,* pp. 5–183. Cuzzi y Cía, Arequipa, Peru.

Netherly, P. 1978. *Local Level Lords on the North Coast of Peru.* Ph.D. dissertation, Department of Anthropology, Cornell University, Ithaca, New York.

Nielsen, A. 1991. Trampling the archaeological record: An experimental study. *American Antiquity* 56(3):483–503.

Nielsen, A., and W. H. Walker. 1999. Conquista ritual y dominación política en el Tawantinsuyu: El caso de Los Amarillos (Jujuy, Argentina). In A. Zarankin and F. Acuto, editors, *Sed non satiata: Teoría social en la arqueología Latinoamericana contemporánea,* pp. 153–169. Ediciones del Tridente, Buenos Aires.

Niles, S. 1977. *Reflexiones sobre la ciudad pre-Colombiana de Iskanwaya.* Publicación 24. Instituto Nacional de Arqueología, La Paz.

Niles, S. 1987a. *Callachaca: Style and Status in an Inca Community.* University of Iowa Press, Iowa City.

Niles, S. 1987b. The temples of Amantaní. *Archaeology* 40(6):30–37.

Niles, S. 1988. Pachamama, Pachatata: Gender and space in Amantaní. In V. Miller, editor, *The Role of Gender in Pre-Columbian Art and Architecture,* pp. 135–152. University Press of America, Boston.

Nordenskiöld, E. 1953. *Investigaciones arqueológicas en la región fronteriza del Perú y Bolivia*. La Paz.

Núñez, M. 1994. Tiwanaku en la bahía Puno. *Gaceta Universitaria, Universidad Nacional del Altiplano* 1(2):5–6.

Nuñez, L. 1992. Ocupación arcaica en la puna de Atacama: Secuencia, movilidad y cambio. In B. Meggers, editor, *Prehistoria Sudamericana: Nuevas perspectivas*, pp. 283–307. Taraxacum, Washington, DC.

Nuñez, L., and T. Dillehay. 1979. *Movilidad giratoria, armonía social y desarrollo en los Andes meridionales: Patrones de tráfico e interacción económica*. Universidad del Norte, Antofagasta, Chile.

Nuñez Mendiguri, M., and R. Paredes. 1978. Estévez: Un sitio de ocupación Tiwanaku. In R. Matos M., editor, *III congreso Peruano del hombre y la cultura Andina* 2:757–764. Lima, Peru.

Onuki, Y. 1993. Las actividades ceremoniales tempranas en la cuenca del Alto Huallaga y algunos problemas generales. *El mundo ceremonial* 37:69–96. Lima.

Orlove, B., and G. Custred 1980. Agrarian economies and social processes in comparative perspective: The agricultural production unit. In B. Orlove and G. Custred, editors, *Land and Power in Latin America*, pp. 13–54. Holmes and Meier, New York.

Ortloff, C. 1996. Engineering aspects of Tiwanaku groundwater-controlled agriculture. In A. Kolata, editor, *Tiwanaku and Its Hinterland: Archaeology and Paleoecology of an Andean Civilization*, pp. 153–167. Smithsonian Institution Press, Washington, DC.

Ortloff, C., and A. Kolata. 1992. Climate and collapse: Agro-ecological perspectives on the decline of the Tiwanaku state. *Journal of Archaeological Science* 20:195–221.

Osgood Brooks, S., and M. Glascock. 1996. Colca Valley obsidian quarries: A primary source of obsidian to the Lake Titicaca area. Paper presented at the 36th Annual Meeting of the Institute of Andean Studies, Berkeley.

Palka, J. 1997. Reconstructing classic Maya socioeconomic differentiation and the collapse at Dos Pilas, Peten, Guatemala. *Ancient Mesoamerica* 8:293–306.

Paredes, R. 1985. *Excavaciones arqueológicas en Pukara-Puno*. Master's thesis, Universidad de Cuzco, Peru.

Parsons, J. 1968. An estimate of size and population for Middle Horizon Tiahuanaco, Bolivia. *American Antiquity* 40:259–282.

Parsons, J. 1971. *Prehistoric Settlement Patterns in the Texcoco Region, Mexico*. Memoirs of the Museum of Anthropology, University of Michigan, Ann Arbor.

Parsons, J. 1976. Settlement and population history of the Basin of Mexico. In E. Wolf, editor, *The Valley of Mexico: Studies in Prehispanic Ecology and Society*, pp. 69–100. University of New Mexico Press, Albuquerque.

Parsons, J., and R. Whalen. 1982. *Prehispanic Settlement Patterns in the Southern Valley of Mexico: The Chalc-Xochimilco Region*. Memoirs of the Museum of Anthropology, University of Michigan, Ann Arbor.

Pärssinen, M., and A. Siiriäinen. 1997. Inka-style ceramics and their chronological relationship to the Inka expansion on the southern Lake Titicaca area (Bolivia). *Latin American Antiquity* 8:255–271.

Pauketat, T. 2000. The tragedy of the commoners. In M.-A. Dobres, and J. Robb, editors, *Agency in Archaeology*, pp. 113–129. Routledge, London.

Paul, A., and S. Turpin. 1986. The ecstatic shaman theme of Paracas textiles. *Archaeology* 39(5): 20–27.

Paz Soría, J. 1999. Excavations in the Llusco Area. In C. Hastorf, editor, *Early Settlement at Chiripa, Bolivia*, Contributions of the University of California Archaeological Research Facility, number 57, pp. 31–36. Archaeological Research Facility, Berkeley.

Paz Soría, J. 2000. *La transición Formativo-Tiahuanaco en el valle Mesothermal de Tambo Kusi*. Licenciatura de Facultad de Ciencias Sociales, Carrera de Arqueología, Universidad Mayor de San Andrés, La Paz.

Pease, F. 1982. Formation of Tawantinsuyu: Mechanisms of colonization and relationship with ethnic groups. In G. Collier, R. Rosaldo, and J. Wirth, editors, *The Inca and Aztec states, 1400–1800: Anthropology and History*, pp. 173–198. Academic Press, New York.

Perrin Pando, A. 1957. Las tumbas subterraneos de Wakuyo. In C. Ponce Sanginés, editor, *Arqueología Boliviana (Primera Mesa Redonda)*, pp. 172–205. Alcaldía Municipal, La Paz.

Platt, T. 1982. *Estado Boliviano y ayllu Andino: Tierra y tributo en el norte de Potosí.* Instituto de Estudios Peruanos, Lima.

Platt, T. 1986. Mirrors and maize: The concept of Yanantin among the Macha of Bolivia. In J. Murra, N. Watchel, and J. Revel, editors, *Anthropological History of Andean Polities*, pp. 228–259. Cambridge University Press, Cambridge.

Platt, T. 1987a. The Andean soldiers of Christ. Confraternity organizations, the mass of the sun and regenerative warfare in rural Potosí (18th –20th Centuries). *Journal de la Société des Américanistes* 73:139–192.

Platt, T. 1987b. Entre ch'axwa y muxsa: Para una historia del pensamiento político Aymara. In T. Bouysse-Cassagne, O. Harris, T. Platt, and V. Careceda, editors, *Tres reflexiones sobre el pensamiento andino*, pp. 61–132. Hisbol, La Paz.

Plourde, A. 1999. The role of interregional exchange in Pukara and Tiwanaku state formation and expansion, northeastern Titicaca Basin, Peru. Paper presented at the 64th Annual Meeting of the Society for American Archaeology, Chicago.

Plourde, A. 2004. Prestige goods and their role in the evolution of social ranking: A costly signaling model with data from the Late Formative Period of the Northern Lake Titicaca Basin, Peru. Manuscript in possession of author.

Plourde, A., and C. Stanish 2001. Formative period settlement patterning in the Huancané-Putina River Valley, northeastern Titicaca Basin. Paper presented at the 66th Annual Meeting of the Society for American Archaeology, New Orleans.

Ponce Sanginés, C. 1961. *Informe de labores.* Centro de Investigaciónes Arqueológicas en Tiwanaku, La Paz.

Ponce Sanginés, C. 1969. *Descripción sumaria del Templete Semisuterraneo de Tiwanaku.* Academia Nacional de Ciencias de Bolivia, No. 20. Academia Nacional de Ciencias de Bolivia, La Paz.

Ponce Sanginés, C. 1970. *Las culturas Wankarani y Chiripa y su relación con Tiwanaku.* Publicación No. 25. Academia Nacional de Ciencias de Bolivia.

Ponce Sanginés, C. 1971. La cerámica de la época I de Tiwanaku. *Pumapunku* 2:7–28.

Ponce Sanginés, C. 1977. *Reflexiones sobre la ciudad pre-Colombiana de Iskanwaya.* Publicación No. 24. Instituto Nacional de Arqueología, La Paz.

Ponce Sanginés, C. 1981. *Tiwanaku: Espacio, tiempo y cultura. Ensayo de síntesis arqueológica.* Editorial Los Amigos del Libro, La Paz.

Ponce Sanginés, C. 1990. *El Templete Semisuterraneo de Tiwanaku.* Editorial Juventud, La Paz.

Ponce Sanginés, C. 1991. El urbanismo de Tiwanaku. *Pumapunku (nueva época)* 1:7–27.

Ponce Sanginés, C. 1992. El modelo integrador del estado prehispánico de Tiwanaku. *Enfoques* 16:26–27.

Ponce Sanginés, C. 1993. La cerámica de la época I (aldeana de Tiwanaku). *Pumapunku (nueva época)* 4:48-49.

Ponce Sanginés, C. 1995. *Tiwanaku: 200 años de investigaciones arqueológicas.* CIMA, La Paz.

Ponce Sanginés, C., J. Reinhard, M. Portugal, E. Pareja, and L. Ticlla. 1992. *Exploraciones arqueológicas subacuáticas en el Lago Titikaka.* Editorial La Palabra Producciones, La Paz.

Portugal Ortíz, M. 1981. Expansión del estilo escultórico Pa-Ajanu. *Arte y Arqueología* 7:149–159.

Portugal Ortíz, M. 1989. Estilo escultórico Chiripa en el peninsula de Santiago de Huata. *Textos Antropológicos* 1(1):45–78.

Portugal Ortíz, M. 1991. La prospección efectuada en zonas de la Provincia Camacho del Departamento de La Paz. *Textos Antropológicos* 2:9–42.

Portugal Ortíz, M. 1992. Aspectos de la cultura Chiripa. *Textos Antropológicos* 3:9–26.

Portugal Ortíz, M., H. Catacora, J. Inchausti, A. Murillo, G. Suñavi, R. Gutiérrez, V. Plaza, W. Winkler, S. Avilés, and J. Portugal. 1993. Excavaciones en Titimani (Temporada II). *Textos Antropológicos* 5:11–191.

Portugal Ortíz, M., and M. Portugal Zamora. 1975. Investigaciones arqueológicas en el Valle de Tiwanaku. *Arqueología en Bolivia y Peru*, Vol. 2, pp. 243–283. Instituto Nacional de Arqueología, La Paz.

Portugal Ortíz, M., and M. Portugal Zamora. 1977. Investigaciones arqueológicas en el Valle de Tiwanaku. *Arqueología en Bolivia y Peru: Jornadas Peruano-Bolivianos de estudio científico del altiplano Boliviano y del sur del Perú*, Vol. 2, pp.

243–283. Casa Municipal de la Cultura "Franz Tamayo," La Paz.

Portugal Zamora, M. 1967. Un ídolo más en Tambo Tusi Khana. *Revista Municipal de Arte y Letras* 38:238–241.

Portugal Zamora, M. 1977. Estudio arqueológico de Copacabana. *Arqueología en Bolivia y Peru*, Vol. 2, pp. 285–323. Instituto Nacional de Arqueología, La Paz.

Posnansky, A. 1912. Guía general ilustrada para la investigación de los monumentos prehistóricos de Tihuanacu é Islas del Sol y la Luna. *Revista de la Sociedad Chilena de Historia y Geografía* 2:467–479.

Posnansky, A. 1938. Simillake o Ayakewia. In *Antropología y sociología de las razas interandinas y de las regiones adyacentes*, pp. 106–113. Editorial "Renacimiento," La Paz.

Posnansky, A. 1945. *Tihuanaco: The Cradle of American Man*, Vols. I and II. Translated by J. F. Shearer. J. J. Augustin, New York.

Posnansky, A. 1957. *Tihuanaco: The Cradle of American Man*, Vols. III and IV. Translated by J. F. Shearer. J. J. Augustin, New York.

Pozorski, S., and T. Pozorski. 1997. Chronology. In J. Haas, S. Pozorski, and T. Pozorski, editors, *The Origins and Development of the Andean state*, pp. 5–8. Cambridge University Press, Cambridge.

Pozorski, T., and S. Pozorski. 1996. Ventilated hearth structures in the Casma Valley. *Latin American Antiquity* 7(4):341–353.

Protzen, J. P. 1993. *Inca Architecture and Construction at Ollantaytambo*. Oxford University Press, New York.

Proulx, D. 1999. Nasca headhunting and the ritual use of trophy heads. In *Nasca, Geheimnisvolle Seichen im Alten Peru*, pp. 79–87. Museum für Volkerkunde, Vienna.

Ramenofsky, A. 1987. *Vectors of Death: The Archaeology of European Contact*. University of New Mexico Press, Albuquerque.

Ramos Gavilán, A. 1988 [1621]. *Historia del santuario de Nuestra Señora de Copacabana*. Facsimile edition. Gráfico P.L. Villanueva S.A., Lima.

Rasmussen, K. 1998. *Exploring the Origins of Coastal Sedentism in the South-Central Andes*. Ph.D. dissertation, Department of Anthropology, University of California, Santa Barbara.

Rasnake, R. 1988. *Domination and Cultural Resistance: Authority and Power among an Andean People*. Duke University Press, Durham, North Carolina.

Ravines, R. 1967. El abrigo de Caru y sus relaciones culturales con otros sitios temprano del sur del Perú. *Ñawpa Pacha* 5:39–57.

Ravines, R. 1972. Secuencia y cambios en los artefactos liticos del sur del Perú. *Revista del Museo Nacional* 38:133–185.

Reinhard, J. 1991. Tiwanaku: Ensayo sobre su cosmovisión. *Pumapunku (nueva época)* 2:8–66.

Reinhard, J. 1992. Sacred peaks of the Andes. *National Geographic* 181:84–111.

Reinhard, J. 1995. House of the sun: The Inka temple of Vilcanota. *Latin American Antiquity* 6(4): 340–349.

Revilla Becerra, R., and M. Uriarte Paniagua. 1985. *Investigación arqueológica en la zona de Sillustani-Sector Wakakancha-Puno*. Bachelor's thesis, Universidad Católica Santa María, Arequipa, Peru.

Rice, P. 1987. *Pottery Analysis: A Sourcebook*. University of Chicago Press.

Rick, J. 1980. *Prehistoric Hunters of the High Andes*. Academic Press, New York.

Riddell, F., and L. Valdez. 1987. Hacha y la ocupación temprana del valle de Acarí. *Gaceta Arqueológica Andina* 16:6–10.

Rivera, M. 1991. Pre-Tiwanaku developments in northern Chile. Paper presented at the 56th Annual Meeting of the Society for American Archaeology, New Orleans.

Rivera Casanovas, C. 1994. *Ch'iji Jawira: Evidencias sobre la producción de cerámica en Tiwanaku*. Tésis de licenciatura, Carrera de Antropología, Universidad Mayor de San Andrés, La Paz.

Rivera Casanovas, C. 2003. Ch'iji Jawira: A case of ceramic specialization in the Tiwanaku urban periphery. In A. Kolata, editor, *Tiwanaku and Its Hinterland: Archaeology and Paleoecology of an Andean Civilization*, Vol. II, pp. 296–315. Smithsonian Institution Press, Washington, DC.

Rivera Sundt, O. 1978. Arqueología de la peninsula de Copacabana. *Pumapunku* 12:69–86.

Rivera Sundt, O. 1984. La horca del Inka. *Arqueología Boliviana* 1:91–106.

Rivera Sundt, O. 1989. Resultados de la excavación en el centro ceremonial de Lukurmata. Manuscript in possession of author.

Rodman, A. 1992. Textiles and ethnicity: Tiwanaku in San Pedro de Atacama, North Chile. *Latin American Antiquity* 3(4):316–340.

Roper, D. 1976. Lateral displacement of artifacts due to plowing. *American Antiquity* 41(3):372–375.

Rowe, J. 1944. An introduction to the archaeology of Cuzco. *American Archaeology and Ethnology* 27(2). Peabody Museum, Harvard University, Cambridge, Massachusetts.

Rowe, J. 1946. Inca culture at the time of the Spanish Conquest. In J. Steward, editor, *Handbook of South American Indians,* Vol. 2: *The Andean Civilizations,* pp. 183–330. Bureau of American Ethnology, Washington, DC.

Rowe, J. 1956. Archaeological explorations in southern Peru, 1954-1955. *American Antiquity* 22(2):135-150.

Rowe, J. 1960. The origins of creator worship among the Incas. In S. Diamond, editor, *Culture and History: Essays in Honor of Paul Radin,* pp. 408–429. Columbia University Press, New York.

Rowe, J. 1962. Stages and periods in archaeological interpretation. *Southwestern Journal of Anthropology* 18(1):40–54.

Rowe, J. 1963. Urban settlements in ancient Peru. *Ñawpa Pacha* 1:1–27.

Rowe, J. 1982. Inca policies and institutions relating to the cultural unification of the empire. In G. Collier, R. Rosaldo, and J. Wirth, editors, *The Inca and Aztec States 1400–1800,* pp. 93–118. Academic Press, New York.

Rowe, J., and C. Brandel. 1969. Pucara pottery designs. *Ñawpa Pacha* 7:1–16.

Russell, G. 1994. Cerro Mayal, Peru: Moche ceramic workshop excavated. *Backdirt* (spring): 6-7. Institute of Archaeology, University of California, Los Angeles.

Rydén, S. 1947. *Archaeological Researches in the Highlands of Bolivia.* Elanders Boktryckeri Aktiebolag, Göteborg, Sweden.

Rydén, S. 1957. *Andean Excavations I: The Tiahuanaco Era East of Lake Titicaca.* Ethnographical Museum of Sweden, Stockholm.

Rydén, S. 1959. *Andean Excavations II: Tupuraya and Cayhuasi, Two Tiahuanaco Sites.* Ethnographical Museum of Sweden, Stockholm.

Saignes, T. 1987. New sources on the demographic history of the southern Andes (sixteenth to eighteenth centuries). *Latin American Population History Newsletter* 13:16–21.

Salomon, F. 1986a. *Native Lords of Quito in the Age of the Incas: The Political Economy of North Andean Chiefdoms.* Cambridge Studies in Social Anthropology 59. Cambridge University Press, New York.

Salomon, F. 1986b. Vertical politics on an Inka frontier. In J. Murra, N. Wachtel, and J. Revel, editors, *Anthropological History of Andean Polities,* pp. 89–118. Cambridge University Press, Cambridge.

Sampeck, K. 1991. *Excavations at Putuni, Tiwanaku, Bolivia.* Master's thesis, Department of Anthropology, University of Chicago.

Sánchez-Albornoz, N. 1978. *Indios y tributos en el Alto Perú.* Instituto de Estudios Peruanos, Ediciones, Lima.

Sánchez-Albornoz, N. 1979. *The Population of Latin America.* University of California Press, Berkeley.

Sandweiss, D., K. McGinnis, R. Burger, A. Cano, A., B. Ojeda, R. Paredes del Carmen, M. Sandweiss, and M. Glascock. 1998. Quebrada Jaguay: Early South American maritime adaptations. *Science* 281:1830–1832.

Sandweiss, D., J. Richardson III, E. Reitz, J. Hsu, and R. Feldman. 1989. Early maritime adaptations in the Andes: Preliminary studies at the Ring Site, Peru. In D. Rice, C. Stanish, and P. Scarr, editors, *Ecology, Settlement and History in the Osmore Drainage, Peru,* pp. 35–84. British Archaeological Reports International Series No. 545. Oxford.

Santoro, C. 1989. Antiguos cazadores de la puna. In J. Hidalgo, V. Schiappacasse, H. Niemeyer, C. Aldunate, and I. Solimano, editors, *Culturas de Chile: Prehistoria desde sus origenes hasta los albores de la Conquista,* pp. 33–56. Editorial Andrés Bello, Santiago, Chile.

Santoro, C., and J. Chacama. 1984. Secuencia de asentamientos precerámicos del extremo norte de Chile. *Estudios Atacameños* 7:85–103.

Santoro, C., and L. Nuñez. 1987. Hunters of the dry and salt puna in northern Chile. *Andean Past* 1:57–109.

Sanz, R. 1886. Historia de Copacabana y de la milagrosa imagen de su Virgen. In *Compendio de la obra de Ramos Gavilán*. Imprenta de "La Union" Católica, La Paz.

Sarmiento de Gamboa, P. 1988 [1572]. *Historia de los Incas*. Facsimile edition. Biblioteca de Viajeros Hispánicos No. 4. Miraguano/Polifemo, Madrid.

Schaedel, R. 1978. Early state of the Incas. In H. J. Claessen and P. Skalnik, editors, *The Early State*, pp. 289–320. Mouton, The Hague.

Schaedel, R. 1988. Andean world view: Hierarchy or reciprocity, regulation or control? *Current Anthropology* 29(5):768–775.

Schiappacasse, V., and H. Niemeyer. 1984. *Descripción y análisis interpretivo de un sitio Arcaico Temprano en la Quebrada de Camarones*. Publicación Ocasional 41. Universidad de Tarapacá, Arica, Santiago de Chile.

Schobinger, J., and M. Constanza Ceruti. 2001. Arqueología de Alta Montaña en los Andes Argentinos. In E. Berberián and A. Nielsen, editors, *Historia Argentina prehispánica* 2:523–559. Editorial Brujas, Córdoba, Argentina.

Schreiber, K. 1987. Conquest and consolidation: A comparison of the Wari and Inka occupations of a highland Peruvian valley. *American Antiquity* 52(2):266–284.

Schreiber, K. 1992. *Wari Imperialism in Middle Horizon Peru*. Volume 87 of *Anthropological Papers of the University of Michigan Museum of Anthropology*. University of Michigan Museum of Anthropology, Ann Arbor.

Schultze, Carol. 2000. Tiwanaku expansion into the Puno Bay region of southern Peru. Paper presented at the 65th Annual Meetings of the Society for American Archaeology, Philadelphia.

Seddon, M. 1994. Lithic artifacts. In C. Stanish and L. Steadman, editors, *Archaeological Research at Tumatumani, Juli, Peru*, volume 23 of *Fieldiana Anthropology*, pp. 65–71. Field Museum of Natural History, Chicago.

Seddon, M. 1998. *Ritual, Power, and the Formation of a Complex Society: The Island of the Sun and the Tiwanaku State*. Ph.D. dissertation, Department of Anthropology, University of Chicago.

Seltzer, G. 1990. Recent glacial history and paleoclimate of the Peruvian-Bolivian Andes. *Quaternary Science Reviews* 9(2/3):137–152.

Seltzer, G. 1993. Late-Quaternary glaciation as a proxy for climate change in the Central Andes. *Mountain Research and Development* 13(2):129–138.

Seltzer, G., P. Baker, S. Gross, S. Fritz, and R. Dunbar. 1998. High-resolution seismic reflection profiles from Lake Titicaca, Peru-Bolivia: Evidence for Holocene aridity in the tropical Andes. *Geology* 26(2):167–170.

Service, E. 1962. *Primitive Social Organization*. Random House, New York.

Service, E. 1975. *Origins of the State and Civilization*. W. W. Norton and Company, New York.

Shea, D. 1969. *Wari Wilka: A Central Andean Oracle Shrine*. Ph.D. dissertation, Department of Anthropology, University of Wisconsin, Madison.

Shimada, I. 1991. Pachacamac archaeology: Retrospect and prospect. In I. Shimada, editor, *Pachacamac: A Reprint of the 1903 Edition, by Max Uhle*. University of Pennsylvania, Philadelphia.

Shott, M. 1997. Stones and shafts redux: The metric discrimination of chipped-stone dart and arrow points. *American Antiquity* 62:86–101.

Sillar, W. 1988. Mud and firewater: Making pots in Peru. Report submitted in partial fulfillment of the requirements for the degree of MSc in Archaeology, Institute of Archaeology, University College, London.

Silverman, H. 1996. The Formative Period on the south coast of Peru: A critical review. *Journal of World Prehistory* 10(2):95–146.

Sitio del Cuzco. 1934 [1539]. Relación del sitio del Cuzco y principio de las guerras civiles del Perú hasta la muerte de Diego de Almagro 1533–1539, Madrid [1879]. Facsimile edition published in *Colección de libros y documentos referentes a la historia del Perú* 2(10):1–133.

Smith, C., W. Denevan, and P. Hamilton. 1968. Ancient ridged fields in the region of Lake Titicaca. *Geographical Journal* 134:353–367.

Smith, M. 1987. Household possessions and wealth in agrarian states: Implications for Archaeology. *Journal of Anthropological Archaeology* 6: 297–335.

Smith, M. 1994. Social complexity in the Aztec countryside. In G. M. Schwartz and S. E. Falconer, editors, *Archaeological Views from the Countryside: Village Communities in Early Complex Societies*, pp. 143–159. Smithsonian Institution Press, Washington, DC.

Southall, A. 1988. The segmentary state in Africa and Asia. *Comparative Studies in Society and History* 30:52–82.

Spahni, J.-C. 1971. Liex de culte precolombiens et actuels de departement de Puno (Perou). *Zeitschrift für Ethnologie* 62(2):217–233.

Spalding, K. 1984. *Huarochirí: An Andean Society under Inca and Spanish Rule*. Stanford University Press, Stanford.

Squier, E. 1877a. *Peru, Incidents of Travel and Exploration in the Land of the Incas*. Macmillan, London.

Squier, E. 1877b. *Peru: Incidents of Travel and Exploration in the Land of the Incas*. Harper Brothers, New York.

Stanish, C. 1989a. Household archaeology: Testing models of zonal complementarity in the South Central Andes. *American Anthropologist* 91:7–24.

Stanish, C. 1989b. Tamaño y complejidad de los asentamientos nucleares de Tiwanaku. In A. Kolata, editor, *Arqueología de Lukurmata*, Vol. 2, pp. 41–57. CIAT, La Paz.

Stanish, C. 1989c. An archaeological evaluation of an ethnohistorical model in Moquegua. In D Rice, C. Stanish, and P. Scarr, editors, *Ecology, Settlement and History in the Osmore Drainage*. pp. 303-302. British Archaeological Reports, Oxford.

Stanish, C. 1991. *A Late Pre-Hispanic Ceramic Chronology for the Upper Moquegua Valley, Peru*. Volume 16 of *Fieldiana Anthropology*. Field Museum of Natural History, Chicago.

Stanish, C. 1992. *Ancient Andean Political Economy*. University of Texas Press, Austin.

Stanish, C. 1994a. The hydraulic hypothesis revisited: Lake Titicaca Basin raised fields in theoretical perspective. *Latin American Antiquity* 5(4):312–332.

Stanish, C. 1994b. A new view of the Upper Formative period in the Titicaca Basin. Paper presented at the Northeast Conference of Andean Archaeology and Ethnohistory, Pittsburgh.

Stanish, C. 1997. Nonmarket imperialism in the Prehispanic Americas: The Inka occupation of the Titicaca Basin. *Latin American Antiquity* 8:195–216.

Stanish, C. 1999. Settlement pattern shifts and political ranking. In B. R. Billman and G. M. Feinman, editors, *Fifty Years after Viru*, pp. 116–128. Smithsonian Institution Press, Washington, DC.

Stanish, C. 2000. Negotiating rank in an imperial state: Lake Titicaca Basin elite under Inca and Spanish control. In M. Diehl, editor, *Hierarchies in Action: Who Benefits?*, Center for Archaeological Investigations Occasional Papers, pp. 317–339. Southern Illinois University Press, Carbondale.

Stanish, C. 2001a. The origin of state societies in South America. *Annual Review of Anthropology* 30:41–64.

Stanish, C. 2001b. Regional research on the Inca. *Journal of Archaeological Research* 9(3):213–241.

Stanish, C. 2001c. Formación estatal temprana en la cuenca del lago Titicaca, Andes surcentrales. *Boletín de Arqueología PUCP* 5:189–221. Pontificia Universidad Católica del Perú, Lima.

Stanish, C. 2002. Tiwanaku political economy. In W. H. Isbell and H. Silverman editors, *Andean Archaeology I: Variations in Socio-political Organization*, pp. 169–198. Kluwer Academic, New York.

Stanish, C. 2003. *Ancient Titicaca: The Evolution of Social Power in the Titicaca Basin of Peru and Bolivia*. University of California Press, Berkeley.

Stanish, C., and B. Bauer, editors. 2004. *Archaeological Research on the Islands of the Sun and Moon, Lake Titicaca, Bolivia. Final Results from the Proyecto Tiksi Kjarka*. Monograph 52. Cotsen Institute of Archaeology at UCLA, Los Angeles.

Stanish, C., B. Bauer, O. Rivera, J. Escalante, and M. Seddon. 1996. Report of Proyecto Tiksi Kjarka on the Island of the Sun, Bolivia, 1994–1995. Report submitted to the National Institute of Archaeology of Bolivia, La Paz.

Stanish, Charles, R. Burger, L. Cipolla, M. Glascock, and E. Quelima. 2002. Evidence for early long-distance obsidian exchange and watercraft use from the southern Lake Titicaca Basin of Bolivia and Peru. *Latin American Antiquity* 13(4):444-454.

Stanish, C., E. de la Vega, and K. Frye. 1993. Domestic architecture on Lupaqa area sites in the Department of Puno. In M. Aldenderfer, editor, *Domestic Architecture, Ethnicity and Complementarity in the South-Central Andes,* pp. 83–93. University of Iowa Press, Iowa City.

Stanish, C., E. de la Vega, L. Steadman, C. Chávez, K. Frye, L. Onofre Mamani, M. Seddon, and P. Calisaya. 1995. Archaeological survey in the southwestern Lake Titicaca Basin. *Diálogo Andino* 14/15:97–143.

Stanish, C., E. de la Vega, L. Steadman, C. Chávez Justo, K. Frye, L. Onofre Mamani, M. Seddon, and P. Calisaya Chuquimia. 1997. *Archaeological Survey in the Juli-Desaguadero Region of Lake Titicaca Basin, Southern Peru.* Volume 29 of *Fieldiana Anthropology.* Field Museum of Natural History, Chicago.

Stanish, C., E. de la Vega, L. Steadman, L. Onofre Mamani, K. L. Frye, C. Chávez Justo, and M. Seddon. 1992. Archaeological research in the Juli-Pomata region of the Titicaca Basin, southern Peru. Final report submitted to the National Science Foundation, Washington, DC.

Stanish, C., and E. de la Vega M. 1991. The Tiwanaku occupation of the southwestern Titicaca Basin, Peru. Paper presented at the 47th International Congress of Americanists, New Orleans.

Stanish, C., and A. Plourde. 2000. Archaeological survey in the Huancané-Putina Valley, Peru. Final report submitted to the National Institute of Culture, Lima.

Stanish, C., and L. Steadman. 1994. *Archaeological Research at Tumatumani, Juli, Peru.* Volume 23 of *Fieldiana Anthropology.* Field Museum of Natural History, Chicago.

Steadman, D. 1997. Animal bone. In C. Hastorf, M. Bandy, D. Blom, E. Dean, M. Goodman, D. Kojan, M. Montaño Aragón, J. Luis Paz, D. Steadman, L. Steadman, and W. Whitehead. Taraco Archaeological Project: 1996 Excavations at Chiripa, Bolivia, pp. 48-49. Report submitted to the Instituto Nacional de Arqueología, Bolivia.

Steadman, L. in press. The ceramics from Quelcatani. In M. Aldenderfer, editor, *Quelcatani and the Evolution of Pastoral Societies in the Titicaca Basin.* Smithsonian Institution Press, Washington, DC.

Steadman, L. 1994. Ceramic artifacts. In C. Stanish and L. Steadman, *Archaeological Research at Tumatumani, Juli, Peru,* Volume 23 of *Fieldiana Anthropology,* pp. 19–64. Field Museum of Natural History, Chicago.

Steadman, L. 1995. *Excavations at Camata: An Early Ceramic Chronology for the Western Lake Titicaca Basin, Peru.* Ph.D. dissertation, Department of Anthropology, University of California, Berkeley.

Steadman, L. 1997. Ceramics. In C. Hastorf, D. Blom, E. Dean, M. Goodman, D. Kojan, M. Montaño Aragon, J. Paz, D. Steadman, L. Steadman, and W. Whitehead, editors, Taraco Archaeological Project: 1996 Excavations at Chiripa, Bolivia, pp. 37–42. Report submitted to the Instituto Nacional de Arqueología, Bolivia.

Steadman, L. 1999. The ceramics. In C. Hastorf, editor, *Early Settlement at Chiripa, Bolivia,* Contributions of the University of California Archaeological Research Facility, number 57, pp. 61–72. Archaeological Research Facility, Berkeley.

Steadman, L. 2002. The Yaya-Mama Religious Tradition at Chiripa. Paper presented at the 67th Annual Meeting of the Society for American Archaeology, Denver.

Steadman, L., and C. Hastorf. 2001. Construction for the ancestors: The creation of territory and society in the Middle Formative at Chiripa. Paper presented at the 66th Annual Meeting of the Society for American Archaeology, New Orleans.

Stein, G. 1994. Segmentary states and organizational variation in early complex societies: A rural perspective. In G. Schwartz and S. Falconer, editors, *Archaeological Views from the Countryside: Village Communities in Early Complex Societies,* pp. 10–18. Smithsonian Institution Press, Washington, DC.

Stern, S. 1982. *Peru's Indian Peoples and the Challenge of Spanish Conquest.* University of Wisconsin Press, Madison.

Stuart-Macadam, P. 1987. Porotic hyperostosis: New evidence to support the anemia theory. *American Journal of Physical Anthropology* 74: 521–526.

Stübel, A., and M. Uhle. 1892. *Die Ruinenstatte von Tiahuanaco im Hochlande des Alten Peru*. Verlag von K.W. Hiersemann, Leipzig.

Stuiver, M., and G. Pearson. 1993. High precision bidecadal calibration of the radiocarbon time scale, A.D. 1950–500 B.C. and 2500–6000 B.C. *Radiocarbon* 35:1–23.

Sutherland, C. 1991. *Methodological, Stylistic and Functional Ceramic Analysis: The Surface Collection at Akapana East, Tiwanaku*. Master's Thesis, Department of Anthropology, University of Chicago.

Tambiah, S. 1977. The galactic polity: The structure of traditional kingdoms in Southeast Asia. *Annals of the New York Academy of Sciences* 293: 69–97.

Tapia Pineda, F. 1978. Investigaciónes arqueológicas en Kacsili. *Pumapunku* 12:7–38.

Tello, J. 1935. Las civilizaciones pre-incaicas, su antigüedad y sucesión cronológica. *La crónica*. Lima, 30 de mayo.

Thomas, R., and B. Winterhalder. 1976. Physical and biotic environment of southern highland Peru. In P. Baker and M. Little, editors, *Man in the Andes*, pp. 21–59. Dowden, Hutchinson & Ross, Inc., Stroudsburg.

Thompson, L., M. Davis, E. Mosley-Thompson, and K.-B. Liu. 1988. Pre-Incan agricultural activity recorded in dust layers in two tropical ice cores. *Science* 336:763–765.

Ticlla, L., and A. Vranich. 1997. Informe preliminar sobre los trabajos realizados en Pumapunku entre las fechas 28 de Julio hasta 23 de Diciembre, 1996. Report submitted to the Dirección Nacional de Arqueología y Antropología. La Paz.

Toledo, de F. 1975. *Tasa de la Visita General de Francisco de Toledo*. Universidad Nacional Mayor de San Marcos, Lima.

Tolstoy, P., and S. Fish. 1975. Surface and subsurface evidence for community size at Coapexco, Mexico. *Journal of Field Archaeology* 2:97-104.

Torres, C. 1985. Estilo e iconografía Tiwanaku en la cultura de San Pedro de Atacama. In M. Rivera, editor, *La problematica Tiwanaku Huari en el contexto panandino del desarrollo cultural*, Edicion del Diálogo Andino 4, pp. 247–259. Universidad de Tarapacá, Arica.

Trimborn, H. 1967. Archaölogische studien in den Kordilleren Boliviens. *Baessler Archiv, Beitrage zur Volkerkunde*, Neue Folge (supp) 2(5). Berlin.

Tschopik, H. 1946. The Aymara. In J. Steward, editor, *Handbook of South American Indians*, Vol. 2: *The Andean Civilizations*, pp. 501–573. Bureau of American Ethnology, Washington, DC.

Tschopik, H. 1950. An Andean ceramic tradition in historical perspective. *American Antiquity* 3: 196–219.

Tschopik, H. 1951. *The Aymara of Chucuito, Peru*. Volume 44 of *Anthropological Papers of the American Museum of Natural History*. American Museum of Natural History, New York.

Tschopik, M. 1946. Some notes on the archaeology of the Department of Puno, Peru. *American Archaeology and Ethnology* 27(3). Peabody Museum, Harvard University, Cambridge, Massachusetts.

Urton, G. 1990. *The History of a Myth: Pacariqtambo and the Origin of the Inkas*. University of Texas Press, Austin.

Vaca de Castro, C. 1908 [1543]. Ordenanzas de tambos de Vaca de Castro. Facsimile edition published in *Revista Histórica* 3. Lima.

Valcárcel, L. 1932. El personaje mítico de Pukara. *Revista del Museo Nacional* 4:18–30.

Valcárcel, L. 1935. Litoesculturas y cerámica de Pukara. *Revista del Museo Nacional* 4:25–28.

Valera, B. 1950 [1589]. *Relación de las costumbres antiguas de los naturales del Perú*. Facsimile edition. Editorial Guaranía, Asunción.

Van Buren, M., P. Bürgi, and P. Rice. 1993. Torata Alta: A late highland settlement in the Osmore Drainage. In M. Aldenderfer, editor, *Domestic Architecture, Ethnicity and Complementarity in the South-Central Andes*, pp. 136–146. University of Iowa Press, Iowa City.

Van de Guchte, M. 1990. *Carving the World: Inca Monumental Sculpture and Landscape*. Ph.D. dissertation, Department of Anthropology, University of Illinois, Urbana-Champaign.

Vásquez, E. 1937. Las ruinas de Kachakacha. *Revista del Museo Nacional* 6(1):52–57.

Vásquez, E. 1939. Ruinas arqueológicas de Puno, Qutimpu. *Revista del Museo Nacional* 8(1):117–123.

Vásquez, E. 1940. Itinerario arqueológico del Kollao. *Revista del Museo Nacional* 9(1):143–150.

Vranich, A. 1999. *Interpreting the Meaning of Ritual Spaces: The Temple Complex of Pumapunku, Tiwanaku, Bolivia.* Ph.D. dissertation, Department of Anthropology, University of Pennsylvania.

Vranich, A. 2001. La pirámide de Akapana: Reconsiderando el centro monumental de Tiwanaku. In P. Kaulicke, editor, Huari y Tiwanaku: Modelos vs. evidencias (Segunda parte), *Boletín de Arqueología PUCP* 5:295–308. Pontificia Universidad Católica del Perú, Lima.

Vranich, A., J. M. López B., J. Yaeger, and M. Maldonado V. 2002. Informe de los trabajos arqueológicos realizados por el Proyecto Arqueológico Pumapunku-Akapana: Gestión 2001. Project report for the 2001 field season submitted to DINAAR. La Paz.

Wallace, D. 1957. *The Tiahuanaco Horizon Styles in the Peruvian Highlands.* Ph.D. dissertation, Department of Anthropology, University of California, Berkeley.

Wallace, D. 1980. Tiwanaku as a symbolic empire. *Estudios Arqueológicos* 5:133–144.

Wassén, S. 1972. *A Medicine-Man's Implements and Plants in a Tihuanacoid Tomb in Highland Bolivia.* Göteborgs Etnologiska Studier, Göteborg, Sweden.

Weber, M. 1947. *The Theory of Social and Economic Organization.* The Free Press, New York.

Weber, M. 1958. The city. In D. Martingale and G. Neuwirth, editors, *The City,* pp. 65–230. The Free Press, New York.

Wenke, R. 1975. *Imperial Investments and Agricultural Developments in Parthian and Sussanian Khuzistan: 150 B.C. to A.D. 640.* Ph.D. dissertation, Department of Anthropology, University of Michigan, Ann Arbor.

Wheeler, J., and E. Mujica, J. 1981. Prehistoric pastoralism in the Lake Titicaca Basin, Peru. Final project report for the 1979–80 field season submitted to the National Science Foundation, Washington, DC.

White, J. 1995. Incorporating heterarchy into theory on socio-political development: The case for Southeast Asia. In C. Crumley, R. Ehrenreich, and J. Levy, editors, *Heterarchy and the Analysis of Complex Societies,* pp. 101–124. American Anthropological Association, Arlington, Virginia.

Whitehead, W. 1999a. Paleoethnobotanical evidence. In C. Hastorf, editor, *Early Settlement at Chiripa, Bolivia,* Contributions of the University of California Archaeological Research Facility, number 57, pp. 95–104. Archaeological Research Facility, Berkeley.

Whitehead, W. 1999b. Radiocarbon dating. In C. Hastorf, editor, *Early Settlement at Chiripa, Bolivia,* Contributions of the University of California Archaeological Research Facility, number 57, pp. 17–22. Archaeological Research Facility, Berkeley.

Whitelaw, T., and J. Davis. 1991. The Polis center of Koressos. In J. Cherry, J. Davis, and Z. Mantzourani, editors, *Landscape Archaeology as Long-Term History: Northern Keos in the Cycladic Islands,* Monumenta Archaeologica 16, pp. 266–284. Institute of Archaeology, University of California, Los Angeles.

Wiener, C. 1880. *Perou et Bolivie: Recit de voyage.* Librarie Hachette, Paris.

Wilk, R. 1983. Little house in the jungle: The causes of variation in house size among the modern Kekchi Maya. *Journal of Anthropological Archaeology* 2:99–116.

Wilk, R., and R. Netting. 1984. Households: Changing forms and functions. In R. Netting, R. Wilk, and E. Arnold, editors, *Household: Comparative and Historical Studies of the Domestic Group,* pp. 1–28. University of California Press, Berkeley.

Wilk, R., and W. Rathje. 1982. *Archaeology of the Household: Building a Prehistory of Domestic Life.* Special Issue of American Behavioral Scientist 25(6). Sage Publications, Beverly Hills.

Williams, S. R. 1990. *The Skeletal Biology of Estuqiña: A Late Intermediate Period Site in Southern Peru.* Ph.D. dissertation, Department of Anthropology, Northwestern University, Evanston, Illinois.

Williams, S.R., K. Forgey, and E. Klarich. 2001. *An Osteological Study of Nasca Trophy Heads Collected by A.L. Kroeber during the Marshall Field Expeditions to Peru.* Volume 29 of *Fieldiana Anthropology,* Field Museum of Natural History, Chicago.

Wirrmann, D., and L. Fernando de Oliveira Almeida. 1987. Low Holocene level (7700–3650 years ago) of Lake Titicaca (Bolivia). *Pa-*

leogeography, Paleoclimatology and Paleoecology 59:315–323.

Wirrmann, D., and P. Mourguiart. 1995. Late Quaternary spatio-temporal limnological variations in the Altiplano of Bolivia and Peru. *Quaternary Research* 43:344–354.

Wirrmann, D., P. Mourguiart, and L. F. de Oliveira Almeida. 1988. Holocene sedimentology and ostracod distribution in Lake Titicaca: Paleohydrological interpretations. In J. Rabassa, editor, *Quaternary of South America and Antarctic Peninsula*, Vol. 6, pp. 89–127. A.A. Balkema, Rotterdam.

Wise, K. 1993. Late Intermediate period architecture of Lukurmata. In M. Aldenderfer, editor, *Domestic Architecture, Ethnicity, and Complementarity in the South-Central Andes*, pp. 103-113. University of Iowa Press, Iowa City.

Wright, H. 1977. Recent research on the origin of the state. *Annual Review of Anthropology* 6:379–397.

Wright, H., and G. Johnson. 1975. Population, exchange and early state formation in southwestern Iran. *American Anthropologist* 77:267–289.

Wright, M., C. Hastorf, and H. Lennstrom. 2003. Pre-Hispanic agriculture and plant use at Tiwanaku: Social and political implications. In A. Kolata, editor, *Tiwanaku and Its Hinterland: Archaeology and Paleoecology of an Andean Civilization*, Vol. II, pp. 384–403. Smithsonian Institution Press, Washington, DC.

Zubrow, E. 1990. The depopulation of native America. *Antiquity* 64(245):754-765.

Zuidema, R. 1978. Shafttombs and the Inca Empire. *Journal of the Steward Anthropological Society* 9(1–2):133-178.

Zuidema, R. 1990. *Inca Civilization in Cuzco*. University of Texas Press, Austin.

Index

Note: Page numbes in bold italics indicate illustrations or tables.